THE WAR
OF THE TWO
EMPERORS

THE WAR OF
THE TWO
EMPERORS

THE DUEL BETWEEN
NAPOLEON AND ALEXANDER:
RUSSIA, 1812

CURTIS CATE

RANDOM HOUSE   NEW YORK

Library of Congress Cataloging in Publication Data
Cate, Curtis, 1924–
The war of the two emperors.
Bibliography: p.
Includes index.
1. Napoleonic Wars, 1800–1814—Campaigns—Soviet
Union. 2. Napoleon I, Emperor of the French, 1769–1821.
3. Alexander I, Emperor of Russia, 1777–1825. I. Title.
DC235.C35 1985   940.2′7   84-42506
ISBN 0-394-53670-3

Manufactured in the United States of America

2 4 6 8 9 7 5 3

First Edition

MAPS BY JEAN PAUL TREMBLAY

TO BAJA

PREFACE

THE WRITING of a book—save for those gifted mortals who already have everything worked out to the last comma in their heads—is almost always a voyage of exploration over vaguely, and sometimes totally, uncharted seas. This is true not only of novels, which, as Thomas Mann remarked more than once, tend to take on a life and a will of their own in seeming defiance of the author's original intent; it is also true of biographies, and even of books of "factual" history. The author sets out along a preestablished course, headed like Columbus for a distant Cathay, and ends up unwittingly discovering an entire new continent.

Such, at any rate, has been my experience in the writing of this book. When I began it, it was with the vague intuition that 1812 was one of those crucial years that mark the end of one historical period and the start of another. For Americans, of course, 1812—the year that saw the fledgling republic of the United States embroiled in a war with England—has an entirely different connotation; but it was not the momentous twelvemonth it proved to be for the future development of Europe. For everything that ensued in Europe in the immediate aftermath of 1812—the chain of events leading from Napoleon's initial defeat at Leipzig to the final battle of Waterloo—was little more than a convulsive epilogue, the protracted death agony of a regime which was never able to recover from the debacle in Russia. And the collapse—one is tempted to say the premature collapse—of this regime profoundly altered the subsequent development of the European continent.

The Anglo-American war of 1812 is often looked upon as an absurd anomaly in the two-hundred-year history of our relations with Great Britain. One has the same feeling in approaching the Franco-Russian war of 1812, which could so easily not have happened. Napoleon's needless invasion of Russia is generally regarded as proof of his incurable megalomania, a historical anticipation of Adolf Hitler's later folly in launching a blitzkrieg against the Soviet Union in 1941.

It is indeed curious how history at times takes a malicious pleasure in repeating itself, as though to prove how incorrigibly obtuse certain human beings can be. Before invading Russia in 1941, Adolf Hitler was warned by his ambassador in Moscow, Count Friedrich von der Schulenburg, not to underestimate the formidable strength of the Red Army. The German military attaché in Moscow, General Ernst Koestring, was even blunter. When asked if the Third Reich could win a war against the Soviet Union, he answered, "Yes, but on one condition," and when asked what that condition was, he added, "That we get the Russians to fight the Russians." But the mere suggestion that his Wehrmacht might be too weak to accomplish its "historic task" unless aided by anti-Bolshevik Russians and Ukrainians was enough to unleash one of the Führer's furious tantrums.

Much the same treatment—though of a less demented kind—was accorded to all those who, during the autumn of 1811 and the early months of 1812, sought to warn Napoleon of the hazards he was running in planning an invasion of Russia. But Napoleon, who could not conceivably have written a book like *Mein Kampf,* was not a frustrated veteran of trench warfare thirsting for revenge, still less the Slavophobic addict of a crazy ideology proclaiming the preordained superiority of an Aryan Master Race. For years, as I have tried to show in this book, he regarded Russia as a natural ally rather than as an enemy of France, and it was only when his hopes turned sour that he began to develop a petulant distaste for "those barbarians of the North," who had to be "pushed back into the ice from which they have come." His reasons for invading Russia were eminently rational—or so at least I thought before I began my study of the problem. I believed naïvely that the campaign of 1812 was merely one aspect of his continuing war against his principal foe, England, and that it was essentially motivated by Napoleon's grim determination to force a mulish Russia to abide by the boycott-of-British-goods restrictions of his Continental System.

Far be it from me to belittle the crucial importance of this particular motive, even though I have never been an adherent of the Marxist school of political interpretation, according to which all important historical developments must be traced back to economic root causes. It would doubtless be a mistake to swing from one extreme to the other and to claim that Napoleon's extraordinary career, from beginning to end, is comprehensible only in psychological terms. But I must confess that it was a surprise for me to discover to what extent his highly personal feud with his imperial "brother," Alexander of Russia, was influenced by an element of *dépit amoureux,* as the historian Serghei Tatishchev once put it: that is, by his jilted hope of being able to marry into the Romanov dynasty.

No less surprising to me was the discovery of how important to the genesis of this momentous conflict was the perennial problem of Poland. Before the Solidarity trade movement was launched at Gdansk in December of 1980 all too little attention was paid in the West to what was going on in Poland, and the same basic lack of interest seems to have affected students of history. In London, where I began the research for this book, I came upon a biography of Prince Joseph Poniatowski written by the famous Polish historian Szimon Askenazy. This particular edition was a German translation, published in 1912.

Just when it had been acquired by the prestigious lending library where I found it, I have no idea; but it had probably been lying on the shelf for half a century or more without any of its pages having been cut. Later, in Paris, I had a similar experience when I went to the Bibliothèque Polonaise on the Ile Saint-Louis and asked for a copy of Abel Mansuy's *Jérôme Napoléon et la Pologne en 1812*. The library possessed two copies—a tribute to the importance the librarian had accorded to this fascinating if somewhat prejudiced book about Napoleon's youngest brother and his relations with the Poles—but nobody had bothered to read the copy I was brought, for here too the pages were uncut.

It is probably fair to say that the idea most people have of Napoleon's ill-starred campaign in Russia has either been influenced by or directly derived from Tolstoy's *War and Peace*. That film directors and TV producers should have pounced on this epic novel for their own purposes is understandable; it is full of fascinating battle scenes as well as of glimpses of social and family life in Petersburg, Moscow, and the Russian provinces. Yet the fact remains that the picture Tolstoy has given us of the war of 1812, particularly when viewed as a military campaign, is fundamentally bogus and in places little more than a caricature of what actually occurred.

Tolstoy's case is particularly interesting because it is a classic example of how one author can claim to have been influenced by another while pursuing a totally different objective. We have his word for it that in his treatment of battle scenes he was above all influenced by Stendhal's description of Waterloo in *La Chartreuse de Parme*. Stendhal's novel, most of which takes place in Italy, is the story of two curiously intertwined love affairs, and if the battle of Waterloo figures in it at all, it is to bring out the frustrated idealism of the young Fabrizio del Dongo, thirsting to take part in the battle directed by his hero, Napoleon, but condemned by accidental circumstances only to witness the dusty hustle and bustle, the chaotic movement of men, sutlers, horses, wagons, and cannon rushing back and forth in unintelligible confusion behind the lines. This was the aspect of war with which Stendhal was personally most familiar, as an employee in the French quartermaster service, which was long headed by his kinsman Count Pierre Daru, whom he accompanied to Moscow.

That Tolstoy should have wished to be inspired by Stendhal in this respect is all to his credit. No one who has been near a battlefield can have failed to be impressed by the degree of confusion that is apt to reign when large bodies of men are pitted against each other. Once, when he was describing what he had personally experienced during the first couple of days of the Normandy invasion of June 1944, General James Gavin, commander of the 101st Airborne Division, was asked, "General, if things went as badly as you say, how was it that we finally managed to establish a foothold in Normandy?" "Well," answered Gavin, "I guess it must have been because one army was fighting another army." The answer was a rigorously honest one, but it would have ceased to be so had Gavin tried to elevate this sobering realization about military mismanagement to the level of a general historical truth or axiom of warfare.

Yet this, curiously enough, was more or less what Tolstoy set out to do in

War and Peace. Unlike *The Charterhouse of Parma,* which contains no moral or lesson, *War and Peace* is a didactic novel with a message which grows increasingly strident as the action progresses toward the climax of 1812. The message is repeatedly interrupted by family and salon scenes, where Tolstoy is at his best, yet it keeps returning like the sound of a howling wind heard each time a door is opened, when the focus is shifted from those oases of tranquillity back to the disorderly turbulence of the "front." The gist of this message is that battles, because they involve the individual actions of thousands of human beings, are basically unintelligible to those who take part in them, since all any particular participant can see is only a tiny fragment of what actually takes place. Generals therefore delude themselves when they fancy they are controlling an unpredictable flux of events made up of many disparate elements. This was a "truth" Tolstoy further applied to all leaders, and particularly to politicians, who claim to be leading masses of human beings in this or that direction, when in fact they are like blind rams acting as bellwethers for the equally blind sheep that follow them.

For Tolstoy generals—in this respect no different from statesmen and politicians—are fundamentally vain creatures, and never more so than when they take to theorizing about matters of strategy and tactics and other aspects of military "science." His particular bête noire was General Karl von Phull, the Prussian armchair strategist who devised a totally impractical scheme for defending Russia against a Napoleonic assault through the construction of a single, supposedly impregnable fortified camp at Drissa. It is certainly no accident that his sarcastic portrayal of Phull in *War and Peace* was a fairly accurate one, corresponding to what he knew of Phull's character and foibles from Clausewitz's account of the campaign, Toll's posthumous notes (as edited by General von Bernhardi), and other first-hand sources. Because Phull was nothing but an armchair theorist and thus a living caricature of true military competence, he was an ideal sitting duck, a perfect target for the darts and arrows of Tolstoy's savage irony. With the single, significant exception of Kutuzov, all the Russian generals who appear in this epic novel remain more or less shadowy figures, and to that extent they are caricatures—as is the archvillain, the very prototype of military vainglory, that self-deluding and deluding conqueror and leader of men, Napoleon Bonaparte.

Writing in 1868—the year that saw the publication of the last and most didactic part of the novel—Prince Pyotr Vyazemsky, who, unlike Tolstoy, was actually present at the battle of Borodino, observed that *War and Peace* was in reality a "protest against the year 1812." Persuaded as he was that this war was an absurdity, which assuredly it was, Tolstoy was moved by a kind of populist, antileadership bias to portray almost all of its leading protagonists in more or less absurd terms. Even Tsar Alexander was treated with a certain irony—as in the scene, during his visit to Moscow in July 1812, where he is described, stepping out onto the balcony of his Kremlin Palace still munching a biscuit, the falling crumbs of which are seized and fought over by the adoring crowd below. This scene, Vyazemsky claimed, was a piece of Tolstoyan fabrication from start to finish; for Alexander was far too meticulous and fussy about his public appearances to have allowed himself such an offhand gesture. The great novelist's portrayal of Alexander was thus basically unfaithful, as was, to a far greater degree, his savage delineation of the "mad" governor of Moscow, Rostopchin, whose posters and proclamations were less idiotic and far closer to the popular mood than Tolstoy would have us believe. Nor was Rostopchin the coward he was made out to be.

Equally fanciful was Tolstoy's portrayal of Kutuzov—the only general on either side who found any real favor in his eyes. As Isaiah Berlin has written in his remarkable essay "The Hedgehog and the Fox," "Such heroes as Pierre Bezukhov or Karateev are at least imaginary, and Tolstoy had an undisputed right to endow them with all the attributes he admired—humility, freedom from bureaucratic or scientific or rationalistic kinds of blindness. But Kutuzov was a real person, and it is all the more instructive to observe the steps by which he transforms him from the sly, elderly, feeble voluptuary, the corrupt and somewhat sycophantic courtier of the early drafts of *War and Peace,* which are based on authentic sources, into the unforgettable symbol of the Russian people in all of its simplicity and intuitive wisdom."

This mythical representation of Kutuzov as the embodiment of his country's peasant wisdom, as a kind of canny folk hero, has persisted right down to the present. It suited Tolstoy's purpose to falsify the facts in this way because the real heroes of the 1812 campaign—Barclay de Tolly and Colonel Friedrich von Toll—were both of them of Baltic German rather than of pure Russian stock. This made them, like Phull, automatically suspect to Tolstoy, who had little appreciation for Germanic culture and a virulent dislike of its all too abstract and nebulous philosophers. Yet if there are two definite conclusions that can be drawn from an impartial study of the 1812 campaign, they are, first, that Napoleon was the loser—something few would venture to deny; and second, that Kutuzov was *not* the winner, but rather the hesitant, dilatory general who let Napoleon escape from Russia, thus engaging his country and much of Europe in another round of bloody battles.

The absurd thesis—blown up to the proportions of a philosophical theory of history in the long epilogue to *War and Peace*—that individual military leadership really counts for little in the waging and winning of wars and battles, makes the campaign of 1812 quite simply unintelligible. For if ever there was a campaign in which the element of individual leadership was all-important, it was surely this one. This totally unnecessary campaign could never have taken place—particularly in the face of so much hostility and lukewarmness in France itself—but for the stubborn insistence of one man, Napoleon. His opponent, Tsar Alexander, can be and has been criticized for many things —among others, for having helped to precipitate the war by making the French occupation of Oldenburg and Napoleon's retention of certain Prussian strongholds such personal issues. He also complicated his generals' tasks by wanting to play the part of commander in chief, for which he was not fitted, either by temperament or by training. But we should nonetheless give Alexander his due for *not* having made a mistake that could have sealed his country's doom. For if he had heeded the prevailing sentiment in Petersburg and had chosen the popular Prince Bagration to be his minister of war and the commander of his First Army of the West, rather than the less flamboyant but infinitely more clearheaded Barclay de Tolly, then one thing is virtually certain: Napoleon at the very outset of the 1812 campaign would have destroyed most of Alexander's army near Vilna, and this would have opened the road to St. Petersburg. Its capture by the French, in August of 1812, would have dramatically altered the military situation, even if Alexander had then fled to his other capital, Moscow, and thereby lured part of Napoleon's forces to pursue him into the heart of Russia. For by occupying all of the Courland "hump" as well as Livonia—something Marshal Macdonald was never able to accomplish with his single corps—Napoleon would have established a solid logistical base for future operations, reposing on the elaborate network of waterway supply lines he had so carefully prepared in East Prussia.

Even if Alexander had refused to sue for peace, thus prolonging the war by a year or two, Napoleon, faced by scattered Russian forces, would have been able to develop the defenses of a semi-independent Lithuania, while Poniatowski could have pursued his dream of adding Podolia and Volhynia to what would inevitably have become a new Kingdom of Poland. The British, with their naval supremacy, would have continued to dominate the Baltic, but with the French occupying all of the Courland and Livonian littoral from Memel to Petersburg, there would have been no easy way in which English guns and money could have been brought in to finance and supply the continuing Russian war effort. Bernadotte in Sweden would have been neutralized, while the Turkish sultan would certainly have denounced the Treaty of Bucharest (of May 1812) and have resumed military operations along the Danubian front.

This, I realize, may sound a bit fanciful. But it is far from being idle speculation, still less a form of intellectual charlatanism, as Tolstoy believed. Nations do not develop, rise, or fall according to some preordained but unknown chain of circumstances, if only because they are led by human beings, who at any particular moment are offered a choice—sometimes broad, sometimes terribly restricted—of policies to be pursued, of decisions to be taken or not taken. This situation of being condemned to be free, as Albert Camus put it, is the essence of the human condition and the nub of human history. Only with relation to what *might have been* can *what was* properly be judged. The ability to do the wrong thing—as Napoleon clearly did in 1812—is the first, awesome privilege of human existence; but this ability can be judged only in terms of an imaginary criterion—the course of action that in those given circumstances would have been right. This is the fundamental morality underlying all of human history, and were we to be denied this right (and indeed this necessity) to construct alongside what happened an imaginary schema of what might otherwise have happened, the study of the past would cease to have any significance at all.

At least two questions, therefore, clamor for an answer if one is to attempt to judge the real significance of what took place in 1812: first, what would have happened if Kutuzov had finished off Napoleon and the remnants of his army at Krasnoye, as should logically have happened; and second, what would have happened if Napoleon had heeded the wise counsels of Caulaincourt, Cambacérès, and many others who sought to deter him from invading Russia, and had remained in Paris, preferring to exercise the métier of kingship rather than the craft of generalship, as he had often insisted was his basic wish?

The first possibility was actually envisaged, with a certain trepidation, by Harold Nicolson in his book *The Congress of Vienna*—except that he assumed that it was on the banks of the Berezina rather than at Krasnoye that Napoleon should logically have been trapped by the Russians. Nicolson felt that such a "premature" finale to the campaign of 1812 would probably have led to the reconstitution of a Kingdom of Poland "from Danzig to Cracow" under the auspices of a Russian Empire which, having triumphed single-handedly over the "Corsican ogre," would not have had to share the rewards of victory with anybody else. In effect, this would have advanced the western borders of the Russian Empire almost as far as the Oder River—a situation that would undoubtedly have aroused great concern in the rest of Europe and which would greatly have facilitated Talleyrand's task of forging an anti-Russian coalition. Thus would have been forged a new alignment of European powers, which might well have included a still considerably diminished Prussia. For, contrary to what Nicolson suggests, a Kingdom of Poland stretching almost to the Oder could have been established only at Prussia's expense.

What actually happened—thanks to Kutuzov's failure to trap Napoleon, and Alexander's later insistence on pursuing Napoleon all the way to Paris— was substantially different. It is indeed one of the great ironies of this period that the chief territorial winner at the Congress of Vienna in 1815 was not Russia, which had made the first significant military contribution to Napoleon's downfall; it was Prussia, which, as a reward for the part played by its generals in the allied war effort, was allowed to regain most of its previous Polish territories (though this time excluding Warsaw), as well as two-fifths of Saxony, including the Lutheran heartland of Thuringia. The Treaty of Vienna—and this despite the efforts of Castlereagh and Talleyrand—thus sanctioned the historical injustice committed in the previous century by the dismemberment of Poland, and paved the way for the showdown battle between Prussia and Austria which was to end with the former's triumph (at Königgrätz in 1866) and to the creation, in 1871, of the Bismarckian Reich.

The second question—what would have happened if Napoleon had never invaded Russia?—opens up even more fascinating vistas. The loosely knit coalition of anti-Bonaparte powers of 1813—including England, Russia, Prussia, and Austria, each of whom had reasons for distrusting some of the others—could never have been formed, if only because King Frederick William III and Metternich were convinced that Napoleon on the field of battle was invincible, while Tsar Alexander was persuaded, like his minister of defense, Barclay de Tolly, that Russia could not "go it alone" and hope to succeed in an offensive war fought west of the Niemen River. The only organized military force Napoleon would have had to contend with would have been Wellington's army in the Iberian peninsula, which was in actual fact forced to evacuate Madrid after failing to take Burgos during the autumn of 1812 (that is to say, during the French debacle in Russia). The British almost certainly would have been driven back into Portugal, and Marshal Suchet could have continued the policy of intelligent cooperation with the local inhabitants which had begun to produce such extraordinary results in Aragon, where French soldiers could already move about freely without being set upon and murdered by patriotic *guerrilleros*. Unpopular though he was, the well-meaning Joseph Bonaparte would have had more time to introduce reforms, which in the long run could only have been of benefit to the Spanish people (as had already happened in equally backward and priest-ridden Naples). Wellington would never have been able to reach the Pyrenees, still less Bordeaux, as finally happened early in 1814, and the continuation of the peninsula war would have placed a steadily increasing strain on the English exchequer, with very little to show for it. (We should not forget that in 1812 the population of Great Britain barely exceeded 15 million, whereas France—not including the annexed territories of Belgium, Holland, and northern Italy which had been added to the Napoleonic Empire—was a land of close to 27 million inhabitants.)

There is thus good reason for believing that Napoleon could have continued to reign right up until his death in 1821. With its imperial family now linked to France's by a marital tie, Austria, under Metternich's cynical guidance, would probably have regained most of its Illyrian possessions in exchange for some minor territorial losses in Polish Galicia. The Grand Duchy of Warsaw —supported by France, Saxony, and Austria, which (under Metternich) was basically suspicious of Russian designs on Poland—would have remained a focus of international tension and intrigues; but there can be little doubt that if Alexander and his generals had finally tried the preemptive strike they had envisaged in the spring of 1811, they would have been sent reeling back in even more panicky confusion than in May of 1813 (when Napoleon, at the head of a drastically weakened army, trounced them at Bautzen, northeast of Dresden). To support the Grand Duchy of Warsaw Napoleon would certainly have retained his grip on Danzig and the Oder River fortresses of Küstrin and Glogau; and an unhappy King Frederick William III, at the head of a seriously diminished Prussia of less than five million souls, would have had no choice but to swallow his ruffled pride and wait for a brighter day. The universities of Germany, like the drawing rooms of Berlin, would have continued to seethe and simmer in a stew of anti-Bonapartist fervor, but with the French emperor's prestige untarnished and his military might intact, there is not much that the students, with their new *Burschenschaften* (fraternities) and *Turnvereine* (gymnastic societies), could have done but go on occasional rampages and demonstrate their Germanic patriotism by sporting "Teutonic costumes."

With his death in 1821 the fragile Napoleonic structure would have begun to collapse, but less swiftly and completely than actually occurred in 1814–1815. Joseph Bonaparte would almost certainly have been driven from the Spanish throne, and the restive Dutch, supported by the British, would have revolted against their unnatural incorporation into an oversize imperial France of 128 departments. The luxury-loving Jerome Bonaparte would have been forced to give up his stately residences in and around Kassel, but his departure and that of his bashful wife, Catherine (daughter of the king of Württemberg), would almost certainly have been regretted by the lower strata of Hessian society, and probably by many officers and soldiers, who had no burning desire to see their harsh, penny-pinching despot of 1804 make a belated and vindictive comeback. The Confederation of the Rhine would have withered into oblivion, but the kings of Saxony, Bavaria, and Württemberg would have clung tenaciously to the crowns they had been given by Napoleon. Hanover would have continued to be a bone of contention between England and Prussia, and in the general confusion of the moment (after Napoleon's death) King Frederick William III and his restive Prussian officers might well have mounted an invasion in an effort to obtain the long-coveted province before the English could land an expeditionary force.

In France itself the vast majority of the population would almost certainly have rallied to Napoleon's ten-year-old son. The restoration of the Bourbons, which Tsar Alexander did not relish in 1814, would have been out of the question in 1821—particularly if Caulaincourt, who actually became Napoleon's foreign minister in 1814, could have retained the French emperor's confidence to the end of his life. This level-headed soldier-diplomat, who had earned the sincere respect of Alexander of Russia, might well have been called upon to act as a kind of mentor and regent during the adolescent years of Napoleon II. In this case he, rather than Talleyrand, would almost certainly have been called upon to represent his country at the international congress that would have been convened—in 1821 instead of 1814—to decide what could and should be done to prevent the outbreak of a new European war over the perennial Polish problem. If it had been decided, in the interests of peace, to retain the Duchy of Warsaw as a kind of buffer state—a policy that England would probably have supported as eagerly in 1821 as Castlereagh did (unsuccessfully) in 1815—then the Polish uprising of 1830 might never have taken place.

The period of Metternichean reaction, which actually began in 1815, could not have been ushered in until 1821, giving the continent a fruitful respite of six years. The Karlsbad Decrees of 1819, which set off a witch-hunt against liberal professors and teachers in most German universities, might never have been promulgated, and Heinrich Heine and Karl Marx might not have felt the need to emigrate from Germany to less intolerant lands.

But it is perhaps in Russia itself that the consequences might have been the most far-reaching—if only Napoleon had not invaded in 1812. Moscow, with its five hundred treasure-filled palaces and townhouses, would have remained one of the architectural wonders of the world, and Alexander, not having had his soul "ignited" by the frightful conflagration of September 1812, would not have succumbed so easily to the mystical illusion that he was the chosen instrument of Divine Providence for saving the established order in Europe. He would have had more time and latitude to concentrate on his own country's pressing problems. There is indeed a tragic irony in the fact that Napoleon, representing a supposedly "more civilized" and unquestionably "more advanced" form of society, should have invaded Russia at a moment when its ruler was toying with the idea of reforming and modernizing a hidebound system of autocratic government by introducing representative councils at various district and provincial levels, rising to an apex in the form of a national parliament, or Duma—a reform that was introduced only in 1905, close to ninety years later! This thoroughgoing overhaul of a paralyzing system of administration ("Orders from above, obedience from below"), as prepared by the tsar's state secretary, Mikhail Speransky, was to have been accompanied by another of Alexander's long-dreamed-of reforms: the gradual abolition of serfdom.

But 1812, and a spontaneous xenophobic hostility to all foreign influences, and particularly to "French ideas," kindled by Napoleon's invasion, killed all that. Speransky, as I have shown in Chapter 7, was dismissed and exiled to Siberia, the reform plans were shelved, and all of the Russian Empire's resources were mobilized for the war against the invaders. Nor did this effort stop with the precipitate retreat of the once proud Grande Armée. Alexander insisted on pursuing Napoleon all the way to the gates of Paris, and it was he, more than any other, who insisted on obtaining his abdication (at Fontainebleau in April 1814), although he was magnanimous enough—toward his former "brother"—to have him exiled to Elba, in the Mediterranean, rather than to some more distant, truly godforsaken isle.

The price that Russia, and ultimately Europe, had to pay for this personal triumph, was heavy. Speransky's ambitious reform projects were allowed to gather dust while Alexander busied himself with the affairs of the continent. Weather, geography, and the implacable hatred of the Russian people having contributed more to Napoleon's undoing in 1812 than had the genius of Russia's generals, a new myth was born—one deliberately belittling the power of individual genius and exalting the mystic strength, fortitude, and wisdom of the people. Tolstoy's *War and Peace* bears eloquent tribute to the strength of this "populist" myth, which was to achieve its sinister apotheosis in the Bolshevik revolution of 1917, with its individual-belittling cry "All Power to the Soviets!"

It is, indeed, difficult to resist the conclusion that the subsequent history of Europe would have been profoundly different if serfdom in Russia had been abolished forty years earlier. A no longer "unchanging" Russia could not have been held up to public ridicule by Marx and Engels as the very prototype of reaction. The introduction of a more representative system of government would have given the Russian aristocracy a social raison d'être it so signally lacked under the age-old autocracy (whence the scorn poured on this idle class by Pushkin and other poets). Anarchists and revolutionaries would have found it more difficult to thrive and multiply in a society that seemed less obtusely attached to the maintenance of a perennial, immutable status quo.

But for 1812 there might never have been a Bakunin, nor a Plekhanov, nor a Lenin, nor a Trotsky. Yes, but for 1812 . . .

CONTENTS

LIST OF ILLUSTRATIONS

. . .

Most of the portraits of Russian officers here shown were painted by the English artist George Dawe, with the help of two Russian assistants, Alexander Polyakov and Vassily Golike. Their 330 paintings of Russian officers involved in the campaign of 1812 hang in the War Gallery of the Winter Palace, in what was once St. Petersburg and is now called Leningrad. The photos were provided by the Bibliothèque Nationale's Cabinet des Estampes.

MAPS

THE WAR
OF THE TWO
EMPERORS

CHAPTER 1

ON THE EVE:
MARCH 1812

ONCE AGAIN it was snowing, the flakes falling with soft, cat's-paw soundlessness on the white carpet of the Neva. Spring this year was laggard, and given the abundance of late snowfalls, floods could be expected when the ice began to crack. Long since vanished were the frame-supported ice hills down which the fur-capped inhabitants of Petersburg liked to toboggan onto the yard-thick floor of the frozen river—makeshift products of the midwinter carnival festivities which traditionally preceded the start of the "austere" Lenten season, when marriages were banned and theater plays, replaced by concerts, were forbidden. But another month would have to pass before the ice, thawed by the swiftly lengthening daylight hours, would finally split with a loud report, and broad floes would begin to move slowly downstream toward the Gulf of Finland. For a full week at least, both banks would then resound with hollow thuds as broad chunks of loosened ice floating down from Lake Ladoga crunched noisily against each other or pounded against the granite quays. All traffic across the main branch of the estuary, which at its narrowest was almost three hundred yards wide, was then momentarily halted—save for those hardy souls who still ventured out upon the moving ice and sought to gain the opposite bank of the Vassilevsky Island by hopping nimbly from one slab to the next.

Finally would come the day, in early or mid May, when the cannons of the Peter and Paul Fortress would fire a few ritual rounds to indicate that the river once again was open to navigation. Rowboats large and small, many of them as colorfully festooned, canopied, and crewed as ornate Venetian gondolas, would replace the jingling horse-drawn sleighs that had slid back and forth across the ice during the cold midwinter months; the double windows would be removed from all public and private edifices, and the wealthier merchants and nobles would prepare to move, like the imperial family, to their park-surrounded dachas or palaces scattered over the north-bank islands of the isthmus or spread out along the southern, Bay of Finland, shore. Only in one respect would the brusque transition from winter to summer differ from what it usually was at this season. This year, 1812, the *Gosudar* (sovereign) of all the Russias would not be present to receive the glass of cold water that the governor of the Peter and Paul Fortress traditionally brought over and handed to him on the quayside before the Winter Palace. For long before then, Emperor Alexander would have left his capital to oversee the deployment of the six army corps (including the Imperial Guard) that were now arrayed along the Russian Empire's western border, in uneasy anticipation of a new war with France.

Probably no city in Europe, not even the Paris of Napoleon, had been more spectacularly expanded and embellished over the previous two decades. What, at such a stupendous cost in material and in human lives, Peter the Great had willfully begun and Catherine the Great no less ambitiously continued had by now been largely rounded out and completed by her grandson Alexander and the great princely families that had established new residences on the sea-fronting isthmus of the Neva. Some thirty months before, when the recently arrived American envoy, John Quincy Adams, had presented his credentials to the emperor, he had remarked that he hardly recognized the city in which he had spent a winter during the reign of Catherine II; that compared with New York and Philadelphia, elegant cities built to suit the simpler tastes of the citizens of a republic, Petersburg looked like a city of princes and was now indeed the most magnificent city in Europe, or for that matter, the world.

Nor was this said just to flatter the less widely traveled Emperor Alexander, who admitted somewhat ruefully that in his thirty-one years he had had occasion to visit but two foreign capitals—Berlin and Dresden. Even the normally phlegmatic British were moved to superlatives in trying to describe the impression made upon them by the "glory of the fairest city in the world." To the experienced artistic eye of Sir Robert Ker Porter, who came to paint portraits and naval battle scenes for the Grand Council Chamber of the new Admiralty building, London looked positively plain and shabby in comparison with Petersburg. "Such grandeur and symmetry in building, I never before beheld in any of the different capitals to which my fondness for travel has conducted me. Every house seems a palace, and every palace a city . . ."

The Russians, led by their emperor, were in the process of completing for their own country what Louis XIV of France had tentatively begun at Versailles: the construction of a new, carefully planned, broad-avenued court city. And whereas Versailles had never become more than a stately suburban appendage and grandiose country seat for the kings of France, to which favor-seeking nobles and their fan-wielding spouses could repair in carriages from their provincial châteaux or elegant townhouses in the traditional capital of Paris, Petersburg had become in every sense the residential center of Russia's administrative rulers, aristocrats, and traders.

Its grandest monument was the recently refaced Admiralty building, with its gilded spire and its jutting, statue-studded porches, whose stately white columns stood out in handsome contrast to the bright chrome-yellow stucco of its walls. Almost 400 meters long with wings reaching back 180 meters from the waterside promenade (known as the Angliskaya Naberezhna, or "English

Quay"), this huge edifice was more than twice as long as the rococo Winter Palace (a mere 152 meters long and 117 wide), to which Catherine the Great had added her more "intimate" Hermitage—itself large enough to contain three palace courts, a private theater, a profusion of winter gardens and flowering verandahs, and a collection of paintings (everything from Rembrandt, Rubens, and Van Dyke portraits to seascapes by Wouwerman) so vast that many of them had remained uncrated during her restless lifetime.

Petersburg now even boasted a cathedral, a neoclassical basilica with a pillared rotunda (inspired by Soufflot's Panthéon in Paris), which, unlike so many of the capital's other edifices, was entirely the work of Russian masons, stonecarvers, and sculptors, directed by a former serf named Voronikhin, who had been freed and sent abroad to study architecture by his kindly master, Count Serghei Stroganov. Just two weeks after the solemn consecration of the Cathedral of the Virgin Mother of Kazan, celebrated the previous September, the octogenarian count had suddenly died of pneumonia. His death, mourned by all who had known him, had also been treated as a national event.

Not long thereafter the extraordinary conjunction in the northern skies of two comets had aroused a holy dread in thousands of superstitious souls, who had crossed themselves as they scurried to the churches to light a candle and implore the mercy of the Almighty against the momentous calamities that the new year threatened to bring with it. In Petersburg's French-speaking high society, as in that of Paris, the start of the carnival season had been untroubled by such portents, even though the pre-Lenten gaiety enlivening the long winter nights had been seriously dampened long before it could reach its giddy climax during the traditional *masslenitsa* (Shrovetide) festivities. On the occasion of a parade held in front of the Winter Palace to honor Empress Elisabeth's thirty-fifth birthday, all of the officers of a battalion from an Imperial Foot-Guards Regiment had been placed under arrest for sloppy wheeling and maneuvering. By mid-February the mood of the capital had turned frankly glum, as two regiments left for Russia's western borders. The announcement that new taxes were being imposed provoked much grumbling and worried gossip about the prospects of a war with France.

Over the next four weeks eight more regiments left Petersburg. Their departure was expedited by the detailed information about French troop movements which the tsar's young aide-de-camp Count Alexander Chernyshov had recently brought with him from Paris. But by mid-March these were almost superfluous, so blatantly threatening had Napoleon's behavior grown. To the American minister, John Quincy Adams, whom he met during one of his early-morning walks along the granite quay, the emperor remarked sadly in French, "And so it is, after all, that war is coming which I have done so much to avoid."

Adams seemed surprised by the forthright pessimism of this forecast, coming from someone who normally expressed himself in far more cautious terms. "But are all hopes vanished of still preserving the peace?"

"At all events we shall not begin the war," replied the thirty-four-year-old emperor, a wan smile illuminating his ruddy cheeks, framed by reddish sideburns. "My will is yet to prevent it, but we expect to be attacked. . . . All the indications point to war. And then, HE"—he meant Napoleon—"keeps on advancing. He began by taking Swedish Pomerania, and now he has just occupied Prussia—he can't advance much farther without attacking us." A little later, in response to Adams's expressed hope that this eastward movement might somewhere stop, he added, "Ah yes, I fully hope that he won't come as far as here."

Perhaps never in the eleven years of his reign had the well-meaning, exquisitely well-bred, but somewhat insecure and irresolute tsar found himself more baffled by events he was unable to control than at this moment. Unlike his predecessors, he felt himself caught in the meshes of an international entanglement from which he could no longer escape. His shrewd grandmother Catherine the Great, while encouraging Austria and Prussia to strangle the revolutionary "bastard" in its cradle by attacking the young French Republic, had carefully refrained from committing any Russian forces to the First (anti-French) Coalition. His cranky father, Paul I, who had been the prime mover behind the formation of the Second Coalition in 1798, had managed to ally himself with Britain, Austria, Naples, Portugal, and the Ottoman Empire. The results had been a bitter disappointment: he had quarreled with the Austrians and the English and in a temperamental volte-face, had allied himself with France and had dispatched a horde of Cossack horsemen eastward in a crazy assault on British India (which had petered out in the steppes of Kazakstan). In 1805, when Alexander had joined the Third Coalition, Russia had had England, Austria, Sweden, and finally Prussia as allies. In terms of manpower and resources it should have been invincible. Instead, this alliance too had collapsed, shattered by Austerlitz and half a dozen later battles (from Jena to Friedland), which had brought Napoleon's soldiers to the very borders of the Russian Empire, along the river Niemen. If Russia had fared so badly when supported by an empire (Austria) and three important monarchies (England, Prussia, and Sweden), what hope was there now that she was isolated and alone, without a single ally?

Each attempt to extinguish the revolutionary élan that had made republican, then consular, and finally imperial France such a menace to the monarchical status quo in Europe seemed only to have made it more mighty and invincible. In 1806, when the Kingdom of Prussia had boldly flung down the gauntlet, it had been swiftly overrun by Napoleon's fast-moving soldiery, had lost half of its possessions and almost four and a half million subjects—to the dismay of its downcast sovereign, King Frederick William III, who now seemed ready to do almost anything, even to ally himself with the devil, to keep from losing his throne. The Austrians, who had tried to go it alone in 1809, had been defeated at Wagram; and since then, under the supremely opportunistic guidance of a cynical foreign minister, Prince Clemens Metternich, they had decided that it would be wiser to throw in their lot with the conqueror—the result being an extraordinary marriage, concocted in February 1810, between the Habsburg emperor's eighteen-year-old daughter, Marie-Louise, and a forty-year-old Napoleon. The Swedes, having had Finland torn from them by an invading Russian army in the spring of 1808, were still a potential threat. In the south some ten Russian divisions had been tied down for several years in a desultory war with the Turks, who might at any moment be encouraged by the French to try to regain the recently "liberated" Romanian provinces of Moldavia and Vallachia.

Finally there was England—England, against which Russia (yielding to French pressure) had made a token declaration of war in December 1807. Although it had been at war with France almost uninterruptedly for the past two decades, this island kingdom was more than ever an unknown quantity in any European equation. Its septuagenarian monarch, George III, was already in his dotage, while the Tory prime minister, Spencer Perceval, was confronted by a restive opposition, who blamed the country's economic woes on the continuation of a seemingly endless war. To some, it even looked as though Britain were about the go the way of revolutionary France, as bands of desperate "Luddite" textile workers, in Nottingham, Cheshire, Lancashire, and the Scottish lowlands, went on a rampage, pillaging houses, and smashing looms, frames, and other modern machinery, which had caused a massive glut of cheap manufactured goods for which there were no longer any markets, either at home or abroad.

Of the four thousand English bankers and merchants who had once inhabited the port of Kronstadt, at the mouth of the Petersburg isthmus, only a handful remained. The cordial relations that had existed between the two countries during the early years of Alexander's reign had never really recovered from the crisis of December 1805, when the British government had abruptly suspended its financial assistance (one and a quarter million pounds for every hundred thousand men the Russians could put into the field) after discovering that Alexander was ready to support Prussia's claim to Hanover —still officially a possession of the British Crown, although actually occupied by the French. Many were the Russians who now believed that whenever the English intervened militarily in northern Europe, it was invariably too little and too late. Admittedly, this island folk had at last produced a soldier of some merit—in the person of Arthur Wellesley, now Duke of Wellington—but he had yet to prove himself another Marlborough, still less a Nelson. He and his valiant expeditionary force had managed to save Lisbon behind the impregnable trenchworks of the Torres Vedras lines, and since then they had even advanced into Spain. But they had been unable to prevent the French from occupying Asturias and Valencia, nor had they been strong enough to keep Napoleon from withdrawing many of his finest regiments and commanders to serve in the multinational Grande Armée which, for the past twelvemonth and more, he had been steadily reinforcing and deploying for action in eastern Europe.

The mere fact that such an army could be formed at all was a token of Napoleon's steadily growing might. From a republic of close to ninety departments, which it had been in 1796, France had swollen into a Gargantuan empire of 130 departments, including fifteen in Italy, nine in Flanders and the Belgian lowlands, another six in Holland, ten in Germany, two in Switzerland,

and several more along the Dalmatian coast. Napoleon's oldest brother, the compliant Joseph, was now seated on the throne of Spain, while his youngest brother, Jerome, had been married to the king of Württemberg's daughter and given a new Kingdom of Westphalia (mostly composed of Hessians and Hanoverians) to administer. The most ambitious of his sisters, the delicately fair-skinned and rosy-cheeked, though somewhat squat-necked and broad-hipped Caroline—of whom Napoleon had once said that there was more political intelligence in her little finger than in the entire body of her swarthy, curly-haired husband, Joachim Murat—had become a truly Machiavellian queen of Naples. Pope Pius VII, who had dared to excommunicate Napoleon in 1809 after helping to crown him emperor in Notre-Dame cathedral five years earlier, was now a prisoner at Savona, on the Italian Riviera. The provinces of northern Italy that had belonged to the Austrian Habsburgs until the end of the previous century had been formed into a kingdom, ruled by a viceroy —Prince Eugène de Beauharnais, son of Napoleon's first empress, Josephine, by a previous marriage. Its sovereign, however, was Napoleon, who here too had decided to follow Charlemagne's example by assuming the iron crown of the Gothic kings of Lombardy, while the designated heir was the French emperor's infant son, the now barely one-year-old king of Rome. Piedmont, with its capital of Turin, had been incorporated into the French Empire, and its ruler, King Victor Emmanuel, had been forced to take refuge in Sardinia. A similar fate had overtaken the self-indulgent Bourbon monarch Ferdinand, king of the so-called Two Sicilies; he had had to abandon his magnificent palace at Caserta, near Naples, and flee with his hysterically anti-French wife, Queen Maria Carolina (sister of the tragically guillotined Marie-Antoinette of France), to Palermo, in Sicily, where they were protected by British frigates from the molestations of Napoleon's soldiery.

Along the French Empire's eastern borders, which now stretched down the Rhine from Basel to Cologne, and on to Hamburg, on the Elbe, no less than fourteen German duchies, principalities, and kingdoms, including Bavaria and Saxony, had been pressed into joining a Confederation of the Rhine, the rulers of which were pledged to levy fixed quotas of conscripted soldiers for potential service in Napoleon's Grande Armée. The Danes, being seafarers rather than landlubbers and having a distinctly Nordic, singsong language of their own, had not been forced to join this Germanic *Rheinbund;* but they had had to pay a bitter price for their loyalty to Napoleon—by having their fleet twice destroyed or captured by the British.

Nor was this all. Between the Oder and the Niemen a new Grand Duchy of Warsaw, of about four million souls, had been created from the Polish provinces that had recently been freed by the French from Prussian or Austrian rule. Nowhere in Europe were the inhabitants more rabidly pro-French and—as Tsar Alexander was chagrined to realize—so disturbingly anti-Russian.

That the map of Europe could have been so radically redrawn in half a dozen years seemed well-nigh miraculous. But then, had Alexander himself not once said to the French ambassador in Petersburg that that extraordinary man

Napoleon could accomplish in one year what it would take another individual twenty years or even a lifetime to complete? It required no particular sagacity to understand that these dazzling triumphs of war and diplomacy had been made possible by the disunity and lack of coordination of his enemies. Acting in real unison against him, they could long since have triumphed over him. Instead, they had acted in a hesitant and piecemeal fashion, and one after the other they had gone down in defeat. Now it seemed by an implacable fatality to be Russia's turn to have to go it alone against the greatest military power the continent of Europe had ever seen. It would be a war for which Russia was not properly prepared, but which, her sovereign felt, could no longer be avoided.

In Paris, some fourteen hundred miles to the west and south of Petersburg —a distance it then took a hard-driving courier a good two weeks to cover— the prevailing mood was less despondent, at any rate among the young, and those relatively privileged souls who were not totally absorbed in a daily struggle to keep body and soul together. Here the pre-Lenten carnival season had been more than usually carefree, in tune with the overconfident insouciance of so many young French officers, who seemed to think that the coming campaign against Russia was going to be as painless and enjoyable as a protracted hunting party. The mere thought that this was likely to be Napoleon's *last* campaign was enough to precipitate a wild scramble for aide-de-camp and junior general-staff posts on the part of the capital's *jeunesse dorée* and of less pampered students who had recently been graduated with distinction from the Ecole Polytechnique and other military schools. "We are leaving for Moscow; we'll be back soon!" was the general cry, uttered by young subalterns, some of whom laughingly declined the offer of a fur pélisse as "quite unnecessary." Possessed of a blind faith in their emperor's invincibility, they were ready to follow him, if necessary, to the ends of the earth. Quite a few, indeed, were persuaded that the main purpose of this expedition was not to make war against the Russians, but to force them and their reluctant emperor (with whom the French were still officially allied) to join them in an overland assault on India—the invasion of which, it was reckoned, would suffice to bring an obdurate Britain to her knees!

It would be too cut and dried to speak in this case of a "generation gap." But inevitably it was among the older and the wiser heads that the gravest misgivings were professed about this stupendous enterprise, far and away the most ambitious and demanding of Napoleon's momentous career. One of these wise skeptics, a former captain named Leclerc who had been assigned the task of preparing a demographic and statistical analysis of Russia, had had the temerity to predict that "if the emperor were to have his army penetrate into the interior of Russia, it would be annihilated, as was that of Charles XII [of Sweden] at Poltava, or forced into a precipitate retreat. I think that only the Russian can wage war in Russia."

Similar warnings were expressed by Jean-Jacques Régis de Cambacérès, the food-and-wine-loving bachelor who had helped to draft the Code Napoléon and who, as arch-chancellor, presided over the vitally important Council of State when the emperor was not present; by the sallow, hollow-cheeked, and distinctly saturnine Joseph Fouché, the former minister of police, who, though he had lost his job, had still retained his new title of duke of Otranto; and by the grand equerry of the imperial court, the somewhat austere but ruggedly honest General Armand de Caulaincourt, who had served for three and a half years as ambassador extraordinary in Petersburg but whom the French emperor had recently been cold-shouldering.

From the distant seaport of Danzig, on the Baltic, the already gray-haired and gray-whiskered Alsatian cavalryman Jean Rapp, who had been given the job of reinforcing this "northern Gibraltar," had with his usual bluntness given free rein to his misgivings, warning that anti-French secret societies were mushrooming all over Germany and that major trouble could be expected were Napoleon to suffer a reverse in Russia. A similar warning had been sent in by Count Jean-Jacques Beugnot, who had been sent as a kind of proconsul to Düsseldorf, at this time still a quaintly walled-in Gothic town overlooking the Rhine. Napoleon's youngest brother, the somewhat frivolous Jerome, had even felt obliged to leave his charming Residenz-Schloss at Kassel, where he had made his mark as a prodigal but not unpopular king of Westphalia, and to travel all the way to Paris in an abortive attempt to dissuade Napoleon from embarking on this fateful enterprise.

Of all these warning voices the most eloquent was probably that of Count Louis-Philippe de Ségur, an ancien régime aristocrat who was the living embodiment of that social "amalgam" (of nobles and bourgeois plebeians) which Napoleon had consciously sought to promote in order to heal the terrible wounds of the French Revolution. He had spent five years in Petersburg as Louis XVI's ambassador, and notwithstanding his young age, he had so charmed Catherine the Great by his lively wit that she had invited him to accompany her on her famous journey to the Crimea in 1787. Since 1804 he had been the grand master of ceremonies of Napoleon's imperial Court, an honorific post that was normally devoid of any real political significance. But when consulted about the feasibility of waging another war against the Russians, Ségur had freely spoken his mind. The kind of whirlwind campaign that Napoleon had so brilliantly conducted since 1805—in which fast-moving armies regularly outstripped their slower-moving baggage trains—had turned his soldiers into marauders, and this had aroused an intense hatred of the French throughout Germany. It was an illusion to believe that such grievances could be forgotten overnight. Yet here he was, proposing to establish the longest line of communications ever, across a sullen, restive land which could suddenly erupt with volcanic force behind him and his advancing army. And what could be the purpose of these never-ending wars, which led to the dethronement of established kings and their replacement by lieutenants who, like Alexander the Great's generals, were sooner or later bound to shake themselves free, thereby undermining the very empire Napoleon was bent on consolidating? Whereas the Russians would be fighting for their homeland and their national independence, all the French would be fighting for would be an added glory. Already they were losing their sense of national identity in an ever-expanding conglomeration in which customs, habits, and languages were hopelessly mixed up. "One cannot extend oneself in this way without weakening oneself, for if France were ever to become Europe, there would no longer be a France." The mere departure of the emperor on this distant enterprise was going to leave France "solitary, deserted, without a leader, without an army, accessible to any diversion. Who will then defend her?"

"My renown!" was Napoleon's immediate rejoinder. "I leave behind my name and with it the fear an armed nation inspires." And with that he was off again on what by now had become a well-rehearsed oration—to the effect that, being master of the fortresses of Stettin, Küstrin, Glogau, Torgau, Magdeburg, etc., he held Prussia in his iron grip, while the marriages he had contracted with the reigning houses of Baden, Württemberg, Bavaria, and Austria had firmly tied all of these states to France.

None of these proffered warnings had been able to shake Napoleon's confident conviction that, if it ever came to that, he could win a "quick war" with Russia. He dismissed the prospect of a mass uprising beyond the Rhine, comparing the Germans to "little dogs that bark but do not bite." As a race, the Germans were too stolid, too cautious and methodical in their Teutonic ways to pose a serious threat. Their phlegmatic character, he never tired of repeating, differed radically from that of the fanatical Spaniards, of the "ferocious Catalonians."

As for the Russians, they had to be taught a lesson once and for all, for having gone on trading with the English in brazen defiance of the boycott provisions of the Continental System, and for having added insult to injury by imposing a heavy tax on the import of French luxury products. This was no way for an "ally" to behave in what was supposed to be a common struggle to force the British to end their war with France and to recognize the freedom of the seas for ships of all nations. Several times already Napoleon had roundly defeated the Russians on the field of battle, and if he could not bring their mulish and at the same time devious emperor back to the negotiating table, then he would trounce them once again, hurling the Russians "back into Asia" —so that they could no longer throw their weight around, as they had recently been doing, and would cease to dictate policy to the frightened states of central Europe.

In January, when news had reached him that the duke of Wellington had just forced the defending French to surrender the town of Ciudad Rodrigo, considered by the Spaniards to be the key to Portugal, and by the Portuguese to be the key to Spain, Napoleon had refused to be impressed. From the very outset the fighting in the Iberian peninsula, because of its irregular guerrilla-warfare character, had struck him as being a messy business and little more than a question of "pacifying" and "policing," which he preferred to leave to certain of his marshals and generals. Spain, formerly governed by a worthless Bourbon monarch who had been easily deposed, and not having an army worthy of the name, could not be regarded as a military power, while Wellington's expeditionary force, though admittedly a nuisance, had too often been beset by shortages of money, munitions, and food supplies to constitute a serious threat to his empire and its continental alliances.

Russia, however, was different. It was a strongly constituted state, with a popular emperor and an aristocratic officer corps that controlled an army which, next to the French, was perhaps the foremost in Europe. Against such a foe it was possible to fight a *guerre des braves* and to win a clear-cut victory. Stubborn and devious though he had shown himself to be, his imperial "brother," Alexander, was not lacking in common sense; he was a chivalrous being who, when confronted by an unprecedented massing of military might, would surely "see the light." That the coming war might not end even before it had begun, that it might not be solved through a quick lightning stroke, that it might indeed drag on and ultimately degenerate into the messy, unclean, ungentlemanly kind of warfare that had so baffled and exasperated his troops in Spain, was a prospect the French emperor imperiously dismissed from his mind as unthinkable.

And so during this month of March 1812, Napoleon's couriers kept leaving Paris, galloping north and east toward Germany, and even southward to Prince Eugène de Beauharnais's headquarters in Milan, with orders that were intended to coordinate the complex movements of the greatest military force that anyone since Hannibal had sought to muster on the continent of Europe.

New forces were recalled from Spain, including four Regiments of the Vistula, which had been engaged south of the Pyrenees for the past three to four years. Not a few of their Polish officers and soldiers frankly regretted having to say good-bye to the bright blue skies, the neatly irrigated orange and lemon groves, the strong red wine, the dazzling white teeth and black mantillas of the smiling damsels of Valencia and Murcia. Though they were now home-ward-bound, they already knew that their ultimate destination was Russia, and it filled some of them with frank forebodings. Old-timers who had seen action against the Russians at Pultusk, Ostrolenka, Eylau, and Friedland—in the winter, spring, and early summer of 1807—said that the sieges and battles they had had to fight at Teruel, Santa Fe, Tudela, and Sagunto were like "children's games" in comparison. "Now we shall see who really are the soldiers and who are not," declared General Chlopicki, the veteran commander of one of these regiments.

On March 21 they finally reached Versailles, after a six-week march which had taken them across the uplands of Aragon and Navarre and over the Pyrenees to Bordeaux. In Versailles they had no time for sightseeing, for the very next day they had to march into Paris to be reviewed by Napoleon. It was a crisp spring day, agreeably warmed by a still low-circling sun. The paved square of the Carrousel, which then separated the Louvre from the Tuileries Palace to the west, was filled to overflowing with carriages as well as troops, as they marched in, looking as smart as they could, with their frayed and tattered cloaks carefully rolled up above their packs. Among the ladies gathered on the palace balcony, they had no trouble recognizing the young blond empress, Marie-Louise, whose high-bodiced Austrian plumpness was offset by her above-average height. Standing conspicuously nearby, his brocaded uniform agleam with diamond-studded star-clusters, was the Russian ambassador, Prince Alexander Kurakin, who talked incessantly to the ladies and paid not the slightest attention to the parade.

Finally Napoleon appeared, dressed in the blue-and-white uniform he normally wore in Paris. He looked distinctly dumpy next to his chief of staff, Alexandre Berthier, his Polish aide-de-camp, Vicenz Krasinski, and the other generals of his suite. Frequently pausing, as was his wont, to interrogate a decorated officer or soldier, he stopped in front of Lieutenant Heinrich von Brandt (who has left us a detailed description of the scene) and asked him how often he had been wounded.

The reply was "Twice, along with a contusion"—caused by the bruising passage of a cannonball.

"Fine," commented Napoleon. "You are still young, later you will be a captain."

Farther on he stopped to ask a Polish soldier where it was that he had managed to grow so fat. His aide-de-camp, Krasinski, had to translate the question.

"In France," replied the stout Polish trooper.

"*Très bien.*" Napoleon nodded. "You did well to stuff yourself. For the time will come," he added, addressing himself to the assembled company, "when you will all have to fast."

Of all Napoleon's prophecies, uttered on the eve of an evitable war, which even he would have preferred to avoid, this one, at least, was to be fulfilled to the letter.

CHAPTER 2

PETERSBURG AND THE
POLISH POWDER KEG

IN MARCH 1801, when the twenty-three-year-old Alexander had suddenly found himself entrusted with the destiny of his vast empire, probably no one in Europe could have foreseen the tortuous ups and downs through which Franco-Russian relations would have to pass, still less the dramatic climax of 1812. In Petersburg, as in virtually all of Europe's princely Courts and capitals, the First French Republic was commonly regarded as a historical aberration, a crime perpetrated by revolutionary hotheads against the God-ordained monarchical order of things, which would as surely come to grief as had Cromwell's short-lived dictatorship in England.

This sentiment was only partly shared by the young tsar, an almost schizophrenic embodiment of the conflicts and contradictions of this tempestuous, topsy-turvy epoch. In his youth—he was born the day before Christmas of 1777 —his strong-willed grandmother Catherine the Great had given him a Swiss tutor, Frédéric-César La Harpe, who had taught the somewhat indolent young prince to revere the republican virtues of ancient Greece and Rome. This was during the twilight years of the ancien régime, when Catherine—like the Austrian emperor, Joseph II, and other "enlightened despots"—was flirting with the liberal ideas propounded by Voltaire, Diderot, Melchior Grimm, and the French *philosophes*. But after 1793—the fateful watershed year which saw the guillotining in Paris of Louis XVI and Marie-Antoinette—Catherine had jettisoned all of her earlier liberal enthusiasms (which at one point had moved her to consider the possibility of doing away with serfdom) and had declared an imperious anathema on all dangerous "new ideas." A disheartened La Harpe had been told to pack his bags and return to his native Geneva.

This abrupt about-face in ideology, combined with Alexander's precocious marriage to the sensitive, romantically inclined Princess Luisa of Baden, had left him with a deplorably unfinished education at the still-malleable age of sixteen: a circumstance aggravated by the crazy behavior of his Prussian-admiring father, who, after his accession to the throne as Emperor Paul I in November 1796, had gone Catherine the Great one better by declaring war on all forms of "modernism." During his erratic four-year reign, watchmen armed with long sticks had been ordered to patrol the streets of Petersburg and to knock the round hats from the heads of carelessly clad strollers—this new "plebeian" form of headdress being regarded, along with top boots, frock coats, pantaloons, and straight-across-the-forehead hairlines, as subversive imports from revolutionary France. Any courtier daring to appear before His Imperial Majesty with his wig improperly powdered ran the risk of being dismissed from his post and banished to his lands in the country, or, if he was less fortunate, to the western confines of Siberia.

Four years of wildly capricious rule, which saw some twelve thousand Russians arrested and punished for the most trivial misdemeanors, had been enough to open the young Alexander's eyes to the evils of "unenlightened despotism." The deplorable as well as predictable result had been one more palace revolution, which reached its grim climax during the night of March 23–24, 1801, when a group of Court officials and Guards officers, led by a general of Hanoverian origin named Levin Bennigsen, had pushed their way into Emperor Paul's bedroom in his new Mikhailovsky Palace—its façade recently repainted a garish red, as though in anticipation of his gory end—had knocked him to the ground with one of his heavy snuffboxes, and then had strangled him with his own silk scarf.

That this macabre murder had a traumatic impact on Alexander's impressionable mind, there can be no doubt. For years thereafter he lived under the oppressive fear that he too might suffer the fate that had overtaken his father, and also his grandfather (Emperor Peter III, deposed and later murdered in another palace plot, masterminded by Catherine the Great in 1762), if he failed to retain the loyal support of the leading nobles of the realm. This was greatly to affect his dealings with Napoleon. But it is no less true that, once he had recovered from the initial shock, Alexander came to view his father's murder as a necessary evil. The ecstatic behavior of his subjects, who danced, sang, and embraced each other in the streets when they heard news of their "deliverance," offered dramatic proof of how universally detested the cranky, unstable Paul had been. For days the boyish new emperor—as tall, statuesque, rosy-cheeked, blue-eyed, beautifully mannered, and benevolent as his father had been short, sallow-faced, simian, pug-nosed, rude, and irascible—was mobbed by rapturous subjects. He could not go for a stroll along the Neva quay or over the well-raked alleys of the Summer Garden without having his shoes and garments kissed. This too was an unforgettable experience. "Anarchy succeeded the strictest of reigns," Countess Varvara Golovine, one of the ladies-in-waiting of his Court, was later to recall. "Costumes of all kinds reappeared. The carriages raced wildly back and forth. I myself saw a hussar officer gallop along the quayside pavement, shouting, 'At present one can do what one wants!' This change was frightening, but it was merely founded on the extreme confidence that was inspired by the new emperor's kindness. . . . Never was the start of a reign more brilliant."

In France, too, another reign had got off to a brilliant start: that of a dynamic Corsican general who seemed bent on consolidating a republican regime founded on the humanitarian ideals of liberty, financial equity, and equality before the law. For Alexander, as for his former tutor, La Harpe, France's First Consul was an essentially stabilizing element who had put an end to the feverish demagogy, mob rule, and revolutionary agitation which had kept Europe in a turmoil for close to a decade.

The sheer romantic excess of this admiration doubtless explains the violence of Alexander's reaction when he learned that his hero, Bonaparte, had had himself elected Consul for life in August of 1802. The sweeping plebiscite endorsing this change—with more than 3.5 million Frenchmen voting for it, over and against 8,374 No's—did nothing to mitigate the former hero-worshipper's sense of grievous disappointment. As he wrote to his idealistic mentor, the equally disillusioned La Harpe, ". . . the veil is now fallen. Since then, things have gone from bad to worse. He has begun by depriving himself of the finest glory reserved to a human being and which alone remained to be plucked: that of proving that he had worked, without any personal view, solely for the happiness and glory of the fatherland, and, faithful to the constitution to which he had sworn allegiance, to relinquish after ten years the power that was in his hands. Instead of that, he has preferred to ape the Courts while violating the constitution of his country. Now he is one of the most egregious tyrants History has produced."

Coming from someone who was officially a *samoderzhets*—an autocrat responsible to no parliament, who had no constitution to contend with—this sweeping anathema was a curious condemnation. It reflected the Anglophilic sentiments of Alexander's closest political advisers. Being, all of them, from wealthy land-owning families, they were suspicious of the republican "experiment" in France, far too radical and Jacobin to inspire any long-standing confidence, and were more favorably disposed toward England, to them a model of the orderly, aristocratic, parliamentary system of government that they would have liked to see progressively introduced in Russia.

Had Alexander been a person of greater mental toughness and consistency, he would not have let himself be deflected from the main task he had set himself at the start of his reign: that of reforming a chaotic system of administration and of modernizing his vast country in other ways. Russia at this time was a heterogeneous empire of 35 million to 40 million souls, 90 percent of whom were more or less illiterate peasant serfs who were dependent in one way or another on the bounty of their masters, or, as was more often the case, on the cruel whims of their bailiffs, who acted as both tax collectors and recruiters. Since the time of Peter the Great, the first European monarch to introduce a rudimentary form of military conscription (to bolster the regular, partly mercenary army), these peasants had been made to pay an unpopular "soul tax" (usually levied on the proceeds of their harvests) and had been subjected to an even more detested, though extremely haphazard, manpower draft. Russia, though it already extended as far as the Pacific, bordering on the "Middle Kingdom" of the Manchus and the empire of the Persian shahs, had virtually no manufacturing industry, save for a few foundries, arsenals, and cotton mills. Its middle class, compared with those that had enriched Prussia, France, and

Britain, was embryonic, and for much of its trade and commerce it was still dependent on German (and other) merchants in Moscow, and on English traders and bankers in St. Petersburg. So backward and inefficient was a system of government based almost exclusively on the caprices of Court favoritism that, prior to Alexander's accession to the throne, the empire had been haphazardly administered without any clearly defined ministries.

Painfully aware though he was of all that needed to be done, Alexander was by nature hesitant, discreet, diplomatic, and he lacked the will to introduce reforms with the savage impetus of a Peter the Great. Like Hamlet, he also seems to have felt that rightly to be great means greatly to find quarrel in a straw. The straw in this case was one of those trifling accidents that can derail an entire historical process.

The abduction of the duc d'Enghien, in March of 1804, was one more episode in a series of more or less violent incidents that had marked the uncertain progress of the First French Republic. On Christmas Eve of 1800 Napoleon Bonaparte, his wife, Josephine, and her daughter (by a previous marriage), Hortense de Beauharnais, had narrowly escaped death when a barrel filled with gunpowder was detonated near their passing carriages as they were being driven to a concert at the Paris opera house. The attempted assassination was thought to have been masterminded by the late Louis XVI's brother, the comte d'Artois, and other ancien régime émigrés living in England, who were hoping to overthrow the Consulate and restore the Bourbon monarchy. In February 1804 another plot, fomented by Breton royalists and again financed by the British, was uncovered before it could mature. The resulting police inquiry indicated that a key role in this new conspiracy was to be played by a Bourbon prince, who was to proceed posthaste to Paris once Bonaparte had been assassinated and to proclaim the restoration of the monarchy. This scheming Bourbon, Napoleon was given to understand, by his foreign minister, Talleyrand, and others, was the young duc d'Enghien, sole surviving grandson of Prince Louis-Joseph de Condé, who had led the ill-fated "Army of the Princes," which had tried to invade France from its base in the German Rhineland in 1792. An attractive auburn-haired officer who had served with Suvorov's forces in Italy, the thirty-one-year-old Louis-Antoine de Condé-Bourbon, now known as the duc d'Enghien, had established residence in the Rhineland castle of Ettenheim, where he spent his time hunting and flirting, making occasional trips to Strasbourg and others to the Baden capital of Karlsruhe, where he was very much *persona grata* to Princess Amélie (mother of Empress Elisabeth of Russia).

Determined to put a stop to all this British-financed plotting, Bonaparte in mid-March of 1804 ordered one of his generals to proceed at once to Strasbourg and to seize the suspect prince. Rowed across the Rhine during the dead of night, some three hundred French dragoons surrounded the castle of Ettenheim, dragged the protesting prince from his bedroom, and brought him to Strasbourg, from where he was dispatched in a well-guarded carriage to Paris. Napoleon had originally intended to have him locked up as a kind of hostage and as a warning to his Bourbon enemies; but yielding to the pleas of his impetuous brother-in-law Joachim Murat, who argued that exemplary punishment had to be meted out to deter his scheming foes, Napoleon agreed to let the duc d'Enghien be summarily tried and condemned by a military tribunal for attempting to undermine the French state by fomenting civil war. With equal dispatch the young Bourbon prince was executed by a firing squad at two-thirty in the morning of March 21, 1804, in the waterless moat of the fortress of Vincennes, in the eastern outskirts of Paris.

This hasty judicial murder unleashed an extraordinary wave of indignation in all the capitals of Europe, but nowhere more so than in Petersburg. The fact that Bonaparte had callously violated the territorial integrity of Baden, still a constituent part of the Germanic Empire and linked by marriage ties to the Russian imperial family, reinforced the already well-entrenched conviction that France's First Consul was an unprincipled bandit. Alexander, who had been charmed by the young Bourbon prince's unaffected ways when they had met seven years before in Petersburg, regarded his execution as a personal affront. His delicate wife, Empress Elisabeth, broke down and wept when she heard the news, as did her much tougher-minded mother-in-law, Dowager Empress Maria Feodorovna. A full week of mourning was prescribed for the Russian Court.

But for the accidental fact that the duc d'Enghien was kidnapped from the principality of Baden, with which the tsar was linked by marriage, it is doubtful if Russia would have displayed such readiness to sign treaties with Austria (November 1804), Sweden (January 1805), and England (April 1805), which forged a new anti-French coalition.

The Russian foreign minister at this time was the thirty-one-year-old Adam Czartoryski, a distinguished Polish prince whose almost equine features—a long nose, arched eyebrows, heavy-lidded eyes, and determined mouth muscles —were as sharply cut, resolute, and faintly sardonic as his friend Alexander's were softly contoured, luminous, and bland. As the most forceful, though not the most successful, of Alexander's foreign ministers, he deserves a special mention; for it was he, more than any other, who pushed Russia into participating in the campaign that led to the crucial battle of Austerlitz—the first act in a drama which reached its tragic climax in Moscow in the autumn of 1812.

Although Russia, under Czartoryski's guidance, played a leading role in the formation of the Third anti-French Coalition, Napoleon could still not bring himself to believe that Tsar Alexander was implacably opposed to him. Unlike his subtle foreign minister, the elegantly silk-stockinged Charles Maurice de Talleyrand-Périgord, who had been trying to persuade him to buy off Austria's hostility by offering her emperor, Francis I, extensive acquisitions in the Balkans as compensation for the territories France had freed from Habsburg rule in northern Italy, Napoleon clung stubbornly to his conviction that Russia, rather than Austria, was France's natural ally in Europe. There was no good reason why the Russians and the French, situated as they were at the opposite confines of the continent, should be fighting each other, since there were no territorial conflicts dividing them; and if the idealistically inclined Alexander seemed so unfavorably disposed toward France, it was, Napoleon felt, because the young Russian emperor had succumbed to the baleful influence of ministers and courtiers who had been bribed by English agents in Petersburg into assuming an attitude of intransigent hostility toward him and his regime. This, it is pertinent to add, was to remain an idée fixe with Napoleon, despite much evidence to the contrary, fatally influencing his behavior in 1812.

Twice during the month of November 1805, which preceded the battle of Austerlitz, Napoleon sent one of his aides-de-camp, General René Savary, to propose a peace parley and a personal meeting between the Russian and French emperors. The offers were contemptuously greeted by the younger members of Alexander's entourage—a coterie of splendidly epauleted, chest-decorated dandies who made no secret of their scorn for the older, battle-hardened veterans, led by the paunchy, one-eyed General Mikhail Hilarionovich Kutuzov, who were cautiously suggesting that it would be wiser to wait for reinforcements before engaging the French, particularly since the Prussians had recently agreed to join the fray. Spoiling for battle, these young hotheads were convinced that they could thrash the living daylights out of Bonaparte's overrated Frenchmen and gallop on triumphantly into Paris!

Four days later the young Russian hotheads who had been so cocksure that the outnumbered French would be a pushover were galloping wildly away from the corpse-strewn battleground of Austerlitz in a disorderly retreat toward the east. The wary Kutuzov, who had vainly counseled caution, had received another wound—this time in the cheek—and Alexander himself had seen several of his officers bite the snow when their horses were shot out from under them. His own famous chestnut mare had almost thrown him from the saddle when an incoming French cannonball had spattered both of them with slush. As the magnitude of the disaster began to dawn on him, he had broken down and wept, saying, "We are infants, in the hands of a giant!"

One of Napoleon's first actions, after the battle was over, was to dispatch a particularly distinguished prisoner—Colonel Repnin, of the Russian Imperial Guard—with a personal message to Alexander. "Tell him that if he had heeded my proposals and accepted an interview between our outposts, I would have submitted myself to his lovely soul. He would have declared to me his intentions to give Europe a respite, and I would have agreed to them." Alexander was invited to send a plenipotentiary to Vienna (now occupied by the French), but it had to be some responsible person, "not one of those courtiers who make up his general staff. The truth is [kept] distant from sovereigns," Napoleon concluded. "Alexander was born for the throne; I myself reached it, and my former comrades, my present-day commanders, no longer dare tell it to me"—that is, the truth.

This extraordinary message, expressing a continuing confidence in Alexander's idealistic magnanimity and a profound distrust of his Anglophilic advisers, never reached its destination. By the time Repnin had galloped into the cathedral town of Olmütz, Alexander was on his way across the Carpathian mountains, bound for distant Petersburg. Adam Czartoryski, who had vainly sought to dissuade the young Russian emperor from assuming personal charge of military operations, simply pocketed the message and let the matter die.

The offhand treatment of this olive branch, tendered by Napoleon for a third time, had two far-reaching consequences. To begin with, it excluded Russia from the peace-making process—in effect a new Napoleonic order—which the victor of Austerlitz was intent on imposing upon Europe. With his capital, Vienna, occupied by the French, the crestfallen Habsburg emperor, Francis, was forced to swallow the humiliating Treaty of Pressburg, signed the day after Christmas of 1805, which put an end to the Holy Roman Empire, stripped Austria of its Adriatic possessions in Venetia, Istria, and Dalmatia, recognized the title Napoleon had recently assumed as king of Italy, and made monarchs of the prince-electors of Bavaria and Württemberg.

The other, no less momentous, consequence was to revive a war that could easily have been ended without further upsetting the status quo in central and eastern Europe. The key factor here was Prussia, which at this time was ruled by the thirty-five-year-old Frederick William III, a shy, solemn-faced monarch who was even more hesitant, insecure, and vacillating than his friend Alexander of Russia. So inarticulate in his mode of speech that he tended to speak in infinitives—his favorite word, typically enough, was *kalmieren* (to calm)—he was a chronic fence-straddler whose fearful disposition seemed to have found facial expression in the diminutive split-triangle mustache separating the overly long nose from the oafish mouth.

In Berlin a powerful pro-French faction, led by the king's private secretary, felt that there was much to be gained by making a private deal with Napoleon. A rapprochement with France would enable Prussia to consolidate its grip on northern Germany by taking over Hanover, with the permission of the French, who had overrun it in their continuing war with the English, and by annexing the stretch of Pomeranian coast running from Greifswald to the mouth of the Oder, which still belonged to the Swedish Crown. This prospect was particularly appealing to Frederick William III—that dedicated "man of peace"—since it promised a significant aggrandizement of Prussian territories without the necessity of firing a shot.

Radically different and of a far more determined disposition was Frederick William's wife, Luise, an ardent supporter of the "war party" in Berlin, which was all for pushing Bonaparte back into the "mire" from which he had emerged. Regarded by the Prussian war party as responsible through his devious inertia for the defeat of Austerlitz, the guilt-stricken Frederick William III spent the spring and summer of 1806 fussing and fretting indecisively in the despairing hope that Napoleon would agree to hand over Hanover as a price for his ambiguous neutrality. But when he realized that Napoleon did not value him highly enough to make him such a present, indeed, that he was quite prepared to have Hanover returned to British rule in exchange for peace with England, the frustrated Prussian king yielded to the clamor of the war hawks in Berlin. In September he finally gave the signal, launching his country into a reckless assault on Napoleon's forces in southern Germany.

Three devastating defeats followed—first at Saalfeld, then at Jena, and finally at Auerstädt, where Marshal Louis Nicolas Davout utterly routed Blücher's famous Red Hussars, hitherto regarded as the finest cavalrymen in Europe. Shortly afterward Berlin was occupied by the victorious French, as was every other Prussian fortress except Danzig (which managed to hold out for six more months). By early December French cavalrymen and soldiers were triumphantly trotting and marching into Warsaw, where they were hailed as liberators by a deliriously happy populace.

To understand why this introduced a new and profoundly unsettling element into French-Russian relations, one must go back for a moment to the first half of the eighteenth century, when the Kingdom of Poland, with twelve million inhabitants, was still an independent, though turbulent, state. This kingdom, which in the fifteenth century had been the most extensive in Europe, had originally been forged from the union of two entities—the Crown lands of Poland proper and the even more extensive Grand Ducal territories of Lithuania. As a result of the three partitions of Poland—which a ruthless Catherine II of Russia had embarked upon with the cynical Frederick the Great in 1772 and had completed with his successor, King Frederick William II of Prussia, in 1793 and 1795—the enormously expanded Russian Empire had absorbed all of Lithuania, the northern hump-shaped Duchy of Courland, Polish Livonia, and Ruthenia, as well as the more southern, Ukraine-bordering provinces of Volhynia and Podolia. To the Austrians—on the whole, the least predatory and greedy of the three butchers—had gone the southern Polish provinces of Galicia, while the Prussians took possession of the traditional Polish Crown lands, including the autonomous seaport of Danzig (until then a kind of "free state" near the mouth of the Vistula) and the capital at Warsaw. Thus 140,000 square kilometers of Polish lands had been absorbed into the greatly enlarged Kingdom of Prussia, whose population rose dramatically from six to nine million—with the result that from then on one "Prussian" in every three was in reality a Pole.

What Adam Czartoryski had most feared in the early autumn of 1805, and had vainly sought to avert by trying to persuade Alexander to espouse the Polish national cause, was now consummated sixteen months later by Napoleon and the French. From all parts of the previously Prussian-ruled territories, Polish noblemen came streaming into Warsaw, eager to offer their services and to raise battalions and regiments of peasant troops for the French. Within weeks a Polish army was being formed under the grudgingly accepted leadership of Prince Joseph Poniatowski, nephew of the country's last king, and by early February of 1807 a provisional Polish administration was beginning to function in what was soon to become the Grand Duchy of Warsaw.

This momentous development not only shattered the fragile status quo in central Europe; it in effect undermined Napoleon's long-cherished hope of befriending Russia and its seemingly enlightened emperor. Hitherto there had been no serious territorial issue to divide the two countries. But from now on the troubling question of Poland's future was to poison the climate of friendship Napoleon would have liked to establish between his and Alexander's empire. More than any of the other provisions contained in the treaty that was signed in July of 1807, the establishment of the Grand Duchy of Warsaw turned the "peace of Tilsit" into an armed truce—one that finally collapsed in blazing ruins in June of 1812.

After the inconclusive snow-blinding battle of Preussisch-Eylau—fought in early February 1807 between the French and the Russians (supported by a small Prussian contingent)—many Russian Guards officers, led by their commander, Grand Duke Constantine, began arguing that there was no point in continuing a war that was being fought not to defend any vital Russian interests, but for the king of Prussia and even more for the beautiful blue eyes of his lovely Queen Luise. The grumblings rose to a clamor four months later, after the crushing defeat of Friedland, which cost the Russians twenty thousand more casualties. Danzig, after a long siege, had finally surrendered; the East Prussian capital of Koenigsberg had been hastily evacuated by its sovereign before being invested by the French; and the only unconquered territory of this once far-flung kingdom was a tiny tongue of coastal land extending northward toward Memel, where a panicky Frederick William III and the crestfallen remnants of his court were now lodged in distinctly cramped quarters. It was the Prussians, more than anyone else, who had egged on the "slow and incompetent" General Bennigsen, encouraging him to take the offensive against Napoleon, and the result had been a disaster. But so far the French had not set foot on Russian imperial soil.

At Alexander's military headquarters in the little Lithuanian town of Olita, now teeming with a multinational swarm of English, Swedish, Prussian, and French émigré officers and civilian officials, the impulsive Grand Duke Constantine (who had inherited some of his father's mercurial instability as well as of his pug-nosed ugliness) heatedly upbraided his brother in French—a language all present could understand: "If you do not wish to make peace with France, then give a loaded pistol to each of your soldiers and ask them to blow their brains out! You will obtain the same result as will a new and final battle, which will unfailingly open the gates of your empire to French troops, trained for battle and always victorious."

With what was left of his army now profoundly demoralized and weakened by the antagonisms of rival generals, Alexander felt obliged to heed his younger brother's advice. But it was galling to have to open negotiations with a man whom the Synod of the Russian Orthodox Church had publicly stigmatized in an unprecedented barrage of homilies and sermons as "the raving foe of mankind," a worshipper of "idols and whores," a friend of Mahometans and Jews who was now bent on having himself recognized and hailed as a new Messiah!

The extraordinary meetings that followed with the world's foremost self-made man were so fantastic that the young tsar wondered at times if he was not dreaming. For the sake of face-saving protocol, the first encounter had to take place on "neutral" ground. A barge was accordingly constructed and attached by ropes to one of the central piles of the recently destroyed wooden bridge across the Niemen. Here, after being rowed from their respective banks, the two emperors met for an exclusive tête-à-tête conversation in the larger of two pavilions, one side of which was decorated with an ornate green *A* (for Alexander), the other with an ornate green *N* (for Napoleon). We have Alexander's word for it that during those two hours he was so transfixed by the piercing glance of Napoleon's bright blue-gray eyes that he frequently had to avert his own. Napoleon, for his part, was favorably impressed by the Russian emperor, half a head taller than himself, who in addition to being "right handsome, good and young," as he wrote to his wife, Empress Josephine, "is more quick-witted than is commonly thought."

After a second meeting on the style-cramping barge, the little East Prussian town of Tilsit, on the river's left bank, was declared to be neutral territory, and the two emperors moved into their allotted areas with their Court officials, generals, aides-de-camp, Guards officers, and sentinels. To Alexander's plea that Frederick William III be included in the peace negotiations, Napoleon readily assented. The disconsolate Prussian monarch was allowed to take up residence in a disused mill on the outskirts of the town of which he was still the titular ruler.

From the substantive negotiations—conducted for the French by Talleyrand and for the Russians by Princes Kurakin and Lobanov-Rostovsky—the Prussians were quite simply excluded. Nor did Napoleon, who had developed a withering contempt for Prussia and its lackluster ruler, let himself be disarmed by the blond beauty of the lovely Queen Luise, who was hastily summoned from Memel and allowed to attend several banquets, where she vainly pleaded for a less harsh treatment of her downtrodden country.

Throughout the negotiations, which lasted two weeks, the Prussian monarch was pointedly excluded from the long after-dinner talks which Alexander and Napoleon carried on alone in their respective residences into the wee hours of each morning. His imagination fired by his mesmeric ability to fascinate his young imperial "brother," Napoleon made sweeping promises, encouraging him to conquer Swedish-ruled Finland. Alexander was also invited to help himself to large chunks of the Turkish-occupied Balkans along the Black Sea littoral, in exchange for the recognition of French supremacy in the Adriatic regions. Nor was this division of the Ottoman Empire's European possessions to stop there. For if their common enemy, the British, refused to accept their new alliance and to make peace at last, then, declared Napoleon, in a particularly visionary flight of fancy, they should extend this partition to the Turkish sultan's Asiatic lands and mount a joint assault on British India!

Although Alexander was frankly skeptical about the feasibility of this extraordinary scheme for "bringing England to her knees," his vanity was flattered by the privileged treatment he was accorded by the emperor of the French. "God has saved us," he wrote in almost rhapsodic terms to his nineteen-year-old sister, Catherine. "In the midst of sacrifices we emerge from the struggle with a kind of luster."

The giddy euphoria of the moment did not last long. Officers and soldiers of the elite Preobrazhensky Guards Regiment, who had been given the task of protecting their emperor at Tilsit, made little effort to hide their feelings of hostility toward the French, refusing to follow the example of the flighty Grand Duke Constantine, who was soon on such good terms with the dashing Joachim Murat that he had his tailor cut him a pair of Cossack breeches, in which the plume-and-braid-loving cavalryman could swagger around with his usual panache. In Russia the prevailing reaction was one of shocked bewilderment. When the news began to filter back that their beloved *Batiushka* (Little Father) had agreed to meet the detested "Antichrist" on a raft in the middle of the river, the idea seemed so preposterous to many peasants that word spread that the encounter had been thus arranged so that the "heathen" Bonaparte could undergo a cleansing baptismal immersion in the river waters before being allowed to appear before their sovereign.

Far from permitting Russia to advance its western border as far as the Vistula—as Alexander's sister Catherine and other optimists in Petersburg had fondly hoped—the Treaty of Tilsit, which was largely the work of Talleyrand (no friend of the Russians), established a new Grand Duchy of Warsaw, composed of the four Polish provinces Prussia had acquired through the partitions of the previous century. It gave official sanction to the creation of a new Kingdom of Westphalia, granted the French the right to maintain garrisons in certain North Sea and Baltic ports, and even stipulated that the Russians were to evacuate the recently overrun Danubian provinces of Moldavia and Vallachia once a peace treaty—thanks to French "mediation"—had been drawn up with the Ottoman sultan in Istanbul. Even more ominous for the future were the terms of a secret agreement, supplementing the formal Treaty of Alliance, according to which Russia was pledged to support the continental boycott against British shipping, which Napoleon had formally decreed the previous November, and to declare war against England if the latter refused to make peace by December 1, 1807.

Although Alexander's "chivalrous" championship of Prussia's cause enabled the Hohenzollerns to retain their throne, the browbeaten Frederick William III had to agree to the loss of about half his lands (in western Germany as well as in Poland), and he was even forced to cede the region of Bialystok (north of the Narew River) to Russia—enough to provoke cries of "betrayal" from the outraged Prussian Court when he returned to his refuge in Memel.

The success of any treaty of alliance depends as much on the spirit animating the signatories as on the terms themselves. In this respect the Treaty of Tilsit was from the start a misalliance between suspicious partners, each of whom begrudged the other's territorial gains and acquisitions. Napoleon was irked to see the Russians drive the Swedes from Finland in four brief months, instead of being tied down for several years of warfare in its "frozen wastes," as he had expected. Alexander, for his part, was loath to evacuate the Danubian provinces of Moldavia and Vallachia, which Russian soldiers had expended so much blood and sweat to free from the yoke of the "barbaric" Turks.

So pronounced was the hostility of the Russian Court, where the tone was set by Alexander's prim, pomp-loving, etiquette-minded mother, Dowager Empress Maria Feodorovna, that it would probably be no exaggeration to claim that there were only two persons in all of Petersburg who sincerely believed in the virtues of this Franco-Russian alliance. The first was the ambassador whom Napoleon sent to Russia in December 1807, the second the new minister who was chosen by Alexander to implement an unpopular foreign policy.

The Frenchman chosen by Napoleon to represent him in Petersburg was none other than his grand equerry, the thirty-four-year-old General de Caulaincourt, destined to play the role of devil's advocate in the mighty drama of 1812. Born into an ancient military family from Picardy in northern France, Count Armand de Caulaincourt, who had narrowly escaped imprisonment at the height of the Robespierre Terror of 1794, was one of the many thousands of ci-devant noblemen who had rallied to Bonaparte out of patriotism and the belief that if he were swept from the scene, the catastrophic result for France would be a bloody civil war, with the country fatally torn asunder between the revolutionary mob rule of the Jacobins and the obtuse despotism of the Bourbons. Partly brought up at Versailles, where his mother had served for a while as lady-in-waiting to one of Louis XVI's brothers, Caulaincourt was better suited than his immediate predecessor, the more humbly born General Savary, to disarm the outspokenly anti-Bonapartist sentiments of Petersburg's high society.

It was months and indeed years, however, before this calm, courteous, but somewhat reserved Frenchman could overcome local prejudices. Splendidly lodged in one of Petersburg's grandest townhouses—a proudly colonnaded palace overlooking the Neva which Tsar Alexander had bought for him from the Volkonsky family—Caulaincourt felt it to be his duty, as Napoleon's grand equerry and ambassador extraordinary, to be served by forty lackeys, chambermaids, and ostlers, to maintain a stable of more than fifty horses, and to be driven around in gleaming equipages. Alone of all the foreign envoys in the capital, he was permitted to ride with Emperor Alexander's suite during parade-ground reviews in front of the Winter Palace, and at diplomatic receptions and the exclusive soirées at the little Hermitage theater he was accorded the unique distinction of being seated with the imperial family. So marked was his preeminence that John Quincy Adams, in his diary entries, regularly referred to him as "the Ambassador"—in a separate category, superior to that of the other diplomatic "ministers" accredited to the imperial Court of St. Petersburg. In keeping with this status, which he was very punctilious in respecting, Caulaincourt spent every centime of the 800,000 (later one million) francs he was allotted by Napoleon for his annual salary and upkeep, treating his guests to succulent repasts prepared by his celebrated chef, Tardif, whom the poet Pushkin was later to extol as a grand master of the art of gastronomy.

Notwithstanding the exceptional favors accorded to Caulaincourt, it was soon clear that Alexander's views differed radically from Napoleon's when it came to deciding how the "division of the world" so euphorically envisaged at Tilsit was to be carried out in practice. The massive "reparations"—

amounting to 140 million francs—which Napoleon had imposed on Frederick William III of Prussia as a penalty for having started the war of 1806 so far exceeded the limited capabilities of his drastically shrunk realm that they virtually gave the French occupying forces the right to maintain garrisons in Berlin and other Prussian cities indefinitely. The newly formed Grand Duchy of Warsaw, though it was placed under the nominal sovereignty of the aging and harmless King Frederick Augustus of Saxony, now a grateful ally of France, was in fact a French protectorate, guided as well as guarded by Napoleon's ablest field commander, the formidable Marshal Davout, who was busy recruiting a fledgling Polish army imbued with an ardently pro-French and anti-Russian esprit de corps. Whereas, in Napoleon's eyes, Danzig and other Prussian fortresses had to be maintained in French hands in order to protect the three million inhabitants of the Grand Duchy of Warsaw, for the Russians the presence of French soldiers hundreds of miles east of the Rhine constituted a standing threat to the territorial integrity of the Russian Empire, which had only managed to absorb all of Polish Lithuania a dozen years before.

Alexander's strong feelings on this subject were even more emphatically shared by the man he chose, after Tilsit, to be his foreign minister—Count Nikolai Petrovich Rumiantsev. A gentleman of the old school, who still wore the wig, silk stockings, and satin breeches of the eighteenth century, this privileged inheritor of a vast fortune was the son of a famous field marshal who had particularly distinguished himself by his vigorous campaigns against the Turks. Like his prestigious father and the strong-willed empress he had served, Rumiantsev was persuaded that it was his country's mission to free the Slavic inhabitants of the Balkans from the grip of the Ottomans—"an empire ready to die without making a will," as he put it. In the townhouse located on the "English quay" where he lived with an aged aunt, he had begun amassing a notable collection of ancient Russian and Slavic manuscripts and books even before Alexander had appointed him minister of commerce in 1802. Almost alone among Alexander's ministers, this Slavophilic bachelor had from the very start favored making peace with Bonaparte, believing that this was the surest way of hastening the dismemberment of the Ottoman Empire and of fulfilling Catherine the Great's "Greek project" by occupying what, for "geographical reasons," must be part of Russia's "heritage"—Constantinople and the Bosphorus. He was willing to allow Napoleon a relatively free hand in western Europe, but what happened on Russia's western borders could not be a matter of indifference. In the interests of European peace, as he made bluntly clear to Caulaincourt, he and the emperor, his master, were willing to accept the existence of a Grand Duchy of Warsaw, but neither of them could tolerate a significant enlargement of this relatively small state leading toward a possible restoration of the ancient Kingdom of Poland.

No less upsetting for the future of this fissured misalliance between ostentatiously friendly but basically distrustful sovereigns was Napoleon's belief that, once he had divorced the childless Josephine, it could best be cemented through a grandiose marriage pact linking the Bonaparte and Romanov families. When the two emperors met again at Erfurt in the autumn of 1808, Caulaincourt was accordingly instructed to sound out Alexander's reaction to the idea of Napoleon's marrying his sister Catherine.

The one Russian to whom the idea of such a marriage had a certain, momentary appeal was, interestingly enough, the Grand Duchess Catherine herself. Of Alexander's remaining sisters—for the three eldest had by this time died—the dark-haired Catherine, now in her twentieth year, was far and away his favorite. There was something irresistibly mischievous and naughty in her bold dark eyes, saucy mouth, plump cheeks, and the delightfully pudgy nose about which he had so often teased her, playfully kissing it or pressing its fleshy tip with a finger. In the often stuffy Court atmosphere of Petersburg, for which the fun-loving Alexander had never much cared, this uninhibited sister, who spoke her mind and dared to talk back to their august, etiquette-minded mother, was like a breath of fresh air. As politically ambitious as her mother, Catherine would have been quite willing to marry the "old, ugly, dirty" Emperor Francis of Austria after the death of his second wife, persuaded as she was that she could take him in hand and cleanse him, if given the opportunity. With the same forthright bumptiousness she seems to have believed, for a brief moment at any rate, that she could "tame" Napoleon, were she to become his bride. Doubtless it flattered her adolescent vanity to fancy that she could do what no woman, or for that matter, man, had so far been able to accomplish.

The illusion, at any rate, seems to have been of brief duration. Just five weeks after the final mid-October meeting between Alexander and Napoleon, on the road leading from Erfurt to Weimar—where the two emperors had embraced and sworn to meet again in a year's time to settle the affairs of Europe—Caulaincourt was forced to report from Petersburg that the temperamental Grand Duchess Catherine had suddenly decided to marry her first cousin, Prince George of Oldenburg.

Catherine's sudden decision to marry this undistinguished princeling from a distinctly minor duchy probably owed little to her brother Alexander's prodding. She had never let herself be swayed in sentimental matters by good looks alone, and had not hesitated to plunge into a hot love affair with one of Russia's most prestigious warriors, the swarthy, hawk-nosed, and repellingly ugly Prince Pyotr Ivanovich Bagration. It may well have been the vehemently anti-Bonapartist Bagration, who had fought the French in Italy and later at Austerlitz and other battles, who helped rid her of the illusion that Napoleon was someone who could be "tamed." For by January of 1809 she was openly declaring to her friends in Petersburg that she would rather be "the wife of a *pop* [Orthodox parish priest] than the sovereign of a country under the influence of France."

A few weeks later the Austrians—who had refused to recognize Joachim Murat's new title of King of Naples and Joseph Bonaparte's right to be King of Spain—threw down the gauntlet by invading France's ally, Bavaria. Swift though Napoleon's reaction was—by May 13 the Austrians had been driven down the Danube valley and the French were once again masters of Vienna

—it could not keep the spirit of rebellion from spreading to Germany.

This eight-week war was also an embarrassment to Alexander, who found himself duty-bound as an "ally" to put an army into the field against the Austrians. The Russian emperor repeatedly assured Caulaincourt that he would live up to his Tilsit treaty obligations by sending an army corps into eastern Galicia, but he had already hinted privately to the Austrian general, Prince Karl Schwarzenberg (who had been dispatched to Petersburg to sound out his intentions), that he would do everything possible to avoid major confrontations between Russian and Austrian troops.

This proved to be no hollow promise. When the Russian commander, Prince Sergei Golitsyn, finally crossed the Bug in early June—three weeks after Napoleon had entered Vienna—the forward movement of his thirty thousand soldiers was so leisurely that it took them six weeks to approach the Galician capital of Cracow. What Napoleon had hoped would be a vigorous campaign aimed at tying down many Austrian units turned out instead to be a remarkably peaceful march, in which a couple of Cossacks lost their lives!

By this time events had assumed a momentum which neither Napoleon nor Alexander could control. Realizing that they had little to fear from the Russians, the Austrians sent an army of forty thousand northward to occupy Warsaw. Seriously outnumbered, the Polish minister of war, Prince Joseph Poniatowski, was forced to abandon his capital, but he avenged himself by mounting a diversionary attack on Austrian-occupied Galicia. One Galician town after another was thus liberated from Habsburg rule, to the delight of the local inhabitants, and in mid-July Poniatowski took possession of the venerable university city of Cracow, to the dismay of the Russian commanders, who were finally obliged to accept a joint occupation and the establishment of a Polish municipal administration, headed by a Polish commandant.

An article in a Hamburg newspaper reporting that Poniatowski was going to be named viceroy of Poland brought the effervescence in Petersburg to a new boil in mid-August. To Napoleon, once again installed in the Habsburgs' Schönbrunn Palace, near Vienna, a worried Caulaincourt reported that "the emperor [Alexander] alone is calm amidst the general agitation. . . . No restraint is shown in remarks made about the Emperor Alexander; people speak openly of having him assassinated. Never since the start of my sojourn in Petersburg have I seen people so worked up. All who surround the sovereign, even those who are the most attached to him, are appalled. . . . Everything we hear from Moscow and the provinces confirms that this agitation is general: one must die with weapons in one's hands, it is said, rather than suffer that Galicia should be reunited to the Grand Duchy [of Warsaw], or be in any way under the influence of France."

The Treaty of Schönbrunn, finally signed on October 14, 1809, after three months of diplomatic wrangling, did little to calm Russian apprehensions. Austria was allowed to retain most of Polish Galicia, but four-fifths of the rest —including one and a half million Poles and the key city of Cracow—were added to the Grand Duchy of Warsaw.

Alexander and Foreign Minister Rumiantsev made no effort to conceal their disenchantment over this new settlement, from which they had excluded themselves by refusing Napoleon's invitation to join him at Schönbrunn. For weeks thereafter it was the subject of bitter recriminations. To placate their aggrieved ally, the French foreign minister wrote to Rumiantsev to say that Napoleon was ready to eliminate the name of Poland from all public acts, while in Petersburg Caulaincourt was authorized to draft and sign an informal convention spelling out the restrictions that were to be imposed on the Grand Duchy of Warsaw and its tutelary sovereign, the king of Saxony. In early December Napoleon, in opening a new session of his Legislative Corps (the name given to his submissive parliament), publicly expressed his joy that his "ally and friend" (Alexander) should have added Finland, Moldavia, Vallachia, and "a district of Galicia" to his "vast empire." His minister of the interior (Montalivet) was even more explicit in declaring that most of Galicia had been allowed to remain under Austrian sovereignty so as not to offend the emperor of Russia; after which he added, in a phrase that caused consternation when it was repeated in Warsaw: "His Majesty [Napoleon] has never had in view the reestablishment of Poland."

In Petersburg the feeling of relief induced by these official declarations lasted barely one week. Alexander had just returned from a swift sleigh trip to wintry Moscow when he was jolted by the impact of a new Napoleonic thunderclap. In a private after-dinner conversation at the Winter Palace Caulaincourt said that he had been instructed to inform him that Napoleon was bent on divorcing Empress Josephine, who had been unable to give him an heir, long hoped for and essential to the stabilization of his young dynasty. The French emperor was casting around for a suitable new wife, and of all the possible matches he could make, the one he distinctly preferred was with a grand duchess of the Russian imperial family. By this was clearly meant the tsar's youngest, still unmarried, sister, Anna Pavlovna, who was due to celebrate her fifteenth birthday in a few days.

Alexander, who by now had become a past master in the art of diplomatic dissembling, feigned to be delighted by the news, saying that the idea of such a match appealed to him very much. Unfortunately, his authority in such matters was limited; for an imperial ukaz, based on the specific wishes of his late father, Emperor Paul I, had given his mother, the Dowager Empress Maria Feodorovna, an absolute right to decide her children's marital arrangements as she chose.

Alexander's real feelings were betrayed by the worried look on his face when he turned up at the snowbound castle of Gatchina (south of Petersburg) shortly before the Russian Orthodox Christmas, to discuss the matter with his mother. A courier had just brought a dispatch from the Russian embassy in Paris informing him that Napoleon's divorce from Josephine had been agreed upon at a council of war held by the Bonaparte family. Though most of the others wanted him to marry his niece, the daughter of his brother Lucien, Napoleon himself was said to "have views" on the Grand Duchess Anna Pavlovna of Russia.

This news threw the normally serene Dowager Empress Maria Feodorovna into a state of nervousness bordering on panic. The mere idea that her "poor Annette" could thus become a "holocaust sacrificed for the good of the State" and that she could be wedded to a man "with the character of a scoundrel for whom nothing is sacred" was utterly abhorrent to her. But what were they to do? If they were to reject Napoleon's bid, as she wrote in despair to her daughter Catherine, "the consequences of the refusal will be bitterness, ill will, nagging over petty trifles," and so on. And if, to avenge his wounded pride, Bonaparte chose to marry the Habsburg Archduchess Marie-Louise, "he will join himself with Austria and raise her up expressly to harm us." Yet thanks to the convention that had been laboriously drafted and just signed by Caulaincourt and Rumiantsev—pledging France, Russia, and the Kingdom of Saxony to expunge the words "Poland" and "Polish" from all official texts concerning the "parts that previously constituted that kingdom"—there was every reason for their remaining on good terms with France.

No less appalled by this marriage proposal was Count Nikolai Rumiantsev, whom the tsar had recently raised to the dignity of chancellor. "As a friend of the alliance, as a man who has devoted his whole life to the system [i.e., Napoleon's]," he told Caulaincourt, "I would have liked not to have had this idea put forward."

By the time these wise words were uttered, it was too late. In a second and far more peremptory dispatch from his foreign minister in Paris, Caulaincourt was ordered to demand a "categoric answer" from Emperor Alexander to Napoleon's request, within just two days. Acting with customary impatience, the strong-willed emperor of the French was now issuing an ultimatum.

For four weeks Alexander kept reassuring Caulaincourt how much he personally favored a match between the French emperor and his sister, and how much he regretted that the final decision was not his. Finally, on February 4, 1810, he told the increasingly insistent French ambassador that his mother, the dowager empress, had refused to yield to his entreaties and would not allow her daughter Anna to risk her health and life by being rushed into a premature marriage before she was eighteen years old. Much as he regretted this intransigence—here Alexander even pretended to be angry with his mother—he remained personally as committed as ever to the alliance between France and Russia.

Unlike the ingenuous Caulaincourt, who was completely taken in by Alexander's artful game, Napoleon had already concluded that his bid for the Grand Duchess Anna's hand was going to be rejected. At another extraordinary conclave, held in Paris during the night of February 6–7, it was decided that in view of the procrastination in Petersburg, a formal proposal would be made for the hand of the Archduchess Marie-Louise, the eighteen-year-old daughter of Emperor Francis of Austria. The request was promptly transmitted to the Austrian ambassador—the same Prince General Karl Schwarzenberg who had been sent to Petersburg one year before in a vain endeavor to secure Russia's military cooperation in the coming conflict with the French. Schwarzenberg gave his immediate consent, and the very next day he and the French foreign minister, Champagny, signed the marriage contract in Paris.

It took more than two weeks for news of this *coup de théâtre* to reach Petersburg, where it exploded like a bombshell. The normally tactful Alexander made no effort to conceal his conviction that the French, in this instance, had been less than honest in carrying on two simultaneous negotiations. A day or two later a clearly upset Caulaincourt had to deliver a second piece of bad news: the draft convention so laboriously worked out between himself and Rumiantsev—which was to have provided the Russians with a written pledge that the Kingdom of Poland would not be restored and that the words "Poland" and "Polish" were never to be employed in official texts—had been rejected out of hand by Napoleon. "No matter how powerful may be the empires of France and Russia," he declared in a memorandum dictated to his foreign minister, "they are nevertheless not so powerful that things may not happen against their volition." But the real reason, unstated, for this second impulsive action was his ruffled pride over the rejection of his marriage bid.

A little more than two months later, on May 23, 1810, the French ambassador in Petersburg gave a splendid ball in his colonnaded palace on the banks of the Neva, to celebrate his emperor's marriage to Archduchess Marie-Louise of Austria. Emperor Alexander, his mother, the Dowager Empress Maria Feodorovna, his wife, the Empress Elisabeth, his brothers, the Grand Dukes Constantine, Nicholas, and Michael, were all present, as was the tsar's youngest sister, the fifteen-year-old Grand Duchess Anna Pavlovna. The Volkonsky townhouse, as John Quincy Adams noted in his diary, "was elegantly illuminated. . . . As the imperial family were at the ball, it was necessary to go early. We went at nine o'clock, but it was daylight as at noon, so that the illumination made scarcely any show at all. It was past two in the morning when the Court retired, after which we immediately came home. It was then again broad daylight, and, by the time I got to bed, almost sunrise. The Emperor was gracious to everybody, even beyond his usual custom, which is remarkable for affability. . . . The rooms," concluded James Madison's representative, "were excessively warm, and a very small part of the company took real pleasure in the fête. I heard the Ambassador himself say to some one that he gave the ball because he was obliged to do it—it gave him no pleasure."

It certainly did not. Indeed, the host on this occasion may well have been the unhappiest individual in all that glittering throng. The bright hopes Armand de Caulaincourt had once entertained of helping to forge an enduring alliance between his own country and Russia had paled, like the glowing lamps and chandeliers of this brilliantly illuminated palace, to the point of insignificance in the harsh daylight of this precocious summer. The alliance, as the French saying has it, *avait du plomb dans l'aile*—it had a slug of grapeshot in one wing—and from this crippling wound, he sensed, it might be unable to recover.

CHAPTER 3

THE LOOMING STORM

SOME ELEVEN MONTHS after this gala ball, news reached Petersburg that the new French empress, Marie-Louise, had given birth to a son and heir. The thirty-three-year-old tsar must have experienced a twinge of envy. His own wife, the delicate Empress Elisabeth, whom he had often callously neglected, had only been able to bear him two daughters, both of whom had died. By Maria Antonovna Naryshkin—the voluptuous, dark-haired wife of the Grand Master of the Imperial Hunt—he had also had two daughters, who were presumed to be Alexander's. But now Napoleon, who had already had a son by his lovely Polish mistress, Maria Walewska, had succeeded for a second time in doing what his imperial "brother" and rival had been unable to achieve. Like his Francophilic chancellor, the tsar was duty-bound to add his signature to a formal note of congratulation; but unlike Rumiantsev, he did so without joy.

The relations between France and Russia, which had still been fairly cordial in May of 1810, had by the following April soured. Three things had greatly contributed to this growing estrangement. The first was Napoleon's high-handed determination to tighten the continental garrote on trade with England. The second was an imperial ukaz imposing taxes on imports of French luxury goods, and the third, also a Russian initiative, was the tsar's decision to move a number of divisions up to his empire's western borders, where they posed a standing threat to the fledgling Grand Duchy of Warsaw.

When Alexander had agreed at Tilsit to declare war on England and to cooperate in a continental boycott on British goods, it was almost certainly in the belief that the English, now confronted by a formal alliance between the two mightiest powers on the continent, would finally sue for peace. The Continental System must have seemed to him a somewhat abstract notion, to which he and his government could pay the necessary lip service, rather than an oppressive economic reality which would end up crippling Russia's foreign trade.

Initially, France's protracted conflict with England had been, as far as merchant shipping was concerned, an essentially bilateral affair. English warships could seize any French merchantman they encountered on the high seas and bring it back to a British port, where its cargo was confiscated or the master was forced to pay an exorbitant ransom to obtain the crew's and the vessel's release. In retaliation the French had closed their ports to British shipping and had ordered the seizure of British subjects caught in any part of the French Empire. But the leading European countries with which England at one time or another was allied in the First, Second, or Third Coalition—Prussia, Austria, and Russia—being none of them maritime powers, they were not much affected by the trade war between the English and the French.

The imperial decree that Napoleon issued from Berlin in November 1806 altered this situation dramatically—by outlawing the importation of English goods in *all* the continental countries allied to France or occupied by French troops. This sweeping edict—perhaps the most fateful and obnoxious in Napoleon's imperial career—internationalized France's war with Britain. It turned a bilateral trade war between two countries into an international trade war between England and the unwilling continent of Europe. It led, by an inexorable process of escalation, to the relentless expansion of the French Empire, which Napoleon had originally envisaged as being limited to the Italian peninsula, France, Switzerland, and Holland (including the German-speaking territories on the left bank of the Rhine), and linked by marriage pacts to Bavaria, Württemberg, and Baden. It was to force Portugal to cooperate in a total boycott on trade with Britain that Napoleon dispatched General Andoche Junot over the Pyrenees and all the way to Lisbon—the first step in the fateful process that was to embroil France in a savage guerrilla war over most of the Iberian peninsula. It was his determination to force a recalcitrant Pope Pius VII to cooperate in his continental embargo against England which led the French emperor to order the invasion and annexation of the Papal States in central Italy and ultimately, in July 1809, the pope's arrest—a high-handed action which alienated many Italians and further enraged the fervently Catholic Spaniards. It was his determination to halt the flourishing trade in Turkish cotton and other "colonial goods" that were brought up the Adriatic in merchant vessels escorted by British frigates to the very harbor mouths of Fiume and Trieste, as much as his desire to punish the Austrians for launching the war of 1809, which moved him to add the Dalmatian coast (the provinces of "Illyria") to the already extensive French Empire. Finally, it was his insistence that the Russians, too, cooperate unreservedly in the maintenance of this anti-British "system" which led, most calamitously of all, to the campaign of 1812.

To the sweeping Berlin decree of November 1806 the British government replied by issuing several Orders in Council, which authorized British warships to halt, visit, and if necessary bring to port and subject to tariff payments *all* vessels (even those flying the flags of neutral, friendly, or allied countries) suspected of carrying goods from colonial lands to the continent of Europe. To these high-handed measures, which were to prove so vexatious to United

States merchant vessels (and eventually to lead to the Anglo-American war of 1812), Napoleon retaliated in his turn by closing North Germany's ports to British shipping, and then, even more drastically, by declaring in his Milan decree of December 17, 1807, that any vessel that had been inspected by a British man-of-war or been forced to put in to a British port was henceforth to be regarded as an English ship, regardless of the flag it might be flying.

The British, who had first sought to harass their French enemies in the North Sea by blocking the mouths of the Weser and the Elbe, soon realized that it would be far cleverer to open these and other German bays and estuaries to a massive ingress of British vessels, and later, when this became too blatantly risky, of neutral or supposedly neutral merchantmen. Indeed, it would be no exaggeration to say that the four years 1807–1810 were a golden age for European smugglers—and for counterfeiters and customs officials as well. The forging of ship's papers, to prove that neither the vessel nor the cargo was of English origin, became a major industry. Protected by powerful coastal batteries and the guns of Britain's invincible warships, the rocky island of Helgoland, situated thirty or more miles out to sea beyond the estuaries of the Weser and the Elbe, became a vast depot of British cloth, woven fabrics, and manufactured goods, as well as of cane sugar, tea, coffee, and colonial spices, which could be quickly loaded on to sloops and skiffs and directed to this or that "neglected" cove, bight, or inlet when the coast was clear.

It is a tribute to Napoleon's tireless energy and vigilance, and the fear of God he could inspire in so many of his subordinates, that he was able to get himself obeyed at all in enforcing such unpopular measures. His own brother Louis —whom he had had proclaimed king of Holland in a carefully stage-managed ceremony at the Château de Saint-Cloud in June 1806—finally got so fed up with having to heed directives that were ruinous to his trade-dependent Dutch subjects that in June 1810 he abruptly abdicated his throne: an action which led inexorably to the "union" (Bonapartese for annexation) of the two-centuries-old Kingdom of Holland with the French Empire and the transformation of its lowland provinces into six new departments.

To perpetuate a blockade which had so far benefited smugglers, commodity speculators, forgers, and defrauders of every kind while sending honest traders to the wall, Napoleon, as the historian Jean Tulard has pointed out, became a contrabandist in his turn. Unable to suppress a now continent-wide black market, he decided to run it himself—by granting licenses to French traders dealing in vital imports and exports. Enormous import duties of up to 50 percent—800 francs on a bale of Georgia cotton, 400 francs on a bushel of coffee or of Turkish or Egyptian cotton—were to bring in millions in customs revenue to the hard-pressed imperial treasury. While other countries kept their ports closed to unauthorized vessels, the French, through their licensing system, were to become the chief distributors of vital imports, and thus the quartermasters of the continent. Unlicensed English goods, on the other hand, were to be seized and even burned—as happened in Frankfurt, where to the dismay of its outraged inhabitants French customs officials put the torch to vast stocks of British merchandise during four dreadful days in mid-November of 1810.

In essence, this new economic strategy, like so many of Napoleon's initiatives, was of military inspiration. France, at the center of this continental system, was to use its inner lines of communications (roads, riverways, canals, etc.) to keep everyone supplied, while the frustrated English, reduced to occasional coastal "probes" and beachhead skirmishes, were confronted with an impregnable "front." But even theoretically this extraordinary system could work only if the coasts of the European continent were made absolutely hermetic and impervious to the infiltration of unlicensed British goods. The sealing off of the Dutch coast, finally achieved with the annexation of Holland, could not by itself secure such a gigantic objective. All it did, in fact, was to shift the center of gravity of the "smugglers' war" from the North Sea into the Baltic. The port of Göteborg, on Sweden's western coast, replaced the inhospitable island of Helgoland as a strategic point where vast quantities of English or colonial merchandise could be stocked and shipped to some eastern Baltic harbor, or transported overland through Finland to Russia, and from there southward across the Lithuanian provinces and the Duchy of Warsaw all the way to the German trade center of Leipzig.

On October 23, 1810, a French courier set out from Paris with one more letter addressed to Alexander in Petersburg. In it Napoleon reiterated his pet theme: the English, with their leading merchant houses going bankrupt, their factories reduced to partial or total idleness, their warehouses clogged with unexportable goods, were on the brink of economic collapse. He had just ordered the seizure of "immense quantities of English and colonial merchandise" in Frankfurt and Switzerland—yet another crippling blow to a country whose doddering monarch (George III) now seemed at death's door. All that was needed, therefore, was the delivery of a final, "terrible" blow to those increasingly desperate, discontented islanders—by seizing the 600 merchantmen which, barred from the shores of Pomerania and Prussia, were now anxiously headed for Russian ports in which to unload their cargoes. "It is up to Your Majesty to have peace, or to make the war last," declared Napoleon roundly. "Whatever papers they may have, under whatever name they may be masked—French, German, Spanish, Danish, Russian, Swedish—Your Majesty may be sure that they are English."

Before the month was up, however, Napoleon's Corsican blood was brought to a new boil by the news that 1,200 English or "masked" ships had managed to dock in Russian ports, bringing the year's total to around 2,000! It was too late to do anything about it now. But he could at least make Alexander realize that he was in deadly earnest and grimly determined to enforce his continental boycott on unauthorized English goods, in the Baltic as well as in the North Sea. And so, on December 13, he issued another sweeping decree annexing the entire coastal region from the estuary of the Ems, on the North Sea, to the Hanseatic port of Lübeck, on the Baltic. Three new departments were thus added to the French Empire.

Included in this imperious incorporation was the Duchy of Oldenburg, a hollow, pear-shaped expanse of marshy flatland situated west of Bremen and the Weser River. It belonged to the Holstein-Gottorp family, of which Emperor Alexander was now the titular head (his great-great-great-grandfather

Karl Friedrich of Holstein-Gottorp had married Peter the Great's daughter Anna). Its present ruler, furthermore, Duke Peter of Oldenburg, had married Dowager Empress Maria Feodorovna's sister Frederike of Württemberg; and last but by no means least, his second son, Prince George of Oldenburg, had married Alexander's favorite sister, Catherine.

Napoleon had rashly assumed that neither Duke Peter of Oldenburg nor his nephew-by-marriage, Tsar Alexander of Russia, would make too much fuss over this "trivial" annexation. On both counts he was grievously mistaken. When approached by a French emissary, the fifty-five-year-old Duke of Oldenburg flatly refused to leave his ancestral domain and to move himself, his family, and his personal belongings to the Lilliputian territory of Erfurt (41,000 inhabitants, compared with Oldenburg's 170,000). Marshal Davout, whom Napoleon had appointed supreme commander of all French forces in northern Germany, thereupon had his soldiers occupy the little town, where they laid hands on the treasure chest and made the helpless duke a prisoner in his own castle.

Several weeks later (January 22, 1811) Napoleon formally endorsed this military coup by transferring the family's ducal rights to the much smaller principality of Erfurt. Both actions were flagrant violations of the Tilsit accords, which had specifically guaranteed the Duchy of Oldenburg's continuing independence. They proved totally unacceptable to the harassed duke's nephew, Emperor Alexander of Russia. The issue, on which he displayed the kind of mulish stubbornness that Napoleon had found so troubling during the "congress" of Erfurt, was to remain unresolved and to smolder like a sizzling fuse throughout the year 1811, finally helping to detonate the war of 1812.

While Napoleon was thus trying to plug another gaping hole in the leaky breastworks of his Continental System, his partner and imperial "brother," Alexander, was moving in a contrary direction. Russia's declaration of war against England in December 1807, combined with the irksome restrictions of the continental embargo, had crippled the country's traditional trade in hemp, flax, furs, and wood. They had proved equally ruinous to the provinces of Russian Lithuania, which had long depended for their welfare on cereal exports to the British Isles. Russian merchants were increasingly vehement in their complaints. Equally alarming was the decline in the exchange value of the ruble, which had lost almost half of its purchasing power in just four years; worth 2 francs 90 in 1807, it was now worth little more than 1 franc 50, owing to Russia's inability to pay for its imports through its normal export trade. Since Napoleon had forced the French to forgo coffee, tea, cane sugar, and other "colonial products," Alexander decided that he too had a right to impose a regime of austerity on his own Russian subjects. Accordingly, on the last day of 1810, he issued a ukaz authorizing the importation of colonial products transported in merchant vessels flying the American flag, and subjecting the importation of all luxury goods—such as the lace, silks, and satins that had been flooding in from the textile factories of Lyon and other French towns—to heavy import duties.

In issuing this ukaz Alexander was fully aware of the hostile reaction it was certain to arouse in Paris. But it was a risk he felt he could take at a time when more than half of Napoleon's divisions were tied down in the Iberian peninsula.

Assisted by his close friend Prince Pyotr Volkonsky, who headed the Russian army's quartermaster-general department (in fact, if not in name, a general staff that was housed in a neoclassic edifice facing the Winter Palace), Alexander had long been pondering the problem of how to defend Russia's vulnerable western frontier: seven hundred miles of monotonously flat land which offered no natural obstacles to an enemy assault save for several rivers and the swamplands of the Pripet Marshes between Brest and Bobruisk. The conclusion they had come to was that this could best be achieved by constructing a cordon of formidably defended fortresses anchored at the northern end by the medieval bastion which the Livonian Knights had built at Riga, and at the southern end by the mighty Pechersk fortress overlooking the Dnieper River near Kiev. But the new minister of war—a Baltic baron of partly Scottish, Swedish, and German Lutheran extraction named Mikhail Barclay de Tolly—pointed out that with Russia's military and financial resources already strained to the limit by a smoldering war with Turkey in the lower Danube region and the need to defend the Caucasian province of Azerbaijan from Persian attempts at reconquest, it would take a good twenty-five years to complete a really effective chain of strongholds. He therefore proposed that Russia, as a measure of self-defense, launch what today would be called a preemptive strike—by overrunning the ill-defended Grand Duchy of Warsaw and establishing a new border along the Vistula River with the active aid of the Prussians, who were burning to avenge their recent defeats and humiliations by rising up en masse against the French.

Coming from anybody else, such a bold proposal could have been rejected out of hand. But no one could have been less hotheaded than this calm, pale-faced general, whose imposing silhouette, crowned by its distinctive high-domed forehead and balding head, seemed to grow even taller and more arresting in the heat of battle. His Scottish phlegm and coolness under fire had made him something of a legend and an object of hero worship to the troops he had commanded—first at Preussisch-Eylau, where he had been severely wounded in one arm by a charge of grapeshot while fighting to retake a vital churchyard, and later during the campaign of 1808 in Finland, which he had first helped to conquer and later administered with remarkable sagacity.

That Alexander was seriously tempted by Barclay de Tolly's bold proposal for a preemptive advance to the Vistula, there can be no doubt. To strengthen Russia's forces on its western borders, one division was ordered to march south from Finland, while four of the nine divisions engaged on the Turkish front were sent northward.

Just six days after issuing his ukaz severely taxing the import of luxury goods, Alexander sent a letter to Prince Adam Czartoryski, who had left Petersburg six months before and gone into retirement on one of his family's estates near Grodno, in what had become the French-protected Grand Duchy of Warsaw. The Russian army, the emperor explained to his old friend, now had 21 infantry and 8 cavalry divisions, as well as 32 Cossack regiments, available for action in the West. All told, they composed a first, front-line army with an approximate strength of 100,000 men, supported by a second, reserve or backup army numbering 124,000. If to this first-line army of 100,000 Russians one added the 50,000 Poles who were now being trained in the Grand Duchy of Warsaw, 50,000 Prussians, and 30,000 Danes, one reached a total of 230,000 men, who could quickly be reinforced by another 100,000 Russians. Over and against this number all Napoleon could muster was 60,000 French troops (46,000 stationed in various parts of Germany, bolstered by 14,000 more that could be drawn from recently annexed Holland), 30,000 Saxons, 30,000 Bavarians, 20,000 Württembergers, 15,000 Westphalians and other miscellaneous forces of Germanic origin—or a total of 155,000 men. The military odds, in other words, were very definitely in favor of the Russians and their "allies." Included in the latter category were the Poles, whom Alexander hoped to wean away from Napoleon and the French. This he proposed to do by promising them a "regeneration of Poland"—by which was meant (for even now Alexander shrank from clearly specifying it) a restoration of their old kingdom under Russian auspices.

The naïveté of this letter must have left Adam Czartoryski slightly open-mouthed. Five eventful years had passed since the memorable fortnight in September-October 1805 which Alexander, at the invitation of his friend and then foreign minister, had spent at the Czartoryskis' grandiose castle overlooking the Vistula at Pulawy (some seventy miles upstream from Warsaw). Here, while Napoleon was moving his divisions by forced marches across the Rhine and toward Bavaria, two leisurely weeks had been spent in a beguiling round of dinners, gala balls, musical and theatrical soirées, as well as visits to the famous "Gothic House" where Adam's mother, Princess Isabella Czartoryski, had assembled a priceless collection of parchment scrolls, caskets, swords, shields, banners, and other mementos of Poland's glorious past. While her venerable husband, Prince General Adam Casimir (former commander of the Polish Military Academy in Warsaw), had looked on approvingly, his forceful wife, who made no secret of her antipathy for Prussia, had used every artifice in her power to try to induce her imperial guest to move two Russian army corps across the Niemen and into Prussian Poland. She had even thrown herself at Alexander's feet with a melodramatic plea that he issue the momentous order and proceed to Warsaw with his "liberating" soldiers, there to be offered the crown of the kings of Poland. Instead, to the bitter dismay of his Polish hosts, Alexander had preferred to heed the counsels of the Prussophiles in his entourage, led by the brash Prince Pyotr Dolgoruky, and had made the hurried trip to Potsdam, which had so fatefully embroiled Russian foreign policy ever since.

The bold course that Princess Isabella and her son had advocated in the autumn of 1805 was admittedly a gamble. What Adam Czartoryski most feared was that if the Polish national cause was not in some way encouraged by Russia, it would inevitably be promoted by the French, who enjoyed great prestige among the Poles because they had not been a party to the surgical mutilations of the previous century. In 1805 Tsar Alexander was still something of an unknown quantity on the European chessboard and was invested with an aura of liberalism which, Adam Czartoryski felt, would make him acceptable to his Polish countrymen. (His idea was that the Kingdom of Poland should be revived and made a constituent part of a Slavic confederation, under the aegis of the Romanovs, much as the ancient kingdoms of Bohemia and Hungary had been incorporated into the Germanic empire of the Habsburgs.) But since then his worst forebodings had been confirmed. The tsar's pro-Prussian leanings had alienated whatever sympathy he may once have enjoyed west of the Niemen, while Napoleon's continuing victories had fired the patriotic fervor of the highly inflammable Poles. In Warsaw the anniversary of the anti-Russian uprising of Good Friday, 1794—when several thousand about-to-be-disbanded officers and soldiers had seized the arsenal, stormed the townhouse of the detested Russian ambassador, killed more than 2,000 Russian officers and men and taken as many prisoners—was now celebrated as a national memorial day, with persons of every walk of society, the wealthier in carriages, the humbler on foot, going from church to church to offer alms to the poor. No less alive was the searing memory of what had ensued six months later when, after the defeat of Kosciuszko's hopelessly outnumbered forces, Suvorov's furious foot-sloggers and saber-slashing Cossacks had stormed the Warsaw suburb of Praga, gutted hundreds of houses, and slaughtered more than 10,000 victims. Though some of the sting of this bitter memory had later been assuaged by Emperor Paul I's clemency in ordering the release of Kosciuszko and the 12,000 other Polish patriots who had been imprisoned in Petersburg or banished to Siberia, few were the Poles who still placed much faith in the liberal intentions of his son Alexander, who now, and in far less favorable circumstances, was belatedly proposing to undertake the bold move that Adam Czartoryski and his mother, Princess Isabella, had vainly pressed upon him in October 1805.

In replying to the Russian emperor's confidential query, Czartoryski had to tell him quite frankly that the obstacles to his scheme were just about insuperable. Napoleon, no matter what his ultimate intentions or sentiments might be, had established the Grand Duchy of Warsaw and cleverly persuaded most Poles that he sincerely desired the restoration of the old Kingdom of Poland —something which would inevitably result from any full-scale rupture between France and Russia. Between the Poles and the French there had been established a genuine *camaraderie d'armes*. If the Poles, at this late date, were to throw in their lot with the Russians—in exchange for a promised "regeneration" of their country—they would be jeopardizing the lives of 20,000 Polish soldiers, fighting with the French in Spain, whom Napoleon could seize as hostages, as he could the many young Polish children who had been sent by their parents to Paris to perfect their education. No less tellingly, Czartoryski pointed out that if the 50,000 Poles whom Alexander had so readily listed in his lineup of "allies" were to be transferred to the French camp, the forces at Napoleon's disposal would total 205,000, compared with only 180,000 for

Russia and her allies. He further doubted Alexander's tranquil assumption that Napoleon could draw no more than 14,000 soldiers from Holland to bolster the French forces stationed in various parts of Germany; for the latest French conscription order involved a publicly proclaimed levy of 115,000 men. Dutifully, however, as someone who had long been one of the Russian emperor's close friends, Czartoryski promised that he would travel to Warsaw to sound out Joseph Poniatowski, the Grand Duchy's minister of war, who was unquestionably the Pole who currently enjoyed the greatest influence and prestige with his countrymen.

As Czartoryski had suspected, Joseph Poniatowski's reaction to his discreet overture was totally negative. The preemptive Russian strike idea was quietly shelved by Alexander, who explained in a second secret letter to Czartoryski that he would never embark on such an enterprise without an absolute assurance of wholehearted Polish support from its leading citizens, and that he had no intention of letting Napoleon goad him into an open breach of their alliance, so that he could be branded in the eyes of the world as the aggressor.

The only practical result of this clandestine exchange of letters was to confirm reports that Poniatowski and his French mentors in Warsaw had already begun receiving from Polish informants in Lithuania about Russian troop movements and other military measures. Napoleon himself was well aware that something was brewing, for on December 5, 1810—one month before the start of Alexander's secret correspondence with Czartoryski—he instructed his ambassador in Petersburg to find out why the Russians were building forts on the Dvina and Dniester rivers. If it was the Russians' intention, after making peace with the Turks, to make peace with England, too, then Caulaincourt was to inform Emperor Alexander that this would be an immediate cause for war. On the same day his foreign minister (Champagny) was ordered to provide him with a detailed appraisal of the military situation existing in each one of the member states of the Confederation of the Rhine, and in the Grand Duchy of Warsaw. He was also ordered to prepare two order-of-battle booklets on the present state of the Russian and Austrian armies—reports, which, from here on out, were to be updated and improved at fortnightly intervals.

In early January 1811 the tempo quickened. Napoleon dictated a whole series of directives and dispatches—some addressed to his submissive minister of war, a fat-faced military bureaucrat of Irish ancestry named Henri Clarke, others to Marshal Davout, commander of the French forces in northern Germany, who had established his headquarters in Hamburg. A new Grande Armée was to be formed, composed of four different army corps. The first, commanded by Davout, was to consist of two light cavalry brigades and five infantry divisions. Two of these were to be moved forward rapidly—one as far eastward as the Prussian seaport of Stettin (at the mouth of the Oder) while another took up positions at and around the Baltic seaports of Wismar and Rostock, in the still independent Duchy of Mecklenburg, ostensibly to guard the "threatened" coast against an English seaborne assault. A second corps,

known as the Corps d'Observation de l'Elbe, initially composed of three infantry divisions and two brigades of light cavalry, was to be concentrated at
Münster and Osnabrück, under the command of Marshal Oudinot, now officially ennobled as the duc de Reggio. A third corps, drawn from French troops
that had been serving in Belgium and northern France, was to be assembled
at the key Rhine crossing-points of Düsseldorf and Mainz, under the command
of Marshal Ney, while a fourth, the Corps d'Observation d'Italie, was to be
mustered at Bolzano, Trentino, Verona, and Brescia, ready to march over the
Alpine passes and across Austria to Saxony and southern Poland, under the
command of Napoleon's former stepson, Prince Eugène de Beauharnais. Davout's First Corps (which was eventually to reach a total strength of six
divisions and 90,000 men, including Swiss and North German units commanded by German-speaking French officers) was given the vital front-line
mission of rushing forward to help the hard-pressed Poles and Saxons should
the Russians invade the Grand Duchy of Warsaw.

To facilitate these movements, a new paved road was to be built by French
engineers between the Rhine stronghold of Wesel and the North Sea port of
Hamburg, while other engineers discreetly prospected the possibility of extending this major artery along the Baltic coastline as far east as Stettin.
General Count Baston de La Riboisière, commander of the Imperial Guard's
artillery, was ordered to bring back all of the units and supply trains that had
been left at Bayonne, near the Spanish border, in order to bring its strength
up to a full complement of 132 cannon and howitzers, so that the Guard—in
itself an army corps composed of three formidable divisions—could march,
north and east, at a moment's notice. The strongholds of Küstrin, on the Oder,
and Glogau, in Silesia, were to be greatly strengthened, while General Rapp's
small force of 6,000 men in Danzig was to be massively reinforced with the
dispatch of French artillery and Polish cavalry units, as well as contingents
from Saxony, Bavaria, Württemberg, and Westphalia. Eventually this key
seaport, located at the mouth of the Vistula, was to be protected by a garrison
of 16,000 men, backed up by a formidable stock of powder, cannonballs,
muskets, munitions of all kinds, pontoons, planks, and other bridge-building
equipment, not to mention 800,000 biscuit rations—enough to sustain a two-
year siege!

No detail in this vast deployment of forces was too minor for Napoleon.
Typical was a directive specifying the need to construct a new and lighter
artillery caisson, less likely to get bogged down in the muddy roads and
quagmires of Poland, as had so often happened during the cold, wet, winter
campaign of 1806–1807. Similarly, to forestall the possibility of a Prussian
insurrection while his forces were battling the Russians in Poland, the French
emperor gave his artillery chief, General de La Riboisière, the top-secret task
of preparing surprise assaults on the Spandau fortress in Berlin and the mighty
stronghold of Kolberg, located northeast of Stettin on the Baltic coast of
Prussian Pomerania.

Napoleon himself discounted the rumors of impending war, which by now
were racing wildly across Poland. The key to his thinking was expressed in two

long letters to Davout, dictated on March 24. "Nothing leads me to think that the Russians wish to line up with the English and to make war on me; they are too busy with the Turks, but I have reason to believe that once they have finished with the Turks and their army is back and [concentrated] in force on the frontiers of Poland, they could become more exacting; . . ."

It was not his intention, he went on, to make any more troop movements this year, provided that the Russians did not begin hostilities. But he wanted to be ready just in case. It must be made clear to Poniatowski that large quantities of artillery and munitions were to be stored not in Warsaw, but farther back (i.e., to the west) in the fortress of Modlin. The stocking of large quantities of cannon and munitions in Warsaw might well tempt the Russians into launching a preemptive seizure—which was precisely what he wished to avoid. "I do not want a war with Russia," he concluded, but "it is evident that if these movements were to be made when the Russians have all of their forces available, they would no longer wish to believe my explanations and would march immediately to seize Warsaw."

Some six weeks after these instructions were dictated a new French ambassador arrived in Petersburg to replace the excessively Russophilic Caulaincourt. This too was one more straw in an increasingly chill wind. General Jacques de Lauriston was a self-made man who owed his recent title of count to the valor and ingenuity he had displayed in 1807 in storming the key Dalmatian port of Ragusa and in successfully defending it against the repeated assaults of 15,000 Russians and Montenegrins. The time for diplomatic niceties was clearly past. The kind of person Napoleon now needed in the Russian capital was a battle-hardened soldier capable of impressing Alexander by his prowess and of furnishing Paris with precise reports on Russian troop movements, frontier fortifications, and other vital military information.

Alexander himself can have harbored no illusions as to what Lauriston's appointment really meant. In a personal letter he thanked Napoleon for his choice of a new ambassador, declaring that "the so superior genius I recognize in Your Majesty leaves me no illusion as to the difficulty of the struggle that could arise between us." But having made this humble admission, he added without equivocation, "I repeat that if war takes place, it is Your Majesty who will have willed it, and having done everything to avoid it, I shall then know how to fight and to sell my existence dearly."

When, after Lauriston's arrival in mid-May, Caulaincourt came to present his official letters of departure to the tsar, Alexander gave him a diamond-studded replica of the Order of Saint Andrew as a token of his personal esteem. He was invited to dine at the emperor's table several times and was given, as a final farewell gift, an exquisitely enshrined medallion—this miniature "portrait likeness" of himself being, as Alexander put it, "the present of a friend."

Caulaincourt was so touched by these and other marks of friendship from the hosts and hostesses of Petersburg, who had more or less grudgingly admitted him to their salons, that he could not hold back his tears when saying good-bye. "Charming weeper!" commented the doyen of the diplomatic corps, the erudite as well as penniless Joseph de Maistre, in a characteristically ironic dispatch penned for his royal master, Victor Emmanuel, King of Sardinia, now living in the island's tiny capital of Cagliari, under the protection of British naval guns. "He spent 1,200,000 francs [a year]. . . . He was the first and foremost, and constantly favored at the Court, etc. All of which was doubtless better than having to hold Napoleon's horse, or perhaps being killed by a Catalonian bullet."

His successor, as the rock-ribbed Savoyard went on to note, "has neither the same tone nor the same character, and he will surely not exercise the same sway over the sovereign"—a judgment in which John Quincy Adams was more than ready to concur. "He began by committing a great mistake; for when, during the parade, the Emperor singled out some movement of the military drill, Lauriston replied, 'Those are trifles to which we pay no attention in Paris.' I have been assured that at the following parade His Imperial Majesty did not speak to him even once."

The Paris to which Armand de Caulaincourt returned in June of 1811 was, like Petersburg, also undergoing a process of transformation, although it had yet to acquire some of its most distinctive monuments and edifices. The Champs-Elysées were still a wood, divided by an avenue that had only recently been paved, while the Arc de Triomphe, which now crowns its western slope, was only just beginning to rise from the ground, amid an excrescence of ungainly scaffolding. The broad Place de la Concorde—on which, eighteen years before, "le citoyen Louis Capet" (Louis XVI) had been ignominiously guillotined—had already acquired the two splendidly columned buildings that line its northern side (the Hôtel Crillon and the present-day Ministry of the Navy), as well as its rearing horses and the stony-bottomed goddesses representing French provincial towns; but the obelisk of Luxor had not yet been erected over the central spot, where (prior to the Revolution) an equestrian statue of the "well-loved king" Louis XV had stood. To the south, beyond the Seine, one could admire the pedimented façade of the still-far-from-completed building which now houses the National Assembly, but the northern end of the Rue Royale was still open, so that one had a clear view over scattered rooftops, cultivated fields, and vineyards to the Mount of Mars (Montmartre), whose sleepy hilltop hamlet continued to bask in its tranquil suburban torpor. The grillwork gates of the Tuileries Gardens—through which Napoleon and his new empress, Marie-Louise, had been driven one year before in a gleaming glass-and-gold carrosse—were now permanently closed to the public. The Louvre, half a mile to the east, had yet to acquire the second of its two distinctive arms (the one stretching along the Rue de Rivoli, which was completed by Napoleon's nephew), while the small arch of triumph of the so-called Carrousel, incongruously surmounted by the four bronze horses of Byzantium, which the French had unceremoniously removed from Venice's San Marco basilica fifteen years before, stood in the middle of a square which was regularly used for parades and troop reviews. Today's long vista—up the central alley of the Tuileries Gardens, past the obelisk of Luxor, and as far as the distant Arc de Triomphe—was then blocked by an edifice almost as majestic in scale as the Louvre itself: the Renaissance palace which Philibert Delorme had built for Catherine de Médicis in the late sixteenth century.

It was from here—or from his other palaces at Saint-Cloud, Fontainebleau, and Versailles—that Napoleon now ruled much of Europe, with a ceremonial and a pomp which had grown even stiffer and more stilted since the bashful Marie-Louise had replaced the more outgoing and gracious Josephine as empress of the French. The relatively relaxed atmosphere of the Consulate, which had been marked by the reopening of the churches (many of which had been turned into makeshift prisons, barracks, or armories by the anticlerical fanatics of the Revolution) and by the return to France of thousands of previously proscribed aristocrats, had long since yielded to a new imperial solemnity, graphically reflected in a new style of mahogany furniture, ponderously overlaid with gilded bronze motifs. Each day now began with a formal *lever,* ministers and Court officials coming to pay their morning obeisance to the sovereign, as their ancien régime predecessors had once done at the royal Court of Versailles. Although Napoleon often regretted the simpler etiquette of the past, when he was only a division general—whence the evident pleasure he derived from talking to individual soldiers during military reviews—he was now the prisoner of the imperial image he was bent on projecting everywhere. Even with his oldest and closest friends—most of whom by now were princes, dukes, or counts—there was little left of the familiar camaraderie that had marked their earliest campaigns, and exceeding rare was the marshal who still dared use the second-person singular, *tu* (rather than the plural, *vous*), in speaking to the emperor, who was now addressed as "Sire"—the ceremonial form reserved for royal or imperial sovereigns.

All forms of Court protocol are to a certain extent intimidating. But Napoleon's appearances at diplomatic receptions or at the evening *Cercle*—where the beautifully satined ladies sat stiffly on their chairs while the gentlemen, carefully attired in the breeches, silk stockings, and buckled shoes of the ancien régime, remained standing behind them—seem to have been awe-inspiring enough to induce an uncomfortable silence which even Talleyrand, when he was grand chamberlain, was not prepared or could not be bothered to break. Once, when the French emperor paused in front of the pregnant Madame Fabre de l'Aude and asked her when she expected to be delivered of her next child, all the expectant mother could blurt out beneath the steady gaze of those piercing blue-gray eyes was "Whenever Your Majesty may wish."

"As long as Josephine shared the throne," as Count Jean-Jacques Beugnot observed, "her presence sufficed to preserve the memory of previous times, which is to say of an elegant equality. . . . The arrival in her place of Marie-Louise was the signal for a change that struck me: Austrian stuffiness seemed to have succeeded French elegance. . . . This Court has grown in officials, chamberlains, ladies-in-waiting, equerries; a hitherto unknown luxury has sprung up on all sides, but boredom too has crept in along with the magnificence." After noting that the marshals and heads of administrative departments on whom Napoleon had bestowed large fortunes now resided in lavishly furnished townhouses, where "these spoiled children of the Revolution feel obliged to show off in the midst of their marbles and their bronzes," he added a bit wistfully, "Nowhere do I encounter that cordiality which, six years earlier when I entered the Conseil d'Etat, used to bring together at unpretentious dinners and family feasts the great man's soldiers and the wise drafters of his Codes."

For this insidious change of atmosphere, for this ponderous pomp and circumstance, for this corruption through a sudden plethora of wealth and honors, Napoleon, not Marie-Louise, was of course responsible. He had unwittingly contributed to this process through his wish to develop an "intermediate" aristocracy—one based on merit and achievement rather than on mere nobility of birth—and thus to heal the social wounds of the recent past by reconciling the elevating impulses of the ancien régime with the egalitarian ideals of the French Revolution. In this new "fusion," as it was called by some, the title of marshal, which he had begun to confer on his leading generals from 1804 on, was no longer sufficient; something grander was needed as a form of recompense and recognition for services rendered to the State.

The first to be so honored was Napoleon's hypernervous but indefatigable chief of staff, Alexandre Berthier, who in 1806 was elevated to the title of prince de Neuchâtel (a Swiss province which the Prussian Crown had recently ceded to the French). The following spring François-Joseph Lefebvre, an Alsatian miller's son who had fought his way up from the ranks to the very summit of the military hierarchy, got the surprise of his life, after forcing the surrender of a septuagenarian Junker, General Count Friedrich Adolf von Kalkreuth, and close to 20,000 Prussians, when Napoleon personally informed him that from now on he was "Monsieur le Duc de Dantzig." The ruddy, ginger-haired, and once stoutly republican Michel Ney—like Lefebvre of modest origins (his father was a cooper from Sarrelouis, in Lorraine)—was similarly honored by being made duc d'Elchingen, in recognition of his bold crossing of the flooded Danube River and the successful storming of an Austrian-held monastery, which had completed the encirclement of General Mack's army and hastened his subsequent surrender at Ulm (October 1805). In the same way that stern and oddly bespectacled taskmaster Louis Nicolas Davout—who, unlike the two previously mentioned warriors, was descended from a noble Burgundian family—was made duc d'Auerstädt, to commemorate his extraordinary feat in repulsing the furious onslaught of 60,000 Prussians, led by Blücher and his famous Red Hussars, who, along with other Prussian squadrons, were considered (until October 1806) the finest cavalrymen in Europe.

That Napoleon should have chosen to reward his marshals with titles derived from the battlegrounds on which they had particularly distinguished themselves had a certain logic to it. But the logic had its limits, as was bound to happen with this ambitious attempt to forge a new imperial meritocracy— one that eventually led to the ennoblement of half a dozen princes (not including members of Napoleon's own family), thirty-one dukes, four hundred counts, and more than a thousand barons. The locality associated with an extraordinary feat of arms was often too obscure to support the creation of a ducal title. It was also Napoleon's intention to reward civilian as well as military merit. Dukedoms were thus created from localities with which the recipients had little, if any, connection.

If Armand de Caulaincourt, whom Napoleon had named Duke of Vicenza to exalt his status as his ambassador extraordinary in St. Petersburg, felt any uneasiness or apprehensions as he was driven into Paris on June 5, 1811, he made no mention of it in the fascinating memoirs he later wrote on the basis of detailed notes and diary jottings (which make them one of the half dozen surest sources for this period of Napoleon's life). The French capital seemed, outwardly at any rate, in a festive mood. Many façades and windows were festooned with flowered wreaths, honoring the forthcoming baptism of Napoleon and Marie-Louise's son, the eleven-week-old king of Rome.

The returning duke of Vicenza had little time to admire these leafy decorations as his carriage sped him along the curving bank of the Seine to the Château de Saint-Cloud. It was eleven in the morning when he finally dismounted inside the cobbled courtyard. As the Imperial Court's Grand Equerry he needed no introduction; but the speed with which he was ushered into Napoleon's presence, after he had been accompanied upstairs, was indication enough of how anxious the French emperor was to see him.

Coming out from behind the heavy mahogany desk, overwrought with the sphinx-breasted giltwork and other Egyptian motifs of the ponderous Empire style, Napoleon shook hands briefly with his former ambassador and invited him to take a seat in one of the equally ornate armchairs. Now approaching the end of his forty-second year, Napoleon was no longer the lean, long-haired general he had been when he had led his Army of Italy over the St.-Bernard Pass in May of 1800. His hair, which now lay flat on the top of his head according to the dictates of the new Caesarian style he had helped to introduce, seemed to have grown less dark as it had thinned over the brooding forehead, with no more than a faintly curved forelock to suggest the windswept wildness of the previous mode. The once gaunt cheeks were fuller now, and there was a perceptible middle-age spread beneath the blue-and-white waistcoat, which made him look shorter than, at five feet, he actually was. (At this time a man whose height was five feet six inches was relatively tall.)

Restless as ever, the French emperor preferred to remain standing. His face was severe, unsmiling, and there was no trace of the warmth and affability which in the past he had so often shown to his grand equerry. Speaking with the torrential volubility he was apt to exhibit when worked up, he launched without further ado into a long litany of grievances against his "ally" Alexander, who had added insult to injury by imposing a tax on the importation of French goods, after quietly refusing to cooperate further in the maintenance of the Continental System. As though this were not enough, Alexander had been even more patently displaying his animosity by moving Russian divisions up from Moldavia to reinforce the line of the Dvina River.

To these various accusations Caulaincourt replied by pointing out that the tsar had no choice but to issue his ukaz to keep the exchange value of the ruble from falling below its present level. He had done everything that could humanly be expected of a Russian ruler in trying to uphold the boycott on English goods, but he could not reasonably accept restrictions that the French were now circumventing by the issuance of special licenses authorizing a minimum of trade with England. He had been greatly disturbed by Napoleon's refusal to ratify the convention on Poland which Caulaincourt had personally drafted with Chancellor Rumiantsev, and he had finally been persuaded by recent French troop movements that Napoleon was bent on threatening him and on reestablishing the Kingdom of Poland.

"You are the dupe of Alexander and the Russians!" exclaimed Napoleon.

Stung to the quick by this reproach, Caulaincourt declared that he was ready to be arrested on the spot and to place his head on the scaffold block if the reports sent back from Petersburg by Lauriston did not justify everything he had just stated.

This impassioned cri de coeur took Napoleon by surprise and reduced him, momentarily, to silence. Five, ten, fifteen minutes passed as he paced nervously up and down without proffering a word.

Finally Napoleon stopped his pacing and gazed at Caulaincourt intently with his piercing blue-gray eyes, which seemed to grow darker and bluer whenever he was angry. "So you believe that Russia does not want war and that she would remain in the alliance and would take measures to support the Continental System if I were to satisfy her over Poland?"

"The issue is no longer only about Poland," Caulaincourt replied. "Still, I have no doubt, Sire, that one would be most satisfied if Your Majesty were to withdraw from Danzig and Prussia at least the greater part of the forces that are thought to have been concentrated there against Russia."

"So the Russians are frightened?"

"No, Sire, but being a reasonable people, they prefer an openly declared war to a situation which is not a real state of peace."

"So they think they can dictate terms to me?"

"No, Sire."

"Nonetheless, it is dictating to me to demand that I evacuate Danzig for Alexander's good pleasure."

"Emperor Alexander has not designated anything, doubtless lest it be said that he is threatening. Nevertheless, he . . . finds that Your Majesty's armies, posted three hundred leagues in advance of his frontiers and on the frontiers of Russia, have not come there in the spirit of the maintenance of the alliance."

"Soon," snorted Napoleon, "I'll have to ask Alexander for permission to hold a parade in Mainz!"

"No, Sire," retorted Caulaincourt, "but a parade held in Danzig is for him a slight."

"The Russians have become mighty proud," observed Napoleon acidly. "They think they can kick me around like their king of Poland! I am not Louis XV; the French people would not suffer such a humiliation."

He repeated this phrase several times before lapsing into another long silence. It was followed by a new exchange, in which Caulaincourt pointed out that while in Petersburg Alexander and his government were respecting the Continental System and being true to the spirit of Tilsit, the French were violating both by letting specially licensed French ships return to port laden with British goods.

Breaking into a sudden smile, as was his way when he wished to cajole after unsuccessfully trying to browbeat his interlocutor, Napoleon came up to Caulaincourt and gently tweaked his ear. "So you are in love with Alexander?"

"No, Sire, but I am in love with peace!"

"So am I!" agreed Napoleon. "But I don't want the Russians to order me to evacuate Danzig."

Caulaincourt then repeated what Alexander had said to him during their final conversations in Petersburg: the alliance, to be maintained, had to be of benefit to both parties. If the alliance could not achieve its principal objective —bringing England to the negotiating table and thus guaranteeing the peace of the world—the whole question had to be reconsidered.

"You have been taken in by these reasonings because he envelops them in flattering terms," Napoleon upbraided his former ambassador. "I am an old fox. I know the Greeks."

Caulaincourt now decided to state the fundamental issue in its simplest, most diametric terms. "Sire, I dare repeat it to Your Majesty, I see only two courses to be taken: to reestablish Poland and to proclaim it in order to have the Poles on our side . . . or to maintain the alliance with Russia, which will bring peace with England and will finish your Spanish affairs."

"Which course would you take?"

"The maintenance of the alliance, Sire! It is the course of prudence and of peace."

"You always speak of peace!" objected Napoleon irritably. "But peace is only something when it is enduring and honorable. . . . For peace to be possible and lasting, England must needs be convinced that she will no longer find auxiliaries on the continent. The Russian colossus and its hordes must therefore no longer be able to threaten the South with an invasion."

From this Caulaincourt inferred that Napoleon favored the Polish option. In which case, he pointed out, it behooved the emperor to speak another, distinctly different language.

"I don't want war, I don't want Poland!" insisted Napoleon once again. "But I want the alliance to be useful to me, and such it is no longer when one" —he meant Russia—"receives the neutrals" (i.e., vessels flying non-English flags). The alliance, he added, had in effect ceased to be when the Russians had failed to march resolutely to his aid during his war with Austria in 1809.

The conversation continued in this inconclusive vein for some time, with Caulaincourt playing the part of Alexander's advocate, while Napoleon reproached him for so extravagantly singing the Russian emperor's praises. ("If the ladies of Paris heard you, they would be even more enraptured over Emperor Alexander. What they were told about his manners, about his gallantry at Erfurt, quite turned their heads.") But he quickly abandoned this bantering tone when Caulaincourt told him frankly that Alexander was not afraid of him, as Napoleon seemed to think. "While paying due respect to your military talents, he has often said to me that his country is large, that your genius could give you many advantages over his generals, but that . . . there was plenty of margin to cede ground and that to draw you away from France would already be to combat you successfully . . . Your Majesty will be obliged to return to France, and then all the advantages will be on the side of the Russians, the winter, the harsh climate, and above all else, Emperor Alexander's firmly proclaimed intent to prolong the struggle and not to be so weak as to sign a peace in his capital, as so many other sovereigns have done."

Napoleon then launched into a digression, saying that if it ever came to war, the Russian nobles, fearing for their palaces, would, "after a good battle," force Alexander to sue for peace.

"Your Majesty is in error." Caulaincourt undertook to disabuse him. He then repeated the things that Alexander had said to him in several private conversations, which he had later written down, so as to be able to repeat them, almost word for word. "If Emperor Napoleon wages war against me," Alexander had said to him, "it is possible, even probable, that he will defeat us if we accept combat, but this will not give him peace. The Spaniards have often been defeated, and they are neither vanquished nor subdued. Nevertheless, they are not so far removed from Paris as we are; they have neither our climate, nor our resources. . . . I shall not be the first to draw the sword, but I will be the last to return it to the scabbard. . . . Were the fortunes of war to prove contrary to me, I would rather withdraw to Kamchatka than yield provinces and sign treaties in my capital that are no more than truces. The Frenchman is brave, but prolonged privations and a bad climate wear him down and discourage him. Our climate, our winter will wage the war for us. With you, prodigies are wrought only there where the Emperor is, and he cannot be everywhere and absent from Paris for years."

Napoleon's face, as he listened intently to this detailed recapitulation, betrayed considerable surprise. Then its stern expression seemed to soften as he plied Caulaincourt with questions and spoke of Alexander, his army, his administration, and Russian society with no trace of his previously manifested bitterness.

The respite, however, did not last long. Alexander, he claimed, was "false and feeble," with the character of a Byzantine intriguer; he was ambitious, he was pursuing some subtle, secret design in preparing to make war on him, and so on.

Caulaincourt was unwilling to endorse any of these charges. Alexander was stubborn rather than sly, prepared to yield on trifling matters, but there was a line he had drawn beyond which he was not prepared to retreat. Caulaincourt even startled Napoleon—when the latter complained that it was his failure to marry one of Alexander's sisters that had spoiled everything between them— by bluntly informing him that his marriage to an Austrian princess, in solving this particular problem, had been greeted by the government and Court circles in Petersburg with a genuine sigh of relief. He followed up by declaring that the issues of war and peace were in the French emperor's hands, and he beseeched him to give due thought to his own welfare, as well as to that of France, in choosing a prudent course.

"You speak like a Russian" was Napoleon's crisp rejoinder.

"Rather as a good Frenchman, as a faithful servant of Your Majesty," answered Caulaincourt.

"I repeat it once again, I don't want war. But I cannot keep the Poles from wanting me and waiting for me. Davout and Rapp inform me that the Lithuanians are up in arms against the Russians; they keep sending them deputies to press and decide us."

These reports, Caulaincourt replied, were misleading. The Russian system of government, by virtue of its constitution, was, he argued, the one that best suited the Polish nobles. Already well treated by Emperor Paul, they had benefited even more under Emperor Alexander. Caulaincourt had personally talked to many Lithuanian landholders who, much as they regretted their former national independence, were more than dubious about the prospects of a successful resurrection of Poland as an independent state. The present far from prosperous condition of the Grand Duchy of Warsaw had not made them as favorably inclined to Napoleon as he seemed to think. The great families of Poland, furthermore, were divided among themselves by bitter rivalries, which, combined with a certain *légèreté* (light-headedness), impeded any effective joint action on their part. After which he added, with the kind of frankness that almost no one in Napoleon's imperial entourage still dared to exhibit, that in Europe it was now only too well understood that the French emperor wanted countries for himself rather than for their own interests.

"Do you really believe that, Monsieur?"

"Yes, Sire," came the uncompromising answer.

"Then you are not pampering me," said Napoleon, breaking into a sudden smile. "But now it is time to go have dinner."

So ended a conversation that had lasted five full hours, and which may well have been the most momentous either of them had ever had or would have in the future. Over the next few weeks Caulaincourt was twice invited to dine with the French emperor, and he had several long talks with Napoleon's devoted confidant, Duroc, and with his former secretary, Hughes-Bernard Maret, who in March had replaced the colorless Champagny as minister of external relations. Each time the same arguments were marshaled, the same assurances given: Napoleon did not want war; he cared little for the Poles, whom he regarded basically as a *"nation légère."*

Charmed though he had been by the touching fidelity of the beautiful but brainless Maria Walewska, Napoleon was nettled by the fact that Tadeusz Kosciuszko—hero of the uprising against the predatory Prussians and Catherine the Great's even more unscrupulous suborners—had preferred to go on living quietly in a modest house in the southern suburbs of Paris rather than return to now "liberated" Warsaw to serve his country once again. If this was not simply ingratitude, it displayed a disturbing lack of confidence in Poland's future. How could one reasonably expect a ruler of France to be more ultra-

Polish in his aims than the most illustrious of living Poles? Had he not made it clear to these quarrelsome, intriguing, unmanageable people that the regeneration of Poland depended first and foremost on their own united efforts?

At a moment when, as Caulaincourt had pointed out, it behooved the French emperor to choose one clear-cut course or the other (pro-Polish or pro-Russian), Napoleon remained curiously undecided. And this indecision, as we shall see, was to prove absolutely fatal to the most ambitious and perilous of all his undertakings.

CHAPTER 4

THE FINAL SQUEEZE

FOR MONTHS Napoleon had vainly tried to persuade Armand de Caulaincourt to become his foreign minister. He had also been repeating a proposal which soon became an idée fixe. If only the Russian tsar were willing to send a plenipotentiary to Paris, an envoy expressly empowered to negotiate the troublesome issues dividing them, all of their outstanding quarrels could be resolved overnight.

To Alexander, as to his foreign minister and later chancellor Rumiantsev, this reiterated proposition was understandably suspect. Given his forceful and even magnetic personality, there was no telling what lopsided new "accord" Napoleon might not be able to wring out of a Russian ambassador who had been granted plenipotentiary powers. Nor could there be any question of having a rare bird like Rumiantsev—who enjoyed Napoleon's confidence but who was needed to maintain an unpopular alliance at home—leave Petersburg for Paris. Rumiantsev being unavailable, it was finally decided that the person best suited to be the tsar's representative in France was Prince Alexander Kurakin, a senior member of the Russian foreign service whose father had been the grand marshal of Catherine the Great's Court.

That Alexander could have found no one better fitted to represent him in Paris than this vainglorious peacock of a diplomat was in itself dramatic proof of how difficult it was in Bonaparte-hating Petersburg to find somebody who had a good word to say for the emperor of the French. At Tilsit Kurakin, like Grand Duke Constantine, had practically blessed Napoleon for agreeing to an immediate suspension of hostilities rather than marching his victorious armies forward to occupy Vilna and the ill-defended provinces of Russian Lithuania. As a reward for this sudden Francophilia he had first been sent as Russian ambassador to Vienna to replace Prince Andrei Razumovsky, the music-loving patron of the arts whose name is revered by connoisseurs of chamber music for his generous support of Beethoven, but whose much-frequented drawing rooms were even better known at this time as centers of virulently anti-Bonapartist gossip.

A bachelor, like Rumiantsev, Prince Alexander Borisovich Kurakin was also fabulously rich, but those were about the only qualities they had in common. Whereas the first was prudent, retiring, and discreet, the second was inordinately vain, exhibiting such a love of ostentatious luxury in his manner of dress and mode of entertaining that he was known to the French-speaking nobility of Petersburg as "le prince Diamant." Marie-Elisabeth Vigée-Lebrun, who painted two portraits of Kurakin, has left us a memorable description of his immense Moscow palace, filled with a seemingly interminable succession of drawing rooms, embellished by full-length or chest-high portraits of himself. The corridors leading to the dining room were lined on both sides by a small army of serf-servants, dressed in impeccable liveries and holding flaming torches, as though participating in some solemn pharaonic rite. But surpassing everything in splendor—and this too was typical—was the master bedchamber of this palatial mansion. "The bed, upraised on steps covered with superb carpets, was surrounded by richly draped columns. Two statues and two flower-vases were placed at the four corners of the dais, and pieces of furniture of exquisite taste, and magnificent divans, made this chamber worthy of being inhabited by Venus." The goddess herself never visited this sanctum, but many persons of her sex, from the very highest to the lowest levels of society, had. Indeed, so enterprising had the lusty prince proved himself, particularly in his younger years, that it was reckoned he had sired close to seventy bastard children—a number of whom he unconcernedly brought along with his numerous household flunkeys when he moved from Vienna to Paris in 1809.

Such was the Muscovite grandee, almost a living caricature of the Russian grand seigneur, who became Emperor Alexander's official representative at Napoleon's Court. At six and fifty years he had little left of the good looks that had once swept so many willing females into his bed, and with his small head and fluffy hair (carefully powdered in the eighteenth-century style), his narrow, half-smiling, half-scheming eyes, and a dimpled chin, he had the look of an old roué. But his love of ostentation remained as vigorous as ever. His sorties from his Paris townhouse—in a huge gilded coach drawn by six horses and preceded by liveried footmen and runners—were as spectacular as the diamond-studded decorations adorning the heavy brocade coats he wore on ceremonial occasions. It was indeed the very thickness of one of these embroidered brocade coats which saved the prince from being burned to death in the terrible fire that broke out at the Austrian ambassador's residence, in June 1810, on the occasion of the gala ball given to celebrate Marie-Louise's marriage to Napoleon. Even so, his powdered hair and eyebrows were burned to a crisp, while the skin of his left hand was so seared that it could practically be peeled off like a glove.

This unfortunate mishap inevitably impaired Kurakin's usefulness as an ambassador. There could be no question therefore of making him a plenipotentiary. Nor did Alexander or Rumiantsev at all like the idea of seeing the center of the decision-making process transferred from the isthmus of the Neva to the banks of the Seine.

The deaf ear which Alexander turned to his reiterated proposal in turn convinced Napoleon that his "ally" was being not only mulish but deceptive. He was subtly raising the negotiating stakes and concealing his real aim: a cession of more Polish territory, as an "equitable" compensation for the French annexation of Oldenburg.

The feeling of frustration induced by this diplomatic foot-dragging built up ever greater pressure as the summer weeks of 1811 passed. Finally it erupted in a major explosion in mid-August. The auspicious conjunction of Napoleon's birthday with the Catholic feast of the Assumption of the Virgin—August 15 —made this a very special occasion, commemorated by a solemn mass in the once royal (now imperial) chapel of the Tuileries Palace and an elaborate audience accorded to the leading grandees of the realm, distinguished foreigners, and members of the diplomatic corps.

At midday on this particular August 15, while outside the cannon boomed their window-shaking salvoes, Napoleon, dressed in the satin breeches he now wore on state occasions, walked briskly into the Throne Room of the Tuileries and took his place on the dais. After he had received the bowing homage and the birthday wishes of the princes, cardinals, government ministers, and leading dignitaries of his imperial Court, the members of the diplomatic corps were ushered into the hall.

Stepping down from his gilded throne, Napoleon began to make the usual rounds, pausing to exchange a word or two with the newcomers, who on this day included three citizens from the United States and a Bavarian general. This laborious ceremony completed in an oppressive canicular heat, most of those who had been presented began to drift away, leaving a few members of the diplomatic corps and several government ministers behind. Among them, as splendidly attired as ever in a gold-embroidered brocade coat which sparkled with gleaming star clusters and other diamond-studded decorations, was the Russian ambassador, Prince Alexander Borisovich Kurakin.

"Well, Prince," began Napoleon in a bantering tone, "you have certainly brought us news!" He was referring to what the Russians claimed had been a victory won by their general Kutuzov over the Turks at Routchouk, on the lower Danube, a "feat of arms" that the Turks no less insistently claimed to be theirs. There followed a ten-minute lecture on military tactics, which the inexperienced Kurakin had to listen to in deferent silence. He did, however, hazard the opinion that his imperial master, the tsar, had decided for financial reasons to withdraw some of his troops from the Turkish front—which explained why their commander had been forced to abandon the captured fortress of Routchouk.

"My dear friend," said Napoleon, determined to make the most of this admission, "if you are speaking to me officially, I must pretend to believe you or make no reply at all; but if we are speaking confidentially, then I shall tell you that you were defeated, that this was so because you lacked troops, and that you lacked them because you sent five divisions of your Army of the Danube to Poland, and this not because of any disarray in your finances, which would have been better served if those troops had lived off the enemy, but in order to threaten me."

With that Napoleon launched into a monologue, which grew increasingly heated as he progressed. How else, he claimed, could he have acted than by concentrating French forces in Poland when beyond its borders he saw troop movements for which no rational explanation was forthcoming? "I am not foolish enough to believe that it is Oldenburg that matters to you; I see clearly that it is Poland. You imagine that I harbor projects in Poland's favor, while I am beginning to believe that it is you who wish to seize it, thinking perhaps that there is no other way of securing your frontiers on this side." But if the Russian emperor believed that he could thus find compensation for the Duchy of Oldenburg, then he was very much mistaken. "No," cried Napoleon, his eyes flashing in anger, "even if your armies were camped on the heights of Montmartre, I would not yield an inch of Warsaw territory! I have guaranteed its integrity. . . . You will not have a single village, you will not have one mill! I am not thinking of reconstituting Poland; the interest of my peoples is not linked to that country. But if you force me into war, I will use Poland as a weapon against you. . . . I have no taste for waging war in the North; but if this crisis is not over by November, I will raise another one hundred and twenty thousand men. I shall keep this up for two or three years, and if I find that this system is more tiring than war, I shall make war on you . . . and you will lose all of your Polish provinces.

"You are counting on allies, but where are they?" he went on caustically. "Is it Austria, from whom you took three hundred thousand souls in Galicia? Is it Prussia? Prussia will remember that at Tilsit Emperor Alexander, its good ally, took away the province of Bialystok. Is it Sweden? It will remember that you half destroyed it in wresting Finland from it. None of these grievances can be forgotten; all of these insults will be paid back in kind. You will have the entire continent against you."

Against this gushing torrent of threats and reproaches Kurakin repeatedly sought to protest. His master, Emperor Alexander, wished nothing so much as an end to the present misunderstandings. Well, cried Napoleon, if that was really so, then he too was ready to negotiate. But, he added pointedly, "do you have the necessary powers to negotiate?"

The embarrassed Kurakin had to admit that he did not. But he would hasten to transmit the French emperor's peace-desiring wishes to his superiors in Petersburg.

"Write, by all means write!" Napoleon encouraged him sarcastically. "I have nothing against it. . . ."

And so the diatribe continued, as an increasingly flustered Kurakin sought to stem the flood. Not before three-quarters of an hour had elapsed was Napoleon at last willing to relent, ending his harangue with a few conciliatory words to Alexander's overawed and tongue-tied ambassador. Mopping his moist brow, Prince Alexander Borisovich Kurakin had barely strength to mutter, "It is very hot in His Majesty's palace," as, red-faced and puffing, he beat an inglorious retreat.

The day after this extraordinary outburst Napoleon decided to review the post-Tilsit history of his relations with Alexander with his new foreign minister, Maret, officially ennobled as the Duke of Bassano. Hugues-Bernard Maret, now in his forty-ninth year, was one of those indispensable assistants whom great leaders need to implement their policies and who are inevitably overshadowed by the giants they serve. His relatively undistinguished looks—flattish eyebrows, a dimpled chin, an air of affable tranquillity—were reassuring rather than inhibiting, and thus markedly different from the upturned, almost impish nose, the cold, mocking, from-under-the-eyelids glance, and the mask of imperturbable hauteur which had made Talleyrand such an arresting figure. No one has ever thought of attributing a sarcastic bon mot to Maret. He was a person of tact and discretion rather than biting wit.

Unflagging industry, a first-class memory, a rare ability to record the words and to distill the essence of other persons' speeches had been the cardinal virtues Maret had displayed—first during his two years of service under Louis XVI's foreign minister, Vergennes, and later, during the early years of the Revolution, as a recorder of parliamentary debates. Diplomacy, however, had remained his first love. In less troubled times he would probably have made his mark as an able ambassador.

It was as much for Maret's diplomatic expertise as for his stenographic-journalistic skills that Bonaparte, after returning from Egypt in 1798, had made him a leading member of his secretariat. As secretary of state, to which in 1804 was added the title of minister, Maret was privy to all of Napoleon's secrets. In particular, he was entrusted with the compilation and updating of the secret register (confidential files of biographical information) which Napoleon kept on all monarchs, princelings, diplomats, and leading generals he had to deal with in Europe. Nobody had been closer to Napoleon than this discreet assistant, who had accompanied him on almost all of his campaigns and trips abroad.

It has often been claimed that Napoleon's decision to make war on Russia was really taken on August 16, 1811, the day on which he dictated a long memorandum on the subject of Russian-French relations to Maret. This, however, is an oversimplification of the case. Essentially, this memorandum examined the existing alternatives and the possibility of a war with Russia. Its conclusions may be briefly summarized as follows: There could be no question of trying to appease Alexander for the loss of the Duchy of Oldenburg by offering to cede territory close to Russia's borders, with the transfer to Russian sovereignty of 500,000 to 600,000 Poles; that would fatally undermine Polish confidence in France and hasten the collapse of the fragile Grand Duchy of Warsaw. Still less could there be any question of abandoning the Grand Duchy to its fate; for if the Russian Empire were to advance its western borders to the Vistula, this would make it far and away the greatest power in Europe. A war against Russia should be envisaged primarily as a preventive measure, aimed at keeping it from drifting away from the Continental System toward an open alliance with England. The next six months should suffice to determine if this really was the direction in which Russia was headed. During this interval the Grande Armée's strength in Germany and Poland would be steadily reinforced, to take care of any eventuality. It was already too late in any case to launch an invasion of Russia now; the proper moment would come in the early summer of 1812, when the ripened wheat fields of Poland and Lithuania would supply the needed fodder for the horses of the Grande Armée's enormous cavalry forces and supply trains.

In actual fact, as we have seen, Napoleon's first military measures had been taken as early as December of 1810 and January of 1811. Though initially inspired by a fear of a Russian invasion of the Grand Duchy of Warsaw, they assumed a less defensive character when Napoleon decided to send Lauriston, a military man, rather than a civilian diplomat, to replace Caulaincourt as his ambassador in Petersburg. This increasingly offensive disposition was spurred by the Russian ukaz of December 31, 1810. Its progress can be charted step by step with almost mathematical precision from the orders issued to or from the Dépôt de la Guerre, a highly specialized rear-echelon staff which acted as the French army's "memory" (with a library of 9,000 volumes of military history) and as its probing eyes (with a large stock of maps and 90 engineer corps officers carefully trained in the techniques of military cartography).

On April 13, 1811, General Nicolas Sanson, commander of the Dépôt de la Guerre, was ordered to provide Colonel Albert Bacler d'Albe, the head of Napoleon's personal topographic staff, with everything it possessed concerning Prussia and Poland. Just four days later Sanson had to appeal to Maret for the loan of one of the French Foreign Ministry's two maps of Russia—available in 106 separate sheets. Napoleon had decided that the existing military map was inadequate and that a new one, blown up to three times its scale, needed to be engraved. The preparation of this new map, covering European Russia and comprising 54 sheets, was made a top-priority assignment. It was followed by the preparation of a 21-sheet map covering Poland, Livonia, and Estonia, the drawing of which was pursued on the same round-the-clock basis, with two engravers relaying each other in alternating shifts.

The first two sections of the new map of Russia were ready for presentation to Napoleon on July 1—six weeks before his public diatribe against Kurakin. In August other sections were presented to him. The Dépôt de la Guerre was then ordered to provide large-scale city maps of Petersburg and Moscow—to the considerable embarrassment of General Sanson, who had to write to Lauriston in Petersburg, asking him to send back whatever he had available.

The transliteration into French of the names of towns located in the Baltic provinces of the Russian Empire also seems to have created unforeseen difficulties, incidentally revealing how shockingly ignorant were the "linguistic experts" hired for the job. For when Marshal Davout finally received the maps for Estonia, Livonia, and Courland, he was incensed to find a tongue twister like "Neiahaouzen" where "Neuhausen" should have been written, simply because the former was the closest Russian approximation of the Germanic vowel sounds.

Nowhere in Europe did the relentless buildup of French military might engender more furious gnashing of teeth than in Berlin. The city, which at this time numbered barely two hundred thousand souls (less than half of Paris's population), had not recovered from the numbing shock of November 1806, when Marshal Davout's seasoned First Corps troopers had marched in through the Hallischer Tor with their caps askew and hardly bothering to keep in step, and had later broken into a double-time jog-trot—an unheard-of feat for the stiffly gaitered and rigidly drilled soldiery of Prussia. The French garrison had finally been withdrawn in the autumn of 1808, to the intense relief of most Berliners. But though their sovereign had been able to return at last to his capital, his despondent face now seemed longer, gloomier, and less inspiring than ever.

In the summer of 1810 Prussia had lost its popular heroine, the radiant Queen Luise (who had died of pneumonia)—but the harassed, hamstrung kingdom had acquired a hero, one refreshingly different from the doddering septuagenarian generals who had been responsible for the disasters of 1806. The hero was a dauntless hussar officer named Ferdinand von Schill, who had managed to drag himself, though wounded, from the battlefield of Auerstädt. In June of 1809, when Napoleon was tied down in Austria, he had boldly raised the standard of revolt, had raised a "free corps" of saber-swinging volunteers, and had succeeded in defeating the French in several minor engagements. Pursued by a Dutch division all the way to the Baltic seaport of Stralsund, the quixotic cavalry captain had finally been killed while leading one more desperate sortie. His death, far from dampening the anti-French ardor of his countrymen, had merely stimulated the patriotic cause. In Berlin he became a martyr overnight. Miniature portraits of his manly face, or the magic letters *FvS*, were reproduced on hundreds of medallions and boldly strung from ironwork necklaces over the décolletés of many leading Berlin ladies. "It is with iron," as the fashionable slogan went, "that Prussia will rise again, and it must be used everywhere—even on the bosoms of our womenfolk."

While such was the prevailing mood in most of the salons of Berlin, caution was more than ever the watchword at King Frederick William's Court, haunted by the panic dread that Napoleon might be planning to carry out his oft-repeated threat to do away with the Hohenzollern dynasty. Never had the Prussian government been more Janus-faced than at this moment. Ostensibly the nervous monarch had succumbed to the influence of a pro-French coterie. In secret, however, King Frederick William was pursuing a different policy of anti-French resistance with the connivance of his chancellor, Baron Karl August von Hardenberg, and the head of the Prussian General Staff, General Gerhard von Scharnhorst. So hush-hush was this latter policy that there was not an official in the Prussian foreign office, from the foreign minister on down (and including the Prussian ambassador in Paris), who knew anything about it.

To circumvent the crippling restrictions of Tilsit and Erfurt, which had limited to 42,000 the number of men under arms, Scharnhorst had developed a clever *Krümpersystem* (literally "shrinkage-system") of enrollment, whereby new recruits, after being taught the rudiments of infantry maneuvering and musket-loading without resort to the savage beatings of the past (which had so depressed the morale of the Prussian rank and file), were quietly released from service into a readily available reserve. Other recruits could then be enrolled and given training in their turn without exceeding the prescribed manpower quotas. More difficult to conceal, however, were the entrenched camps, which Scharnhorst wished to arm with a new model of rapid-firing cannon, and the moats, redoubts, and glacis that were already being added to the Vistula fortress of Graudenz, to the Baltic strongholds of Pillau and Kolberg, and to the forbidding red-brick turrets of Spandau, near Berlin.

Persuaded by the late spring of 1811 that war between France and Russia was inevitable and that Prussia would have to side with one or the other, the shrewd chancellor, Hardenberg, decided that the best way of making these military measures more palatable to the suspicious French was to enter into an "honorable" alliance—in return for the guaranteed integrity of the Prussian state, the evacuation by the French of the fortress town of Glogau (on the Oder), and the scrapping of further "contributions" (punitive reparations) once hostilities had started. Napoleon, however, was in no mood to relax his iron grip on any of the Oder River fortresses, nor prepared to lighten the burden of the financial reparations that he had imposed on Frederick William's groaning subjects.

Fearing the worst for his shriveled kingdom, the uneasy Prussian monarch decided in July to make new overtures to his former friend and ally, Tsar Alexander of Russia. The person entrusted with this top-secret mission was the close-lipped chief of staff, General von Scharnhorst. To allay suspicions as to what he was really up to, Scharnhorst first journeyed to Silesia on "personal business," before going to spend a few days in a country house he owned in East Prussia. He then headed secretly for the Russian border, where a Jaeger (light cavalry) officer was waiting to escort him by carefully chosen side roads to the "imperial village" of Tsarskoye Syelo, near Petersburg. Here he was lodged in the house of a retired chamberlain, from which he always emerged with his arm in a sling, to sustain the illusion that he was a wounded colonel, recently returned from the Turkish "front."

From the start Tsar Alexander showed himself exceedingly wary, even allowing a week to pass before he would receive the Prussian general. In the interim Scharnhorst was able to present his arguments to the Russian minister of war, General Barclay de Tolly, with whom he quickly established an excellent rapport. Prussia, Scharnhorst pointed out in his densely argued memorandum, was now reduced to a kingdom of four and a half million—the number of subjects Frederick the Great had had at the start of the Seven Years War in 1756. But, though terribly vulnerable to a massive French attack, Prussia was not done for as a military power. Thanks to their secret *Krümpersystem* of recruiting and training, the Prussians could now double their military forces overnight. By withdrawing to eight carefully prepared fortresses and three entrenched camps—some located in mountainous Silesia, the others along the Baltic—80,000 Prussian soldiers could harass the exposed flanks and rear of Napoleon's Grande Armée and thus tie down 100,000 Frenchmen as they moved across the Grand Duchy of Warsaw. But to be able to fall back successfully and to concentrate their scattered forces around these strongpoints, the Prussians had to have Russian help. Otherwise Prussia was certain to be overrun and eliminated as a fighting force in the opening weeks of the campaign.

The vital question, therefore, was: how much effective Russian help could the Prussians count on in the event of a war with France? The answer given to Scharnhorst was disappointing. Of the six front-line divisions guarding the Niemen River, the Russians could dispatch only one to reinforce the defenses of Koenigsberg, while the other five advanced westward to seize the key Warsaw fortress of Praga and to aid the embattled Prussians in the other Vistula stronghold of Graudenz (some 70 miles south of Danzig). Three to four more weeks would be needed to move up the other eleven divisions of Russia's second line—which meant that they could not offer the Prussians any prompt help in Silesia.

A hard-headed realist, Scharnhorst decided that this aid, though limited at the start to six divisions, was better than nothing. For his part, Tsar Alexander, albeit reluctant to abandon the defensive military strategy to which he was personally committed, was sufficiently impressed by Scharnhorst's claim that 80,000 Prussians could tie down 100,000 of Napoleon's Grande Armée forces to authorize his minister of war to draft a military convention with the Prussian chief of staff. By its terms Russia pledged itself to come to Prussia's rescue if the latter country was overrun by the French, it being further agreed that, once hostilities began, neither of the two countries would sign a separate peace.

This draft convention, amounting in effect to a full-scale military alliance, was duly signed by Scharnhorst (for Prussia) and by Chancellor Rumiantsev and Barclay de Tolly (for Russia) on October 18. But it was two weeks before the Prussian chief of staff could have it brought back to Berlin for submission to his king. In the interim, under relentlessly mounting French pressure, Frederick William III had again caved in, ordering a halt to all further ditch-digging and bastion-strengthening at Spandau and the dismissal of the vehemently anti-French General Leberecht von Blücher from his post as governor of Pomerania.

Chancellor Hardenberg, having abandoned his earlier hope of being able to reach an "honorable" alliance with Napoleon's France, now decided to make overtures to England. But to his dismay, his tormented sovereign, Frederick William, simply could not bring himself to sign a letter addressed to the prince regent requesting British help—even though a number of English ships loaded with muskets, gunpowder, and cannon were already in the Baltic, and prepared to reinforce the Prussian strongholds of Kolberg, Pillau, Koenigsberg, and Memel.

After studying the treaty draft Scharnhorst had signed in Petersburg, King Frederick William decided that, with only six Russian divisions pledged to help her in the crucial first weeks, Prussia would be doomed in any future conflict with France unless Austria could be persuaded to come to her rescue in Silesia. Although he personally doubted that Emperor Francis and his foreign minister, Metternich, would be willing to join them in a triple alliance, he finally agreed to let Scharnhorst undertake a second top-secret trip to Vienna. The alternative, as he now saw it, was simple: "Either a definite and positive contribution from Austria, or an honorable, albeit unhappy, alliance with France."

Frederick William's gloomy conviction that this second mission would come to nothing was confirmed even before Scharnhorst reached the Austrian capital in late November (traveling this time disguised as a privy councillor from Prussian Pomerania). The moment Emperor Francis learned that the Prussian emissary was Scharnhorst, he went into a nervous flap. The name of Scharnhorst was associated in his exceedingly simple mind with the Tugendbund, the so-called League of Virtue, which a number of Prussian patriots had launched in 1807, at a time when King Frederick William and his panic-stricken Court had taken refuge in the East Prussian capital of Koenigsberg. The Tugendbund had in fact been officially dissolved not long after its creation, but the mere fact that it had once existed as a secret society made it extremely suspect to the arch-conservative and devoutly Catholic Emperor Francis, who regarded all secret societies and Masonic lodges with holy horror, as agents of revolutionary agitation.

Metternich himself had other and more serious reasons for not wishing to ally Austria to Prussia and Russia. He was instinctively suspicious of Protestant Prussia, which in the previous century had frequently created trouble for the Austrians in the Catholic Rhineland, and which, under Frederick the Great, had wrested the rich province of Silesia, with its precious mines and workshops, from Habsburg rule. He was even more suspicious of Russia—a country which, under the fumbling leadership of its present ruler, had upset the status quo in Europe by speeding the collapse of the Holy Roman Empire, by rashly egging on the Prussians, and then by effecting a "monstrous" alliance with France. And as though this were not enough, Russia was further upsetting the balance of power in the Balkans.

If war broke out between France and Russia, Metternich was convinced, Napoleon would proclaim the restoration of the Kingdom of Poland. This was bound to unleash a wave of popular fervor and unrest among the Polish inhabitants of Austrian-ruled Galicia: unrest which a ruthless Napoleon was certain to encourage if Austria chose to remain neutral. Even if Austria opted reluctantly for a limited participation on France's side, she would probably be obliged at the conclusion of the war to surrender Galicia to the new Kingdom of Poland. For the already drastically shrunk Habsburg Empire this would mean another serious territorial amputation, but it could be compensated by the reacquisition of all or most of Prussian-ruled Silesia.

On the other hand, for Austria—already four times defeated by Napoleon in successive wars—to ally itself with Russia struck Metternich as suicidal folly. Russia, under Alexander's wobbly guidance, could not hope to win a war against Europe's greatest soldier. All Austria would gain by joining the losing side would be another French occupation of Vienna, new and more drastic amputations (an independent Bohemia? an independent Hungary?), which would put a shattering end to the Habsburg Empire. A Russian defeat, furthermore, might not be such a bad thing, since it would throw "this Empire back into the steppes of Asia"—as Metternich had recently put it in a long memorandum presented to his emperor. It would help to shore up the strife-torn Ottoman Empire, which Metternich was bent on preserving at all costs, and keep the already vast empire of the tsars from laying greedy hands on Constantinople and the Bosphorus.

At their final meeting, held the day after Christmas, the Austrian foreign minister was careful to conceal these underlying sentiments from Scharnhorst. Instead, he repeated what he had already told the general: the Austrian government believed that it was in Prussia's interest to sign a military alliance with Russia, and that the best way of postponing the outbreak of war would be for the governments of those two countries to issue a joint proclamation making it clear that any French aggression against Prussia would be considered a casus belli in both Berlin and St. Petersburg. If Prussia, on the other hand, chose to sign an alliance with France, this would surely precipitate the war that the emperor of Austria, as much as the king of Prussia, was anxious to avoid. The important thing was to play for time. Austria, though "morally" committed to the Prussian cause, could not, however, provide any immediate military help, given the parlous state of its finances and the months it would need to form a new army capable of making itself respected on the field of battle.

This subtle answer effectively killed all hope of forming a triple alliance against Napoleon. It dealt a death blow to all of Scharnhorst's hopes. Prussia and Russia would have to go it alone, and given King Frederick William's fearful disposition, it was well-nigh certain that he would finally knuckle under to French pressure.

The way was now open for Napoleon to achieve through threatening coercion what the German general had been unable to obtain through simple powers of persuasion. The softening-up process began in January of 1812, when one of Davout's divisions invaded Swedish Pomerania. In early February his soldiers occupied three Prussian towns along the Baltic coast—a clear warning of what lay in store for Frederick William III and his drastically reduced kingdom if he made the slightest effort to cross Napoleon's plans.

Next came the news that General Charles Gudin, commander of the 3rd Infantry Division in Marshal Davout's First Corps, had left Magdeburg and was marching northward with 16,000 men. Hardenberg at this point suggested that the Court leave Berlin and head for Silesia with all available Prussian troops. But before they could move, a courier arrived from Paris with the news that Foreign Minister Maret had informed the Prussian minister in Paris, General Friedrich Wilhelm von Krusemarck, that the time for fence-straddling was over. If Prussia wished to survive as a state, it would have to side with France in the looming conflict with Russia. Napoleon had summoned Krusemarck to a midnight meeting in his office, where he had bluntly told him that his French forces would have to be granted a right-of-transit through Prussian territory, and that for their failure to pay the rest of their arrears in punitive "contributions," the Prussians would now be obliged to provide 30 million francs' worth of food, horses, and supplies. Of the 42,000 officers and soldiers Prussia had been allowed to maintain, 20,000 were to be incorporated into the Grande Armée for the coming campaign.

The next day another courier arrived with the text of a partly open, partly secret treaty, which a thoroughly browbeaten Baron von Krusemarck had been forced to sign under duress in Paris. This treaty opened all of Brandenburg, Pomerania, and Prussia to French occupation, with the sole exception of upper Silesia and two fortresses (Kolberg and Graudenz), over which the French were officially to have no jurisdiction. In effect, this treaty turned the once proud kingdom of Prussia into a puppet state.

For Scharnhorst these were intolerable terms. He therefore proposed that the entire kingdom be placed on a war footing and that the army be increased overnight to a strength of 120,000 men—which could be done by calling up the trained reserves, distributing arms and munitions, and concentrating all available manpower in five fortresses and in the three entrenched camps that had been readied for the long-awaited day of national renovation.

Six months earlier, Hardenberg had proudly told the French minister in Berlin that King Frederick William and his subjects would prefer to go down fighting with weapons in their hands rather than submit to further humiliations. But that was before Davout had moved his six divisions forward. Now the Prussian Court was trapped. And so, on March 5, King Frederick William, once again the loser in his continuing duel with Napoleon, was forced to put his signature to a treaty that consummated Prussia's military humiliation by forcing her to contribute 20,000 men to the French emperor's Grande Armée.

Shortly thereafter several French artillery officers turned up on an "inspection tour" and managed to seize the massive Spandau fortress by infiltrating a few companies of infantrymen and then expelling the Prussian garrison. Marshal Oudinot could now ride triumphantly into Berlin with the headquarters staff of his Second Corps, who were invited to dine at Potsdam with a helpless monarch. Unwilling to go on serving, close to one quarter of the officers in the Prussian army resigned their commissions. Some of them headed south and eastward, persuaded that Russia was their stricken country's last remaining hope.

With his father-in-law, Emperor Francis of Austria, and his foreign minister Napoleon had fewer problems, though he did not get everything he wanted. Acting with the same slick rapidity he had shown in negotiating Marie-Louise's marriage to the "Corsican ogre," Metternich authorized the Austrian ambassador in Paris, Prince Karl Schwarzenberg, to offer Napoleon an auxiliary force of 30,000 Austrian soldiers—substantially fewer than the 40,000 to 50,000 the French emperor had originally requested. It was to be an independent entity—unlike the 20,000 Prussians (who were finally enrolled in Marshal Macdonald's Tenth Corps).

The treaty of alliance, signed in Paris on March 14, went some, though not all, of the way toward satisfying Metternich's hopes and wishes concerning Austria's eventual rewards for participating in the coming war. Austria's continuing sovereignty over Galicia was specifically guaranteed, even were a Kingdom of Poland to be established. An eventual cession of those Polish provinces was, however, envisaged in exchange for a return to Austrian rule of the Illyrian provinces of Dalmatia, Fiume, and Trieste. In the case of a "happy outcome of the war," Napoleon also promised Austria indemnities and territorial aggrandizements; but whether they were to come from the Russian provinces of Volhynia and Podolia or from Prussian-held Silesia was not specified. Having browbeaten the Prussians into allying themselves with him, the French emperor could not further dismember their hard-pressed kingdom. It was indeed essential to his war plans that the future of Silesia be held in abeyance and suspense—an ominous question mark, a sword of Damocles suspended over the head of the fearful Frederick William III, as a warning of what might happen if he or any of his generals committed the slightest "transgression."

In France, throughout this winter and early spring of 1812, there were rumblings of discontent on the part of town dwellers, dismayed to see the price of a sack of flour rise from 70 to 120 francs (because of the terrible drought and devastating hailstorms of the preceding summer, which had ruined much of the wheat crop). In a number of cities (including The Hague, Antwerp, and Rotterdam) there were serious riots to protest the forced induction of thousands of new recruits. But in Paris, where the press was sufficiently well controlled to muffle the report of these distant explosions of popular wrath, one fancy-dress ball followed another in a round of carefree entertainment. Not to be outshone by a stately "Quadrille des Incas" which Louis Bonaparte's wife, Hortense (the former "Queen of Holland"), put on to celebrate her happy return from the "northern fogs" of The Hague, Napoleon's sister Caroline undertook to stage a ball celebrating the newly established friendship between "Rome and France." This provided the beautiful Princess Pauline with an ideal occasion for adorning her lustrous Pompeian-styled hair with a metal headband and ostrich feathers and her voluptuous arms with golden, cameo-embossed bracelets, while the queen of Naples (Caroline) could exhibit her virile regality in a plumed Roman helmet and a long white robe edged in embroidered gold and purple.

One of the male adornments of these carnival festivities deserves special mention because he inadvertently helped to fan a burst of anti-Russian xenophobia on the eve of Napoleon's departure for the East. This was the tsar's aide-de-camp Colonel Alexander Ivanovich Chernyshov, a young cavalryman who had helped his stunned emperor to find Kutuzov during the disorderly twilight retreat from Austerlitz, and who had later distinguished himself at Friedland (June 1807) by finding a ford across the Alle River when all of its bridges were ablaze, enabling thousands of trapped Russians to escape to the farther bank.

Napoleon, at their first meeting in January 1808, had appreciated Chernyshov's forthright judgments on the tactical skills of various battlefield commanders. He had been even more impressed, two months later at Bayonne, by the young emissary's ability to bring him another imperial letter from Petersburg in just sixteen days. For this exploit and others, which were to earn him the nickname of *l'éternel postillon,* the twenty-five-year-old aide-de-camp was granted the rare privilege of being invited to stay on at the French emperor's military headquarters through the decisive weeks of the Austrian campaign of 1809.

The detailed military information that Chernyshov was able to bring back to his imperial master so impressed Alexander that he decided to send the "eternal postilion" on repeated missions to Paris, where his primary and ostensible purpose would be to deliver a new letter to Napoleon, while his secondary and no less important duty would be to keep the Russian tsar informed about the mood of the French capital.

In this latter task Chernyshov seems to have been eminently successful. A member of one of Russia's most distinguished families, he had impeccable manners and a breathtaking virtuosity in waltzing, which quite literally swept women off their feet. They found his curly dark hair and sideburns, his neatly twirled mustache, his scimitar-sharp nose and indrawn nostrils, and above all his gleaming, coal-black eyes utterly irresistible. Laure d'Abrantès, in her garrulous memoirs, was probably not exaggerating much in thus describing the effect that Chernyshov's presence at a Court ball at the Tuileries Palace was capable of producing on members of the female sex: "All looked like wild cats when the Lovelace of the North appeared among them. . . . Everything about him, including his costume, the wasp-waisted tight-fittedness of his attire, that hat, that plume, that hair surging out in large tufts, and then that Tartar physiognomy, those almost perpendicular eyes . . .—all this put together . . . made for an original and curious type."

While much of Chernyshov's time was devoted to charming the ladies, a significant part of it was reserved for conversations of a more serious nature, which revealed how widespread were the misgivings felt in many quarters about the future of the ever-expanding French Empire.

For a while, acting in conjunction with Prince Kurakin's diplomatic assistant, Karl von Nesselrode, Chernyshov had tried to find ways of helping those who were opposed to the Napoleonic regime in Germany and France. But since these contacts had begun to arouse the attention of the French police, he had concentrated his unofficial efforts on obtaining as much information as he could about the strength and latest movements of different units in Napoleon's Grande Armée.

It would be doing this Cossack Don Juan too much honor to claim that his remarkable achievements in this field were all of his own doing. The initial spadework had been accomplished six years before, in 1806, when the Russian chargé d'affaires, Pierre d'Oubril, had made the acquaintance of a French clerk named Michel, who was employed in the military-movements section of the Ministry of War. Although his superiors often praised him for having the "finest hand" in the ministry, they do not seem to have esteemed Michel's talents as a copyist so highly as to pay him the kind of salary he felt entitled to. This oversight had been promptly remedied by Pierre d'Oubril, who had thoughtfully offered him a "present," with a promise of more to come if every now and then he could slip him a spare copy of the reports he was duty-bound to pen in his elegant script.

After the signing of the Tilsit Treaty, in July 1807, Michel does not seem to have felt that he was committing any serious offense in providing the Russian embassy with such reports. But once launched on this slippery slope, he discovered that there was no easy turning back; and as the relations between France and Russia began to sour, he found himself in an increasingly desperate situation, under the pressure his Russian paymasters could bring to bear on him by threatening to expose his activities.

Since this kind of shady business could not be conducted too directly or at too high a level, the job of maintaining contact with Michel had been delegated to the gatekeeper of the Russian ambassador's townhouse, a former Viennese named Wustinger. Prince Alexander Kurakin seems to have had no inkling of these goings-on, but at least two of his subordinates were "in the know." One of them was his deputy, the short and almost repellently obsequious Karl Robert Nesselrode, of whom Metternich was later to remark that "if he were a fish, he would be carried away with the current."

In the autumn of 1811 the young Nesselrode had been recalled to Petersburg, supposedly to be briefed by Tsar Alexander and Chancellor Rumiantsev, and then sent back to Paris with the "plenipotentiary powers" needed for a "decisive" negotiation with Napoleon. In his absence someone was needed to maintain contact with the invaluable Michel. The job was turned over to the young Chernyshov.

That the tsar's aide-de-camp was up to some kind of mischief, Napoleon had long ago begun to suspect. Foreign Minister Maret was accordingly instructed to keep a sharp eye on this Cossack colonel, who, after being sent back to Paris in December 1811 with another message from his imperial master, had been asked to cool his heels for a while in the French capital before returning to Petersburg.

What neither Napoleon nor his new minister of police, General Savary, knew was the extent to which the Russians had been able to penetrate to the very heart of the French military establishment. When Chernyshov had taken over from Nesselrode, the once invaluable Michel was no longer employed in the vital military-movements section, having been transferred to the uniform-and-clothing department of the quartermaster service. There the conscience-stricken informer would have preferred to pursue a career of bureaucratic anonymity, but he was not allowed this respite. With the remorselessness of a bloodhound, Chernyshov tracked the poor scribe down to his humble lair in an obscure Paris street and put the fear of God—or more probably of Satan —into him with the dangerous gleam of his white teeth and the stiletto glitter of his dark eyes. The terrified copyist managed to recruit three employees in the war ministry whose job it was to have the loose report pages on latest order-of-battle movements taken to a bookbinder to be properly boxed before being presented to the emperor.

On February 25 Chernyshov was asked to call on Maret, who then took him in his carriage from the Ministry of External Relations across the Seine to the Elysée Palace, which Napoleon had recently taken back from former Empress Josephine for his own use. In the conversation that followed Napoleon renewed his familiar complaints about the restrictions imposed on Kurakin's negotiating powers, and restated his own conditions for a settlement of the outstanding issues. Chernyshov was asked to transmit the gist of these statements to his imperial master, even though, Napoleon pointedly added, he knew that the tsar's aide-de-camp was in Paris only "for military information."

The hint did not fall on deaf ears. On returning to his place of residence, Chernyshov went through his papers, throwing everything he could discard into the fireplace, where he put a match to them. The rest, compressed into a tight packet, were slipped in behind the breast buttons of his tunic, giving his chest a more than usually impressive bulge above the shapely wasp waist when, the next morning, he climbed into the post chaise for his return to Petersburg.

An hour or two after his departure several Paris police agents broke into the apartment where he had been staying. A few letters, carefully torn into tiny shreds, were all he appeared to have left behind, along with a pile of ashes in his bedroom fireplace. But in pulling back the small fireplace rug in order to rummage in the ashes, one of the policemen came upon a slip of paper addressed to "Monsieur le comte"; it indicated that at seven o'clock the next morning the sender would be bringing him some surprising information about the "Grande Armée of Germany," of which the Imperial Guard was to be an integral part. The note was signed "M."

It took the investigators four days to discover that this mysterious "M"—betrayed by the excessive elegance of his script—was the clerk, Michel. He and his three accomplices were arrested. The Vienna-born janitor of the Russian embassy, after being lured to a café rendezvous, also disappeared behind the bars—to the bewildered dismay of Prince Kurakin.

Napoleon now had the proof he needed that his onetime ally, his dear "brother" Alexander, had been acting in bad faith. But having reached the conclusion that the Russians were not going to upset all of his carefully calculated plans by invading the Grand Duchy of Warsaw before he himself reached the scene, he ordered the "Michel affair" to be turned over to the normal judicial authorities, knowing that it would take the examining magistrate a good month to complete his investigation.

In mid-April Michel and his three accomplices were duly placed on trial for "high treason" amid a blaze of publicity provided by the *Gazette de France*. The public prosecutor delivered a lengthy comminatory harangue, in the course of which he unfolded a tale of sordid bribery and corruption. The unfortunate Michel was finally sentenced to death and guillotined; one of his accomplices was publicly pilloried as well as fined; the other two were exonerated.

Outraged by all these charges of devious behind-the-scenes doings of which he knew absolutely nothing, Prince Kurakin drafted a vehement note of protest, calling on the French government to issue an official denial. This fatuous request was ignored, whereupon the irate ambassador began packing his belongings and sending home some of the illegitimate members of his vast family.

On April 24 another of his bastard sons, an official named Serdobin, arrived from Petersburg with a message from the Russian government that seemed to have been designed to render tit for tat. It indicated that the Russian emperor was prepared to enter into negotiations, provided that France began by evacuating Prussia and agreed not to raise the question of neutral ships being allowed to put in to Russian harbors.

It was now Napoleon's turn to blow his top. In an interview granted to Kurakin on April 27 he angrily declared that these conditions were an insult and that the Russian government was in effect "putting a knife" under his throat. The stage-managed "treason trial" of Michel had been answered by an ultimatum.

Both sides by this time had passed the point of no return. Foreign Minister Maret had intimated as much on February 25, 1812, in a letter addressed to General Lauriston in Petersburg. The French ambassador was informed that Napoleon "places no confidence in any kind of negotiation, unless the 450,000 men whom His Majesty has put into motion and their immense baggage-train should move the Saint Petersburg cabinet to serious rethinking, bring it back sincerely to the system that was established at Tilsit, and place Russia back in the situation of inferiority in which she was then . . . Your only aim, Monsieur le Comte, should be to gain time." Time to mount another, even more spectacular mise-en-scène, destined to be held this time in Dresden: a lavish diplomatic show calculated to emphasize the isolation of Napoleon's impressionable but so mulish "brother," Alexander, and to persuade him that it would be better to agree to a second Tilsit rather than face annihilation by daring to pit his woefully inferior forces against the mightiest military host the continent of Europe had ever seen assembled under one commander.

CHAPTER 5

DRESDEN

AT FIVE-THIRTY in the morning of May 9, Napoleon and Marie-Louise finally left the Château de Saint-Cloud and headed eastward along the northern bank of the Seine. Their green-upholstered berlin was accompanied by a score of other carriages, carrying officers, chamberlains, and ladies-in-waiting of the two imperial households—not to mention the 40 mules, 200 spare horses, and 70 eight-horse-drawn wagons loaded with uniforms, dresses, and other essentials of Court attire that had preceded them. Nothing could have seemed less militant than this long file of postilion-guided equipages clattering and rumbling over the cobblestones of Paris, and as one of the French emperor's private secretaries, Baron Jean-François Fain, was later to write, "Never has a departure for the army more resembled a journey of pleasure."

That this was no more than an agreeable illusion, no one knew better than Napoleon. One of the officers he had consulted—a colonel of the engineer corps named Ponthon, who had spent some time in Russia after the signing of the Tilsit Treaty—had actually got down on his knees and begged the emperor *not* to attempt an invasion of Russia, given that country's immensity, the sorry state of its roads, the abundance of its marshes, the shortness of its summers, and so on. Though he had dismissed him with a brusque gesture, Napoleon had been so struck by the colonel's anguished plea that during several days of brooding meditation he had seemed about to call a halt to everything. But to give up, after having devoted so much time and effort to his elaborate preparations, would, he realized, make him look ridiculous in the eyes of all those resentful European sovereigns who were watching, like buzzards, for the first telltale sign of weary weakness, of faltering determination. To Baron Etienne-Denis Pasquier, whom he had appointed to the important post of prefect of police shortly before leaving Paris, he admitted that this was "the biggest, the most difficult enterprise I have yet attempted," adding almost ruefully, "but one must finish what has been begun."

Just how long he would be away, there was no telling. But this was the least of Napoleon's worries. Administering France from abroad was no new experience for a highly mobile ruler who, wherever he might be, was kept constantly informed of what was happening at home by couriers and *estafettes,* who passed on their locked dispatch boxes at designated relay stations. Since he had become emperor he had spent the winter of 1805–1806 in Bavaria, Moravia, and Austria, the following autumn, winter, and spring (ten months in all) in Saxony and Prussia, and the entire summer and early autumn of 1809 in Austria.

In his absence the portly Jean-Jacques de Cambacérès, who had served with him as Second Consul at the turn of the century, would continue to preside with his customary imperturbability over the sessions of the Conseil d'Etat, a carefully handpicked body of legal, financial, and administrative experts which was the real "brain" of the Napoleonic system. The threat of a seaborne invasion had been parried in advance by the addition of formidable batteries of cannon and heavy mortars to the defenses of France's major Mediterranean and Atlantic seaports, now secure from a surprise English assault. And to make them doubly safe more than 100,000 Frenchmen had been recruited into National Guard units, ready to be rushed to any threatened stretch of coast.

Not least of all, in a country that had recently been plagued by food riots and rampant draft-dodging, there was the Ministry of Police. Here, the French emperor knew, he had nothing to fear, for it was controlled more firmly than ever by the vigilant watchdog who had headed his secret-police bureau since 1800, General René Savary, now Duke of Rovigo. Indeed, so meddlesome had Savary's police surveillance grown that it had precipitated the flight from France and Switzerland of Europe's foremost *femme de lettres,* the incorrigibly anti-Bonapartist Germaine de Staël.

No, what preoccupied Napoleon was not the familiar problems he was leaving behind him, but the troubling uncertainties that lay ahead. In December he had asked his Tuileries Palace librarian, Barbier, to gather together all the books he could find about Lithuania and Russia. They included several accounts (one of them by Voltaire) of King Charles XII's fateful invasion of Russia, which had ended so disastrously for the Swedes at Poltava in July 1708; a 500-page description of Russia's countryside, geography, and resources; and at least two manuscript translations of books that had recently been written about the Russian army.

No one could accuse the French emperor of not having done his homework before embarking on this campaign. With Charles XII's misfortunes present in his mind, he had written to Eugène de Beauharnais, in Milan, on the eve of the new year, to point out that the coming "Polish war" would bear no resemblance to the "Austrian war" of 1809, when the French and their Bavarian allies had been able to live off the land. "Without means of transport, all is useless. Each military supply battalion must have 771 men, 1227 horses, and 252 wagons," he had decreed, adding a little farther on that some of the larger wagons could now carry 4,000 rations of flour (enough to supply 4,000 men with bread for one day), and that Prince Eugène's soldiers should set out with a thirty-day supply of foodstuffs.

It was not simply the immense distance separating the north Italian region of Verona, Vicenza, and Treviso from Poland and the Niemen River—some 1,200 miles—but even more the many mountainous roads they had to follow, which made it necessary for the 65,000 men of Prince Eugène's Armée d'Italie to start their long march several weeks before the other corps of the Grande Armée. When they began their arduous trek over the Alps into the Tyrol during the last week of February, the Brenner Pass and other passes were still partly blocked by snowdrifts, which had laboriously to be cleared.

Having several hundred fewer miles to travel, the 40,000 men of Marshal Ney's Third Corps, who had been assembling in the Rhineland area between Stuttgart and Mainz, did not set out until the second week of March. But the warm spring sun, which had first speeded them on their way, suddenly disappeared when they reached the wooded mountains of Thuringia, and they were then beset by such thick snowfalls that the riders had to dismount, while the weary foot-sloggers staggered forward, carefully using the footholes of the men preceding them to keep from sinking waist deep into the drifts.

Among the last to leave their depots and assembly points, along roads that had been clogged for weeks with infantrymen and cavalry squadrons, were the 50,000 men of the greatly expanded Imperial Guard, who had been concentrated in the Paris area. To reinforce the mustachioed veterans of what was now called the Vieille Garde, three Young Guard divisions (one of them entirely Polish) had been formed and placed under the command of the big-boned Marshal Edouard Mortier, whose towering bulk—"a big mortar has a small range" was one of the cruel epigrams concerning him—now often seemed as out of place in the stuffy antechambers of the Tuileries or Saint-Cloud as his hearty, Falstaffian gusts of laughter. More fortunate than others who had to march with fifty-pound packs all the way to the Rhine, many soldiers of the Old and Young Guard had been bundled into fiacres, assembled in the northern Paris suburb of La Villette, and had been driven posthaste as far as Meaux, where requisitioned peasant carts were waiting to carry them at the same nonstop, day-and-night pace across the rolling plains of Champagne toward the brooding pine forests of the Saar.

It was over the same splendidly paved road, lined on both sides by trees that had been planted to provide welcome shade during the hot summer months, that Napoleon and Marie-Louise now traveled with their extensive retinue. They spent their first night at Châlons (arrival at six in the evening, departure at four the next morning) and the second one at Metz (arrival at five, departure at two in the morning). But two full days and nights were needed for their next stop, Mainz—the central and in many ways the most important of the military supply bases Napoleon had established along the Rhine.

Of the ninety-seven German states that had existed on the left bank of the Rhine in the eighteenth century, the Archbishopric and Electoral Principality (Kurfürstentum) of Mainz had been the richest, the most prestigious, and one of the most reactionary. When the French Revolution had begun to take an ugly turn in 1792, the old walled city had become a haven for French émigrés who were bent on reestablishing Louis XVI's divine right to undisputed rule;

at Baron von Erthal's banquet table elegantly crinolined ladies had vied with each other in offering a few feet of their carefully tressed hair for the making of rope needed to hang the Jacobin "dogs," while gentlemen officers boasted of the sackfuls of revolutionary heads they were going to bring back from a chastised and chastened Paris. A few weeks later the ill-inspired Duke of Brunswick and the fatuous "Army of the Princes" had been ignominiously routed as they sought to advance into Champagne. But the stout burghers who had refused to join the panicky exodus of Jesuit fathers and noble ladies had been as dumbfounded by the revolutionary rabble which had tramped into their city—with chunks of bread and meat impaled on their gleaming bayonets —as they were by the *grand seigneur* air of its leader, the marquis de Custine, a veteran of Rochambeau's expedition to the New World who had returned imbued with the humanitarian ideals of the young American republic.

Since that memorable October day of 1792 the French had swept the left bank of the Rhine clean of Prussian, Hessian, and Austrian soldiery, and the electoral principality had been transformed into a French department with the curious name of Donnerberg, or Mont-Tonnerre (Thunder-Mount) in French.

After crossing the Rhine on a bridge of boats Napoleon and his empress moved on to nearby Frankfurt. Here, in the old Gothic city where Marie-Louise's father, Francis of Austria, had been crowned twenty years before as the last of the Holy Roman Kaisers, the new Charlemagne of Europe and his young wife were offered a "brilliant welcome" by the municipal authorities and the populace massed along the crowded streets. Brilliant it may have been, but that it was sincere may be doubted. To be sure, the venerable "free city" had greatly benefitted from the enlightened rule of Karl Theodor von Dahlberg— a subtle as well as supple prelate who had helped Talleyrand redraw the map of Germany by "secularizing" close to seventy ecclesiastical states. The medieval ramparts had been transformed into tree-lined promenades, the serfs had been emancipated along with the ghetto Jews, who previously had been confined at night behind chains stretched across the shabby Judengasse, and who had been made to doff their hats in daytime each time a Gentile passed. But for many Frankfurt burghers the sight of all those confiscated goods (supposedly of British origin) being put to the torch by French customs officials in the grim November of 1810 was too searing a memory to be easily forgotten.

Continuing their eastward progression in clouds of gritty dust—for in still-fragmented Germany paved roads were unknown beyond the limits of any major town—the imperial cortège reached Würzburg on the evening of May 13. The old vineyard-surrounded bishopric had been "secularized" in 1801 and four years later made a grand duchy for the benefit of the emperor of Austria's younger brother, Ferdinand, who had recently been dispossessed of his native province of Tuscany. Now magnificently housed in the eighteenth-century palace which Balthasar Neumann had designed and Tiepolo decorated with exquisitely frescoed ceilings, Marie-Louise's gracious, music-loving uncle could entertain his imperial guests with an affability that was not feigned.

Totally different in character as well as physiognomy was another of Napoleon's protégés, King Frederick of Württemberg, who had specially displaced his portly bulk from his Swabian capital at Stuttgart to pay his royal homage to his imperial benefactor. Known to many of his contemporaries as "the wittiest of European monarchs," the brother of the Dowager Empress Maria Feodorovna of Russia was also the most obese, with a protruding girth of such Gargantuan proportions that an extraordinary concave dining table—a real masterpiece of baroque craftsmanship—had had to be fashioned to permit him to approach within arm's length of his food. (Divine Providence, as Napoleon liked to say, had specially created him to "show to what extent the human skin is capable of being stretched.") For the forthcoming campaign against Russia, the callous monarch—who thought it quite natural to employ convicts in ankle chains to pick and shovel dirt for the enlargement of his city palace gardens —had managed to recruit (and in some cases dragoon) more than 400 Württemberg officers, 15,600 noncoms and soldiers, and close to 600 cavalrymen for service in the Grande Armée—enough to cause Napoleon to overlook his grudging vassal's tyrannical quirks and embarrassing family connections.

Leaving Würzburg and its hillside vineyards behind them, the French emperor and empress journeyed on the next morning to the old cathedral town of Bamberg, which had recently been added to the new Kingdom of Bavaria. There were further stops at Bayreuth, Hof, and Plauen, as the increasingly hilly road took the long procession of carriages northeast along the wooded fringes of Bohemia. Over this same road more than 40,000 Frenchmen had already marched or ridden, led by General Grouchy's cavalrymen and the black-busbied, white-waistcoated grenadiers of the Old Guard, commanded by the duke of Danzig (the former Alsatian miller's son who had slashed and sabered his way up to fame and decorations as Marshal Lefebvre). They had been followed by 19,000 Italians, 12,000 Bavarians, 2,000 Dalmatians, 1,500 Croats, and as many Spaniards—soldiers belonging to Prince Eugène de Beauharnais's Fourth and Sixth Corps. The incessant movement of foot-sloggers, horsemen, artillery caissons, and supply wagons had for weeks kept the inhabitants of upper Saxony in a state of uproar and expectation. It now reached its crescendo with the passage of Napoleon and his imperial cortège.

Uncertain as to just when his distinguished guest would be reaching Dresden —he had been expecting him since March—King Frederick Augustus of Saxony and his queen, Marie Amélie, had driven out as far as the silver-and-lead-mining town of Freiberg, where, to keep from being surprised by the sudden arrival of the unpredictable Napoleon, the Saxon foreign minister, Count Senfft von Pilsach, had sat up all night in an antechamber armchair. Not until five o'clock on the following afternoon did Napoleon and Marie-Louise finally reach Freiberg, where they were offered a quick dinner and a picturesque march-past by miners armed with lamps.

Five years before, after the signing of the Tilsit Treaty, Napoleon, approaching from the northeast, had made his entry into Dresden over the sixteen-arch stone bridge spanning the river Elbe—which in this pre-metal-bridge age was one of the architectural wonders of Europe. Now, approaching from the opposite direction, he and Marie-Louise made an even more triumphant entry at eleven at night on this festive Pentecostal Saturday of May 16. Church bells pealed, the cannon thundered. From the Freiberg city barrier to the royal castle the mile-long route was lined with a double row of saluting soldiery (one row French, the other composed of the local militia), while portals and windows blazed with flaming torches and lit candles. Preceded by cuirassiers of the Saxon household cavalry, in their striking white uniforms, black breast-plates, and plumed helmets, the line of carriages seemed endless, for in addition to half a dozen dukes and forty other members of Napoleon's imperial household, "the Empress's suite numbered no less than 177 persons."

Rounding the northeast corner of the Royal Schloss, Napoleon's gleaming carriage, immediately followed by the Saxon king's, drove in through the so-called Green Gate beneath the 300-foot tower into the main forecourt. Pages in heraldic dress blared forth a fanfare on their tasseled trumpets, while on the steps two ascending rows of Swiss Guards, clad like the Beefeaters of London Tower in bouffant pantaloons of blue and yellow (but with plumed tricorne hats covering their powdered wigs), drew up their halbards in ceremonious salute.

Elsewhere—at the duke of Würzburg's baroque residence or the king of Württemberg's imitation-Versailles palace in Stuttgart—this medieval touch might have seemed out of place. But here, in an old ducal (now royal) Schloss which had retained the rambling informality of some of the French châteaux of the Loire, the pageantry seemed perfectly attuned to the antiquated charm of walled-in Dresden and the conservative temper of its pacific, punctilious, tradition-honoring ruler. (It was only in the preceding year that the ladies of this Court, the most rigidly old-fashioned in Europe, had finally abandoned the bell-shaped, basket-ribbed dresses of Madame de Pompadour's generation, causing one of the officers in Napoleon's suite, the young Boniface de Castellane, to note in his diary, "Saxony is fifty years behind France.")

The celebrated adage generally attributed to Louis XVIII—"L'exactitude est la politesse des rois" (Punctuality is the courtesy of kings)—could just as easily have been pronounced by Frederick Augustus of Saxony. A sober, soft-spoken, studious individual who had taken the trouble to master Polish as well as French and Italian during his adolescent years, he was the very antithesis of his overpowering great-grandfather Augustus the Strong, who liked to demonstrate his Herculean might by crumpling silver banquet-hall plates into compact balls between his two massive hands, and whose appetite for the fair sex was so insatiable that he is estimated to have sired three hundred bastard children.

During the stately drive in from Dresden's city limits, Duroc, the grand marshal of the French imperial household, informed Saxony's foreign minister that Napoleon insisted on being lodged, together with Empress Marie-Louise, within the confines of the royal castle. The commotion that this must have introduced into the normally placid, meticulously regulated life of the Saxon Court is easy to imagine. But there was absolutely nothing that the king or his equally submissive queen could do about it.

The next morning, May 17, the castle windows rattled yet again as the cannon boomed and the bells pealed for the Whitsunday mass celebrated in the baroque Hofkirche. This "Court chapel"—an architectural wedding cake covered from oval nave to triple-tiered spire with a post-Bernini profusion of gesticulating saints—was in every sense an anomaly. It was the only Catholic church in fanatically Lutheran Dresden, whose rulers had abandoned the reformed faith of their predecessors in the late seventeenth century, when Augustus the Strong had had himself elected king of arch-Catholic Poland; and to permit the members of the reigning family to reach this sanctum with a minimum of ostentation, a lovely five-windowed archway had been thrown across the intervening pavement, linking castle to chapel, like a Saxon "bridge of sighs."

There was more wild pealing of church bells and another 101-cannon salute on Whitmonday when the Austrian emperor, Francis, and his empress reached Dresden in their turn shortly after noon. Although the same strict ceremonial was observed—with an official welcome at the city limits and an escort of household cavalry preceding the imperial carriage past cheering throngs and windows flower-boxed with candles—nothing could have differed more from Napoleon and Marie-Louise's seemingly endless procession of vehicles than the Austrian emperor's modest suite. Faithful to the *kleinbürgerlich* qualities which had made him such a homely sovereign and his Hofburg Court (in aristocratic eyes) a deplorable example of gala-shunning simplicity, Francis I seemed bent on making a low-keyed entry into the city. In lavish ostentation, as in so many other respects, the last and most totally divested of Holy Roman Emperors knew that he could not compete with Napoleon.

The first evening Napoleon and Marie-Louise had been invited to dine *en famille* with King Frederick Augustus, his wife, their only daughter, and the king's brothers and sisters-in-law. The following evening it was the queen of Saxony's turn to act as hostess at a large half-moon table, where the two emperors, the two empresses, and the leading members of Frederick Augustus's family ate off golden plates and were entertained by songs sung by the royal choir. Outside, to mark the occasion, the castle square was illuminated by six lampion-girt obelisks on which were inscribed the initials of the two visiting emperors—*N. I.* and *F. I.* (Napoleon, Franz, followed by the Latin "Imperator"). In the distance, beyond a necklace of lamps on the bridge spanning the dark, glimmering waters of the Elbe, a seventh illuminated obelisk rose like a ghostly beacon from the darkness of the city's northern bank.

From this second banquet, as from the first, all lesser fry were formally excluded—to the spluttering indignation of Karl August of Saxe-Weimar, one of a score of German princelings who had come to Dresden to pay obeisance to Napoleon. The outraged duke returned in a huff to the quaint Gothic town on the banks of the humble Ilm which, in welcoming Goethe, Schiller, Wieland, and Herder, had long since eclipsed Dresden as a home of the Muses.

For the rest of his two-week stay Napoleon insisted on acting as host at the eight o'clock dinner, held in the private dining room that had been placed at his disposal. Wishing to please his son-in-law at one of these evening repasts, the Austrian emperor informed Napoleon that a Viennese genealogist had discovered that the Buonaparte family had once exercised its "sway" over the town of Treviso, north of Venice, before moving on to Tuscany. Napoleon needed no genealogist to remind him how modest had been the origins of the Bourbon dynasty, founded by Henri of Navarre, a native of the equally humble town of Pau, in the Pyrenees. That a descendant of the Trevisan or Tuscan Buonapartes should now have stepped into the silk stockings and slippers of the Bourbons seemed to him so natural that, in speaking of the horrors of the French Revolution, he calmly declared—to the stupefaction of his listeners— that things in France could have taken a different and far less tragic turn "if only our poor uncle had shown more firmness." The "poor uncle" was the luckless Louis XVI, married to the equally ill-fated Marie-Antoinette, Emperor Francis of Austria's aunt and thus the great-aunt of Marie-Louise!

Nothing indeed could have been more deliberately Bourbonic than the way in which Napoleon, at Dresden, began each new day. The nine o'clock *lever* was almost as solemn and as stilted as those of Louis XIV at Versailles. After being helped into his court attire by his valet, while fawning dukes and princes paid their morning respects, the French emperor would repair to Marie-Louise's bedchamber, where an even more elaborate ritual graced the young empress's *toilette*. At the sight of all the glittering necklaces and bejeweled brooches and tiaras from which Marie-Louise could pick and choose, her less pampered stepmother could not conceal her envy: an admission of "poor cousin" inferiority which must have flattered Napoleon's marital vanity, coming as it did from the small, vivacious, dark-eyed Maria Ludovica of Modena d'Este, whom Emperor Francis had married in January 1808. Rightly regarded as one of Bonaparte's most determined enemies, she had ardently championed the "war party" in Vienna and had even sought to arouse a sense of Germanic patriotism by launching a new "Teutonic" style of feminine attire to counteract the glamor of Parisian haute couture.

To the relief of the Saxon hosts, who had dreaded this encounter, Napoleon went out of his way to be affable to his captivating foe. Displaying the coquettish charm he liked to concentrate on persons he knew to be opposed to him, he gallantly offered the Austrian empress his hand in escorting her into the banquet hall, and moved his chair closer to hers in order to engage her in dinner-table talk.

It is true, of course, that as a conversationalist the literature-loving Maria Ludovica was in quite another class from her uninspired, paper-shuffling and document-stamping husband, whose distinctly drawn features and lanky frame had once moved Napoleon to dismiss him as a "skeleton whom the valor of his ancestors has placed upon the throne." Nothing could have seemed more tedious to Napoleon than having to pace up and down the tapestried drawing room in the evening with the tongue-tied emperor of Austria, who could obviously not keep up with his son-in-law's torrential discourse.

It would of course be wrong to think that during these two weeks all of Napoleon's time was taken up with ceremonial dinners, concerts, and other gala entertainments. The amount of time he was willing to devote to such agreeable (or disagreeable) distractions was, as usual, strictly limited. While Marie-Louise was encouraged to go out for drives with her stepmother in an open calèche, Napoleon remained closeted in his wainscotted cabinet, poring over maps, perusing the diplomatic dispatches personally brought in or sent to him by Foreign Minister Maret, and studying the reports prepared by his chief of staff, Berthier, who was entrusted with the formidable task of coordinating the complex movements of the nine army corps, additional reserve detachments, and enormous supply trains that were now moving slowly eastward, to the Vistula and beyond that to the Niemen.

In real terms there is little doubt that this extraordinary Dresden "congress" was a diplomatic flop. While it impressed or intimidated the groveling German dukes and princes in attendance (without disarming the distaste most of them felt for the Corsican upstart of an emperor), it failed in its two main purposes.

The first of these objectives, for Napoleon, was to emphasize the solidity of his recently established ties with Austria and to assure himself of the wholehearted support in the coming campaign of its auxiliary corps, commanded by the former ambassador in Paris, Prince Karl Schwarzenberg. This wholehearted participation might possibly have been obtained if Napoleon had offered to return Trieste, Fiume, and mountainous Dalmatia (the so-called Illyrian provinces) to Habsburg rule *before* the outbreak of hostilities—which is what Metternich had hoped for. Instead, all the latter had obtained in the March 14 treaty was a vague promise that Austria would regain Trieste and the Dalmatian coastline in exchange for the eventual handing over of part or all of Galicia to the reestablished Kingdom of Poland. For the canny, cautious Metternich—the scion of a noble Rhineland family who basically detested everything Napoleon stood for—this casual promise was far too imprecise to be convincing. At Dresden, where they had ample opportunity to discuss these territorial problems, Napoleon preferred to talk of other matters: of how the overly voluble French needed to be governed ("no windbags, no ideologues, no hollow showiness"), or of how, if he had to cross the Niemen, he would conduct a patient, methodical campaign, aimed at reaching Smolensk and Minsk; at which point his Grande Armée would go into winter quarters while he attended to the administrative reorganization of a liberated Lithuania. Since the outcome of this looming conflict seemed anything but certain—at any rate to Metternich—it was imperative that Prince Schwarzenberg's 30,000 Austrians not get too deeply involved, letting the two formidable adversaries wear each other down while the Habsburg Empire quietly rebuilt its own forces for the later day of diplomatic and, possibly, military, reckoning.

The second of Napoleon's objectives at Dresden was to emphasize Russia's isolation, in the hope that this spectacular concourse of crowned and coroneted princes, whose forces had been incorporated into the most gigantic military apparatus the world had ever seen, would overawe the tsar into agreeing to another Tilsit-style negotiation on the Niemen. Here too the result was a fiasco. Alexander refused to be impressed. One Tilsit was quite enough; he could not risk another without endangering his throne, and indeed his life. Dresden, as far as he was concerned, was like an iridescent rainbow, dazzling but ephemeral. If Napoleon really wanted peace, he would have to begin by making a real gesture, by withdrawing the vast forces now gathering in Poland and East Prussia. The rest was mere words, Bonapartist sophistry, which left him quite unmoved.

The first inkling Napoleon had that such might be his prospective adversary's attitude came on May 25, when the Saxon ambassador in Petersburg, General von Watzdorff, returned to Dresden. He was immediately accorded a long audience in Napoleon's private study. What Watzdorff had to say did not much differ from the warnings Caulaincourt had been obstinately repeating about the tsar's supposedly "indecisive" character: Alexander could not be forced to yield on matters of vital national interest.

The next morning King Frederick William III of Prussia made a relatively discreet entry into Dresden, after a French protocol official had informed him when he reached the outskirts of the Saxon capital that he could not be accorded a 101-gun salute, such as had greeted the French and Austrian emperors. This slight was one more drop from the cup of bitterness he had been made to drink, after being "invited" to remain at Potsdam with his royal Court, while Marshal Oudinot and the staff officers of the Grande Armée's Second Corps took over the administration of Berlin. But Napoleon, who had never concealed the contempt he felt for this "sergeant instructor," now surprised the members of his entourage by calling on King Frederick William shortly after he had been shown to the suite of rooms reserved for him. This unusual gesture was intended to express the French emperor's gratitude toward a sovereign who had, albeit grudgingly, agreed to furnish his Grande Armée with a contingent of 20,000 men.

The event that eclipsed all others on this May 26 was the arrival in Dresden of a distinctly dust-covered but still debonair Count Louis de Narbonne—already well known to King Frederick Augustus and his Court because of his long sojourn in the Saxon capital as a French émigré refugee in the 1790s. Now it was as a kind of ambassador extraordinary that he was returning from a ten-week trip that had taken him to Berlin and then to Vilna, in Russian Lithuania, where he had been instructed to tender the olive branch of peace to Tsar Alexander.

Of the many aides-de-camp who were to accompany Napoleon to Moscow, not one was to display more imperturbability and graciousness than this ancien régime gentleman, whose black eyes had lost little of their youthful luster, even though his carefully powdered hair was now almost completely white. Born in 1755, he was—with the single exception of Chief of Staff Berthier—the oldest member of Napoleon's entourage and the one who had replaced Talleyrand as the French emperor's favorite conversational partner. An illegitimate son of King Louis XV, Louis de Narbonne had been brought up in the climate of elegant depravity that had characterized the Court of Versailles during the Madame Du Barry years and before the accession to the throne of the prim Louis XVI had ushered in a kind of puritanical reaction. But the scintillating gay blade who liked to live it up with Comédie Française actresses had also received an excellent grounding in the classics, and being an assiduous reader, he acquired a remarkable knowledge of history, and not least of all of diplomatic history, which years later was greatly to impress Napoleon. Able to move with perfect ease in aristocratic circles, he had speeded up the peacemaking process in the autumn of 1809 by quietly agitating the specter of a Magyar revolt against Habsburg rule, and later he had played a key behind-the-scenes role in arranging Marie-Louise's marriage to Napoleon. By the spring of 1812 he had acquired such a reputation for diplomatic fence-mending that Napoleon had picked him to hurry to Berlin to mollify a stunned King Frederick William of Prussia and the mortified members of his Court. Having by that time crossed almost half of Europe, it was he who was logically chosen to move on to Vilna with a personal letter to Emperor Alexander.

Napoleon, with whom Narbonne was immediately closeted, paced nervously up and down as he listened to what his tall, white-haired aide-de-camp had to tell him about the Russians' reactions to the two letters he had been given to deliver. In the first, addressed to Chancellor Rumiantsev, Foreign Minister Maret had explained that the French had made another peace overture to the English in March, but it had been swiftly rejected by Lord Castlereagh. The onus of blame for the "needless" prolongation of the war was thus placed on the English (rather than on Napoleon for refusing to have the Spanish throne returned to its Bourbon rulers). In his own much briefer letter, addressed to "Monsieur mon Frère," Napoleon had reiterated his desire to avoid war and to remain faithful to "the sentiments of Tilsit and Erfurt," and had concluded, in a sentence which was a curious mixture of compliment and threat, "that if fatality should render inevitable a war between us, it would in no wise change the feelings that Your Majesty has inspired in me and which are safe from every vicissitude and alteration."

Neither letter had cut any ice with the Russians. The ailing Chancellor Rumiantsev, his speech but not his·mind affected by a recent attack of apoplexy, sent Napoleon's envoy on to the tsar. What Alexander told Narbonne did not differ substantially from what he had said to Caulaincourt one year earlier—except that he had new complaints to add to his earlier grievances, since Napoleon had managed to enlist the military cooperation of Austria, Prussia, and indeed of most of the continent for a crusade against Russia. But, Alexander added, "the Russian nation is not one which recoils before danger. All the bayonets in Europe on my frontiers will not make me alter my language."

The next morning Narbonne was invited to watch a military parade, then invited to dine at the emperor's table. At the conclusion of the meal Alexander had offered him a small diamond-encrusted box containing a miniature medallion of himself. He added, as a final farewell warning, "Tell the Emperor that I will not be the aggressor. . . . He can cross the Niemen, but never will I sign a peace dictated on Russia's territory."

Narbonne had come with several letters addressed to Poles living in the immediate vicinity of Vilna. But the Russians, who suspected him (quite rightly) of wishing to see as much as possible of their military dispositions, did not allow him to deliver them. He had hardly returned to his lodgings when the Russian minister of the interior, Viktor Kochubey, and the tsar's diplomatic factotum, Nesselrode, turned up to say good-bye. His Most Gracious Majesty, the emperor, they informed him, had most thoughtfully provided him with a plentiful supply of food as well as horses for the return trip to the Polish border. It was five o'clock in the evening, and time for Monsieur de Narbonne to be on his way.

Napoleon must have been less than pleased to discover that Narbonne, like Caulaincourt before him, had been impressed by Tsar Alexander's courteous comportment—"dignified without swagger or dejection"—and by the firm, frank manner with which he had explained, in front of an unfurled map, that Napoleon would have to pursue him to the uttermost confines of his empire before he would consider making peace with him once his soldiers had crossed the Niemen.

Narbonne was instructed to repeat the gist of this conversation to the Austrian emperor and Metternich, who had made no secret of their belief that Alexander could have avoided war by being more supple in his dealings with Napoleon. Since diplomacy had failed, the outstanding issues had to be settled on the battlefield.

The next day Napoleon staged a final ceremonious sortie, mounted on one of his striking white horses, with the distinctive red shabrack underneath the saddle emblazoned in gold with his imperial eagle. He paused on the way, to see how work was progressing on the demolition of Dresden's medieval ramparts, before riding on across the pontoon bridge his engineers had thrown over the Elbe and then returning via the city's northern suburbs to the stately bridge leading to the castle.

On May 28 the doleful king of Prussia said good-bye to his Saxon hosts and to the two visiting emperors, and left for Berlin with his unhappy chancellor, Hardenberg, and the seventeen-year-old Kronprinz, whose smiling sprightliness contrasted markedly with his father's somber mien. The two emperors were to leave the next day—Napoleon headed north for Poznan, his father-in-law, Francis of Austria, southeast for Prague. Marie-Louise, it had been decided, would tarry for a month in Dresden before proceeding, with due pomp and ceremony, to the fashionable watering place of Toeplitz, and from there to the Bohemian capital, where she was to be her father's guest. Each detail of her trip was worked out in advance with extraordinary punctiliousness, Napoleon being very strict in his insistence that the somewhat inhibited Marie-Louise be treated everywhere not as the emperor of Austria's daughter but as the empress of the French, and thus the First Lady of the Continent.

The French emperor's departure was particularly painful for the somnolent King Frederick Augustus of Saxony, who had a way of nodding and even of sleeping through the final part of the evening meal. Kept guessing up to the very last moment as to just when the bustling Napoleon was going to move on, he had to stay up half the night to be able to bid farewell to his imperial guest and benefactor at four o'clock in the morning.

Probably the saddest Frenchman to leave Dresden was the twenty-four-year-old Boniface de Castellane, one of the youngest and most enterprising aides-de-camp in Napoleon's suite of officers. After a week of searching, the adventurous young captain had found a grocer's pretty daughter who spoke French and who was willing to risk a five o'clock assignation in her bedroom while her unsuspecting parents were still asleep. One hour later, after some passionate embraces, the gallant heartbreaker had to tell her that he would be leaving Dresden within an hour or two—which was enough to make her weep. "I came back at seven," he later noted in his diary, "to throw her a ring through the window, without her mother noticing it. I left Dresden at nine, much sadder than I would have been if it had been the previous day."

CHAPTER 6

ONWARD TO DANZIG

ESCORTED ONCE AGAIN by a detachment of the Saxon household cavalry rather than by his own Imperial Guard chasseurs—a token of his trust in King Frederick Augustus and his soldiers—Napoleon left Dresden at dawn on May 29. Up front, next to the coachman who held the reins to the six trotting horses, the dark-skinned Mameluke bodyguard, Roustam, in his plumed turban and scarlet bolero jacket, added a touch of exotic color to the yellow-hued coupé. Inside this remarkable conveyance there was a kind of traveling desk complete with inkwells and quills, drawers for the storing of maps and state papers, a miniature bookcase, mirrors and soap-holders, a small washbasin, a night lamp to read by, and even a mattress, which could be pulled out from under the seat so that the emperor could, if he so wished, stretch out for a catnap.

Seated next to him, as usual, was his small-bodied, large-headed chief of staff, the distinctly unprepossessing but tireless Alexandre Berthier, who was probably chewing his fingernails with more than customary nervousness. At the age of fifty-nine, he had seen more than enough of warfare on several continents (for he too had accompanied Rochambeau to America), and he would much have preferred to remain in Paris. Duroc and Caulaincourt occupied another carriage just behind, itself followed by others carrying imperial aides-de-camp and members of Berthier's headquarters staff.

Traveling at a steady seven miles an hour—several miles per hour less than on the paved highways radiating out from Paris—the imperial cavalcade proceeded over dirt roads in a northeasterly direction to Bautzen, Görlitz, and on across Silesia. At two-thirty in the morning of May 30 they stopped at Glogau, on the Oder River, an old walled city whose normally placid streets were patrolled at night by watchmen armed with long sticks, but which in recent weeks had been so crammed with French, Bavarian, Westphalian, Polish, and other passing troops that the city commandant in desperation had taken to closing the gates at six o'clock in the evening.

After five hours of sleep inside his carriage, Napoleon dashed off a second letter to Marie-Louise, saying that the previous day "I went very fast, only a little bit of dust," and that he expected to reach Poznan that evening. She was not to be depressed by his absence, but to appear "gay and reasonable" during her stay in Dresden, and she must be sure to give each officer bringing her a letter from him a small diamond-encrusted ring, and so on. Accustomed as he was to dictating to his two hard-pressed secretaries, Napoleon detested having to pull out a quill himself, but in the case of his own wife he had no choice. The quaint spelling, like the erratic handwriting, in these brief missives must often have brought a smile to Marie-Louise's lips; for even the simplest words —*senté* for *santé* (health) or *eccelent* for *excellent*—were consistently misspelled.

At eight-thirty in the morning the imperial cavalcade resumed its journey. To his secretary, Baron Fain, who had retained a bitter memory of endless wastes of snow stretching off to a blank horizon, the now verdant plains of Poland, checkered by dark-green woods and clusters of peasant houses, were an agreeable surprise. Considerably less enchanted was the much younger Captain Boniface de Castellane, who had not had to endure the freezing rigors of the winter campaign of 1806–1807. He found the roads winding in and out of pine forests as "execrable" as the one-story, wood-and-mud houses with their boarded-in garden enclosures, which, as he put it in his diary, "are what in Poland one calls a town." Even the fields of ripening wheat and barley found scant favor in his eyes, any more than did the crowded town of Poznan, which they reached at eight-thirty in the evening.

For several days the capital of the Grand Duchy of Warsaw's westernmost province had been preening itself for this moment by stretching transparent streamers across window fronts and house façades and erecting triumphal arches. Met at the city's southern gate by the Polish prefect and military governor, Napoleon and his suite were greeted by noisy acclamations as they were driven or rode up the thronged streets toward the Prefecture building, where he was to spend the night. The towered gate of the old Jesuit college (which it had once been) was festooned with a brilliantly illuminated transparent streamer, on which had been inscribed the Latin words *"Grati Poloni Imperatori Magno"* (Grateful are the Poles to the Great Emperor). Bonfires blazed in a number of squares, and their sparkling light, added to that of so many candle-lit façades, turned night into day. Joyous crowds surged through the streets, including many happily drunk souls who tottered along unsteadily, not wishing to miss the glorious fun. For much of the night an orchestra, cleverly assembled in the town-hall tower, dispensed a kind of celestial music from on high, providing a soothing lullaby for the hundreds of old Polish soldiers who had been encouraged by members of the local gentry to tramp in from the countryside and to bivouac under the stars in the now teeming Sapieha Square.

For Captain Heinrich von Brandt, a twice-wounded and twice-decorated hero of the war in Spain, there was something painfully artificial about this elaborate mise-en-scène. Already irritated to find themselves now commanded by a brusque French general (Claparède), he and other returning Polish veterans were further disheartened by the condition in which they found their country. Deprived of their traditional export markets abroad (England and Scandinavia) by the Continental System, the local peasants and land-owning gentry had seen the price of wheat decline to an absolutely rock-bottom level, which no longer covered basic farming costs. French quartermaster commissioners had taken advantage of this situation to amass huge stocks of grain, to the detriment of current consumption in the larger towns and cities. The once flourishing cattle trade had been hard hit by an outbreak of foot-and-mouth disease, and everywhere there were complaints and lamentations about near-starvation levels of subsistence.

Because agricultural conditions were so wretched, Polish and French recruiting officers had had little trouble rounding up young farmhands, many of whom had never yet tasted a cup of coffee, smoked a cigarette, or eaten a breakfast roll (as opposed to peasant bread). Offered an unexpected chance to earn a few extra gulden, the peasants' womenfolk had pulled out their needles and gone to work with astounding speed on the military cloth provided. But after donning their smart white-blue-and-red uniforms, many of the new recruits disappeared into the night, heading back to the villages from which they had been drawn in order to dazzle the local lasses with their newly acquired finery. Most of them were easily rounded up and marched back to the parade-ground squares, where they were administered a public thrashing (fifty to sixty blows across the buttocks) to deter them from further desertions.

Two out of every three of these raw recruits were still not fully uniformed when they were ordered, on May 31, to march into Poznan to stand review before the emperor. After lining up on Sapieha Square with their bayoneted muskets, they were reviewed by Marshal Mortier, commander of the Jeune Garde. True to his jovial form—he was as quick to laugh as Napoleon was to frown—the big, hearty marshal had nothing but praise for the speed with which these new Polish battalions had been formed. But as they were about to be marched back to their training centers in the countryside, Napoleon himself appeared, looking much displeased. "I find these people too young," grumbled the emperor. "I need people in a condition to endure fatigue— fellows who are too young merely fill up the hospitals."

Napoleon had just received a message from his foreign minister, Maret, who had stayed on in Dresden to wind up his diplomatic business: the price Bernadotte in Stockholm was now exacting for his cooperation with Napoleon (in a joint attack on Russia) was his imperial permission to occupy Norway, which at this time was not an independent country but a possession of the Danish Crown. (Napoleon's reaction was sharp and unequivocal: "There is nothing to be gained by sacrificing a loyal friend in order to gain an untrustworthy ally.")

There were other reasons too for Napoleon's discontent. After being offered private mass by the bishop of Poznan, the emperor formally received leading members of the local gentry in the great refectory hall of the former Jesuit college. The sight of their satin breeches and silk stockings immediately raised his dander. "Gentlemen," he declared, "I would have preferred to see you spurred and booted, each with a saber at his side, as were your ancestors at the approach of Tartars and Cossacks. We are living at a time when one must be armed from head to foot and have one's hand on the hilt of one's sword."

The elegantly gowned ladies were just as gruffly treated. One of them—Countess Mycielka, who looked considerably older than her eighteen years because of her outlandish height and rotundity—was asked how many children she had.

"Sire, I don't have any."

"So you are divorced?"

"Sire, I am not married at all, I am still a demoiselle."

"Ah!" decreed Napoleon, who made little secret of his Corsican conviction that a woman's prime function was to bring children into the world. "You must not be too choosy, you don't have much time to lose."

Napoleon, of course, had more important things to worry about than the feelings of the local gentry. The provincial city of Poznan was simply not made to accommodate an enormously inflated general staff. As one of Napoleon's aides-de-camp, Raymond de Montesquiou-Fezensac, was later to recall, "each officer had at least one carriage, and the generals each had several; the number of servants and horses was prodigious." So too must have been the clouds of gritty dust that were raised each time a galloping courier or a trotting equipage passed over the unpaved streets.

From Poznan Napoleon should logically have headed eastward to Warsaw, which was now in the grip of an extraordinary effervescence. But at Dresden he had decided to bypass the Polish capital, fearful as he was of having his subtle calculations swept away in an avalanche of patriotic fervor. Instead, he had decided to appoint an ambassador to supersede the well-intentioned but insufficiently prestigious Baron Edouard Bignon, who for the past fifteen months had been acting as his proconsul in the Grand Duchy of Warsaw. The person Napoleon had originally had in mind for this ambassadorial post was Talleyrand, whose *grand seigneur* manner had greatly impressed the Polish capital's nobility during the winter and spring months of 1807, when he had been called upon to oversee the administration of the city while the French emperor was away campaigning in the field. But the appointment, which Napoleon had wished to keep secret for as long as possible, had been subtly sabotaged in Paris in the early spring of 1812 by a calculated indiscretion committed by one of Napoleon's aides-de-camp, Count Philibert de Rambuteau, who, in addition to being Louis de Narbonne's son-in-law, was on very friendly terms with Talleyrand's successor and enemy, Foreign Minister Maret.

It seems odd that in casting around for someone else to fill this key diplomatic post Napoleon should have overlooked Louis de Narbonne, who was also well known for his pro-Polish sentiments. But it was precisely this, as much as the prospect of losing his scintillating company, that must have ruled him out. Napoleon at this moment did not wish to proclaim a formal, full-scale restoration of the old Kingdom of Poland because he knew that this would at one stroke destroy all hope of making a quick peace with Emperor Alexander of Russia.

In August of 1809, when he was at Schönbrunn trying to negotiate an end to his war with Austria, the French emperor had frankly told a delegation of distinguished Poles that, though the restoration of a Polish kingdom was needed to establish a proper balance of power in Europe, he did not know how it could be accomplished without involving him in a protracted war with Russia. "One would first have to push through four conscription levies ahead of time, ruin France," he had told them, ". . . and then, you have seen how difficult warfare is for my Frenchmen in your country: the climate does not suit them, my troops lack wine, without which they contract illnesses; in short, the French have a repugnance for campaigns in the North—so, gentlemen, I do not wish to draw upon myself an eternal war with Russia. . . ."

What Napoleon had said in August of 1809 was no less valid for June of 1812. None of the basic factors had changed, yet he was now preparing to launch a war for which French soldiers, by his own admission, were not really suited. His answer to this seemingly insoluble conundrum had been to beef up his French forces through the creation of an enormous pan-European army. Since the Poles, who now had 70,000 men under arms, were already making far and away the largest non-French contribution to this polyglot host, it was absolutely vital to fire their martial spirit and patriotic fervor—or, as Napoleon put it in a long memorandum of detailed instructions which he dictated during his last day in Dresden, to "put the entire nation in a state of drunkenness." It was up to the Poles to convene a Diet, and, if they felt so inclined, to announce their wish to see the old Kingdom of Poland reestablished. The French ambassador's hand was to guide the issuance of successive manifestos and proclamations, but to remain invisible throughout. In this way, Napoleon reckoned, he could stir up a maximum of trouble for Alexander in his Lithuanian provinces without committing himself irrevocably to a French-sponsored restoration of the Kingdom of Poland. He was still keeping his options open.

To conjure up this stimulating simulacrum, this exalting mirage, a master of the written and spoken word was clearly needed, a kind of superior rabble-rouser capable of electrifying the Poles through the issuance of inspiring proclamations. Such a man, Napoleon suddenly decided, was none other than the new grand almoner who had accompanied his imperial Court to Dresden —the former Abbé de Pradt, later bishop of Poitiers and then archbishop of Malines (in Belgium), to whom had been entrusted the august responsibility of conducting high mass in Dresden's baroque Hofkirche, and who had acquitted himself of the task with eloquent distinction.

That the archbishop of Malines was possessed of a facile gift for florid speech, nobody has ever doubted. But as the historian Adolphe Thiers was later to write about this intriguing prelate in words it would be difficult to improve on: "Without sense of coherence, devoid of tact, devoid of the art of moving skillfully among parties, without any of the administrative knowledge needed to help the Poles, solely capable of dazzling repartees and withal something of a coward, he could only add to the confusion of a patriotic uprising the confusion of his own mind."

After two busy days spent in overcrowded Poznan, Napoleon continued in a northeasterly direction across rolling plains and stretches of sandy pine forests. Stragglers from various Grande Armée units were overtaken all along the dusty highway, and at each stop he heard reports about the ruthless way in which the countryside was being pillaged.

When Captain Heinrich von Brandt made a brief detour from this road to visit his parents' estate near Thorn, his father, whom he had not seen in four years, raised his arms in a gesture of despair, saying, "My son, today you are entering the house of a beggar!" First Marshal Ney, and then Crown Prince Wilhelm of Württemberg had spent several days and nights in the country house, while a battalion bivouacked in the spacious forecourt. When they had left, they had taken most of the horses—needed for artillery trains—and all of the accumulated forage, leaving absolutely nothing for the few horses they had been kind enough to leave behind. The military coupons issued in exchange were absolutely worthless, merely legalizing this form of plunder. In a word, Poland was being treated not as an allied but as a conquered country.

By the time Napoleon reached the Vistula, close to six o'clock in the evening of June 2, he was in a state of high dudgeon. After crossing the river he found himself in the middle of a vast bivouac encampment, with rows of tents stretching all the way to the old city walls of Thorn. Prince Wilhelm of Württemberg, whom he met shortly afterward, was treated to a stiff dressing-down for the predatory behavior of his troops. History has not recorded what excuses the browbeaten crown prince sought to make on behalf of his soldiery, but one thing is certain: Napoleon and more specifically the *commissaires* and *ordonnateurs* who had to administer the magazines and stocks of food and fodder were as much to blame for the existing lawlessness as the thirty-one-year-old crown prince, who was totally lacking in battlefield experience. From the moment that the 14,000 Württembergers had crossed the Saxon border into Poland, the food situation had grown dramatic. The poverty of the peasant villages through which they passed was harrowing, while the arrogance of the *Mehlwürmer* ("mealworms," as the Württembergers called the French commissaries responsible for issuing food supplies in the larger towns and cities) was such that they practically had to draw their swords and fight to obtain the stingiest of rations.

In Thorn, now as crammed to bursting as had been Poznan, the commander of the Grande Armée's Third Corps was taken to task in equally vigorous terms. This was none other than the rough, red-haired, tobacco-chewing Marshal Ney, well known for his simplicity of manner and his personal readiness to share the hardships of his men. At forty-four—he was almost exactly Napoleon's age—this fearless front-line soldier who had risen from the ranks had lost none of the fire that had earned him the title "the bravest of the brave." But the heterogeneous corps he now commanded was a far cry from the splendid Sixth Corps he had led in so many battles and campaigns, from

Ulm and Elchingen in 1805 to Guttstadt and Friedland in 1807. Alas, this new Third Corps was not in the same class. Though it included a nucleus of 23,000 Frenchmen, many of them battle-hardened veterans, it also included 3,000 Portuguese, an almost equal number of "Illyrians" (or Yugoslavs, as we would say today), picturesquely clad in bright brown jackets with scarlet facings and shakos of an incredibly bent form, as well as 14,000 Württembergers.

The last named, though now formed into the Grande Armée's 25th Division, were not all of them South Germans. Many of their officers were Pomeranians or Mecklenburgers who had been forced to look for military employment in other parts of Germany when Prussia's army was forcibly reduced by the terms of the Tilsit Treaty of July 1807 to one quarter of its previous size (from 160,000 to 40,000 men). Ney, who spoke fluent German—not for nothing had he been born the son of a cooper from Sarrelouis in Lorraine—thus found himself commanding officers and noncoms whom, not six years before, he had ignominiously chased from Jena across Thuringia, Brandenburg, and Pomerania all the way to East Prussia.

Incredible as it may sound, many of the Württembergers had never had to spend more than one night actually bivouacking in the field. Their king was none too happy about his troops' departure for the East. Frederick of Württemberg had spent several years in Russia during his younger days, and he harbored no illusions as to the formidable obstacles his soldiers were likely to encounter. His somber apprehensions were shared by many of the older officers, in marked contrast to the younger—like the lieutenant who had boasted at a farewell banquet in a country inn, "As far as I'm concerned, taking part in such a Russian campaign is as easy as eating a slice of bread and butter."

Ney, who in his previous, almost exclusively French corps, had known many of the junior officers by name, was so unfamiliar with those of his new Third Corps that many Württembergers caught a glimpse of him for the first time at a review held near Lübben, about fifty miles southeast of Berlin. His two guiding maxims in all of his previous campaigns had been "March fast! Shoot straight!"—maxims he had picked up from Bonaparte himself. At Thorn it must thus have seemed a bit paradoxical to find Napoleon trying to reverse the principles of Blitzkrieg warfare that had ensured the spectacular success of his earlier campaigns. Marching at top speed without waiting for the lumbering supply trains, and living off the land, or "marauding," had been an inherent feature of Napoleonic strategy and tactics from the very start; and it was asking a lot of the Germanic newcomers now moving forward alongside his prestigious imperial eagles to forfeit a right that the French old-timers had enjoyed, very often at their own or at least their fellow countrymen's expense.

It is more than a little ironic that this campaign, the most carefully planned of all Napoleon's military expeditions, was also the one that occasioned the greatest chaos and confusion, not least of all in the vital field of food supplies. A more rapid advance across the Polish plains would have left the country less cruelly ravaged than the slow, almost creeping movement which gradually washed over it like a tide. Certain of the Grande Armée's corps, furthermore, entered Poland earlier than was necessary for a planned invasion of Russia. For this premature forward movement there was, however, a reason. Napoleon, who had carefully studied Voltaire's and other authors' accounts of King Charles XII's incursion into Russia in 1708, had concluded that if a major battle had to be fought to bring Alexander "to his senses" and to the negotiating table, it would be strategically preferable to have it take place in Poland rather than in Lithuania.

At Dresden he had told Metternich that he was convinced that the Russians would be the first to attack. What he did not say was that this was his secret hope. Twice before, he had crushingly defeated the Russians when they had taken the offensive. At Austerlitz, by evacuating the central Pratzen plateau, he had lured them into imprudently attacking him rather than waiting for the reinforcements with which they could have overwhelmed him. A year and a half later, Bennigsen had rashly moved his army across the Alle River and had been dealt a stunning blow at Friedland. If the Russians could be lured once again into advancing—this time toward Warsaw and the Vistula—then an even more shattering defeat was virtually certain to follow. While the surprised right wing of the Grande Armée began a hasty retreat, Napoleon would order the far more powerful left wing, composed of Davout's six elite divisions and Oudinot's Second Corps, to curl southward from the Baltic littoral and push the advancing Russians into a giant dragnet formed by the Narew and Vistula rivers, Poniatowski's Poles, and his own Imperial Guard.

In the hope that he could bait the Russians with the prospect of an easy initial victory, Napoleon had accordingly ordered one of his weaker units— the Seventh (Saxon) Corps, commanded by an ill-starred general named Reynier—to cross the Vistula in the region of Pulawy, while the far stronger and more combative Fifth (Polish) Corps, under Prince Joseph Poniatowski, was repositioned east and northeast of Warsaw, to hold the vital center should the Russians begin hostilities by advancing westward from Grodno and Brest.

As a final touch to this artifice of simulated weakness Napoleon decided to entrust the overall command of these two corps to his youngest brother, Jerome. Only twenty-eight years old and in military matters a novice, the young king of Westphalia did not apparently realize that he was being used as a decoy.

Ever since Frédéric Masson, in his many-volumed history of Napoleon and his family, undertook to chronicle Jerome Bonaparte's amorous escapades, boyish whimsies, and careless prodigality, he has generally been dismissed as an irresponsible playboy who, most unpardonably of all, left his older brother in the lurch during the first weeks of the 1812 campaign. That this spoiled child of fortune, who had rocketed upward from the modest rank of naval lieutenant to that of monarch in just five years, was inordinately vain and casual about financial matters cannot be denied. The luxury of his wardrobe, the number and richness of his equipages (Florimond de Rambuteau once counted 92 carriages in the mews and forecourts of his royal palace), the dazzling splendor of his gala balls and other entertainments offered in elaborately redesigned parks and gardens had all made the little Court of Kassel a byword for prodigality throughout Europe. Yet, curiously enough, his two million subjects do not seem to have been too much put out by Jerome's ostentatious extravagance. Few Hessians lamented the forced departure of the detested Landgraf (later Prince Elector) Wilhelm, an avaricious martinet who had been ever ready to clap his remorselessly caned and cudgeled soldiers into irons if the length and thickness of their pigtails were not exactly as prescribed.

Jerome, whose juvenile ego had been flattered for a while with the idea that he might become king of Poland, had by 1811 abandoned this ambition. He would have been quite content to remain in Kassel, one of Germany's most charming princely cities, with his popular German-speaking wife, Catharine, daughter of the king of Württemberg. He frankly did not like the prospect of a war with Russia—as he had made clear to Napoleon, during the summer of 1811 and again in December. Indeed he was so irked that he had written in a huff to Foreign Minister Maret to say that he was going to give up his kingship and return to France.

It is unfortunate that at this critical juncture Jerome's nerve failed him. Had he abdicated his throne, as his brother Louis had done eighteen months earlier, his action might well have shaken the Confederation of the Rhine to its foundations and have forced Napoleon to postpone his military mobilization against Russia. Jerome would have secured for himself a tiny niche in History as a person not totally lacking in resolution and common sense, instead of making himself an object of ridicule to future generations as a feather-brained popinjay.

In March, however, Jerome had been summoned to Paris by Napoleon and informed that he was to be placed in overall command not only of the Eighth (Westphalian) Corps, but also of General Jean-Louis Reynier's Seventh (Saxon) Corps and Prince Poniatowski's Fifth (Polish) Corps. It was now Jerome's duty, with the aid of a capable chief of staff (General Jean-Gabriel Marchand, personally selected for him by Napoleon), to assure the defense of Warsaw should the Russians begin hostilities by driving westward toward the Vistula.

For Jerome this was more than a promotion; it was implicitly a promise that if all went well and he distinguished himself in the field, his kingdom of Westphalia would be enlarged—though at just whose expense was anything but clear.

Accompanied by his splendidly uniformed Royal Guard, in their smart white uniforms, scarlet revers, and bearskin busbies, Jerome had accordingly left Kassel in early April, traveling in a ponderous coach, which he had to abandon momentarily after their passage through Silesia when it sank up to its axles in soggy sand. His appearance on Polish soil immediately set tongues wagging, and it was assumed in many Warsaw salons that he was being groomed by Napoleon to become king of Poland.

In more favorable circumstances the size of his royal suite—254 all told, including bakers, butchers, postal clerks and dispatch riders, pharmacists and physicians, Court chamberlains and pages, general staff officers and royal household officials—would probably not have seemed excessive, particularly if their upkeep had been entirely covered by Westphalian funds. But the coffers of the Westphalian treasury being empty, Jerome and his suite had to be billeted and fed at local expense. Soon they were being described as an "army of locusts" battening off the blood-sucked land of Poland like the tens of thousands of Grande Armée soldiers who had preceded them or who were now ominously approaching.

When he finally entered Warsaw—which, like the rest of the country, was full of striking contrasts between lordly mansions and shabby wooden dwellings—the young king of Westphalia took up residence in the baroque Brühl Palace. There, the unswept carpets were found to be full of fleas and the mattresses unsatisfactory. To provide one broad enough to suit His Royal Majesty's exacting tastes, the prefect of Warsaw, Count Nakwaski, had to strip his wife's bed and offer the king of Westphalia the mattress she normally slept on—enough to damn Jerome in the eyes of many a salon hostess. Every day flocks of curious onlookers gathered near the handsome pillars of the statute-ornamented gate to gawk at the number of carriages crowding the ample forecourt. His Majesty, the gossips claimed, insisted on taking two baths a day; according to some it was in rum in the morning and in milk in the evening; according to others it was in wine, in eau de cologne, or even, according to the most inventive, in champagne! All of these luxuries being provided, of course, by the hard-pressed municipality.

If Napoleon had come to Warsaw, where a suite of apartments had been specially prepared for him in the royal castle, Jerome and most of the reproaches heaped upon him, as an indolent, self-indulgent parasite, would soon have been forgotten. But in the absence of the ardently awaited emperor, it was inevitable that this "rabbit kinglet" (as the playwright Julian Niemcewicz called him), who liked to sally forth from his palace on a white Arabian horse and wearing a green uniform and small hat similar to Bonaparte's, should become the focus and target of a multitude of woes and frustrations.

Meanwhile, at Thorn, Napoleon had once again been displaying the tireless energy that made him such an exacting master. Rising at three in the morning on June 5, he rode out beyond the rampart glacis, which thousands of ditch-digging and stone-carrying workers had been laboring to reinforce, to a sandy plain by the Vistula. Here five regiments of his Old Guard—12,000 men in all—were drawn up for inspection.

Accustomed though he was to reviewing troops, even he must have been moved by the sight of so many splendid grenadiers drawn up, row after impressive row, in their impeccable gold-buttoned waistcoats and white breeches, dark-blue jackets crisscrossed with straps holding cartridges and scabbards, their scarlet-pomponned bearskin busbies pushed down over their eyebrows. According to Heinrich von Brandt—whose word carries some weight since he later rose to become a general—nowhere in Europe was a more imposing body of troops to be seen than these solemn giants (each had to be 5 feet 11 inches tall, have served for ten years, and have been wounded at least once), whose grim miens were made even more awe-inspiring by their long muttonchop sideburns and bushy mustachios. Equally impressive were the mounted grenadiers on their jet-black horses, led by officers seated on gray-white steeds in their gold-embroidered sky-blue jackets trimmed with crimson epaulets. Also mounted on black horses were the green-uniformed dragoons, looking even more fearsome in their reddish-bronze helmets with dark pony tails, and their formidable accoutrement of holstered muskets and sheathed sabers. And this is not to mention the most colorful and special of Napoleon's personal bodyguards: the 125 Mamelukes in their plumed turbans, Venetian-red pantaloons, and multicolored sashes into which was thrust a pistol, a dagger, and even a scimitar, who were all of them—save only for Roustam and a couple of others—dark-featured Frenchmen in Turkish disguise.

Napoleon stopped before many a battle-scarred veteran, asking questions "in the paternal tone which makes him so dear to us"—as Captain Fantin des Odoards noted in his journal. The latter, a rugged infantry officer who had fought under Ney in East Prussia and Spain, had only recently been appointed aide-de-camp to Marshal Lefebvre, the more-than-middle-aged commander of the Vieille Garde. Having never attended a function of this kind before, he was startled to hear Napoleon ask him, *"D'où es-tu?"* (Where are you from?). This use of the second-person singular—distinctly odd on the part of an emperor —was, the newcomer discovered, a practice Napoleon always followed with his Guards officers, to make them feel that they were members of one close-knit family.

That evening a clearly exhilarated Napoleon seemed in no hurry to go to bed. While downstairs in the orderly room a number of exhausted aides-de-camp lay stretched out on benches or slumped in their chairs, a Polish duty officer heard the boards creaking overhead as the emperor continued to pace up and down. Then suddenly, to his amazement, he heard Napoleon burst, like a teenager, into the opening verses of *"Le Chant du Départ"*:

> *Et du nord au midi la trompette guerrière*
> *A sonné l'heure du combat.*
> *Tremblez, ennemis de la France!*

(And from the North to the South the warlike trumpet has sounded the hour of combat. Tremble, enemies of France!)

The following afternoon, after dashing off another brief letter to Marie-Louise ("I am leaving in an hour for Danzic, all is very quiet on the frontier . . ."), he was in such a hurry to get away from the congested town of Thorn that he abruptly advanced his departure by several hours, riding off ahead of his staff on one of his dozen saddle horses. It was hours before a flustered Berthier, traveling alone in the yellow coupé, was finally able to catch up with his impatient master. The journey was continued at the same breathless pace right through the evening and the night until six o'clock the following morning, when the forward shaft of the emperor's carriage suddenly split after he and his suite had crossed a pontoon bridge across the Vistula.

At the key bridgehead fortress of Marienburg, on the river's right bank, lunch was spoiled by a violent altercation between the chief of staff, Berthier, and Marshal Davout, the tough, painstaking, scrupulously honest though often pitiless commander of the Grande Armée's First Corps, who was nettled by the suggestion that an insufficient number of ambulances had been assigned to his six crack infantry divisions. Fanatically loyal to his emperor, Davout resented having to receive orders from a chief of staff who, though seventeen years his senior and gifted with a prodigious memory, enabling him to pinpoint the location of every major unit in the Grande Armée, had never commanded a regiment in the field.

At eight-thirty in the evening of June 7, Napoleon's imperial cavalcade finally trotted and rattled through the towered gates and over the cobblestones of Danzig. His decision to make a sixty-mile detour to this major Baltic seaport was prompted by one overriding worry: the problem of transport logistics. He had come to the conclusion that to keep his enormous Grande Armée properly supplied with foodstuffs and munitions, transportation by road, whether in heavy ox-pulled wagons or the lightweight horse-drawn carts that had been specially designed for this campaign, would not suffice. Pack horses and bullocks have to be well fed to be able to pull their loads, and over long distances this requires a great deal of fodder. He had therefore decided to have much of the supply of flour, rice, biscuits, wine, and brandy shipped by boats and river barges.

On walking into the drawing room of General Rapp's gubernatorial townhouse in Danzig, the French emperor was startled to find himself confronted by a bust of the late Queen Luise of Prussia. Napoleon, who had often taken Rapp to task for not bearing down more harshly on his Danzig "subjects," this time simply wagged his finger, declaring with a smile, "Maître Rapp, I warn you that I am going to write to Marie-Louise about this infidelity."

A brief barrage of questions followed. What were the merchants of Danzig doing with the money they were making (from a more or less clandestine trade with England) and the money Napoleon was now spending on them, to improve the port's formidable ramparts and outer fortifications? The honest old Alsatian had to repeat what he had so often said before: the Danzigers were anything but prosperous; in fact, their economic situation was well-nigh desperate.

"All that will change" was Napoleon's good-humored answer. "It's understood. Now that the war is about to start, I'll take them under my wing."

If Rapp was at all reassured by these words, which seems doubtful, he was less visibly peeved than another of his guests, Joachim Murat, who had been waiting for several days for Napoleon's arrival. With his horizontally striped chamois-hued vest, a short cloak of gold-embroidered green velvet, amaranth-red trousers, polished yellow boots, and a quarter-moon marshal's hat magnificently plumed with aigrettes and ostrich feathers, the intrepid cavalryman had lost none of his inimitable panache. But his usually jaunty features, rendered even swarthier by his sojourns in Madrid and Naples, were now glum.

Napoleon, who had decided to retire early—even he was a bit worn out by twenty-nine hours of dusty travel—summoned Rapp to his bedroom after his valet had helped him out of his boots and riding breeches and into his night-clothes.

"Have you noticed how sickly Murat looks? He seems ill."

"Ill? No, Sire," answered Rapp, "but he is chagrined."

"Why chagrined? Isn't he happy to be a king?"

"He claims that he isn't."

"Why does he play the fool in his kingdom?" snorted Napoleon. "He should be a Frenchman and not a Neapolitan."

For the past three years Murat and his imperial brother-in-law had been carrying on a running feud which had oscillated wildly between opera buffa and tragic farce. Thwarted in his ambition to become king of Poland, the impetuous Joachim had decided to make himself a heroic king of Naples by forging a redoubtable expeditionary force and personally leading it across the Straits of Messina to conquer Sicily. To this end he had formed an army of 40,000 Neapolitans (twice as many as Napoleon felt was necessary)—as though this exhibition of Mediterranean muscle-flexing would be enough to cow the British into removing their frigates from the intervening waters.

To clip the wings of the restless Murat, who had been encouraged by a group of Neapolitan intriguers to believe that he had been designated by Providence to become the unifier of the peninsula and Italy's first king, Napoleon had placed the local military forces under the independent command of a reliable French general, and had then named his and Marie-Louise's newborn son (Napoleon) king of Rome—a blunt warning to Murat that this first step could easily be followed by the annexation, pure and simple, of the Kingdom of Naples to the steadily expanding French Empire.

Openly opposed and thwarted by his infinitely shrewder and less hotheaded wife, Caroline, who had sided with her brother in this battle of royal and imperial wills, Murat by the end of 1811 was so wing-clipped and debt-ridden that he had been forced to sell four million francs' worth of Spanish crown jewels (surreptitiously removed from Madrid in 1808) in order to be able to maintain his Royal Neapolitan Guard, in their gold-braided red breeches and short white cloaks. It was thus a singularly chastened monarch—a king in little more than name—who had agreed in March of 1812 to come northward to command the cavalry reserve, which was to screen and spearhead the Grande Armée's advance into Russia. But to mask his multiple discomfitures, he continued to exhibit the trappings of kingship, being accompanied in his yellow-and-gilded coach by a resplendent retinue of guardsmen and several trunkfuls of plumed shakos, dolmans, and pelisses.

He had hardly crossed the Alps when his ruffled pride was subjected to a new mortification: his brother-in-law's imperious refusal to allow him to appear at the Dresden congress of crowned heads, where he would have liked to flaunt his finery and that of his brilliantly uniformed Neapolitan Guard. New insult was thus added to past injury. Napoleon once again was treating him like a puppy. He was denying him the recognition due his royal rank.

The next morning in Danzig Napoleon was up again and stirring by three o'clock. Murat, as gloomy-faced as ever, had to accompany him, along with

Rapp and other members of the imperial suite, as he visited bastions and forts, inspected food depots and powder magazines, and reviewed five of the garrison's battalions.

That same evening Berthier, Murat, and Rapp were invited to dine at Napoleon's table. Berthier on this occasion was no more loquacious than the sullen Murat. The Grand Armée's chief of staff had never liked the idea of fighting another war against the Russians. A man of stronger character would have resigned rather than agree to take part in a war he did not believe in. But character was the one quality Alexandre Berthier had never possessed. "Of this little goose I made an eagle," Napoleon once remarked to one of his secretaries, and there was much truth in this withering observation. Everything Berthier had acquired—his marshal's baton, his decorations, his titles (prince de Neuchâtel and later prince de Wagram), his income-providing *dotations* (now amounting to one and a half million francs), his fine townhouse in Paris, his even handsomer red-brick-and-white-stone château, his honor guard of Swiss soldiers in their *ventre-de-biche* (doe-hued) uniforms and luxurious red linings —he owed to Napoleon. Even his wife—the gentle, rosy-cheeked, and wonderfully complacent Marie-Elisabeth of Bavaria, whom Berthier had been browbeaten into marrying in order to strengthen France's ties with Bavaria—he owed to this human whirlwind whom he had so obediently and ably served. The one thing he did not owe to Napoleon, the thing—more exactly, a person —whom he treasured above all others, was the Junoesque Giuseppina Carcani, whom Berthier had first met in 1796 at a time when she was married to a Milanese marchese named Visconti. Like a beautiful prize of war, she had later been brought back to Paris and accorded a homage that fell just short of full marital status—an unusual situation which had been transformed into an extraordinarily harmonious ménage à trois when Berthier had been forced to marry his Bavarian princess. Had he dared to cross Napoleon by refusing to have any part in this Russian invasion project, he might not have lost his Paris townhouse or even his château, but an imperious decree could have sent Giuseppina back to her native Italy. To the love-smitten Alexandre Berthier this would have been like a sentence of death.

It was finally Napoleon who broke the long, uncomfortable silence at this singularly cheerless meal by asking Rapp how far it was from Danzig to Cadiz.

"Too far, Sire," replied the incorrigible Alsatian, his lips pursed beneath the venerable white mustache.

CHAPTER 7

PLOTTERS, DREAMERS, AND INTRIGUERS

WHILE NAPOLEON was thus marshaling his forces, his prospective adversary, Alexander, had been anything but idle. "Never have I led such a dog's life," he had already begun complaining during the previous November, in a letter to his sister Catherine. "Often during the week I get up from bed and sit down at my desk," the Russian emperor continued, "and I only leave it to eat a bite all by myself, and then I return to it until the moment comes to go to bed. . . . We are on a continual *qui-vive;* the circumstances are all so thorny that hostilities could start at any moment."

Seven weeks later he had written yet again to his favorite sister to apologize for his silence—he simply hadn't had a moment to himself. "This confounded politics goes from bad to worse, and the infernal being who is the scourge of the human race"—he meant, of course, Napoleon—"becomes more detestable with each passing day." And shortly after New Year's Day, in an even shorter and more hastily scribbled note, he had repeated a by now familiar phrase: "I find myself more than ever like a sentinel, for the horizon darkens more and more."

Throughout January puffing horses in jingling harnesses had continued to trot briskly up and down the Nevsky Prospect and along the frosty quays, whipped on by purple-nosed coachmen, as they carried their fur-enveloped charges to gala balls and masquerades. A few of these Tsar Alexander felt duty-bound to attend. His consolation, more than ever, was Petersburg's most celebrated beauty—Maria Antonovna Naryshkin, the anything but faithful wife of the Grand Master of the Imperial Hunt, who had been the Russian emperor's mistress for close to a dozen years and who had borne him two daughters, the older of whom had died in 1810. Maria Antonovna had recently returned from a long sojourn in Odessa, where plenty of warming sun and Black Sea baths had cured her of a consumptive cough which had greatly worried Alexander during the preceding winter. Now, looking more ravishing than ever, she could make her discreet but not unnoticed appearance in a ballroom, almost invariably clad in a white evening gown and displaying a minimum of jewelry. "Lost in the crowd," as Countess Edling (one of Empress Elisabeth's ladies-in-waiting) was later to recall, the strikingly dark-haired beauty would be gratified by her imperial lover with "a glance that was more expressive and flattering to her than all the distinctions in the world. Silent, lonely (for few persons approached her), she kept her eyelids lowered in order to hide from the curiosity of the assembled company what was going on inside her. This artfulness, if such it was, gave her a particular charm, and engendered more passions"—the plural here was not inaptly used—"than would have the liveliest coquettishness."

In early February Alexander had had to tear himself from his "little family" (Maria Antonovna and their young daughter, Sophie) and leave Petersburg for a quick sleigh tour of border fortresses. The trip, made in sub-zero weather over the blindingly white countryside to fortifications buried deep in snow, was more symbolic than of real military significance. The tsar was anxious to maintain an outward serenity, to reassure his anxious subjects that peace was still possible. Knowing the vehemence of their feelings, he feared that one of them might publicly vent his animosity on the unpopular and increasingly ostracized French ambassador (Lauriston) or on one of his subordinates, thus giving Napoleon another chance to denounce Russia for its hostile attitude and "duplicity."

The sight of elite regiments being reviewed in front of the Winter Palace by their emperor before tramping and trotting out of the still snowbound capital aroused more concern than elation. In this respect the Petersburg of 1812 bore little resemblance to the Petersburg of 1805, when arrogant young dandies had placed bets with each other as to just how many days it would take them to gallop their way victoriously across Germany and France and into a cowed and subjugated Paris. As Alexander wrote on April 1 to his old friend Adam Czartoryski: "There is no longer that swagger which caused one to scorn the foe. On the contrary, one appreciates his full strength, one feels that reverses are quite possible, but in spite of that one is disposed to uphold the honor of the empire to the bitter end."

Bitter, too, was the beginning of, or more exactly the prelude to, the momentous hostilities of 1812 for Russia's leading bureaucrat, the seemingly irreplaceable Mikhail Speransky. His sudden fall from favor, during the last week of March, though few could have realized it at the time, marked the end of an era in Alexander's life, ushering in a period of reaction, which was to continue almost unabated for the next fifty years and to retard a process of reform which might have saved Russia from the Bolshevik revolution of 1917.

Unlike the majority of Alexander's administrative assistants, Speransky was a self-made man who owed nothing to the privileges of noble birth. The son of a humble village priest—whence his derogatory nickname, "the *popovich*" —he was first known as Mikhailo Mikhailovich (at this time few Russian peasants possessed family names), to which was later added the name of Speransky, based on *spes,* the Latin word for "hope." As assiduous in his studies as he was later to be in his bureaucratic functions, the "hopeful one" had gained admission to the Saint Alexander Nevsky seminary in Petersburg, had mastered Latin as well as French, had then taught mathematics, rhetoric, and philosophy, and after tutoring several of Prince Alexander Kurakin's bastard children, he had been given a post in the imperial administration.

Married to the daughter of an English governess who had come to Russia to tutor the sons and daughters of the Petersburg nobility in the unfamiliar tongue of William Shakespeare, Speransky was an interesting example of the Anglophilia which had begun to infiltrate once Gallomanic Petersburg as a reaction to the excesses of the French revolutionaries and of their masterful successor, Bonaparte. His respect for things British was carried to the point of breakfasting in the morning off eggs, roast beef, and tea, and he had even learned English—then an almost unheard-of accomplishment in the French-speaking capital.

In addition to the moist quality of his heavy-lidded eyes, the "ethereal pallor of his face," the soft whiteness of his hands—all of them qualities Tolstoy was careful to note in *War and Peace*—Speransky was distinguished by a high-domed and increasingly balding cranium, which was so crammed with knowledge that it could not but impress (or irritate) anyone who came into contact with him. Among those who were impressed was the tsar, who soon realized that here was the ideal bureaucrat he needed to introduce some badly needed order into the tangled jungle of past imperial decrees and judicial regulations.

The crowning achievement of Speransky's six-year collaboration with his sovereign was the creation of a Council of State composed of thirty-five members. In the *popovich*'s ambitious scheme of reform this was intended to be the apex of a vast pyramid of elected and selected assemblies, which were to constitute a coherent structure capable of transmitting the requests and complaints of the emperor's subjects to the supreme consultative council in the capital. The construction of such an elaborate edifice should logically have begun at the lowest levels of provincial government. Instead, because Alexander's attention was increasingly absorbed by military and diplomatic concerns, this attempt to invigorate a lethargic system of administration was begun from the top. The result was a kind of exotic bud which, lacking stem and roots, could not properly fulfill its modest legislative function. Few of its appointed members seem to have had any clear idea as to just what purpose the Council of State was supposed to serve, though most of them agreed to make donations for the embellishment of the hall graciously selected for their august deliberations. One of them, the waspish Fyodor Rostopchin, who was soon to achieve a curious immortality as the most eccentric governor Moscow had ever known, contributed a richly enshrined crucifix, inscribed below (in Old Church Slavonic) with the words "Father, forgive them their sins, for they know not what they do."

By a simple process of association the ultraconservative nitwits in Petersburg concluded that their own emperor's Council of State was a servile imitation of Napoleon's Conseil d'Etat. Had they had a less jaundiced view of France's strong-willed ruler, they could have laid these fears to rest. Napoleon, who had a deep-rooted distrust of parliamentary assemblies—mere "talking shops," where demagogic windbags vied with and intrigued against each other

—had never intended his Conseil d'Etat to be an elected body; its members were handpicked lawyers, financiers, and administrators whose opinions he was willing to listen to (but not necessarily to heed) because they were persons of experience and proved competence in their respective fields. But in Petersburg, the mere suspicion that this "new-fangled" institution was an alien, and particularly a French, importation was enough to damn the Council of State and its bureaucratic author, Speransky, in the eyes of many prominent persons who detested the parvenu *popovich* precisely because he was bent on replacing the system of Court favoritism which had thrived in the "good old days" of Catherine the Great with a pedantic system of government in which noble birth and wit would eventually count for nothing.

Of all his bitter enemies the most dangerous for Speransky was Tsar Alexander's sister Catherine. Thwarted in her adolescent desire to become an empress, or failing that a queen, she had decided to offset her lackluster marriage to George of Oldenburg by turning their country house near Tver into a provincial "Court" dedicated to the preservation of Russia's age-old culture. Its proximity to Moscow, on the road leading northwest to Petersburg, made it easy of access for aristocratic Muscovites, many of whom resented their venerable city's eclipse by the far younger, more cosmopolitan, and less "authentic" capital on the banks of the Neva.

The most brilliant of these malcontents was Count Fyodor Rostopchin, the onetime enfant terrible of the Petersburg Court, who had enjoyed a brief moment of glory as a combination foreign minister and grand vizier to Emperor Paul I. Since his fall from favor he had sought to relieve his frustrations by importing Scottish farmers to improve the agricultural methods of his serfs, establishing a school, pharmacy, and hospital for peasant children at his estate at Voronovo (near Moscow), and adding new volumes to his impressive collection of French, Italian, English, and German, as well as Russian, books. Like many others, he had felt deeply wounded by Napoleon's victory at Friedland and the "unholy" alliance Alexander had been forced to accept at Tilsit. His characteristically caustic response had been the publication of an incendiary pamphlet in which he deplored the fact that his fellow Russians should continue to ape those "monkeys," that "diabolical race, the scourge of mankind" —the French, a nation of scheming windbags who had proved themselves "in business felons, and in warfare brigands," and who were led by a man who had been running "from one corner of Europe to the other like a scalded cat." To such a mortified superpatriot someone like Speransky—that admirer of Napoleon who dabbled in mystical "illuminism" and frequented Masonic lodges (those dangerous hotbeds of revolutionary speculation)—was a highly suspect person who should be removed as soon as possible from his high office.

Another frequent visitor to Grand Duchess Catherine's provincial "Court" at Tver was Nikolai Mikhailovich Karamzine, a gifted essayist and writer of folk tales who had developed a historian's passion for Russia's medieval past. Russia, he was persuaded, owed its greatness to autocrats like Ivan III and his grandson, Ivan the Terrible, whose iron fists had kept the country from disintegrating under the impact of foreign invasions from East and West. The establishment of constitutional government was certain, on the contrary, to undermine the power and prestige of the nobility, fatally weakening the empire's strongest pillar and exposing it to the dangers of disruption. In a private epistle, which Grand Duchess Catherine sent on to her brother in Petersburg, Karamzine suggested that Speransky had been bribed by the French to subvert the country's traditional institutions. He even hinted darkly that if the power of Russia's nobility was not soon restored to what it had once been, Alexander might well suffer the fate of his father, Paul I.

Alexander's initial reaction to this unsolicited admonition was one of irritation. He did not like to be reminded of the grim circumstances of his father's death. But on a second reading many of Karamzine's arguments began to strike a responsive chord.

The seeds of doubt once sown, it only remained to stimulate their germination. Being by now pregnant and unable to leave her country house, Grand Duchess Catherine was not able to participate in the final stages of the drama, a minor masterpiece of Court intrigue. Its chief Petersburg protagonists were two émigrés. The first, the Chevalier de Vernègues, a diehard believer in the divine right of kings to rule as they please, was the semiofficial representative in Petersburg of the already doddering Comte de Provence (who in little more than two years was to replace Napoleon in the throne room of the Tuileries as Louis XVIII). The other and far more influential fomentor of the anti-Speransky plot was a Swedish adventurer named Gustaf Mauritz Armfelt, whose turbulent life would have offered ideal material for an Alexandre Dumas novel. Dazzlingly good-looking, with romantic waves of blond hair, eyes that twinkled like sapphires, a small but beautifully shaped mouth that seemed specially designed for passionate embraces, and a physique worthy of a Tarzan, Armfelt was one of those men who radiate a robust joie de vivre which makes them irresistibly attractive to many men as well as women.

Being something of a ladies' man himself, Alexander seems to have been fascinated by Armfelt's adventurous career as a dedicated anti-Jacobin and itinerant Don Juan, and impressed by the forceful way in which he ventured to press his opinions upon him. In questions relating to Napoleon the handsome Swedish baron was what today we would call a hawk, believing that the inevitable war with France could best be won by a frankly aggressive strategy. He had vigorously endorsed the idea of a preemptive advance to the Vistula in the spring of 1811, and he had later made no secret of his scornful disapproval of the defensive strategy—a deliberate withdrawal eastward and an avoidance of a major battle with the French—which Barclay de Tolly, the minister of war, was now advocating as the surest way of wearing down Napoleon's forces, should he choose to invade Russia.

In addition to his general detestation of everything the dangerously "liberal" Speransky stood for, Armfelt harbored a personal grudge against the all-too-powerful *popovich* because he had made himself the state secretary for Finnish affairs, thus undercutting the dominant role he himself had hoped to play in the administration of the newly annexed territory. He suspected (quite rightly) that Speransky wished to make the Grand Duchy of Finland a proving ground for the far-reaching reforms he was hoping to be able to introduce one day into other regions of the Russian Empire.

Speransky was thus *l'homme à abattre*—the man who had to be "felled" by hook or by crook. To aid him in this enterprise Armfelt enlisted the cooperation of General Alexander Dimitrevich Balashov, an uninspired but not unambitious garrison commander who had served as "grand master of the police" *(Oberpolizeimeister)* in Moscow and Petersburg before being appointed minister of police in 1810. Little eloquence was required to persuade the not particularly intelligent Balashov that the unwieldy Council of State could be vastly improved if it were to be run by a "triumvirate" to be composed of State Secretary Speransky, Minister of Police Balashov, and Armfelt, acting in his capacity as one of the tsar's leading military advisers. His vanity flattered by this prospect, Balashov ingenuously agreed that it was worth considering. But when the third member of the prospective "triumvirate" was approached, he indignantly rejected the idea. So absurd did Speransky find it that he did not bother to mention it to Alexander, considering it unworthy of his sovereign's august attention.

This was a fatal tactical blunder, one quickly exploited by Armfelt and Balashov. The Russian emperor was accordingly given their own, subtly twisted version of what had happened: it was they who had been approached by Speransky with the ruling "triumvirate" proposal. Dumbfounded by this preposterous travesty, Speransky at first was speechless. His spluttering protestations of loyalty left Alexander less than satisfied. Balashov was now authorized to keep an eye on Speransky. But to make sure that he was not being double-crossed by his own minister of police, Alexander ordered the head of the secret-police department to spy on both Speransky and Balashov.

The culminating factor in Speransky's downfall was the discovery by Balashov's police spies that the state secretary, behind his imperial master's back, had been exchanging carefully coded letters with mysterious correspondents in Paris. The police agents had stumbled on one of the most closely guarded secrets of the realm. It was in fact with Speransky's full knowledge and cooperation that the emperor had sent Karl Robert Nesselrode to Paris to establish contact with Talleyrand and other Frenchmen critical of Napoleon, the reports that he sent back in cipher being kept secret not only from Prince Kurakin, his immediate superior at the Russian embassy, but from the official head of the diplomatic service, Chancellor Rumiantsev, in Petersburg. Alexander had opened a similar channel of confidential information with an informant in Vienna, again without the knowledge of the local Russian ambassador or of Rumiantsev in Petersburg. In so doing he was merely seeking to multiply and cross-check his sources of information. But it was more than a little embarrassing for Alexander to discover that his trusted state secretary had been taking highly confidential reports, which were for "imperial eyes only," back home with him in the evening and leaving them casually lying on his desk. This was not simply a case of *lèse-majesté;* it was, at such a critical moment, a serious case of *lèse-sécurité,* and thus even harder to forgive.

On the last Sunday of March, 1812, Speransky was ordered by an imperial messenger to proceed immediately to the Winter Palace. More than two hours later he emerged from the emperor's private office, looking visibly distraught. A moment later the door opened, and to the astonishment of those present the Tsar of all the Russias came out with tears in his eyes and embraced Speransky, saying, "Once more, Mikhailo Mikhailovich, farewell!" Returning to his office, he closed the door behind him. Shortly afterward an usher informed those waiting in the antechamber that His Majesty the Emperor would not be receiving any more visitors that night.

That same evening, Speransky was met in front of his house by General Balashov, who told him that he was under arrest and that his papers were being impounded. Several hours later the crestfallen Mikhailo Mikhailovich took his place next to a police officer in the *kibitka* that was waiting to carry him to Nizhny Novgorod, on the Volga, where the exiled *popovich* would be safe from his Petersburg enemies, capable, Alexander knew, of having him assassinated during his future absence from the capital.

The news of Speransky's downfall took the diplomatic community completely by surprise. The French ambassador, Lauriston, was reduced, like his colleagues, to random speculations as to just what this signified. "The death of a tyrant could not have provoked so widespread a joy!" noted the chronicler Fyodor Fyodorovich Viegel, adding with the wisdom of belated revelation that whenever he had approached Speransky he had always sniffed sulphur, and had seen in his pale eyes "the bluish flicker of the underworld."

"What a great day for the fatherland and for all of us is this 17th of March!" exclaimed the pious Varvara Bakunin in her diary. (It was the twenty-ninth, according to the Western calendar.) "God has manifested His benevolence towards us, and our enemies are fallen. . . . It is probable," she went on, repeating the accusations that were now on everybody's lips, "that Speransky intended to yield our fatherland and sovereign to our foe. It is asserted that at the same time he wanted to foment a sudden uprising in all corners of Russia, and by giving the peasants freedom, to hand them a weapon for the destruction of the gentry."

Overnight the once all-powerful *popovich* became a monster of iniquity, an object of shuddering reprobation, even among the lower classes, which might have seen in his vertiginous ascension a welcome harbinger of their own betterment. He became the scapegoat for all the ills and burdens under which the country was laboring. Hostile crowds gathered on the snow-covered pavement in front of Speransky's house, hissing and even spitting at the frightened members of his family as they climbed into the sleigh that was to take them in their turn to Nizhny Novgorod.

Repellent to his sense of justice and fair play though these manifestations were, they confirmed Alexander in his conviction that he had done the right thing. A sovereign was not free, like an ordinary mortal, to follow the dictates of his heart; there were moments when he had to put aside all humanitarian considerations and act according to a cruel *raison d'Etat.*

If, judged by its long-term effects, Speransky's disgrace was a serious setback for Russia, it was offset in the short run by two diplomatic successes, which did much to enhance Alexander's self-confidence in his ability to rule, if need be, single-handedly.

The first was a secret pact of cooperation, signed in early April by Chancellor Rumiantsev and Count von Löwenhielm, a Swedish Court chamberlain whom Bernadotte had sent to Petersburg as his unofficial ambassador. This agreement effectively destroyed one of the props of Napoleon's grand strategy, which had been based on the confident assumption that the recently humiliated Swedes would take advantage of Russia's military predicament to invade and reoccupy their former Finnish provinces.

The second diplomatic breakthrough took longer to mature. But it was to prove an even greater setback to Napoleon's expectations. For some months past a number of Alexander's subordinates—Barclay de Tolly, Alexander Chernyshov, Karl Robert Nesselrode, and even the somewhat senile Prince Alexander Kurakin—had been pleading with the emperor to make peace with the Turks, so that more divisions from the Army of the Danube could be rushed northward to reinforce the Russian army corps stationed along or near the Polish border. Desperately anxious to maintain the unpopular alliance with France, Chancellor Rumiantsev, on the other hand, had repeatedly warned the tsar that a quick peace with the Turks and a northward movement of Russian forces would be interpreted by Napoleon as a hostile act and might help to precipitate the war they wished to avoid. Alexander, true to his hesitant temperament, had thus kept on temporizing. Loath to renounce Russia's claim to the Danubian province of Moldavia, he was still obstinately hoping that by combining threats and cajolements he could browbeat the new, insecure sultan in Istanbul into accepting a formal offensive and defensive alliance with Russia, similar to the one he had signed with England in 1809. Nothing, the tsar was persuaded, could give Napoleon greater pause than a diplomatic coup of this nature.

There is little doubt that if Napoleon, in the early spring of 1812, had made a serious effort to improve France's sour relations with the Sublime Porte, he could have created a lot of trouble on Russia's southern front—with military consequences that would greatly have limited the scope of the ultimate French debacle. From 1798 until early 1806 relations between Paris and Constantinople had frequently been strained—first because of Bonaparte's incursion into Egypt and then Syria (both provinces of the Ottoman Empire), and later because of the sultan's refusal to recognize the "upstart" Bonaparte's imperial title. But Napoleon's dramatic triumph at Austerlitz, as galling to the Russians as it was to the Austrians, had brought about a complete reversal of opinion. The sultan (Selim III) had hastened to recognize the imperial pretensions of the new Charlemagne of the West, and for the next year and a half the "French party" in Istanbul had carried all before it.

But then, in July of 1807, had come the *coup de théâtre* of Tilsit. It had provoked as much consternation in Istanbul as in Petersburg. The sudden about-face in Napoleonic policy, culminating in an "unholy alliance" between former enemies, had at one stroke destroyed the soaring prestige of the French. In now blatantly allying himself with his onetime enemy, Napoleon, in Turkish eyes, had made mincemeat of his earlier pledges to do everything he could to preserve the Ottoman Empire, in the Balkans as in the Caucasus. An "emperor" he might claim to be, but this double-crosser was in reality no better than a liar and a cheat. Among Istanbul's one million inhabitants passions quickly rose to fever pitch. The French embassy was stormed by an infuriated mob; the ambassador came close to having his throat cut by an assailant; and in a later riot a number of Frenchmen were massacred, while others were seized and brutally tortured by Ottoman police officials.

These sanguinary upheavals confirmed Napoleon's low opinion of the Turks, already influenced by the overthrow, in early June of 1807, of Sultan Selim III, who had been trying to develop a more modern and better-disciplined army by curbing the power of the unruly Janissaries and of the fanatically Moslem *ulemas* (interpreters of the Koran), violently opposed to all attempts at Western-style reforms. Selim's murder, engineered by his ruthless cousin and successor, Sultan Mustapha IV, and the massacre of seventeen leading dignitaries, whose severed heads were impaled on pikestaffs by the gates of the seraglio, convinced Napoleon that there was no curbing the fratricidal barbarism of the "unspeakable" Turks and consequently no further point in trying to shore up a moribund empire.

By 1809, after another sultan, Mahmoud II, had been placed on the throne, the British were able to score a decisive comeback by signing a full-fledged treaty of alliance. This, coming on the heels of more bloody upheavals in Istanbul, in which flaming torches and boiling oil, as well as scimitars and pikes, were used by contending factions, further disgusted Napoleon. By withdrawing his earlier offer to "mediate" a peace settlement between Turks and Russians, he in effect gave the latter carte blanche to resume their war against the Ottomans in the Balkans and the Caucasus.

In the early summer of 1810 the Russians, commanded by an able young general named Nikolai Kamensky, advanced in force across the Danube into what is now Bulgaria, at one point coming close to Varna, on the Black Sea coast. After forcing the Turks to surrender the important stronghold of Routchouk, on the southern bank of the Danube, Kamensky was preparing to mount a new offensive in the spring of 1811 when four of his divisions were removed and sent northward to be concentrated near Russia's Polish border. Shortly afterward he died—probably from some sort of malignant fever, very common in the marshy regions of the Danube estuary, although rumor had it that he had been poisoned by the Turks.

The general chosen to replace Kamensky had neither his youth nor his dynamism, but he made up for it by being plentifully endowed with guile. This was Mikhail Hilarionovich Kutuzov, who hoped to refurbish his military reputation, badly smudged by the rout of Austerlitz, by winning a decisive victory against the demoralized Turkish army. Unfortunately, the forces under his command had been so weakened that he was finally obliged to evacuate Routchouk and to conclude an armistice with the Turks in October 1811.

Throughout the following winter it was Tsar Alexander's hope that the mere prospect of a massive revolt of Orthodox Christian Bulgars against the Ottoman authorities would be enough to persuade the Turks to agree to an offensive and defensive alliance, similar to the one they had concluded with the British. Instead, the new and surprisingly stubborn sultan, Mahmoud, raised new conditions; and as the weeks and then the months went by, the prospect of a Christian uprising gradually faded, replaced by groans of discontent from the recently "liberated" Vallachians and Moldavians, bitterly protesting the off-hand way in which they were being treated by the new commander of the Danubian "front," Kutuzov, who was now holding court in Budapest in conditions of almost pasha-like luxury.

Although the one-eyed general (who had twice been wounded by bullets in the head) was now approaching seventy, he had retained a lusty appetite, and not merely for good food. His personal means could not be compared to those of Catherine the Great's favorite, Prince Grigory Potyomkin, who had taken along an entire orchestra and a small harem of dancing girls and pretty princesses to stimulate his martial energies during his campaign against the Turks in 1790. But Kutuzov, who had not served under Potyomkin for nothing, had long since decided that a veteran commander, and particularly one of his age, had a right to enjoy first-class meals served on silver plates engraved with the imperial crest and to find relief from the hardships of war in the arms of any wench who could be induced to share his couch. All of this was known to Alexander, who felt that these pleasant distractions were keeping Kutuzov from actively waging war or making peace, particularly since the sybaritic general's latest "conquest"—a captivating Vallachian damsel—was reported to have been infiltrated into Russian headquarters by the wily Turks.

Such was the situation when, in late March, Alexander received word that Austria had signed a formal treaty of alliance with France. This news, which exploded in Petersburg with the force of a thunderclap, added a new dimension to Russia's troubles. but it also opened a new horizon of military opportunity —or so at least it seemed to Alexander in discussing his empire's increasingly precarious situation with his minister of the navy, Admiral Chichagov.

Pavel Vassilievich Chichagov, who was destined to play a crucial part in the culminating weeks of the 1812 campaign, was in every sense an odd duck in the turgid backwaters of Petersburg politics. Although his father had been an admiral, he himself had risen from the ranks, had distinguished himself in several naval battles against the Swedes in 1790, and had finally been appointed a fleet squadron commander on the basis of his exceptional seamanship. A scathing critic of his country's backwardness—in shipyard construction, ad-ministration, tax-collecting, education, military conscription and prepared-ness, and not least of all serf-based agriculture—he had made no secret of his antipathy for the swaggering Court dandies who owed their fancy general's uniforms and decorations to their aristocratic preeminence. For having been "unpatriotic" enough to wish to marry the daughter of a Chatham naval base commander he had met during a term of service in England, he had incurred the wrath of the mercurial Emperor Paul I, who had had him locked up for a while in the Peter and Paul Fortress. Yet Chichagov's subsequent marriage to this English lady had not turned him into a rabid Anglophile; for though as a seaman he admired Nelson and British naval prowess, he had long harbored an even greater veneration for Napoleon.

In the autumn of 1809 the forty-two-year-old admiral had requested a leave of absence from his ministerial post. In the hope that a few months of sunshine on the French Riviera would revive his ailing wife, he had taken her to Paris, where Napoleon, duly alerted by Caulaincourt's dispatches—here was that rarest of Russian surprises, a genuine admirer of France and its imperial ruler! —had received him at the Tuileries Palace, and had even invited him to spend a hunting weekend with him and Empress Josephine at Malmaison. This flattering attention, however, had not had the expected effect. The pomp and ceremonial of the Napoleonic Court recalled only too vividly the ceremonious fatuities of Chichagov's own imperial Court and the not so distant past when he, like other senior officials of the Russian administrative departments, had been required to stand like flunkeys behind the chairs of their ministers.

The death of his wife, whom he adored, only increased the admiral's embitterment. The sarcastic wit he had once employed against his own hopelessly "backward" countrymen was now turned with a vengeance against Napoleon and all his works. In a humble but characteristically forthright letter, in which he frankly confessed his altered views, he requested Emperor Alexander's permission to bring his wife's body back to Petersburg and to return to his service. The permission was immediately granted.

As human as it was princely, the welcome offered by Alexander to the returning admiral in the autumn of 1811 was almost like that of a forgiving father to a prodigal son—and this though Chichagov was ten years his senior. The emperor had always appreciated his naval minister's *franc parler,* and he now demonstrated his continuing trust by reinstating him in his ministerial post and frequently consulting him.

Rising from these discussions like smoke from a bubbling hookah came a scheme of breathtaking audacity. His lively imagination fired by his now bitter hatred of his former idol, Chichagov conjured up the possibility of mounting a massive Balkan diversion aimed at the "soft underbelly" of the Napoleonic Empire. While the Turks were pressured into signing a full-scale offensive and defensive alliance, which would open the straits and permit Russia's Black Sea fleet to join the British in the Adriatic, a partly Russian, partly Balkan-Christian expeditionary force should be assembled in Vallachia, from where it would march westward over the mountains to join the Serbs. With the Montenegrins, equally devoted to the Russian cause, they could then stage a surprise attack on the French-occupied Dalmatian coast. The massive assault that Napoleon seemed bent on mounting in the north against Russia could thus be countered by a sweeping flank attack aimed at his possessions from the south.

To Alexander, who had always dreamed of becoming a great military commander, this strategic pipe dream seemed of a grandiose audacity. Getting him to head a pan-Slavic crusade was what his friend Adam Czartoryski had really had in mind when he had urged him in 1805 to proclaim himself king of Poland. Even if the cautious British could not be persuaded to go along with this bold enterprise, the mere threat of a pan-Slavic uprising in the Balkans could be suspended like a sword of Damocles over the head of the government in Vienna, as a reminder of the contagious mischief the Russians could foment among the Habsburg Empire's Slovene and other Slavic subjects, should the Austrians display too much zeal in cooperating with Napoleon's Grande Armée.

Far less impressed by this scheme was Chancellor Rumiantsev, who had staked his personal prestige and career on the maintenance of peace with France. If one wished to make peace with the Turks, he pointed out, arousing Slavic national feelings in the Balkans was a singularly clumsy way of going about it. Instead of intimidating, such a project might well exasperate the Austrians as well, pushing them even further into the Napoleonic camp. There was a heated exchange on the subject between the two men, who had once stoutly championed the unpopular cause of peace with France, and at the height of the altercation the volatile Chichagov accused Rumiantsev of treason.

A compromise was finally reached, to the grudging satisfaction of the two antagonists and their master, the emperor. The Turks were to be browbeaten into signing an offensive and defensive alliance, Russia's Black Sea fleet being used, if necessary, for a direct attack on the Bosphorus and Constantinople, while uprisings were fomented in Greece and other Balkan territories inhabited by Orthodox Christians. Admiral Chichagov was to replace the lethargic Kutuzov as commander of Russia's Danubian army; he was to put an end to abuses and reform the scandalously slipshod and corrupt administration of Vallachia and Moldavia, and he was invested with plenipotentiary powers to negotiate a satisfactory peace with the Turks.

It was the stubborn Rumiantsev, however, who had the last and decisive word. Knowing that, as a member of Alexander's suite, he would be leaving Petersburg before Chichagov, he deliberately removed part of the admiral's guiding instructions—as though by oversight—and then had them sent from Vilna by express courier. An accompanying note addressed directly to Kutuzov warned that if he did not immediately sign a peace agreement with the Turks, Admiral Chichagov, who would soon be on his way, would do it in his place and garner all the glory. (Thus forewarned, Kutuzov lost no time opening serious negotiations with the Turks, who agreed one month later to sign a formal peace treaty in Bucharest. The news, as we shall see, reached Napoleon only after he had invaded Russia. Although it greatly annoyed him, he rashly disregarded its future military significance: releasing more Russian divisions to combat his Grande Armée.)

All of these last-minute machinations, carried out in early April shortly before Tsar Alexander's departure for his field headquarters at Vilna, were shrouded behind a dense diplomatic smokescreen, apparently designed to fool the French ambassador, Lauriston, and reassure the uneasy mothers, fathers, uncles, aunts, and sisters who had watched their menfolk march off with their regiments to unspecified destinations near the country's western borders. Even Rumiantsev's departure was enveloped in a cloak of mystery. The day after he had left, John Quincy Adams received an official notification to the effect that the chancellor had left the capital to accompany His Majesty the Emperor on an *ordinary* tour of military inspection in the provinces; in the interim, his deputy, Count Alexander Saltykov, would be running the department of foreign affairs. When, a little later, the Swedish envoy, Count Löwenhielm, asked his American colleague, who had been around somewhat longer than he, what motive a "great Court" could have to "lie for nothing," Adams explained that it was simply "from the power of habit."

CHAPTER 8

THE HORNETS' NEST
OF VILNA

ALEXANDER HIMSELF left Petersburg in the early afternoon of
April 21 (Western calendar), after attending a special good-bye service at the
Holy Mother of Kazan Cathedral, where he was blessed by the local metropolitan. The beautifully echoing chants of choir and congregation sounded more
than usually doleful, and seldom had the flickering light from a multitude of
candles more poignantly expressed the tenuous nature of human life and the
somber uncertainties of the morrow. Though no war had yet been declared,
the word was in everybody's mind, if not on everybody's lips—and they knew
that if it came, it would be fought against a commander of satanic genius who
twice already had humbled their winsome, well-meaning, kindhearted *Gosudar*
(sovereign).

The tsar was so moved by this solemn leave-taking that he wept. So did all
those present. As he came out onto the steps of the colonnaded porch, the
thousands of devoted subjects massed on the cathedral square broke into
deep-throated acclamations of *"Oorah!"* Quickly climbing into the waiting
calèche, to hide his emotion, Alexander nodded to his faithful coachman. The
latter cracked his whip and sent the horses galloping down the avenue toward
the city's southern gate, pursued by hundreds of running spectators, who kept
shouting *"Oorah!"* and "For God and our sovereign!" until they finally had
to give up for lack of breath.

The Russian emperor's first stop was at Tsarskoye Syelo, some fifteen miles
south of the capital. With its two rococo palaces, set in a rambling park filled
with artificial grottos, neo-Gothic ruins, gloriettas, and triumphal arches,
Catherine the Great's "imperial village" was about as genuinely rustic as the
Grand Trianon at Versailles or Frederick II of Prussia's Sans-Souci at Potsdam. But here, even if briefly, Alexander could enjoy something closer to the
privacy that was denied him at the Winter Palace. Working till three o'clock
in the morning, he penned a long letter to Bernadotte, the prince regent of
Sweden, who had recently urged him to make peace with the Turks as quickly
as possible. Napoleon's former marshal had also suggested that he try to wean

Austria away from Napoleon by promising her a return of the (now Bavarian) Tyrol and the cession to Archduke Charles of Napoleon's "Kingdom of Italy." To keep their correspondence a dark secret, Alexander had offered not to show their letters to his own chancellor, Rumiantsev—a precaution that now permitted him to unfold his own quite different plan for the formation of an "imposing ensemble" of "bellicose" Slavs, who, allied with the malcontents of Hungary, could mount a "mighty diversion against Austria and the French possessions of the Adriatic."

Four days later Alexander finally reached Vilna, the progress of his jolting carriage being slowed by muddy ruts and slush and the swollen streams of a late spring thaw. He was met four miles from the city by his minister of war, General Barclay de Tolly, recently appointed commander of the First Russian Army of the West, and, as they rode toward Vilna, by the echoing boom of cannon and the reverberation of Palm Sunday bells.

Spread out along a curve of the ravine-enclosed Vilia River, with a semicircular ring of fir- and birch-covered hills cushioning the southern bank, Vilna at this time was a picturesque city of thirty thousand souls, full of narrow, undulating streets lined with palatial residences, burgher houses, and humbler dwellings that were little more than hovels. Its noblest landmark was the remaining octagonal red-brick tower of the now mostly ruined medieval castle which Guedymin, founder of the Jagellon dynasty of Polish kings, had erected on the highest of the surrounding hills in 1323. But what more immediately struck the approaching traveler's eye in this year of 1812 was a plethora of spires and onion-bulb cupolas attesting the old town's heterogeneous composition. Placed at the confluence of conflicting religions, Vilna had long served as the outpost of a militant Catholicism.

The traditional offerings of bread and salt were made to the incoming sovereign. This was Alexander's second visit in eleven years to the Lithuanian capital, and those who had never before laid eyes on the emperor were determined to do so, even if it meant having to peer down on him from rooftops, domes, and belfries. Curiosity rather than genuine enthusiasm was the dominant sentiment with most of these spectators.

Far less reserved and almost fawning in their welcome were many prominent members of the Lithuanian nobility, who had long since thrown in their lot with the Russians. The day after the tsar's arrival they were received by him in the archbishop's palace, along with representatives of the artisan and merchant guilds, leading prelates, and professors from the recently founded university. To disarm the hostility of those who were suspicious of or hostile to the Russians, Alexander unleashed all the resources of his many-sided charm. Decorations and orders of varying importance were lavished on the men, while a number of privileged daughters and nieces were appointed ladies-in-waiting to the absent Empress Elisabeth. "The emperor," wrote Gustaf Mauritz Armfelt to a friend in Sweden, "is making himself adored by everyone and completely turning the heads of the Polish womenfolk."

Among those whose heads were turned was the nineteen-year-old Sophie von Tisenhaus, who was as captivated by Alexander's exquisite manners as his roving eye was arrested by her tall, svelte figure and dark, flower-decorated hair. Years later she could still vividly recall the "cloudless" blue of Alexander's smiling eyes, the soft golden brown of his carefully arranged hair, the delicate, healthy flush of his rosy cheeks, the lavender scent of the lotion he used on his hands and face, the arch glances he would direct at her through the lorgnette he nonchalantly carried tucked into the sleeve of his blue-lapeled uniform, and the graceful way in which, to overcome his partial deafness, he would turn his head, the better to be able to listen with his good right ear. At thirty-five he looked younger than his age, even though his hairline had begun to recede. His head might not have been specially formed to receive "the triple crown of laurel, myrtle, and olive leaf," as she wrote in a characteristic gush of neoclassic prose, but it would be hard to improve on her acute perception of "the infinity of nuances in his tone and manners. If he was speaking to men of distinguished rank, it was at once with much dignity and affability that he addressed them; to persons of his suite [he spoke] with an almost familiar air of kindness; to women of a certain age with deference; to young persons with infinite grace, a subtle, seductive air, and a look full of expressiveness."

If all Alexander had had to do at this tense moment was to captivate leading members of the Lithuanian gentry, his two-month stay in Vilna would have been a resounding success. But there were more urgent problems, which could not be resolved by effusions of personal charm. In his brief letters to his sister Catherine he wrote of reviewing troops under drenching downpours, of galloping or being driven for miles from one army post to the next. But the impression one gets is that this expenditure of martial energy was distinctly dilettantish. In Petersburg, shortly before Speransky's downfall, he had told Karl Robert Nesselrode that he would need the services of a young man capable of handling his political correspondence and of accompanying him on horseback—something the ailing Rumiantsev could no longer do—since he had decided to place himself "at the head of the armies" in the field. He was thus repeating the mistake he had made in the autumn of 1805, when he had disregarded Adam Czartoryski's urgent plea that he delegate the operational command of his armies to an experienced military soldier, which he could not claim to be.

It would be oversimplifying the case to say that in the six years since Austerlitz Alexander had learned absolutely nothing about the art of war. But it is also true that he had remained stubbornly unchanged in one significant respect—his inordinate regard for foreign "experts" as opposed to Russian commanders. On the eve of Austerlitz he had insisted that the formulation of the general battle plan for a combined Russian-Austrian advance against the outnumbered French be entrusted to the Austrian general Franz von Weyrother, rather than to the more cautious Kutuzov. The result had been a disaster. But this had not kept him from later shifting his personal trust to two Prussians. The first, Colonel Schoeller, had been acting as a secret liaison officer between himself and King Frederick William III. The second was now regarded in Berlin as a "renegade" and a "deserter": Karl Ludwig von Phull, whom Alexander had promoted to the rank of lieutenant general in the Russian army and made one of his aides-de-camp.

Of a somewhat short, almost spiderish build, with a wrinkled face and shoulder blades protruding bonily beneath the back of his stiff-collared uniform, Phull was an academic caricature of his hero, Frederick the Great. Unlike the resourceful Frederick, Phull had never won a victory in more than thirty years of military service. But his ability to expatiate at length on the principles his inspired model had elaborated in his *L'art de la Guerre* and illustrated in his many campaigns was absolutely spellbinding—at any rate to some. Frederick William III considered him a genius—whence his wrath when Phull had left his defeated sovereign in the lurch during the grim winter of 1806–1807 and placed his intellectual baggage at the disposal of the tsar. The equally amateurish Alexander seems to have shared this veneration. In Petersburg, too, this learned Teuton was regarded as a genius, and indeed as a kind of self-effacing genius, to judge by this curiously revealing sentence in John Quincy Adams's *Memoirs:* "There was present at table a Prussian General Pfuhl, who, Mr. Six said, was one of the ablest men in the world, who had lately published in German some remarks upon the system of conscription, though he did not acknowledge himself as the author."

It is only proper to add that this was not the opinion of the military professionals. To the superpatriots, like General Alexander Ivanovich Ostermann-Tolstoy, who was appointed commander of the First Army's Fourth Corps in the spring of 1812, Phull was anathema because he could express himself only in German or a guttural kind of French, having never bothered to learn Russian, which he more or less disdained as a language of barbarians. To the cooler heads, like Barclay de Tolly, who himself spoke Russian with a Baltic-German accent he could never quite get rid of, Phull was a nuisance because his strategic "planning" made no sense. To still others—like the blond Hercules, Armfelt, or the dark, fire-eating Bagration—Phull was an academic crackpot, stubbornly committed to a cowardly defensive policy. But by one and all Phull was disliked because of the baleful spell he had managed to cast over the vacillating emperor's will and imagination.

The "master plan" Phull had devised for trapping and defeating Napoleon was a classic example of the penchant general staff officers so often display for wishing to refight the last war. In this case the war that had inspired Phull was Frederick the Great's summer campaign of 1761, when, forced to retreat into Silesia before the advancing Russians and Austrians, he had withdrawn into the entrenched camp of Bunzelwitz and successfully defied the two opposing armies, which outnumbered his own forces by a ratio of three to one. Guided by what seemed to him a memorable feat of arms, Phull proposed to "save" Russia by establishing a Russian equivalent of Bunzelwitz in some central spot defending the routes to Petersburg and Moscow. This formidable strongpoint was to act like an "abscess of fixation," irresistibly drawing Napoleon toward it like a magnet. While they wore themselves out in vain attempts to storm it, the besieging French were to be cleverly enveloped by two giant pincers. The northern arm was to be composed of General Barclay de Tolly's First Army of the West, while the southern arm, composed of Prince Bagration's Second Army, was to move northward from its preestablished position near the Pripet Marshes and thus to "close the trap" on the French invaders.

Grandiose in its conception—as prefabricated schemes of this kind are apt
to look when demonstrated on large-scale maps or blackboards—this "master
plan" appealed to Alexander because of Wellington's successful defense of the
fortified lines of Torres Vedras, north of Lisbon. In fact, the Wellingtonian
"triumph" in Portugal was as misleading a precedent as the Frederickian
"victory" at Bunzelwitz, because there was nothing even remotely resembling
a mountain range or rugged hill country in the key area between the Dvina,
Berezina, and Dnieper rivers where, according to the Phullian doctrine, this
formidable stumbling block was to be erected.

The site eventually chosen for the entrenched camp—Drissa, 140 miles
northeast of Vilna, near the Dvina River—was anything but ideal, and indeed
an open invitation to disaster. This probably explains why the actual work of
construction, belatedly begun in November 1811 and delayed by accumulating
snowdrifts and midwinter blizzards, was undertaken at a snaillike pace rather
than at the feverish, round-the-clock tempo which might have given the plan
some substance. At the Ministry of War in Petersburg no one except Phull had
any faith in the project.

If Phull's master plan was disliked because of its excessively abstract character, Barclay de Tolly's own strategy aroused even stronger feelings among
many Russian generals. Phull's plan might seem glaringly impractical, but it
did at least call for a major stand to be made at some point against Napoleon
and his Grande Armée. Barclay's strategy, on the other hand, was to avoid
a major battle with Napoleon's forces and to keep withdrawing ever farther
into the depths of the Russian hinterland, while harrying the flanks of the
advancing French columns. The farther he advanced, so Barclay argued, the
more surely Napoleon would seal his doom, since more and more of his
Grande Armée would have to be detached and left behind to guard his supply
depots in the rear. Russia's vast expanse could thus be used to complete what
Russia's existing armies were still too weak to accomplish on their own. As
the prospect of war drew ever closer, Barclay even issued instructions calling
for the implementation of a scorched-earth policy similar to the one Wellington had used to such devastating effect against the French in Portugal. General
Alexander Tormassov, a veteran cavalryman who had recently been recalled
from Georgia (where he had been battling the Persians) to command a Third
Army of the West being formed south of the Pripet Marshes, was thus ordered
to "tear down everything, especially hospitals, that may serve the enemy; rob
him of every chance to lay hands on provisions or conveyances; burn and
destroy bridges, boats, and powder-stores . . . carry off or wreck all available
carts and harnesses; leave the inhabitants only what they need for their own
sustenance. . . ."

The man who conceived this coolly calculated plan could not rationally be
accused of lacking courage or intelligence. In December 1806, when he was
covering the retreat of General Bennigsen's divisions in Poland, Barclay de
Tolly had persuaded a few hardy Cossacks to leap and swim their way across
the Vistula from ice floe to ice floe, and to drag back some half-frozen French

prisoners, who admitted under questioning that the central French army corps was not planning an immediate pursuit. The Russian commander in chief had then halted his retreat, and in the ensuing battle of Pultusk, Barclay had mounted a furious bayonet charge which had forced Marshal Lannes's French forces to retreat—the first military setback Napoleon had suffered in ten years of warfare.

At Hof, in early February of 1807, Barclay had fought an even bloodier battle and shown extraordinary skill in maneuvering his infantry, cavalry, and artillery units so as to delay the massive French advance and to give Bennigsen time to draw up his combined Russian-Prussian armies for a major stand. It was he who had been picked to hold the central town of Preussisch-Eylau in the terrible battle that followed. Driven back at first in bitter house-to-house fighting to the frozen gardens at the edge of the town, Barclay's tired and half-starved men had bayoneted their way back through musket smoke and blinding snow to the town's central square, killing and wounding hundreds of soldiers of Soult's corps and taking five hundred prisoners.

This grim struggle, which proved crucial in preventing Napoleon from winning a clear-cut victory, had culminated, just as dusk was falling, in a final cavalry charge which had cleared the last French soldiers from the church and its snowbanked graveyard. Barclay, leading the charge on horseback, had been hit in the right arm by a round of grapeshot and knocked unconscious by the blast. He might have been trampled to death by the charging horses behind him had not a brave sergeant gathered him up, slung him over the saddle, and galloped him off to the nearest dressing station. Moved by sledge to Koenigsberg and then to Memel, where his wife, Auguste, and a foster daughter turned up to take care of him, Barclay had had to endure the painful extraction (without anesthetics) of not less than forty separate bone fragments splintered by the grapeshot blast. The fifteen months of disability that followed, before the wound was completely healed, had kept him away from the disastrous battlefield of Friedland—thus perhaps saving his life—and left him with a partially immobilized right arm and hand, which thereafter made it difficult for him to write.

All of this was known to Alexander. Impressed by Bennigsen's glowing accounts of Barclay's tactical skill and courage in the field, he had personally visited his Memel sickroom (in April of 1807) and had his Scottish surgeon remove the last bone splinters. Everything about Barclay pleased the tsar: his sober assessment of the Russian army's military deficiencies; a total absence of the swaggering bravado and intriguing sycophancy displayed by so many of his generals, forever vying with each other for more medals and promotions; the orderly neatness of his surroundings; and not least of all, his Spartan readiness, derived from his strict Lutheran upbringing, to share the hardships of his soldiers by bivouacking in the open and sleeping on cottage floors or barn-stored straw. For Alexander, who always traveled with a straw-stuffed leather mattress and pillow, on which he slept at night, this abstemious simplicity and self-discipline—so different from the luxury in which Kutuzov liked to wallow—was a particularly valued trait. It helps to explain the tsar's growing confidence in this phlegmatic commander, who was adored by his soldiers because of the concern he showed for their welfare, but who was hated by many of his fellow generals for the decorations and promotions he kept receiving from their sovereign.

In June of 1809, when Alexander had named him commander in chief of the Russian forces in Finland, as a reward for the ingenuity Barclay had shown in leading a hazardous surprise assault against the Swedes across the fissured ice floes of the Kvarken (the narrowest part of the then frozen Gulf of Bothnia), there was an uproar in Petersburg. Half a dozen outraged generals had tendered their resignations. Barclay de Tolly's principal drawback, in the eyes of many of them, was that he was insufficiently Russian (having been born a Baltic baron in the once Polish province of Courland), and, worse still, that he came from a relatively obscure rather than from a leading noble family.

In January of 1810, when Barclay had been appointed minister of the Military Ground Forces (as the Ministry of War was then officially called), the same rumblings of discontent were heard again. This time his modest origins could not be held against him, since his immediate predecessor, General Alexei Andreyevich Arakcheyev, was of even humbler birth and infinitely more uncouth. The "bulldog," as he was often called—because of the systematic rudeness Arakcheyev displayed in barking out orders and remonstrances to the quaking members of his staff, and even to senior generals—had been grudgingly accepted, even if disliked, because he was the country's foremost artillery expert. Even the most hot-blooded saber-draggers in the land—like Prince Pyotr Ivanovich Bagration—no longer dared to claim that they could win battles against Napoleon and the French without the help of cannon, bombards, and mortars. Barclay de Tolly, however, was not this kind of "expert."

Lacking in prestige and glamor though the tall, laconic, unpretentious minister of war might seem to foreigners (like Lauriston) and to the elite of Petersburg society, he could not be accused of that most unpardonable of military offenses: underestimating the enemy. The situation Barclay found confronting him when he assumed his office at the start of 1810 was positively disheartening. In spite of the vast changes that had occurred in the field of warfare over the past hundred years, Russia's ground forces were still guided by army regulations laid down by Peter the Great in 1716. These had encouraged a deplorable laxity at virtually all levels of the officer corps, because unit commanders were not held rigorously responsible for the carelessness or misdemeanors of their subordinates. The gambling, drunkenness, and dissipation in which so many Russian officers indulged was only one aspect of this general *laissez-aller*. An iron discipline was clearly needed to control serf-soldiers who, once they had been selected by their gentry owners' bailiffs or other recruiting officers, were forced to serve for a period of twenty-five years (and who, in Catherine the Great's time, had their heads half shaved so that they could easily be recognized, like convicts, if they tried to desert). But nothing had more shocked Barclay than the callous indifference of so many Russian officers, from generals down to subalterns, to the proper feeding of their men, who were often reduced to near-subsistence levels and so physically weakened that they were unfit for strenuous marches and maneuvers, and easily fell prey to sickness and epidemics. Appalled by the number of undernourished soldiers filling the military hospitals, Barclay de Tolly had enlisted the support of Alexander's Scottish surgeon, James Wyllie, who had presented the emperor with a report in which he declared that a major cause of this malnutrition was the inability of the rank and file to buy meat to supplement the bread, vegetable soup, and biscuits that were their daily diet. Infantry soldiers were thereafter granted the right to devote three days in each week to any odd jobs or menial work they could obtain to earn the three to four rubles needed to buy themselves some meat.

One of the reasons why Russian conscription figures tended to be so fanciful was the fact that many raw recruits never reached their assembly points; exhausted by the enormous distances they were forced to cover, they simply perished en route. Because the existing system of revenue-collecting—in a country dominated by a tax-exempt gentry and an undeveloped middle class —was woefully inefficient (one of the ills Speransky had hoped to remedy), the pay for junior army officers was the lowest in Europe. Rapid promotion to higher ranks being virtually reserved to the more nobly born and subject to the whims of nepotism and Court favor, lieutenants and captains were on the whole a wretched lot, often tempted to drown their frustrations in alcohol or to enrich themselves at their soldiers' expense by selling army stores or padding their quartermaster accounts.

Even in the field of artillery, where, thanks to the strenuous efforts of Arakcheyev, a formidable number of cannon, bombards, and mortars had been manufactured by the great metalworks at Tula and the lesser arsenals located at Briansk, Moscow, and Petersburg, the situation left a great deal to be desired; for it was current practice on the eve of battle to entrust the command of field-artillery batteries to high-ranking favorites who knew absolutely nothing about ballistics, azimuth direction-finding, and the proper employment of powder charges, but who hoped to earn a coveted decoration without having to risk their lives in sordid hand-to-hand fighting.

Since nothing is more difficult than to reform military habits overnight, Barclay de Tolly had reached the pessimistic conclusion that the Russians stood little chance of besting Napoleon and his well-trained and -officered divisions in pitched battles. The elastic defense strategy he had accordingly formulated was no spur-of-the-moment intuition. He had conceived it in the wake of the Friedland disaster and expounded it, as he lay on his Memel sickbed, to Barthold Georg Niebuhr, who was then the director of Prussia's National Bank. Niebuhr, who was to become the first of the great German historians of ancient Rome, was struck by the analogy between Barclay's withdrawal strategy and the tactics that Quintus Fabius Maximus, surnamed "Cunctator" (the Delayer), had successfully used between 217 and 214 B.C. to wear down Hannibal's Carthaginian invaders in the Italian peninsula. So vividly did he recall these conversations that five years later, in April 1812, he was able to repeat Barclay's explanations almost verbatim to General Mathieu Dumas, whom Napoleon had sent to Berlin to take over the direction of the

Grande Armée's administrative and logistics staff. "The Russian general," as Dumas later wrote in his memoirs, "hoped to lure the formidable French army into the heart of Russia, as far as Moscow and beyond, to wear it down, to draw it far from its operating base, and to have it use up its resources and matériel, while husbanding Russia's reserves until, aided by the rigors of the climate, he could take the offensive and have Napoleon suffer a second Poltava on the banks of the Volga."

Dumas, who, like his superior, Alexandre Berthier, had accompanied Rochambeau to America, had not forgotten the lesson of the Yorktown surrender. He was sufficiently disturbed to feel it his duty to transmit what he had heard of Barclay de Tolly's war plans to Napoleon's chief of staff when he joined the Grande Armée's imperial headquarters at Poznan in late May. Whether Berthier passed the information on to Napoleon we do not know, for he never lived to write his memoirs. But if he did, Napoleon ignored the warning, as he had so many others.

There were at least two reasons why Barclay de Tolly's strategy was not systematically carried out from the beginning. First of all, it ran counter to Phull's master plan, to which the vacillating tsar was more or less committed. Secondly, Barclay's strategy was vehemently opposed by many members of the suite Alexander brought with him to Vilna. The idea of having to withdraw for hundreds of miles without fighting a major battle against the invading French was regarded as ignominious: it was a defeatist policy, it was a gutless strategy—in short, it was thoroughly un-Russian.

According to the dispositions of Phull's master plan the Russian forces stretched out along the Polish border had been divided into two separate Armies of the West. The First Army, because it was assigned the major task of defending the "impregnable" entrenched camp at Drissa, was composed of more than 100,000 men placed under Barclay de Tolly's direct command. The Second Army, being assigned a "supporting" role according to the Phullian strategy, was far smaller and probably did not exceed 35,000 men. For its fiery commander, Prince Bagration, this humiliating disparity in strength was an insult he had difficulty swallowing. Although Barclay de Tolly was four years older, Bagration, who had fought under the "invincible" Suvorov and covered the Russian retreat at Austerlitz, had been made a general half a dozen years before him, and he thus outranked Barclay in terms of strict military seniority.

During his two years at the Ministry of War in Petersburg, where he was surrounded by trusted subordinates and was able to work in a general staff building that was conveniently close to but also separate from the Winter Palace, Barclay de Tolly had been able to accomplish a great deal (the preparation of a new set of military regulations, the restructuring of the ground forces into army corps, etc.) without getting sucked into the maelstrom of Court intrigue. But from the moment he was named commander of Russia's largest army and forced to move to more cramped quarters in Vilna, he found himself suddenly projected into the very center of a storm.

Along with Chancellor Rumiantsev, Minister of the Interior Viktor Kochubey, and his new diplomatic secretary, Karl Robert Nesselrode, Alexander had brought with him to Vilna a number of military dilettantes. They included his uncle Prince Alexander of Württemberg, his brother-in-law Prince George of Oldenburg, the flamboyant Gustaf Mauritz Armfelt, and another gifted troublemaker named General Marchese (for he too had a title) Filippo Paulucci. This last-named gentleman, who originally came from Modena, in Italy, had finally drifted to Petersburg after his sovereign, the unfortunate King of Sardinia, had been driven out of Turin by the French. Paulucci's Latin gift of gab, spiced by flashes of sarcastic wit, had so impressed Alexander that he had sent him to the Caucasus to deal with the troublesome Persians. Here the shrewd Modenan had soon discovered a surefire recipe for military success. It consisted of sending out a regiment or two to "bait" a Persian outpost and to unleash a lot of noisy musketry—enough to claim that a significant battle had been fought and that an extraordinary number of valiant Russian officers and soldiers had distinguished themselves in action. Soon fast-driving couriers were traveling back and forth between the Caucasus and Petersburg, bearing portfolios stuffed with reports of heroic actions and returning with packets full of cordons and decorations.

Having to run a large army composed of five separate corps posed new problems for Barclay de Tolly, who had left the Ministry of War in Petersburg in the hands of his trusted deputy, General Alexei Gorchakov. When it became apparent that the First Army's chief of personnel, General Lavrov, was not up to the task, the emperor suggested that Barclay replace him with Paulucci. The glib Italian marchese was allowed to retain the post for exactly ten days. An increasingly exasperated Barclay then dismissed him in favor of Alexei Yermolov, a thirty-five-year-old general with the broad-shouldered build of a rugby tackle and a bullying disposition to match. Yermolov—destined to become the future "conqueror of the Caucasus"—proved a forceful improvement on his predecessor. But the substitution did nothing to ease Barclay's burden as the advocate of a detested military policy. A good friend of Bagration, Yermolov was as resolutely committed to a "Let's make a stand and fight it out" philosophy. As for Paulucci, still attached to Alexander's personal staff, he never lost an opportunity to exercise his caustic tongue at the expense of the undiscerning blockhead who had had the temerity to forgo his inestimable services.

Also present in Vilna was the frustrated "bulldog" (some even called him "the ogre") Arakcheyev, who had tried but failed to run his former Ministry of War by remote control from his "superior" position as chairman of the Council of State's military committee. There was also Barclay's former commander, General Levin August Bennigsen, who had retired to his country estate near Vilna after his crushing defeat at Friedland. Now the aging Hanoverian was back with a vengeance and burning, for all his sixty-seven years, to supplant the subordinate he had once so lavishly praised. Phull, being a theorist more than an intriguer, did not wish to supplant anyone; but he was no less grimly determined to trample underfoot all military plans at variance with his own inspired brainchild.

Even more troublesome for Barclay de Tolly was the man whom Alexander had chosen to take Speransky's place as the state secretary responsible for the issuing of rescripts, manifestos, and ukazes. This was Admiral Alexander Semyonovich Shishkov, an eccentric, somewhat wild-looking character, with unruly white hair, piercing dark eyes, and a shrewd peasant face which never seemed to stay still, as though the muscles were perpetually agitated by the restless cogitations seething within him. As stubbornly opinionated as was his fellow mariner Chichagov, with whom he had had a major row not long after Alexander's accession to the throne, this retired sea dog had gradually withdrawn in time as well as space, seeking refuge from the insidious floodtide of a French language he abhorred on the solid bedrock of Old Church Slavonic, the uncorrupted kernel of the Russian language. His was a typical, if somewhat comic, reaction to the rationalistic Gallomania of Catherine the Great's day, a Russian version of the Gothic revival which was now sweeping the Europe of Walter Scott and Chateaubriand. The difference, and it was an immense one, was that whereas Scott and Chateaubriand were writing in languages that had been the instruments of change, the Russian language of the early nineteenth century was still so backward and undeveloped that it was ill adapted to a truly intelligent discussion of contemporary political and economic problems.

Compared with the masterpieces of poetry and fiction that Alexander Pushkin and his successors were soon to be producing, Shishkov's literary efforts were laughable productions. Even his *Dissertation on the Love of One's Fatherland*—the work that brought him to Emperor Alexander's attention—would have been quickly forgotten but for the general climate of exasperation and the intensely anti-French war fever of 1812.

The same circumstances that had brought about Speransky's downfall thus contributed to Shishkov's surprise promotion to the post of state secretary—responsible for patriotic propaganda (which is what his job really amounted to). This kind of nationalistic xenophobia did nothing to ease General Barclay de Tolly's task, since the admiral was the kind of fervent superpatriot who felt that to yield one inch of national territory was tantamount to treason. His emotional Russian voice, added to those of other members of the tsar's entourage, merely aggravated the polyglot cacophony. The young Friedrich von Schubert, recently appointed chief of staff of a nearby cavalry division, later wrote that Barclay de Tolly needed all of his sangfroid "not to lose his head completely" in this welter of conflicting plans, projects, and proposals that were gratuitously thrust forward by "advisers" bent on showing off their military savvy and the lamentable shortcomings of the minister of war.

CHAPTER 9

FORWARD TO
THE NIEMEN!

NEWS OF THESE paralyzing dissensions and intrigues took some time getting back to Petersburg, where May Day was celebrated with the traditional promenade of hundreds of handsome equipages, vying with each other in the elegance of their horses, harnesses, and liveries. The carriages seemed to be almost as numerous as they had been the previous year—an illusion perhaps fostered by the fact that because of the lateness of the spring, the bridge of pontoon boats across the ice-filled Neva had not yet been constructed, so that the participants were restricted to the crowded English Quay and Admiralty Boulevard, and could not cross over to the islands of the isthmus. Nothing seemed to presage the advent of a war, except for the abnormal number of troops that continued to stream out of the capital (including quite a few now being withdrawn from Finland).

This eerie calm lasted until early June, when the more devout inhabitants of Petersburg—particularly those who had seen in Speransky's downfall a sign of divine *misericordia*—learned to their dismay that in Vilna the officers, from old-timers to mere youths, were all living it up with parades, balls, and philandering. "The young officers," wrote the deeply shocked Varvara Bakunin, "drink, gamble, and so on. . . . There are daily *orgies,*" she went on, writing the word in French, since (as she explained in her diary) no one had yet felt the need to enrich the Russian vocabulary with an expression so alien to the "purity" of Russian mores. "Everything is in a state of inertness, one might almost call it one of stupor. When one thinks that the enemy, the most cunning, the most fortunate, the most skillful commander in the world, is approaching our borders step by measured step, that there are 300,000 soldiers under his leadership; it is claimed that we for our part have no fewer, but it is the unknown, inexperienced Barclay, who has not merited the trust of our armies, who commands them. . . . Of his common sense, of his virtues, of his noble feelings, of the elevation of his mind, nobody has ever heard, but to him has been entrusted the fate of Russia. Oh, my poor country!"

If it is often difficult for general staff commanders to know exactly what is going on at the "front," it is even more difficult for civilians residing hundreds of miles farther back to have any accurate idea of what is going on at a distant military headquarters. This was certainly the case with Petersburg's high society in this spring of 1812. The Lenten season was less strictly observed in Catholic Vilna than in Orthodox Petersburg. Friedrich von Schubert, who made frequent visits to the Lithuanian capital as the recently appointed chief of staff of the 2nd Cavalry Division, was offered a virtually nonstop succession of balls, festivals, plays, and not least of all, musical soirées, at which the stars were the virtuoso cellist Bernhard Heinrich Romberg—the Pablo Casals or Mstislav Rostropovich of his day—and an amateur diva with an unusually fine operatic voice named Madame Frank, who was married to a professor from the local Faculty of Medicine. That quite a few Russian officers in Vilna indulged in drinking and gambling, while others flirted with the local *paninki*, there can be no doubt. But the talk about "orgies" was almost certainly the miasmic emanation of the xenophobic fever now gripping Petersburg—as though the normally "virtuous" officers of elite Guards and other regiments were being "corrupted" by foreign hussies in a way that never occurred at home.

Meanwhile the "most cunning, fortunate, and skillful commander in the world" was, as Varvara Bakunin had rightly noted, approaching the western frontier of the Russian Empire step by measured step. From Danzig Napoleon had continued his journey of inspection along the coastal road to Koenigsberg, where he took up residence in the royal palace of the kings of Prussia. He spent the next four days (June 13–16) reviewing French, Dutch, and Westphalian regiments, visiting supply and artillery depots and port installations.

Although his final plans were still uncertain, Napoleon wanted his Grande Armée to be in a position to cross the Niemen at short notice. He was waiting for news from General Lauriston, who, despite the rebuff Louis de Narbonne had met with, had been instructed to hurry to Vilna for a last-minute interview with Alexander. If the Russian emperor refused to change his tune, then the signal would be given for the mighty offensive to begin—with a lightning assault on the Lithuanian capital, intended to destroy the First Russian Army of the West. What happened thereafter would depend on the direction Alexander and his shattered forces took in their panicky flight—assuming that he had not been captured or persuaded to enter into immediate negotiations.

In the meantime Napoleon was increasingly preoccupied with the staggering problems posed by the concentration of more than 400,000 soldiers in East Prussia and the Polish provinces situated between the Vistula and the Niemen. His brother Jerome, to whom he wrote on June 15, was told to keep spreading the rumor that he was on his way to Warsaw—a ruse intended to keep the patriotic fervor in the Polish capital at fever pitch—but immediately afterward he added, "Do not touch your twenty days of food supplies."

The order, issued to all corps commanders, that every battalion and company was to maintain an untouched "reserve" of flour, rice, and biscuits amounting to twenty days of rations for each soldier was intended to give the

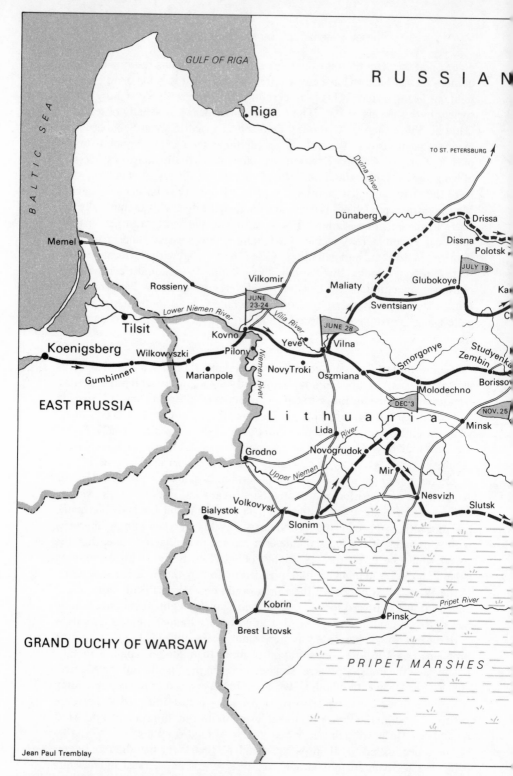

RUSSIAN EMPIRE

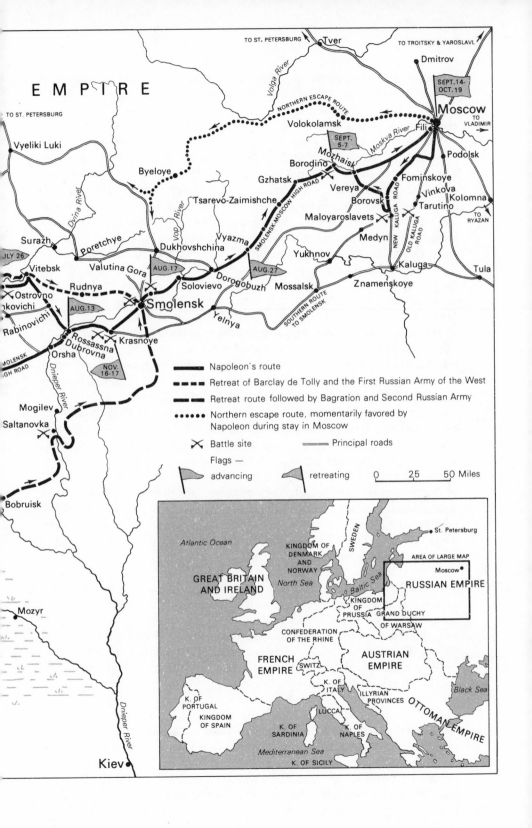

TO ST. PETERSBURG Tver

TO TROITSKY & YAROSLAVL

Dmitrov

EMPIRE

SEPT. 14-
OCT. 19

NORTHERN ESCAPE ROUTE

Volokolamsk

Moscow

TO
VLADIMIR

TO ST. PETERSBURG

Moskva River Fili

SEPT.
5-7

Podolsk

Vyeliki Luki

Byeloye

Mozhaisk

Borodino

Fominskoye

Dvina River

Tsarevo-Zaimishche

Gzhatsk

Vereya

Vinkova

Kolomna

SMOLENSK-MOSCOW HIGH ROAD

Borovsk

Tarutino

TO
RYAZAN

Vop River

Vyazma

Maloyaroslavets

NEW KALUGA ROAD

OLD KALUGA ROAD

Surazh

JLY 26

Poretchye

Dukhovshchina

Valutina Gora

Vitebsk

AUG.17

Medyn

Yukhnov

Ostrovno

Rudnya

AUG.13

Dorogobuzh

AUG.27

Mossalsk

Znamenskoye

Kaluga

Tula

kovichi

Smolensk

Solovievo

Rabinovichi

Yelnya

SOUTHERN ROUTE
TO SMOLENSK

Krasnoye

MOLENSK

Rossassna

Dubrovna

Orsha

Dnieper River

NOV.
16-17

Napoleon's route

Retreat of Barclay de Tolly and the First Russian Army of the West

Mogilev

Saltanovka

Retreat route followed by Bagration and Second Russian Army

Northern escape route, momentarily favored by
Napoleon during stay in Moscow

Bobruisk

Battle site

Principal roads

Flags —

advancing

retreating

0   25   50 Miles

Mozyr

Atlantic Ocean

SWEDEN

St. Petersburg

KINGDOM OF
DENMARK
AND
NORWAY

AREA OF LARGE MAP

Moscow

GREAT BRITAIN
AND IRELAND

North Sea

Baltic Sea

RUSSIAN EMPIRE

KINGDOM
OF
PRUSSIA

GRAND DUCHY
OF WARSAW

CONFEDERATION
OF THE RHINE

AUSTRIAN
EMPIRE

FRENCH
EMPIRE

SWITZ.

K. OF
ITALY

ILLYRIAN
PROVINCES

Black Sea

K. OF
PORTUGAL

LUCCA

OTTOMAN EMPIRE

KINGDOM
OF SPAIN

K. OF
SARDINIA

K. OF
NAPLES

Dnieper River

Mediterranean Sea

Kiev

K. OF SICILY

Grande Armée a maximum of mobility and independence during the opening days of the campaign. Twenty days of rations would be enough to carry his men to Vilna and even as far as the fortified camp of Drissa, in the unlikely event that the Russians chose to give up the Lithuanian capital without a fight.

The only trouble was that the Grande Armée had not yet reached the Niemen River, and in the meantime it had to be fed. In none of his campaigns was Napoleon's famous dictum that "an army marches on its stomach" put to a more cruel test than in this one, the most ambitious and carefully planned of them all. Every cavalryman had been ordered to equip himself with a sickle, and for every twenty horsemen in a cavalry squadron there was to be a scythe (usually carried on an accompanying supply or baggage cart), to cut whatever grass, rye, wheat, oats, or barley might be found along the route of march. But since the invasion could not begin until the wheat, rye, and barley fields beyond the Niemen were ripe enough to feed the Grande Armée's huge cavalry forces (more than 60,000 strong), as well as the tens of thousands of other horses needed to drag 1,200 artillery pieces and caissons, countless supply carts and officers' carriages, the practical effect of the twenty-day-ration order was to force local units in the interim to live off the land. No matter how much he might rant against the "laxity" of discipline and the "excesses" committed in allied countries by detachments of his Grande Armée, Napoleon was now the captive of the gigantic military instrument he had fashioned.

He was also the captive of climatic conditions which were to upset all of his meticulous calculations. Already in 1810 the harvest had been poor. In 1811—known all over Europe as the "year of the great comet"—the summer heat, which in Germany had produced fabulous wines, had parched the Polish plains and resulted in an even lower harvest yield. Reserves of grain, as well as fodder, were thus abnormally low even before Napoleon's voracious Grande Armée began to swarm over the countryside. Just to complicate matters, the early months of 1812 were harsh and the warm spring weather was three to four weeks late in coming. The new cereal crops, which Napoleon had expected to be ready by mid-June, were still unripe.

Some eighty-five miles of occasionally foggy but mostly dusty road, traversing fertile meadows and woodlands of birch and larch as it followed and occasionally crossed the Pregel River, separated Koenigsberg from Gumbinnen, the last important East Prussian town on Napoleon's itinerary. Frequently dismounting from his carriage to inspect the waterway's facilities, the emperor continued his busy journey eastward, anxious to verify as much as he could with his own eyes.

Gumbinnen was, like the other towns on his itinerary, so crammed with soldiers that many of them had taken to bivouacking in the streets. Here, on the morning of the nineteenth, Napoleon's last remaining doubts about Emperor Alexander's dispositions were dispelled when a courier brought the news that General Lauriston had been refused permission by the military governor to leave the Russian capital and to travel to Vilna. "So that is that," declared Napoleon to his secretary, Fain, and other members of his suite. "The Russians, whom we have always defeated, are now assuming a tone of conquerors; they are provoking us, and we shall doubtless have occasion to thank them."

Further proof of this "provocative" attitude was provided by the latest number of the German-language *Petersburgische Zeitung* (Petersburg Gazette), which a French embassy official had brought with him. It explained in some detail just how Russia's forces were spread out along the frontier—from Riga on the Baltic all the way to Slonim, 120 miles south of Vilna. This curious indiscretion confirmed Napoleon in his conviction that he could score a lightning victory over Barclay de Tolly's First Russian Army by driving straight for Vilna with the first three corps of his Grande Armée, spearheaded by Murat's cavalry reserve (six mounted divisions) and backed up by the Imperial Guard—a total force of between 220,000 and 240,000 men. Two other army corps—the Fourth and the Sixth, composed of French, Italian, Bavarian, and Croatian troops commanded by Prince Eugène de Beauharnais—would follow hard on the heels of the others, using the same pontoon bridges or perhaps throwing another across the Niemen a few miles to the south. Three more corps—the Fifth (Polish), Seventh (Saxon), and Eighth (Westphalian), under the overall command of Napoleon's younger brother Jerome—would cross the Niemen some ninety miles farther south in order to pin down Prince Bagration's Second Army of the West and to keep him from moving northward to assist Barclay de Tolly's beleaguered First Army. Yet another corps —the Tenth, composed of two Prussian divisions and a recently added French one, commanded by Marshal Macdonald—was to cross the Niemen at Tilsit and to clear the river's right bank, making it navigable for French supply boats and barges; after which it was to overrun Courland and lay siege to Riga— a diversionary movement intended to tie down more Russian troops in the north, just as Prince Schwarzenberg's Austrian corps was supposed to keep General Tormassov's Third Army occupied in the region of the Pripet Marshes.

Vilna, as the crow flies, was about 110 miles almost due east of Gumbinnen. But instead of aiming the thrust of his assault at the border point closest to Vilna, Napoleon had decided to stage the main river crossing farther to the north, near the town of Kovno, where the undulating Vilia River empties into the Niemen. This, he calculated, would shorten the distance of overland transport between the Pregel's upper tributaries and the Niemen, as well as the distance for waterborne supplies moving up the Niemen from the Kurisches Haff (the protected Courland bight northeast of Koenigsberg).

The five elite divisions of Davout's First Corps, almost exclusively composed of Frenchmen, were accordingly strung out along a slightly curving east-northeastern line of march. Napoleon spent much of Sunday, June 21, reviewing these admirably drilled soldiers, who everywhere greeted his appearance with shouts of *"Vive l'Empereur!"* Their martial enthusiasm was on a level with their state of readiness; for in his meticulous drill work and planning for the coming campaign, Davout had seen to it that each of his infantry companies had its complement of expert swimmers, cobblers, tailors, blacksmiths, armorers, bakers, and even masons—to build makeshift kilns for baking bread.

Anything but squeamish about the means employed to keep his men properly supplied, he had ordered his infantrymen to fill out their twenty-day quota of emergency rations by seizing all the flour, rice, and bread they needed from the terrified inhabitants of the East Prussian towns and villages through which they passed. Every available horse, cart, and carriage was commandeered in the same ruthless manner.

Proceeding onward in irksome clouds of dust, Napoleon reached the little town of Wylkowyszki on this same Sunday evening. The next day Davout, Murat, and the three marshals commanding the infantry and cavalry regiments of the Imperial Guard were summoned to a conference in a rustic pavilion which had been turned into a general staff map room by Berthier and his topographical aides. At the conclusion of the conference Berthier was ordered to read out a singularly vainglorious order of the day, which is worth quoting in full for the fateful consequences it was soon to have:

Soldiers!
The second Polish war has begun. The first was ended at Friedland and Tilsit: at Tilsit Russia swore an eternal alliance with France and war against England. Today she is violating her pledged word. She is unwilling to give any explanation for her strange conduct until the French Eagles have crossed back over the Rhine, leaving our allies there to her discretion. Russia is led on by fatality! Her destiny must be accomplished. Does she then believe us to be degenerates? Are we then no longer the soldiers of Austerlitz? She places us between dishonor and war. The choice cannot be doubted, so let us march forward! Let us cross the Niemen! Let us carry the war on to her territory. The second Polish war will be glorious for French arms, like the first; but the peace we shall conclude will carry with it its guarantee, and put an end to that proud influence Russia has exercised for fifty years over the affairs of Europe.

This bombastic piece of rhetoric could hardly have been more ill conceived. Though it announced the start of a second Polish war, it significantly failed to say that this war was being fought to reestablish an independent Kingdom of Poland. Worse, in declaring, "Let us carry the war on to her territory," it implied that Lithuania, to say nothing of Volhynia and Podolia, belonged to Russia, and could therefore be indiscriminately plundered and pillaged as enemy lands. Finally, in exalting the glory of French arms instead of stressing the European character of the Grande Armée, it indicated that for Napoleon the other contributing nations were simply providing cannon fodder for his country's personal quarrel with Russia.

The effects of this proclamation were to prove absolutely catastrophic. It compounded a whole series of strategic, tactical, and psychological blunders which were to seal the doom of the Grande Armée. The first error had been made during the previous summer when Prince Joseph Poniatowski, during a three-month stay in Paris, had vainly pleaded with Napoleon, in the event of a war with Russia, to aim his first thrust at Kiev and the rich breadbasket of the Ukraine. This had been followed some months later by Napoleon's decision to detach a number of Polish regiments from Poniatowski's Fifth Corps and to place them under separate French commanders—an unpopular move that had been bitterly resented by the Polish rank and file. Finally and most devastatingly, there had been the French emperor's devious decision to avoid Warsaw, while its misled inhabitants were encouraged to believe that he was about to arrive at any moment to proclaim what they were all ardently hoping to hear.

Writing years later, when he was an old general and could not be suspected of juvenile exaggeration, Friedrich von Schubert expressed the opinion that if Napoleon at this point had proclaimed the reestablishment of the Kingdom of Poland, "Russia would have been irretrievably lost. Poland could without excessive effort have raised an army of 200,000, would have done so with pleasure, and many of our Polish provinces would have risen in revolt against us if Napoleon had only promised this conceited nation that it would be formed into a separate kingdom and would have its own king." The financing of such a military effort would not have been easy, and the addition of Lithuania, Volhynia, and Podolia to the Grand Duchy of Warsaw—forming a kingdom of fourteen million Poles—would have involved Napoleon in a two- to three-year war with Russia. But there is little doubt that Schubert was right in thinking that the conflict, in such conditions, would have proved more disastrous for Russia than for France. In offhandedly neglecting to obtain the enthusiastic cooperation of the Poles who had been forcibly incorporated into the Russian Empire during the second half of the eighteenth century, Napoleon made the same overconfident miscalculation that Adolf Hitler was to make, 130 years later, in scorning the aid the White Russians and Ukrainians would have brought to his Wehrmacht had they been entrusted with a genuine liberating mission.

The rest of this sweltering Monday, June 22, was devoted to the issuing of march orders to the various corps commanders of the Grande Armée, most of whom had set up their headquarters in villages or towns located a certain distance from the Niemen, so as not to give the Russians any advance warning of their proximity. By five o'clock Napoleon, mopping the perspiration from his brow, decided he had had enough. Leaving his staff officers to dispatch the final couriers to their respective destinations, he climbed into his yellow coupé with Berthier and took off in a cloud of dust. He was now in such a hurry to determine for himself exactly where the Niemen could best be crossed that it was several hours before Caulaincourt, the young Boniface de Castellane, and a Polish officer interpreter could catch up with him. At eleven at night and thirty-five miles farther on, they stopped at a village with the tongue-twisting name of Skriavdziai, where Napoleon invited his hard-riding companions and General Exelmans (from Murat's staff) to join him for an informal supper in the garden of the local priest.

After supper, finished as usual in a brisk twenty minutes, Napoleon climbed back into his coupé and had himself driven on with his two calèches and two closed wagons, filled with maps, field-tent equipment, and other personal effects, as far as Nogaraidski, where the imperial headquarters were set up in a small country house bordered by pine forests on one side and wheatfields on the other. Five miles to the east, but hidden by the crest of the intervening slope, was the Niemen River.

By this time it was one-thirty in the morning (of June 23)—a perfect moment for a nighttime reconnaissance under the light of a nearly full moon. Joined by Davout, who had ridden over from his nearby headquarters, Napoleon climbed onto one of his white horses, this time simply saddled without the conspicuous red-and-gold shabrack. To make sure that he would not be recognized after they had ridden over the crest of the hill—for in midsummer at this northern latitude the sun rises early—Napoleon took off his familiar green riding coat (the one he always wore as colonel of his Imperial Guard's Chasseurs) and donned the darker-hued jacket and black-silk kalpak worn by Polish lancers. His companions—Berthier, Davout, Caulaincourt, and General François Nicolas Haxo (the First Corps' chief of engineers)—did the same.

Their first destination was the village of Alexoti, where they left their horses in the courtyard of a doctor's house, which had a fine view over the old walled town of Kovno, to the east. Leaving the others to examine the farther bank with their spyglasses, Napoleon, guided by a Polish lieutenant, rode down the escarpment with General Haxo and followed the water's edge for some distance along a curve leading on and around a kind of hump-shaped promontory. Then, turning northward, they rode back over a distance of four miles, past the wooden bridge leading to Kovno, which the Russians had partly destroyed, and back up the escarpment to the doctor's house at Alexoti. On the farther bank the unsuspecting inhabitants of Kovno slumbered on as the huge, bloodshot globe of the sun emerged over the northeastern horizon. Along this stretch of the Niemen the left-bank escarpment is higher than the slope on the other side, so that it was easier for the eastward-looking French to observe what was going on on the other bank than it was for the westward-looking Russians. Of these there were none to be seen, save for an occasional Cossack, recognizable in the distance by his distinctive long pike.

The logical site for the pontoon bridges, Napoleon decided, was the tip of the hump-shaped promontory, which could be covered by several artillery batteries placed on its sandy hillocks. Returning to his Nogaraidsky field tent, he treated himself to a few hours of sleep before rising to dictate new orders. Murat and his chief of staff, Belliard, were his guests for lunch, along with his inseparable companions Berthier, Duroc, and Caulaincourt. The French emperor, normally cheerful and expansive on the eve of major military operations, was this time in a pensive, somber mood. As he was galloping back across the wheatfields toward his headquarters, a startled hare had streaked past, causing his horse to shy. Suddenly unbalanced, he had lost his seat and fallen to the ground, which fortunately was soft. He was on his feet and back in the saddle before any of his companions could ride up to help him. But to Berthier, as to Caulaincourt, this was an inauspicious portent—the kind of omen that would have given a Roman general pause.

Napoleon, however, had other worries on his mind. He was bothered by the lack of reliable intelligence as to just what the Russians were up to. None of the scouts or Polish spies recently sent across the river had come back. From the headquarters of Ney's Third Corps at Marianpole, some thirty miles to the southeast, came the report, gleaned from a Jewish merchant who had just returned from Lithuania, that the Russians were pulling their forces back from the Niemen, leaving a few Cossacks behind to keep an eye on the French. To Napoleon this was both good and bad news: bad in that he would have preferred to find Barclay de Tolly's divisions massed close to the Niemen, where it would have been easier to envelop them in a pincer operation; good in that it meant (for this was his interpretation) that the Russians were withdrawing to the lakes and hill-surrounded marshlands of Troki, where they apparently intended to make a major stand to defend Vilna.

There was not a moment to be lost. The faster his troops could be flung across the Niemen, the greater would be his chance of catching the Russians by surprise before they had completed their defenses, or while they were in the midst of a retreat—much as he had caught and crushed Bennigsen's forces at Friedland five years before.

In Vilna, some sixty miles to the southeast, the Tsar of all the Russias seems to have been blissfully unconscious of the danger. In May of 1807, a few weeks before the decisive battle of Friedland, Adam Czartoryski had been dismayed by the otiose example set by his sovereign, who (as he described it in a letter to a friend) "strolls around Tilsit, nods and salutes to right and left, knows and ogles all the young ladies in town, and spends his day in the greatest idleness." Had the Polish prince been in Vilna in June of 1812 he would have had the impression of something déjà vu, of history curiously repeating itself. For Alexander, who had been toying for some weeks with the idea of making Lithuania a semi-independent grand duchy, thinking that this might blunt the pro-French sentiments of so many of its inhabitants—had chosen this singular moment to buy the nearby property of Zakret, in which General Bennigsen and his lively young wife had been living for the past few years.

Of all the happenings in Vilna during the tsar's two-month stay, none caused more critical gossiping in Petersburg than this real-estate venture, followed as it was by the holding of a gala ball. As Varvara Bakunin was to write, citing an old Russian proverb: *igoomenya za charkoo, syostry za kovshi*—which may be translated very roughly, "When the mother superior reaches for the goblet, the nuns go for the pitchers." How could one expect Russian officers to behave with more propriety when their own sovereign was setting such a deplorable example?

The explanation later given in Petersburg was that the tsar bought this relatively modest country mansion in order to become a Lithuanian squire and to be able to wear the uniform of the local gentry. One thing is certain: The *galantuomo* side of his complex personality had again got the better of his political and military judgment. To reciprocate the hospitality that Count Pac and other Vilna noblemen had shown him and members of his entourage, Alexander and two of his close friends—Count Nikolai Tolstoy and Prince

Pyotr Volkonsky—decided that he needed a place of his own wherein to entertain the local aristocracy. Arrangements were promptly made to hold a ball in the newly acquired estate. It was further decided to make the occasion something of a *fête champêtre*—or a "Vauxhall," as it was then commonly known—by erecting a flower-decorated dance pavilion on the lawn leading down to the river.

The construction of this makeshift ballroom was entrusted to a local architect with the Germanic name of Schultz. Probably because the whole business was undertaken in far too great a rush, the round wooden pillars supporting the pavilion roof were not sunk sufficiently deep into the ground. Around noon on the day of the projected ball the structure suddenly collapsed with a shuddering rumble. Fortunately most of the workers were having lunch, so that only one of them was trapped beneath the wreckage.

The terror-stricken architect, appalled by the number of illustrious victims such a disaster would have crushed and maimed if it had happened in the evening, completely lost his head. Rushing down to the riverbank, he threw himself into the Vilia and was drowned as the current swept him downstream. The poor man fearfully imagined that some hideous fate, probably including torture, was in store for him for this "attempt" on the emperor's life. Nor was this fear entirely fanciful. So hated was Napoleon in Russian army circles that soon the rumor was galloping from one headquarters unit to the next—to the effect that the diabolical Bonaparte had hired a German agent to assassinate their sovereign.

Working at a frantic pace, the workers managed to clear away the wreckage in time for the gala fête, planned to begin that same evening at eight o'clock. Though the sky was slightly overcast, there was not a drop of rain to spoil the outdoor preparations and the now roofless parquet floor on which the dancing was to take place. Crowds of curious onlookers swarmed out from Vilna to watch the emperor's arrival and the start of the festivities. From different points in the park came the brassy sound of wind instruments, blown by musicians of the Russian Imperial Guard.

Sophie von Tisenhaus, who was one of the privileged guests, has left us a lyrical description of this crepuscular tableau—with a circle of flower-bedecked ladies seated in the center of the open-air ballroom floor, framed farther back by smartly uniformed officers and the fragrant orange trees that had been dragged out in their greenhouse pots to replace the fallen pillars. "The variety and sparkle of the colors glittering on their attire; those ancient trees forming clumps of greenery; the Vilia, reflecting in its sinuous course the azure of the skies and the rosy hues of sunset; those mountains whose tufted heads disappeared on the vaporous horizon—everything offered a ravishing vista. Then the Emperor appeared, and he was all one saw!"

Dressed in the blue-lapeled uniform of the Semyonovsky Guards Regiment, which he had once personally commanded (in the days of his grand ducal youth), Alexander graciously made the rounds, begging the ladies to be seated and to help themselves to the available refreshments. He exchanged a few pleasantries with a number of gentlemen present; then, offering his arm to

General Bennigsen's pretty wife, he opened the ball with a traditional polo-naise. He next danced with the wife of his minister of war, Madame Barclay de Tolly, and then—to the astonishment of most of the ladies present—with the young Sophie von Tisenhaus, who, having learned something of his tastes, had carefully selected a high-waisted white percale gown elegantly hemmed with gold and garlanded with pearls. ("It is you the butterfly is after," as General Bennigsen's sprightly wife later whispered to her, en passant.)

These preliminaries completed, the guests ascended the stairs to the indoor ballroom, where other musicians were waiting to entertain them. Later the emperor returned to the garden to enjoy a light supper under the stars and the rising moon. It was a warm midsummer evening and there was not a breath of wind to stir the candle flames in their little glass lampions. Nothing could have seemed more idyllically untroubled than this alfresco scene, brightened by the soft flush of illuminated boughs and branches, the phosphorescent foam of the rapids, the quicksilver shimmer of the moonlit water gliding past the shadowy silhouettes of tiny river islands.

Not long afterward General Balashov, the minister of police, approached the emperor and whispered into his good right ear. Alexander exchanged a few words with him, then sent him on his way, as though nothing had occurred. Later, after paying his respects to Countess Bennigsen, the acting hostess, he discreetly withdrew, followed by his grand marshal, Count Tolstoy, his chief of staff, Prince Volkonsky, and Barclay de Tolly, his minister of war. The guests were encouraged to go on dancing, drinking, and flirting under the full moon and the stars.

Only later did they discover the reason for the emperor's early departure. A breathless Cossack cavalryman had just galloped into Vilna with the news that units of Napoleon's Grande Armée were now crossing the Niemen on several pontoon bridges that had been thrown across the river not far from Kovno. The diplomatic skirmishing was over. The real war had begun.

CHAPTER 10

AN OMINOUS BEGINNING

A T   S I X in the evening of Tuesday, June 23, Napoleon had climbed back into the saddle, for a last-minute inspection of General Eblé's bridge-building *pontonniers*. The night once again was clear, illuminated by a rising moon. More than 100,000 men were now gathered in the large Pilwiszki forest, with strict orders not to light bivouac fires.

Shortly after eight o'clock the first French boats were carried down the sandy slope to the water's edge by several companies of musket-armed *voltigeurs* (light reconnaissance infantrymen), who had orders to paddle across the Niemen to secure the bridgeheads on the farther side. After they had landed, an officer commanding a Cossack patrol rode down to the riverbank to ask who they were and what they were doing. *"Français!"* came the reply. Turning his horse, the Cossack commander cantered back toward the wood from which he had emerged, followed by a couple of French gunshots.

Annoyed by this unnecessary shooting, Napoleon continued to ride up and down the left-bank escarpment, his eyes trained in an easterly direction. Along the riverbank below, the bridge-builders pushed and paddled their pontoons out across the water, expertly knitting them into three wood-planked filaments, two hundred yards apart. By midnight their work was completed.

At last dismounting from his horse, Napoleon personally supervised the emplacement of the cannon covering the three bridges on the northernmost hump of the promontory. But no troops showed up on the other side to contest the passage of the light cavalry units from Davout's First Corps, who clattered across the bridge of boats shortly after midnight. Napoleon's tent, and next to it Berthier's, were now brought forward and pitched on the highest elevation overlooking the promontory.

At three in the morning Napoleon rode down to the water's edge for a closer look at the infantrymen who were tramping across the pontoon bridges, each carrying a pack with three extra pairs of shoes, three shirts, a rolled-up uniform, and twenty pounds of emergency rations (flour, rice, and biscuits). A little later he rode across the pontoon bridge himself. At the sight of the familiar figure, seated on a white horse in his green riding coat and under his small half-moon hat, the passing soldiers broke into cries of *"Vive l'empereur!"* Napoleon seemed to share their jubilation.

By this time General Claude-Pierre Pajol's light cavalrymen had galloped into Kovno, after dispersing several hundred Cossacks. The eastern bridgehead was secure. There was no further need for any quietness or stealth, and each regiment's buglers and drummers, in their colorful page-boy costumes, could break into stirring music as they trudged, slid, or steered their gaily caparisoned horses down the sandy slope toward one of the three bridges.

For virtually all of those who emerged from the fringes of the crowded Pilwiszki forest and suddenly found themselves with the Niemen just below them and the broad plains on the other side already streaked with advancing columns, it was an unforgettable sight. But the bright summer sun, whose darting rays were so vividly reflected off the breastplates of the cuirassiers, the crested helmets of the dragoons, the pennanted spearheads of the lancers, the musket barrels of the infantrymen, must have made this a painfully hot day for many of them.

Not all of those who contemplated this imposing spectacle were taken in by its polychrome pageantry. When the Dutch general Anton Gijsbert van Dedem, commanding a cavalry brigade in one of Davout's divisions, happened to approach the sun-baked imperial tents, he was struck by the brooding silence of Napoleon's entourage. He made some sprightly comment to the governor of the corps of pages, General Auguste de Caulaincourt (a younger brother of the grand equerry, Armand), only to hear him answer in a low voice, "This is a great day, but . . ."—with a finger pointed to the Niemen's farther bank—"there yonder is our grave."

The sight of waiting detachments puffing out like snakeheads before being compressed into thin columns for the actual bridge crossing already offered a foretaste of what was to follow. After Napoleon, in the early afternoon, had crossed the Niemen for a second and final time, the conflicts between unit commanders degenerated into anarchy.

It had apparently not occurred to Berthier, or for that matter to Napoleon, that someone invested with supreme authority should remain behind to orchestrate all these converging movements of gun caissons and carriages, horses, mules, and livestock. The congestion soon assumed such proportions that Napoleon had to send back two of his staff generals—Jomini, the Swissborn writer-tactician, and Guilleminot, one of his senior topographers—to try to restore some badly needed order. Neither seems to have been prestigious enough to make much of an impression.

In the late afternoon of this fateful June 24 the radiant skies darkened and black clouds closed in over the river. The marching and riding columns dissolved into a dusky mist, lit by a lurid gray-green glow and the first flickers of lightning. The oppressive air was stirred by a breath of wind, quickly followed by the rumble and crash of thunder and blinding flashes eerily illuminating the river and the darkling plain. Then came the first heavy drops, falling in ever denser sheets of rain. They drenched every inch of the landscape, as they drenched Napoleon and the members of his suite who had gone forward to watch the *pontonniers* build another makeshift bridge across the Vilia River, to replace the wooden one that the departing Russians had destroyed.

To the superstitiously inclined, this sudden storm was like the wrath of God, one more somber warning, one more portent of disaster. But worse, far worse, was soon to follow.

No one will ever know for sure just how many men actually crossed the Niemen in the vicinity of Kovno during those three days of June 24–26, 1812. The estimates range from 200,000 to 240,000. The number, not only of men but of horses, was prodigious. General Jomini, who, being Swiss-born, was not given to fanciful exaggeration, later estimated that the total number of horses assembled by the Grande Armée was around 200,000, while the wagons, carts, gun caissons, and carriages of every kind it had brought along numbered at least 20,000.

Not all of these horses, carts, and carriages plodded or clattered across the three pontoon bridges near Kovno. The 30,000 men of Macdonald's Tenth Corps went across at Tilsit, the 70,000 men of Prince Eugène de Beauharnais's two corps crossed the Niemen at Pilony, and the 65,000 men of the three corps under the command of Napoleon's brother Jerome crossed in the region of Grodno in early July; all had sizable cavalry and artillery units, not to mention slower-moving supply trains. But since half of the Grande Armée's artillery (600 cannon) and more than half of Murat's cavalry reserve crossed the river near Kovno, one can reckon the number of horses suddenly pouring out over the plains and forests of Lithuania in this region at close to 100,000. As Jomini aptly remarked, one could without exaggeration apply to such a stupendous host "the hyperbole used to describe Xerxes' army, after the passage of which one looked in vain for a trace of the lands it had traversed."

In an attempt to limit plundering, which had been so flagrantly rampant in Poland, Napoleon had issued strict instructions setting up military tribunals in a number of cities, and he had ordered General Louis Saunier, from Davout's First Corps, to proceed with fifty of his gendarmes to Kovno, to maintain law and order. Any soldier caught marauding or pillaging was to be brought before the nearest provost marshal's court, summarily tried, and executed within twenty-four hours. These instructions seem to have had little deterrent effect, if only because the gendarmes were so few. The total number for the entire Grande Armée, incredible as it may sound, was 520: a figure which Napoleon, no less incredibly, considered quite sufficient. Among the worst offenders were the soldiers of his own Imperial Guard, who, after occupying Kovno, broke into every shop and raided every cellar they could enter.

Napoleon, though he took a dim view of pillaging and pillagers, was too busy with his immediate strategic and tactical problems to have time to deal with the unruly behavior of his troops. From his imperial headquarters, now established in a monastery just outside the walls of Kovno, a number of Polish staff officers were dispatched in different directions to find out where the Russians were massing their forces for the defense of Vilna. Still persuaded that Emperor Alexander would be unwilling to give up Vilna without a major fight—for why otherwise had he made this his headquarters for the past two months?—Napoleon had Oudinot cross the Vilia River with his two infantry divisions and supporting cavalry to deal with any Russian reinforcements moving down from the north; Murat's cavalrymen and Davout's five infantry divisions were ordered to advance down the main road to Vilna, some sixty miles away.

If Murat's lancers, hussars, cuirassiers, and even more their mounts, had been in top-notch condition, they could have reached Vilna in three days. But their horses, for lack of oats and other fodder, were already in a sorry state even before the Niemen crossing. From then on most of them were reduced to grazing off the still-unripe rye and wheat—a pernicious diet which bloated their stomachs and weakened them still further.

No less harrowing were the strains imposed on the infantrymen, and particularly on those of Ney's Third Corps. Unlike Davout's troopers, who were fairly close to the pontoon bridges when they were put together during the night of June 23–24, Ney's foot-sloggers had had to cover from thirty-five to fifty miles to reach the Niemen crossing-point in just two days. Some of them were forced to march for forty out of forty-eight hours, and for part of the distance through a forest fire probably ignited by careless bivouackers. But their ordeal, they now discovered, was only just beginning. For Napoleon, determined to outflank the Russians or to cut off their retreat if they sought to make a stand in the hilly lake district of Troki (west of Vilna), now ordered Ney's three divisions to continue their advance at the same grueling pace.

What most struck Lieutenant Karl von Suckow, of the 25th Division, after he and his fellow Württembergers had crossed the Niemen, was the "stillness of the grave" they everywhere encountered. Not only was there not a trace of life in any of the hamlets they passed, but even the birds seemed to have fled from the scorching, sunlit skies. Afraid of being surprised by Russians emerging from the nearby forests, the troops had to maintain a semiopen formation in order to be able to close ranks rapidly to repel a sudden flank attack. The interval between advancing ranks was not enough to allow the dust to settle. Foot-sloggers and cavalrymen thus found themselves tramping or trotting through blinding clouds of dust, which blurred and even blotted out the sun. To many soldiers wearily advancing through this man-made sirocco the only thing to steer by was the rhythmic beat of an invisible drummer-boy marching or riding somewhere up ahead. A few, crazed by hunger and fatigue, staggered off toward the nearest woods, where an occasional gunshot indicated that one more infantryman had shot himself in a moment of despair.

The news that the French were crossing the Niemen near Kovno, as we have seen, took the Russians completely by surprise. Hurrying back from the Zakret ball to his imperial headquarters in Vilna's archiepiscopal palace, Alexander spent a sleepless night and the early morning of June 25 discussing with members of his entourage what should be done. With the aid of his new secretary, Admiral Shishkov, he drafted a rescript which, compared with Napoleon's bombastic proclamation of war, was a model of restraint. It made no reference to Russia's alleged "destiny," but invoked instead the aid of "the Almighty, witness and avenger of the truth," declared that the tsar would not lay down his arms "so long as one enemy warrior remains in my empire," and ended quite simply with two staccato sentences: "I am with you. God is against the aggressor."

At imperial staff headquarters the dominant feeling was one of consternation. No one in Vilna had expected Napoleon to be able to strike so fast. The detailed order-of-battle reports on the strength and movements of the Grande Armée that the resourceful Chernyshov had managed to smuggle out of Paris were by now four months out of date. Alexander's generals were reduced to more or less inspired guesswork as to just how great were the forces Napoleon had mobilized for this new war. All of their estimates were wide of the mark —from the highest, those of Barclay de Tolly and Phull, which credited Napoleon with having mustered close to 250,000 men on Russia's western borders, to the lowest, those of Bagration and Bennigsen, who put the figure at 200,000 and 169,000 respectively. In reality, the Grande Armée was almost twice as massive—with nine infantry and four cavalry corps (totaling 400,000 men), an auxiliary contingent of 30,000 Austrians, and two reserve corps (commanded by Marshals Victor and Augereau), which were gradually moving forward from the Elbe to the Vistula and East Prussia.

In the midst of the consternation and confusion prevailing at imperial headquarters in Vilna, one man at least had not lost his phlegm. This was the close-lipped minister of war, Mikhail Barclay de Tolly. After a hastily convened staff conference presided over by the tsar, he sent couriers racing off to the five corps commanders of the First Russian Army of the West, whose forces were stretched in a shallow arc from Rossieny, in the north, to Lida, in the south, instructing them to begin an orderly withdrawal toward the Dvina River and the fortified encampment at Drissa. Other couriers were dispatched southward to Bagration and Ataman Matvei Platov, commander of fifteen independent Cossack regiments attached to the Second Army of the West, ordering them to move northward to harry the right flank of Napoleon's invading force.

There remained the all-important question of whether Vilna itself should be given up without a fight. With only one corps (General Nikolai Tuchkov's) stationed directly west of Vilna at Novy Troki, and Grand Duke Constantine's Imperial Guard positioned between Vilna and Sventsiany—a total force of 40,000 men—Barclay knew that it would be folly to try to hold the Lithuanian capital against a master tactician like Napoleon. Two other corps—General Baggovut's Second Corps, to the north, and General Shuvalov's Fourth Corps, to the south—were likely to be attacked by the French even before they could draw back toward Vilna. Since most of the city extended like a crescent along the southern bank of the Vilia, any defending forces positioned on its surrounding ring of hills could be trapped between the French and the river, and with only one bridge behind them, could be even more devastatingly crushed than had been Bennigsen's army at Friedland. But so overpowering was the prevailing superpatriotic sentiment—to retreat at once would be an act of un-Russian cowardice!—that it was not until Barclay had sent out scouts in all directions and had ridden out on several personal reconnaissances that he could finally draft a letter to the tsar saying that the French were rapidly approaching and that they had no choice but to evacuate the city.

Unwilling to precipitate a panic, Alexander left Vilna at three o'clock in the morning of June 27. Few members of his suite were able to leave so surreptitiously. Soon the streets were blocked with vehicles carrying not only Russian officers, but pro-Russian aristocrats fearful of reprisals, who left in carriages piled high with precious objects as well as incongruous assortments of sheets and blankets, baby cribs, and cages filled with nervously twittering birds. Every available horse was requisitioned by the departing Russians, deaf to the howling protests of owners, who barricaded themselves inside their houses. One venerable Vilna lady, to keep her own horses from being seized, had them led up the stairs of her townhouse and stabled for a few hours in the attic!

Barclay de Tolly, typically enough, was one of the last to leave. Refusing to be rushed in the midst of this unseemly pandemonium, he had the municipal archives carefully packed and bundled into carts, while his soldiers worked frantically to remove as much flour, grain, fodder, and munitions as they could from local warehouses into waiting wagons. Finally, as the sound of gunfire began to be heard coming from the western hills, he ordered all the grain stores to be fired. As cool and unemotional as ever, he then walked down the street and climbed into his carriage. It was one of the last to cross the wooden bridge, which a rearguard detachment of Russian sappers was then ordered to burn.

With his departure a strange stillness descended on the city's cobbled streets, where not a hoofbeat nor a jolting wheel rim was any longer to be heard, but only the sound of voices anxiously discussing what was going to happen next.

At dawn on June 27 Napoleon had left the Kovno monastery and moved his headquarters forward to a handsomely pillared country house near Yeve, slightly more than thirty miles from Vilna. Murat and his leading cavalry regiments had bivouacked a few miles farther on. It was evident by now that the Russians were not planning to make a major stand in the swampy, lake-filled vicinity of Troki, as Napoleon had originally expected. But the next morning, after breasting the ring of hills surrounding Vilna, a regiment of French hussars was trotting down toward the city when it was assailed, not far from General Bennigsen's Zakret estate, by an elite Cossack squadron of the Russian Imperial Guard. The attack so surprised the overconfident Frenchmen that a number of them were taken prisoner, including their wounded squadron commander, Captain Octave-Henri de Ségur, the older son of Napoleon's grand master of ceremonies. He was the first noteworthy Frenchman to be captured during this campaign. He was not to be the last.

The first to gallop into Vilna were a squadron of Polish lancers, led by their ardent young commander, Colonel Dominik Radziwill. Heir to an immense fortune—150 villages and 120,000 "souls" (serfs)—the twenty-six-year-old prince had disregarded the friendly warnings of the Grand Duchy of Warsaw's minister of war, Joseph Poniatowski, who knew that the price the young man would have to pay for his Polish patriotism would be the confiscation by the Russian tsar of his vast Lithuanian properties (which was exactly what had happened). At his personal expense he had recruited and equipped 200 lancers —something it was not difficult to do in a horse-loving country where usually even the humblest farmhand was an agile rider.

Another, larger force of Polish lancers chased several companies of Russian rearguard soldiers right out of the city and forced 500 of them to surrender in a nearby wood. At the sight of these intrepid riders, galloping past on their small horses and carrying lances adorned with the split red-and-white pennant of Poland, there was jubilation in the streets. The men cheered, while the women flocked to the open windows to wave their handkerchiefs. Even Sophie von Tisenhaus, who had been so smitten by the blond beauty and exquisite manners of Emperor Alexander, found her young heart beating faster and had tears of joy in her eyes.

By the time Napoleon entered the city, around two in the afternoon, the façades of many townhouses were adorned with carpets in festive recognition of Vilna's "liberation." Biscuits as well as flowers rained down from above, tossed from windows and balconies by ladies who had donned their finest dresses to honor the occasion. Their enthusiastic welcome delighted Murat and his cavalrymen, but Napoleon did not let it distract him from his immediate military concerns. Once inside the city walls he had himself led straight down to the river and the smoldering bridge. Soldiers of his Imperial Guard were trying to put out the flames with the help of local artisans and workers, some of whom waded out into the water to retrieve the muskets that the withdrawing Russians had hastily tossed into the river. Sitting down on a log, Napoleon drank a glass of beer, declared that it was *"Dobre piva!"* (good beer), and then requested that more be distributed to the perspiring workers and soldiers, who received the foaming tankards with shouts of *"Vive l'empereur!"*

At seven in the evening, when he returned from an inspection tour of the city's northern suburbs to take up residence in the archiepiscopal palace, which the tsar had vacated only thirty-six hours before, wisps of smoke were still rising from the charred grain stores, but the flames had been extinguished. Throngs of jubilant artisans and workers, many of them now proudly armed with Russian muskets pulled from the bottom of the Vilia River, paraded through the streets, shouting patriotic slogans and throwing their bonnets in the air.

The euphoria, however, was of brief duration. That night an extraordinary electric storm, extending north and south over a front of several hundred miles, broke over Vilna and the surrounding countryside. It lasted, not for minutes, as had the previous thunderstorm over the Niemen, but for hours on end. For the tens of thousands of Grande Armée soldiers who could not find shelter in the forests and had to bivouac in the open, it was a night of unforgettable woe. Everywhere campfires were extinguished in a deluge of increasingly chill water, mixed with sleet and hail. Captain Fantin des Odoards, who had endured many hardships in a dozen years of military service, later confessed that he had never known anything like it. One lightning flash, falling among the Old Guard veterans with whom he was serving, killed a grenadier.

Sergeant François Coignet, commanding one of the Young Guard's baggage-train detachments, was barely able to make it to a ravaged hamlet, many of whose huts had already been knocked down to supply wood for campfires. His horses were so panic-stricken by successive lightning flashes that, after unbridling them, he had to keep them hitched to the wheels of their wagons, while he and his men went out with sickles to cut clumps of soaked grass to feed them. He himself was so frozen by the falling hail and snow that he finally took refuge inside one of his covered wagons. On climbing out the next morning, he was confronted by the gruesome sight of hundreds of dead horses littering the ground of a nearby cavalry encampment. Three of his own horses had died of cold during the night. "The unfortunate animals were shivering so violently that they broke everything once hitched, rearing up wildly in their harness-collars and kicking out in frantic fits of rage. If I had delayed one hour longer I would have lost every one of them."

Later, when his unit resumed its advance, they passed the bodies of hundreds of soldiers who had died of cold and exhaustion during the night. Heinrich von Brandt noted that in places the bodies were piled in "heaps" along the roadside. The death toll among the horses was even more appalling. Murat's chief of staff, General Belliard, estimated that no fewer than 8,000 ill-fed horses perished in the vicinity of Vilna during this fiendish night and the two days of freezing rain that followed. Many of them were artillery horses; being subjected to greater strains and having to subsist on the same diet of wet grass and unripe rye, they were in an even poorer condition to resist this onslaught of the elements.

No less devastating for the Grande Armée was the despair induced by this brusque change of climate. The number of marauders and deserters was doubled in a couple of days. When Marshal Mortier reached Vilna on the last day of June, he was no longer in his usual laughing mood: two of his three Young Guard divisions had been decimated by deaths and desertions, and he put the number of marauders now swarming over the countryside in search of food and booty at not less than 30,000. Entire villages had vanished, as soldiers tore down the wooden walls for firewood and fed the straw roofs to their horses. To the Polish veterans of General Claparède's division, now forming the rear echelon of Napoleon's Imperial Guard, it was more than discouraging to be approached by haggard Lithuanians, who had been so ruthlessly plundered that they were reduced to begging for a crust or two of bread.

Although the mansion's stone walls were still intact, at Zakret there was no trace left of the candlelit enchantment which had cast its magic midsummer spell over the evening ball given in Emperor Alexander's honor. When Heinrich von Brandt walked over from his nearby bivouac to visit the estate, he found that doors as well as window frames had been torn from their hinges to supply firewood, while the trampled lawns were a quagmire. Inside the house, now filled to bursting with French officers and administrative officials, someone, to amuse himself, had knocked the bust of its former owner, General Bennigsen, from its pedestal, and neck and shoulders lay headless on the mud-soiled floor.

Many were the plundered Lithuanians who sought refuge in Vilna from lawless Grande Armée bands now roaming the countryside. A few looters caught red-handed were summarily condemned. Marched off to their firing squads, they displayed an insouciance which left Sophie von Tisenhaus open-mouthed. Inside the archiepiscopal palace Napoleon took his marshals severely to task: "Messieurs, you are dishonoring me!" But all that these browbeaten gentlemen could do was bow their heads and wait for the storm to blow over.

In Vilna itself hunger soon stalked the streets. For three days there was no bread, even for the soldiers, the luckier of whom could stretch out on the stone floors of townhouse vestibules, while the less fortunate slept outside on the cobbled pavements. To feed his Polish lancers the ever-generous Dominik Radziwill had food supplies brought in from one of his Lithuanian estates. When the sun finally reappeared, after three days of diluvial rains, it brought with it the stench of rotting horse flesh, sweeping in from the surrounding hills and plains. Quite a few unburied carcasses were casually pushed into the Vilia —so polluting the river that more than one chef employed by a noble family refused to serve his masters with the river trout and crayfish that had so often graced their silver platters.

All this cast a chill on the carefree rapture with which the inhabitants of Vilna had at first greeted their "liberators"—a chill so marked that soon Napoleon was complaining to Caulaincourt that "these Poles are not like those of Warsaw."

On the morning of June 28 Murat's cavalrymen had met General Alexander Balashov, who had been ordered to stay behind and to deliver a personal letter from the tsar to Napoleon. The Russian minister of police was courteously greeted by Murat, and then brought to Vilna by a roundabout route, to keep him from seeing the sorry state of the Grande Armée's horses.

Not until July 1 did Napoleon consent to receive him. "My brother Alexander, who was so high and mighty with Narbonne, would already like to negotiate," he exulted to Berthier. "He is afraid. My maneuvers have upset the Russians. Within a month's time they will be at my knees."

He was nevertheless annoyed by the contents of Alexander's letter, which asked the reasons for this undeclared war and expressed the tsar's willingness to resume negotiations once the French had withdrawn behind the Niemen. "Alexander takes me for a fool," he declared to Berthier, Duroc, and Caulaincourt. "Does he think I came to Vilna to negotiate commercial treaties? I have come once and for all to finish off these barbarians of the North. The sword is now drawn. They must be pushed back into their ice, so that for the next twenty-five years they no longer come to busy themselves with the affairs of civilized Europe."

Received after breakfast in the very same chamber in which, five days before, the tsar had given him his instructions, Balashov was accorded a hot-and-cold treatment of mingled threats and cajolements. During this private audience, as at the seven o'clock dinner which the Russian minister of police was invited to share with Berthier, Duroc, Caulaincourt, and Bessières (the commander of the Imperial Guard's cavalry forces), Napoleon kept stressing his own army's numerical superiority. "Your infantry numbers a hundred and twenty thousand men and your cavalry from sixty to seventy thousand men. In short, less than two hundred thousand. I have three times as many." He couldn't understand how Alexander, in military matters a novice, could have chosen to make himself supreme commander; for if things went badly, he would be held personally responsible. As for the tsar's commanders, except for Bagration, to whom he was willing to accord a certain prowess, they were all mediocre. What was the point of building up supply depots and later putting them to the torch instead of using them for what had been originally intended? "Aren't you ashamed?" he taunted Balashov, using arguments similar in tone to those that Bagration and Admiral Shishkov had been using in the Russian camp to denounce a policy of withdrawal. "Since Peter the Great, since the time when Russia has been a European power, never has the enemy penetrated onto your lands; yet here at Vilna I conquered an entire province without a fight."

When Balashov protested that the Russians would fight like tigers to defend their homeland, Napoleon made light of it. He stressed the patriotic fervor of the Poles, who were now fighting with the French, whereas the Russians this time were without allies. "How can one conduct operations through a council?" he went on. "All wars conducted in that fashion end in misfortune. In the middle of the night, at two or three o'clock in the morning, when I am struck by a good idea, the order is given in a quarter of an hour and in half an hour it is put into execution by the advance outposts; whereas with you, Armfelt proposes, Bennigsen examines, de Tolly deliberates, and Phull opposes, and all of them together do nothing but waste their time."

Later he told Balashov that if Emperor Alexander continued to surround himself with his (Napoleon's) personal enemies, "I am going to chase all of his Württemberg, Baden, and Weimar relatives from Germany, he can prepare quarters for them in Russia." Noting the look of disapproval on Caulaincourt's face, he added jokingly, "Emperor Alexander treats his ambassadors well. He thinks he can conduct policy with cajoleries. Here is one of your emperor's chevaliers. He has made a Russian of Caulaincourt."

"It is doubtless because my frankness has too much proved that I am a good Frenchman that Your Majesty now seems inclined to doubt it," protested Caulaincourt with some heat. "The marks of kindness with which I was often honored by Emperor Alexander were intended for Your Majesty. As your faithful subject, Sire, I shall never forget it."

Napoleon hastily changed the subject. But later he could not help twitting his grand equerry again, when asking if General Balashov's horses were ready: "Well, so you say nothing, you old courtier of Saint Petersburg?"

Managing to control his temper, Caulaincourt escorted Balashov to his carriage and begged him to transmit his respectful homage to his master, the tsar. After he had returned upstairs, Napoleon continued to upraid his grand equerry for being so patently upset "at the harm I am doing to your friend" —he meant, of course, Alexander. "His armies do not dare to wait for us; they no more save the honor of arms than that of the government. Before two months are up, Russia's nobles will force Alexander to sue for peace."

Caulaincourt could contain himself no longer. Heatedly he told Napoleon that he had proved himself a better Frenchman by warning against this war than those who, wishing to please him, had encouraged him to embark on it. He didn't mind being made fun of in the presence of his fellow countrymen, but it was insulting to have his loyalty called into question in the presence of a foreigner. He was not ashamed to have declared himself against this war, but since his advice and services were no longer appreciated, he asked to be given another command in Spain and allowed to leave the next day.

"Who is casting doubt on your loyalty?" answered Napoleon, who seemed more surprised than irritated by his grand equerry's outburst. "I know full well that you are a brave man. I was only joking. You are too susceptible. You know perfectly well that you enjoy my esteem. Right now you are talking nonsense."

Seizing hold of his riding coat and trying to pull him back, Berthier and Bessières sought in vain to calm Caulaincourt, who continued his heated expostulations. Napoleon turned on his heel and walked back into his office. Still spluttering with rage, Caulaincourt returned to his billet and packed his belongings. The next morning he failed to appear for the emperor's habitual *lever*. Berthier and then Duroc were sent to reason with him. Caulaincourt told both of them that he wished to be relieved of his post as grand equerry and permitted to go to Spain. Finally, after making another tour of Vilna and its ring of surrounding hills and visiting the three new pontoon bridges, Napoleon ordered Caulaincourt to be brought to him. Unable to disobey a formal order of this kind, Caulaincourt rode over to the other side of the river, where Napoleon was reconnoitering the terrain.

"Are you mad enough to want to leave me?" said Napoleon, leaning over and gently pinching Caulaincourt's ear. "You know I esteem you and had no wish to wound you." And with that he set off at a gallop, leaving his grand equerry no time to say a word.

Still persuaded that Alexander could eventually be brought to the negotiating table, Napoleon could not afford to lose the services of a man who had won the tsar's respect and who might, when the moment came, be an ideal interlocutor. But in this, as in so much else, he was destined to be mistaken.

In the early hours of June 29 two of Murat's cavalry divisions were ordered to cross the river, after only a few hours of respite. They were followed by one of Davout's infantry divisions and some artillery pieces, which were hauled up to the plateau immediately north of Vilna, where a palisaded camp was to be built to guard the suburbs from a possible Cossack assault.

The next day two more of Davout's infantry divisions crossed the Vilia to join Murat's cavalrymen in their pursuit of Barclay de Tolly's retreating forces, which now seemed headed for Sventsiany, fifty miles to the northeast. Like the three infantry divisions of Ney's Third Corps, which were ordered to cross the undulating Vilia River at a point twenty miles northwest of Vilna, the foot-sloggers placed under Murat's overall command wore themselves out in a vain pursuit of the withdrawing Russians, who, being better fed and rested, had little trouble outmarching them, protected by a rearguard screen of cavalry.

Davout, with his two remaining divisions, was dispatched in a southeasterly direction down the highroad leading from Vilna to Minsk. His task was to intercept the troops of Bagration's Second Army of the West, so that the Poles of Poniatowski's Fifth Corps and the Westphalians from General Vandamme's Eighth Corps, advancing from Grodno, could catch the retreating Russians from behind in a battle of annihilation.

For the commander of the crack First Corps this must have been a bitter pill to swallow. Of the six elite divisions he had personally trained, one had already been detached to bolster the two Prussian divisions of Macdonald's Tenth Corps, operating in the Tilsit region. Three more of his divisions had now been detached to strengthen Murat's pursuit of the main Russian force, leaving Davout with just two infantry divisions and several cavalry brigades to deal with Bagration's Second Army of the West. That Davout's enemy, Berthier, had encouraged Napoleon to break up the once massive First Corps there can be no doubt; it was his petty revenge for Davout's heated outburst against him at Marienburg three weeks before. But it was to prove a costly tactical mistake. For if Davout had been left with four instead of two divisions for his drive on Minsk, he could probably have dealt Bagration a crippling blow when their forces finally met near Mogilev, on the Dnieper.

At the start of this campaign, however, Napoleon had only the haziest notion as to just where Bagration and his forces were. A few days before crossing the Niemen he had received a report that Bagration had moved his headquarters north from Slonim to the town of Lida, almost fifty miles due south of Vilna. From this he concluded that the fiery commander of Russia's Second Army of the West had been ordered to march northward to join Barclay de Tolly's First Army in a concerted defense of the Lithuanian capital.

Psychologically, Napoleon's reasoning was sound. Had Bagration been in supreme command of the First and Second Russian armies, he would have done exactly what Napoleon was hoping for—by concentrating the two Armies of the West for a major battle to save Vilna. On June 26, when news reached him that Napoleon had crossed the Niemen unopposed, he wrote a furious letter to the former minister of war, Arakcheyev (obviously hoping that he would convey his bitter feelings to the tsar), to complain about a senseless military strategy which had first forced him to stretch out his forces "like disemboweled tripe" and then, after the enemy had invaded without a shot being fired, to "retreat without knowing why. You will not be able to convince anybody in the army that we have not been betrayed"—he meant, of course, by Barclay de Tolly and his "German" entourage. "Russians should not flee. We have become worse than the Prussians."

On the evening of June 30 a detachment of retreating Russian troops ran into Davout's advancing cavalry and infantry forces twenty-five miles southeast of Vilna, on the road to Minsk. Their commander, realizing that his line of march was cut, hastily retreated southward, but a few of his soldiers were captured by the French. Interrogated by Davout's Russian-speaking interpreters (most of whom were Poles), they explained that they were part of General Dmitri Dokhturov's Tenth Corps. This corps had originally been placed under Bagration's command, but, unknown to the French, it had recently been reassigned to the left wing of Barclay de Tolly's First Army. Davout's soldiers had thus intercepted a rearguard unit of the retreating First Army rather than the advance guard of Bagration's Second Army—as Napoleon and his chief of staff, Berthier, erroneously assumed.

Shortly after midnight on July 1 Napoleon dictated two sets of orders to Davout, asserting his conviction that Bagration and his Second Army were trying to cut across the Vilna–Minsk road. Several hours later the three Polish regiments of General Claparède's Young Guard division were marched at top speed from the vicinity of the ravaged manor of Zakret around the crescent of wooded hills until they reached the highlands east of Vilna, where they fixed bayonets and prepared for battle. The sun, which had burst through the clouds at last—to the delight of the soaked and mud-caked infantrymen—soon vanished once more behind sheets of blinding rain. Suddenly Napoleon appeared, mounted on one of his white horses, his little half-moon hat looking curiously rain-soaked and misshapen as water trickled from its guttered rims onto his green chasseur's uniform. Beating his right boot with his riding crop, he vainly tried to see through the downpour with his spyglass. Finally he gave up, exclaiming impatiently to General Claparède, "But this is a terrible rain!" After which he dug his spurs into his horse's flanks and cantered on, followed by an equally disgruntled and soggy Berthier.

All hope of catching the Russians and bringing them to battle had in fact been washed away in the deluge of rain, sleet, and hail that had inundated Lithuania during the last days of June. When Ney's dog-tired and half-starved soldiers reached the abandoned village of Kirgaliszky, twenty miles northwest of Vilna, they found the swirling waters of the Vilia so swollen that only with great difficulty were they able to construct a makeshift bridge. From the opposite bank the road led up a steep, tree-studded incline. The tired infantrymen managed to slog their way up, but the grade was too much for many undernourished horses.

By the time Faber du Faur, an artillery major serving with the 25th (Württemberg) Division, reached the rickety, rain-soaked bridge, the opposite slope was streaked with transversal tracks up which pathetically slobbering horses strove to pull their cannon. Each new gun carriage deepened the ruts along which the following caisson lurched and slithered and finally bogged down, axle-deep in mud. Even doubling the teams—using eight hitched horses instead of the usual four—did nothing but multiply the number of exhausted horses. After seeing several hundred horses die of overexertion, the Württembergers decided to leave behind an entire battery of 12-pounders, which were rerouted to Vilna along with one-half of the Third Corps's artillery reserve.

Informed by a courier that Ney was moving forward with only half of his artillery, Napoleon ordered the marshal to halt his advance until the rest of his cannon could be brought to him via the long detour through Vilna. Beyond the swampy lake district of Maliaty (forty miles north of Vilna), where they marked time for several days, new woes descended on Ney's men, in the form of acute dysentery. Crown Prince Wilhelm, whom Napoleon had taken to task at Thorn for the undisciplined behavior of his troops, succumbed to typhus and had to relinquish the command of his Württemberg division. During a review of the remaining troops, Lieutenant Karl von Suckow ruefully reported that his company, which had set out from Württemberg with 150 men, was now down to exactly 38 soldiers still able to carry packs and weapons. Not one of them had yet seen action against the enemy. So far the only shots fired had been aimed at a steer or heifer trying to escape from the herd of cattle they had rounded up during forages along the route of march and which for much of the way had been their only source of subsistence.

Ney, like Murat, was ordered to slow down the rate of his advance. Other corps commanders, however, were blamed for excessive sloth. On July 2 Berthier sent off a sharp dispatch to Prince Eugène de Beauharnais, expressing the emperor's displeasure that his Fourth (partly Italian) and Sixth (partly Bavarian) Corps should have remained at Pilony, a dozen miles upstream from the Kovno crossing-point, paralyzed by the news that between 30,000 and 40,000 Russians were about to assail their left flank. In reality, Prince Eugène had reached the Niemen only on June 29 and had not been able to put his half-starved Fourth Corps across it until the thirtieth. They were then engulfed in the freezing downpours which wreaked such havoc everywhere.

On July 4, when they finally emerged after hours of weary tramping through soggy woods, Eugène de Beauharnais's soldiers were gladdened by the vista of a lake, dominated by a forest-covered mountain with a monastery on its summit. Rising from the middle of the gleaming waters, like some fairy-tale enchantment, was an old ruined castle, now darkly illuminated against a flaming sunset. This was Novy Troki, on whose wooded slopes the Russians were supposed to have gathered for a major battle to defend Vilna. The town itself, like every village through or near which Italians, Spaniards, Croatians, Bavarians, and Frenchmen had passed, had been abandoned by its inhabitants —save for a few black-bearded Jews and their wailing families, who fell on their knees, imploring the mercy of this new band of plunderers.

Long before their comrades-in-arms had reached this idyllic landscape, recalling the green-girt lakes of their Alpine homeland, quite a few homesick Bavarians had preferred to abandon this interminable march toward an increasingly evanescent glory. The next day, when he went into Vilna for a meeting with Napoleon, Prince Eugène brought him the news that the trek from Kalwariya to Novy Troki had cost his two corps 4,000 horses. Exactly how many of his men had fallen by the wayside or chosen to desert, he did not say; but the figure of those remaining was certainly nowhere near the 80,000 he had mentioned in a letter to his wife three weeks before.

· · ·

A number of contemporaries later felt that Napoleon had made a serious mistake in spending more than two weeks in Vilna. The charge seems unjustified because of the all-important question of supplies and depots, which had to be properly organized before he could move on ahead to join Murat or Davout. His highly centralized system of government also made it imperative that he devote a certain amount of time to reading the reports that were daily sent to him by express couriers from Paris.

No less urgent was the need to set up a provisional government for Lithuania. Here, as he had done in Warsaw in 1807, Napoleon formed a seven-man committee drawn almost exclusively from members of the nobility. Although they included the rector of Vilna's university, none of these gentlemen seem to have been persons of marked administrative ability or energy.

Like Alexander, whom he had so brusquely displaced, Napoleon went out of his way to woo Vilna's aristocracy by holding an official reception in the archiepiscopal palace. Among them was the young Sophie von Tisenhaus, who had had to appeal to a Polish general (Aksamitowski) on Murat's staff to keep the latter's servants from making off with her family's fine damask mattresses when the yellow-booted and splendidly plumed King of Naples had been ordered to leave his luxurious quarters and to resume his pursuit of the Russians. At the unusual hour of five in the morning she was informed by a French emissary that she was to be ready by noon to be presented to the emperor.

What most impressed her after she had taken her place in the hall, where an altar had been set up for the preliminary celebration of mass, was the speed with which Napoleon made his entry—"like a cannonball," she later described it. She was surprised by his shortness—we should not forget that he was only five feet tall—and also by his corpulence (so marked by now, as Boniface de Castellane noted in his journal, that he had trouble swinging himself up from his left stirrup into the saddle unless aided by Caulaincourt).

The religious ceremony completed, Napoleon left with the same nervous rapidity; after which the ladies present were ushered into another hall for the official presentations. To Sophie von Tisenhaus there was a lack of delicacy in the pointed questions he put to many of the ladies as he made the ritual round: "Are you married? . . . Do you have children? . . . Are they fat and healthy?" She was surprised by the flatness of his hair—so different from Emperor Alexander's reddish curls—and the almost marmoreal pallor of his face, which was, however, mysteriously softened when he smiled and exhibited two rows of fine white teeth. Full of restless energy, he had a curious way of shifting his weight back and forth from one leg to the other, which again contrasted sharply with the unhurried grace of Emperor Alexander's movements.

Sophie von Tisenhaus's friends and relatives had been horrified to see her turn up for this reception with the diamond-studded decoration Tsar Alexander had given her boldly pinned onto the bodice of her dress. But when it was her turn to be interrogated, Napoleon merely peered at it intently and then asked her what it was; after being told that it was the *chiffre* (the intertwined initials) of the two Russian empresses, presented to her as an honorary lady-in-waiting, he nodded and moved on. "One can be a good *Polonaise* and still wear the cipher," he added a moment later, turning back with a friendly smile.

One of the troubles with this wartime "visit" to Vilna, as Napoleon probably realized, was that it had come five years too late. Even the most rabidly pro-Russian among the Lithuanians were willing to admit that if the French had crossed the Niemen after the battle of Friedland in June 1807 the population would have risen in spontaneous revolt and have greeted them with joy and exultation. Instead there had followed the major shock of the Tilsit Treaty, which had left them to the tsar's devices and aroused a widespread distrust of long-term French intentions.

Equally inhibiting, because left deliberately unsettled, was the question of exactly how the new Lithuanian duchy, with its local provisional government, was to be linked to the Grand Duchy of Warsaw. In the Polish capital the news that the Grande Armée had finally crossed the Niemen had been greeted with transports of delight. Later, recalling the moment in his memoirs, the French Resident, Edouard Bignon, described this city of 80,000 inhabitants as being in the grip of an exaltation that was "strange, almost sublime." For a brief intoxicating moment the persistent grumblings about food shortages were forgotten, and even the most acerbic critics seemed prepared to forgive the "voracity" of French, German, and Italian "plunderers," who had requisitioned so many of the city's carts and horses. Weeks before the Niemen was actually crossed there was hardly a salon in Warsaw worthy of the name in which circles of ladies were not to be found seated at tables preparing lint and gauze, so that every Polish soldier could set out for the battlefield with a roll or two of bandages in his kit. "Neither Russia's threats nor the fears and calculations of parents could halt this patriotic élan," Anna Potocka (herself the great-niece of Poland's last king) was later to recall. "A new generation was replacing that which had partly disappeared into the ranks of the French army. Children listened with feverish curiosity to the tales of their elders and were consumed with ardor. . . . Those who did not wear uniforms no longer dared to show themselves in the streets, for they risked being insulted by urchins."

This spontaneous upsurge was exactly what Napoleon had hoped for. But it was soon to be seriously dampened by the pompous inanity of the man he had chosen to keep this spirit of patriotic effervescence at fever pitch—His Grace, the archbishop of Malines.

The archbishop's first concern, when he reached Warsaw on June 5, was to be lodged in a manner truly becoming to his new title of French ambassador extraordinary. When he discovered that he could not be lodged in the Brühl Palace because it was still occupied by the young King Jerome of Westphalia, he put up a terrible fuss and was only with difficulty persuaded to establish temporary residence in the "small house" (as he witheringly described it) that Talleyrand had been quite willing to occupy in 1807, which had since been the home of two French Residents. For several days the Polish municipal authorities and even the Council of Ministers were kept in a dither over this all-important question, as emissaries traveled back and forth in a vain attempt to persuade King Jerome to move out of the Brühl Palace to an apartment in the royal castle.

While this petty quarrel further diminished Jerome's waning prestige, it inevitably tarnished the lustrous "image" of the incoming ambassador extraordinary. As the caustic playwright Julian Niemcewicz noted in his diary exactly six days after the archbishop of Malines's arrival in Warsaw: "That the rabbit-kinglet should not wish to give up a house destined for the great ambassador; that the latter, not finding another suitable house in a city in ruins, should install himself in the drawing-rooms of [Stanislaw] Potocki is belittling. But that having money"—Napoleon, before leaving Dresden, had given his ambassador a 200,000-franc allowance for housing and entertainment—"instead of buying a bed, linen, chinaware, he should demand all of these things, including servants, is simply outrageous. . . . Avarice and indelicacy are what characterize the French people today."

These words were written on June 11, less than two weeks before the crossing of the Niemen River. According to Napoleon's plan the start of hostilities in Lithuania was to be accompanied in Warsaw by the convening of the Polish Diet and the solemn proclamation of the "reestablishment" of Poland. The *Sejm,* furthermore, was to remain in extraordinary session for as long as might be necessary to galvanize the country and to ignite the combative ardor of Lithuanian "insurgents."

What actually transpired differed sharply from this imagined scenario. The fault was ultimately Napoleon's, for having bypassed Warsaw while encouraging its expectant inhabitants to believe that he would be arriving at any moment. During his two-day sojourn (May 31–June 2) in Poznan he had received an urgent visit from the Grand Duchy of Warsaw's finance minister, Thaddeus Matuszewicz, sent by the Council of Ministers to draw Napoleon's attention to the country's harrowing plight and the grinding poverty to which it was being reduced by the ceaseless passage across its territory of predatory troops. His quick wits, fine voice, and argumentative persuasiveness had greatly impressed Napoleon when they had met in Paris during the previous summer; and they seem to have impressed him again during this second encounter in Poznan. For when he returned to Warsaw on June 2 Matuszewicz informed his ministerial colleagues that Napoleon had given his imperial blessing to the idea of inviting old Prince Adam Casimir Czartoryski to preside over the opening session of the Diet.

The venerable "Prince General"—as Adam Czartoryski's father was addressed—was now almost eighty years old. Though still sprightly for his age, this gentleman, who spoke or at least read eight or nine languages (including Arabic and Turkish) and whose library at Pulawy was one of the wonders of Europe, had virtually retired from politics more than twenty years before. Although highly esteemed, he was clearly too old to be much more than a figurehead for the coming parliamentary convocation. But Napoleon seems to have been beguiled by the prospect of winning over to his cause the father of a son—Prince Adam Czartoryski—who had once served as the tsar of Russia's foreign minister.

Flattered to be summoned from his lordly retreat in the statue-and-temple-studded gardens and woods of Pulawy, the aged prince general journeyed to Warsaw, where he was duly elected a deputy by the members of the assembled *szlachta* (gentry). Overcome by emotion, the old prince faltered in his speech, many of the onlookers wept, and the carefully stage-managed ceremony ended in a tumult of joyful acclamations.

The Diet, originally supposed to meet five days later, did not open until June 26. The reason for the delay was the archbishop of Malines's insistence on personally redrafting the report of the parliamentary commission charged with presenting the country's woes, and the various proclamations that were to announce the restoration of the Kingdom of Poland. The texts submitted seemed insufficiently grandiloquent to suit the lofty tastes of the ambassador extraordinary and were accordingly rewritten in a more florid style.

When the Diet finally convened on June 26 in the parliamentary hall of the royal castle, where all meetings of the *Sejm* traditionally took place, the designated grand marshal of the Diet, Prince General Adam Casimir Czartoryski, committed the fatal blunder of appearing in the gray-blue uniform of an Austrian field marshal—the dignity that had been conferred on him a quarter of a century earlier by his good friend Emperor Joseph II. His powdered white wig already made him look like a relic of the past rather than a herald of a glorious future, but his choice of costume was an even more galling reminder of the partitioned kingdom's past misfortunes.

His opening speech was equally ill-inspired. After having begun with a vibrant appeal to the heroic sentiments of his compatriots and stressed the sacrifices they would have to make, he went on to speak of the patriotism which Polish women would also have to display as mothers, wives, and sisters. At these words his wife, Princess Isabella, and his two daughters, who were seated in the gallery, broke into ecstatic cries of approbation and began tossing out red-and-white cockades to the assembled deputies. A shudder of emotion swept through the hall when the old prince general uttered the climactic words, "Poland exists; the Kingdom of Poland and the body of the Polish nation are reestablished." But the unseemly tumult that followed destroyed the solemnity of the occasion. The archbishop of Malines then took the floor, delivering an oration which was so full of high-flown phrases and nebulous ambiguities that nobody present could make out what it really meant—except that the French emperor's ambassador, and thus the French emperor himself, seemed unwilling to commit himself to anything specific.

The inauspicious opening of this new parliamentary session might have been happily forgotten if the Diet had been allowed to go on functioning through the rest of the summer as a galvanizing symbol of the Polish nation's renascence. But after exactly three days the archbishop of Malines took it upon himself to prorogue the Diet—without consulting his superior, Foreign Minister Maret. He was afraid, he explained in a letter to Maret, that these parliamentary sessions were going to get completely out of hand and breed endless chaos and confusion. But the real reason was that he knew he could not control a lively parliamentary body, whereas he was confident of his ability to master the small "council of confederation" he had established in its place.

News of this abrupt suspension reached Napoleon in Vilna on July 5. It angered him as much as it flabbergasted Foreign Minister Maret, who had now joined him in the Lithuanian capital. For a moment Napoleon was tempted to dismiss his ambassador extraordinary, who had done the very opposite of what had been intended.

The damage might have been partially repaired if Napoleon had fired Malines and sent Louis de Narbonne to Warsaw with orders to have the Diet immediately reconvened. Instead, the pompous prelate was allowed to remain in Warsaw, where his meddling arrogance, his penny-pinching insistence on being lavishly housed and fed at the expense of the virtually bankrupt Polish exchequer, and not least of all his rank vulgarity and cowardice—for he was ready to believe that the Cossacks were about to invade Poland—made him an object of abomination and ridicule.

From this mace stroke delivered to it just as it was about to take wing, the cause of Polish patriotism was unable to recover. It was further stricken by a second blow delivered by Napoleon himself.

On July 11 a delegation of eight Poles, whose carriages had been held up several times by menacing marauders demanding food and money, finally reached Vilna with an official petition that had been drafted in Warsaw. The delegation was headed by the most prestigious of Polish senators, the now sixty-six-year-old Joseph Wybicki. A jovial, warmhearted optimist who had reacted to Kosciuszko's crushing defeat in 1794 and the final partition of Poland by composing the verses to *"Ieszce Polska nie zginela"* ("Poland has not yet succumbed")—which are still sung today as a kind of national anthem —Wybicki had worked tirelessly to unite his often divided and feuding countrymen behind the banners of France. A more devoted champion of the French was nowhere to be found among the Poles than this indomitable patriot, who, barely six weeks before, had been one of the three Polish notables sent to the Silesian border to welcome Napoleon's entry into their country. Yet now, in reply to the white-haired senator's vibrant appeal for open French support— "Sire, say the word, say that Poland exists, and your decree will be for the world the equivalent of reality"—Napoleon once again refused to commit himself. He explained that in his particular situation he had many interests to conciliate and many duties to fulfill. "I like your nation. For sixteen years I have seen your soldiers at my side on the battlefields of Italy, as on those of Spain. I applaud everything you have done. . . ." But then came the dispiriting caveat: "In lands so distant and far-spread, it is above all in the unanimity of efforts of the population inhabiting them that you should place your hopes of success. . . . I should here add that I have guaranteed to the emperor of Austria the integrity of his domains, and that I can sanction no maneuver or movement that tends to trouble the peaceful possession of what remains to him of the provinces of Poland."

Roman Soltyk, whose father was a member of the delegation, later wrote that he could not understand how a great man like Napoleon could have failed to realize that in adopting this equivocal attitude he was throwing away an opportunity to recruit another 110,000 men, who in six months could have been added to the 70,000 Poles already serving with the Grande Armée, since the territories now occupied by the French included nine million inhabitants.

Wybicki and the fellow members of his delegation saw their hopes further dashed during the dinner they were invited to share with the French emperor. During the quick, half-hour repast Napoleon made little effort to learn more about what was going on in Warsaw and the rest of the Grand Duchy. Virtually all of his questions, shot forth between rapid mouthfuls of food and wine, concerned Russia and his immediate military plans. "If I go to Saint Petersburg, I take Russia by the head," he declared. "If I march on Kiev, I take it by the feet; but if I go for Moscow, I shall strike it in the heart." He asked Wybicki the distance from Vilna to Moscow, giving him the answer— 250 leagues (about 625 miles)—before the old man could reply.

At the ball which was given the next day by Count Pac, recently appointed aide-de-camp to Napoleon, many persons present were struck by the French emperor's irritable disposition. In taking his place upon the makeshift throne at one end of the ballroom he impatiently kicked aside the cushion that had been intended as a footrest. While his marshals and Imperial Guard officers were encouraged to dance, Napoleon, who liked to say that he had outgrown the age for such pastimes, made a ritual tour of the hall, addressing a word or two to many of the ladies, and then left, amid the usual cries of *"Vive l'empereur!"* His officers stayed on to finish the elaborate buffet supper, which their host, for all his affluence, had had some trouble preparing, while outside on the pavement by the gates of the splendidly chandeliered townhouse a pauper died that night of hunger.

CHAPTER 11

THE ELUSIVE FOE

ONE REASON for Napoleon's irritability at Count Pac's ball was his mounting dissatisfaction with the performance of the Grande Armée's right wing, which he had rashly placed under the overall command of his militarily inexperienced brother Jerome. This error had been compounded by a serious miscalculation of the distance that Jerome's Polish and German soldiers would have to cover before reaching the Niemen River in the region of Grodno. As a result the main body of the Grande Armée, under Napoleon's personal guidance, began its invasion of Lithuania almost one week before the right wing could cross the Niemen in its turn.

In mid-June, nine days before the first crossings took place near Kovno, Prince Poniatowski's Fifth (Polish) Corps and General Vandamme's Eighth (Westphalian) Corps were spread out like a crescent curving from a point slightly northeast of Ostrolenka, on the Narew River, down past Warsaw to the region of Gora, more than twenty miles south of the Polish capital. From the northeastern tip of this crescent, formed by a Polish light cavalry division, it was about 120 miles to Grodno, along a line of march which curved up toward Augustowo and then veered east and slightly southward toward the Niemen; but the distance from the southern end of the crescent, formed by the Grande Armée's 24th (Westphalian) Division, was more than 200 miles. To move two entire army corps, totaling upward of 55,000 men, over such a distance in less than ten days would have been no mean feat in the most favorable of circumstances. But as it happened, the condition of the men, almost as undernourished as their horses, was far from perfect, while the climatic conditions were disastrous.

One of the great, lingering myths regarding the 1812 campaign is that Napoleon could have dealt the Russians a crushing blow at the outset by catching and destroying Bagration's Second Army of the West—if only his bungling brother Jerome had not ruined all his plans by his lethargic leadership. This legend has persisted to this day because of the penchant so many armchair strategists have of viewing divisions and army corps as abstract entities or chessboard pieces that can be moved forward, sideways, or backward, across fixed distances and at "normal" rates of march, regardless of topographical and climatic circumstances. In reality, neither the Poles, who were in the van, nor the Westphalians, who were just behind them, stood a reasonable chance of catching up with Bagration's retreating Russians—for the simple reason that Napoleon, stung by the Russian rebuff administered to his ambassador, Lauriston, "jumped the gun" at Gumbinnen on June 22, in ordering the main body of his army to prepare itself for an immediate crossing of the Niemen. Had he waited three to four days longer, the right wing of his army could have reached its jumping-off point on time, and it might then have been able to carry out its otherwise unfulfillable assignment.

According to Napoleon's suddenly accelerated timetable, Poniatowski's Fifth Corps was supposed to reach the Russian border on June 26—three days after the start of his own Niemen River crossing—and to have invested Grodno by the twenty-seventh. In fact, its three Polish divisions did not reach the Niemen, near Grodno, until June 29. They covered the 120–135 miles at an average speed of about eighteen miles per day. This may seem slow, but they had to make repeated stops to enable their cavalry and artillerymen to scythe down any grass or rye they could find along the road, which led through one of Poland's poorest and least populated regions.

Fortunately we have several detailed accounts of the hardships Jerome's men had to endure on their weary trek toward the Niemen. One of them is that of Friedrich Giesse, a twenty-four-year-old lieutenant in a Westphalian line regiment. After a blisteringly hot march past fields still littered with skulls and bones from the December 1806 battle of Pultusk, he saw a number of his parched-lipped infantrymen die after gulping down too much river water in the region of Ostrolenka. From then on, to avoid the dreadful heat, they marched at night for the next five days with virtually nothing to eat. According to Lieutenant Eduard Rüppell, who traveled by a slightly different route, the prevailing hunger was so great that he and his companions of the Second Westphalian Hussar Regiment were glad when they were able to receive a small roll of bread and a spoonful of honey. Lacking salt—essential to keep from fainting in the intense summer heat—these hussars were soon reduced to sprinkling their meat with gunpowder!

As they approached the Niemen, the Westphalians, like the Poles ahead of them, entered a pine forest so filled with impenetrable underbrush that Giesse had the impression of traveling up a mine shaft. Along the narrow track there was room enough for only one infantryman on each side of the creaking artillery caissons. When Rüppell, during a brief halt, pushed through a thicket to pick some berries, he suddenly found himself face to face with a bear.

The dreadful heat of the first days was then followed by the same cold rains that had drenched all of Lithuania. The forest road became a ribbon of mud, in which soldiers had to struggle at every step to keep from losing their boots. Here, as elsewhere, hundreds of artillery horses had to be unhitched and left to die.

Not until the morning of June 30—four days behind the Napoleonic schedule—did the first of the three Polish divisions cross the Niemen, after scattering several thousand rearguard Cossacks with a few cannon puffs. The next day King Jerome was able to establish his headquarters in Lithuania's second city, where he and his officers and soldiers were greeted by a wild ringing of bells. But Grodno, with its quaint whitewashed churches and golden domes, soon revealed itself to be a logistical embarrassment rather than a genuine prize; for though it had been garrisoned, the Russians had carefully refrained from stocking magazines and food depots this close to their western border. Dismayed to discover that their "liberators" were penniless as well as famished, the increasingly sullen shopkeepers boarded up their fronts, and to keep the old medieval town from being further plundered, King Jerome was obliged to place it off-limits to all but his Royal Westphalian Guard.

Jerome decided to give his weary, half-starved soldiers a day or two of rest, while masons built new ovens and the bakers worked overtime turning out more bread. There is little doubt that this was a wise decision—even though his "procrastination" aroused Napoleon's wrath in Vilna. From spies and Polish scouts sent out from Grodno it was learned that Bagration had left Volkovysk with the headquarters staff of his Second Army on June 28. Since Volkovysk was almost fifty miles southeast of Grodno, this meant that by July 2 he was already four march-days away. To send on his weary, ill-fed troops in immediate pursuit, before they had replaced the many artillery horses they had lost, struck Jerome, as it did his chief of staff, as foolhardy.

At this point there occurred an incident that later was to have a fateful bearing on the outcome of the battle for Smolensk. The man whom Napoleon had chosen to command the Eighth (Westphalian) Corps was a gruff soldier named Dominique Vandamme, who had already had several tiffs over poor food supplies with Jerome's more gentlemanly chief of staff, General Jean-Gabriel Marchand. Appalled by the haggard look of his 24th (Westphalian) Division, as they marched past the royal balcony at Grodno on July 2, and outraged by a quartermaster order restricting his famished men to half the normal bread ration and a half bushel of rye per horse, General Vandamme addressed an indignant letter to Jerome, vehemently protesting the "violence" and disorder that were now everywhere in evidence.

It was apparently Vandamme's hope that this forthright protest would sting Jerome into action, and that he would bring the plight of his famished soldiers to Napoleon's immediate attention, so that more food supplies would be diverted to the cruelly neglected right wing. Instead, Jerome treated Vandamme's complaints as a personal affront. The truculent general was relieved of his command and "authorized" to proceed to Warsaw.

Stunned by this unexpected adversity, the disconsolate Vandamme wrote a personal letter to Napoleon, requesting another command. He also wrote to Berthier, with equal lack of success. Instead of summoning Vandamme to Vilna for a personal explanation, Napoleon let this rough but competent commander return to France. This mistake—which assuredly it was—deprived the Grande Armée of a general who had distinguished himself at Austerlitz and helped Davout win a decisive victory over the Austrians at

Eckmühl in 1809. It was one more proof of the extent to which the French emperor's better judgment was now overweighed by family considerations.

Within a week of Vandamme's disgrace, it was Prince Joseph Poniatowski's turn to be treated to a similar rebuff. Appalled, like Vandamme, by the famished condition of his troops, he wrote to Berthier to say that his officers, who had voluntarily accepted a one-third cut in their salaries, had received no further pay at all—which made it impossible for them to buy even the barest necessities, while his soldiers were now trying to subsist on half rations.

Napoleon's answer to this plaintive missive was a stinging rebuke, delivered via Berthier, who was instructed to inform the commander of the Fifth Corps that "His Majesty was very discontent that you should speak to him of pay and bread when it is a question of pursuing the enemy. . . ." The soldiers of Napoleon's Imperial Guard had come all the way from Paris by forced marches, and far from obtaining half rations, they had even had to do without bread and live on meat alone, yet "they do not grumble. The Emperor could not but be pained to see that the Poles should be such bad soldiers and that they should be so wrongly minded as to hark upon such privations, and that His Majesty hopes that he will hear no more of such talk."

The same man who had once declared that "an army marches on its stomach" now chose to regard such down-to-earth considerations as unworthy of a valiant officer's consideration. Napoleon's sharp rebuke and his manifest impatience with Jerome's "dilatory" maneuvering prodded the humiliated Poles into rash acts of gallantry, which depleted their cavalry forces to no good purpose. The first to suffer was a newly formed regiment of Polish lancers, who were sent riding pell-mell down the road leading due east to Lida (more than sixty miles from Grodno). They were severely mauled in a bloody skirmish with the Cossacks, whose dexterity in wielding their extraordinarily long, light pikes was on a par with the Poles' skill in handling their pennanted lances.

The Poles, though as famished as the others, were at least sustained by a crusading élan and the patriotic feeling that they were liberating their Lithuanian "brothers" from the yoke of the hated "Muscovites." But for quite a few Westphalians, now banished to a bivouac encampment some distance from the city walls of Grodno, the continuing privations were just too much. Knowing that they would be rounded up by gendarmes and shot by a firing squad if they tried to desert, they preferred—"in full forgetfulness of God," as the former theological student Friedrich Giesse later put it—to put an immediate end to their misery with a self-inflicted gunshot in head or heart.

On July 5, when the 24th (Westphalian) Division resumed its forward march, the cold rains were over and the summer heat, sometimes reaching 26 degrees centigrade (79 degrees Fahrenheit), had returned with a vengeance. This was particularly oppressive for soldiers clad in heavy flannel uniforms and forced to carry packs on their sweating backs. According to Giesse, only one-third of the Eighth Corps—already reduced to less than half of its original strength of 29,000 men when it had set out from Kassel—was able to complete the first day's march (some 17 miles) across fertile plains absolutely bereft of any shade. The road was lined with men who had collapsed under the strain and lay gasping on the ground for lack of water and, one suspects, for lack of salt. Half of the officers in Giesse's own regiment thus fell by the wayside, and when the count was made that evening of those who had managed to reach the assigned bivouac area, by the soggy edge of a lake, there were exactly 210 men left in a regiment that had originally numbered 1,980 men and 81 horses.

The astonishing thing about this phase of the 1812 campaign is not, as has so often been written, that Bagration and his Second Army were able to escape from the trap Napoleon wanted to set for them, when he sent Davout's two infantry divisions and Grouchy's Third Cavalry Corps down the road toward Minsk, to block Bagration's eastward retreat. The astonishing thing is that the Polish vanguard of the Grande Armée's right wing was ever able to catch up with the Russians at all.

At the start of the campaign Barclay de Tolly had urged Bagration to head from Volkovysk for Minsk, which his advance guard could almost certainly have reached before Davout's if he had followed the instructions of the minister of war. But acting in his capacity as commander in chief, Tsar Alexander had taken it upon himself to countermand Barclay's instructions. Instead, Bagration was ordered to move in a northeasterly direction toward the fortified camp at Drissa. As a result of that ill-conceived imperial order Bagration and his retreating Russians lost three precious days crossing the upper reaches of the Niemen in order to cross the Vilna–Minsk highroad some 25 miles southeast of the Lithuanian capital. When the Russians reached the highroad, they ran into Davout's troopers, who were headed for Minsk. Not realizing that Napoleon had reduced Davout's First Corps to one-third of its original strength, Bagration assumed that he had 60,000 Frenchmen to deal with— more than a match for his small corps of 35,000 men. To avoid being trapped in the swampy forests west of Minsk, Bagration then veered again, this time heading southeast toward Nesvizh, so as to be able to move from there to Slutsk, along the northern fringe of the Pripet marshlands, and from there to the fortress town of Bobruisk, on the Berezina River.

It was these two successive changes in the direction of the Russians' retreat (first a northeasterly, then a southeasterly) which finally enabled several squadrons of Polish cavalry to catch up with Ataman Platov's rearguard Cossacks not far from Mir on July 9. Without waiting for artillery or infantry reinforcements, which were a good day's march behind, the Poles charged the Cossacks with their lances, only to find themselves attacked on both flanks by other Cossack horsemen they had not seen. After some furious fighting, most of the Poles managed to fight their way free, leaving several hundred wounded prisoners behind.

The next day, after his men had passed through the town of Mir, the commander of the Polish vanguard, General Rozniecki, sought to avenge this setback by throwing his entire cavalry division—3,000 lancers in all—at the Cossacks, who had been reinforced by three cavalry regiments, backed by infantry. The result was an even bloodier defeat for the impetuous Poles.

News of this upset—which the Russians played up as their first important "victory" in the campaign—increased Napoleon's irritation against his brother Jerome. But since he had been demanding that Jerome's two corps relentlessly harry and pursue Bagration's retreating forces, *l'épee dans les reins* (the sword in their backside), he was ill placed to blame those "bad soldiers," the Poles, for advancing at too headlong a pace.

The truth, which Napoleon was unwilling to admit, was that he had given the wretchedly supplied and undernourished right wing of his Grande Armée an impossible assignment. One day, toward the end of his stay in Vilna, he complained to Louis de Narbonne about the "lack of firmness" shown by Emperor Alexander and his retreating armies, a wobbliness which seemed to him neither politically nor militarily sound. "Sire," Narbonne reminded him, "this is the kind of war of time and space that we were promised."

While Bagration and his Second Army were moving southward in an effort to outrace Davout's advancing columns, the First Russian Army of the West had continued its retreat in a northeasterly direction, headed for the entrenched camp at Drissa, on the Dvina River. The distance between the two armies was thus steadily increasing—a situation that seemed deplorable to most Russian generals but which was ultimately to prove their vast country's salvation.

For the two southernmost of the First Army's six corps, which had been stationed south of Vilna, the withdrawal involved a number of forced marches, but for the others the pace was almost leisurely, rarely exceeding fifteen miles a day. Barclay de Tolly refused to be rushed—to the dismay of General Karl Ludwig von Phull, an inveterate pessimist, who was by now convinced that the French would reach Drissa before them.

The sublime Prussian "strategist," who in Vilna had found himself deprived of maps as well as of office space in which to elaborate his abstract theories, was more than ever out of touch with reality now that hostilities had begun. As an aide-de-camp to the tsar, he was attached to imperial headquarters, where his presence was barely tolerated by most members of Alexander's entourage, who were little disposed to let this detested foreigner know just how far and fast Napoleon's forces had advanced. Barclay de Tolly, on the other hand, had insisted on keeping his First Army headquarters one day's march behind the tsar's. He was thus closer to Russian rearguard units, who kept him regularly informed as to just where Murat and his cavalrymen were and what was the condition of their horses.

The sheer size of Alexander's imperial headquarters—with its plethora of aides-de-camp, government and Court officials, "advisers," and relatives, all of them accompanied by liveried servants, ostlers, coachmen, cooks, and so on —afforded Barclay de Tolly a convenient pretext for keeping his own First Army headquarters separately located. He could thus see to it that the remaining military stores and magazines were efficiently gutted at each stage of the retreat. But his real reason for maintaining a separate headquarters was the realization that his ability to command at all would have been paralyzed by Alexander's entourage. As he wrote to his wife on July 8, "I find myself regarded as an enemy by the troops, and I am almost never present at the main [imperial] headquarters, because it is a veritable den of intrigues and cabals which render our fine sovereign irresolute and distrustful."

A week before these lines were written the prevailing confusion had reached new heights thanks to a distinctly lukewarm report about the defensive capacities of the entrenched camp at Drissa. The officer entrusted with the drafting of this report was a thirty-two-year-old colonel, Carl von Clausewitz, who was destined to become one of the most celebrated military theorists of all time. A Prussian patriot who had made a name for himself in Berlin as a war college lecturer, Clausewitz was one of a number of German officers who had bitterly opposed King Frederick William's last-minute alliance with Napoleon and who had come to Russia in the hope of serving in a "Russian-German Legion" (a pet idea of Alexander's which never got off the ground). Placed under the orders of his fellow German, Phull, he had been ordered to leave Vilna on June 23, and to go examine the state of preparedness of the entrenched camp at Drissa.

Its glaring weaknesses sprang instantly to his eyes. Designed like a convex arc bulging out from the Dvina at a point where the river described a 90-degree angle, the entrenched camp consisted of several concentric rings of redoubts built along a five-mile perimeter. Connecting trenches had been dug, wooden embrasures for riflemen constructed, and artillery emplacements readied for the defense of the various redoubts and the central "bastion." Opposite the camp's southeastern rim, a stretch of swampy woodland had been chopped down to afford Russian sharpshooters and gunners a better field of fire against enemy soldiers suddenly emerging from the nearby forests. But none of these ostensibly formidable dispositions made the slightest military sense, simply because the Dvina River, along whose western and southern bank the camp rested, could be forded at almost any point, notwithstanding its fifty-foot escarpment of sandy soil.

According to Phull's master plan some 50,000 men, supported by 120 cannon, were to hold the entrenched camp against all assaults, while another 70,000 were poised beyond the Dvina to hit Napoleon's forces as they attempted their encirclement. In effect, this entailed the splitting of Russia's First Army of the West into two distinct entities, which Napoleon could easily dispose of with his vastly superior forces. After scattering or crushing the more mobile 70,000, he could then starve the 50,000 trapped defenders into surrender or force them to launch desperate sorties against French *tirailleurs* and gunners positioned in the nearby woods. The Drissa camp was a perfect prescription for disaster.

When Clausewitz returned on June 28 to the little town of Sventsiany, he was received by the tsar in the presence of his mentor, Phull. He tried to be as diplomatic as possible, but he could not conceal his misgivings. His report, reinforcing the vehement hostility which the adventurous Armfelt, the sarcastic Paulucci, the emotional Admiral Shishkov, openly manifested to the whole "Phullian" scheme, must have shaken Alexander to the core. His despondency during his two-day stay at Sventsiany was so marked that Countess Mostowska later claimed that the tsar had spent all of his time in a tent pitched at the farther end of her garden, "seeing nobody and plunged in the most somber meditations."

Not until July 8, when the tsar made a personal horseback reconnaissance of the fortified encampment, was the Drissa scheme finally abandoned. There were tears in Alexander's eyes as he viewed the hundreds of yards of trenches, wooden and earthen embrasures, and the reinforced redoubts which several thousand serf-soldiers had spent half a year preparing—all for nothing! No one in his suite was more outspoken in condemning the defensive site than Colonel Michaud, a former French officer from the Kingdom of Sardinia, whose opinion carried great weight since he was by profession an engineer. At a staff conference held the next day Barclay de Tolly delivered the *coup de grâce* by pointing out that the Drissa camp could not possibly be held without the assistance of Bagration's Second Army of the West. Until the two armies were united it would be sheer madness to engage a battle against Napoleon's superior forces.

The decision to scrap the Drissa scheme left wide open the problem of where the First Army should next head. The union of Russia's scattered military forces seemed a top-priority objective. Perhaps the most reasonable suggestion was put forward by the tsar's fifty-five-year-old uncle Duke Alexander of Württemberg, a cavalry general who for the past several years had been governor of Vitebsk. The hilly terrain around this town of twenty thousand souls, crisscrossed by ravines and woods and resting on the southern escarpment of the Dvina River, offered a very strong—he even claimed an "impregnable"—position against the enemy.

This proposal was finally adopted, more by default than deliberate design. No one could say for sure just what Napoleon's intentions were, but Vitebsk, one hundred miles to the east and south, was clearly a better place to station the First Army if the French emperor chose to aim his main thrust at Smolensk. The one thing Barclay de Tolly was determined to thwart was a French outflanking movement aimed at cutting his line of communications with Russia's fertile "breadbasket," located beyond the curving Dnieper River. While 25,000 men were left behind to enable General Wittgenstein to oppose Marshal Oudinot's Second Grande Armée Corps, the rest of the Russian First Army (about 80,000 men) could move up the Dvina River, ready to backtrack and to hit Napoleon's exposed right flank if he chose to direct his main thrust at St. Petersburg.

Alexander now decided to scrap the Illyrian invasion scheme for which he had developed such an intemperate enthusiasm several months before in Petersburg. Instead, Admiral Chichagov was ordered to move northward with most of the Army of the Danube to link up with General Tormassov's forces south of the Pripet Marshes, and to threaten Napoleon's line of communications by invading the Grand Duchy of Warsaw.

To General Mikhail Miloradovich, the military governor of Kiev, was entrusted the important task of training 55 infantry battalions—enough to provide Russia with an entirely new army corps. Even more significant for the immediate future was Alexander's reluctant agreement to leave the "front" and to proceed to Moscow in order to rouse the patriotic fervor of its population and to accelerate the levying of new recruits. In a cleverly drafted letter which was jointly signed by Shishkov, Balashov, and Arakcheyev, it was argued that their sovereign would be doing himself and his country a disservice if he let himself be inspired by the misleading precedents of Peter the Great (personal creator of a regular Russian army) and Frederick II of Prussia (who had militarized his kingdom). Alexander, being (unlike Bonaparte) emperor by birthright, did not need to sustain his legitimacy on the battlefield.

It is very much to Alexander's credit that he finally heeded this sound advice, also given to him by his sister Catherine. From his imperial headquarters, now located in the old walled city of Polotsk—once a Jesuit stronghold defiantly planted on the banks of the Dvina River, the demarcation line between Catholic Lithuania and Orthodox Russia—the tsar had himself driven back past columns of perspiring soldiers until he reached the simple barn which his minister of war had chosen for his command post. Barclay de Tolly was seated at a table, poring over maps and dispatches, as the emperor walked in. Just what was said during their hour-long conversation we do not know, but Alexander made it clear that his minister of war still enjoyed his confidence. After publicly embracing him before climbing into his carriage, he held out his hand to Barclay, saying, "Good-bye, General, once again farewell and good-bye. I recommend my army to you. Do not forget that I have only this army. May this thought be ever present with you."

The departure of the tsar's extensive governmental and diplomatic suite (including Chancellor Rumiantsev, Nesselrode, Arakcheyev, Balashov, the Prussian ex-minister and exile Baron vom Stein, and Prince Volkonsky) did little to lighten the heavy cross Barclay de Tolly had to bear as the increasingly unpopular commander of the First Army of the West. While the troublesome Paulucci was dispatched to Petersburg and later given command of the embattled port of Riga, the Swedish giant Armfelt, the abstract theorist Phull, Duke Alexander of Württemberg, and other "authorities" stayed on to give Barclay the benefit of their professional "advice." Most importunate of all was the continuing presence of the recently appointed chief of staff, General Alexei Yermolov, who was as hostile as ever to Barclay's withdrawal strategy.

Nor did the tsar ease Barclay's command problems when he denied him specific authority over the Second Army and its irascible commander. For the time being, even though he was leaving the front, Alexander remained supreme commander of Russia's scattered armies. These were now more than ever disunited, in spirit as well as geographically, as Bagration made clear in this characteristic fulmination to his friend Yermolov: "I am ashamed to wear this uniform—it kills me. . . . What an imbecile! . . . The Minister Barclay flees while ordering me to defend the whole of Russia. We were brought to the frontier, then scattered everywhere like pawns, then they stayed put, openmouthed, and strewing shit all along the border, off they fled. . . . It all disgusts me so much that it is driving me mad. . . . God preserve you; as for me, I'm going to swap my uniform for a peasant's blouse!"

. . .

On July 7, when his senior bridge-building officer, General Jean-Baptiste Eblé, expressed his dismay at the number of horses the Grande Armée had lost, Napoleon reassured him, "We shall find fine coach horses in Moscow." It was the first inkling any of his staff officers had that Napoleon seemed inclined to head for Moscow.

In reality, the French emperor had taken no firm decision about this or any other strategic movement. For if ever there was a general who liked to "play it by ear," it was Napoleon Bonaparte. Twenty years of experience in the field had taught him at least one thing: in a campaign the most elaborate advance planning can be reduced to nothing overnight by some fortuitous occurrence.

Several months before, one of Berthier's chief cartographers, General Armand Guilleminot, had been given the task of studying the various roads leading from Russia's western borders to St. Petersburg and Moscow. After reaching Vilna Napoleon was still undecided as to which should be his target. Strictly speaking, neither was his goal. His overriding aim was to bring the Russians to battle and to destroy their main army in a decisive super-Austerlitz.

This explains Napoleon's extreme annoyance with Oudinot when he learned that, yielding to his natural impetus, the marshal had raced northward after surprising a Russian rearguard unit on June 29 at Vilkomir, where he seized an undestroyed bridge as well as a sizable quantity of unburned food stocks. Having reached Dünaburg, on the Dvina River, this ruddy-cheeked brewer's son had been stopped by a furious cross fire from the entrenched camp on the farther side of the river. At this point he was almost eighty miles northwest of the main Russian camp at Drissa and dangerously exposed to a possible flank attack by Barclay de Tolly's First Army of the West.

Napoleon's intention, as he made clear in his rebuke to Oudinot, was not to make a frontal assault on the entrenched camp at Drissa, but to attack it from the rear by crossing the Dvina River at some point upstream between Dissna and Polotsk. If Barclay de Tolly and his First Army chose to make a stand at Drissa, they would find themselves as hopelessly surrounded as had been General Mack's Austrians at Ulm. If, instead, the Russians chose to evacuate the Drissa camp and to retreat northward toward Petersburg, Marshal Macdonald was to cross the Dvina with his two Prussian divisions and to hold up the withdrawal of the Russian First Army while Napoleon, with Oudinot's Second Corps and the main body of his army, harried the Russians' other flank and rear. The Russians' precipitate withdrawal would lead to the liberation of all of Courland and Polish Livonia—a liberation which would be as exhilarating to the Poles in Warsaw as it would be humiliating to the tsar and the *haute société* of Petersburg.

On July 15, two days before Napoleon left Vilna, 3,000 Russian horsemen staged a dawn crossing of the Dvina River and surprised two cavalry regiments commanded by General Horace Sébastiani, a cousin of Napoleon's. The Russians captured 145 prisoners, including a French general, before recrossing the Dvina River. In the belief that this might be the prelude to a general counteroffensive, Napoleon issued orders to prepare for a major battle.

Only three days later did Napoleon realize that this was no more than a feint action intended to disguise the movements of Barclay's First Army of the West. The Russians, as he had expected, had decided to abandon the entrenched camp at Drissa. But instead of heading north toward Petersburg, they were now headed in a southeasterly direction along the northern bank of the Dvina River.

By traveling nonstop through the night, Napoleon, who left Sventsiany at ten o'clock on the night of July 17, was able to reach the equally humble town of Glubokoye by two in the afternoon of July 18. Frequent changes of horses, at relay stations prepared in advance, made it possible for him to cover the last eighty-five miles in sixteen hours. By this time, the vanguard of Barclay's army was less than fifty miles from Vitebsk, whereas Murat's undernourished cavalrymen and the three divisions of Prince Eugène's Fourth Corps, which had been assigned a roughly due-east line of march from Vilna, were still seventy to eighty miles away.

The four days Napoleon spent at Glubokoye, housed in a Carmelite convent, were thus anything but happy. "The Emperor is ill-humored," noted the young Boniface de Castellane in his diary. "The manner in which the Russians are having us wear ourselves out pursuing them does not amuse him at all." To make up for the devastating losses in artillery horses, Napoleon had decided to replace them, wherever possible, with oxen, which, having tougher stomachs, can get along without oats. But this expedient was bound to slow the pace of the Grande Armée's advance, since bullocks move much more slowly than horses.

The most spectacularly successful in rounding up local bullocks and horses were the advance cavalry units and the two leading infantry divisions under Davout's command. Their success was not due solely to the drive and energy of their commander. The line of advance Napoleon had assigned to Davout —from Vilna southeast to Minsk—took him through an intermediate region situated between the operational zones of the First and Second Russian armies. At Minsk, where Davout was met by the "district marshal"—an old Polish gentleman who drove up with a handsome four-horse equipage, accompanied by ostlers and liveried lackeys and with his splendidly uniformed chest dazzlingly adorned with Russian decorations—the French were able to seize 22,000 bushels of badly needed oats, 6,000 hundredweights of straw, and twenty vats of vodka. Fifty miles farther on, at Borissov, located on one of the upper branches of the Berezina River, they captured 16 Russian siege guns, 18 artillery pieces, 200 carts and carriages of various kinds, 60,000 pounds of gunpowder, as well as 200 cannoneers and 600 draft horses.

Davout was able to move so fast because his soldiers were advancing through mostly undefended regions. But these favorable circumstances were quite exceptional. Almost everywhere else French and foreign commanders had great trouble keeping their men properly supplied and fed. Sent by Napoleon to deliver a message to Marshal Ney at his headquarters near the Dvina

River, Boniface de Castellane found the Württembergers of his 25th Division literally dying of hunger. "The Emperor," he noted in his diary, "reproached the Crown Prince of Württemberg because his troops were committing dreadful horrors and pillaging. The officers, full of honor, keep the soldiers from wandering from the road, preferring to die with them." This was doubtless the impression these disciplined Germans wished to give. In fact, as we know from Karl von Suckow, the Württembergers, like everyone else, sought to keep body and soul together by fanning out in search of food and fodder. Marshal Ney himself made no bones about it. He asked Castellane to tell Napoleon that his "corps, marching behind the others, lived by seizing half of the carts loaded with flour driven by soldiers from other corps who cross his columns; they share like brothers, for otherwise his army would die of hunger."

It was during his brief stay at Glubokoye that word reached Napoleon of a major row that had broken out between the commander of the First Corps, Davout, and his own brother, King Jerome of Westphalia. Jerome, after reaching the town of Nesvizh on July 13, had dispatched one of his aides-de-camp on a seventy-five-mile trip through the dense woods and marshlands separating him from Minsk to inform Davout of the positions reached by his leading units. Acting with his customary tactlessness, Davout sent back the aide-de-camp with a copy of the confidential instructions he had received from Napoleon, indicating that when a junction between their forces had been effected, Davout, as the more experienced of the two, was to assume supreme command of the Grande Armée's Fifth, Seventh, and Eighth corps. Napoleon, in issuing this tersely worded authorization, had neglected to explain to Davout that it was only to be used when his own and Jerome's three corps had joined forces for a battle with Bagration's Second Army. He had also neglected to breathe a word about this to Jerome, aware as he was of his brother's intense dislike of Davout—a dislike that was cordially reciprocated.

Jerome lost his temper. For several weeks he had been bombarded by stern reprimands from imperial headquarters, blaming him for the clumsiness of his maneuvers and the deplorable slowness of his advance. This new insult was more than he could take. He drafted a letter to his older brother, informing him that he had been honored to assume command of troops under His Majesty, the emperor, but that he could not agree to command them under anyone else. Such being the case, he felt it better to withdraw.

Without even waiting for his brother's reaction, the irate young king left Nesvizh in a huff and set out with his Royal Westphalian Guard for Grodno. "*Quelle incartade!*" (What a peevish outburst!), exclaimed Napoleon after reading Jerome's letter. Berthier was instructed to send Davout a sharp rebuke for his peremptory behavior, but the damage was done. Unable to soothe his brother's ruffled feelings, Napoleon ordered the immediate return to the front of the Royal Westphalian Guard. Jerome, with the remaining members of his suite, proceeded to Warsaw, while his Westphalian soldiers, having already lost General Vandamme, continued their demoralizing march eastward toward the Berezina River.

· · ·

On Thursday, July 23, leading detachments of the First Army of the West aroused the 20,000 inhabitants of Vitebsk from their midsummer somnolence by trotting and clattering across the Dvina bridge. They were soon followed by Barclay de Tolly and members of his staff. Since the brick-built town could not possibly accommodate the sudden influx of close to 80,000 men, Barclay had the advance units march through and bivouac on the plain to the south and west.

Bordered on the north by the rocky escarpment of the Dvina, which at this point was so high and steep as to be virtually unscalable, Vitebsk presented certain topographical advantages for a spirited defense, even though it was far from constituting an "impregnable" position, as the town's military governor, Duke Alexander of Württemberg, had glibly claimed at Drissa. Two miles to the west the plain—in effect a plateau—was cut by the deep scrub-brush-filled ravine of the Luchiosa River, which was little more than a broad stream flowing northward and finally emptying into the Dvina. To the south there was a range of low hills on which, if a battle had to be fought, the Russians could rest their left wing. West of the Luchiosa the ground was wooded, offering convenient shelter to enemy troops advancing up the main road from Beshenkovichi and Ostrovno. But the position's gravest drawback—enough for Clausewitz later to term it "detestable"—was the lowness of the hills to the south, which the French could all too easily bypass, cutting off the main road leading southeast to Rudnya and Smolensk.

Dubious though he was about the defensive strength of this position, Barclay realized that he would have to make a stand, if only to still the mounting clamor against his tactics of ceaseless withdrawal. Those favoring a bolder course—and they included virtually every senior officer in the First Army— were greatly heartened by the news that the commander of Russia's Third Army, General Tormassov, had surprised and defeated a small Saxon force (part of the Grande Armée's Seventh Corps) not far from Brest Litovsk, on the northwestern fringe of the Pripet Marshes.

This minor success—hailed as a major victory and celebrated in Vitebsk's largest church with a Te Deum service—was of little help in solving Barclay's most pressing problem: the dangerous disparity in strength between the 75,000 men under his command and the 120,000 or more men whom Napoleon could now throw against him. To be able to take on the French with some hope of success it was imperative that his First Army be reinforced by the 35,000 men under Bagration's command. But Barclay's repeated pleas urging Bagration to move northward at top speed from his fortress headquarters at Bobruisk had so far had no effect.

By early Sunday, July 26, the growl of cannon fire could clearly be heard in Vitebsk—enough to precipitate the panicky exodus of the town's wealthier inhabitants. The road leading northeast to Surazh, on the Dvina River, was soon jammed with equipages, sometimes traveling two or even three abreast. They were joined by the numerous vehicles and baggage trains of the imperial headquarters staff, which Barclay dispatched eastward toward Moscow so as to be less of an encumbrance in any future retreat. This order, threatening to deprive them of their fancy uniforms and carriages, hastened the departure of many senior officials, whose presence and unsolicited advice had been more a hindrance than a help.

The gunfire heard by the inhabitants of Vitebsk came from the direction of Ostrovno, a town located twenty miles west of Vitebsk at a point where the main road from Kamen and Beshenkovichi (to which Napoleon had by now advanced) makes a 90-degree turn from north to east. In an effort to gain time so that he could be joined by Bagration's Second Army, Barclay had ordered the commander of his Fourth Corps, General Alexander Ostermann-Tolstoy, to hold up the French advance as long as possible. During two days of confused fighting personal courage seems to have played a more important role than tactical brilliance on the part of the commanders.

Had another, tactically more astute Russian commander—General Pyotr Konovnitsyn—not come to the rescue with a fresh division, Murat's cavalrymen and Prince Eugène's infantrymen might have turned Ostermann-Tolstoy's holding action into a rout. Instead, the French, Poles, Croatians, and Italians composing this multinational force were held up by a withering fire from Russian soldiers hiding behind tree trunks as they retreated slowly through the woods toward Vitebsk.

Not until the late evening of Sunday, July 26, did Napoleon, along with his brother-in-law Joachim, king of Naples, and his former stepson Eugène, now viceroy of Italy, finally reach the eastern fringe of this forest. Spread out before them like a terrestrial constellation, like a glittering array of rubies covering the darkened earth, were hundreds of glowing campfires—visible proof that Barclay de Tolly's First Army was deployed across the plain for battle.

If Napoleon could have launched the full might of his army at the Russians the next morning, there is little doubt that he would finally have won a crushing, though bitterly contested, victory. But he needed time to deploy his forces, which had been held up by the colossal confusion farther back created by the sudden convergence on the town of Beshenkovichi, located on the southernmost dip of the Dvina River, of Ney's three infantry divisions, moving down from Ula, of the three Davout divisions that had been temporarily placed under Murat's command, and of the regiments of Napoleon's Imperial Guard, to say nothing of its cavalry.

During this same Sunday evening (July 26), which saw the fighting around Ostrovno gradually peter out into twilit silence, Barclay de Tolly in Vitebsk received two disturbing messages informing him that Bagration had suffered a setback south of Mogilev, on the Dnieper. Not realizing that Davout's First Corps, reduced to half of its original strength, had been further weakened by the need to leave a regiment behind at Minsk, the normally fearless Bagration had not dared risk more than one of his divisions in a frontal assault on the carefully fortified roadblock which Davout had mounted behind a barricaded bridge at Saltanovka, athwart the main road leading northward along the western bank of the Dnieper. In a fierce day-long battle the Russians had been repulsed, with a loss of more than 3,000 men, and had been forced to beat a humiliating retreat. Bagration had accordingly decided to cross the river some distance farther south in the hope of being able to outmarch the French and to reach Smolensk before them.

This news was all Barclay de Tolly needed to scrap his battle plans. At a hastily convened staff conference everyone present, with the sole exception of the military governor, Duke Alexander of Württemberg, agreed that Vitebsk had to be abandoned. Otherwise Napoleon, with a sweeping right-flank movement (which Marshal Ney's divisions were already preparing), could cut off their direct retreat route to Rudnya and even the longer route via Poretchye, and the Russians might find themselves completely encircled or forced to flee northeastward to Surazh, with no hope of joining up with Bagration's Second Army at Smolensk. But to mask his next retreat, Barclay ordered one of his rearguard generals, Count Pahlen, to stage a diversionary advance beyond the Luchiosa River against the French left wing, while Russia's senior cavalry commander, General Fyodor Ouvarov, was sent out with another sizable force to harass Napoleon's southern flank.

From the early dawn of Monday (July 27) and all through that morning there were repeated cavalry charges and mêlées on both sides of the main road leading across the ravine of the Luchiosa River to Vitebsk. Toward noon, the Russian cavalry squadrons that had been engaged in heavy skirmishing drew back onto the plateau east of the Luchiosa River. The two armies now faced each other across the intervening ravine. But to the surprise of the Russians, who had expected to be more vigorously attacked, the French fire slackened, though exchanges of cannon fire and musketry continued at sporadic intervals.

Napoleon spent the rest of the afternoon on horseback, reconnoitering his troops' positions and those of the Russians, in preparation for the major attack he was going to launch the next morning. All trace of his previous glumness, so apparent at Glubokoye, had disappeared, and his pale features now radiated joyous anticipation. Night had already descended on the plain, again lit by Russian campfires, before he was ready to retire to his blue-and-white-striped tent, pitched near a gutted mill. "Until tomorrow, at five o'clock, the sun of Austerlitz!" were his parting words to Murat.

Three and a half hours later he was once again in the saddle, as he rode past his soldiers' campfires for last-minute consultations with Murat and Prince Eugène. The night was troubled by the moans of wounded soldiers and the pathetic whinnying of stricken horses left to languish in the ravine. But farther to the east all was strangely quiet, as though the Russian army had sunk into a deep sleep, neglecting to keep up the campfires, which no longer glowed like rubies across the darkened plain. The only sign of light was a reddish glow, which seemed to come from beyond the walls of Vitebsk, some four miles distant, and which Napoleon, like Berthier and his aides-de-camp, probably took to be the first glimmerings of a rosy dawn.

Not until several hours later did they begin to grasp the truth. Above the distant roofs, church towers, and domes of Vitebsk columns of brownish smoke could be seen, soon reddened by the sun's first rays. The Russians, under cover of darkness, had slipped away during the night, taking all their gear with them and setting fire to the remaining military stores in Vitebsk and the wooden bridge leading northward across the Dvina to the St. Petersburg road. Not a cart, not a cannon, not a caisson, not even a musket had been left behind in a surreptitious movement so faultlessly executed as to seem the work of a sleight-of-hand magician.

CHAPTER 12

LET US PLANT
OUR EAGLES HERE!

NAPOLEON'S RESPONSE to this extraordinary vanishing act was one of mingled disbelief and wariness. Fearful at first that the elusive Barclay might have set a giant trap for him, he spent several hours carefully examining the Russians' recently abandoned bivouac area, trying to ascertain from artillery tracks and other telltale signs how numerous had been their forces and in which direction they had fled.

Although Napoleon did not know along which routes Barclay's Russians had retreated (in fact they were split into three columns, using three different roads), he must have suspected that some of them had marched along the road to Rudnya—the most direct route to Smolensk. Ney was ordered to push his advance guard forward to see if he could catch up with them.

When Boniface de Castellane rode into Vitebsk with a company of Imperial Guard chasseurs, he came upon two Cossack squadrons waiting to open fire with carbines beyond the town's eastern gate. Armand de Caulaincourt's younger brother, Auguste, rounded up some Polish lancers and two squadrons from Prince Eugène's Royal Italian Guard, and they set out in pursuit. A five-mile chase ensued, punctuated by random carbine shots, but Caulaincourt and his riders finally had to give up for fear of being lured into an ambush. It was well they did so. For another, less cautious body of French cavalrymen, after galloping for fifteen miles through clouds of stifling dust, discovered that they had been led on a wild-goose chase up the northeast road leading to Surazh. So worn out were their mounts—it was swelteringly hot—that many of the French horsemen were unable to gallop back to safety when the Cossacks gave up the pretense of fleeing and suddenly turned on them.

Later in the day Napoleon set off in the same direction after receiving a delegation from Vitebsk's Jewish community and making a brief reconnaissance of the half-empty town. He finally halted his carriage and had his tents pitched for the night in a field some sixteen miles northeast of Vitebsk. Altogether, it was a disappointing day. At a staff meeting attended that evening by Berthier, Prince Eugène, Murat, and his chief of staff, General Belliard, the last-named bluntly informed Napoleon that their horses were exhausted and that if the cavalry were asked to continue at such a pace, in five or six days' time there would be no cavalry left.

At six o'clock on the morning of July 29, when one of his duty officers, Anatole de Montesquiou, came into the imperial tent with a message from Murat, he found Napoleon slumped in an armchair with his small half-moon hat on his head and his brows knitted in that air of brooding concentration which the painter Horace Vernet was later to make so famous. Shortly afterward the disgruntled emperor decided to call off the vain pursuit and to return to Vitebsk to give his army corps, and in particular his cavalry and artillery horses, the rest they badly needed. From the governor's small wood-pillared palace, recently vacated by the tsar's uncle Alexander of Württemberg, he scribbled another brief note to Marie-Louise, who by this time had returned to Paris: *"Mes affaires vont bien. Ma senté* [sic] *est bonne"* (My affairs are going well. My health is good), he wrote, using a ritual formula that now recurred in almost every letter. But the truth, which he could perhaps be forgiven for wishing to conceal from his worried wife, was that nothing was going according to his plans and that even his health left something to be desired, since he was beginning to be troubled by dysuria (a form of uremia).

The two weeks he spent at Vitebsk—from July 28 to August 12—were unquestionably among the most nerve-wracking Napoleon had ever experienced. The heat, to begin with, was oppressive—as bad as the most stifling days he could recall from his youthful days of service in Marseille and Toulon. Though not addicted to siestas, he often felt so listless by the early afternoon that he would collapse limply onto the iron camp bed he had had installed in his private apartments (which, like the rest of the gubernatorial mansion, seem to have been very poorly furnished).

For the first couple of days he was kept fully occupied by a host of immediate problems that claimed all of his time. The most pressing of them all was the need to reestablish a minimum of discipline in an army that had gradually degenerated into an immense horde of predatory marauders. Though better supplied than other Grande Armée corps, Napoleon's own Imperial Guard had succumbed to the general *laissez-aller*—with the result that many abandoned Vitebsk houses were plundered even more shamelessly than had been the case in Kovno. Caulaincourt's younger brother, Auguste, recently appointed commandant of imperial headquarters, was ordered to take whatever measures might be needed to reestablish order. A few plunderers were caught red-handed, tried, and shot, as a warning to others, and to keep the various Guard regiments on their toes, a different brigade had to stand review in full dress uniform each morning at six. The square in front of the governor's mansion being cluttered by a number of wooden huts and houses, Napoleon ordered his sappers to demolish them in order to open up a more imposing parade ground.

Less easily solved was the problem of assuring regular distributions of foodstuffs from meager stocks, which often had to be defended from the assaults of hungry soldiers by sword-wielding sentinels. In Vitebsk all of the Russian magazines and warehouses had been methodically reduced to smoking cinders, so that the French had to rely on their own supply trains or on what they could garner from the countryside. Thirty-six brick ovens were hastily constructed, capable of furnishing 30,000 pounds of baked bread with each loading, but it was no easy matter to keep them operating at full capacity in a region where wheatfields were not particularly abundant and before the harvest was in. The idea of using canals, protected waterways, and the lower part of the Niemen to transport large quantities of flour by sailboats and river barges might commend itself on paper, but in practice this mode of transport proved most laborious and time-consuming, if only because the boatmen had to work their way *upstream* from the Niemen's river mouth to Kovno. In advancing to Vitebsk and beyond, the central corps of the Grande Armée had put 300 miles between themselves and the Niemen. For horses and oxen advancing at a maximum rate of 15–20 miles a day, that meant a journey of two weeks or more, during which the draft animals, to be able to do their work, had in addition to be fed. At Vitebsk, as he had done at Thorn, Napoleon placed all the blame for poor provisioning on General Mathieu Dumas and the civilian officials of his quartermaster corps. But this facile resort to demagogy, calculated to please the old-timers of his Imperial Guard, who felt a soldierly contempt for the civilian *ordonnateurs,* did nothing to solve the underlying problems.

Even more scathing were the reproaches leveled at the Grande Armée's woefully understaffed medical corps. "You do not deploy enough activity, Messieurs les docteurs," declared Napoleon in one such diatribe. "I shall send you back to Paris to take care of the inhabitants of the Palais Royal. You do not understand the sacred nature of your mission. You, whom I have charged with the task of tending to the needs of our soldiers, you want to sleep in white sheets! But it is out in the open, in the mud, that one must sleep; for glory is not to be found in softness, it is only to be found in privations."

To no one can this criticism have seemed more galling than to Dominique Larrey, a dark-haired Pyrenean who for the past eight years had been the chief surgeon of Napoleon's Imperial Guard. A revolutionary innovator, Larrey had broken with tradition by insisting that military surgeons and doctors follow the infantry into battle rather than remain several miles to the rear. Experience had taught him that the sooner a wounded officer or soldier could be operated on, the greater were his chances of surviving the onset of gangrene. To this end he had personally set up six companies of *ambulances volantes,* composed of military surgeons and assistants who could be directed to any part of a battlefield to take care of the wounded and to amputate on the spot. These mobile medical units had become a standard feature of the Imperial Guard, but elsewhere they seem to have been regarded as a luxury which less privileged corps could not afford.

The sad fact of the matter was that both the quantity and the quality of the French army's medical corps had been declining for the past three or four years, as surgeons with valuable battlefield experience were dismissed for reasons of economy. Friedrich Giesse, who had access to official figures, later claimed that the quota prescribed for each army corps (which at the beginning varied from 20,000 to 45,000 men) was 23 doctors and pharmacists, and that the total for the Grande Armée was exactly 719. Even assuming that not more than 450,000 men actually crossed the Niemen, that represented a catastrophic ratio of one doctor or pharmacist for every 625 men.

During the three days of fighting immediately preceding their entry into Vitebsk, the French had accumulated about 750 wounded, and the Russians a roughly equal number. Larrey, who managed to supervise forty-five leg and arm amputations during the final day, soon found himself so short of lint and bandages that he and his fellow surgeons had to use the soldiers' linen and strips torn from their own shirts to bandage wounds. In Vitebsk four makeshift "hospitals" were set up, but in the most appalling conditions. Most of the wounded were parked on the stone or dirt floors of churches or warehouses, usually without even a bed of straw to lie on. The sick and the wounded were indiscriminately mixed together, spreading infections everywhere. Because all available draft horses had been rounded up to pull top-priority cannon and artillery caissons, many wagons loaded with surgical instruments and medicines had been casually left behind.

Already desperately short of nails, horseshoes, and blacksmith work tools, many Grande Armée units were further plagued by the scarcity of healthful drinking water during this hot midsummer season. Lacking bread (needed to balance a preponderantly meat diet), reduced to slaking their thirst with polluted water from the lakes and swampy streams they passed, tens of thousands of soldiers and officers had by now come down with dysentery. Heinrich von Roos, a thirty-one-year-old doctor serving with a Württemberg hussar regiment in Murat's cavalry reserve, tried everything from chamomile and mint infusions to thick soups and flour mashes in an effort to check attacks of acute diarrhea, which, as we know from others, plagued Davout's infantry divisions as well as those of Ney's Third Corps. At a camp near a town southeast of Vitebsk diarrhea, according to Roos, "had assumed such violent scope that it was impossible to assure normal service, let alone indulge in any kind of drill. The houses were all filled with sick men, and in the camp itself there was such a continuous running back and forth behind the front that it was as though purgatives had been administered to entire regiments."

Exactly how many soldiers and officers were thus momentarily disabled, there is no way of telling, but there is good reason for believing that it ran into the tens of thousands. Murat's chief of staff, Belliard, later reckoned that by the time the First and Second French Cavalry corps reached the vicinity of Vitebsk, they had lost between 8,000 and 9,000 men—one-half of the number that had crossed the Niemen some four weeks earlier. The rate of attrition in infantry units was probably just as high. When General Anton Gijsbert van Dedem made a tally of the officers and soldiers in his brigade, he found that they had fallen from 4,000 to 2,500; but when the Dutchman reported this to his division commander, General Friant, the latter, wishing to shine in Napoleon's eyes as a commander who took good care of his men, insisted on reporting an effective brigade strength of 3,280 men.

During a visit to Vitebsk Dedem told Napoleon's aide-de-camp General Georges Mouton—a much feared officer whose job it was to recommend promotions and decorations—how the figures for his infantry brigade had been deliberately inflated. Mouton must have passed on the complaint. For Napoleon now took the unprecedented step of ordering Mouton to look into the effective strength of each infantry brigade, while another of his aides-de-camp was ordered to do the same for the cavalry. These measures might have done some good had Napoleon really been willing to face the increasingly disturbing facts and figures. But, as Dedem had already discovered, this was not the case. When he dared to voice his admiration for the masterly way in which Barclay de Tolly and his generals had carried out their quiet and disciplined withdrawal from Vitebsk without leaving a horse or a wagon behind, his obviously nettled French superiors informed him coldly that "the word *retreat* is unknown in the dictionary of the French army."

There remained the prospect of trying to make up for the Grande Armée's staggering manpower losses by delving into the local "reservoir." In Lithuania, as in Poland, wealthy landowners and country squires had traditionally armed their serfs and formed *pospolite* companies of lance-wielding horsemen to deal with foreign incursions and invasions. But the curt reception Napoleon had accorded to the Wybicki delegation in Vilna had chilled the pro-French ardor of many Lithuanian noblemen. Friedrich von Schubert later scathingly dismissed the military contribution provided by Lithuanian noblemen as consisting essentially of the confection of picturesque uniforms in which self-appointed "colonels" swaggered around with a dazzling retinue of aides-de-camp and gave wild parties, where the waltzes and mazurkas were played by military bands in gala dress.

Another deterring factor was the widespread fear among Lithuanian nobles that the French, who had already begun to introduce the Code Napoléon in the Grand Duchy of Warsaw, were going to subvert the established order by liberating their serfs. A number of peasant uprisings did in fact occur during Napoleon's stay in Vitebsk. Frightened noblemen and ladies, some of whom sought momentary refuge in the town, came almost daily to knock on the door of the newly appointed governor, General Charpentier, with requests for help against serfs who had gone on a rampage and ransacked their country castles and estates. These revolutionary uprisings were promptly suppressed by French and other soldiers: proof that the Grande Armée of the Emperor Napoleon in 1812 was quite different from the ardent "army of the Republic" which the twenty-seven-year-old General Bonaparte had led into northern Italy in 1796. Tempting though it might at times have seemed, Napoleon eschewed any determined effort to ignite a wave of revolutionary unrest in Russia by promising freedom to its serfs. As he had explained to Louis de Narbonne in Paris, he was not now going to start a social conflagration that could spread like wildfire to other parts of Europe, once again unleashing the kind of revolutionary passion which had wreaked such havoc in France and which his empire had been designed to contain. His quarrel with Alexander was a quarrel between rulers, between imperial "brothers." It was not a giddy endeavor to accelerate the "course of history"—with all of the incalculable convulsions such a deliberately mischief-creating policy might have brought in its wake.

Pressing though these various problems were, they could not dispel the ever-recurring question which haunted Napoleon's nights, as it did his early-afternoon catnaps: what exactly should he do next? Most of his senior staff officers and advisers, beginning with Berthier, Duroc, and Caulaincourt, were all for ending the campaign at Vitebsk and not penetrating farther into far more hostile Russian territory. The oldest of his aides-de-camp, the urbane, white-haired Louis de Narbonne, had never concealed his misgivings about a march on Moscow, while believing it to be France's mission to repair the scandalous injustices of the eighteenth century by reconstituting a strong Poland "from Poznan to Danzig to Vilna," capable of providing a rampart of 200,000 soldiers against a predatory and overly ambitious Russia. Generals Mouton and Durosnel, who had been ordered to furnish Napoleon with precise indications of the real strength of each of his cavalry and infantry brigades, were also in favor of not advancing farther. Such too was the opinion of Count Pierre Daru, the precise, unemotional, efficient quartermaster general whom Napoleon had promoted to the rank of minister secretary of state. He made no bones about it: the already staggering problems of keeping the Grande Armée properly supplied and fed could only grow more awesome if it continued its forward march.

For a moment it looked as though the older and wiser heads in his imperial entourage had won out. Every day Napoleon climbed onto his horse and rode out to examine the gullies and ravines guarding Vitebsk's southern and western approaches. He crossed the pontoon bridges his engineers had put together on the Dvina in order to admire the cliffs and precipices falling sheer to the water's edge on the town's northern side. By erecting palisaded trenchworks, bastions, and artillery emplacements, he could build a solid bridgehead on the Dvina's northern bank to offer additional protection. By fortifying Polotsk and other points along the river, he could protect the northern edge of the giant arrowhead he had driven into the flank of the Russian Empire. Seated firmly astride the Dnieper and Berezina rivers, Davout's and Poniatowski's corps could anchor the southern edge on the natural barrier of the Pripet Marshes. Since the intervening area between the Dvina and Dnieper rivers was largely wooded country, it would not be difficult to block the few roads passing through it at their western extremities.

When his brother-in-law Murat came in to protest against his enforced inactivity, Napoleon smiled and said: "The first Russian campaign is over. Let us plant our eagles here. . . . 1813 will see us in Moscow, 1814 in Petersburg. The Russian war is a three-year war." Later that same day he told members of his staff that they would have to get used to the idea of staying in Vitebsk, since he had no intention of repeating the "follies" of King Charles XII of Sweden.

To enliven the monotony of the long winter months, he even spoke of having a troupe of Comédie Française actors and actresses travel all the way from Paris. But as the days passed, his natural impatience returned and he grew increasingly restless at the idea of having to remain holed up in this *masure* —this wretched "hovel" of a town.

Unable to sleep during the hot nights, he would get up without bothering to dress and spend hours poring over candlelit maps, as though they could yield him the secret of what he should do next. During the day he would surprise his three secretaries by suddenly interrupting a letter he was dictating to some minister in Paris or to Maret, who had stayed behind in Vilna with his foreign ministry staff. Walking to the window, he would peer up at the sky. He would pace back and forth, his hands clasped behind his back, return to resume his dictation, then break off as suddenly again, to ask the time or to resume his meditative pacing.

With the members of his staff, and particularly with Berthier, he became increasingly brusque. Well, and what did it matter if unit commanders now had to send out foraging expeditions twenty, thirty, or even forty miles from their bivouac encampments to procure the food and forage they needed? Had he ever said that this would be an easy campaign? His generals, like his quartermasters, surgeons, and doctors, were becoming soft; they were developing cold feet. They wanted featherbeds, an easy life; they hankered after the urbane pleasures of their townhouses in Paris.

Ingenious as ever in conjuring up arguments to justify his pent-up cravings, Napoleon scoffed at the idea that the Russians, in withdrawing to Smolensk, might have been pursuing a calculated plan. They had abandoned Vilna because they had been surprised and outnumbered. They had fled from Drissa because they knew it to be indefensible. They had abandoned Vitebsk because they could not hold it without a union of their forces. The long-awaited moment of battle was thus approaching.

"How can I go into winter quarters in July?" he asked rhetorically. The question, posed in such sarcastic terms, could only be answered in the negative. He himself had no ambition to become another Wellington. It wasn't in his temperament to fight defensive battles. The same went for the French. "Our troops are glad to advance. A war of invasion is something they like. But a prolonged and stationary defense is alien to the French genius. To halt behind rivers, to remain encamped inside huts, to maneuver every day only to be in the same place still after eight months of privations, is it thus that we are wont to wage war?"

Submitted to an implacable logic based on contrary premises, his earlier arguments collapsed. It was an illusion to believe that effective defensive lines could be established along the Dvina and Dnieper rivers. "Once the winter comes, you will see them fill with blocks of ice and disappear beneath the snow."

Those familiar with his ways of thought could recognize the old, familiar obsession, the fear that Europe would treat him "like a little boy," which so often in the past had made it impossible for him to offer concessions to humbled monarchs. All the past arguments and reports which General Rapp in Danzig, Count Beugnot in Düsseldorf, his own brother Jerome in Kassel had earlier submitted, warning of the growing unrest in Germany that prolonged war in Russia was certain to revive, now became reasons for resuming the offensive. To stop now, halfway, would be to court disaster. It would encourage the fatal ferments, which a dazzling victory, on the other hand, would stifle. And so, as Philippe de Ségur was so aptly to put it, Napoleon persuaded himself that "for him the only prudence lay in audacity."

Why stop in Vitebsk for eight months when twenty days would suffice to reach the goal? What did he mean by that? A further advance to Smolensk? No, that would no longer be enough. With his northern flank now threatened by Wittgenstein and new Russian troops sent down from Finland, with his southern right wing under pressure from Tormassov, who could soon be reinforced by Russian troops from the Army of the Danube, it was time to strike hard and fast at the vulnerable heart of Russia. "Let us forestall winter and further reflections! We must strike promptly, for fear of compromising everything. We must be in Moscow in one month, or risk never entering it at all!"

CHAPTER 13

THE BATTLE FOR SMOLENSK

WHILE NAPOLEON was thus debating with himself and with members of his entourage as to the course to follow, a somewhat similar debate was raging in the Russian camp—except that the roles were virtually reversed. For here it was the voice of caution—that of Barclay de Tolly, sarcastically dubbed by Napoleon *le général de la retraite*—which was a lonely voice over and against the hue and cry of the war hawks, led by Bagration, who were all for taking the offensive. Their clamor obscured the basic fact that it was the initial separation of the First and Second armies and their inability to join forces during the first few weeks that had lured Napoleon so far eastward and saved them from a premature and probably catastrophic battle. Indeed, this ironic truth can be pushed even further. Had Napoleon been less intent on keeping the two armies separated—by driving Davout's two-division wedge toward Minsk, Borissov, and Orsha—the Russians might have joined forces at Vitebsk; and then Barclay and his jealous rival Bagration would have had to fight an uncoordinated battle, which they most certainly would have lost.

After slipping out of Vitebsk during the night of July 27–28, Barclay de Tolly reached the northern suburb of Smolensk on August 1. From here one had a fine vantage point for viewing the old fortress city, situated on the Dnieper's southern bank, with its bright-green domes and cupolas, its crenellated battlements, and its many square and polygonal towers. While the various divisions of his First Army bivouacked along the wooded hilltops, Barclay took up residence farther down in the governor general's mansion, located closer to the river and the single bridge joining the northern, residential suburb and the old walled city.

Two days later Bagration came clattering across this bridge in an open carriage, accompanied by an imposing escort of bemedaled generals and aides-de-camp. Apprised by an aide-de-camp of the cavalcade's arrival, Barclay de Tolly hastily donned his ceremonial sash, picked up his sword and general's hat, and came out into the antechamber to greet his rival. A few conciliatory words to the effect that he had been about to go call on Bagration sufficed to break the ice. Soon the two generals were exchanging courtesies, as Bagration praised Barclay's "faultless" withdrawal from Vitebsk, and Barclay complimented Bagration on the skillful manner in which he had eluded the giant trap Napoleon had sought to spring on him. Disarmed by the minister of war's tact, Bagration swallowed his ruffled pride and intimated that he was prepared to place his Second Army under Barclay's overall command.

For several days the old walled city, frequently besieged in the past by Poles as well as Tartars, was so crammed with soldiers of every kind that, as an innkeeper explained to the patriotic German poet Ernst Moritz Arndt, "a mouse could hardly squeeze its way in." Like a number of his fellow countrymen who had decided to seek refuge in Russia, Arndt—whose *Geist der Zeit* (The Spirit of the Times) in 1806 had first sounded the trumpet call of Germanic nationalism against Bonaparte—had clandestinely fled from his native Pomerania and proceeded from Breslau to Prague and from there to Kiev and Smolensk. Eager to promote the formation of a German Legion to be recruited from Grande Armée deserters, he was understandably fascinated by the colorful, Oriental character of the heaving throng of riders he encountered at Smolensk—"handsome Tartars from the Kabarda and Crimea, stately Cossacks from the Don, Kalmucks with flat noses, board-hard bodies, sharp legs and sharp eyes, . . . and maliciously squinting Bashkirs with their bows and arrows. But most splendid of all were a squadron of Circassian cavalrymen, in their breastplates and steel helmets with waving plumes, the finest, slimmest men on the finest horses."

On August 6 an important conference was held in the governor's palace between the commanders of the First and Second armies, assisted by their respective chiefs of staff and quartermasters-general. Grand Duke Constantine, commanding the Imperial Guard, was also present, as was Tsar Alexander's aide-de-camp Baron Ludwig von Wolzogen.

The first to speak at this meeting was Grand Duke Constantine, who had vainly tried to persuade Barclay to have a petition circulated among senior officers soliciting their opinions as to how the war should be conducted—which would have totally undermined the controversial minister of war's grudgingly accepted authority. The grand duke insisted that the two Russian armies, now at last combined, had to go over to the offensive, to counteract the devastating slump in morale pervading all ranks caused by a ceaseless five-week retreat.

This plea was energetically supported by Barclay's acting chief of staff, Colonel Karl von Toll, a competent though somewhat abrasive Estonian who shared the widespread belief that the victor in battle is the one who can establish "internal" (shorter) lines of communication—which now seemed to be the case for the reunited Russians. Bagration, predictably, was all in favor of a bold offensive strategy, as were his two senior staff officers and his friend and former subordinate General Alexei Yermolov. Barclay alone demurred, carefully repeating the tsar's parting words to him at Polotsk, and stressing the point that if his only army was destroyed, Russia would be lost. But realizing how unpopular his withdrawal strategy was at all military levels,

Barclay tentatively agreed to an offensive strategy provided that it was undertaken "with the greatest caution."

When asked by Grand Duke Constantine to state his own opinions, Wolzogen went Barclay one better in expressing reservations. Despite their serious manpower losses, there was good reason to believe that the six infantry and three cavalry corps now under Napoleon's immediate command far outnumbered the 116,000 men available to the two Russian armies of the West. Even more of a drawback was the terrain over which the intended counteroffensive was to be launched. Wolzogen had carefully reconnoitered it during the previous year, and it did not lend itself to a war of maneuver since it was full of woods and swamps.

In the end, a compromise was reached. A general of engineers was ordered to look into the matter of modernizing Smolensk's defenses, while a plan for a concerted attack was rapidly worked out between the assistant chiefs of staff of the two Russian armies and submitted to Barclay de Tolly on the evening of August 7. Although dubious of its merits, he gracefully acquiesced, insisting, however, that the advance against the French be of limited extent and that the two Russian armies maintain a sizable body of their troops not more than three march-days' distance from Smolensk.

That same evening the First Army's five corps moved north and northwestward in the direction of Poretchye and Rudnya, while the Second Army advanced westward along the northern bank of the Dnieper. The news that the Russians were at last taking the offensive was greeted with such elation that the Cossack commander, Ataman Platov, decided to attack immediately. Shortly after daybreak on the eighth a swarm of Cossack and Bashkir horsemen pounced on an unsuspecting French hussar unit at Inkovo, creating such chaos and confusion that the commanding general, Sébastiani, had barely time to jump on his horse and gallop away. But for a spirited flank attack by Prussian uhlans, a valiant holding action by a regiment of Polish lancers, and the last-minute arrival of cavalry and light-artillery reinforcements personally commanded by the prestigious General Montbrun, Sébastiani's cavalry division would have been cut to pieces and surrounded.

Instead of trying to exploit this initial success by mounting a major attack on the French center at Rudnya—which was what had been planned—Barclay de Tolly now ordered a countermarch and moved his forces eastward toward the Poretchye–Smolensk road. He had long believed—and in this, as Clausewitz later pointed out, he was correct—that the greatest danger to Smolensk lay in a strong French drive down this highway, from which Napoleon's forces could branch out eastward to cut the even more vital Smolensk–Moscow road.

The sudden calling-off of the planned attack on Rudnya aroused feelings of dismay in virtually every Russian unit. Russian soldiers had already coined a sarcastic appellation for their aloof and seemingly indecisive minister of war with the strange foreign name—Boltai i tolko—which may be translated roughly as "All talk and nothing more." Just to complicate matters, the Cossacks who had surprised and almost captured General Sébastiani had found among his briefcase papers a message from Murat warning him that the

Russians were preparing a surprise attack. This raised an embarrassing question: how could Murat have been so quickly informed of the Russians' battle plan? Obviously somebody had "talked" and probably deliberately.

It was soon being bruited that the offender was Wolzogen, already a notorious object of suspicion as a foreigner and a supporter of Barclay's defensive tactics. The word "traitor" was soon on everybody's lips, and the hue and cry against him was led by Grand Duke Constantine, who, true to his impulsive form, now turned on the very man he had until recently favored. Barclay himself was not spared, not even by his own chief of staff, Yermolov, who made no secret of his contempt for his commander's sudden "collapse of nerve" and panicky retreat. The retreat grew even more confused when it was learned that Bagration, acting on his own initiative and without informing Barclay, had decided to pull back some of his forces toward Smolensk. (Only years later did Wolzogen learn that the "leak" had come from one of Alexander's aides-de-camp, a Polish prince named Lubomirski, who, after accidentally overhearing several generals discussing the Russian attack plans in the street, had hurriedly sent a message to his mother, in whose country house Murat was billeted, urging her to pack her bags and move elsewhere as quickly as possible.)

While in the Russian camp all was now uproar and confusion, the springs were being methodically wound up to propel the Grande Armée on another forward lunge. News of the sudden Cossack attack on General Sébastiani's advance detachments, far from annoying Napoleon, filled him with elation. So the Russians were now going over to the attack! So much the better. This was just what he wanted to hear. At last they were prepared to do battle. But this battle would be fought on his terms; it would be fought where the Russians least expected it—not in front of them but in their rear.

While Bagration's and Barclay's armies fanned out west and northwest from Smolensk, he would have Ney's Third Corps, his own Imperial Guard, and most of Murat's cavalry proceed by forced marches to the Dnieper, where Davout was now stationed with his five infantry divisions, backed up by Poniatowski's Poles and the Eighth (Westphalian) Corps. Protected from enemy observation by an extensive forest, they stood a good chance of reaching Rossassna and of crossing the Dnieper before Barclay and Bagration realized what was happening. Using the Minsk–Smolensk highway, which was broader than the roads north of the Dnieper, they should be able to reach the "holy" city of Smolensk before the Russians could rush back to defend it.

Once this decision had been made, all traces of the French emperor's previous irritability disappeared. The harassing uncertainties were banished, and he seemed once again supremely confident and serene.

As luck would have it, there was now a change of weather. The stifling heat of the first nine days of August was followed by three days of cooling rains, which made the forced marches more endurable, even if uncomfortably moist.

On August 13 Napoleon himself left Vitebsk with Berthier and the other members of his staff, to join his Imperial Guard divisions on the Dnieper. The sudden convergence on the two chosen crossing-points—Rossassna and

Khomino, a few miles farther east—of more than 100,000 men created the kind of *chacun pour soi* confusion that had marked the second and third days of the Niemen River crossing. There was the same impatience to get across, accompanied by the same casual disregard for priorities. The shallow river was forded with ease, but in the absence of anyone to direct the cannon and caissons moving down the steep embankment ramps, there was endless jostling and confusion. Tempers became so frayed that furious duels were fought between mounted officers, refusing to yield their "right of way."

The disorder rose to a crescendo when the sound of cannon fire up ahead indicated that Ney's leading infantry division had come to grips with the Russians near the town of Krasnoye. To keep an eye on Davout's First Corps units, Bagration had left a division south of the river to guard the approaches to Smolensk. Though undermanned (7,000 soldiers) and composed mostly of raw recruits recently arrived from Moscow, this infantry division was commanded by an able general named Neverovsky.

Driven from the town of Krasnoye by one of Ney's infantry divisions, Neverovsky realized that his only hope of salvation lay in an orderly retreat along the main road leading northeast toward Smolensk, some thirty miles away. This splendid highway, so broad that it could accommodate six to eight carriages traveling abreast, was bordered on each side by a ditch and by two rows of white-barked birch trees, which had been planted there some thirty years before by Catherine the Great's minister, Potyomkin. Already half harvested, with haystacks dotting the landscape, the wheat and rye fields to right and left were ideally suited to cavalry charges, and here Neverovsky's outnumbered dragoons could easily be sabered or lanced down by Murat's horsemen. The Russian dragoons were accordingly called back from the fields and interspersed between the marching columns of infantrymen. Each time Murat ordered another of his squadrons forward, the cavalrymen would charge, the Russian ranks would open as soldiers took refuge behind the trees and ditches lining the highway, reloading and firing as they did so. After a lot of wild but largely ineffective sabering, the French riders would gallop off, leaving a few wounded men and horses. The Russian column would reform and continue its retreat.

The simplest way of dealing with this situation would have been to employ the horse-drawn artillery of Ney's leading division to open deadly breaches in the retreating Russian columns. But as we know from the Württemberger Faber du Faur, who was serving with Ney's 25th Division, each time his 2nd Light Artillery Battery unlimbered its cannon and was about to let fly, Murat would imperiously wave his bejeweled saber, shout *"En avant!"* and send another squadron of horsemen galloping up the highway, obstructing the cannoneers' field of fire.

As a result of Murat's impetuous obtuseness, Neverovsky's infantrymen were able to escape total annihilation on the evening of August 14, when they finally reached the cover of a wooded ravine. Forty successive cavalry charges, each cleverly "absorbed" by opening ranks, had failed to scatter the retreating Russian columns, even though the Russians lost 5 cannon, 700 killed and

wounded, and several thousand prisoners. But the rest—close to 4,000 men—
were able to make it back to Smolensk in time to reinforce its garrison. The
French "victory" at Krasnoye—as it was described in the ninth *Bulletin de
l'Armée*—was in reality a setback for Napoleon. He admitted as much to
certain members of his staff, remarking that Murat in this engagement had
behaved like a student cadet from the officers' training school at Saint-Cyr. As
Tsar Alexander was later to declare, it was Napoleon's flamboyant brother-in-
law who destroyed the French cavalry during the 1812 campaign, long before
the wintry snows set in.

Meanwhile both Bagration and Barclay de Tolly had received express messages from Neverovsky saying that he was being attacked by powerful French
forces. Bagration immediately ordered the most rear-line of his divisions to
march back without delay, cross the bridge into the old city of Smolensk, and
then to march southwest along the Minsk highway to succor Neverovsky.

For the next twenty-four hours the two adversaries continued to have mis-
taken notions about the other's whereabouts and intentions. The Russians,
alerted by reports of troop movements west of the Rabinovichi forest, had
concluded that the French emperor was preparing to celebrate his birthday,
August 15, with a major attack centered some distance north of the Dnieper.
For his part Napoleon, on the basis of information obtained from captured
Russian prisoners, was persuaded that Smolensk was undefended and that
Barclay de Tolly by this time had moved too far north to be able to come to
the city's rescue.

On the evening of the fourteenth drums throbbed, horns and bugles blared
for miles along both sides of the Minsk–Smolensk highway, as bivouacked
regiments celebrated the eve of Napoleon's birthday with repeated cries of
"*Vive l'empereur!*" Using Russian gunpowder from the captured caissons of
Neverovsky's small artillery battery, cannoneers of the French Imperial Guard
marked the occasion with a 101-gun salute. To Murat, Ney, and Davout, who
rode up to convey their birthday greetings, Napoleon declared, "We are going
to take Smolensk. We will cross the Borysthène"—Herodotus' name for the
Dnieper, one commonly used by the French—"in order to fall on the enemy
army, which we shall take from behind."

On the morning of August 15, troops of General Nikolai Rayevsky's corps,
after crossing the Dnieper River bridge and then marching out through the old
city's western gate, met up with Neverovsky's retreating infantrymen several
miles from Smolensk. Not until four o'clock that afternoon did the first French
cavalrymen appear, at which point the Russians prudently drew back to the
old walled city so as not to be outflanked. Together with the small garrison
the Russians now had more than 15,000 men ready to defend Smolensk.

It was with a feeling of joyous relief that Murat's cavalrymen, followed by
Ney's three infantry divisions, finally breasted the tree-dotted slopes lying to
the west and south of Smolensk during the early hours of August 16. A serious
shortage of water had begun to make itself felt for men as well as horses, and
the previous day's march through clouds of dust so thick that "one could cut

it with a knife" (as Heinrich von Brandt later described it) had been extremely painful to reddened eyes and parched lips. In the Dnieper River, here compressed between high banks to a narrowness of 70 yards, there was an abundance of fresh water, but access to it was blocked by the fortress city.

Spread out over a mile-long swell of land, the "holy" city of Smolensk lay in the center of an unevenly shaped bowl formed by a semicircle of hummocks to the south and an even higher range of hills to the north. From their southern vantage point the French could see the trees rising from the old town's many gardens, next to the green and golden cupolas of its dozen churches. Encompassing them like a loose knobbed belt was a line of crenellated battlements extending unbroken from the visible riverbank of the Dnieper to the west to the invisible riverbank farther to the east, hidden by the sharp turn of the ramparts. Eighteen feet thick and between thirty and forty feet high, these walls, composed mostly of poorly whitewashed bricks, were embossed at irregular intervals by bastions—some square, some twelve- or even sixteen-sided —whose polygonal dovecot roof coverings (made of wood) looked distinctly oriental. In all, twenty-nine of these towers were still standing, though only seventeen of them—something Murat and Ney did not know—could still be used for purposes of defense. A dry moat protected the base of the three-mile stretch of ramparts, while a jutting five-sided citadel—known as the "royal bastion" because it had been built by King Sigismond III of Poland in the early seventeenth century—guarded the western approach. Additional protection for the walls was provided by five suburbs, composed of houses, huts, tree-filled orchards, and vegetable gardens, which had spread down the slopes west, south, and east of the city.

Beyond the construction of a wedge-shaped redan, jutting out in front of one of the five gates, little had been done to improve Smolensk's medieval defenses. A few artillery pieces had been positioned behind the citadel's parapets, others had been placed behind points where the old walls had begun to crumble, forming jagged indentations, while one of the gates, as the French were later to discover, was covered from the inside by a horseshoe arc of cannon. But aside from that, everything had to be improvised from scratch.

The Russians' first reaction to the appearance of the French was one of characteristic bravado. A division commander insisted on deploying a few squadrons of dragoons on a slope between the eastern and southern suburbs. Murat, looking more theatrical than ever in his many-feathered musketeer's hat, green velvet dolman, and crimson riding breeches, promptly sent several French cavalry regiments to assail them. The Russian dragoons were finally forced from the field, but, typically enough, they suffered more as they withdrew from a few well-aimed rounds fired at them by General Lubin Griois's artillerymen than from the wild saber-slashing that had preceded the cannonade.

Ney, believing that Smolensk was defended only by the remnants of Neverovsky's division, marched his men forward along the Minsk road and toward the western gate, only to find himself attacked by Russian riflemen posted in the western (Krassny) suburb, bordering the Dnieper. While his *tirailleurs* were assigned the task of driving the Russian marksmen from the suburb, he decided to mount a frontal assault on the pentagonal citadel with an infantry battalion. The attack was repulsed by a hail of bullets and a lethal barrage of cannon fire. Ney, who, as usual, was up front directing operations, was slightly wounded in the neck by a stray bullet, which pierced his stiff, gold-embroidered collar.

From the first captured Russians Ney's interrogators learned that Smolensk was now defended not by Neverovsky but by General Rayevsky, commanding between 15,000 and 20,000 men. This sobering news was soon given visible confirmation in the early afternoon when clouds of dust were spotted moving along the western crest of hills beyond the Dnieper River. The joyous cheers from the Württemberg artillerymen of Ney's 25th Division soon died out when they realized that the dusky columns were neither French nor Westphalian, but another of Bagration's army corps, marching to the relief of the threatened city.

By one o'clock, when Napoleon himself reached the scene, it was clear that Smolensk could no longer be taken by surprise. After a rapid reconnaissance of the uneven terrain, scarred by small gullies and ravines, he had his imperial tent pitched on a birch-shaded knoll about a mile and a half from the city's southeastern extremity. Exchanges of rifle fire and smoky cannonades continued inconclusively throughout the afternoon.

As the sun began to set, advanced detachments of the First Russian Army appeared on the crest of hills above the northern suburb. Setting out at dawn, they had made a forced march of thirty miles. Shortly afterward Barclay de Tolly reached the northern suburb via the Petersburg–Poretchye road. He and Bagration immediately conferred. Barclay's fear once again was that Napoleon might try a right-wing flank attack aimed at cutting the main road to Moscow. He therefore suggested that Bagration march his Second Army eastward to guard the vital bridge at Solovievo, twenty-five miles away, where the Smolensk–Moscow highway recrossed the undulating Dnieper, while leaving a strong rearguard force to guard the highway in the vicinity of Smolensk. Since this left him more or less on his own and not directly subordinated to Barclay, Bagration willingly agreed to the proposal.

During the night Rayevsky's hard-pressed riflemen were quietly withdrawn and replaced by First Army regiments commanded by General Dmitri Dokhturov. Leaving the old walled city via the permanent bridge and two recently erected pontoon bridges, Rayevsky's men wheeled right and marched out of the northern suburb along the Moscow road, to join the rest of Bagration's Second Army. To Barclay and his 75,000 soldiers was now entrusted the fate of Smolensk.

By the early hours of Monday, August 17, three of the Grande Armée's corps, backed up by five divisions of the Imperial Guard, three cavalry corps, and some 500 cannon, howitzers, and mortars, had taken up their positions in a kind of semicircular arc, anchored at each end by the steep cut of the Dnieper River. The left wing was composed of Ney's three infantry divisions; the center, Davout's five infantry divisions; the right wing, Murat's cavalrymen and two of Prince Poniatowski's three infantry divisions (the other having been sent south to besiege the Berezina river fortress of Bobruisk). Prince Eugène's Fourth Corps had been left some distance behind to guard supply trains moving up the Minsk–Smolensk highway, while the Eighth (Westphalian) Corps, which was supposed to back up Poniatowski's Poles, was led by its new commander, Junot, over such an incredibly circuitous route that it failed to show up until the evening of this crucial Monday.

The hostilities began at eight in the morning, when General Dokhturov ordered his infantrymen to stage a surprise sortie and to drive French skirmishers from the southern and southwestern suburbs of Rosslavl and Mstislavl. Napoleon, thinking that the Russians were going to sally forth en masse for a pitched battle, waited all morning, as the sun rose ever higher and the burning heat grew more intense and his waterless soldiers more cruelly wracked by thirst. Finally, his patience exhausted, he ordered a general attack at two in the afternoon.

If the assault had been launched three to four hours earlier, the outcome by the end of this hot, dry day might well have been far more favorable to the French. The frontal assault, in any case, revealed an unusual lack of imagination on the part of Europe's most resourceful military commander.

Soon the entire "front" was ablaze with musketry and cannon fire, as Ney's *tirailleurs* fought their way into the huts and gardens of the Krassny suburb, near the well-defended citadel, while Davout's seasoned troopers, advancing through orchards and scrub brush, pushed the Russian riflemen back from the central suburbs toward the walls and gates of Smolensk. Even more intrepid, to the point of recklessness, were Poniatowski's Poles, who undertook to clear the eastern (Razenka) suburb of the Russians defending its warehouses. It became a point of honor among competing Poles to be able to say that one had advanced all the way to the dry moat and had actually touched the city's walls. But in the absence of scaling ladders there was little these daredevils could do once they had reached such advanced positions, except to withdraw a little later to the safety of some undestroyed warehouse wall or building, in the hope of not being shot in the back by a Russian marksman firing down from one of the crenellated battlements.

Losses were heavy on both sides, and for the French particularly severe on the western and eastern flanks, where Ney's Third Corps soldiers and Poniatowski's Poles were exposed to the devastating cannonades of Russian artillery pieces, set up across the Dnieper in the gardens and promenades of the northern suburb. So thick were the clouds of smoke billowing up from the contested suburbs and battlements that great chunks of the city—including domes, spires, tall trees, and rooftops—disappeared at times from view. To the practiced eye of Captain Fantin des Odoards, who was watching from the hill on which his Imperial Guard grenadiers were bivouacked, this frontal assault resulted in a pointless carnage, which it was painful to hear as well as see. "Drunk on *eau-de-vie*"—by which he presumably meant vodka—"the Russians added their ferocious cries to this dreadful din," he later noted, adding that Dante, had he been present, could have found plenty of inspiration here for his imagined inferno.

Napoleon cantered back and forth, stopping every now and then to peer through his spyglass at a stretch of wall or a gate and to issue another order to one of his duty officers. Davout, acting under his instructions, brought up thirty-six 12-pounders, which began booming away, albeit to little effect. Each cannonball would chip away a few bricks, but the walls being eighteen feet thick, the only result was to set off a "slide" of rubble, which did little to reduce the height of those awe-inspiring battlements. Finally Napoleon called off the wasteful cannonade. The artillery pieces were aimed instead at the crenellations, which disintegrated into streaks of masonry, leaving a more or less toothless ridge, from which Russian marksmen continued to blaze away.

The only significant success was obtained on the right flank when one of Murat's corps commanders led his light cavalry men in a bold attack on a small plateau situated between a patch of wooded ground and the Dnieper. Sixty cannon were brought up, to pound away at the Russian batteries which, from the other bank of the river, had been raking the Polish positions with their fire. The French gunners soon realized that from this newly won position they could aim cannonballs at the bridges which the Russians were using to pour in fresh troops and to evacuate the wounded.

The Russians, realizing the danger, brought up more cannon, and a furious cross-river duel ensued. Later both the French and the Russians claimed that their cannoneers had got the best of it. But by early evening Barclay de Tolly had come to the conclusion that Smolensk could not be held much longer. Daylight passage across the bridges was becoming increasingly hazardous, and if the French gunners managed to destroy them, the 10,000 men defending the old city would have no choice but to surrender.

At the prospect of giving up Smolensk so soon many senior Russian officers began furiously cursing the "cowardly" minister of war. Their leader once again was Grand Duke Constantine. This time he was supported not only by General Bennigsen, but by a recently arrived British hothead, General Sir Robert Wilson, a veteran "observer" of the battles of Eylau and Friedland who now proposed that the Russians stage a massive sortie from the old city, while Ataman Platov's Cossacks crossed the Dnieper a few miles to the west and pounced on the Grande Armée's supposedly unprotected baggage trains. Accompanied by a throng of malcontents, Grand Duke Constantine proceeded to Barclay's headquarters and sought to have him rescind the withdrawal order. But Barclay, refusing to be cowed by a move which came within an ace of mutiny, was adamant. He was not going to indulge in foolhardy sorties, nor was he prepared to write off the lives of 10,000 men in a grim but foredoomed effort to hang on to Smolensk. Already French artillerymen, seeking to silence a Russian cannon that had been firing through an aperture, had opened an alarming breach in one of the bastions. Once they discovered the truth—that the walls of these bastions were only eight feet thick, half as thick as the rest of the ramparts—French gunners were certain to train their fire on these vulnerable points in the old city's fortifications, opening breaches through which their assaulting infantrymen could storm.

Almost punch-drunk from the heady feeling that victory was in their grasp if only they attacked, the rebels were not prepared to listen to rational argu-

ments. Barclay had to remind them crisply that he was in command and that
if he needed their advice, he would call upon them individually to offer it.
Turning to Grand Duke Constantine, he added that he had documents of such
importance to send to the emperor in Petersburg that he felt he could entrust
them only to his brother. This polite way of informing the grand duke that his
disruptive presence was no longer desired and that he was sending him back
to the capital effectively silenced all opposition, though it did not keep a fuming
Ataman Platov from later snarling at Barclay, "You see, I wear only a cloak.
I will never again put on a Russian uniform, since it has become a disgrace."

Toward nine o'clock in the evening the cannon fire began to slacken. But
the deep-blue twilit air continued to be crossed by the reddish arcs of glowing
shells and bombards lobbed by French howitzers and mortars. The Russian
musketeers posted behind the darkening crenellations were now silhouetted
against the glow of rising flames, which made them look "like devils in the
middle of hellfire" (to Major Jean-François Boulart, of the Imperial Guard
artillery). But as the French besiegers, both enthralled and horrified by its
macabre beauty, gazed in wonderment at this pyrotechnic spectacle, it dawned
on them that the flames were too tall and brilliant to have been caused by the
random explosions of their shells and bombards. "The sheaves and ears of corn
which rose with a fiery swoosh and, glowing dark-red, fluttered to and fro in
the black smoke, then gradually paled and finally fell back to earth as exhausted ashes, could only remind one of the eruptions of a fire-spouting
mountain," Heinrich von Brandt was later to write. Others were struck by an
extraordinary blue glow, amid the red and orange—coming from an invisible
depot where a large quantity of sugar had been stored. It was soon joined by
greenish flames, as sacks of salt which had been piled up to barricade one of
the city's gates were also put to the torch.

Soon the entire town was blazing, throwing sparks and ashes and volcanic
pillars of dark smoke into the soft night air, and eerily illuminating the tree-
shadowed hills for miles around. Many, like the artistically inclined Württemberg artillery officer Faber du Faur, were too spellbound by its dramatic beauty
to grasp its full portent. Even Napoleon was momentarily carried away. Accompanied by Berthier and the commander of the Imperial Guard's cavalry,
Marshal Bessières, he watched for a while by his imperial tent, then walked
forward to a campfire, by which an exhausted Caulaincourt had sat down to
warm himself—for though it was mid-August, the nights at this latitude were
cold.

"It's an eruption of Vesuvius!" exclaimed Napoleon, arousing Caulaincourt
from his slumber with a friendly slap on the shoulder. "Is it not a fine sight,
Monsieur le Grand Ecuyer?"

"Horrible, Sire," the grand equerry answered, staggering to his feet.

"Bah!" said Napoleon. "Remember, gentlemen, this adage of a Roman
emperor: 'The corpse of a dead enemy always smells good.' "

Berthier, whose glance crossed Caulaincourt's, raised his eyebrows but said
nothing. Only a few hours before, Napoleon had assured Caulaincourt that if
the Russian generals chose to evacuate Smolensk, "one of their holy cities,"

they would disgrace themselves in the eyes of their countrymen. This would make it possible for him to halt his advance, to fortify Smolensk, to "put Poland under arms," and at a later date of his own choosing to strike at either Petersburg or Moscow. But when Caulaincourt had repeated this to Berthier, urging him to do everything he could to maintain Napoleon in these "wise dispositions," Berthier had answered sadly, "You'll see, they won't outlast the capture of Smolensk."

At dawn the next morning, when the first French scouts clambered over crumbled masonry and blackened bodies and penetrated into the gutted city, there was no one left to defend it. The rubble-littered streets, bordered by still-smoking houses, were empty. The few panic-stricken inhabitants had taken refuge in the churches, from which, still traumatized by the previous night's holocaust, they long refused to budge. Above them the whitewashed tower walls were hideously smudged, but the green and golden cupolas continued to glow like Christmas-tree ornaments against the pale blue sky. The three connecting bridges had vanished—two of them dismantled, the third blown up by departing sappers. Gone too was the Cathedral of the Assumption's most cherished treasure, the "miraculous" ikon of the Virgin, said to have been painted by Saint Luke and brought to Russia by a Byzantine princess. Everything of possible value to the enemy—stocks of grain, sugar, salt—had been systematically gutted, and even the apothecary shops had been emptied of their precious contents by Barclay's retreating soldiers.

Once again Napoleon had been cheated of his prey. He had added one more city—and this time an authentically Russian one—to his list of conquered towns, but it was no more than a burned-out shell.

CHAPTER 14

BLOOD AND DUST

THE NEXT MORNING, after a few brief hours of sleep, Napoleon gave orders to have Smolensk formally invested by his "victorious" regiments. Thousands of French and Russian corpses, many of them hideously charred, littered the gutted suburbs and the dry moat, where they had fallen. From all sides came the yelps and barking of homeless dogs and the clamor of the wounded, trying to make their pathetic voices heard above the martial sound of drums, fifes, trumpets, and the sporadic boom of cannon. Heaps of bodies had to be removed before the old town's gates could be opened, and even then the troops had to watch their step, as they zigzagged around smoldering beams fallen from still-burning houses.

"Never, since the start of operations, had we encountered such a sight," Laugier de Bellecour, an Italian officer of Piedmontese extraction, was later to recall. "Preceded by our musicians, proud but frowning, we passed these ruins where wounded Russians lay covered in blood and dirt. . . . How many men were burned and asphyxiated! . . . On the thresholds of spared dwellings the wounded beseeched us to help them. . . . The dead, the dying, the wounded, the living, men, bearded ancients, women, and children filled the cathedral. Entire families clad in rags, their terror-stricken faces streaked with tears, were clustered around the altars, weakened, famished, worn out. Everyone trembled at our approach."

Napoleon himself chose to ride into the scarred city via a breach on the eastern side, later dismounting to enter a bastion overlooking the river. Here he spent several hours training his spyglass on the northern suburb, still solidly held by rearguard units of Barclay de Tolly's First Army. Major Jean-François Boulart, of the Imperial Guard artillery, also headed for the northern ramparts, which, unlike other stretches of wall, were relatively undamaged. When he and his companions reached the gate leading to the bridge across the river, they found it closed. Beyond they could hear the sound of musketry. He climbed the stairs to a kind of garret above the gate, and looking out through an oval window, which one had to approach with care, he spied the river, the remains of the gutted bridge, and the northern suburb spread out over its upward-sloping hill. Russian marksmen, concealed behind ruined walls and riverbank willow trunks, were returning the fire of French soldiers firing from the parapets of the old city. Near him Boulart saw a French officer, wearing a colonel's epaulets, post himself by an embrasure and begin blazing away. He asked who this marksman was, and was amazed to be told that it was Marshal Davout.

Among the first to reach this gate had been the Württembergers of the 25th Division and several Portuguese battalions of Ney's Third Corps. They were now ordered to ford the Dnieper some distance downstream from the city. Holding their muskets in the air, they managed to wade through the chest-high water, urged on by French staff officers, who preferred to remain on the dry ground. The previous day the Württembergers had been decimated by Russian artillery pieces firing from the other bank as they stormed the cemetery of the western (Krassny) suburb. Now they were subjected to a no less withering fire from Russian musketeers, shooting from windows and house corners, and from behind garden tree trunks. "Well, Herr Leutnant," Karl von Suckow heard his brigade commander say to the sassy young officer who, at the farewell banquet, had dared predict that the coming campaign would be a walkover, "how goes it with your picnic?"

Marshal Ney, taking personal charge, had his Württemberg artillerymen drag their cannon up through the corpse-strewn streets of the Krassny suburb and reposition them between two bastions along a tumbledown stretch of the old city's wall. Here they were able to rake one of the northern suburb's main thoroughfares with grapeshot, while crouching to avoid Russian bullets whistling overhead.

To the heat of the afternoon sun was soon added the torrid crackle of blazing houses. By seven in the evening the first French pontoon bridge was strung across the Dnieper slightly downstream from the city. But large sections of the northern suburb were now burning so fiercely that the Württembergers had to fall back to protect the bridgehead. As the flames licked relentlessly forward along the wood-paved street, they engulfed the writhing bodies of the wounded.

The fire did nothing to dampen the ardor of Russian gunners farther up the hill, who kept spraying the riverfront area with shells and bombards. Seated in the courtyard of a suburban house that had recently been commandeered for his quartermaster staff by Napoleon's minister secretary of state, Pierre Daru, his kinsman Henri Beyle (the future novelist Stendhal) watched half a dozen grenadiers of the Imperial Guard punch holes in the shingle roofing, and then, emerging like "pulpit preachers," lay about them with long poles to scatter the red-hot embers that threatened to ignite it.

This second major conflagration provided a flaming smokescreen behind which Barclay de Tolly's First Army could begin its planned retreat. All Napoleon had been able to determine, after several hours of intense spyglass-scanning from various observation points, was that Barclay's troops were withdrawing northward up the road to Poretchye, apparently headed for Petersburg.

· · ·

Napoleon was not the only one to be mystified by Barclay de Tolly's tactics. Carl von Clausewitz later confessed that he could not understand why Barclay had not dispatched most of his First Army eastward along the Moscow highroad during the morning and early afternoon of August 18. But Barclay seems to have decided that he could not risk exposing his marching columns to the fire of French artillery batteries posted east of the old city of Smolensk along the two-mile escarpment commanding the Moscow highroad, which at this point ran perilously close to the Dnieper's northern bank. He also seems to have felt that his First Army soldiers needed a rest, after the grueling forced march they had made on the sixteenth and the exhausting battle many of them had had to sustain in the suburbs of Smolensk through much of the seventeenth. By the evening of the eighteenth the Moscow highroad could no longer be approached directly, so furious was the blaze engulfing the riverfront area of the northern suburb through which it passed.

Moving 70,000 men and close to 500 artillery pieces over a single road requires a great deal of time. Barclay therefore decided to split his First Army into two columns and to have them march north and then east along two separate, curving routes to join up with the rear guard of Bagration's Second Army. Two of his five army corps, along with the First Army's reserve artillery, were accordingly sent up the Petersburg road for a distance of seven miles and ordered to veer toward the right and to follow a series of minor roads that would eventually bring them out onto the main Smolensk–Moscow road near the Dnieper River crossing at Solovievo. The three other infantry corps, with Barclay and his headquarters staff, were to set off two hours later (nine that evening) along a shorter, semicircular route branching off from the Petersburg highway two and a half miles beyond the northern suburb's limits.

Distrusting Bagration and not knowing how strong a rearguard force he had left behind to guard the Smolensk–Moscow road, Barclay decided to send out an advance detachment of six infantry battalions, two Cossack regiments, and several light-artillery batteries under the command of one of his brigade generals, Pavel Tuchkov, and of his operational chief of staff, Colonel Toll. Following the shorter route, they were to secure the village of Lubino, where it joined the Moscow highroad, eight miles east of Smolensk. But for this wise precaution, the First Army would have been in very serious trouble, and a good part of it might have been destroyed.

If Barclay had been more familiar with the hilly ground northeast of Smolensk, he would have thought twice before dispatching three of his army corps via this shorter route. The primitive country road cut across four successive valley streams and ridges as well as stretches of soggy marshland, which made passage at night extremely hazardous for cannon and artillery caissons. During the descent of the first steep hill four two-wheeled ammunition carts and two 12-pound cannon plunged out of control, carrying the struggling horses to their death. Ropes gripped by soldiers had to be hitched to all succeeding caissons and gun-carriages to keep them from gaining too much downhill momentum, and to limit further accidents the cannoneers had to wait till daybreak to continue the descent. In the soggy valley bottoms the rickety wooden bridges had to be buttressed with beams torn from the nearest peasant huts. General Tuchkov's 4,000 men were repeatedly forced to halt, and it took them some thirteen hours to cover a distance of thirteen miles.

When they finally came out onto the main Moscow road at eight in the morning on August 19, there was another surprise in store for them. Instead of posting a strong rearguard force across this vital highway and ordering it to stay put until it had been joined by the vanguard of the First Army, Bagration had casually instructed its commander to march eastward toward Dorogobuzh as soon as the leading First Army detachments came into view. It was as though, to keep his Second Army from being contaminated, he had willfully decided to put as much distance as he could between it and Barclay's First Army of the West.

But this, as it turned out, was only the beginning of the Russians' tribulations. One corps, commanded by General Ostermann-Tolstoy, set out along the shorter route four hours later than scheduled, and then, followed by another corps, lost its way during the early stages of the night march. The two corps made a 180-degree instead of a 90-degree turn, their nocturnal march describing a loop that brought them back at daybreak to within a mile or two of Smolensk's northern suburb.

Clearly audible to the dismayed Russians was the sound of bugle calls and drums, coming from the direction of this suburb. The march music was French, and the tirailleurs who soon appeared formed the vanguard of Marshal Ney's three infantry divisions.

At this point Barclay de Tolly fortuitously appeared. Worn out by the nervous strain of the past three days—on Tuesday, the seventeenth, the only food he had had to sustain him was a bowl of milk—the commander of the First Army had fallen asleep in his carriage, guided by a driver who was as lost as the others. Only now did the general realize how far he and his men had gone astray. Immediately he altered the line of march of his regiments, redirecting them northeastward toward Gorbunovo. Then, in a move designed to lure the French away from the Smolensk–Moscow highroad, he ordered Tsar Alexander's cousin, Prince Eugen of Württemberg, who though only twenty-four had already proved himself an able battlefield commander, to stage a diversion with three infantry regiments, half a squadron of hussars, and a battery of four field guns.

Thinking that the Russians were preparing a major flank attack on his advancing columns, Ney halted his advance guard and began to deploy his forces for battle. Though this was the sensible thing to do, it was a tactical mistake, delaying by several hours the eastward march of his soldiers. Bitter fighting followed—the first stage of what the French later called the battle of Valutina Gora. For more than an hour Prince Eugen's Russians managed to repulse repeated French attacks, each time forcing Ney to commit more men. In so doing they slowed down the French advance along the Moscow highroad, gaining precious time for Barclay.

Not until midday did Ney's infantrymen, advancing eastward up the highway, begin their attack on General Pavel Tuchkov's small rearguard force of

4,000 men. The latter had spread themselves out along an undulating crest of hills, which cut across the west–east highroad, eight miles from Smolensk. By this time the marching columns of the First Russian Army's Third Corps had finally reached the highway. Immediately they were dispatched westward to keep Ney's forces from breaking through to the junction of Lubino—which would have spelled disaster for a good part of the First Army, including the almost certain loss of sixty artillery pieces, immobilized in a narrow valley.

When news was brought to him that thousands of Grande Armée troops were pouring across the Dnieper five miles upstream from Smolensk and that they would soon be in a position to cut the Moscow highroad, even Barclay de Tolly seemed to lose his iron nerve. "All is now lost," he admitted to Friedrich von Schubert, the operational chief of staff of one of his rearguard units. But then, with a courage born of desperation, he galloped to the next command post and took personal charge of the defense. From then on, "he was here, there and everywhere until sunset," as his former critic, Sir Robert Wilson, was to write in a belated burst of admiration. "Overwhelmed with shells, shot and musketry," a Russian detachment "flew back behind the crest of the hill"—at which point "General Barclay opportunely arrived . . . and seeing the extent of the danger to his column, galloped forward, sword in hand, at the head of his staff (including myself . . .) . . . and rallying fugitives, and crying out, 'Victory or death! We must preserve this post or perish!' by his energy and example reanimating all, recovered possession of the height, and thus, under God's favour, the army was preserved."

By mid-afternoon Ney's infantrymen were finding the going increasingly rough across a series of north–south hills, each more fiercely defended than the last. With the exception of the broad Smolensk–Moscow highway, the few country roads in the area, like the hills and valleys, ran from north to south, greatly impeding the deployment of French artillery pieces. Napoleon, who that morning had traveled up the Petersburg road in pursuit of Barclay de Tolly, had since joined Ney's and Murat's command post on a hill slightly north of the Moscow highroad four miles from Smolensk. To assist Ney's hard-pressed troopers, he ordered two of Davout's infantry divisions to join the battle. But at five o'clock, he rode impatiently back to his headquarters in Smolensk, apparently convinced that Ney, with the help of Davout's veterans, would soon rout this obstinately resisting Russian rear guard. Little did he guess that an entire Russian army corps was now pitted against the French, and that two other corps were debouching onto the highway just behind.

Murat, meanwhile, had been having trouble with the new commander of the Eighth (Westphalian) Corps, Napoleon's old friend and comrade-in-arms, Andoche Junot. General Junot, whose soldiers were relatively fresh and rested, had been ordered to cross the Dnieper some five miles upstream, near the village of Pruditchino, and to threaten the Russians' line of retreat. This was the outflanking movement Barclay de Tolly had so rightly feared, which had caused him to say, "All is now lost!" What Barclay could not have foreseen is that once across the Dnieper, Junot, so fearless in the past, would suddenly refuse to advance any farther.

There is a mystery here that has never been properly elucidated. Junot's wife later claimed that he had received so many saber cuts around neck, cheeks, and ears that he was no longer quite right in the head. This may well have been the case. Two days before, when he had finally turned up at imperial headquarters after wandering for hours in the forests south of Smolensk, he had looked singularly glassy-eyed as he begged for water and complained of sunstroke. But there may have been other reasons for Junot's indecisiveness during this crucial afternoon of August 19. A Livonian hussar officer, Carl von Martens, who had been sent by Barclay to reconnoiter the vulnerable spots where the Dnieper could be forded east of Smolensk, happened to stumble on a formidable concentration of enemy troops—almost certainly the soldiers of the Eighth (Westphalian) Corps, who were about to cross the Dnieper. Hurriedly recrossing the river, Martens had his trumpeters sound their bugles for an "assembly call," hoping to persuade the enemy that the hillside woods immediately north of the Dnieper were alive with Russian soldiers. In his memoirs he claims that this ruse helped to save the Russian army from disaster.

One thing is certain. When Murat, whose cavalrymen were having trouble deploying over this hilly and heavily wooded terrain, came galloping up to Junot's command post and implored him to advance, crying: "This is the chance of a lifetime. Seize it! You are sure to win your marshal's baton!" Junot stubbornly refused to budge. The only Westphalians willing to follow Murat's lead were the horsemen of General Hans Friedrich von Hammerstein's cavalry brigade. But before they could be properly deployed for a charge against the elite hussar units opposing them, the Russians had positioned a few artillery pieces along the Smolensk–Moscow highway. Several furious mêlées ensued in clouds of blinding dust, as the fast-riding Russians, simulating retreat on their fleet mounts, led the Westphalians past their gunners, who maintained a deadly fire "with the precision of a parade-ground exercise," as Eduard Rüppell was later to describe it. Lacking the artillery support that Junot's infantrymen should promptly have provided, Hammerstein and his cavalrymen could do no more than beat an inglorious retreat.

By five that evening upward of 50,000 men were locked in a battle for the final crest guarding the Gorbunovo–Tishinino road, down which the columns of the First Army continued to stream. For a while the Russians managed to push back the French attackers. General Gudin, at the head of one of Davout's divisions, had one entire leg and the shin of another torn off by a cannonball as he led his men across a bridge raked by Russian artillery fire. (He died three days later.) His bayonet-wielding soldiers finally stormed the height, wounding and capturing the valiant General Tuchkov after nine successive charges. But this belated triumph came too late to matter. Junot, whose idle soldiers could have wreaked havoc with a devastating flank attack, still refused to budge.

When the sun finally set at nine o'clock, the French were astride the last of the wooded ridges, but Barclay's First Army, having escaped destruction, was withdrawing eastward in good order along the Moscow highway. It was already midnight when Napoleon's aide-de-camp Gaspard Gourgaud returned to imperial headquarters in Smolensk to report on what had happened. The news that Junot had let everybody down provoked an outburst of anger. "I don't want him to go on commanding the Westphalians," exclaimed Napoleon to Berthier. "He must be replaced by Rapp, who speaks German and will lead them well."

What he did not say was that here too the blame was ultimately his. Had he restored Vandamme to his original command of the Westphalians after his own tiff with Jerome, there is little doubt that that truculent, bullheaded general would not have stopped until he had put his Westphalians across the Moscow highroad and had seriously mauled at least one of Barclay de Tolly's retreating army corps.

Early the next morning Napoleon rode out again to the scene of the previous day's battle to decorate the officers and soldiers of Ney's and Davout's infantry divisions. The hills for miles around were strewn with upset wagons, scattered weapons and utensils, cannonballs, torn uniforms, dismembered limbs, and the corpses of dead horses, which, as they grew rigid, rolled onto their backs, with their stiff legs sticking up into the air. The Russian dead could be distinguished from the French, for their peasant heads were shaved. Many corpses were half naked, having been stripped during the night of their uniforms and finery by marauding Cossacks, and, if General Anton Gjisbert van Dedem is to be trusted, by some of Murat's cavalrymen, who were ordered to strip away as many French uniforms as possible in order to conceal the magnitude of French losses. If this is true, then the ruse worked brilliantly. For to General Etienne Gérard, who had succeeded the mortally wounded Gudin as commander of the Third Division, Napoleon declared, "This is how I like a battlefield to look: four Russians to every Frenchman!"

To what extent Napoleon here was indulging in wishful thinking, it is not easy to say, so great was the subsequent discrepancy in the estimates of losses reckoned up on either side. Squadron Leader Eugène Labaume, who entered the old city of Smolensk the day after it was taken, claimed that for every French corpse he saw there were five or six Russian dead. Less adept in concealing themselves than the more agile and experienced French, the Russians were further handicapped by the stiff slugs of vodka they imbibed before rushing into battle, which made them recklessly brave but wildly inaccurate in shooting.

In his memoirs Napoleon's chief surgeon, Dominique Larrey, put the number of French casualties during the battle for Smolensk at 1,200 killed and 6,000 wounded, or a total of 7,200, which was probably close to the truth. Wolzogen, on the other hand, claimed that the August 17 battle for Smolensk cost the French 12,000 dead and wounded, compared with 7,000 Russian casualties, while the August 19 battle at Valutina Gora–Lubino cost the French 9,000 killed and wounded, compared with only 5,000 for the Russians. Clausewitz, citing even more inflated figures, reckoned that in the two battles the Russians lost 30,000 men, while the French lost 36,000 (including stragglers and marauders who were left behind or ambushed by Cossacks when the Grande Armée resumed its forward march). But whereas the Russians, during their continuing retreat, were reinforced with 20,000 fresh troops from various recruiting centers, Napoleon's forces were further weakened by the need to send one of Prince Eugène's Italian divisions (8,000 men) back to guard Vitebsk, and to leave another, Young Guard division (6,000 men) behind to garrison Smolensk.

Although Clausewitz's figures for battlefield losses were almost certainly inflated, his overall estimates help to explain how an army that numbered close to 182,000 before the battle of Smolensk had been reduced to some 130,000 three weeks later (his figures). Whereas the Grande Armée enjoyed an incontestable superiority in numbers prior to the battle for Smolensk, this was no longer the case on the eve of the battle of Borodino. For the French, therefore, Smolensk and Valutina Gora could at best be considered Pyrrhic victories— the real victors in each case being Barclay de Tolly and the retreating Russians.

On August 21 it was the Poles' turn to be honored by Napoleon for the exemplary valor they had displayed during the battle for Smolensk. But their ranks, like those of Ney's Third Corps, looked woefully thinned as they stood for review, behind their white-eagled flags and banners, near their bivouac area beyond the old city's eastern battlements. A no longer grudging and grumbling French emperor was this time lavish in according promotions and awarding decorations, including eighty-six crosses of the coveted Légion d'Honneur.

To the Poles this seemed to be Napoleon's day of atonement, in which he sought to make up for the harsh, unjustified reproaches of the past. But to their often troubled and tormented commander, Prince Joseph Poniatowski, the gratification was distinctly short-lived. For before the day was over, it was marred by another acrimonious altercation, which showed how obdurate, short-tempered, and obtuse Napoleon could be when his "superior wisdom" was questioned. Once again the commander of the Grande Armée's Fifth Corps was forced to submit to the dictates of his suzerain, who, in preferring the dazzling and "sublime" (the capture of Moscow) to more mundane considerations (of food and fodder), seemed more than ever to have forgotten that an army marches on its stomach.

Relations between the two had been distinctly strained since early July, when Poniatowski had dared to complain of the dire condition of his unpaid and undernourished soldiers, and had been stingingly rebuked by Napoleon. To the sensitive Polish prince, who was subject to fits of depression, this must have seemed a cruel reward for loyalty. In June, shortly before the outbreak of hostilities, Tsar Alexander had sent Colonel Karl Friedrich von Toll from Vilna to Poniatowski's headquarters with a secret message offering him the highest office in a future Polish kingdom (to be set up under Russian auspices) if he would renounce his command of the Grande Armée's Fifth Corps and take no part in the invasion of Russia. Poniatowski had told the tsar's confidential emissary that there could be no question of his betraying Napoleon.

Too often in the past he had been suspected by his fellow countrymen of favoring one or another of Poland's territorial "partitioners" to be able to embark again on this slippery path. Thanks to the strange circumstances of his birth (he was born in Vienna, son of a Czech countess) and to his equivocal kinship to Poland's last, weak-willed king (he was the favorite nephew of Stanislaw Augustus Poniatowski), Prince Joseph was the only living Pole to have served an Austrian emperor as colonel and aide-de-camp, to have been awarded the most prestigious of Prussian decorations, the Black Eagle, and to have been named lieutenant general and honorary commander of the Kazan Cuirassier Regiment in the Russian army. Each of the occupying powers had thus sought, at one time or another, to make a "client" of him.

Lucid enough to realize that Napoleon was Poland's only hope, Poniatowski could not easily forget that he had once called him "the murderer of the Polish legions" (a reference to the 2,000 Poles whom the French first consul had sent to their deaths in Santo Domingo in 1802). Thousands of other Poles had been consumed in the four-year war in Spain without tangible benefit to their partitioned country. What guarantee was there that Napoleon might not again be using Poles for his own imperial purposes rather than for the restoration of their bygone kingdom?

The auspices, during the early weeks of the 1812 campaign, were anything but bright. During his three-week stay in Vitebsk Napoleon had treated one of Poniatowski's aides-de-camp to a tirade in which he and his Polish soldiers were dismissed as slow-moving bunglers. There had been a later flare-up when the French emperor, dismayed to learn that the Fifth Corps had only 15,000 men left for the assault on Smolensk, had angrily exploded, "You are only good for living it up with your Warsaw *danseuses!*" (Some Polish officers present even claimed that Napoleon had used a stronger word, *putains,* meaning "harlots.") Poniatowski and his infuriated suite had returned to their bivouacs in a seething rage. The next day they had shown the mettle they were made of by driving the Russians from the eastern (Razenka) suburb and seizing the strategic Dnieper embankment, from which their fusiliers could train their flintlocks on the old city's bridge. The bitter fighting had cost them sixty officers, including a brigade general (Grabowski), and 2,000 dead and wounded soldiers.

Napoleon's belated recognition of the Poles' fighting qualities did nothing to calm Poniatowski's misgivings about the future course of the campaign. The idea of heading for Moscow did not appeal to him at all. The Poles in the late sixteenth and early seventeenth centuries, when their kingdom was at the apex of its glory, had occupied Moscow for a few years, but had soon been forced to relinquish it. On the other hand, the fertile plains of Volhynia and Podolia, west and south of the Pripet Marshes, had been Polish for several centuries, and Poniatowski was persuaded that if they were now invaded, their inhabitants would rise in revolt against their Russian masters, just as the Galicians had done against the Austrians in 1809.

General Jan-Henrik Dombrowski, whose 16th Division had been sent down the Berezina to lay siege to Bobruisk, had long favored such a course. But Poniatowski's most powerful ally in this respect was the man who had originally launched the recruiting and training of the Grand Duchy of Warsaw's military forces in 1807–1808, the man who—like his rival and enemy, Murat —had for a brief moment thought he might be made king of Poland, Marshal Louis Nicolas Davout.

Shortly after the review and decorations-dispensing ceremony of August 21, Poniatowski, accompanied by Davout, called on Napoleon and sought to persuade him that the Russian Empire's Achilles' heel was the Ukraine, from which it derived its grain, its fodder, and its horses. If allowed to join Dombrowski in his assault on the fortress of Bobruisk, he felt confident that the Poles of the reunited Fifth Corps could drive on southward to Kiev and foment a massive insurrection against Russian rule, thus significantly expanding the recruiting effort being made in Lithuania and providing the Grande Armée with the grain and forage it needed for its undernourished men and horses.

Napoleon did not take kindly to this suggestion. He reminded Poniatowski that everything had gone well for Charles XII of Sweden's invasion of Russia in 1708 until he had decided to turn south; the result had been Poltava. The imperial Court in Vienna would be understandably alarmed to see a Polish army invade Volhynia and Podolia, fanning a spirit of revolt which was certain to spread by contagion to the neighboring provinces of Austrian Galicia.

The more Poniatowski pleaded, the more annoyed Napoleon became. He was not used to having his corps commanders question his political alliances, and he was infuriated rather than touched when Poniatowski, in a gesture worthy of a medieval vassal, got down humbly on one knee and craved his imperial permission to mount an assault on Kiev. "No," shouted Napoleon angrily, "you are not going to Kiev, and if you dare make any such move, I shall not hesitate to have you shot!"

As ill luck would have it for Poniatowski, news had just reached Napoleon that, some 300 miles away, Prince Karl Schwarzenberg had teamed up with General Jean-Louis Reynier, commander of the Grande Armée's Seventh (Saxon) Corps, to defeat General Tormassov and several divisions of his Third Russian Army near Kobryn (west of the Pripet Marshes). Originally, when Schwarzenberg had volunteered to lead the Austrian military force that was to participate in the campaign, it had been understood that he and his 30,000 men would fight under Napoleon's direct command. Napoleon had in fact wanted the Austrians to join Davout's divisions on the Berezina River. But he had been forced to change his plans after learning that Tormassov, whose Third Russian Army he had always discounted, had surprised a Saxon brigade on the edge of the Pripet Marshes, had forced its commander to surrender, and was poised to invade the Grand Duchy of Warsaw. Schwarzenberg had then been ordered to move back to help General Reynier and his Saxons. His subsequent victory over Tormassov reinforced Napoleon's confidence in the Austrian prince's reliability as a battlefield commander.

This too was an error of judgment Napoleon was to have occasion to regret. It was, as General Pierre Berthezène was to write, a serious psychological error to entrust the defense of the Duchy of Warsaw and the Grande Armée's southern line of communication to an Austrian (Schwarzenberg), naturally antipathetic to the Poles. By the time Napoleon had reached Smolensk, the distance between their respective positions—about 300 miles—made it practically impossible to have the Poles backtrack toward Brest Litovsk, while Schwarzenberg's Austrians proceeded by forced marches to join the rest of the Grande Armée. The Kiev thrust proposed by Poniatowski might have provided a compromise solution. But since the Grande Armée by now was too weak to be able to mount a simultaneous twin-pronged offensive, a choice had to be made between Kiev and Moscow. The die had in fact been cast as far back as Vitebsk, and with Moscow only 260 miles away, all Napoleon needed was some new justification for not remaining in Smolensk.

The week Napoleon spent in Smolensk (August 18 to 24) was one of feverish activity. Simply clearing the streets of human corpses and the carcasses of dead horses took several days. A new military governor had to be appointed to oversee the administration of the ruined city and measures taken to assure its defense. Working round the clock, Dominique Larrey and the doctors and surgeons of his six mobile "ambulance" units tried desperately to tend to the needs of more than 10,000 wounded French, allied, and Russian soldiers, who were dumped more or less pell-mell into fifteen large buildings, transformed into makeshift hospitals. By the end of the first day Larrey and his assistants were reduced to using paper from the local archives on which to lay the sick, parchments to make splints, and cotton derived from birchwood to replace nonexistent supplies of lint.

Once again many Grande Armée soldiers had to make do with whatever they could find in undamaged larders or cellars. Weeks of hardships and privations, forced marches, dire shortages of forage, bread, and even water, the ravages of dysentery, and now the substantial losses sustained in two bloody battles led many, particularly among old-timers, to hope that they would stop at Smolensk, or return to Vilna to prepare the following year's campaign, which would see their triumphal entry into Moscow and Petersburg. "Grumbling could be heard on all sides," Anatole de Montesquiou later recalled. "Several of those very generals whom we had previously found so pliant to the Emperor's orders, so confident in his successes and so full of reverence for his glory, now greeted us harshly when they saw officers bringing them orders. 'Well, so it's *En avant,* is it?' they would say ironically. '*En avant, en avant, toujours en avant!* But hasn't he had enough of it by now? Will he ever have enough of it?'"

After sending off a snorting reprimand to Marshal Oudinot, guilty of entertaining "the most extravagant notions about Wittgenstein's forces," Napoleon was jolted by the news that the intrepid commander of his Second Corps had been seriously wounded by these same contemptible forces and that the town of Polotsk had almost been captured by them. It was in a way unfortunate for the Grande Armée that this had not happened; for the fall of Polotsk might have given Napoleon pause and have forced him to put off his further drive toward Moscow. But Oudinot's temporary reverse had been brilliantly avenged by a surprise counterattack, which had sent a catnapping General Wittgenstein and his unwary Russians reeling back in confusion. In a grateful letter of commendation sent to the austere, unloved, but supremely competent commander of the Sixth Corps, who had engineered this feat, Napoleon informed General Gouvion Saint-Cyr that he was being awarded the coveted marshal's baton.

. . .

On Monday, August 24, Napoleon received word from Murat that the Russians were digging in near the town of Dorogobuzh, some fifty-five miles east of Smolensk. This was all Napoleon needed to order a new advance.

Of the many marches made during the 1812 campaign this seems to have been one of the most painful for pursuers and pursued. There was no letup in the dog-days heat, and once again there was a cruel shortage of water. For the advancing columns of the Grande Armée, as Philippe de Ségur later noted, meat was in less short supply than bread because of the "meat on the hoof" that was prodded along by soldiers armed with whips and sticks in the wake of each regiment and brigade. "But the length and above all the rapidity of the marches caused many of these animals to be lost; they were suffocated by the heat and the dust, and when they encountered water, they rushed at it with such fury that many of them drowned. Others filled themselves so immoderately with it that they swelled up and soon could no longer walk."

The still-warm carcasses of exhausted horses, promptly chopped up and thrown into French caldrons or roasted over campfires, were virtually the only presents that Barclay's retreating Russians left behind for Murat's advance-guard cavalrymen; for all their efforts, they were unable to catch a single prisoner for interrogation. Carabineers as well as breastplated cuirassiers, often mounted on emaciated steeds or incongruously small horses, had been sent forward to beef up Murat's light cavalry, all to no avail. Here, as at Vitebsk, the Cossacks consistently outrode the French, skillfully delaying their counter-charges until late afternoon or evening, by which time they had exhausted their opponents. Each day a few more Grande Armée cavalrymen were thus lost, killed or wounded and forced to surrender.

For the infantry, who enjoyed less freedom of movement, the going was even rougher. Veterans who had fought under Napoleon in Egypt claimed that the heat here was more ferocious than in the valley of the Nile. Years later, in looking back on these dry, canicular weeks, Heinrich von Brandt expressed his amazement at the lack of interest shown by military analysts in the "dust factor." On the basis of his personal experience he could declare that a freezing temperature of 6 degrees or 8 degrees below zero (centigrade) was easier to endure than the thirst and choking grit he and his companions had to put up with during the forced marches eastward from Smolensk. So thick were the clouds of dust that the marchers could hardly see the birch trees lining the broad highroad beyond a distance of thirty yards. By the time they reached Dorogobuzh their eyes were luridly bloodshot. The French soldiers preceding them picked up every scrap of glass they could find, and by enclosing the pieces in makeshift leather "mounts" or by surrounding them with canvas, they fashioned protective "spectacles" to shield their smarting eyeballs. Others, carrying the shako under one arm, bound their heads with towels, leaving an aperture through which to see and breathe. Still others sought to shade their blistering foreheads with wreaths of birch leaves wound over their ears. Each breath of cooling breeze was greeted with cries of grateful relief as this exotically blinkered, turbaned, and garlanded host tramped forward through the dust.

From these various tribulations Napoleon, needless to say, was cushioned by the amenities of his imperial household. Having left Smolensk at one o'clock in the morning of August 25, he was able to reach Dorogobuzh in the middle of that afternoon, after twelve hours spent in a closed carriage. Here he was considerably put out to learn that Barclay's Russians once again had vanished. Murat's claim that they had been digging in to make a stand was just one more Neapolitan mirage. But now that Napoleon had put close to sixty miles between himself and Smolensk, less than ever could there be any question of his turning back. "Peace lies before me," he declared to Berthier and other members of his entourage. "We are only eight days from it. Being so close to the goal, there is no reason to deliberate any further. Let us march on Moscow!"

Napoleon, sketched by
Girodet, March 1812

Military review in the court
of the Carrousel, as painted
by Bellangé

Dowager Empress Maria Feodorovna (mother of Alexander I); engraving from painting by Lampi

King Frederick I of Württemberg, brother of Maria Feodorovna; engraving from painting by von Seele

Prince Alexander Borisovich Kurakin, Russian ambassador to Paris; painting by Borivokovsky

Grand Duchess Catherine (Alexander's favorite sister); miniature by Dubois

Colonel Count Alexander Ivanovich Chernyshov;
painting by Lieder

Count Nikolai Rumiantsev, Russian chancellor;
painting by George Dawe

General Armand de Caulaincourt, French
ambassador to St. Petersburg; portrait by Gérard

Empress Elisabeth (wife of Alexander I), by
unknown painter

Emperor Francis I of Austria (father of Marie-Louise); engraving from painting by Fendi

Marie-Louise, Empress of the French (Napoleon's second wife); portrait by Gérard

View of Dresden, showing bridge across Elbe, royal palace, and baroque Hofkirche; painting by Bernardo Bellotto

Grand Duke Constantine; painting by George Dawe

Bottom left: King Frederick William III of Prussia; engraving from painting by Gérard

Bottom right: Count Louis de Narbonne, aide-de-camp to Napoleon and special diplomatic emissary; miniature by unknown painter

Prince Joseph Poniatowski, commander of Grande Armée's Fifth Corps, minister of war of the Grand Duchy of Warsaw; lithograph by Lemoine

Left: Prince Adam Czartoryski, former Russian foreign minister; painting by Oleshkevich

Jerome, king of Westphalia (Napoleon's youngest brother), commander of Grande Armée's Fifth, Seventh, and Eighth Corps; painting by Gros

Prince Eugène de Beauharnais, viceroy of Italy; painting by Scheffer

Colonel Karl Friedrich von Toll (Barclay de Tolly's acting chief of staff), painting by George Dawe

Crossing of the Niemen; engraving by Faber du Faur

General Mikhail Barclay de Tolly, Russian minister of war and commander of the First Army of the West; painting by Dawe

General Count Peter zu Sayn-Wittgenstein, commander of the Russian army's First Corps; painting by Dawe

General Prince Pyotr Bagration, commander of Russia's Second Army of the West; portrait by L. de Saint-Aubin

Left: Ataman Matvei Ivanovich Platov, Cossack commander; portrait by Dawe

Middle: General Alexei Andreyevich Arakcheyev, former Russian minister of war, later director of imperial chancellery; portrait by Dawe

Right: Admiral Alexander Semyonovich Shishkov, Russian state secretary; painting by Kiprensky

General Alexei Petrovich Yermolov, chief of staff of Russia's First Army of the West; portrait by Dawe

General Count Levin Gottlieb Bennigsen, former Russian army commander; painting by Dawe

Marshall Alexandre Berthier, chief of staff of the Grande Armée; engraving after a drawing by Noireterre

Marshal Nicolas Charles Oudinot, commander of the Grande Armée's Second Corps; portrait by R. Lefevre

Marshal Joachim Murat, king of Naples, commander of the Grande Armée's reserve calvary; painting by Gros

Marshal Michel Ney, commander of the Grande Armée's Third Corps; anonymous portrait from a private collection

Marshal Louis Nicolas Davout, commander of the Grande Armée's First Corps, painting by Marzacchi

Siege of Smolensk, painting by Langlois

General Pyotr Petrovich Konovnitsyn, commander of Russia's 3rd Infantry Division, later Kutuzov's chief of staff; painting by Dawe

General (later Prince and Field Marshal) Mikhail Hilarionovich Kutuzov, Russian commander in chief; drawing by Hopwood

Battle of Borodino; painting by Lejeune

General Karl Fedorovich Baggovut, commander of Russian army's Second Corps; painting by Dawe

Count Fyodor Rostopchin; painting by Kiprensky

Conference of Fili, showing, from left to right, Kaissarov, Kutuzov, Konovnitsyn, Rayevsky, Ostermann-Tolstoy, Bennigsen (with back turned), Barclay, Uvarov, Toll (back turned), Dokhturov, Yermolov; painting by Kivshchenko

Old Moscow street scene, before the fire; illustration from a book by M. I. Pyliayev

Moscow in flames; lithograph after painting by Oldendorf

General Mikhail Andreyevich Miloradovich, commander of the Russian rear guard, later of the advance guard; painting by Dawe

Marshal Edouard Mortier, commander of the Grande Armée's Young Guard and for a brief moment governor of Moscow during Napoleon's stay; painting by Lariviére

Napoleon leaving Moscow; engraving by Faber du Faur

Emperor Alexander I; painting by G. Dawe

The Retreat: scene near Smorgonye; engraving by Faber du Faur

CHAPTER 15

THE TWO CAPITALS

IN MOSCOW there had been scant feeling of alarm during the first weeks of the Napoleonic invasion. The city, which had not let the gathering war clouds cast a shadow over the midwinter carnival festivities, had reacted to the news of the Niemen crossing with disdainful cocksureness. The idea that Napoleon's Grande Armée might advance eastward far enough to threaten Russia's ancient capital struck most Muscovites as preposterous.

No one was more assiduous in encouraging this sublime overconfidence than Moscow's new governor general, the tall, witty, waspish Count Fyodor Rostopchin. Although totally lacking in military experience, this somewhat sallow-faced gentleman with the sharp tongue and the mobile blue eyes made himself a salon oracle by first declaring that "we shall not let him cross the border," and then, after Napoleon had crossed the Niemen and occupied Vilna, by no less blandly assuring everyone that Russia's armies would soon send him reeling back toward Poland.

It might at first seem odd that Grand Duchess Catherine, who had advised the tsar so well in urging him to give up his military command, should have displayed such a lack of judgment in persuading her brother, who had never much cared for him, to appoint the volatile Rostopchin governor general of Moscow. Yet there was a certain logic to this choice. Rostopchin's predecessor, a retired, vodka-loving field marshal familiarly known as "Papa Gudovich," had been popular with the Muscovites because he interfered as little possible in their affairs. But for the Grand Duchess Catherine this benevolent torpor was not what the country's present crisis called for. What was needed was someone able to arouse and inflame the Moscow nobility through the contagious force of his patriotic fervor. Such a person, it seemed to her, was the considerably younger Count Fyodor Rostopchin (now in his forty-seventh year), a good friend of the fire-eating Prince Pyotr Bagration, as well as the sworn adversary of revolutionary Jacobins, Freemasons, and other insidious elements.

The day Rostopchin took office he ordered special prayers to be said before the city's miracle-working ikons to indicate that a new page was being turned and that there was going to be no more of the casual tolerance and *laissez-aller* of the Papa Gudovich era. He was going to wage war on idleness and dissipation by rounding up the tavern wastrels who were disgracing the nocturnal life of the city and by having them forcibly conscripted into the army. He had an officer responsible for distributing food in a military hospital arrested because he was not to be found in the kitchen at breakfast time. He hurried from one quarter of the city to the next as though to make himself seem vigilant, and he let it be known that those who had truly urgent matters to communicate could appear at his governor's residence at any hour of the day.

Moscow at this time had a paper, *Moskovskiye Vyedomosty* (Moscow News), which published regular résumés of the military situation, as well as a weekly, *Russky Vyestnik* (Russian Messenger), edited by a chauvinistic firebrand named Sergei Glinka. But this was not enough for Rostopchin. He felt it to be his personal duty to supervise and set the tone of patriotic discourse and behavior. For having dared to circulate a statement attributed by a Hamburg paper to Napoleon, who was reported to have boasted that he would occupy both Russian capitals (St. Petersburg and Moscow) within six months, a Muscovite named Vereshchaghin was tracked down by the police and thrown into jail. The director of the local post office was likewise arrested, so that Rostopchin could install a henchman of his own to open letters and to report to him on what people were writing. Agents were sent out to counter "subversive" rumors about Russian setbacks in the field, while Rostopchin exercised his polemical verve through the composition of messages and proclamations that were placarded and posted all over the city.

Reactions to these various initiatives were mixed. Some, like the pamphleteer F. F. Viegel, felt that Alexander had been God-inspired in naming Rostopchin governor, going so far as to compare him, "with his frowning eyebrows," to "Jupiter the thunderer." Others were disturbed by a certain absence of scruples in purging "unfit" elements and promoting favorites. Members of the nobility were initially indifferent, persuaded that Rostopchin could do little to change the character of their city. Most of them, besides, had long since left their townhouses and palaces to spend the summer months in their country dachas—an annual exodus which drained Moscow of one-third of its inhabitants.

A city of close to three hundred thousand souls, Moscow, because of its vast spread and the abundance of its trees, parks, gardens, ponds, and rustic wells, seemed to many a traveler "more like a province than a city." The Kremlin, from its tulip-bed of sparkling domes, seemed to have sown a score of satellite towns, each with its panoply of golden cupolas and crosses. They were linked by avenues radiating out like bent spokes, some covered with logs and planks, others totally unpaved. Here, as elsewhere in Russia, most of the houses were still made of wood, but many of them were picturesquely painted in bright yellow, rhubarb-green, and rosy hues, with sculpted porches and glowing ikon niches, which reminded Madame de Staël of "dessert ornaments."

Shadowed by the Kremlin's maroon-red walls, the Krasnaya Ploshchad

(Beautiful Square) looked more like an enormous marketplace than the highly regimented Red Square it has since become. A vast expanse of bumpy ground over which trundled four-horse carriages and peasant carts laden with hampers of vegetables and poultry, sarrazin and sunflower seeds, it was partly enclosed by two long arcades, where slit-eyed Tartars, turbaned Uzbeks, trappers and merchants of every size and hue peddled sables, minks, and fur from Siberia, brilliant shawls and fabrics from India, copper trays and bowls from Turkey, carpets, silverware, earrings, and rubies from Persia.

In the nearby Kitai-Gorod (the so-called Cathay Town, which owed its exotic appellation to the merchants from the Orient who had originally camped there in the Middle Ages) there were many taverns, where wine and vodka were dispensed in terra-cotta goblets. Here each guild—the goldsmiths, the silversmiths, the potters, the ikon painters and frame-makers—had its own busy, sign-strung street. To the north and east was the Byelo-Gorod, or "white town," which took its name from the massive whitewashed walls enclosing the "inner city" of the Kremlin. This had become Moscow's most fashionable quarter. Its principal artery, running due north from the Kremlin and as wide as the boulevards of Paris, was a street curiously named the Kuznetsky Most —the Ironmongers' Bridge—after the skilled artisans who had first made it famous. Its wooden paving (in the form of carefully fitted planks) still justified its original "bridging" or ground-covering function, but the smoking smithies had long since disappeared, replaced by shops selling French lingerie, perfumes, books and fashion reviews, imported wines, leather goods, hats, and lacework.

Still farther removed from the center, and more authentically Russian, was the Skorodom—a log village where anyone could come and order himself a wooden house, which could be put up in just two days (whence the quarter's name, skoro-dom, meaning "fast house").

In 1714 Peter the Great had issued a draconian decree forbidding the use of stone in house construction everywhere in Russia except in Petersburg. This crippling ukaz, intended to enhance the imperial primacy of his new capital, had stunted Moscow's architectural development for close to fifty years. But after 1762, when Catherine the Great's husband, Peter III, rescinded the decree and freed the nobles from obligatory service to the state, counts and princes had sought to make up for lost time. Members of the country's leading families had streamed back to Moscow, and for several decades the Saltykovs, the Orlovs, the Gagarins, the Sheremetievs, the Golitsyns, the Bezborodkos, the Trubetskoys, and many others had vied with each other in the erection of ever grander stone edifices. Among the more spectacular results was Prince Nikolai Yussupov's Arkhangelskoye Palace, with its 30,000-volume library and a picture gallery containing 236 canvasses; the neo-Grecian townhouse of the wealthy merchant Pashkov, with its soaring Corinthian columns and its towering belvedere; and Count Razumovsky's stately mansion, with the close to 500 acres of surrounding parks and gardens, which so astounded Baron vom Stein.

Such was the city, at once intensely cosmopolitan and conservatively Russian, which Alexander decided to rouse from its torpor in the middle of July.

Informed by an imperial aide-de-camp that the sovereign would soon be visiting Moscow, Rostopchin had lost no time sending out messengers to alert several hundred members of the gentry in their dachas. They were expected to return to the city forthwith in order to be personally addressed by His Imperial Majesty.

The following morning (July 23) a vast throng of Muscovites began moving toward the Dorogomilov bridge and barrier and out along the Smolensk road to greet their monarch. It was already late in the afternoon when Alexander and his suite reached the final relay post of Perkushkov, a dozen miles west of Moscow. Waiting to greet the tsar was Rostopchin, who had driven out this far in his carriage. An uneasy Alexander questioned the governor about the state of public opinion in Moscow. Knowing how hostile many of the city's *starodumy*—the rock-ribbed champions of "old thought"—had been to the liberal tendencies and constitutional experiments of the early years of his reign, he was afraid that the nobles might react adversely to his appeal for their patriotic support. They might detect in this unusual démarche a sign of weakness and set about to exploit it.

Rostopchin assured the tsar that he need have no fears. The nobles were not in a rebellious mood and could be counted upon to do their patriotic bit by volunteering to provide serf recruits for the rapid formation of an *opolchenye* (reserve militia). The merchants, delighted to learn that Russia was abandoning the crippling restrictions of Napoleon's Continental System and resuming trade with Britain, were also prepared to make generous donations of money toward the common effort. But to guard against possible "excesses of speech," the governor general was going to have a few police carriages pointedly drawn up in front of the Sloboda Palace, so that any intemperate "hotheads" or "wild tongues" could be whisked away with a minimum of trouble along the road leading to the fortress city of Kazan (more than 500 miles to the east).

If Alexander, who wanted to make a discreet entry into the city, thought that by eight o'clock in the evening the expectant Muscovites who had tramped out and waited all day to greet him would have gone to bed, he was destined to be pleasantly surprised. Thousands had chosen to sit or lie on the roadsides and in ditches by the light of a radiant moon. At each village along the way the imperial carriage was met by candle-bearing devotees and priests holding silver crosses, who ceremoniously blessed the sovereign of all the Russias as he passed. The closer the cortège drew to Moscow, the more numerous were the lanterns until, in the words of an eyewitness, "it was almost as bright as in daytime." The climax was reached on the Sparrow Hill, also known to the Russians as the Poklonnaya Gora—Hill of Respectful Salutation—where the tsar, heeding the age-old tradition, dismounted from his carriage and got down on his knees to kiss the hallowed ground. He then kissed the cross tendered to him by the officiating priest, who in a deep, ringing voice proclaimed, "So may God bless you, and his enemies be scattered!"

It was already past midnight when the imperial cortège finally reached the Kremlin, where to the emperor's dismay everyone except the sentinels was found to be asleep. Rostopchin, who had been so insistent that Alexander be lodged in the "palace of his ancestors," had absentmindedly neglected to tell the servants!

The next morning a solemn service, commemorating the recent signing of a peace treaty with the Turks, was held in the Uspensky Sobor (Cathedral of the Assumption), in which the tsars and tsarinas of Russia were traditionally crowned. The service, announced by the reverberations of countless bells, drew such a multitude of reverent subjects that all of the squares of the Kremlin were soon packed. "*Oorah!*" shouted the heaving mob repeatedly, as it pushed and shoved its way forward. "Batiushka, lead us anywhere you like! Father, lead us! We will die or conquer!" Pressing forward ecstatically, those in front threw themselves down and tried to kiss Emperor Alexander's boots or to touch the ends of his riding coat, while his aides-de-camp struggled to push them back from the red-carpeted cathedral steps.

Unable to attend the service personally because of several cerebral strokes that had impaired his powers of speech, Metropolitan Platon, who had retired to the Troitsky monastery forty miles northeast of Moscow, sent Alexander an ikon of Saint Sergei, which had accompanied Tsar Alexis Mikhailovich into battle against the Poles, and later Peter the Great in his struggle against the Swedes. With the sacred image came a letter in which the stricken prelate compared Alexander to the "humble shepherd" David and Napoleon to the uncouth Goliath. "God is with you!" echoed his deputy, Archbishop Augustine, who greeted the tsar at the entrance to the cathedral with a cross and holy water. "With your voice he will command the storm, and silence will descend on the deep, and the diluvial waves will be stilled."

Although more subdued in its expression, much the same patriotic fervor was manifested the next day when Alexander addressed the two assemblies—of the nobility and of the merchant class—at the Sloboda Palace. The representatives of the gentry listened in respectful silence as the emperor made his plea for more recruits. But after old Marshal Gudovich had risen to reply that the nobles of the Moscow region would gladly contribute one serf recruit out of every twenty-five in their service, several voices rang out in protest, "No, not one in twenty-five, one in ten, uniformed and supplied with food for three months!" This counterproposal was seconded by acclamation.

The representatives of the merchant class proved equally receptive to the tsar's plea, which in this case was for money. When Admiral Shishkov, who had undertaken to back Alexander's appeal with a harangue of his own, declared that the enemy was approaching "with a smile on his lips but with fetters in his hands," many of the bearded members in the hall could no longer restrain their rage, wringing their hands, tearing their hair, and beating their heads on the tables in a biblical exhibition of pious wrath and indignation. The city's lord mayor set a self-abnegating example by making a personal contribution of 50,000 rubles—more than a third of his total capital worth. One of Moscow's wealthiest merchants volunteered to donate one million rubles. That evening, when Rostopchin returned to the Kremlin, he informed the tsar that in addition to the 50,000 recruits whom the gentry had agreed to provide, the assembled representatives of the merchant class had made voluntary contributions totaling 2,400,000 rubles.

A contagious fever of self-sacrificial emulation now gripped Moscow's *haute société*. Count Mamonov, the son of one of Catherine the Great's lovers, magnanimously offered 800,000 silver rubles and a casket full of glittering diamonds worth hundreds of thousands more. Some nobles let it be known that they were going to give up their private orchestras, choirs, and actors, others that they were going to reduce the number of footmen, grooms, and retainers in their employ, since these could more easily be taught the rudiments of warfare than peasant serfs.

Human nature being what it is, however, a number of local shopkeepers and merchants decided to make the most of this patriotic upsurge. Overnight the cost of a sword or a saber, hitherto 6 rubles or less, soared to 30 to 40 rubles. A brace of pistols from the famous Tula workshops, which used to cost 7 to 8 rubles, were now hawked at 35 to 50 rubles, while the sale price of carbines and muskets shot up from 15 to 80 rubles apiece.

Alexander, whose worried look prior to his speech to the nobility had been noted by more than one Muscovite, was in brighter spirits when the time came to leave. Indeed, his change of mood may even have swung too much from one extreme to the other. For when saying good-bye to Rostopchin during the night of July 28–29, he informed the delighted governor that he was giving him full authority to act as he saw fit, whatever might occur. "Who can predict events? I rely on you entirely." But of what those events might be, there was not a hint.

After spending the next night at Tver with his sister Catherine, who, now eight months gone with child, had been rejoined by her husband, George of Oldenburg, Alexander continued his four-day journey to Petersburg. He slipped into his capital at two in the morning, finding it illuminated, not for his arrival, which had been expected two days earlier, but because this August 3 was the name day of Dowager Empress Maria Feodorovna.

The emperor's return had not come a moment too soon. In the absence of a guiding hand and of definite news from the front the wildest rumors had begun to circulate, setting off the first tremors of panic. From Riga came reports that the governor, General Essen, had lost his nerve completely and had set fire to the seaport's suburbs instead of trying to defend them against the French and Prussian besiegers. Even more upsetting was the news that Napoleon had occupied Vitebsk virtually without a fight and that Barclay's First Army was now headed for Smolensk in an effort to save Moscow. For most inhabitants of the capital this meant that Petersburg was being left to its fate, with no more than a tiny army corps, under General Wittgenstein's command, to protect it from the onsweeping French. No more was needed to throw Dowager Empress Maria Feodorovna into such a fluster that she issued orders to have some of her belongings packed, in case the imperial family had to leave in a hurry.

Everyone was now clamoring for Barclay de Tolly's dismissal, some on the grounds that he was a traitor, others because they considered him a madman or a fool. But who was there to replace him? No one could question Bagration's heroic fearlessness, but the tsar had never placed much faith in the hot-tempered Georgian's understanding of strategic matters. Bennigsen he had always disliked—for the murky role he had played in his father's murder. Besides, Bennigsen, born a Hanoverian, was even less Russian than Barclay, who could at least claim to be a product of Russian Livonia.

The universal hue and cry in Court and aristocratic circles, "the one and only thought, the only topic of conversation," was for a savior who was authentically Russian and authentically noble; and here, as Varvara Bakunin noted, "worried women, old and young, in a word, all ages, all classes of society," had but one name upon their lips: that of Mikhail Hilarionovich Kutuzov. The sybaritic ex-commander of the Army of the Danube had re-turned some weeks before to Petersburg in a kind of semidisgrace, associated with the forced relinquishment of his command. He had been given the rela-tively menial task of training the auxiliary militia, which the nobles of Peters-burg, like those of Moscow, had been asked to furnish from among their serfs. Then quite unexpectedly he had been elevated by the tsar to the hereditary rank of prince, as a reward for his achievement in making peace with the Turks. This had accredited the idea that he was back in imperial favor—which was anything but the case. Kutuzov, now in his sixty-seventh year, had grown so corpulent that he could only with difficulty be heaved up onto a horse. For Kutuzov, furthermore, Alexander harbored a tenacious aversion. At Auster-litz the canny old fox with the milky-white eyeball and the deceptively droop-ing lid had wanted to avoid battle pending the arrival of reinforcements. Subsequent events had proved him right and Alexander wrong—a humiliating recollection the young tsar had been unable to forget. Nor had he ever cared for Kutuzov's slovenly and self-indulgent ways, so different from Barclay's methodical efficiency, financial scrupulousness, and Spartan simplicity in the field.

For two troubled weeks Alexander wrestled with the thorny problem of command, going over the reports sent to him by various commanders, reading and rereading letters full of grievances about Barclay de Tolly's "indecisive" leadership and military "incompetence," and listening to oral complaints about him. Almost every evening the emperor's carriage was to be seen, taking him across the bridge of boats to Kamenny Island, where he sought to forget his cares by going for solitary walks in the leafy alleys surrounding his summer residence, or in the restful company of Maria Antonovna Naryshkin.

The news, played up and amplified in the local gazettes, that General Wittgenstein had "totally defeated Marshal Oudinot with great slaughter, and had taken his baggage, artillery, and three thousand prisoners" (as John Quincy Adams recorded in his diary) gave the tsar only a brief moment of encouragement; for it was followed almost immediately by the disturbing tidings, carefully kept from the Petersburg press and public, that the resource-ful French marshal had avenged himself for this setback by luring two Russian divisions across the Dvina and into a lethal artillery trap, capturing fourteen cannon and killing a general in the process.

On August 17, the very day on which Napoleon launched his frontal assault

on Smolensk, the tsar's personal friend and aide-de-camp Prince Pyotr Volkonsky brought him a letter that General Pavel Shuvalov had written five days
before during a visit to the headquarters of the First and Second Russian
armies. A former corps commander who had been obliged to relinquish his
command because of ill health, Shuvalov, who had fought alongside Barclay
during the Finnish campaign of 1808–1809, was not one of the many Russian
generals who had so bitterly resented his appointment as minister of war; but
the fact that he was so unprejudiced made his present testimony all the more
crushing. He painted a devastating picture of a grumbling, demoralized, ill-fed
army, whose soldiers often lacked bread, whose cavalry horses often lacked
oats—all because their commander (Barclay) issued his march orders so errati-
cally that the quartermasters were hopelessly confused. His conclusion was
that "another chief is absolutely necessary, he must command both armies,
and it is indispensable that Your Majesty designate him immediately without
losing an instant, otherwise Russia is lost!"

Although the letter betrayed a certain bias in favor of Bagration, it unquestionably reflected the sentiments of most senior officers in the First and Second
Russian armies. Alexander decided then and there that he could temporize no
longer. But loath to make an appointment that was personally repugnant to
him, he decided to delegate the decision to a six-man committee, headed by
his onetime tutor, Count Saltykov, now chairman of the prestigious but largely
impotent Council of State. Its members included the former foreign minister,
Count Viktor Kochubey, Minister of Police Balashov, and most menacingly
of all for Barclay de Tolly's cause, his unforgiving predecessor as minister of
war, Arakcheyev.

That same evening at seven o'clock the six men met in emergency session.
It was virtually a foregone conclusion that their choice for the post of supreme
commander would be Kutuzov—the "unkillable" old soldier who had twice
had a bullet go through his head without his powers of speech and thought
being in the least affected (though he had lost an eye). But knowing how little
the emperor cared for Kutuzov—the animosity, it might be added, was fully
reciprocated—the six arbiters spent four and a half hours trying to find the
proper words and arguments needed to support their choice without giving
offense to His Imperial Majesty.

At the imperial dacha on Kamenny Island, to which he was summoned to
be given news of his appointment, Kutuzov was informed by the emperor that
he was being made supreme commander of Russia's active forces as well as
of its reserve units and militia. He was given carte blanche to conduct military
operations as he wished, but he was under no circumstances to enter into
negotiations with Napoleon.

True to his sly form—for he knew that this was what Alexander wished to
hear—Kutuzov assured the emperor that the French "will only enter Moscow
over my dead body." He also lived up to his dubious money-grubbing reputation—Bagration liked to say that Kutuzov was ready to sell anything, even his
own country, if he thought it might make him rich—by stopping near the door
as he was about to leave the emperor's office and saying in French, "*Majesté,*

je n'ai pas un sou pour partir" (Majesty, I do not have a penny for the trip). Alexander, who was probably not surprised by this shameless confession, ordered that he be given 10,000 rubles. He now had one more reason for disliking the paunchy generalissimo, as he made clear a little later to his aide-de-camp Komarovsky: "The public wanted his appointment, so I appointed him. As for myself, I wash my hands of it."

The news that Kutuzov had been named commander in chief of Russia's armed forces in the field, made known by an official ukaz on August 20, was greeted with almost delirious relief in most Petersburg salons. The approaches to the house where he had been staying were suddenly jammed with carriages, which disgorged a multitude of gushing congratulators. Wherever he went— and during his last day or two in the capital he pointedly visited several churches, as a token of his pious faith in the succor of Russia's patron saints —he was mobbed. When he left Petersburg his carriage was followed by a cheering crowd of well-wishers, who kept shouting, "Save us, save us! Rout the enemy!" The acclamations were repeated at every stop along the road by townsfolk and villagers, some of whom got down on their knees in naïve homage to the designated "savior."

At the first relay post, while the horses were being changed, Kutuzov learned from a courier that the French had just occupied Smolensk and that the First and Second Russian armies were now withdrawing along the road to Moscow. Other couriers were already on their way to the commanders of Russia's four armies of the West—Barclay, Bagration, Tormassov, and Chichagov—informing them that Infantry General Prince Kutuzov was now in overall control of military operations.

The imperial rescript contained the usual words of exhortation. ("I am confident that your love of the Fatherland and your devotion to duty will clear the way for new exploits by you, which I shall be only too pleased to recognize with appropriate rewards.") But the copy sent to Barclay de Tolly was not even accompanied by a personal note from the tsar. This, even more than the rescript itself, made the sudden blow particularly painful for the commander of Russia's First Army. No one could more faithfully have respected Alexander's parting injunction at Polotsk: "Remember that this is my only army and that I have no other." Yet this was his reward!

The suddenly demoted minister of war could not have guessed how his prestige had been rising in the eyes of certain of his French adversaries. Philippe de Ségur chronicled it well when he wrote, "And so Barclay, alone against all, had right up to the last moment upheld the plan of retreat he had boasted of to one of our generals in 1807, as Russia's only means of salvation. Among us he was praised for having stuck to this wise defensive strategy, notwithstanding the clamors of a proud nation in the face of an aggressive enemy. . . . Everything he had done had been done in a timely manner, whether he had hazarded, defended, or abandoned. Yet he had drawn upon himself a general animadversion! But this to our eyes was his highest praise. We approved him for having disdained public opinion when it was going astray, for having contented himself with observing our movements in order to profit from them; and for having thus known that, as often as not, nations are saved despite themselves."

Barclay wrote back stoically to assure his sovereign of his continuing "eagerness to serve the country in whatever post or assignment" might be granted to him. But he could not keep from adding a note of self-justification toward the end of the letter: "Had I been motivated by blind and reckless ambition, Your Imperial Majesty would probably have received quantities of reports of battles fought, and nevertheless the enemy would still be at the gates of Moscow without encountering sufficient forces able to resist him."

Alexander's only response to this brief plaint was a terse note informing Barclay that, because of his "momentous and manifold" preoccupations at the front, the post of minister of war had been transferred to his deputy, Prince Gorchakov. But there was some consolation to be found in the polite note sent on ahead by Kutuzov, in which he was informed that the generalissimo was retaining his services as commander of the First Army of the West. It was to prove one of the old warrior's wisest decisions.

CHAPTER 16

DIVISIONS AND DISSENSIONS

AMONG THE SKILLFULLY retreating Russians of the First and Second armies there was now a superficial unity of purpose. All, from Barclay on down, were determined to make a stand. But the question was where, and who was to pick the battleground. In the absence of an overall commander there had been nothing to keep the refractory Bagration from refusing to agree to whatever site Barclay de Tolly might suggest.

Never, indeed, had the relations between the two generals been more strained. In another furious letter to Arakcheyev, written on August 19—the very day on which Barclay had to fight unaided to save his First Army from destruction—Bagration accused him of being "cowardly, muddle-headed, sluggish," and a disgrace to Mother Russia, claiming that Napoleon and his thirst-racked Grande Armée would have had to withdraw from Smolensk for lack of water if only the gutless "minister" (his derogatory term for Barclay) had held out for another forty-eight hours.

During the first days of this new retreat he kept exploding into tirades, saying he was going to resign. His friend Yermolov, who, though nominally working under Barclay, was in reality conspiring against him, urged Bagration to write to the tsar directly and boldly suggest that he be named supreme commander of both the First and Second armies of the West. Although this was Bagration's secret ambition, he hesitated to go so far, contenting himself with sending Alexander copies of his recent correspondence with Barclay, as though this would suffice to unmask the latter's weak-kneed incompetence.

While Smolensk was being evacuated, several officers from the First Army's headquarters staff had been dispatched along the Moscow highroad to look for suitable battlegrounds, and after the conclusion of the Valutina Gora–Lubino battle, Barclay's acting chief of staff, Colonel Toll, had been sent on ahead to check their findings. On the basis of this reconnaissance a first possible site was recommended by Toll near the Uzha River, just short of Dorogobuzh. But when Toll presented himself at Second Army headquarters and sought to convince its commander of the tactical merits of this site, he met with hot resistance. Bagration, hitherto a fire-eating advocate of the offensive, would not hear of making a stand near the Uzha River, claiming that Napoleon could easily outflank the combined Russian armies and hurl them back against the Dnieper. The prickly Georgian prince even lost his temper, ranting at Toll and shouting that he deserved to be degraded to the rank of simple soldier "and beaten about the backside with a rifle butt!"

Surprised by this development, Barclay was quite happy to abandon the idea of making a stand near the Uzha River. He was even quicker to scrap the idea of fighting a battle at Dorogobuzh—the "worst" position yet suggested, and one apparently put forward by members of Bagration's entourage as a wily maneuver calculated to force Barclay to order one more withdrawal, thus further blackening his reputation in official eyes as a perpetual "retreater."

In this welter of backbiting intrigue, Barclay had scored at least one clear-cut victory—in persuading Grand Duke Constantine to leave for Petersburg. The emperor's brother was quickly followed by the ambitious Bennigsen, who now realized that his only chance of obtaining a definite military post lay with the tsar. Deprived of his two principal on-the-spot allies, Barclay's chief of staff, Yermolov, assumed the attitude of a "cringing dog," as Major Waldemar von Loewenstern later put it. "All these gentlemen sensed that a man who had had the energy to send away the emperor's brother would not treat the others with kid gloves."

Barclay's triumph lasted less than one week. Two days after Grand Duke Constantine's departure Colonel Toll returned from his latest reconnaissance to say that the only really good position for a major defensive battle was near the town of Tsarevo-Zaimishche, about one hundred miles from Moscow. Bagration promptly found fault with the new site, saying that its defensive properties were worthless. "The poor soldiers are grumbling once again," he wrote in a letter to Barclay. "They can neither drink nor cook their mash. It seems to me that we should leave without delay"—for the nearby town of Gzhatsk, but not retreat "one step" beyond it. "For the rest, do as you wish," the Georgian prince concluded in a tone of sullen resignation, prompted by the news that had just reached him that a new generalissimo—Kutuzov—was about to join them.

Within hours of the Russian rear guard's departure and hot on the heels of Murat's cavalrymen, Napoleon reached the town of Dorogobuzh, where the Smolensk–Moscow highroad briefly joined the winding Dnieper River. He spent the night of August 25–26 in a kind of fortress castle overlooking the town, and here, without waiting for his secretaries, whom he had momentarily left behind, he began impatiently dictating letters to the aides-de-camp on duty. The most important was destined for Marshal Victor, who had just reached Kovno, on the Niemen, with the three fresh divisions of his Tenth Corps (on paper, more than 30,000 men). He was to proceed to Vilna for consultations with Foreign Minister Maret, and to go on from there to Smolensk, destined to become the central link in the Grande Armée's steadily expanding line of communications.

To Maret he wrote that "the country is good"—he meant for the forage, crops, and food it could provide—"and I am assured that it remains very good as far as Moscow. The heat we are experiencing is excessive." But this was not going to slow down his advance, since, after fighting a battle with the Russians, he expected to be in Moscow by September 5.

Such had been the speed of Murat's advancing cavalry that they had managed to occupy Dorogobuzh before the retreating Russians could put it to the torch. But not long after Napoleon's arrival much of it was reduced to ashes thanks to the carelessness of Imperial Guard soldiers, who established their bivouac fires too close to its wooden houses.

The increasing frequency of such fires, accompanied by brazen looting, was one more symptom of a gradual breakdown in discipline which boded ill for the future of the Grande Armée. One person who was well aware of this was that strict taskmaster Davout. His leading infantry divisions, now echeloned along the Moscow highway, had been increasingly hard put to keep up with Murat's cavalrymen, who sometimes covered as many as twenty-five to thirty miles in one day. Davout felt that they were trying to move ahead too fast and carelessly; and on the evening of the twenty-seventh his fears were confirmed when Murat narrowly escaped capture while leading a detachment of light cavalry against a well-entrenched Russian force defending a river-bridge crossing.

The next morning the two leaders, who disliked each other intensely, got into a violent argument in the presence of Napoleon, who had dismounted to examine the terrain of the previous evening's engagement. Murat complained that his cavalrymen were not catching any Russian prisoners (for interrogation) because Davout's slow-moving infantrymen always reached the scene of a skirmish too late to do more than frighten off the enemy. Davout riposted with a blistering critique of Murat's reckless ardor in pressing hasty frontal assaults against enemy rearguard detachments with whatever tirailleurs, horsemen, and light-artillery pieces he could quickly muster, instead of carefully reconnoitering each position with a view to turning it through a clever flanking movement. Such piecemeal assaults used up valuable ammunition, as well as men and horses, and were a source of exasperation to the long columns of cavalrymen behind, who were forced to remain saddled up through the dusty heat of the day to be ready for a major battle that never came. At this rate, Davout concluded, there would soon be nothing left of the cavalry.

Napoleon, who listened in silence while prodding a Russian cannonball with the toe of his boot, was loath to take sides in this altercation. Being ultimately responsible for the haste of the Grande Armée's advance, he could not blame Murat for displaying a combative ardor which was in keeping with his own impatient temperament. He reminded Davout that no one could "unite all forms of merit," told him that he knew more about the fighting of pitched battles than about vanguard operations, adding that if Murat, rather than Davout, had been given the task of pursuing Bagration, he would perhaps not have let him escape—a cruel comment which must have made Davout seethe with rage as he returned to his command post.

The next day a new row blew up when Davout tried to keep his lead division from cooperating with Murat's cavalrymen during another frontal assault on a well-positioned Russian rearguard unit beyond the town of Vyazma. When Murat's chief of staff, General Belliard, galloped up to imperial headquarters to report the incident, Napoleon lost patience. Cursing Davout for his stubbornness, he sent Berthier to inform him that he was placing General Dominique Compans's infantry division under Murat's command, whether he liked it or not. But Murat by this time was in such a state of fury that it was all his friend Belliard could do, when he returned to the king of Naples's tent, to keep him from seizing his jeweled saber and rushing off forthwith to have it out with Davout!

Vyazma itself, like so many places they had passed, was a ghost town, full of lovely green-domed churches but abandoned by virtually every one of its twenty thousand inhabitants. A solitary beggar and a Strasbourg hairdresser who had been hired as French tutor for a well-to-do family seemed to be the only remaining souls, along with the sacristan of a high-walled monastery, who was finally prevailed upon to open the gates to members of Napoleon's staff. In the chapel the candles were lit around an open coffin containing the body of the local archimandrite. On hearing that the "Antichrist" Napoleon was approaching, the old man had suffered a heart attack and died, and the terrified monks had later decamped in a panic before completing the funeral service. To show that he was less satanic than the Orthodox clergy would have everyone believe, Napoleon ordered the funeral service to be conducted by one of his Imperial Guard detachments, with some of his senior general staff officers in respectful attendance.

Although deserted, Vyazma offered welcome relief to the hungry. Its many gardens and cellars provided a variety of vegetables, ample stocks of flour, generous quantities of pickled herring, and hundreds of bottles of much-appreciated vodka.

Equally heartwarming was the news that the Russians were digging in at Tsarevo-Zaimishche, some twenty miles farther up the road. It was accompanied by a burst of rain, which helped to settle the dust and to make the next marches less excruciating for eyes, ears, nostrils, sand-caked hair and faces.

The village of Tsarevo-Zaimishche may not have been a perfect defensive position, but it had several features to recommend it. Located at the edge of a plain with a virtually unobstructed view for miles around, it was dominated by gently rising ground, which provided the Russians with admirable vantage points for observing enemy movements and for the positioning of their artillery batteries in a long defensive crescent, around which the French would have to move if they wished to outflank them. Beyond the ridge the Smolensk–Moscow highroad stretched on across a now-desiccated marshland in a northeasterly direction to the town of Gzhatsk, some ten miles distant, offering an unimpeded avenue of withdrawal if a retreat had to be ordered. Colonel Toll was not the only one to believe that this was one of the very best defensive positions to be found between Smolensk and Moscow. Such too, though after the event, was the opinion of a Prussian major named Blesson, who went as far as to declare that it was only because the Russians gave up this excellent position that Napoleon was later able to enter Moscow.

Barclay de Tolly, who reached Tsarevo-Zaimishche on the early morning of August 29, immediately put his First Army soldiers to work building redoubts and other fortifications to make this defensive site even stronger. The combined strength of the First and Second Russian armies now stood at just under 96,000. Barclay assumed that the Grande Armée still outnumbered the Russians by a substantial margin. But with the addition of the 20,000 to 25,000 men whom General Miloradovich was expected to bring to Gzhatsk the next day, he reckoned that this numerical inferiority would be largely eliminated.

Shortly before noon on this August 29 Kutuzov drove into the pretty market town of Gzhatsk, followed by an impressive suite of carriage-borne officers, led by General Bennigsen. They had met at a relay post approximately halfway along the road to Petersburg, and after listening to the gray-haired Hano-verian's account of what had been going on at the headquarters of the First and Second Russian armies, Kutuzov on the spur of the moment had offered Bennigsen the post of chief of staff. The latter had accepted with alacrity. Too shrewd and worldly-wise not to realize that what Bennigsen coveted above all was his own supreme command, Kutuzov, who basically distrusted him (quite rightly, as events were to prove), probably reckoned that this would be the surest way of insulating himself from the possibly disastrous consequences of the dissensions existing between the commanders of the First and Second Russian armies.

So overjoyed were the inhabitants of Gzhatsk to see the old soldier that several of the town's leading merchants insisted on lending him their finest carriages and horses for the final lap of his journey. As the cavalcade approached the Tsarevo-Zaimishche camp, soldiers broke into ecstatic cheers, everywhere faces brightened, and once more joyous songs were heard around the bivouac fires.

Kutuzov's actions on this first day, particularly when compared with what was to follow, were a model of cunning calculation. He did just the right things and said exactly what was needed to foster the impression that here, so help him God, he was going to stand and fight! After climbing out of his carriage in front of the First Army's headquarters, he nodded his head approvingly at the sight of the honor guard drawn up to greet him, then muttered quite audibly, "How can one go on retreating with young lads like these?" The comment, repeated from mouth to mouth, was on everybody's lips by evening.

His appearance created a sensation, unleashing deep-throated *"Oorah!"*'s as he was led by Barclay from one regiment to the next. Beside the tall, erect figure of the First Army's austere commander, Kutuzov's enormous bulk, placed athwart a lightly bridled horse, looked a trifle obscene but unmistakably paternal. There were no Western-style epaulets on his old-fashioned uniform; instead of a splendidly feathered half-moon hat he wore a cuirassier's white forage-cap with red trimmings; and though the ceremonial scarlet sash was draped from one shoulder across his bulging front, a short Cossack whip was suspended from the other shoulder by a cord. It would have been difficult to look more simply clad, more down-to-earth, more muzhik-like and authentically Russian.

There had been rumors that the old man's sight was failing, and many officers of the First and Second armies were wondering how well he could see with his remaining eye. Well aware of what everyone was thinking, Kutuzov, shortly after his arrival, quietly summoned a Cossack officer and told him to take his detachment out to guard a wood situated about two-thirds of a mile from the main highroad some distance to the east. Later, accompanied by an enormous retinue of generals and staff officers, he set off down the road, and when they came abreast of the wood, he pointed to the horsemen drawn up near the trees, saying, "Who can that be?" Several members of his suite assured him that they were a French cavalry patrol. "No, they are Cossacks," Kutuzov corrected them. "But anyway, make sure who they are." He continued calmly on his way while several aides-de-camp galloped off to identify the horsemen. All doubts about his eyesight were dispelled when they returned to report that yes, indeed, they were Cossacks—just as the prince had said.

Later on this same day, or it may have been the next—for the incident is shrouded in mystery—a bird of prey was seen describing circles some distance above the point where Kutuzov was reviewing troops. Looking up into the air with his one good eye, he doffed his vizorless cap and saluted it. Was it a hawk, a buzzard, or a kite? No one knows. But soon it was being asserted by superstitious soldiers that a huge eagle had soared back and forth above the supreme commander's head throughout that afternoon review. The auspicious nature of the omen needed no explaining, even if this fancied eagle had only one head—unlike the two on the Russian imperial crest. Here, obviously, was a winner of battles, another "invincible," made of the same tough, heroic stuff as the great Suvorov. (This aquiline phenomenon was duly recorded in the Petersburg press, and thus the legend, adopted by later historians as established "fact," became part of Russia's historic folklore.)

Far less pleased by the new generalissimo's performance were Bagration and Barclay, who saw their wings drastically clipped. Bagration's quartermaster-general, a cadaverous nonentity named Vistitsky, was transferred to Kutuzov's headquarters, which was no loss; but Barclay, his protests notwithstanding, was forced to relinquish Colonel Toll, whose youthful drive and competence had attracted Kutuzov's attention years before when he commanded the Petersburg Cadet School.

No less mortifying for Barclay was the reappearance on the scene of Colonel Païsy Kaissarov, an intriguing member of Alexander's imperial staff whom he thought he had managed to get rid of a few days before. Kaissarov now made a triumphant comeback as Kutuzov's senior "duty officer," a position of considerable importance since, like Bennigsen, he was authorized to issue orders in the generalissimo's name at any hour of the day or night. Kaissarov, in fact, was only one of a large number of anti-Barclay malcontents who came swarming back to the front in the wake of their victorious protector and benefactor, Kutuzov. With them came Kutuzov's son-in-law, Prince Nikolai

Kudashev, who, though he held no official position at combined headquarters, was soon blandly issuing orders in his father-in-law's name. All the rules for the regular transmission of orders, which had been carefully codified in Barclay de Tolly's famous Yellow Book, were thus conveniently forgotten, and it soon became difficult to determine just who had issued a particular directive —a chaotic situation aggravated by Kutuzov's well-known preference for issuing instructions orally and his extreme reluctance to draft or even sign a written order.

The first dramatic consequence of these new general staff and command regulations was not long in coming. After inspecting the defensive positions which soldiers of the First and Second armies were working to improve across the long curving hill behind Tsarevo-Zaimishche, Kutuzov nodded approvingly, telling Barclay that they struck him as "very advantageous and solid." But that night, after he had come back to his headquarters and Barclay had retired to his own tent area, Colonel Kaissarov and the young Prince Kudashev went to work on Kutuzov, arguing that it was degrading for a person of his experience and prestige to accept a battle site selected by another. In the case of victory—and as superpatriotic hotheads they could imagine no other outcome—a good part of the credit would go to Barclay, and Kutuzov's personal glory would be correspondingly diminished. The sixty-seven-year-old generalissimo, who was a good deal shrewder than his feather-brained son-in-law, was not easily convinced, but he finally yielded to the call of vanity. Not until the late afternoon of the following day, August 30, were Barclay and Bagration informed that the army was going to withdraw to a fall-back position behind Gzhatsk. A whole day was thus lost in the needless construction of fortifications that were never to be used—a point of some interest, since it helps to explain why the redoubts later hurriedly started at Borodino were unfinished when Napoleon finally attacked.

During the night of August 30–31 the First and Second Russian armies retreated up the Moscow highway and through the town of Gzhatsk to a new position near the village of Ivashkovo. Here they were joined by General Miloradovich, who turned up, not with 20,000 to 25,000 soldiers, as Barclay had hoped, but with 15,600 half-trained recruits. Too inexperienced to be formed into independent units, they were divided up among different companies and battalions of the First and Second armies. They were, however, a welcome addition, raising the total strength of the Russian forces facing Napoleon to slightly more than 111,000 men.

The two Russian armies had hardly begun to entrench themselves in their new battle site when a new crisis arose—this time provoked by Bennigsen, who declared that the position was wretched. An argument ensued in Kutuzov's presence between Barclay, who wanted to know what was wrong with the new site, and Bennigsen, who replied that there was a wood in the middle, behind which the French could concentrate their troops and conceal their offensive preparations.

"If what you think is needed for a good battleground is an area entirely lacking in all woods, then you will have trouble finding one in all of Russia," countered Barclay impatiently. It was all very well to criticize this battle site, he went on, but what else did he have to propose? To this Bennigsen replied that while traveling in his carriage between Mozhaisk and Gzhatsk he had seen several "fine" battle sites that would do very well for their purposes. Kutuzov seemed dubious about this claim, supporting Barclay in his advocacy of the present position. But after Barclay had left, Bennigsen in his turn went to work on the somnolent generalissimo, depicting the various battle sites he had glimpsed from his calèche in such glowing terms that Kutuzov finally let himself be persuaded to order yet another withdrawal.

The decision to undertake this second withdrawal was an enormous gamble, quite at variance with Kutuzov's normally cautious behavior. For at this point no one really knew on the basis of careful reconnaissance if another really first-class battle site existed between Gzhatsk and Moscow. A Lieutenant Colonel Harting was hastily dispatched along the Moscow highroad to inspect the battle sites recommended by Bennigsen, while the two armies resumed their orderly retreat, protected by General Konovnitsyn's rear guard, a now formidable force of ninety-six cavalry squadrons and twenty-five infantry battalions.

On September 2 Kutuzov reached Kolotsky, where he spent the night in a monastery overlooking the Smolensk–Moscow highroad. From here he dispatched a courier to Governor Rostopchin—who, like many other Muscovites, was increasingly uneasy over reports reaching him from the ever-retreating, inexorably approaching "front"—to reassure him that he intended to fight "a general battle and a decisive one for the salvation of Moscow" at a chosen spot near Mozhaisk.

The next morning the generalissimo and his huge suite rolled past the little town of Borodino, with its score or two of wooden houses and its whitewashed church with the two onion domes, turned right over the creaky, planked bridge across the Kolotcha River, and then labored up the mile-long slope to the village of Gorky, lying athwart the Smolensk–Moscow road. The undulating river, now seriously narrowed by the August drought, and the wooded hill extending off to the right may not have seemed to Kutuzov as "splendid" a battle site as had been made out to him; but since this was the spot that Bennigsen and Colonel Harting had settled on, he was willing to go along and to declare, "Here we will stop and make our stand!" They were now seventy-five miles from Moscow, and as Kutuzov wrote the next day to Rostopchin, if he found himself outflanked or was defeated in battle, "I shall go to Moscow and there I shall defend the capital."

On the last day of August Murat's cavalrymen, having covered another fifty miles and passed the halfway mark between Smolensk and Moscow, were at last able to capture a Cossack, whose horse had been killed by a well-aimed carbine shot. Shortly afterward they surprised a black African as he emerged from an abandoned village where he had been scrounging for food, and discovered that they had captured one of the Cossack leader Ataman Platov's cooks. The two captives were immediately sent back to Napoleon's headquarters, to be personally interrogated by the emperor and his chief interpreter, François Lelorgne d'Ideville, a diplomat who had served for years in the French embassy in Petersburg.

Neither of the two captives, who were quite willing to talk, could believe that the short, pale-eyed officer in the small half-moon hat and unpretentious green uniform—so much less impressive than the brilliantly panached Murat—could be the French tsar, Napoleon. To begin with, he was too close to his advance guard for such a thing to be conceivable.

The news they provided—that Barclay, the cowardly *général de la retraite,* had been replaced by Kutuzov—was music to Napoleon's ear. Like Lauriston, who had recently joined his imperial headquarters, he had little esteem for any of Russia's commanders, and that included Kutuzov, whom he had defeated at Austerlitz and whose later performance against the Turks had been dismal. To please the Russian nobility, so that it could not be said that the Russians had been willing to yield Moscow without a fight, the one-eyed general would have to deliver a token battle with a seriously weakened and demoralized army. But when the fighting was over, Alexander, having lost his army as well as Russia's ancient capital, would have no choice but to negotiate.

Equally heartened were the French veterans of the Grande Armée, for whom Kutuzov was *le fuyard d'Austerlitz* (the fugitive from Austerlitz). Morale, which had slumped during the first march-days from Smolensk, now rose with the advent of cooling rain and richer sources of booty. The peasant houses along the way, though often reduced to cinders, were found to have ice-walled larders, sometimes extending eight or ten feet below the ground level of their barns, where butter, milk, eggs, and even meat could be preserved during the hottest summer months.

On hearing that the Russians were now building earthworks and redoubts near the village of Borodino, Napoleon decided to grant his Grande Armée a badly needed rest. He wanted to give Kutuzov time to prepare a strong defensive position, so that he would not have a pretext for slipping suddenly away and shirking battle, as Barclay repeatedly had done.

While the soldiers brushed the wrinkles out of their full-dress uniforms and polished their buttons and brass fittings in preparation for the coming battle, Napoleon issued orders to have all stragglers rounded up and returned to their units as soon as possible, so that an accurate count of available manpower could be taken. He had already instructed General Delaborde to advance by forced marches from Smolensk with the 5,000 men of his Young Guard division, whose garrison functions had been taken over by several Polish units, and 5,000 other infantrymen and cavalry were to follow with the paymaster's "treasury."

At Smolensk, prior to the battle of Valutina Gora, Napoleon's forces had been estimated to number around 160,000 men. But the losses suffered in that battle, added to the many dropouts who were unable to keep up with the rugged pace of the advance, to foragers who were ambushed by Cossacks, and to units that had to remain behind to garrison towns and relay posts along an ever-lengthening line of communication, had further reduced his forces by

25,000 men. Davout's First Corps, which had numbered 80,000 men in early June, was now down to 45,000. But since one of its six divisions (about 11,000 men) had gone to strengthen Macdonald's Tenth Corps, its battlefield and sickness losses amounted to no more than 23,000, or less than one-third of its original strength—a remarkable tribute to Davout's resourcefulness in keeping his men properly supplied. The other corps, however, were all down to half of their original strength or even lower. Ney's corps, originally 35,000 strong, now numbered 10,000. Prince Eugène's Fourth Corps, 52,000 at the start of the campaign, was now down to 18,000. Even allowing for the subtraction of the 9,000 men of the Italian Pino Division, who had been sent to guard the Vitebsk–Smolensk road, this represented a combined battlefield, sickness, and stragglers loss of 26,000 men. Poniatowski's Polish Corps, having suffered the amputation of one division and heavy losses at Smolensk, was now not much more than 10,000 strong. The Westphalians, who had started out with more than 20,000, now numbered 9,000.

The five cavalry corps, more than 40,000 strong at the time of the Niemen crossing, were now down to 20,000, including the 5,000 elite horsemen of Marshal Bessières' mounted Imperial Guard, who had taken no part in any fighting. Certain cuirassier divisions, with a normal strength of 3,500 riders, now had fewer than 900.

During the previous week's precipitate advance Napoleon had given no thought to the setting up of hospitals. He now summoned his chief surgeon, Dominique Larrey, who was appalled to learn that a major battle was imminent. Five of his *ambulance volante* teams had stayed behind to take care of the wounded in Smolensk, while the sixth, after accompanying him out to the corpse-strewn hills of Valutina Gora, had been ordered to take 600 to 700 bandaged soldiers back to Smolensk. On hand to help Larrey were exactly two surgical assistants—for an Imperial Guard numbering more than 20,000! A number of surgeons from different regiments were hastily assigned to a central pool, attached to the general staff. Larrey was thus able to recruit forty-five surgeons and surgical assistants in time for the big battle.

The sight of repeated traffic jams caused by vehicles trying to keep up with their units was particularly irksome to Napoleon. Berthier was instructed to appoint a baggagemaster to restore some semblance of order to the chaotic crush and congestion of carriages, wagons, and rope-pulled Russian *kibitkas* loaded with foodstuffs, military gear, rusting weapons, and booty of all kinds. A special order of the day, issued on September 1, specifically accorded a priority right of way to artillery cannon, caissons, and ambulance wagons for the sick and wounded. All officers were ordered to send their carriages back to join the food and baggage trains, which were forbidden from approaching closer than five miles to the advance guard—by which was clearly meant the battlefield. They were further warned that any offending vehicle would be burned. The emperor himself decided to set a Spartan example by riding everywhere on horseback.

Not long after this draconian order was issued Napoleon was infuriated to see several equipages moving calmly forward next to an artillery train. Dismounting, he ordered the leading carriage, a conspicuous buttercup-yellow calèche, to be burned on the spot. Seeing that his carriage was about to be put to the torch, Louis de Narbonne decided to put in a word on its behalf.

"Sire," he began in his suavest tone, "may Your Majesty forgive me for pointing out that the destruction of this carriage might well deprive of his belongings an officer who could have his leg carried off by a cannonball the next day."

"It would cost me far more if I did not have my artillery tomorrow" was Napoleon's testy answer.

Narbonne watched impassively as his valet removed his belongings and the chasseurs accompanying the emperor brought up straw and bits of wood to set the vehicle alight. The fire lit, Napoleon galloped on, followed by the members of his suite. Narbonne returned a moment later, distributed a few louis d'or coins to the soldiers, who helped the driver put out the blaze. The calèche, now singed to a treacly hue, was reloaded with the count's belongings and sent back to join the baggage train.

"I only wish it had been your carriage," said Napoleon to Berthier, the next time they paused for a halt. "It would have more effect and you deserve it, for I bump into it everywhere."

"Behind Your Majesty's carriage," Berthier reminded him.

Napoleon's relations with his chief of staff were now more strained than ever. At Gzhatsk several days of rain, which turned the roads into quagmires, and the first intimations of autumn—the nights were now cold and the birch leaves turning brown—prompted Berthier to renew his plea that Napoleon halt the Grande Armée's advance. His patience tried by ever-mounting problems, Napoleon blew up.

"Go, be off with you!" he shouted at his chief of staff. "I don't need you. You're no more than a festering sore. Go back to France! I'm not retaining anyone against his will."

Berthier drew himself up solemnly to his full height. "When the army is in front of the enemy," he declared, "the vice-constable does not quit, he takes a flintlock and joins the ranks of the soldiers."

Napoleon, who after scenes of this kind usually went out of his way to mollify his chief of staff, this time made his displeasure felt by no longer inviting Berthier to share his daily dinner with him—a "punishment" which was maintained for the next four days.

Berthier, as it happened, was not the only one who was perturbed by the way things were going. Ney, who was made of stouter stuff, turned up shortly afterward to say that everywhere guns and caissons were bogging down, and that the draft horses were near the end of their tether. His foot soldiers, he added, were almost as exhausted by these constant forced marches.

"All right," said Napoleon, after hearing him out in silence. "If the rain continues all day, tomorrow we shall withdraw toward Smolensk."

But several hours later, as though obeying an imperial order, the rain stopped and a bright sun reappeared, drying out the water-logged roads and fields. By early afternoon the order had been given to break camp. The Grande Armée, again advancing in three columns—with Prince Eugène's Fourth Corps several miles to the left, and Poniatowski's Polish Corps a few miles to the right of the main body—resumed its forward march.

CHAPTER 17

BORODINO

ON SEPTEMBER 3, two columns of militiamen, levied with the help of affluent noblemen in the regions of Moscow and Smolensk, joined the main Russian army. A more ragged host than these 16,000 hastily recruited serfs it would have been difficult to imagine. Most of them were still dressed in peasant belts and blouses, and the only unifying feature among them was the cross that had been sewn into the front of their caps. The pikes they were armed with had not even been given proper lance points. Many of them, however, were put to useful work with picks and shovels to speed the construction of redoubts and other fortifications; and all of them, by and by, were to prove invaluable auxiliaries in bringing up ammunition, and carrying or escorting the wounded from the battlefield.

The terrain Kutuzov and Bennigsen had chosen to defend, east and south of the village of Borodino, consisted of a line of hills whose wooded crests were covered with clumps of pines, birch trees, and alders. Down the indented slopes of these hills ran a number of now dried-up streambeds. They emptied into the Kolotcha, a sluggish river which, after more or less paralleling the Moscow–Smolensk highroad for several miles, flowed under a wooden bridge near Borodino and then wound its serpentine way in a northeasterly direction as far as the much larger Moskva. Stretched out along these hills over a distance of 11,000 yards were the seven Russian corps, lined up in a curving arc which began at its northern tip about a mile from the Moskva River and ended at its southern tip near a partly wooded, partly fallow area overgrown with hazelnut and juniper scrub brush, beyond which was the village of Utitsa, located on the old Smolensk–Mozhaisk post road. The new highway cut through this defensive arc somewhat to the right of center, and it was here, on the sloping ground to left and right of the roadside village of Gorky, that a good half (four full corps) of Kutuzov's forces had been positioned. A fifth corps, comprising elite regiments of the Imperial Guard, had been placed farther back to guard Kutuzov's headquarters. To the two remaining corps, both belonging to Bagration's Second Army, had been entrusted the task of defending the remaining 4,000 yards of front.

Ever since the Seven Years War (1756–1763), Russian commanders in the field had shown a predilection for fighting stand-fast battles, simply because their troops were ill trained for rapid-maneuver warfare. At Borodino a short front had been chosen, which for an army of 104,000 men already provided a dense ratio of 9.5 men per yard. The actual battle area, however, was limited to the terrain between Borodino and the village of Utitsa—an effective "front" of less than 6,500 yards. Here, if the troops concentrated on the overmanned right wing are considered a kind of strategic reserve, the density reached the ratio of 16 men per yard.

In itself this density of manpower need not have been a handicap if Bennigsen and Kutuzov had set out to organize a defense in depth. But unfortunately the terrain made this impossible, for the rearmost Russian lines backed up against the woodlands crowning the hill crests. The distance from these woodlands to the river embankment of the Kolotcha and to the two streambeds behind which the Russians were aligned was in most places little more than 2,000 yards—just 800 yards more than the 1,200-yard range of a normal cannonball.

The lower stretch of the Kolotcha River, between Borodino and the Moskva, into which it emptied, had a steep right bank, which it was easy for the Russians to defend. Bagration's part of the front, on the other hand, was covered only by the waterless gullies of two streams—the Semyonovka and the Kamenka—where the western bank, over which the French would be attacking, was actually higher than the eastern. Such being the case, considerable pains should have been taken to strengthen the left wing, at the expense of the right. But this was not the way Bennigsen had planned it. To one of Bagration's corps—the Seventh, which had already distinguished itself under General Rayevsky during the siege of Smolensk—was entrusted the task of holding the center of the line. To the other of Bagration's corps, the Eighth, was entrusted the defense of the key village of Semyonovskoye and of the open ground sloping gradually down to the edge of the wooded scrub brush, north of Utitsa. As though this were not enough, Bagration was also assigned the task of erecting a redoubt on top of a hummock located near the hamlet of Shevardino, a good mile farther to the west.

With his customary care and thoroughness Barclay de Tolly spent his first day at Borodino going over the First Army's right-wing positions. He had part of a wood chopped down for the positioning of a powerful artillery battery, and he ordered his sappers to construct three open-end redans to make this sector of the line as formidable as possible. Other artillery batteries were stationed in the scrub brush close to the undulating Kolotcha River, opposite the village of Novoye Syelo, which was gutted so that it could not be used by French snipers.

Not until the next day, September 4, did Barclay have time to visit the entire length of the line with Kutuzov. What he saw made him distinctly uneasy. Although sappers and militiamen were hard at work constructing a five-sided earthwork redoubt on the forward Shevardino hummock, nothing had been done to fortify the round hill in the center of the Russian line, as well as the

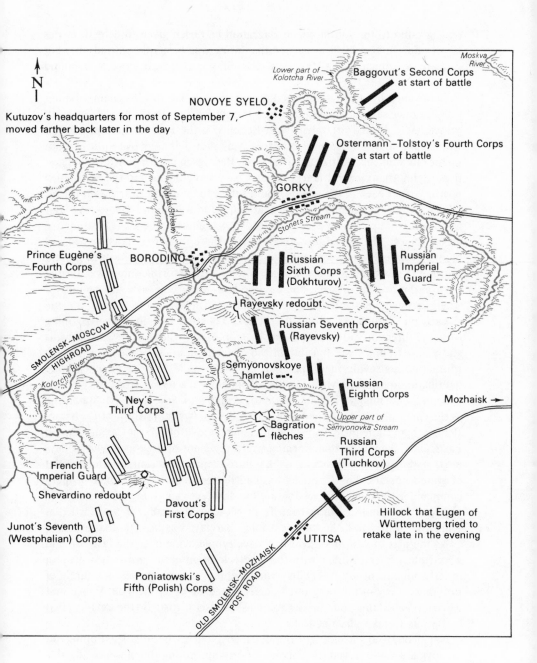

N

Lower part of
Kolotcha River

Moskva
River

Baggovut's Second Corps
at start of battle

NOVOYE SYELO

Kutuzov's headquarters for most of September 7,
moved farther back later in the day

Ostermann–Tolstoy's Fourth Corps
at start of battle

GORKY

Stonets Stream

Volha Stream

Prince Eugène's
Fourth Corps

BORODINO

Russian
Sixth Corps
(Dokhturov)

Russian
Imperial
Guard

Rayevsky redoubt

SMOLENSK–MOSCOW
HIGHROAD

Kolotcha River

Kamenka Gully

Russian Seventh Corps
(Rayevsky)

Semyonovskoye
hamlet

Russian
Eighth Corps

Mozhaisk →

Ney's
Third Corps

Bagration
flèches

Upper part of
Semyonovka Stream

Russian
Third Corps
(Tuchkov)

French
Imperial Guard

Shevardino redoubt

Davout's
First Corps

Junot's Seventh
(Westphalian) Corps

Hillock that Eugen of
Württemberg tried to
retake late in the evening

UTITSA

Poniatowski's
Fifth (Polish) Corps

OLD SMOLENSK–MOZHAISK
POST ROAD

BORODINO BATTLEFIELD

open ground to the south, which Bagration had been given to defend. It was largely due to Barclay's insistence that work was belatedly started on what came to be known as the Rayevsky redoubt, guarded by a score of 12-pound cannon.

Confronted by such capricious dispositions, Barclay and his enemy, Bagration, for once saw eye to eye. During a tour of his lines the unhappy Georgian prince had a heated argument with Bennigsen; the French, he pointed out, would have no trouble turning his excessively short left flank by sending troops up the old Smolensk–Mozhaisk post road. Bennigsen pooh-poohed the suggestion, saying that General Karpov's six Cossack regiments and the militiamen posted farther back in the woods would suffice to take care of any such threat. Like Kutuzov, he seemed to think that Napoleon was bound to aim his major thrust straight up the new Smolensk–Moscow highway, where the Russian line was strongest. He agreed, however, to have three *flèches* (redans shaped like blunt arrowheads and open-ended at the rear) constructed on the open ground south of the Semyonovka streambed. Work on these fortifications was started only on the fourth—at least one day too late—and they were still unfinished when they were assaulted on the seventh.

Early on the morning of the fifth the sound of gunfire could be heard coming from the direction of the vast Kolotsky monastery, whose whitewashed walls and painted domes were visible in the distance, some six miles to the west. Murat and his cavalrymen, spearheading the Grande Armée's advance, were fighting another battle with General Konovnitsyn's rear guard.

Soon Konovnitsyn's infantry battalions came into view of the Russian army as they marched through the village of Valuyevo, two miles short of Borodino. Behind them came the cavalrymen of General Ouvarov's First Cavalry Corps. Particularly happy on this morning was a regiment of dragoons who at daybreak had teamed up with a Cossack unit to surprise and slaughter a regiment of Dutch hussars. The Cossacks too had reason to be happy. Their peppery commander, Ataman Matvei Platov, his dark eyes sparkling with malicious pleasure, had come rushing back from Moscow the moment he heard that Kutuzov, rather than the "unspeakable" Barclay, was now in charge.

As the first of Murat's advancing cavalrymen came over the last rise and were suddenly confronted with the spectacle of an entire army drawn up in orderly alignment on the hills rising behind the two-towered church of Borodino, a cry of joy rang out—one repeated by every Grande Armée unit when it reached this point on the Smolensk–Moscow road. So the long-awaited battle was to take place at last!

Napoleon, who was not far behind, called a halt to the advance. Pulling out his spyglass, he surveyed the Russians' positions, noting the presence of light-infantry Jaegers near the green-domed Borodino church, signs of earthworks and formidable artillery batteries farther up the hill, around the village of Gorky. In the distance, about an hour's march beyond the range of hills on which the Russians were now massively arrayed, he could see a number of church towers and the tall roofs of a many-domed monastery rising from dark woodlands. They were in or near the town of Mozhaisk, where the old Smolensk post road joined the new highway, up which he had been riding. He lowered the focus to examine the Russians' bivouacs and the various concentrations of soldiers, whose weapons, helmets, and breastplates glinted like golden pinheads as they moved about in the rays of the afternoon sun. What most arrested his attention was the fortified hummock he could see over on the right between two villages. A few silhouettes were visible above the redoubt parapet, as were two dark bodies of troops spread across the fields on either side.

It was obvious at a glance that this obtrusive strongpoint would have to be eliminated swiftly, for its guns, from their slightly higher elevation atop the hummock, could sweep the gently rolling ground to the right of the Kolotcha, where Napoleon's forces would have to be deployed to be able to attack Kutuzov's army. French engineers put up two wooden trestle bridges across the Kolotcha, so that General Dominique Compans, commanding the 5th Division of Davout's First Corps, could trundle his artillery over the riverbed behind his advancing columns. A courier was simultaneously dispatched to Poniatowski, instructing him to veer left from the old Smolensk–Mozhaisk post road with his two Polish infantry divisions, supporting cavalry, and cannon, and to move through the intervening woods and scrub brush to assault the Shevardino bastion from the south.

To General Grouchy's artillery commander, Lubin Griois, this late-afternoon attack seemed to glow and glisten like a pageant. "A superb sky and a setting sun added to the beauty of the spectacle. The rest of the army, from their positions, followed with their eyes those marching troops, proud to be the first called upon to have the honor to combat, and accompanied them with their acclamations." Supported by two of Murat's cavalry corps, General Compans's infantrymen drove the Russians from the first two villages they came to and continued their enveloping movement toward the south. From a hillock near the village of Fomkino a battery of six French cannon began bombarding the Shevardino redoubt, while another battery, set up by Poniatowski's Poles, shot roundshot at it over the heads of Compans's advancing skirmishers. The guns of the redoubt riposted, and the hummock disappeared behind puffs of smoke, each followed by a distant boom.

Shaped like a pentagon and some sixty yards in width, the Shevardino redoubt had been so hastily constructed that some of its nine cannon had been inserted into improperly cut grooves (making them incapable of swiveling), while the rest had to fire over the crude earthwork embankment. Its main defense came from eight line-infantry regiments, nine dragoon and cuirassier regiments, two squadrons of hussars, and eight mounted artillery pieces, which Bagration's local commander, Prince Gorchakov, had positioned in the fallow fields, the underbrush, and the woodlands roundabout. The Russian cavalrymen, however, found their ability to charge impeded by field fences, from behind whose wooden slats the French tirailleurs kept up a very effective fire.

The guns on the Shevardino redoubt having been silenced through combined cannon fire and musketry, Compans marched his regiments toward the opposing Russian lines just beyond it. Soon both sides began blazing away at each other at point-blank range.

To put an end to this sanguinary shooting match, Compans brought up a reserve battalion and had it execute a rapid transversal movement. Behind it four light-artillery pieces were suddenly unmasked, which let fly at the Russian line with grapeshot. A bayonet charge followed, straight through the intervening smoke. With its left wing suddenly crumbling, the entire Russian line began to retreat in disorder, allowing the French to occupy the redoubt.

By now it was close to eight o'clock in the evening. Dark clouds obscured the sunset and the light was fading fast. The badly battered redoubt, filled with the bodies of dead or wounded gunners and their stricken horses, had by now lost all military value. But his pride piqued by this French success, Prince Bagration decided to lead the 2nd Grenadier Division into battle to regain it. It was a quixotic venture, typical of his hot-blooded and unreflecting temperament. To the sound of rolling drums and deep-throated *oorah*s the Russian grenadiers of Prince Carl of Mecklenburg's division tramped forward with fixed bayonets and drove out the French infantrymen who had just invested the redoubt. Another of Davout's divisions had to be committed to the fray. In the smoke-filled gloaming it became increasingly difficult to tell friend from foe, as the redoubt changed hands several times in dusky hand-to-hand fighting. An advancing French infantry regiment lost two light-artillery pieces when it was suddenly set upon by Russian dragoons. The survivors were finally rescued by a regiment of Spanish fusiliers, who kept blazing away into the night at the murky silhouettes of blade-flashing cavaliers and neighing horses, garishly illuminated by flaming peasant houses.

The confused nocturnal struggle was still raging at ten o'clock when an emissary arrived from Kutuzov's headquarters, ordering Bagration to recall his men and to leave the exposed redoubt in the hands of the enemy. The French had lost several thousand casualties but the Russians, as Barclay de Tolly later reported to the tsar, lost more than 6,000 dead and wounded, as well as eight cannon—a price he felt was inordinately high.

The loss of the Shevardino redoubt did, however, have one salutary consequence for the Russians. It convinced Kutuzov that Bagration and Barclay de Tolly were right in feeling that the extreme left wing, and in particular the old Smolensk–Mozhaisk post road, could not adequately be defended by six Cossack regiments and a few miscellaneous detachments. Without bothering to keep Barclay or even his chief of staff, Bennigsen, informed of his intentions, Kutuzov now ordered General Nikolai Alexeyevich Tuchkov (brother of the Pavel Tuchkov who had been taken prisoner at Valutina Gora) to move his Third Corps from its right-wing reserve position to the wooded area behind Bagration's left flank. The move was made during the night, so as not to arouse the attention of the French. Had Barclay not happened to send an aide-de-camp to Tuchkov's Third Corps command post—only to learn that the entire corps had vanished without a trace!—he would not have discovered until much later that his available reserves had just been dramatically reduced by some 8,000 men.

During this same night, the Grande Armée's six infantry and five cavalry corps moved into their assigned bivouac positions. The Imperial Guard, forming a hollow square enclosing Napoleon's and Berthier's tents, took up its position left of the Smolensk–Moscow highroad, behind the soldiers of Prince Eugène's Fourth Corps, who stretched out as best they could among the willows and the scrub brush. The 10,000 survivors of Ney's Third Corps were camped on the slightly higher ground to the right of the Kolotcha, while the 40,000 men of Davout's First Corps spread over the area adjoining the recently captured redoubt south of the smoking ruins of the Shevardino and Doronino hamlets. Prince Poniatowski's Poles occupied the woods and scrub-brush area beyond, while what was left of the two Westphalian divisions of the Eighth Corps were bivouacked some distance behind Ney's men. The main Smolensk road for miles back was crammed with cannon, artillery caissons, baggage and supply wagons, as well as herds of livestock, which had to be fed and watered in the nearest fields and streams. For the cavalrymen, in particular, it was a restless night.

Napoleon too got little sleep. At two in the morning (of September 6) he heaved himself up onto one of his white horses and toured the entire camp area from the extreme right wing to the left, and back again. Through the drizzle he could see the Russians' flickering campfires, laid out in neat rows, roughly indicating their assigned battle lines across the hills to the east. By counting them he tried to assess the exact strength of Kutuzov's forces.

From what he had already seen the previous afternoon, it was clear that Kutuzov had established a powerful and well-entrenched right wing, which it would be folly to assault. There was no point in attempting an outflanking movement on this side, which, given the relatively flat ground on which the Fourth Corps was bivouacked, could not be concealed from the Russians' hillside vantage points. Instead, Napoleon ordered Prince Eugène's men to start throwing up earthwork parapets for artillery batteries, to protect his left wing from a possible Russian counterattack. He had already decided to throw the main weight of his assault against the other end of the Russian line, but these gun emplacements on his own left wing might help to mask his real intentions.

When the sun finally rose, Napoleon, and many Grande Armée officers and soldiers with him, were relieved to see that the Russians had not moved and that they were digging in more determinedly than ever. This Friday, September 6, passed off peacefully, with brief outbreaks of gunfire between advance-guard outposts. A bright autumn sun, playing hide-and-seek behind the clouds, contributed to this deceptive tranquillity by "skipping along the murderous steel of bayonets and guns" and darting a "blinding glare" from the burnished bronze of cannon barrels, as the Russian artillery lieutenant Ivan Rodozhitsky put it. All regiments had been ordered to don their full-dress uniforms, as though for a fête.

During the afternoon Napoleon undertook another personal reconnaissance, approaching close enough to the village of Borodino to unleash a blast of grapeshot from some infuriated Russian gunners. The extraordinary density of the Russian lines, drawn up only three hundred yards apart, with the reserves backed up against the hilltop woods, made them vulnerable to a massive artillery bombardment. Davout, however, felt that something bolder was called for than a frontal assault on the redans and redoubts the Russians were still busily reinforcing. Given the shortness of their line and the manifest weakness of its left wing, he boldly proposed that his five First Corps divisions team up with Poniatowski's two Polish divisions in a powerful encircling movement through the Utitsa woods, calculated to bring them out behind Bagration's left flank and onto the wooded crest of the hills where the Russians' backup artillery pieces were massed in an almost unbroken line. Driving across those hills, the French and the Poles could roll up the entire enemy line with one prong of this encircling movement, while another, driving straight down the old Smolensk–Mozhaisk post road, cut off the Russians' retreat. After which Kutuzov's hopelessly disorganized forces could be relentlessly pushed back into the triangular pocket formed by the Kolotcha and Moskva rivers and annihilated, or forced to surrender.

The proposal had a great deal to commend it. But after carefully considering Davout's idea, Napoleon turned it down on the grounds that it was too risky. Taken together, Davout's five and Poniatowski's two divisions, more than 50,000 men in all, amounted to one-half of Napoleon's available infantry. Their joint enveloping movement would open a sizable gap in his own line, which would have to be plugged by moving the entire line over to the right, or by moving up the two largely untested Westphalian divisions of the Eighth Corps as well as his two Young Guard divisions. This would have left Napoleon with virtually no reserves, save for the five grenadier regiments of the Old Guard and the 4,000 elite horsemen of Marshal Bessières's cavalry.

According to Philippe de Ségur, who has left us the most detailed account of this discussion, Napoleon put an end to it by brusquely interrupting Davout: "Ah, you're always in favor of outflanking the enemy! But it's too dangerous a maneuver." Davout returned to his tent in high dudgeon, wondering what on earth had come over Napoleon, whom he had always known in the past as audacious and willing to take risks.

Earlier in the day Jean-François de Bausset, one of the prefects of the imperial palace in Paris, had finally caught up with his master after a carriage ride of thirty-seven days. With him he brought messages and letters from Marie-Louise, along with a recently completed painting of their son, the seventeen-month-old "king of Rome." Napoleon insisted on having the painting immediately uncrated. Executed by Gérard, it showed the infant propped up in his cradle and joyfully clutching a tiny scepter in one chubby hand and a globe in the other.

"Admirable!" exclaimed Napoleon, his pale blue eyes and the expression on his face seeming suddenly to soften. He had the framed painting placed upon a chair near the entrance to his tent. "Gentlemen, if my son were fifteen years old, you may be sure that he would be here among so many brave ones otherwise than in a painting," he declared to his marshals and aides-de-camp. The portrait's timely arrival was regarded as an auspicious omen for the morrow. It was left exposed for the rest of the day, so that the mustachioed *grognards* of his Imperial Guard could also come up and admire it.

But in the evening Napoleon had it returned to its protective crate, remarking almost sadly, "He is too young to see a field of battle." The favorable auspices of the morning had been troubled by a piece of bad news from Spain, brought by an aide-de-camp who reported that Marshal Marmont, having rashly attacked the duke of Wellington without waiting for reinforcements, had been wounded and defeated near Salamanca. This serious setback at the other end of the continent made a decisive victory the next day even more imperative.

In the Russian camp, where the soldiers also spent the day sharpening bayonets, polishing buttons and bronze helmets, whitening scabbards, cross-straps, and leggings, the prevailing mood was one of grim resolve rather than of elation. Certain commanders were as unhappy as was Davout, in the French camp, with the existing dispositions. Prince Eugen von Württemberg, for example, waited all day in vain for Bennigsen to carry out his announced intention of having the bulk of the Second and Fourth corps moved from the right wing to the general reserve in the center.

Kutuzov's main concern during most of this Friday was to maintain the morale and fighting spirit of his troops. As simply dressed as ever, he personally accompanied the robed priests and archimandrites who passed through the ranks, melodiously intoning Old Slavonic prayers as they held aloft the miracle-working Black Madonna ikon of Smolensk, swung their smoking censers, and sprinkled drops of holy water on the shaved heads of the soldiers. "The French will break their teeth on us," he assured his soldiers, in the simple, pithy language he was so skilled in using. "It will be a pity if, having broken them, we can't finish them off."

After Kutuzov had returned to his headquarters, which had been moved forward to the village of Gorky, Barclay de Tolly again sought to persuade him to strengthen the weak left wing. He proposed that under cover of nightfall the entire Russian line be moved to the left so that the First Army's two right-wing corps would be positioned across and to the left of the Smolensk–Moscow highroad, instead of to the right of it, while the left flank of Bagration's Second Army was extended southward through the underbrush and woods as far as the village of Utitsa, where it could properly be anchored, rather than left as at present "hanging in the air." Had this been done, as Barclay subsequently pointed out in a long explanatory letter to the tsar, the army's reserves, instead of being thrown into action at an early stage, "could have been preserved until the last moment, and, not being scattered about, might have decided the outcome of the battle." But once again Kutuzov, while seeming to approve of the suggestion, did nothing to put it into execution.

As dusk fell the final eve-of-battle orders were issued, first of all by Kutuzov, who urged his subordinates to commit their forces sparingly, "for the general who retains his reserves remains undefeated." Barclay de Tolly was more specific in enjoining his commanders to keep their infantrymen from indulging in "random gunfire, which never has much effect," to hold them back at the end of successful attacks, and to forbid them to bellow "*Oorah!*" until they were ten paces from the enemy, when this frightening roar could be used to maximum effect. General Alexander Kutaïssov, the twenty-eight-year-old son of Emperor Paul I's Turkish barber, who had risen through intrinsic merit to become commander of the First Army's reserve artillery, pulled no punches in telling his subordinates what was expected of them: "Insist with all companies that they should not withdraw from their positions until the enemy is on top of the guns. . . . Let them take you with your guns, but fire the last charge of canister at point-blank range. . . ." Bagration, for his part, ordered all of his front-line Jaeger skirmishers to be relieved by others, so that they could enjoy a good night's rest as well as a meal of hot *kasha* (buckwheat gruel) laced with wine before returning to their front-line posts the next morning.

It is doubtful if the Jaegers, or many others in the Russian camp, got much sleep, so tense and full of foreboding was the general atmosphere during this pre-battle night. It was already so cold that many soldiers huddled together in their greatcoats around blazing logs or scraps of wood, singing melancholy folk songs.

Thousands of militiamen were kept up all night digging frantically to reinforce the defenses of the central redoubt. Shaped like a nutcracker opened to an angle of 160 degrees, this redoubt consisted of an earthwork parapet that was some 420 feet in length. Although its nineteen 12-pounders were protected in front by a ditch that was twenty-five feet wide and five feet deep, nothing had yet been done to protect the flanks when at eleven at night Engineer Officer Dementy Bogdanov was summoned by General Rayevsky. Working as fast as they could wield their picks and shovels, under Bogdanov's direction, the militiamen dug two thirty-yard-long ditches, so as to make the open rear or "throat" of the redoubt less accessible to enemy cavalrymen, who would first have to weather the cross fire of powerful batteries positioned to the right near the village of Gorky, and of sixty artillery pieces arrayed to the left.

In the opposing camp too, few soldiers were able to enjoy much more than a brief, fitful sleep. Many, particularly among French veterans, preferred to sit up cracking jokes and telling stories of their adventures in past campaigns. Shortly after sundown there was a burst of rain, which, leaving the fields silvered with heavy dew, added to the general discomfort of a cold, occasionally windswept night for soldiers who had no tents to sleep under. The army doctor Heinrich von Roos, who like his fellow Westphalians spent this night on an empty stomach, was so frozen that in the early hours of the morning he went out to cut juniper branches to try to keep the campfires burning.

To the damp, piercing cold and lack of food and water was added the additional discomfort of noise, as artillery pieces were moved forward to new positions. General Lubin Griois, commanding the horse artillery of Grouchy's Third Cavalry Corps, had a lot of trouble getting his cannon and caissons across "steep-banked and soggy gullies, which had to be crossed without guides, at times in utter darkness, at others in the midst of bivouac fires, which blinded us and caused us to lose all sense of direction." While Griois was laboriously moving his horses and his guns over to the left, to join Prince Eugène de Beauharnais's Fourth Corps, General Jean Sorbier, commanding the Imperial Guard's reserve artillery, was moving 100 guns more or less in the opposite direction. He had been ordered to line up two powerful batteries in front of the charred remains of the Shevardino hamlet. The artillery commanders of Davout's First and Ney's Third corps were likewise kept busy installing two more batteries of 60 guns, somewhat farther to the left. In this way the concentrated fire of 180 cannon and howitzers, in addition to the 30 field pieces that were to accompany the first wave of the assault, were to be concentrated against the earthwork *flèches* that Bagration's sappers and militiamen had erected on the crest of a low rise some 800 yards beyond the streambed gully separating the French and Russian armies. Napoleon had already resorted to massed artillery barrages at the bloody battle of Wagram, but the cannonade he was now preparing for Kutuzov's Russians surpassed everything even he had so far tried.

At two in the morning Napoleon was on his feet again, after an hour or two of sleep. He was suffering from a painful head cold, but he was not going to let this keep him from making sure that everything was proceeding according to his plans. Accompanied by a small suite of duty officers, he crossed the Kolotcha River and rode past the drowsy soldiers of Ney's Third Corps. He had decided to direct the coming battle from the vantage point of the captured Shevardino hummock, opposite Kutuzov's weak left flank. But so as not to reveal his hand too soon, he had deliberately left his tent and the Imperial Guard bivouacked to the left of the Smolensk–Moscow highroad. Only when dawn began to break and everywhere bugles and drums were sounding reveille did these elite grenadiers and cavalrymen move southward in their turn to new positions around and behind the Shevardino redoubt.

The bugle calls were also the signal for the reading by company commanders of Napoleon's order of the day. "Soldiers," it declared, "here is the battle you have so long desired! Henceforth victory depends on you; it is necessary to us. It will give us abundance, good winter quarters, and a prompt return to the homeland! Conduct yourselves as you did at Austerlitz, Friedland, Vitebsk, and Smolensk, and may the most distant posterity cite with pride your conduct during this day; may it be said of you, 'He was at the great battle under the walls of Moscow!' "

Carefully calculated to offer what his hungry soldiers craved—plenty of food and loot, comfortable beds to sleep in, and a rapid homecoming—this terse proclamation in its final sentences echoed the more original and inspiring order of the day preceding Austerlitz. Napoleon had even indulged in geographic hocus-pocus, in making it sound as though the battle were taking place in the vicinity of Moscow, when in fact his army was still more than seventy miles away.

There is general agreement among most participants that the battle started around six in the morning with a signal shot fired by a cannon of General Sorbier's Imperial Guard artillery. The sun at first was veiled and the valley separating the two armies was blanketed in early morning mist. When the sun finally broke through the fog, it was predictably hailed by Napoleon with the words *"Messieurs, voici le soleil d'Austerlitz!"* This time, however, it proved an initial handicap, for the almost horizontal rays momentarily blinded the French and made it difficult to see immediately ahead. But as the fog began to lift, General Sorbier realized that the batteries that had been set up during the night had been placed too far back. The guns were hastily moved forward from their earthwork embankments closer to the Russian lines.

The early morning mist, however, proved an unexpected boon for Napoleon's left wing. To mask the main thrust of his attack, Napoleon had decided to begin operations with an assault on the village of Borodino, which was held by an elite Guards regiment of Russian Jaegers. The task was entrusted to one of Prince Eugène de Beauharnais's divisions, which mounted a two-pronged assault—straight up the Smolensk–Moscow highroad and also from the northwest. The fog-shrouded assault took the Russian Jaegers completely by surprise. They were driven from the church cemetery and the village in a matter of minutes. The gunners had just time to hitch up their 6-pounders and to have the horses drag them back across the main highway's wooden bridge across the Kolotcha and on up the hill toward the village of Gorky.

Farther up the hill Barclay de Tolly had been watching the pandemonium with grimly pursed lips. Instead of going to bed, he had spent the night in a village hut with his young artillery chief, Alexander Kutaïssov, and his new and even younger chief of staff, Colonel Arseny Andreyevich Zakrevsky, finishing a long letter of detailed self-justification intended for Emperor Alexander. His pride deeply hurt by his recent demotion and by the scant attention that had been paid to his suggestions, he was in a frankly suicidal mood and more than ready to court death by exposing himself to enemy cannonballs and bullets. Instead of wearing the inconspicuous gear favored by some Russian generals, he had donned his full-dress uniform and sported all his decorations, including three star clusters flashing on his chest. Now, seated on his horse, he looked down on the still partly mist-shrouded village of Borodino with a feeling of pent-up anger. He had vainly tried to persuade Kutuzov to leave Borodino to the French, realizing the danger of trying to hold it when there was only one bridge linking this exposed position with the rest of the army. But Yermolov, probably for reasons of prestige, had convinced the generalissimo that the town had to be held for as long as possible. As a result an elite Guards regiment was being needlessly decimated.

But soon it was the victorious French who lost their heads. Elated by their easy victory in clearing Borodino of Russian troops, the fusiliers of the 106th Line Regiment charged across the corpse-littered bridge and began to move up the slope in dispersed formation toward the village of Gorky, apparently confident that nothing and nobody could stop them. Coolly Barclay summoned a colonel (Vuitch) known for his courage and told him to mount a counterattack with two Jaeger regiments. Advancing down the hill, the Jaegers fired a first volley at the French infantrymen from a distance of thirty yards, killing the French general Plauzonne, who was trying to hold back his overeager men. A bayonet attack followed, and hundreds of French infantrymen were relentlessly pushed back into the Kolotcha River and across the bridge. The 106th Regiment in its turn was virtually annihilated. The survivors took refuge behind the advancing columns of another French regiment. But the Russian Jaegers, again acting under Barclay's orders, made no attempt to recapture Borodino.

By this time all hell had broken loose south of the Kolotcha River, as 300 French artillery pieces went into action. "Suddenly," as Philippe de Ségur vividly described it, "from this peaceful plain and from those silent hills one saw whirls of fire and smoke erupt, followed almost immediately by a multitude of explosions and the whistling of cannonballs, which tore through the air in all directions."

What the two adversaries were now witnessing, with an uncomfortable mixture of awe and horror, was a new kind of stationary warfare, which was to reach its grim apogee one hundred years later in the pulverizing shellings of Verdun and the battle of the Somme. If the French came out the winners in this artillery battle, it was almost certainly due to the greater ability of their artillery officers, and to the fact that Napoleon was able from the start to concentrate close to 300 guns over and against the 200 that Bagration had available. Kutuzov, with 640 cannon and howitzers, had 50 more artillery pieces than Napoleon had—an advantage enhanced by the fact that almost one-quarter of the total were longer-range 12-pounders, whereas the Grande Armée had only one 12-pounder in every ten artillery pieces, the rest being 3-, 4-, and 6-pounders. But because so much firepower had been concentrated on the right wing, many of these Russian guns could not be brought into action soon enough, or even moved at all, to make this advantage tell.

The intensity of the cannonade may be judged by the difficulty so many of the participants in this battle had in trying to find words to describe it. Friedrich von Schubert, who was serving as chief of staff for a Russian cavalry corps, later said that once it got under way, "it was no longer possible to distinguish one cannon boom from another." He could only compare the infernal din to "several hundred drums" pounded so rapidly that "one can no longer hear them individually." Captain Roman Soltyk claimed that "it bore more resemblance to broadsides fired by men-of-war at sea than to an artillery engagement on land." Bagration's senior duty officer, General Sergei Mayevsky, later wrote that "while galloping over a distance of two versts"—about 1.3 miles—"I was so deafened by the flight of bombards that for two hours I could not clear my ears and close my mouth."

In an official tally drawn up after the battle, General Baston de La Riboisière, inspector general of the Grande Armée's artillery, reported that French and allied gunners had fired 60,000 artillery rounds and that the infantry had expended 140,000 cartridges. Even if one assumes that the Russian volume of fire was slightly less—50,000 artillery rounds and 120,000 cartridges—the combined average rate of fire for a battle that lasted ten hours was three cannon booms per second and more than 430 musket shots per minute.

So thick were the clouds of smoke rising from so many cannon, howitzers, and muskets, not to mention exploding canisters, that the battlefield was soon obscured by a drifting pall, which at times completely blotted out the sunlight. As the day progressed the dew-covered ground of the early morning dried out completely, and bouncing cannonballs and horses' hooves kicked up huge clouds of dust, which greatly impeded visibility and added to the general confusion.

To few military encounters can Wellington's famous dictum "It is as impossible to describe a battle as it is to describe a ball" be more aptly applied than to Borodino. So much was happening simultaneously in a relatively restricted space, there were so many charges and countercharges, so many confused mêlées and hand-to-hand engagements, that no two eyewitness accounts agree exactly as to just what took place at this moment or that. All one can do, therefore, is to retrace somewhat schematically the general evolution of the battle.

The French attack on the Russians' weak left flank, which Napoleon intended to be the main thrust of his offensive, got under way some time after six in the morning. General Compans's 5th Infantry Division was chosen once again to lead the assault—this time against the southernmost of the arrowhead flèches which had been erected on Bagration's sector of the front. Compans divided his division into two columns. The left-hand column, led by himself, was to approach the redan directly, while the other, right-hand column moved forward through the underbrush and the fringe of the Utitsa woods.

This assault ran into far stiffer resistance than Napoleon had anticipated. Poniatowski, who had been ordered to capture the village of Utitsa and to clear the neighboring woods during the first hour of daylight, found the going very difficult through the dense underbrush to the immediate left of the Smolensk–Mozhaisk post road. The Poles, using their 50 cannon, finally drove the Russians from Utitsa. But they were unable to emerge triumphantly through the woods in time to help Compans's right-hand column, which lost its way as it pushed through the pathless underbrush, and then ran into strong musket and artillery fire from the Jaegers of General Tuchkov's Third Corps.

Even fiercer was the resistance encountered by General Compans's prestigious 57th Regiment—nicknamed "le Terrible"—in its direct assault on the southernmost Bagration redan. To approach the flèche, the column had to leave the plateau on which it had been posted, some 600 yards ahead of the Shevardino redoubt, and descend into the scrub-filled gully of the now virtually waterless Kamenka streambed. As they ascended the opposite slope onto the open ground leading to the Bagration flèche, the infantrymen, led by their mounted officers, were met with a barrage of cannonballs and grapeshot fired from several Russian batteries set up near the redan. A number of his officers were hit, and then General Compans himself was felled by three grapeshot slugs in the shoulder.

At the sight of their division commander being carried from the field, the infantrymen of the 57th Regiment began to waver. Davout, notwithstanding his poor eyesight (which forced him to wear spectacles), had been watching the attack through a spyglass. Perceiving that the attack was bogging down, he galloped boldly forward to revive the flagging spirit of Compans's infantrymen. Galvanized by his unexpected appearance, the two converging columns rushed forward across the remaining ground and stormed the redan, bayoneting the remaining Russian gunners by their cannon. But as they did so, a cannonball hit Davout's horse, which rolled over on the ground, carrying the marshal with it.

On the Shevardino hummock, where the French emperor was following the attack through his telescope, there was a moment of consternation—soon followed by immense relief when it was learned that Davout had not been killed but merely badly bruised and shaken up by his horse's rolling fall. Napoleon, who had already dispatched General Jean Rapp to replace Compans as commander of the 5th Division, now called on his brother-in-law Murat to take command of the First Corps, not realizing that the tough, muscular Davout was not *hors de combat* by any means.

As intrepid as ever, the white-whiskered Jean Rapp galloped forward to take command of Compans's 5th Division. But he had hardly reached the redan, which the infantrymen were trying to hold against a Russian counterattack, when within the space of a few minutes he was grazed three times—twice by bullets, once by a cannonball, which ripped the cloth from the sleeve of his riding coat and shirt—and then knocked from his horse by a canister explosion, which lodged a piece of metal in his hip.

Unlike the five-sided redoubt that had been erected on the Shevardino hummock, the chevron-shaped redans, or if one prefers, the arrowhead flèches, which the Russians had thrown up on this slightly inclined open ground, were open at the back. Holding them against a counterattack, after they had been taken, thus proved an even more difficult enterprise than storming them, since once inside the V, the infantrymen were exposed to the fire of marksmen and gunners firing from farther back.

Several hundred yards to the left, the leading division of Ney's Third Corps was finding it difficult to hold the second redan, which it had finally managed to storm after an intensive artillery bombardment shortly after eight o'clock. It was only now that the French discovered that a third flèche had been built a little farther back, beyond the breast of the hill, to cover the first two redans and the streambed gully of the Semyonovka, above which Bagration had established his command post.

Reacting with his customary vigor, the commander of Russia's Second Army threw everything he had into his counterattacks. The infantrymen of Neverovsky's 27th Division managed to push the French out of the southernmost flèche, while those of Count Vorontsov's 7th Combined Grenadier Division sought to evict Ney's troopers from the northernmost redan.

As more and more men were committed to the fray, Bagration found the pressure on his part of the front inexorably mounting. From Tuchkov's Third Corps he borrowed General Konovnitsyn's 3rd Division, a move that seriously weakened Tuchkov's ability to resist the advance of Poniatowski's Poles. From Rayevsky's Seventh Corps to his right Bagration removed most of the second line, gravely weakening the Russian center. Desperate appeals for reinforcements went out—first to Kutuzov, and then directly to Barclay de Tolly, whose two right-wing corps had virtually nothing to do but listen to what was going on elsewhere. Barclay, who had already received a plea for help from

Tuchkov, had not waited for Kutuzov's permission to order General Baggovut to march his Second Corps (composed of two divisions) southward. But given the distance separating the right wing from the left, and the woods through which men and cannon had to pass, they could not be brought into action quickly. Bennigsen, belatedly realizing the weakness of Bagration's Second Army, ordered General Lavrov to move up three crack regiments and two batteries of 12-pounders from the Imperial Guard reserve. Thus, within three hours of the battle's start, and because of lopsided dispositions, the Russian commanders were already forced to commit some of their precious reserves —just what Barclay had hoped could be avoided through a better alignment of forces.

Paradoxically, precisely at the moment (between eight-thirty and nine) when Bagration's situation was becoming increasingly difficult, the atmosphere at Kutuzov's headquarters, now located behind the village of Gorky, was one of heady jubilation. Colonel Toll, who had just galloped back from Bagration's command post, brought the news that the first French assault on the flèches had been repulsed. This was followed by a report that Murat, the king of Naples, had been captured in the first stormed and then recaptured flèche. "The enthusiasm aroused by this news flared like a bonfire," in the words of Carl von Clausewitz, now serving as chief of staff for General Ouvarov, commander of the First Russian Cavalry Corps. The younger hotheads were all for opening the champagne and drinking a victory toast.

In reality Murat had not been captured. He had had several close calls while galloping fearlessly from one redan to the next and personally leading cavalry attacks in his conspicuous sky-blue riding jacket, gold-tasseled sash, and velvet headgear. His narrowest escape came during a charge made by one French and two Württemberg light-cavalry regiments, which were ordered to break up a Russian infantry assault aimed at recapturing one of the Bagration redans, now held by infantrymen of the 25th (Württemberg) Division. During a moment of confusion caused by the appearance on the scene of a Russian cuirassier regiment, Murat found himself suddenly alone with one of his grooms, a Moor as fantastically garbed as himself. Leaping from his richly harnessed horse, he tossed the reins to his faithful attendant and ran into the flèche to keep from being encircled and captured by the upriding cuirassiers. An almost comic scene ensued, as Murat, waving his white-plumed hat and repeatedly shouting "*Scheuss! Scheuss!*" (as near as he could get to the German word *schiess*), urged the Württembergers to *shoot* at the cuirassiers, while the Moorish groom stood pathetically still in the narrow no-man's-land between. The Württembergers must have been amused by this gush of Gascon-flavored *Deutsch,* and at first they were understandably reluctant to open fire, given the closeness of the solitary Moorish groom—who, incredibly enough, emerged unscathed from the eventual salvo, as did Murat's horse.

Not all who saw Murat in action were as impressed as was Napoleon's young aide-de-camp Anatole de Montesquiou, who could not take his eyes off him. "With his thundering artillery and the immense cloud of smoke into which he disappeared entirely, or which his tall stature dominated, he resembled one of those terrible gods of Olympus." General Gijsbert van Dedem, whose infantry brigade twice saved Murat from capture by offering him refuge inside one of its solid squares, later wrote: "It is on great occasions that one sees the difference in character of prominent men. The King of Naples charged forward impetuously in the midst of his squadrons like the boiling Achilles; Marshal Ney rode around on his white horse while taking pinches of snuff with rare calm; he was old Nestor putting himself out to be helpful, encouraging everyone by his example, and giving the best advice to those who were marching with him, and the best orders to those who were serving under him."

Exactly how many times one or another of the three Bagration flèches was recaptured by the Russians, it is impossible to say from the mass of contradictory evidence available. But the fierceness of the fighting may be judged by the comment made by A. A. Shcherbinin, a young member of Kutuzov's staff: compared with what he had witnessed at Borodino, all the later battles in which he (and other Russian survivors) participated during the rest of 1812 and in the two ensuing years of 1813 and 1814 were "like war maneuvers." Chosen to accompany Colonel Toll on a rapid mission to Konovnitsyn's 3rd Division, he found that "shells were pouring in on the village of Semyonovskoye"—a key position just north of the three flèches, and that "the logs were falling and the huts were collapsing like stage sets. The air howled uninterruptedly, and the ground trembled."

The situation for the Russians had taken a sudden turn for the worse. The fearless Bagration, while exhorting his soldiers to launch one more counterattack, had had his shinbone smashed by a shell burst, to the consternation of his staff officers, who saw him suddenly slump forward onto his horse's neck to keep from falling from the saddle. He was carried back to a dressing station, where he was soon joined by his chief of staff, a French émigré count named Guillaume de Saint-Priest, and three of his division commanders—Prince Andrei Gorchakov, Prince Carl of Mecklenburg, and General Dmitri Neverovsky. Another general, Alexander Tuchkov (one of five brothers serving in the Russian army), was killed by a cannonball while preparing to lead his Reval infantry regiment into battle. Indeed, before this bloody morning was over, almost half of Bagration's brigade and regimental commanders were either dead or wounded.

Hostilities in the more central area of the front had also begun with an intense French artillery bombardment, which had cut down many of the first-line infantrymen of General Paskevich's 26th Division, posted south of the Rayevsky redoubt. Two French divisions—one from Prince Eugène de Beauharnais's own corps, the other "borrowed" from a disgruntled Davout—were then ordered to clear the Russian Jaegers from the intervening meadowland and streambed gully, and to storm the central redoubt, whose battery of twenty 12-pounders was taking a heavy toll of French men and horses. Caught in a furious cross fire from Russian artillery batteries positioned around the village of Gorky, the infantrymen who sought to approach the fortified hill up the gully to the left of it had had to retreat. But two regiments from Davout's

1st Division, which tried a direct assault, were more successful, chiefly because the steepness of the slope was such that most of the Russian cannonballs and shells fired from the redoubt sailed harmlessly over their heads once the soldiers had begun the ascent.

The Seventh Corps's commander, General Rayevsky, who was suffering from a wound in the calf, was actually inside the redoubt when it was finally stormed. "Your Highness, save yourself!" he heard one of his officers shout, as a couple of French grenadiers appeared with bayonets fixed. In the ensuing tussle Rayevsky managed to hobble out and to reach his first defensive line, drawn up behind the hollow formed by the redoubt's rearward slope, and climbing painfully onto his horse, he galloped farther up the hill to safety.

His vision obscured by drifting clouds of gunsmoke, Barclay de Tolly once again dispatched his trusted aide-de-camp Waldemar von Loewenstern to find out what was going on. Loewenstern arrived on his white horse just as the first French infantrymen were bayoneting their way into the redoubt. He sent a young lieutenant galloping back to Barclay, then persuaded a battalion commander from Dokhturov's Sixth Corps to launch a counterattack. Obeying Barclay's prebattle directive, the infantrymen advanced silently on the redoubt, only erupting into a blood-chilling *"Oorah!"* when they were ten paces from the French.

Barclay's chief of staff, Yermolov, happened to be passing by with the young general Alexander Kutaïssov and three companies of horse artillery, which were to strengthen the Second Army's left flank, when they saw the French storming into the redoubt while several regiments of Russian jaegers beat a panicky retreat. Galloping over to the nearest infantry unit (the Ufimsky Regiment of Dokhturov's Sixth Corps), Yermolov persuaded them to follow him in a resolute counterattack, rallying the fleeing Jaegers as they came on. Barclay, some distance farther back, now ordered two light-infantry regiments and some dragoons to bear down from the right, in order to cut off the French retreat. Thus supported, Yermolov's and Loewenstern's improvised forces stormed triumphantly into the redoubt. Straight down the hill behind them came six battalions from General Likhachov's 24th Division, their bugles blaring and their drums rolling menacingly as they advanced in perfect order.

Of the 1,300 men of the 30th Line Regiment who had begun the assault, exactly 11 officers and 257 men made it back across the Semyonovka streambed gully to the relative safety of the French line. Their valiant commander, General Charles-Auguste Bonnamy, was captured in the redoubt by a gruff Russian grenadier, who pushed and prodded him with a bayonet and then marched him as a kind of living trophy straight to Kutuzov's headquarters, paying no heed to the trail of blood the wounded general was leaving behind him. When his bloodstained undershirt was removed from his chest and shoulders, it was found that Bonnamy had been wounded in a dozen different places!

For the Russians the recapture of the Rayevsky redoubt was marred by one mishap: the disappearance of General Alexander Kutaïssov. Fired by the example of Yermolov's élan, the twenty-eight-year-old commander of the Russian army's reserve artillery galloped impetuously into the fray, leading a detachment of Russian infantrymen past the redoubt in pursuit of the retreating French. A little later Yermolov was dismayed to see Kutaïssov's horse gallop wildly past with an empty, blood-covered saddle. Just what had happened to his friend, Yermolov was never able to discover. Before the day was over, thousands of corpses were to be added to those already littering this blood-soaked hill, making a later investigation impossible.

At this point the distinction between the First and Second armies had ceased to have much significance, as even the wounded Bagration was ready to admit. When Loewenstern, who had been ordered by Barclay to have his wounded arm bandaged, reached the main dressing station, he found Bagration stretched out on the grass. Emperor Alexander's personal surgeon, James Wyllie, was trying to extract a piece of metal that had pierced the shinbone. His face creased with pain, Bagration looked up, and, seeing Loewenstern, he asked, "What is General Barclay doing?" Without waiting for the answer, he added, "Tell him that the fate of the army is in his hands."

Encouraged by Colonel Toll, who had a fondness for offensive actions, Kutuzov had meanwhile ordered Ataman Platov and the commander of the First Russian Cavalry Corps, General Ouvarov, to stage a diversionary attack on the Grande Armée's left flank. Around eleven o'clock a mass of yellow-uniformed hussars, dark-green-clad dragoons, and Cossacks in colorful red-and-blue tunics swarmed across the Kolotcha some two and a half miles downstream from Borodino and bore down on a Bavarian cavalry detachment. The Bavarians lost two horse-artillery pieces during their precipitate withdrawal. At Fourth Corps headquarters there was a sense of consternation. To repel what was thought to be a major Russian flank attack, Prince Eugène had to postpone his planned assault on the central redoubt and gallop over personally to see what was going on. Napoleon's Imperial Guard was placed on the alert, and the Polish veterans of General Claparède's Young Guard division were hastily marched toward the threatened left flank.

Had Ouvarov been given a few Jaeger regiments and a larger artillery force to back him up, his 2,500 cuirassiers, dragoons, and hussars could have tied down several French divisions for the rest of the day, decisively weakening Napoleon's forces in the center. But after staging several halfhearted cavalry attacks against a French regimental square—instead of peppering it with his dozen horse-artillery pieces, as his chief of staff, Clausewitz, suggested—Ouvarov and his horsemen retreated, overawed by the sight of General Delzons's 13th Infantry Division, solidly arrayed before the village of Borodino. Ataman Platov's 2,000 Cossacks, having been ordered to support the cautious Ouvarov, simply raised a lot of dust cantering in and out of the bushes while trying to avoid salvos of French musketry. Finally they too prudently retired behind the Kolotcha River—confirming Yermolov (and many others) in the opinion that the Cossacks, for all their swagger and bravado, were "of little use in pitched battles."

Compared with the decisive blow that Barclay de Tolly had envisaged—but at a later stage in the battle and with reserves that should have been carefully husbanded—this halfhearted flank attack was pitiful indeed. But in prompting

Napoleon to move General Claparède's Young Guard division from its original position behind Ney's soldiers, it helped to save the center of the Russian line from the breakthrough that threatened it in the middle of the afternoon.

To the north of the redans that Ney's and Davout's corpsmen had so much trouble taking and then holding was a formidable obstacle which still remained to be stormed: a hill, protected on its southern side by the soggy ground and steep embankment of the Semyonovka streambed and on its summit by several powerful batteries, which had been placed there to defend the village of Semyonovskoye, where Bagration had first established his forward command post.

The first French attempt to storm this hilltop village was thrown back by a hail of Russian grapeshot and musketry. Sent by Napoleon with a message for Davout, Colonel Louis-François Lejeune arrived just in time to see a Russian cannonball kill the First Corps's chief of staff, General Romoeuf. "He must be possessed of the devil to want to attack the bull by the horns!" exploded Davout, angrier than ever with Napoleon for adopting such pigheaded tactics. Even Ney, who (to Lejeune) "was admirable to see, quietly standing on the parapet of one of the redoubts and directing the combatants who were pressing forward at his feet," was now so hard-pressed that he kept sending messages to Napoleon requesting reinforcements.

After a murderous artillery duel the key hilltop village was finally taken by a twin-pronged cavalry assault launched by horsemen from two of Murat's four reserve cavalry corps. Those of the left prong, largely composed of Saxon, Polish, and Westphalian cuirassiers, had to charge up a steep bank, trusting to their momentum to carry them over the top. "The hill, viewed vertically, was not more than twenty yards to the top," according to the Saxon lieutenant von Meerheim, "but the slope was such that some, who did not appreciate the advantage of climbing obliquely, tumbled over backward and were trampled on by those following behind." Those who made it to the brow of the hill found themselves only sixty yards from the village, now reduced to a heap of still-glowing logs. The Saxon cuirassiers, charging recklessly forward, did their best to saber down the gunners of a Russian battery and the nearest grenadiers before they could form into bayonet-bristling squares. A number of riders and horses tumbled into hidden pits—underground silos used by peasants to store grain and other foodstuffs.

East of the destroyed village the other prong of the French cavalry attack was badly bent at first when it ran into the massed fire of three elite Guards regiments—the Izmailovsky, Litovsky, and Finland Jaegers—whose checkerboard squares fired volley after lethal volley at the oncoming horsemen and at such point-blank range that, as General Konovnitsyn, who took refuge for a while inside one of these squares, later claimed, "Every bullet, one can say, toppled over a horseman."

The struggle for the shattered hamlet of Semyonovskoye and the vital plateau beyond it was to last for three more hours—as General Gijsbert van Dedem, commanding a brigade in Davout's 2nd Division, soon discovered. His three regimental squares had to sustain five successive cavalry attacks as well as a barrage of Russian cannonballs and canister, which in one regiment alone claimed the lives of 48 officers and 360 soldiers, leaving 92 other officers and 900 soldiers wounded. "Who is the imbecile who placed you here?" exclaimed Ney at one point, appalled by the exposed position in which Dedem's brigade had been ordered to stand fast. Apparently he knew the answer, for a moment later he turned to Murat and said, "Why don't you charge with your cavalry, or have this infantry advance, since one seems so bent on getting it killed off?"

As more and more horse-artillery pieces were hauled up over transversal paths and positioned on the edge of the plateau, the more critical became the situation of the Russian center. From this new position French artillery batteries could rake the Russian lines defending the Rayevsky redoubt to their left as well as those immediately in front of them. Perceiving the danger, Barclay de Tolly ordered Prince Eugen of Württemberg to advance on the French guns with his four line regiments. For Prince Eugen this was like a "step into hell." The "enemy volcano"—a long line of eighty cannon—spewed forth its lava with renewed intensity, taking a heavy toll of Russian infantrymen. Two of his generals were wounded, and he himself had a couple of horses shot out from under him, while a third, offered to him by one of his officers, was killed with its just-dismounted rider before the prince could climb onto it.

Ney, whose three understrength divisions had barely totaled 10,000 men at the start of the battle, was already suffering from a serious manpower shortage, even though Napoleon had placed Davout's 2nd Division and the 24th (Westphalian) Division at his disposal. But these reinforcements were not enough to make possible a decisive breakthrough across the plateau east of the village of Semyonovskoye and as far as the woods, some thousand yards beyond, along the fringes of which the Russians had arrayed much of their reserve artillery. To Ney's repeated pleas for reinforcements Napoleon turned an obstinately deaf ear. All of his available divisions were now committed to the battle, with the exception of those of the Imperial Guard. In the morning he had seemed ready to give him General Claparède's Young Guard division, but then it had been diverted to Prince Eugène's left wing to help deal with the Ouvarov-Platov flank attack.

Davout, though seriously shaken up by his morning fall, was once again directing his divisions—for he was damned if he was going to let them be commanded by Murat! He came back personally to try to persuade Napoleon to commit his other Young Guard division, but he too was rebuffed, as somewhat later was Murat's chief of staff, General Belliard. "The situation is not yet sufficiently unscrambled" was Napoleon's answer. "I must be able to see more clearly on this chessboard."

When Ney was informed of this reply, he blew up, as had Davout earlier in the day. "What's the Emperor doing behind the army?" he cried. "There he is within reach only of reverses, not of successes. Since he's not waging war himself, since he's no longer a general and wants everywhere to play the Emperor, let him go back to the Tuileries and leave us to be generals for him!"

Even Napoleon's most fervent apologists were later forced to admit that this was one of the emperor's off days. Not once during the morning or even in the early afternoon did he mount up and gallop to one part or another of the front, to invigorate his soldiers with his inspiring presence, as had almost invariably been his habit in the past. Instead, after spending an hour or two on top of the Shevardino redoubt, over which an occasional Russian cannonball came whining, he descended to a kind of sandy depression (what golfers would call a bunker) in front of the hummock. Here he paced up and down with his hands clasped behind his back, conferred with Berthier and other members of his suite, occasionally sat astride a chair, steadying his spyglass on its back, and sometimes rested by leaning against the sandy slope in a semi-upright, semi-recumbent position. He was often seen taking coughdrop lozenges from a little box in his pocket, and at ten o'clock he drank a glass of hot punch to combat the sore throat that was beginning to affect his ability to speak.

Finally, as a supreme concession to the combined pleas of Ney, Murat, and Davout, Napoleon ordered General Sorbier to move sixty pieces of his Imperial Guard artillery forward beyond the Kamenka streambed gully and on up to the edge of the Semyonovskoye village uplands. When Berthier's aide-de-camp, Louis-François Lejeune, galloped up to Sorbier with the message, the "boiling" artillery general greeted him impatiently. "We should have done this more than an hour ago!" A few minutes later twenty-four 12-pounders and several dozen cannon of smaller caliber were laboriously dragged forward and deployed along the elbow-shaped southern bank of the Semyonovka streambed, from where the French gunners could plow up the Russian lines with almost lateral (rather than perpendicular) barrages.

Irked by the Russians' recapture of the central redoubt, Napoleon now decided to try a transversal cavalry attack launched from the right wing of Prince Eugène de Beauharnais's Fourth Corps. If it failed to get as far as the redoubt, it would at least serve the purpose of halting Prince Eugen of Württemberg's counterattacking columns.

Barclay de Tolly had just galloped up and ordered the young prince to halt the advance of his 1st Brigade and to turn his 2nd Brigade around, to close a dangerous gap that was opening up in the Russian lines, when they saw a "monstrous" cloud of dust advancing across the slope to their left "like an avalanche." The commander of the 4th Infantry Division ordered his battalions to form squares. Barclay de Tolly had barely time to take refuge inside one of these squares, along with Generals Miloradovich and Rayevsky, before the hurricane swept past. "Children," cried Prince Eugen to the infantrymen of the Kremenchug Regiment, "take your time, take good aim and look the enemy in the eye!" As the French cuirassiers emerged from their dust cloud in a sudden glitter of sun-reflecting armor and came on, looking ever larger, more majestic, more "drunk" with a sense of their invincible impetus, they were met with a volley of musket balls that sent the foremost among them crashing to the ground.

From this moment on, the battle for the central Rayevsky redoubt degenerated into a confused mêlée, as the French cavalrymen were halted and then slowly, very slowly, pushed back. "Someone who did not see it with his own eyes can have no idea of what this disorder was like," wrote Friedrich von Schubert later. "One could no longer speak of general order or leadership.

Each regiment, as soon as it had been halfway reassembled by a new bugle call, immediately returned to the attack. . . . In the midst of it all there were the remains of our infantry divisions, which the officers were trying to reorganize; Paskevich, who in desperation was tearing out his hair, cursing and swearing; and Barclay, whose horse had just been killed and who quite calmly was trying to restore order on foot."

In the course of this furious mêlée, in which the dust was so dense that one could hardly see ten paces in front of one, Yermolov was wounded in the neck and had to retire from the field. Wolzogen had his horse shot out from under him by a cannonball, which removed part of his staff officer's sash. He had to disengage the girth strap from under the body of his dead mount and carry the saddle back to the rear, where he had told his groom to stay with his remaining horse. He was stopped on the way by a cordon of gendarmes, who had been ordered by Yermolov to send all soldiers back to their posts and to allow no one past the picket line on the pretext that they were needed to escort a wounded comrade back to the dressing station. (This was a job reserved for the militia.) It was only with difficulty that Wolzogen managed to persuade them that he was not trying to flee the battlefield. Having finally found his groom, who quickly saddled the waiting horse, he rode back through the woods. When he came out into the open, some distance behind the Rayevsky redoubt, he had the impression of riding through a stormy sea of grit. "Each canister shot kicked up a tiny cloud of dust from the surface of the ground, which had been trampled into a fine powder, and as everywhere these tiny billows were curling over on themselves, they truly looked like moving waves."

During a momentary lull between successive cavalry attacks—when the cannon resumed their murderous salvos—Barclay de Tolly had let Prince Eugen of Württemberg withdraw two of his four regiments from their exposed position north of the Semyonovskoye hamlet, to rejoin the rest of the Second Russian Corps on the extreme left wing, where General Baggovut had now taken over from the seriously wounded General Nikolai Tuchkov. Prince Eugen's infantrymen were replaced by the 11th and 23rd divisions of General Ostermann-Tolstoy's Fourth Corps, who were raked in their turn by the lethal cross fire of General Sorbier's 12-pounders and scores of other guns.

Napoleon meanwhile had decided to renew his earlier effort to storm the Rayevsky redoubt with cavalry. The task was to have been entrusted to General Louis-Pierre Montbrun, commander of the Second Cavalry Corps. This prestigious cavalier had spent a most unhappy morning, watching his men and horses being gradually laid low by Russian cannonballs and canister, simply because Napoleon had decided that they were needed up front to fill the gap between Prince Eugène's Fourth Corps and Ney's Third Corps, which had opened up as a result of the Ouvarov-Platov "diversion."

Why Napoleon and his brother-in-law Murat felt it necessary to expose so much of the cavalry to hours of Russian cannon fire is one of the supreme mysteries of this bloody battle. Colonel Louis-François Lejeune, a member of Berthier's staff who was able to observe this "misfortune" from the relatively safe vantage point of the Shevardino hummock, later suggested that it was probably "through vanity, or rather so as not to give rise to a false interpretation"—i.e., of being cowardly—that so many regiments of Murat's reserve cavalry were not "withdrawn several hundred paces to the rear." General Lubin Griois, commanding the horse-drawn artillery of Grouchy's Third Cavalry Corps, was equally mystified by the sight of cavalry lines being made to stand for hours "without moving" while "large holes" were opened up in their ranks. "The plain was covered with wounded men making their way back to the ambulance carts and of riderless horses galloping about in disorder. I noticed near me a regiment of Württemberg cuirassiers for which the cannon-balls seemed to have a preference; in all ranks helmets and breastplates kept flying apart in shattered fragments."

"A cavalry battle for people who are strong, healthy, and well mounted is truly child's play compared with what Napoleon demanded of his cavalry at Borodino," commented Roth von Schreckenstein, who had strong feelings on the subject after seeing half of his Saxon brigade cut down by Russian artillery fire. "There can hardly have been a man in those ranks and files whose neighbor did not collapse to the ground with his horse, or who, severely wounded, did not give up the ghost while crying out for help."

One of the victims of this wasteful exposure to enemy fire was General Montbrun. The commander of the Second Cavalry Corps was knocked from his horse by a shell burst, which sent a piece of metal through his kidneys, causing his black-bearded face to turn yellow before he died later in the afternoon.

To replace this almost legendary hero of so many past battles and campaigns was well-nigh impossible. After a moment of reflection Napoleon decided to entrust the command of the Second Cavalry Corps to General Auguste de Caulaincourt, his grand equerry's younger brother, a twice-wounded dragoon commander who had distinguished himself at Marengo and in Spain.

"Do what you did at Arzobispo!" said Napoleon briefly. He was referring to the brilliant surprise action which Auguste de Caulaincourt had pulled off in August 1809, when he had forded the Tagus with 5,000 dragoons and attacked the duke of Albuquerque's forces from the rear, seizing the fortified bridge across the river. This time it was the Rayevsky redoubt that he was to take by surprise assault.

The tactics for this new attack, worked out with Murat's chief of staff, Belliard, called for a swerving cavalry attack on the newly aligned troops of Ostermann-Tolstoy's Fourth Corps, to the right of the Rayevsky hill (as viewed by the French), to be combined with other charges from the left. But this time the horsemen were to be supported by the simultaneous assault of three infantry divisions, commanded by Prince Eugène, which were likely to divert some of the Russian fire.

Auguste de Caulaincourt himself seems to have doubted that he would succeed in his mission. The chronic pains occasioned by his past wounds had imbued him with a sense of almost suicidal resignation. Taking leave of his older brother, Armand, he said, "The fighting is so hot that I shall doubtless not see you again. We will triumph or I'll get myself killed."

The assault was finally launched around three in the afternoon by the combined forces (operating in successive waves) of Montbrun's Second, Grouchy's Third, and Latour-Maubourg's Fourth cavalry corps. The last-named included the elite Saxon Life-Guard and Zastrow regiments, as well as Count Malachowski's Polish cuirassiers, whom General von Thielmann had led in the earlier assault on the Semyonovskoye village, while Grouchy's corps included a number of embittered Saxon and Bavarian riders who had been forced to "sweat it out" for close to five uncomfortable hours in a "mousetrap" formed by the junction of the Semyonovka and Kolotcha rivers, where they were like sitting ducks for Russian gunners. This helps to explain the pent-up fury of these riders when they were finally unleashed against the redoubt that had been doing them so much harm.

The redoubt by this time had been so badly battered by French cannonballs that its parapets had been reduced to shapeless mounds of earth. Indeed, the redoubt for much of the time was all but invisible, enveloped in a thick cloud of dust and smoke periodically illuminated, in the words of one German eyewitness, by the "reddish, aurora-borealis glow" of spouting guns. To others, like Louis-François Lejeune (who had started out in life as a painter before joining Berthier's topographic staff), the clouds seemed to be silvered by these muzzle blasts, and there was one dramatic moment when, a shell burst having set fire to a barrel of resin, which the Russian gunners had stored in the redoubt to grease the axles of their gun carriages, purplish flames suddenly spewed out horizontally, "curling and writhing on the ground like an infuriated snake before rising to join the clouds."

Just which squadron first made it to the redoubt, through a hail of musketry and grapeshot, is a matter of some dispute. An assault on its northern side, made by a French cuirassier brigade, was finally beaten back, though some, like General Auguste de Caulaincourt, actually forced their way inside, only to be shot dead. It was thus left to the Saxon and Polish cuirassiers of Latour-Maubourg's Fourth Cavalry Corps to complete the job that Montbrun's Second Corps had begun.

To protect the redoubt General Likhachov had filled the ditches in front and on the sides with bayoneted fusiliers. To the oncoming riders the redoubt thus looked a bit like a porcupine of bristling bayonets, over which the horses had to leap. But as the Saxon cuirassier lieutenant von Meerheim later described it, "notwithstanding the hot stream of whistling lead which poured down on us, nothing could dampen the attackers in their eagerness to triumph, just as the defenders, fired by a desperate rage, did everything to hold their prize possession.

"The fight was terrible! Man and horse, hit by lethal lead, fell backward down the slope and wrestled, dying, with the also-stricken foe, hacking away at each other with weapons, fists, and teeth, while those immediately behind, adding their own wild yells to the dreadful tumult, trampled everything underfoot and charged furiously into the nearest heap, dealing out death and destruction, only to be felled themselves."

Soon the ground around the redoubt was covered with writhing bodies and the carcasses of dead or dying horses, as the Saxon Life-Guards and the Zastrow cuirassiers jumped the ditches and the battered parapets beyond. The savage fighting swept past the beleaguered redoubt and on up the smoke-shrouded hill behind, as more and more cavalrymen joined the fray. At one or two points French carabineers, in their golden breastplates and red-crested helmets, actually managed to hack their way through the Russian lines with their long swords, but elsewhere the Russian infantrymen, contracted once again into formidable squares, held fast, mowing down successive waves of horsemen, including many of those who swept into the redoubt via the rear-end "throat," where they were not protected by any earthwork parapet. But this lethal musketry could not save the redoubt itself, which was stormed and occupied by soldiers of Prince Eugène's three infantry divisions who, momen-tarily outstripped by the cavalry, now surged over the breast of the hill. Inside they captured the commander of the 24th Division, General Pyotr Likhachov, who, less fortunate than Rayevsky, had been wounded and was unable to escape.

At this critical moment Barclay, who was personally directing the defense, found his position threatened by a new attack, launched by two divisions of General Grouchy's Third Cavalry Corps via the gully leading up from Borodino. He had wanted to retain the 1st Russian Cuirassier Division in reserve for such a crisis but now discovered that someone had dispatched it to the left wing of the Russian line. All that was left of the strategic reserve, which at the start of the battle had numbered close to 19,000 men, was two elite Horse-Guard regiments which had been stationed in the woods more than a thousand yards behind the Rayevsky redoubt, where they were safe from French artillery fire. In the absence of its nominal commander, Grand Duke Constantine, the Fifth (Imperial Guard) Corps was commanded by General Nikolai Lavrov, a superannuated gentleman—Waldemar von Loewenstern considered him "incompetence personified"—who was so arthritic that he could hardly ride or walk. Such being the case, Barclay decided to lead the elite black-breastplated cuirassiers into the fray himself.

In his later report to Emperor Alexander, Barclay termed the ensuing cavalry battle "one of the stubbornest ever to have been fought." The Russian Guards horsemen, who were in much fitter condition than their adversaries, covered themselves with "immortal glory," according to the indomitable Loewenstern, who, with an arm in a sling, continued to gallop around with Barclay, ready to offer him his mount if another horse was shot out from under him (as had already happened three times). In the middle of the free-for-all one of Barclay's aides-de-camp, Lamsdorf, was laid out by a pistol shot, and the general himself came near to having his head split in two by a sword-swinging cuirassier, who was shot in the nick of time by a vigilant groom.

In the end Napoleon's cavalrymen, most of whom had been in the saddle for nine hours and who were almost as weary as their exhausted mounts, had to trot back down the hill, leaving Prince Eugène's infantrymen to hold the captured redoubt. Barclay's battered forces were by now so weakened that he dared not risk a costly counterattack, which, had it failed, could have opened a gaping breach in his fragile lines and have resulted in disaster. But his remaining infantrymen, and also his gunners, still had enough firepower left to force Prince Eugène to withdraw most of his men below the brow of the hill, where they were less vulnerable to Russian cannon fire and musketry.

Heinrich von Brandt, who came up this same hill with the Poles of General Claparède's Young Guard division, was horrified by the sight of corpses and carcasses piled six to eight deep in all the ditches and right up to the battered parapets of the redoubt, which was also filled with bodies, some dead, others still pathetically groaning. In the middle of the carnage he saw General Auguste de Caulaincourt's dead body being brought out of the redoubt and carried down the hill on a bloodstained white cloak by several French cuirassiers.

The horsemen on both sides having by now exhausted their last reserves of energy, the cannoneers could resume their murderous duels. Prince Eugène's gunners moved up all of their available horse-artillery pieces until they stretched off in a long line southward from the "anchor" of the Rayevsky redoubt. A deafening as well as deadly cannonade ensued, in which the Russians—according to Brandt, whose impartial testimony can be trusted—gave as good as they received.

Bullets, as well as grapeshot, kept whistling overhead, and Prince Eugène's infantrymen were ordered to lie down to avoid the enemy fire. The mounted officers alone could not do so, in order to be able, as a Polish captain put it, to "meet death upright." Brandt, though he emerged unscathed, had his face splattered by the brains of a nearby grenadier, whose head was torn off by a cannonball just as he was getting up to approach another soldier.

And so the grim battle ended, as it had begun, in the thunder of cannon fire. Russian infantrymen, like their adversaries, took refuge from round shot and canister wherever they could, and where they could not, they simply closed ranks—once again confirming what had already been said about them during the Polish campaign of 1807: "It is not enough to kill a Russian; you still have to push him over."

Although the battle proved less costly than Wagram in the total number of French lives lost, at Borodino Napoleon was not even afforded the satisfaction of seeing the field in his hands at the end of the day. For at four in the afternoon the Russian lines, though hideously depleted and bent back behind the upper stretch of the Semyonovka streambed, were still unbroken.

At his command post near the Shevardino redoubt Napoleon for some time had been in a rare agony of indecision, debating with himself as to whether he should throw the five regiments of his Old Guard and Marshal Bessières's 4,000 elite horsemen into action to deliver the knockout blow for which Ney, Murat, and so many others had been impatiently waiting. Berthier and Bessières are both reported to have counseled against it, and theirs was almost certainly sound advice. The battle had in fact been lost, or at any rate not won, by Napoleon several hours earlier when he had failed to concentrate all of his available forces (including Claparède's Polish division) on a breakthrough across the Semyonovskoye plateau, which would have cut the Russian line in two. It had been Barclay de Tolly's original intention, before the battle was seriously engaged, to throw the Imperial Guard cavalry of the Fifth (reserve) Corps into a powerful flank attack on Napoleon's left-wing forces deployed west of the village of Borodino near the Smolensk–Moscow highway. What was actually undertaken prematurely (in the late morning) petered out into nothing under Uvarov's listless leadership. But though the Russian knockout blow envisaged by Barclay was never delivered, the threat of it kept Napoleon from delivering his own.

Kutuzov thus failed to win a battle which, given the Russians' superiority in artillery, he should logically have won. But this failure, ironically enough —the 1812 campaign is full of such ironies—contributed to the ultimate French debacle. For had Napoleon's forces been stopped in their tracks at Borodino, they would never have made it to Moscow, and from the strictly military point of view this would almost certainly have been a blessing in disguise for a Grande Armée which had already dangerously outreached itself.

Around four in the afternoon Napoleon finally left his sand pit, and mounting a white horse, he rode forward with a large suite of officers to inspect the positions occupied by the infantrymen of Davout's, Ney's, and Prince Eugène's corps. His face was flushed from the head cold and sore throat he was combating, he looked tired, but otherwise it was impossible to tell from the masklike impassivity of his features how he felt about the outcome of the struggle.

By five o'clock the musket fire began to slacken, though the boom of cannon continued to resound with gradually diminishing intensity until nightfall. As dusk was falling Barclay gathered together what remained of a few infantry battalions and tried to mount a surprise assault on the Rayevsky redoubt, in the hope of being able to retrieve some of its captured 12-pounders. But the sneak attack was beaten back, after half an hour's fighting, by some of Prince Eugène's light-infantry skirmishers, supported by the Poles of General Claparède's Young Guard division, who now at last saw action.

What remained of the Russian army was obviously too depleted and battle-weary to be able to regain any of the lost ground—which for most stretches of the front amounted to little more than 1,500 yards in depth. Most units had been reduced to about half their strength, and some had suffered even more.

His portly front swathed by his official sash and the pale blue cordon of the Order of Saint Andrew, Kutuzov throughout this time had hardly stirred from his headquarters behind the village of Gorky, where he was safe from enemy cannonballs. Unable to see the battlefield directly, he had kept himself informed of what was going on by receiving periodic reports, saying, "*Eh bien, faites-le!*" (All right, do it!), each time an officer proposed an action he approved of. Barclay de Tolly had not seen him since early morning, when he had galloped over angrily to protest an order seriously weakening the Imperial Guard reserve. Now he decided to send Wolzogen to his headquarters to ask the generalissimo for instructions as to what to do next. "But be sure to obtain a *written* order," he added, "for with Kutuzov one must be careful."

Wolzogen had to ride a long way back beyond the bombard-blasted village of Gorky before he found Kutuzov and his suite, which was "so numerous that it looked like an auxiliary corps." While Barclay de Tolly, Bagration, Rayevsky, Konovnitsyn, Ostermann-Tolstoy, and so many others had been risking their lives trying to beat back the furious assaults of Napoleon's Grande Armée, Kutuzov had spent the day in the company of wealthy young sons of noble Russian families who had decided that the easiest way to ignore the "dreadful seriousness" of the occasion was to live it up in style. At the sight of the succulent delicacies off which they had been feasting and of the scores of champagne bottles they had emptied, Wolzogen, who had eaten nothing all day, found his dander rising. His marked Silesian accent doubtless made his oral report, delivered in French, sound particularly abrasive, as he painted a somber picture of a badly battered army which had been forced to give up most of its positions. Kutuzov would not let him finish. "With what low-down sutler woman have you been getting drunk, that you should be making such an inane report?" he shouted angrily. "It is I who must needs know best how the battle has been going! The attacks of the French have everywhere been victoriously repulsed, and so tomorrow I am going to place myself at the head of the army in order to drive the enemy from Russia's sacred soil without further ado!" The generalissimo's one good eye swept imperiously over the assembled company, whose beaming faces reflected his own bristling determination.

Whether Kutuzov was really in earnest in delivering himself of this outburst, Wolzogen was at a loss to know. He reckoned that the canny generalissimo was counting on a few hours of respite, lasting through the night, which would enable him to draft an official report to the tsar claiming that his forces still held the field at Borodino, and that they had consequently won a victory. Since there was no point in starting an argument over the army's depleted state, Wolzogen explained that General Barclay wished to be informed, through a written order, whether he was to continue the battle or not.

At this Kutuzov summoned Colonel Toll, who had been busy "devouring a capon" when Wolzogen appeared. Together they walked off to one side to discuss the matter privately. Toll then wrote out a brief penciled order, which Kutuzov signed before handing it to Wolzogen, to be taken back to Barclay. "I can see from all the movements of the enemy," ran the text, "that he is as weakened as we are, and therefore, having already engaged him in battle, I have decided this night to restore order to the army, to supply the artillery with new munitions, and to resume the battle with the enemy tomorrow. For any withdrawal in the present [state of] disorder would bring about the loss of all of the artillery."

After reading this order, Barclay quietly shook his head. "I don't know where he thinks he can find the forces to do this," he commented. He had not waited for Wolzogen's return to start realigning the remaining troops, so as to be able to resist a second onslaught if Napoleon resumed the attack the following morning. He had the artillery pieces spaced farther apart to make them less vulnerable to enemy cannon fire. Two thousand militiamen were put to work building a new redoubt near the bombarded village of Gorky, now also reduced to a heap of smoking timbers. Scouts were sent out to reconnoiter the vicinity of the Rayevsky redoubt, which Barclay's aide-de-camp Alexander Muravyov, searching the darkened battlefield for his vanished brother, had found abandoned by the French. When the scouts returned to report that most of the French forces had been pulled back to the other side of the valley, Barclay ordered General Miloradovich to assemble a few infantry battalions and a horse-artillery battery and to be ready to launch a dawn attack on the redoubt when the fog was at its thickest.

A remarkable change had by now come over many soldiers of Barclay's First Army, who had seen him galloping all day from one danger spot to the next, coolly rallying broken lines and ordering new counterattacks. It seemed well-nigh a miracle that in his full-dress decoration-studded uniform and his bicorne hat he should have escaped without a scratch, particularly since three horses had perished under him. As he returned from a final inspection of the lines, he was greeted by spontaneous *"Oorah!"*'s proffered by soldiers "by way of retribution for the insulting and unfair accusations that had been heaped upon him up till then" (to quote Lieutenant Ivan Timiryazov, of the Imperial Guard Jaegers). But this belated tribute probably afforded Barclay meager solace, when all around him could be heard the groans of wounded men who might have been spared their sufferings by a more intelligent employment. It may even have occurred to him that in a bloody battle such as this there are really no victors, only victims.

On the other side of the valley, too, there was little cause for facile rejoicing. While riding back toward Shevardino with his Royal Saxon Life-Guards, Roth von Schreckenstein heard all around him in the dark the dreadful, repeated cry, *"Au nom de Dieu, gare aux blessés!"* (In the name of God, pay heed to the wounded!).

CHAPTER 18

THE TORRENT AND
THE SPONGE

THE EVENING and the night that the Poles of General Claparède's Young Guard division had to spend on the slopes of the Rayevsky redoubt were probably more grim than any these veteran soldiers could recall. Whereas most of the French, German, Italian, and Spanish regiments of the Grande Armée had been ordered to move discreetly back to their original bivouac positions west of the Kolotcha River and the Kamenka and Semyonovka streambeds, the Young Guard division and other designated units to its right were left to hold the ground they had conquered, so that Napoleon could claim to have ended up master of the field.

A numbing wind, propelling gusts of fog and drizzle, added to the sufferings of the wounded, whose groans could be heard on every side. Their own field packs being empty, the "victors" were reduced to searching for whatever flour, *kasha* grits, and vodka they could find in the food kits and canteens of dead Russian soldiers. Butts were smashed away from musket barrels, and over-turned ammunition caissons were torn into planks and strips of splintered wood to provide firewood for the brewing of soup (with water brought all the way up from the sluggish Kolotcha River) and the roasting of horse meat, of which there was more than a plentiful supply. As the bivouac flames began to rise, like beacons of good cheer, they illuminated the forms of wounded men, desperately crawling or tottering toward the inviting warmth until, in Heinrich von Brandt's words, the entire area "began to resemble a hospital."

From the south, like growls of distant thunder, came the sound of cannon booms and sporadic bursts of gunfire in the region of the old Smolensk–Mozhaisk post road. Here Poniatowski's Poles were still trying to outflank the Russian army's left wing, now held by General Baggovut's Second Corps and the remnants of Prince Eugen of Württemberg's 4th Division. For Kutuzov the continuation of the fighting in this vital area was a matter of serious concern. If the Poles, backed up by French reserves, were to make a break-through during the night, the main body of the Russian army might wake up to find that the enemy had reached Mozhaisk before them, cutting off their main avenue of retreat across the Moskva River.

No less disquieting for the generalissimo was the report brought back to him by Colonel Toll, who, after Wolzogen's departure, had been sent on an inspection tour of the Second Russian Army and its threatened left wing. The Second Army, as far as Toll could judge from a cursory inspection, had suffered 20,000 casualties. The First Army's losses, though proportionately less severe, exceeded 25,000. Battalions that had started out 400 or more strong had shrunk to 160 men or less.

After hearing Toll's sobering assessment Kutuzov shelved his previously announced plans for resuming the battle the next morning. Instead, all corps and division generals were instructed to prepare their men for a 2:00 A.M. withdrawal, while battery commanders were ordered to have their artillery pieces limbered up for immediate departure down the main highway to Mozhaisk.

The pullback Napoleon had ordered for most of his Grande Armée forces greatly facilitated the Russians' withdrawal, even fostering the illusion with many of them that they had really won the day. It made it easier for Kutuzov to dictate a brief and distinctly ambiguous report for the tsar in which, after declaring that the French had suffered heavier losses than the Russians and that "the enemy did not gain a single yard of ground for all his superior forces," he asserted that, his aim "being directed to the destruction of the French army," he had decided to withdraw beyond Mozhaisk, after spending the night on the battlefield. Virtually the same words were used in two letters dispatched to Governor Rostopchin in Moscow, who was first informed of Kutuzov's intention to renew the battle the next day, and then of his curious decision to withdraw a few versts, the better to be able to destroy the French army.

Many Russians were understandably unhappy over this forced abandonment of their positions, which in effect condemned thousands of wounded soldiers to a slow death on the battlefield or to the less than tender mercies of their French captors. But at least it spared most of them the sight of the carnage when the sun rose the next morning on a field strewn with moaning men and horses, shattered lances, breastplates, helmets, and shell fragments "as numerous as hailstones after a violent thunderstorm," in the words of Eugène Labaume. "Most dreadful of all was it to see the interior of the gullies; almost all of the wounded by a natural instinct had dragged themselves thither to seek protection from new gunshots; it was there that these unfortunates, heaped on top of each other and swimming helplessly in their own blood, uttered dreadful groans," repeatedly imploring passersby to put them out of their misery with a final pistol shot.

Napoleon, who toured the battlefield on horseback for more than an hour in the morning, did not let the dreadful groans of the wounded divert him from an almost scientific postmortem of the battle. He stopped repeatedly to note the regimental numbers inscribed on the buttons of dead Russians, to obtain a more precise idea of how Kutuzov's units had been aligned and to estimate their losses. His own losses, compiled from roll-call tallies and reports furnished by his corps and division commanders, were so shockingly high that they had to be concealed—from the Grande Armée's rank and file as well as from the general public in France, Germany, and Austria. According to Berthier's aide-de-camp Baron Pierre-Paul Denniée, who was told to keep the figures secret, the casualties included 49 killed or wounded generals, 27 wounded and 10 dead colonels, 6,547 dead officers, noncoms, and soldiers, and 21,453 wounded.

Officially, the Grande Armée's losses thus amounted to about 28,000 casualties. But there is good reason for suspecting that the real figure was higher. The figure for the wounded (whose chances of survival were slim at best) was inherently deceptive; for we know that most of those who were left behind to recover from their wounds at the Kolotsky monastery (transformed into a vast hospital) later died of starvation after the Grande Armée had moved on. Certain divisions had virtually ceased to exist. This was particularly true of the 25th (Württemberg) Division, whose valiant infantrymen had saved Murat from capture during the struggle for the Bagration redans. Of the 17,000 men who had set out from Württemberg the previous spring, not many more than 600 remained to fight another battle.

While, generally speaking, Russian infantry regiments suffered heavier losses than their adversaries, in the cavalry squadrons the situation was roughly the reverse. The French and allied cavalry—some 70,000 horses strong at the time of the Niemen crossing in late June and early July—had already been reduced to fewer than 30,000 by early September. At Borodino another 15,000 of the Grande Armée's cavalry horses perished—providing some substance for the later Russian claim that here Murat's reserve cavalry was dealt a crippling blow from which it was never able to recover.

So worn out were his surviving horsemen and their ill-fed mounts that not until the late morning of September 8 did they set out in pursuit of Kutuzov's retreating forces, again shielded by Ataman Platov's roving riders. The Cossacks' hit-and-run raids on the French vanguard helped to mask the Russians' somewhat disorderly withdrawal along the two roads leading to Mozhaisk and enabled Kutuzov to get most of his baggage trains through the town without their being intercepted by the French.

More than one Grande Armée officer was impressed by the care with which the retreating Russians stopped along the way to bury their dead, each hastily spaded tumulus being marked with a wooden cross. "In all fairness it must be granted that these people whom we call barbarous take great care of their wounded and have the piety to bury their dead," noted Fantin des Odoards in his diary, "whereas we French, so vaingloriously proud of our civilization, let ours perish for want of succor, and only provide the rest with sepulchres when the stench of their corpses incommodes us."

Thousands of wounded Russians had managed to make it back as far as Mozhaisk, which was only half a dozen miles distant from the Borodino battlefield. But at Mozhaisk they found themselves stranded, for lack of transportation. Kutuzov's repeated pleas for carts and horses had gone unheeded, simply because in Governor Rostopchin's Moscow thousands of coachmen and droshky drivers were now busy transporting church valuables, items of the

Kremlin treasury, and tons of books and documents from various administrative archives to the safety of Kolomna, Vladimir, and more distant Nizhny Novgorod, on the Volga. There were thus no carts or draft horses left for the thousands of wounded soldiers who were too weak to leave Mozhaisk on foot.

On September 9, when two French infantry columns converged on the town from different directions, there was hardly a house in Mozhaisk that was not crammed with wounded Russian soldiers, some of whom were forcibly evicted, notwithstanding Napoleon's orders that they should not be disturbed. The town looked like a gigantic hospital, not to say a mortuary, for by the time the chief surgeon, Dominique Larrey, reached the scene some twenty-four hours later, many of the atrociously mutilated Russians were dead.

For Napoleon quarters were found near the main square in a house that was so new and unfinished that it still lacked doors. But its upper-floor rooms had huge tiled stoves as well as windows, which helped to lessen the chill autumnal damp. The emperor's sore throat had by now turned into laryngitis, so that he could no longer speak. Unable to dictate, he sat down at a table and began to scribble out his orders and dispatches in his all-but-illegible handwriting, imperiously banging a little bronze hammer each time he had finished another sheet of paper.

It was three days before Napoleon felt well enough to climb back into his carriage and to catch up with the main body of his army, which had been ordered to continue its pursuit of the retreating Russians. On the whole this pursuit was a leisurely affair, with advances averaging little more than a dozen miles a day.

It had originally been Tsar Alexander's wish to rejoin his forces in the field. But the military leadership crisis he had had to deal with on his return to Petersburg, and not least of all his sister Catherine's blunt advice that he leave the conduct of the war to his generals, had caused him to change his plans. Instead of returning to Moscow, as he had first intended, he wisely chose to make a far more profitable trip to Finland to meet Sweden's new crown prince and heir apparent, the erstwhile prince of Pontecorvo (Bernadotte).

Alexander's trip to Åbo, on Finland's southwestern coast, consolidated the rapprochement between the two recently hostile countries which had led to the preliminary accord of the previous April. By the terms of this agreement, which had been signed by Chancellor Rumiantsev and the Swedish envoy, Loewenhielm, before it was certain that Napoleon would invade Russia, Alexander had promised to provide Bernadotte with an expeditionary force of 35,000 men, who were to help him launch an attack against the Danes, at this time masters of Norway. The wily Gascon reckoned that the acquisition of Norway would be the easiest way of reconciling the Swedes to the loss of Finland. But the attack on the Danes was only a first step in a far more ambitious scheme, which envisaged a seaborne assault mounted with British help on the Mecklenburg or Pomeranian coast and designed to foment a massive North German uprising against Napoleon (an objective that was effectively achieved in 1813). Now that his country had been invaded and was fighting for its survival, Alexander was in a poor position to honor his pledge of military help, as Bernadotte was well aware. But after being treated to a review of the three Russian divisions stationed in Finland, Bernadotte abandoned the diplomatic sparring and declared quite openly that these "excellent" troops could far more usefully be employed in the immediate future to reinforce Wittgenstein's corps on the Dvina and the garrison defending Riga against Marshal Macdonald's Franco-Prussian forces. For, as he put it, if Russia were to be defeated by Napoleon, it would be the end for both of them.

Thanks to this gracious gesture, which made it clear that Sweden was not going to take advantage of Russia's present plight to wrest Finland from her, Alexander was able to remove another 14,000 Russian soldiers garrisoned in the north. Ferried in ships across the Gulf of Finland to Reval, they were assigned the task of breaking the siege of Riga.

When Alexander returned to Petersburg on September 2, after an absence of thirteen days, he found his capital seething over the loss of Smolensk. Grand Duke Constantine's first action on reaching Petersburg on August 26 had been to go see his mother, now installed in the Tauride Palace, and to explain that with the First and Second Russian armies in a state of leaderless confusion, the only reasonable solution was to make peace with Napoleon. This pessimistic report from her second son again threw Dowager Empress Maria Feodorovna into a dither, convincing her how right she had been to have all the imperial treasures, including the more precious items from her country palaces of Gatchina and Pavlovsk, crated up and made ready for transport eastward.

Many Petersburgers, like the devoutly patriotic Varvara Bakunin, felt that it was an outrage that at such a dire moment French actors and actresses should be allowed to go on playing in the city's only public theater. To signify their disapprobation they began by imposing a boycott, as Sir Robert Wilson discovered when he went to watch the "celebrated Mademoiselle Georges" play the lead role in Racine's *Phèdre*. "She deserves her fame. The house, however, presented a singular spectacle: empty boxes and benches, notwithstanding her attractions. I was much pleased with this patriotic sacrifice of enjoyment. . . ."

The British general, who had reached Petersburg barely a week ahead of the new English ambassador, Lord Cathcart, would have been even more delighted had he witnessed the fate that overtook the talented Mademoiselle Georges a few days later, when some of the theater's usually sedate patrons decided to give more forceful expression to their patriotic indignation. Madame de Staël, who had finally reached Petersburg after a long overland journey from Vienna, which had taken her through Kiev and Moscow, and who was now practically holding court at the Hôtel de l'Europe, where as usual she overpowered everyone with her torrential gush of speech, missed the uproar, being more interested on this particular afternoon in exchanging views with the equally strong-minded Prussian exile Baron vom Stein; but her son, Auguste, and her latest paramour, the twenty-four-year-old John Rocca, were both present. "We others," the German poet-patriot Ernst Moritz Arndt later recorded, "were still seated at table when the two of them came back looking somewhat upset and told us that at the start of the play the Russians had raised such a din and indulged in such ranting and raving against the French actors and the French play that the performance had had to be stopped. . . . And Madame de Staël? She forgot both time and place and had feelings only for her people. She was beside herself, burst into tears, and cried, 'The barbarians! Just imagine—not wishing to see Racine's *Phèdre!*' "

Like Madame de Staël, Sir Robert Wilson was invited to dine at the Winter Palace. After dinner the tsar led him off to his study for two and a half hours of private conversation. He wanted to hear the English general's first-hand impressions of the battle of Smolensk and what he thought of his commanders in the field. Wilson's highly prejudiced account must further have shaken the emperor's waning confidence in Barclay de Tolly.

What his generals were most worried about, as Alexander knew, was his own determination to continue the struggle, no matter what. About this he was categoric when, a day or two later, he again received General Wilson. He was sending him back to Kutuzov with the title of British commissioner appointed to the Russian armies, he told him, and with a message to the effect that never would he make peace with Napoleon so long as there was a single French soldier on Russian soil. He was ready to remove his family to the interior, to undergo any sacrifice, for sooner than make peace with the invader, "I would rather let my beard grow to the waist and eat potatoes in Siberia."

The garrulous Germaine de Staël had left for Sweden, but the brash Sir Robert Wilson was still in Petersburg when a courier came galloping in with news of the "victory" of Borodino. Even Alexander, who was no babe in the woods when it came to seeing through other people's wiles, seems to have been taken in by the generalissimo's affirmation that "the enemy did not gain one yard of ground with his superior forces." All mention of his "necessary" withdrawal was expunged from the text which Alexander released for publication in the *Severnaya Pochta* (Northern Post). It was further announced, at a special anniversary service held in the chapel of the Alexander Nevsky monastery which was attended by the tsar and other members of the imperial family, that as a reward for his extraordinary exploit in defeating the "invincible" Napoleon, the Most Illustrious Prince Kutuzov was being promoted to the rank of field marshal with a lump-sum gift of 100,000 rubles, while every participating soldier was to receive 5 rubles.

News of the "victory" of Borodino was received by the Petersburg populace with rapture. Trumpets blared, drums rolled, church bells pealed forth in joyous acclaim, candles flickered in the windows and porch lanterns of illuminated houses, chains of multicolored lampions festooned the granite quays and vessels riding at anchor in the harbor, and bouquets of fireworks brightened the pre-equinoctial dusk. Many of Count Rumiantsev's enemies were even sufficiently emboldened to snub the unpopular chancellor by pointedly failing to attend the elaborate saint's-day dinner he gave in honor of the tsar.

Whereas in writing to his sovereign he had to be cautious in his choice of words, to his wife Prince Mikhail Hilarionovich Kutuzov felt free to declare, in a terse one-sentence letter: "I, thank God, am fine, my friend, and am not defeated, but won a battle over Bonaparte." Within twenty-four hours of this letter's reception in Petersburg virtually every salon in the capital was ecstatically repeating its contents. Joseph de Maistre, the erudite doyen of the diplomatic corps, whose son, Rodolphe, had taken part in the terrible engagement, dutifully passed on to the Sardinian foreign minister what he had just heard from an officer who claimed to have been present at Borodino: "By the end of the battle the French had completely run out of ammunition, and they were throwing stones." To which "hot" piece of news he added the wry comment that "they"—Kutuzov and the rest—"will give them [the French] time to bring up more cannonballs."

In Moscow all trace of the earlier mood of confident nonchalance had by now disappeared. For the first three weeks after Emperor Alexander's departure in late July the city had assumed a martial air, as squares, streets, and avenues filled up with men in uniform, who flooded in from the surrounding countryside to join their respective "colors." But gradually the streets and squares had emptied as officers and recently recruited militiamen left for the "front," and the city seemed about to sink back into its dog-days torpor when it was aroused by the bombshell news that Smolensk had fallen.

On August 22 the young Natalya Rostopchin, who had been sent into town from the family dacha southwest of Moscow, found her father seated despondently at his desk in the enormous townhouse he had recently bought near the Lubianka, a tributary of the Moskva River. (This townhouse still exists and is now used by senior KGB officials.) Rostopchin had just received a letter from Barclay de Tolly informing him of the French capture of Smolensk. Though he admired Barclay's integrity, he had no great faith in his military talents, and so he glumly concluded that "we are soon going to have the enemy in Moscow."

The problem now facing him was how to get as many of the city's treasures —from churches, convents, public libraries, and museums—safely out of Moscow without arousing a sense of panic among its inhabitants. The problem would probably have been insoluble even for a less mercurial gentleman, but Rostopchin undoubtedly added to the growing confusion by rashly promising miracles and by continuing to whip up patriotic fervor through bombastic announcements.

One of these promised miracles envisaged the destruction of an entire French army corps, or failing that, of Napoleon's imperial headquarters, through aerial bombardment. The "infernal machine" that was to perpetrate this devastating feat was a dirigible sphere, more or less inspired by the hot-air balloons which Montgolfier and others had begun experimenting with during the last years of the eighteenth century. This rudder-equipped aerostat was designed (at least on paper) to lift a gondola capable of carrying fifty men as well as a large crate filled with gunpowder and "inflammable materials," which, when dropped on top of the enemy, were supposed to spread death and destruction on a massive scale. The inventor of this lethal instrument of war was a German named Leppich who was possessed of a gift for inventive gab, if for nothing else. After dazzling the Württemberg minister of foreign affairs, Count Ferdinand von Zeppelin, with the merits of his invention, he managed to have it brought to the attention of Tsar Alexander. The latter, who knew even less about the art of constructing "flying machines" than about the art of warfare, was sufficiently intrigued to be willing to have Leppich—carefully rechristened Schmidt in the finest cloak-and-dagger tradition—installed on an estate near Moscow.

Originally it was to have been a hush-hush project. But since it was impossible, even after locking gates and putting up board fences, to conceal the existence of a workshop where one hundred German artisans were kept busy night and day fashioning steel springs, sewing together pieces of silk and taffeta, and preparing Congreve fuses to detonate charges of powder and vitriol, Moscow's civil governor spread the rumor that this particular "factory" was going to turn out cannon mounts of a bold new design. But in the end it was Rostopchin who let this pseudoscientific cat out of the bag by thoughtfully telling the citizens of Moscow that they were not to take fright if they saw a small air-filled sphere appear in the sky, since this was not a sinister visitation of the "villain" (Napoleon), but on the contrary an instrument conceived "for his misfortune and undoing."

The extraordinary pre–Rube Goldberg contraption which emerged from this Teutonic workshop never got off the ground. Or more exactly, after a first attempt to rise, it relanded with such a thud that it snapped the carefully fashioned springs, causing the crestfallen inventor to request a superior British steel capable of cushioning future shocks. The superior British steel was duly supplied, to no avail. But so heady was the atmosphere of giddy make-believe Rostopchin had helped to create with his inflammatory posters and pronouncements that even sober-minded senators belonging to Moscow's judiciary could be heard assuring their listeners that the death-dealing sphere had been successfully tried out by three "aeronauts" on a flock of sheep, all of which had perished in a deluge of fire and flame.

By the time the final fiasco was uncovered, during the last days of August, Rostopchin had more serious problems to worry about. The daily influx of officers and soldiers who had been wounded in and around Smolensk, added to the sight of wagons transporting city treasures to towns and cities to the east, aroused a growing malaise. Entire households now took to the road in carriages, clogging the city's exits and seriously depleting the number of vehicles available to transport munitions westward.

In an effort to limit this exodus Rostopchin issued one more printed statement—this time to say that, contrary to the circulating rumors, he had not posted sentinels at the city barriers to stop outgoing carriages and carts. He found it perfectly proper that noble *ladies* and merchants' *wives* should seek refuge away from Moscow, adding somewhat uncharitably, "The fewer fearful people there are, the fewer tall tales will be told." He then went on to swear "by all that is holiest" that the "villain" (Napoleon) would never enter Moscow. He was reassured in this conviction by the fact that Kutuzov, in addition to 130,000 men, had 1,800 cannon (almost three times the real figure). But if perchance these formidable forces might seem too small to hurl back the "villain," then "I say, All right, Moscow militia, let us go forward too! We will sally forth, one hundred thousand strong, we will take the Iversk ikon of the Madonna and with 150 cannon we will finish the job together!"

On the same day (August 30) Rostopchin issued an order forbidding the delivery of passports to the adult male members of the "merchant and bourgeois estate." The poorer inhabitants of the suburbs and many peasants in the surrounding countryside soon felt it to be their patriotic duty to stop outgoing carriages, taunting their owners with shouted insults as they passed. "To where are you feeling, Boyars, with your serf-servants? Have you no pity now that Moscow is in danger?"

Scenes disturbingly reminiscent of what the Parisians had experienced during the darkest months of the French Revolution now became commonplace as crowds of "patriots" gathered at the city barriers to mock the poltroonery of fleeing "traitors." Men wishing to leave Moscow put on skirts and hid their heads beneath shawls and bonnets. Even those who managed to pass the barriers unmolested risked being stopped on the open road beyond by irate villagers, who "administered the law" in their own rough fashion by divesting owners of carriages and horses and forcing them to trudge back to Moscow on foot.

It was soon dramatically evident that there were simply not enough vehicles available for the transport out of Moscow of various treasures and state documents. The archives of the War Commission alone filled 10,000 wagons. Those of the law-dispensing Senate and of the department of Foreign Affairs (covering the centuries of Russian diplomatic activity before Peter the Great) were probably just as voluminous, and in addition draft horses and wagons had to be found to evacuate the bulky contents of the Armory and other Kremlin treasures, as well as those of the three patriarchal cathedrals.

Rostopchin also let it be known that there were 10,000 muskets stored in the Kremlin Arsenal and that anyone who wanted to could go there in the morning to buy a gun, a pistol, or a saber for a reasonable price. Although the intent was laudable, the result was farcical; for many of these flintlocks were so old, unused, and rusty as to constitute a hazard to muzzle-loading amateurs who knew little about ramrods and even less about priming pans and cleaning bores.

After several weeks of steadily mounting pressure, Rostopchin was clearly beginning to feel the strain. Then, on September 7, came two dispatches from Kutuzov, the first informing him that an exceedingly bloody battle was being fought at Borodino ("We will stand fast, so far all goes well"), and the second that "the Russian army did not retreat one step" and that "tomorrow, I hope, placing my trust in God and in Moscow's hallowed saints, I shall fight him [the enemy] with new forces."

Rostopchin immediately broadcast these glad tidings in another poster bulletin. "Today he [Napoleon] will be defeated again, and the accursed one and his accomplices will perish through famine, fire, and sword." A thanksgiving Te Deum service was held in the Kremlin's Uspensky Cathedral, while the city was literally rocked by the wild pealing of church bells.

The bells had hardly ceased their ringing and the populace its rejoicing when Rostopchin was shaken by three more dispatches from Kutuzov. In the first he was informed that the Russian army was withdrawing behind Mozhaisk; in the second that Kutuzov was desperately short of horses and carts to replace artillery losses and to transport the wounded back to Moscow; in the third, personally brought by the generalissimo's son-in-law, Prince Kudashev, that he needed all that Moscow could possibly supply in the way of artillery supplies, shells, and caissons.

Soon wounded officers and soldiers were streaming into Moscow, accompanied or followed by thousands of fearful peasants, who declared that everywhere the French were advancing, ruthlessly plundering, pillaging, and burning the villages through which they passed. Panic began to grip the city's remaining inhabitants. Seeking to allay their fears, Rostopchin issued another poster proclamation, which outdid all of his previous efforts in bombastic fatuity: "The Most Illustrious Prince Kutuzov, in order the more quickly to join the troops that are marching toward him, passed through Mozhaisk and set himself up at a strongpoint, where the enemy will not suddenly attack him. Forty-eight guns, along with shells, are going forward to him. But His Serene Highness says that he will defend Moscow to the last drop of his blood, that he is prepared to and will fight even in the streets. Should it come to that, I shall need young lads from both city and country. I will give the call in a couple of days, but right now it is not necessary and I am keeping quiet. It will be fine if you come with axes, not bad at all with pikes, but even better with three-pronged pitchforks: the Frenchman is no heavier than a sheaf of rye."

This proclamation, clearly suggesting that the "villain" and his plundering horde were approaching Moscow and might soon be fighting in its streets, brought local passions to a boil. Several taverns and wineshops were taken by storm, and soon drunken hoodlums were weaving their way through the streets, molesting passers-by and shouting, "Where is the accursed enemy? Just wait till we get our hands on him!"

On this same September 11 Rostopchin received five urgent messages from Kutuzov. They must have left Moscow's military governor thoroughly bewildered. In the first the generalissimo informed him that he was afraid of being outflanked by a French army corps (Prince Eugène's Fourth Corps), and he wondered if Rostopchin could not prepare a hot reception—the word he actually used was "tomb"—for this attacking force by calling out the Moscow militia. In the second dispatch he declared, "We are approaching a general battle near Moscow. But the thought that I shall not have the means for removing the wounded in wagons daunts me. For the love of God, I beg as rapid aid as possible from Your Excellency." In his third message Kutuzov, sounding increasingly frantic, asked Rostopchin to send out as many battery guns from the Moscow arsenal as he could, along with supplies of munitions, if necessary using horses belonging to private owners. The fourth message requested 1,000 axes and 1,000 spades and the immediate dispatch of all convalescents who had recovered from their wounds, as well as the return of "marauders" (he probably meant stragglers), who were to be rounded up and organized into military detachments by army officers. The fifth message, written by Kutuzov's chief duty officer, Colonel Kaissarov, asked Rostopchin to send as much mulled wine as he could. This was followed by a message sent by Barclay de Tolly, who wanted Rostopchin to know that the army's supply wagons were moving up the main road and would soon be reaching a point three versts (about two miles) from Moscow. The military governor was asked to see to it that none of the cart drivers actually entered the city (doubtless to keep them from heading for the taverns).

At ten in the morning of this busy September 11 Sergei Glinka, the firebrand editor of the superpatriotic *Russky Vyestnik* (Russian Messenger), came to call on Rostopchin at his house in the Sokolniki suburb southwest of Moscow. The city was already so empty that he had been unable to hire a droshky and would have had to walk the entire way on foot had he not been given a lift by the friendly owner of a private carriage. Glinka was wearing the simple cap, blouse, and boots of the Moscow militia, while Rostopchin was dressed in his lieutenant general's uniform. They sat down on the sofa together beneath a map of Russia. Glinka said that he was sending his family away; Rostopchin replied that he was doing the same. He seemed deeply upset and there were tears in his eyes.

"Sergei Nikolayevich," he said, "let us speak like sons of the Fatherland. What do you think—will Moscow be surrendered?"

Glinka reminded him of what he had said during the assembly meeting of the Moscow nobility in late July: the prospect had to be faced; Moscow might be occupied by the enemy. "But tell me frankly, Count, how will Moscow be given up—with bloodshed or without bloodshed?"

"Without bloodshed" was Rostopchin's laconic answer.

Glinka stood up and pointed to the map of Russia. "The giving up of Moscow will cut it off from our southern provinces. Where will the army, for their defense, take up its position?"

"On the old Kaluga road," answered Rostopchin, "there where my property of Voronovo is. I will set fire to it," he added simply.

Rising to his feet, Rostopchin walked over to his desk, sat down, and swiftly penned the following proclamation:

> Brothers, our forces are numerous and ready to lay down their lives, defending the Fatherland. We will not allow the villain to enter Moscow, but we need to help and each to do his duty. It is a grievous sin to betray one's own. Moscow is our mother, she nourished us, fed us, and enriched us. I appeal to you in the name of the Virgin Mother to defend God's churches, Moscow, the Russian earth. Arm yourselves with whatever you can, come on horseback or on foot; take bread for three days, no more. Come with your crosses, take the pennants from the churches, and with their banners let us gather on the Three Hills [the Vorobyevo (Sparrow) Hills and the Poklonnaya Gora (Hill of Respectful Salutation), west of Moscow]. I shall be with you, and together we will destroy the villain. Glory in the highest to him who does not lag behind. Eternal remem-

brance to him who falls in battle. Woe until the final Day of Judgement to him who starts to waver.

Laying down his quill, Rostopchin got up and handed the proclamation to Glinka, asking him to have it printed up and distributed as quickly as possible. "Nothing will come of this business on the Three Hills," he added in a tone of disabusement, "but this will make our peasants understand what they are to do when the enemy takes Moscow."

The response to this appeal was at once grandiose and pathetic. The next morning a huge mob of men and women, perhaps as many as thirty thousand, tramped the three miles out to the Three Hills, armed with muskets, sabers, pikes, scythes, pitchforks, axes, carving knives, staves, clubs, and crowbars, ready to defend their threatened city. The human crush, according to Alexei Bestuzhev-Riumin, a senior official of the Patrimonial Records Department, was such that "it would have been difficult, as the saying has it, to drop an apple." But the multitude, worked up to a feverish pitch of patriotic excitement as it chanted, "Long live our Batiushka [Little Father] Alexander!," waited all day in vain. There was no sign of Kutuzov's army, which they were supposed to assist. There was no sign of the hated enemy they were ready to attack. There was no sign of the banner-bearing priests, whose leader, Archbishop Augustine, was hell-bent on decamping while the going was good. Above all, there was no sign of the military governor, who had promised to be present.

As the sun began to set, the musket bearers and the ax wielders began to drift back into the city. That night the western horizon was clearly illuminated by the glow of bivouac fires, from the two opposing armies. Fleeing peasants continued to stream into the city, along with wounded soldiers, who further filled the overcrowded hospitals which Rostopchin was finding it increasingly difficult to evacuate for lack of transportation.

Just what Rostopchin did during this Saturday, September 12, remains something of a mystery. At five o'clock in the morning he bade a tearful farewell to his wife and three daughters, saying that he might never see them again, since he had decided to share the perils of the army and of the people and might die in battle. Accompanied by the historian Nikolai Karamzine and several servants, Rostopchin's wife and daughters then joined the horde of carts, carriages, bullocks, household dogs, cooped hens, lame horses, and bearded elders clutching canes and crutches, which was advancing at a snail's pace along the northeast highroad leading to the Troitsky monastery and Yaroslavl. The governor himself then rode in to his enormous townhouse on Lubianka Street (not far from the Kremlin), where his private quarters were as uncomfortable and cramped as the salons and reception rooms were vast. According to his daughter Natalya, he went to visit the wounded in the hospitals and thereafter "busied himself with different important objects"—a vague description which merely deepens the mystery. Going out to the Three Hills to stoke or temper the bellicose ardor of the multitude he had inspired was apparently not one of those "important objects." But it seems well-nigh incredible that this man, who was anything but stupid, should not have realized that his failure to appear was bound to discredit him forever in the eyes of the tens of thousands who had dutifully responded to his call. If he had actually wanted them to join the panicky exodus that was now emptying the city, he could not have gone about it more effectively.

Before this Saturday, September 12, was over, yet another proclamation had been issued. It was destined to be Rostopchin's last, and in some ways it was the most fatuous of them all. "Early tomorrow I shall ride out to see the Most Illustrious Prince [Kutuzov] in order to talk things over, to act and to help the armies destroy the villains [Napoleon's Grande Armée]. We shall rip the living breath out of them and send these guests to the devil. I will be back for dinner, and we will then apply ourselves to the task, we will do in and finish off the villains."

Certain Russian historians—notably Liubomir Beskrovny—have claimed that Kutuzov wanted to make a second battle stand beyond Mozhaisk. Others, like Yevgheny Tarlé, have argued more convincingly that the old fox was merely indulging in elaborate simulation. One thing at least is certain: moving on ahead of Kutuzov's lumbering headquarters staff, Bennigsen hastily explored the remaining fifty miles, and for lack of anything better, he finally decided that the Russian army could make a stand along the crest of the Poklonnaya Gora and the Sparrow Hills, where thirty thousand Muscovites had recently assembled to "destroy the villain."

Worn out by the tension and fatigue of Borodino, dismayed by the increasing sloppiness of a baggage-encumbered army, which until recently had maintained excellent march discipline, deeply wounded by the lack of consideration shown to him by the generalissimo and the members of Kutuzov's entourage, Barclay de Tolly had succumbed to a feverish chill, which forced him to spend four days under blankets on a wagon-borne camp bed. But the moment he heard of Bennigsen's "find," he climbed onto a horse, still flushed with fever though he was, and rode forward to inspect the ground.

Barclay was appalled by what he saw. His lack of confidence in Bennigsen's military judgment was once again dramatically confirmed. The chosen site, crisscrossed by a "cobweb" of virtually impassable ravines and gullies, was a sure recipe for disaster. In the case of a forced retreat, as Barclay later wrote in a report to the tsar, "the entire army would have been annihilated down to the very last man."

Barclay found Kutuzov on the crest of the Poklonnaya Gora, seated near the main road on a campstool, which a Cossack attendant always carried with him. He was surrounded by the usual swarm of sycophantic aides-de-camp and by a crowd of generals and senior officers who were heatedly arguing the merits and weaknesses of the positions to which their respective troops had been assigned.

With the help of a roughly drawn sketch, Barclay pointed out the grave dangers of the position Bennigsen had chosen. Kutuzov looked surprised, even alarmed by what he heard. Calling over his trusted Colonel Toll, he asked him if he agreed with Barclay's findings. Toll, who had spent a number of exasperating hours the previous day with Bennigsen, trying to get him to decide just where the different corps should be positioned, replied that he himself would never have thought of placing the army in such a perilous position. Kutuzov then turned to Barclay's chief of staff, Yermolov, and asked for his opinion. Yermolov, whose formerly hostile feelings toward Barclay had undergone a radical change since Borodino, fully supported his commander. Indeed, the vehemence with which he declared that the position revealed glaring defects so startled Kutuzov that he took him by the wrist, felt his pulse, and asked, "Are you feeling all right?"

Yermolov, who was feeling fine, was emboldened by this friendly gesture. Deciding that most of the generals present were too abashed to speak their minds, he ventured to predict that His Excellency would not deliver battle here, but that if he did, he would surely be defeated. He then turned to Colonel Jean-Baptiste Crossard, who had recently joined Kutuzov's headquarters, and asked him what he thought of the site. A French émigré officer who had long served in the Spanish and Austrian armies, Crossard had accompanied Toll and the senior engineer officer, Colonel Michaud, during the previous day's reconnaissance. Now asked for his opinion, the émigré colonel declared quite bluntly, "This position seems to me very dangerous." Never, he declared, "has a position been better suited to destroy an army"—a statement which elicited a startled "What?" from Kutuzov. Crossard wound up his devastating critique by asking point-blank, "Do you really wish to fight?" Deliberately evading the question, the one-eyed generalissimo called over his son-in-law, Prince Kudashev, and ordered him to accompany Yermolov and Crossard on another reconnaissance of the terrain.

In the meantime Rostopchin, who had left his Moscow townhouse at six o'clock on the morning of the thirteenth and made his way on horseback through streets crowded with wagons full of wounded soldiers bound for the main hospital, had reached the crest of the Hill of Respectful Salutation. Soldiers were everywhere trying to dig entrenchments, while officers argued ill-temperedly among themselves in an atmosphere of "great disorderliness." When Rostopchin's name was announced, Kutuzov, who had never met Moscow's military governor, left his campstool and the fire by which he had been warming himself and took him off to one side for half an hour of private conversation.

By this time each had developed a scornful distrust of the other. Kutuzov had been annoyed by Rostopchin's failure to deliver all the horses and wagons he so desperately needed, feeling, not unnaturally, that the dire needs of his army should have been given priority over the evacuation of state and other treasures from Moscow. Rostopchin for his part had been outraged by the sly way in which Kutuzov had concealed the real outcome of the "victory" of Borodino. The conclusion he had come to was that the generalissimo was an untrustworthy rogue.

Precisely what was said during this half-hour encounter, we do not know. Rostopchin's account, written some time later, is too succinct to be a truly reliable report. But the one thing it makes clear—and this was fully in keeping with Kutuzov's wary nature—was that the generalissimo had no intention of letting this stranger into secrets he was carefully keeping from members of his own staff.

Finally they walked back to the fire, around which a number of generals and officers were gathered, arguing as busily as ever. Yermolov, returning from his inspection tour with Kutuzov's son-in-law and Crossard, was promptly sent off on a second reconnaissance. He came back to report that he was as much opposed to the position as before. Kutuzov listened in silence, but made no comment.

After Yermolov had delivered his second report, Rostopchin approached him and drew him off to one side. "I don't understand why you are exerting yourselves so much to defend Moscow," he said to Yermolov, "for when the enemy takes it, he will find nothing of any use in it." He explained that all of the state treasures and most of the archives had been removed, and that with but one or two exceptions the churches had been emptied of their most precious ikons and gold and silver ornaments. He hazarded the guess that Kutuzov was anything but eager to do battle—that at any rate was the impression he had been given by their half-hour talk. But, he went on, "if you abandon Moscow without a fight, you will see it blazing behind you."

This affirmation struck Yermolov as so odd that it remained imbedded in his memory.

Kutuzov meanwhile had remained seated on his folding stool, listening to what the others had to say, but himself saying nothing. Finally young Prince Eugen of Württemberg, who knew the generalissimo well—he had served under his orders in Vilna in 1810, at a time when Kutuzov was governor general of Lithuania—approached and whispered in his ear, "You must decide, Prince. Indecision is the worst thing of all."

At that moment, as though to underline the urgency of this appeal, there came the sound of gunfire from the west. Miloradovich's Russian rearguard forces were once again engaged in a skirmish with Murat's advancing cavalry.

Kutuzov looked at his young protégé Prince Eugen and said to him in French, *"Ici ma tête, fût elle bonne ou mauvaise, ne doit s'aider que d'elle-même"* (Here my head, be it good or bad, must rely solely on itself).

Rostopchin, realizing that Prince Eugen was on terms of close familiarity with Kutuzov, then approached him and said, "If I were asked what to do, I would say, 'First destroy the city rather than surrender it to the enemy.'"

That same afternoon, after Rostopchin had returned to Moscow, Kutuzov summoned his corps commanders to a meeting in the little peasant hut he had chosen to occupy at Fili, on the extreme northeastern end of the designated battle line. A glowing red lampion illuminated the ikon placed, according to Russian custom, in one corner of the simply furnished room. As they filed in, the generals—the still fever-stricken Barclay de Tolly, the faintly potbellied Dokhturov, the big, lumbering Ostermann-Tolstoy, the lithe, pipe-loving Konovnitsyn, the fat-cheeked Ouvarov, and the burly Yermolov—were asked to take their places on three benches placed around a wooden table covered with maps. Here they were joined by Kutuzov's two staff assistants, Toll and Kaissarov. The white-haired generalissimo was seated in a wooden armchair.

The meeting, which was supposed to start at four in the afternoon, was delayed by the late arrival of General Rayevsky, who had to come galloping back from Miloradovich's rear guard, and by the even later appearance of General Bennigsen, who had finally got around to inspecting the army's left wing. The latter, realizing that this meeting was a challenge directed against himself, strode in and announced that the question was "whether it is better to give battle beneath the walls of Moscow or to abandon the city to the enemy." He was immediately interrupted by Kutuzov, who declared that what was at stake was not simply the army or the city of Moscow, but the very existence of the state. The question could not properly be decided without a preliminary examination of the position's many shortcomings. If a retreat had to be ordered, it would have to be effected in such a way that the army could continue to receive cannon, powder, munitions, and weapons from the new foundry at Kazan and the new arms factory in Kiev, as well as from the older foundry at Tula, where scrap metal was being used to turn out muskets. As long as the army existed and was in a condition to fight the enemy, he went on, adopting the argument that had been Barclay's all along, there was still hope of successfully ending the war; but if the army were to be destroyed, not only Moscow but all Russia would be lost. So the question he now put to all those present, phrased in a pointedly different way from Bennigsen's, was: "Is it proper to await the enemy's attack in this disadvantageous position or to abandon Moscow to the enemy?"

Barclay de Tolly, who was the first to answer, declared categorically that the position was so bad that the army risked being destroyed. Once that had happened, the army's further retreat through Moscow would complete its annihilation. Painful though it was to abandon the country's ancient capital, it might in the end prove a boon in speeding the enemy's downfall, if the Russian army preserved its strength and ability to maneuver. He accordingly proposed that they withdraw from Moscow to Vladimir (140 miles to the east), where they could maintain links with Petersburg as well as with Kazan, Tula, and Kiev.

Bennigsen, in an attempt to make his arguments sound more impressive, rose to his feet and delivered a speech outlining the immense losses to the Crown and others that a surrender of Moscow would entail, and the shattering effect it would have on the morale of the army and of the nation as a whole. Napoleon's forces, he claimed, had also suffered terrible losses at Borodino. The attempt they were now making to outflank the Russian right wing had seriously distended their forces, and so he boldly proposed that several Russian army corps be moved during the night to the left wing of the Russian line for a surprise dawn attack against the French.

Barclay immediately riposted, pointing out that it was now too late for such a realignment of troops to be feasible. Were it to be tried at night and over such uneven ground, it could result in crippling confusion and leave the army the next morning at the mercy of the French. Kutuzov supported Barclay's critique.

The debate now became general, as Ostermann-Tolstoy, Konovnitsyn, and Rayevsky recommended avoiding battle in such a poor position. Dokhturov, who had earlier complained of the trouble he was having getting his artillery into position, surprisingly supported Bennigsen, as did the cavalry general Ouvarov. Yermolov, going all of them one better, spoke out vehemently against a purely passive stance and declared that there was only one thing to do—attack immediately and all along the line. Toll, for his part, felt that a retreat was unavoidable and that it should be made via the old Kaluga road in a southwesterly direction.

From his introductory remarks it was clear enough what Kutuzov's own sentiment was. But by letting everyone express his opinion freely, he could shrewdly claim not to have been the first to advocate the abandonment of Moscow. And so, after Ostermann-Tolstoy had challenged Bennigsen to come out unequivocally with an assurance that his surprise attack on the French was certain to succeed—an impossible demand which provoked a bristling (but noncommittal) retort from the offended Hanoverian—the white-haired generalissimo wound up the acrimonious debate: "I am aware of the responsibility I am assuming, but I sacrifice myself for the welfare of my country. I hereby order the retreat."

Outside it was already dark. The news that the army was retreating once again, and this time abandoning Moscow, was received with a mixture of pain, bewilderment, and consternation. Some officers broke down and wept, others tore off their riding coats, saying that they could not go on serving under such shameful conditions.

Kutuzov himself seems to have been as unhappy as the others. He paced restlessly up and down the floor of his log cabin and, according to his chief duty officer, Kaissarov, he even shed a few tears. A harsh reality was forcing him to eat the very words he had written, barely a fortnight before, to Rostopchin: "In my opinion, with the loss of Moscow is bound up the loss of Russia." Now he had no choice but to dispatch an aide-de-camp with an urgent message for the military governor. The enemy's outflanking columns had forced the generalissimo "with grief to abandon Moscow." Rostopchin was asked to provide as many police officers as possible to help guide the army through the city and out onto the road to Ryazan.

Although the corps commanders had been ordered to put their forces on the alert for immediate departure, it was probably not until an hour or more later that they learned just where they were headed and which route they were to follow. When one of his staff colonels asked Kutuzov, "But where are we going to stop?" the generalissimo suddenly ceased his nervous pacing and brought his fist down on the table. "That's my business!" he snapped. "But I'm going to see to it, as I did last year with the Turks, that the French end up eating horse meat!"

He then summoned his senior supply officer, General Lanskoy, and informed him that the army's destination was the Ryazan road, beyond Moscow's southeastern periphery. Lanskoy pointed out that there were no military depots in this area, whereas there were plentiful supplies at Kaluga, one hundred miles southwest of Moscow. Kutuzov had probably decided already that the army should move in that direction. But knowing how quickly Napoleon could move when he spotted a strategic opportunity, he realized that unless he disguised his true intention by adopting a roundabout march route, the French could decimate his laboriously marching columns with crippling flank attacks. By pretending to head for Vladimir and Ryazan he was sure to lure Napoleon into Moscow, where anything might happen. Barclay had already hinted that this might be the beginning of the end for Napoleon's Grande Armée, but it was Kutuzov who gave the idea its most graphic formulation, by comparing Napoleon to "a stormy torrent" and Moscow to "the sponge that will absorb it."

CHAPTER 19

THE HOLOCAUST

BEFORE RETURNING to his residence near the Kremlin, Rostopchin called on Archbishop Augustine to transmit Kutuzov's request that he come out the next day to bless the army with Moscow's two miracle-working ikons: the Vladimirskaya Madonna, belonging to the Uspensky Cathedral, and the Iverskaya, which hung in a chapel of that name in the Perervinsky monastery. The archbishop, torn between his personal desire to flee the city and his sense of pastoral duty, had just finished leading the Sunday service in the jam-packed Uspensky Cathedral, where the congregation had groaned and wept with him when he had uttered the doleful words "Will the Lord vouchsafe us again to officiate in this holy place of worship?" Convinced that the battle for Moscow was going to begin the very next day, he did not much relish the prospect of being caught up in the fighting while making his holy-water-sprinkling rounds with the two cherished ikons.

Back at his townhouse Rostopchin sat down to pen a personal letter to the tsar. This extraordinary epistle revealed him at his most exalted—which is saying a lot, given Rostopchin's penchant for high-flown rhetoric. It ended with a supreme appeal to his sovereign: "Sire, may the word 'peace' be banished from you! The history of your reign should not be stained by a disgrace, which would lie on the Russian people like an indelible blot. . . . Sire, do not give way to despondency—you will become the savior of the universe. Much can happen, and it may be that now for the last time I have the good fortune to be writing to you. . . ."

In dashing off this letter Rostopchin was clearly envisaging the following scenario. A battle would be fought before the walls of Moscow—probably in two days, possibly in three. Kutuzov would lose the battle, but some of his forces would manage to escape to the north and east toward Vladimir, others southwestward toward Kaluga. He himself, having joined Kutuzov's army, might well perish in the battle; but thanks to the dispositions taken prior to his departure for the front, Moscow would be an empty, and even a burned-out, shell. Provided Alexander did not at that point cave in and sue for peace,

Bonaparte would find that he had won a second battle for nothing. The Russian people, steeled by the sufferings they had had to endure at the hands of Bonaparte's "brigands," would then wage a war of extermination as pitiless as the one the Spaniards were waging against the French.

There was only one thing wrong with this scenario: Rostopchin's ingenuous assumption that Kutuzov would deliver battle. This was a serious miscalculation, which came near to undoing all of his plans and machinations. For when, sometime after eight on this evening of Sunday, September 13, he received Kutuzov's message informing him of his decision to abandon Moscow without a fight, Rostopchin realized that he had only a few hours, instead of the two days he had been counting on, to complete his supreme gubernatorial mission.

The news threw this inordinately high-strung individual into a paroxysm of despair, which his son, Sergei, had great difficulty calming. His first thought was to dash off a letter to his wife, in which he implicitly denounced Kutuzov's disgraceful duplicity. "The troops are already marching through the city; it will be ransacked and plundered by the Russians. 22,000 wounded are being abandoned. . . . My blood boils in my veins, I think I shall die of grief. . . . "

He then penned a second letter to the tsar, informing him of Kutuzov's decision to give up Moscow without a fight. "All Russia will tremble on learning of the abandonment of a city that is the center of its greatness and where repose the ashes of our ancestors. I shall follow the army; I have put away in safety everything that was in the city, and all that is left for me to do is to weep over my country's lot."

His claim to have "put away in safety" everything of value in this vast city was, of course, a wild Rostopchian piece of rhetoric. In sober fact, many treasures still had to be removed—beginning with Moscow's two miracle-working ikons. So yet another letter had to be dashed off, this time to Archbishop Augustine, who was authorized to leave Moscow with the two precious ikons and the Black Madonna of Smolensk, which had been entrusted to his personal safekeeping.

Rostopchin's next action was to order the departure of all remaining municipal employees. The assistant police chief, Ivashkin, was instructed to have Moscow's 2,100 firemen alerted by their officers and assembled at a designated point with the city's 64 fire pumps. Officers and simple soldiers of the police department were to close the taverns, after smashing any vats of wine or vodka they could find; after which most of them, along with the firemen, were to join the torrent of terrified humanity that was now pouring out of the city's eastern and southern gates. The drivers of the five thousand vehicles that had been requisitioned for this purpose were to pick up the more severely wounded. Quite a few of those who could not fight their way onto one of these vehicles were forced to hobble out of the city on crutches, and many of the more seriously wounded were simply abandoned.

Altogether, it was a hectic night for the military governor. He was besieged by a horde of last-minute suppliants, including a delegation of young Moscow noblemen who wanted him to go plead with Kutuzov to stand fast, and a

number of Georgian princes and princesses who had been left in the lurch—
which is to say, without carriages—by the absconding gentleman to whose care
they had been entrusted. Rostopchin found time, however, to recruit half a
dozen police officers who agreed to remain behind in Moscow disguised as
civilians and to make clandestine trips to the Russian army's headquarters in
the country, with information about what the French were doing in the abandoned capital.

This done, he held a secret meeting in his study with a number of police
agents and patriotic accomplices, who had been recruited by Adam Fomich
Broker, a former naval officer of Swedish extraction whom Rostopchin had
appointed director of the Moscow police force because of his rabid distrust of
Freemasons, mystics, and other "illuminist" groups. The "patriots" included
a significant number of young seminarians who were eager to do their bit in
the grim struggle against the approaching "Antichrist."

The police agents, disguised as beggars or artisans, were to begin by setting
fire to the fire-fighting barges tied up along the wharfs of the Moskva River.
At eight in the morning, the gates of the prisons were to be unlocked and some
eight hundred common-law prisoners were to be released, on the understanding that they would be amnestied for past offenses provided that they per-
formed a "great patriotic deed" by setting fire to buildings occupied by the
French invaders. To this end they were to be given Congreve fuses, brought
in from the large stock of incendiary materials that Leppich and his German
airship-builders had prepared. The first targets were to be the remaining grain
stores and the foodshops near the Kremlin. At five in the morning Rostopchin,
after carefully briefing him, sent one of his senior police commissioners, Voro-
nenko, to the main wine and vodka warehouses, to make sure that the remaining stocks of alcohol were ignited once it was certain that the French had
entered Moscow. But none of these fires were to be started until after the
Russian troops had completed their march through the city.

For several hours already certain Moscow streets and avenues had been
reverberating with the rumble of artillery guns and caissons rolling heavily
over the wooden pavement. For most of those who took part, this march
through unnaturally still and often empty streets was one long torment. Some
soldiers thought they were entering Moscow in order to take up positions
behind the outer walls to defend it; but as the hours passed and no final halt
was called, their spirits sank and they trudged on in a mood of sullen gloom.
The absence of cheering crowds and the monotonous sound of tramping boots
made the march even grimmer. To Wolzogen it seemed like a funeral march,
to Lieutenant Alexander Chicherin of the Semyonovsky Guards Regiment,
like a bad dream haunted by weeping ghosts. Colonel Crossard was struck by
the look of silent rage on the faces of officers and men.

Gradually, as the morning progressed, the deserted city seemed less empty
of inhabitants. Like a mighty flood sucking water from inflowing tributaries,
the seemingly endless column of guns, baggage trains, and soldiers drew
crowds of onlookers, whose joy at seeing these "saviors" soon turned into

despair when they grasped the bitter truth. "In front of the churches," the artillery lieutenant Ivan Rogozhitsky noted, "priests in their ceremonial vestments blessed the crosses they were carrying and sprinkled holy water on the passing soldiers, helping to refresh their flagging spirits. We were greeted by heartrending scenes at every step: women, old men, children wept and wailed, not knowing whither to betake themselves. Some came rushing out of the houses, looking pale and desperate, and bustled about uncomprehendingly: everything was tumbling into ruin before their eyes, and with the approach of the Antichrist doomsday seemed nigh."

In an official report later prepared for the tsar, Barclay de Tolly wrote that if he had not exerted himself to the utmost and had not been present everywhere, fever-ridden though he was, "the army would only with difficulty have been able to get through Moscow." His devoted aide-de-camp Waldemar von Loewenstern was even more forthright in declaring that Barclay managed to save the Russian army from "unavoidable destruction." To begin with, the police guides Kutuzov had requested from Rostopchin failed to show up when and where they were needed. The officers of the quartermaster corps who should have been sent out ahead to check the state of streets and bridges were also nowhere to be seen. To keep the columns of marching infantry from dissolving into the ever thicker throngs of anguished civilians who pressed around and followed them, cavalrymen in close single-file formation were ordered to hedge them in on either side and pitilessly to hack down any soldier or noncommissioned officer who sought to slip away. Barclay even had to dispatch his own aides-de-camp to various squares and intersections to see to it that soldiers did not suddenly hop into a tavern for a "quick nip" or break into abandoned houses.

Less conscientious than Barclay, who spent hours seated on his horse watching the marching columns cross the stone bridge spanning the Yaouza River, east of the Kremlin, Kutuzov sought to pass through Moscow unnoticed. What he evidently feared was a riot, which might erupt at any moment when the Muscovites discovered that the army was leaving the city to its fate. His instinct as regards his countrymen's reactions once again was sound. For when it began to dawn on the dazed populace that all these passing guns, horses, and soldiers were not stopping to defend but simply passing through their city, many of them streamed toward the military governor's townhouse, angrily demanding an explanation. Soon a furious mob had gathered in the forecourt. It was by now close to ten in the morning, and Rostopchin, after a sleepless night, was getting ready to leave his residence with his son, Sergei.

Exactly what happened at this point is anything but clear. Two of the eight hundred prisoners who had been released from their jails that morning were special cases and had accordingly been brought to the military governor's mansion. One of them, the twenty-three-year-old son of a Moscow merchant named Vereshchaghin, had been arrested and condemned by the Senate for circulating written texts in which Napoleon was quoted as saying that he would be in Moscow and St. Petersburg within six months; the other was a Frenchman named Mouton who had been arrested for "seditious talk." Many

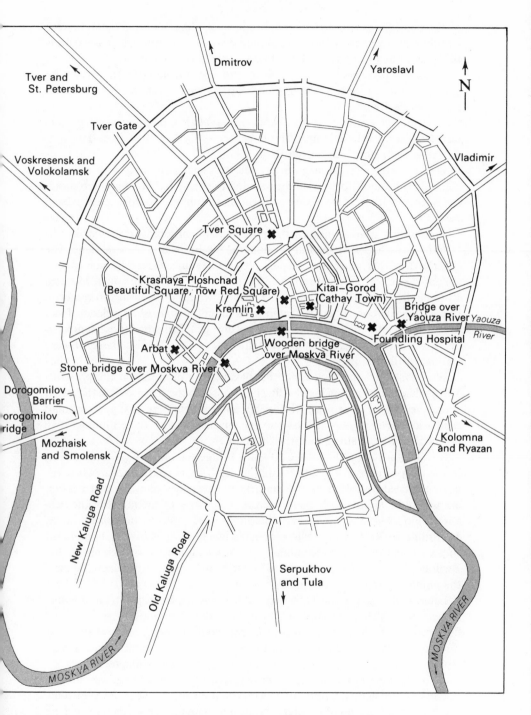

MOSCOW IN 1812

of the clamoring protesters were drunk, and while some of them shouted angrily that they had been lied to and deceived, others wanted Rostopchin to lead them out to the Three Hills to do battle with the enemy.

"Wait, my brothers!" shouted Rostopchin, coming out onto the porch steps and raising his voice to make himself heard above the tumult. "I still have a traitor to deal with."

"A traitor!" roared the drunkards, not realizing that he was trying to distract them. "Where is he? Who is he?"

"He is right here," answered Rostopchin.

The trembling Vereshchaghin, dressed in a sheepskin coat with a fox-fur collar, was brought forward and presented to the mob. "Here is the traitor!" cried Rostopchin. "Here is the man who has brought Moscow to its present pass!"

Summoning one of his orderlies, Rostopchin ordered him to strike the "traitor" who had so shamefully dishonored his family and his fatherland. The orderly drew his saber and slashed Vereshchaghin's face. The young man collapsed to the ground with a moan. Turning to the French prisoner, Mouton, Rostopchin admonished him, saying that he would do well in future not to proffer remarks contrary to the interests of the country that had welcomed him in such a friendly manner. "Now go! I pardon you. But when those compatriots of yours, those brigands, arrive, tell them how we punish those who are traitors to their homeland."

With that he went back inside his palace. The mob fell on the prostrate Vereshchaghin, dragging his bleeding body out into the street. While they went about their bloody business, Rostopchin and his son, Sergei, slipped out into the back courtyard—so at least one version has it—and there mounted two horses that were waiting to carry them away.

Rostopchin rode as far as the crowded bridge spanning the Yaouza River, in the eastern part of the city. Using his leather-thonged *nagaika* whip, the governor tried to hold back civilian drivers and pedestrians, so that the columns could continue their march across the bridge. In the midst of the pandemonium Kutuzov appeared, dumpily seated on his big-boned horse. According to Rostopchin, who may have invented the story later, Kutuzov shot a sarcastic glance at the military governor and said, "I can assure you that I will not move far from Moscow without giving battle"—to which "idiocy" the military governor did not deign to reply.

Later, when Barclay de Tolly decided to move on, Rostopchin and his son, Sergei, joined his suite. Behind them were the thousands of soldiers and horsemen of General Miloradovich's rearguard force, who had to move through an abandoned and increasingly lawless city where hoodlums were already breaking into private homes and going on drunken sprees.

At the Kolomna barrier the human crush was so great that officers and soldiers had difficulty forcing their way out onto the crowded Ryazan road. Their destination was the village of Panki, a few miles farther on, where Kutuzov had decided to establish his new headquarters. Shortly after they had cleared the barrier Rostopchin heard several distant cannon shots, as though specially fired to signal the termination of his military governorship. Reining in his horse, he turned around for a look at the city they were leaving and said to Sergei, "Salute Moscow for the last time, for in half an hour it will be in flames."

Farther on they caught up with a long convoy of covered carts, moving slowly forward under military escort. Wolzogen, who was riding along with other members of Barclay's suite, realized that they were fire pumps. Intrigued, he asked Rostopchin why he had ordered them to leave the city.

"I have my own good reasons" was the enigmatic reply. After which, as though answering an unspoken reproach, he added, "All I have taken from the city is the horse I am riding and this uniform I am wearing."

Not until later did Wolzogen comprehend the full significance of this remark. Unlike many Muscovites, who had taken what they could when they fled, locking up their houses or leaving them in the custody of their serf-servants, Rostopchin had made no attempt to protect his own property or belongings. He was not going to be accused of misusing the facilities at his disposal to save his own belongings at a moment when so much was due to be destroyed. As the military governor of Moscow, he had to set an irreproach-able example, even if it meant sacrificing his own fortune.

Shortly after dawn on this same Monday, September 14, Napoleon sent one of his duty officers, Anatole de Montesquiou, forward to Murat's headquarters to expedite the vanguard's movement toward Moscow. After breakfast they climbed onto their horses and rode forward, preceded by vanguard scouts of General Sébastiani's light-cavalry brigade. Soon they emerged from a wood of birch and pine trees. Ahead of them was a hill, up which they started cautiously, for fear of being ambushed by the Cossacks. A large number of the latter were in fact concentrated on the farther slope, where they were covering the passage of the final baggage wagons and a number of artillery pieces through the Dorogomilov suburb and over its wooden bridge.

Suddenly a Russian officer—Captain Akinfov, of a Life-Guards hussar regiment—appeared on the crest of the hill, waving a white handkerchief. He had been sent by General Miloradovich, who was increasingly worried by the prospect of having to fight a desperate rearguard battle, which might cost him a dozen horse-artillery guns and a few cavalry squadrons. Akinfov was instructed to request a truce, to permit the withdrawing Russians to evacuate nine thousand wounded soldiers and to get their rearguard troops and remaining baggage trains through Moscow unimpeded. Otherwise, the molested Russians would have no choice but to fight to the very last man for every street and house as they retreated, and in so doing they would destroy everything, and the French would be left with a heap of ruins.

Akinfov had no trouble recognizing Murat, whose richly feathered shako and gold-embroidered finery outshone the brightly colored uniforms of his elegantly attired suite.

"Leave us alone," shouted Murat in a stentorian voice, as he galloped forward to meet the Russian emissary. The Russian captain handed him a note from Kutuzov's headquarters and explained the purpose of his mission. About the Russian wounded, Murat replied that there would be no problem: as prisoners of war, they would no longer be considered enemies and would be accorded the same medical care as wounded Frenchmen. About a truce he was more hesitant, though he accepted General Miloradovich's proposal for a cease-fire, in his desire to see Moscow spared. The troops under his command would advance no faster than the Russians withdrew, provided that they were all out of Moscow by midnight.

This gentlemen's agreement, subsequently endorsed by Napoleon, proved an unexpected boon to the Russians. Had Napoleon realized the scorching reception that Rostopchin had been secretly preparing for him, he would certainly not have shown himself so ready to accept this cease-fire proposal. But his overriding concern at this moment was to spare Moscow the fate that had overtaken Smolensk. He even agreed to extend the cease-fire and to delay the Grande Armée's formal entry into Moscow until seven the next morning. In the meantime Murat's cavalrymen were to follow the Russians step by step as they withdrew through the city.

On reaching the crest of the Poklonnaya Gora—where Russians traditionally crossed themselves and knelt before proceeding toward their hallowed capital—Murat and his officers were suddenly confronted with an unforgettable panorama. Spread out before them, less than a mile away, was Moscow, with its oriental multitude of maroon-red, chrome-yellow, holly-green, and blue-tinted spires and towers, the golden cupolas of its innumerable churches, the dark rooftops of its brilliantly whitewashed palaces, rising above the long, low, honey-colored walls like a vision from the *Arabian Nights*. Coiled in a lazy loop across the intervening land, the silvery Moskva wound its serpentine way toward a chink in the ramparts, disappearing in the hidden depths beyond. If not the Promised Land, this was the Promised City, and at the sight many members of Murat's suite clapped their hands and broke into spontaneous applause.

Almost as unbelievable was the strange pantomime that followed, between riders of the two opposing armies. So close were the advancing French to the retreating Cossacks, who were riding ahead of them toward the Dorogomilov city barrier, that they all seemed part of the same host. The French would occasionally halt to let Russian stragglers or baggage wagons move on ahead, riders from the two armies who had frequently met and dueled in the past now saluted each other in the most friendly fashion, and a number of Cossack officers trotted up to have a closer look at the prodigious, larger-than-life warrior-king Murat, who was always to be seen wherever there was a front-line skirmish, fearlessly defying sabers, lances, bullets, and cannonballs in his brazenly flaunted finery and plumes.

Not far behind, the chasseurs of the Imperial Guard and the officers of Napoleon's suite now reached the crest of the Poklonnaya Gora. There were excited cries of "*Moscou! Moscou!*" as the riders spurred their horses forward. Veterans of Bonaparte's Egyptian campaign recalled the shouts of "Thebes! Thebes!" which had greeted the sight of the city of one hundred gates, while the erudite Fantin des Odoards was reminded of the poet Tasso's description of the thousand crusaders roaring their enthusiasm at the sight of Jerusalem the Golden:

> *Ecco da mille voci unitamente*
> *Gerusalemme salutar si sente!*

To Philippe de Ségur, who later needed two pages of inspired prose to recapture the heady exaltation of this moment, the excited riders were like "sailors crying 'Land! Land!' at the end of a long and painful navigation. . . . What a day of glory had arrived! How it was destined to become the greatest, the most dazzling memory of our entire life!"

Finally Napoleon appeared, surrounded by his marshals, several of whom had hurriedly forgotten their earlier grievances and now galloped up in their eagerness to share in the euphoria. The news that the Russians had decided to abandon Moscow without fighting meant that their emperor's proverbial lucky star had not abandoned him.

"So there it is at last, this famous city!" were Napoleon's first words, quickly followed by "It was high time!"

There was an awed hush as the emperor dismounted. He drew his short spyglass from its holder, the better to contemplate this exotic amalgam of East and West, this forest of onion-topped minarets, this "swarm of golden globes" hovering in the warm afternoon air above an immense city of close to three hundred thousand souls. In size as well as polychrome magnificence it dwarfed every other major European city—Milan, Rome, Berlin, Vienna—which had been forced to submit to his imperious dominion.

After a cursory inspection through the spyglass, Napoleon had Caulaincourt summon the page who carried the larger telescope. It was placed on Anatole de Montesquiou's obliging shoulder.

"The barbarians!" exclaimed Napoleon several times, swiveling the magnifying lens from one tall building or tower to another. "They are leaving all of this to us! It's not possible. Caulaincourt, what do you think of it? Tell me, can you believe it?"

"Your Majesty knows better than anyone what I think of it" was the grand equerry's dry reply.

Napoleon's chief interpreter, François Lelorgne d'Ideville, who had served for years with the French embassy in Petersburg, was summoned to identify the principal towers and buildings. But there was one in the Dorogomilov suburb he knew nothing about.

"Montesquiou," said Napoleon, handing the telescope back to the page, "go down there to the left, where you see that strange building, and find out what it is."

Montesquiou cantered down the road to the Dorogomilov barrier and entered the suburb. The streets were absolutely empty. The main gate of the building he had been ordered to identify was open, but there was no one in the courtyard. Hitching his horse to an iron ring anchored in the wall, he undertook a quick inspection. The bare, cell-like chambers and the tall, forbidding walls suggested that this had been a prison, recently emptied of its inmates. As he came back to unhitch his horse, he saw two tall Russians come out and scowl at him. He spoke to them in German, then tried Polish, but the only response forthcoming was the brief phrase *"Frantsouzi kaput!"* ("The French are done for!"), accompanied by gesticulations pointing toward the center of the city.

Montesquiou was not the only one to be sent on an exploratory mission of this kind. Throughout the afternoon of this Monday, September 14, while he waited impatiently to be met by a delegation of municipal officials coming to offer him the keys to their city, Napoleon kept sending in scouts and emissaries to find out what was going on in the nearest suburb by the river and beyond those honey-colored walls. Finally, losing patience, he ordered Murat and his cavalrymen, who had donned full-dress uniform, like his own Imperial Guard, to cross the Moskva River and to follow the withdrawing Russians. Shortly afterward he summoned General Antoine Durosnel, told him that he was appointing him military governor of Moscow, and ordered him to proceed with Colonel Gourgaud to the Kremlin.

Durosnel immediately set out with Gourgaud and a number of staff officers and gendarmes. Those who took part in this cavalcade were struck by the eerie emptiness of the streets. In fact, though it had been abandoned by its aristocracy and merchant class, Moscow was anything but an empty city. The shuttered shops and houses, particularly in the poorer quarters, were filled with Muscovites, as well as wounded soldiers and refugees from burned-out towns and villages, who dared not show their faces.

Some distance ahead, Murat's advance guard was now approaching the Kremlin, passing ever-grander houses, some of them in stone, most of them in wood, on whose balconies watching men and women were occasionally to be seen. The first serious incident occurred around four in the afternoon, shortly after the great Ivan Vyeliki bell on the Kremlin's tallest tower had finished ringing the summons for vespers. Having discovered that the city's police force had vanished, hundreds of Muscovites from the "dregs of society" —as Rostopchin liked to describe them—had invaded the taverns. A number of drunkards had then assembled inside the Kremlin, now abandoned by its garrison, and had helped themselves to weapons from the arsenal. They had then locked and bolted the doors of the Troitsky Gate, while some of the more enterprising among them had climbed up to the parapet, where they were preparing, roaring drunk though they were, to open fire. One of them, who seems to have thought that the superbly plumed general up front was the hated Antichrist in person, actually aimed his flintlock at Murat and came near to hitting Napoleon's aide-de-camp Gourgaud.

A few well-aimed carbine shots quickly cleared the Kremlin walls, and several rounds fired by a mobile field piece smashed open the bolted doors of the Troitsky Gate. The first to enter the Kremlin were several squadrons of Polish uhlans, delighted to efface the historic setback their nation had suffered exactly two hundred years before, in 1612, when the Poles had been forced to

surrender the Kremlin to Prince Dmitry Pozharsky's Russians. Cantering past
the Senate building, they made straight for a small throng of armed "resisters"
gathered near the arsenal, slashing down a dozen of them before they could
use their flintlocks. The rest hastily threw down their weapons and got down
on their knees, imploring mercy. Soon two columns of Grande Armée cavalry,
entering via two different gates, were trotting through the inner city of the
Kremlin, past the Grand Palace and the two cathedrals and out through the
Spassky Gate onto Krasnaya Ploshchad—Beautiful Square, or as we would
say today, Red Square.

Back at the Dorogomilov barrier Napoleon's impatience was mounting by
the minute. Several members of Moscow's French community who had gone
into hiding for fear of being lynched by Moscow's now furiously xenophobic
populace, had confirmed what others had already reported: the city had been
abandoned by its military governor and by all of its administrative officials, and
even its police officers and soldiers had disappeared.

"Moscow deserted! What an incredible happening!" exclaimed Napoleon to
Pierre Daru. "We must enter it. Go, go get me the boyars!"

While Daru and his assistant, General Mathieu Dumas, rode into the city
in search of the Muscovite nobility, Durosnel had found an Italian to lead him
and his gendarmes to the Moscow governor's residence, now empty, like so
many other houses they had passed.

In all the years he had served as his grand equerry, never had Caulaincourt
seen Napoleon so visibly upset. It was already five o'clock, no municipal
delegation bearing the city's keys could any longer be expected, and if he
entered Moscow now, as dusk was falling, it would look as though he were
entering surreptitiously, under the cover of nightfall. To work off his intense
frustration, Napoleon climbed back into the saddle, rode around with Davout
to inspect the disposition of his divisions, and finally took up temporary
residence in an abandoned inn.

Mortier was ordered to send in two of his Young Guard divisions to back
up General Durosnel's handful of gendarmes. Having been urged by Rostopchin to take up their pitchforks and to toss out the French invaders—described
as "no heavier than a sheaf of rye"—some of the city's more simpleminded
inhabitants tried to do just that. As Sergeant François Bourgogne's regiment
marched across the Dorogomilov bridge behind its eagles and its blaring
brasses, its drum major was attacked by a white-bearded Russian in a dirty
sheepskin *touloup* who suddenly emerged from under the bridge like a wrath-
ful Neptune brandishing a three-pronged pitchfork. The splendor of the drum
major's white-and-scarlet uniform and golden trappings must have convinced
the old man that he was attacking a general. The French drum major managed
to dodge the pitchfork, and giving the old man a hefty kick, he sent him sliding
down the bank and into the river.

Other Russians, armed with muskets they had taken from the Kremlin
arsenal, tried to use them against the advancing Young Guard column, but not
knowing how to load them properly, they were easily disarmed and their

flintlocks smashed on the pavement. After a half hour's march up the broad avenue of the Arbat, the Young Guard regiment reached the outer Kremlin wall. Wheeling to the left, the column marched along the Kremlin's northwestern rampart for half a mile, then turned left into a large square, where the soldiers were to bivouac for the night.

Looking out onto this square was the military governor's palace. Inside, after mounting the broad, twin-branched staircase leading to the first floor, General Durosnel and his officers had installed themselves in the paneled conference room, where, watched over by a portrait of Emperor Alexander on horseback, Count Fyodor Rostopchin had been wont to receive his visitors. Of the governor and his staff there was not a trace.

While the new occupants moved through the palace's many chambers, the grenadiers of Sergeant Bourgogne's regiment, assigned to guard the square, were not losing time. The officers, as famished as the men they commanded, turned a blind eye as soldiers and noncoms knocked at the doors of neighboring houses, to ask for food and drink. Finding them empty, they went in and helped themselves to whatever they could find in larders and cellars. Within an hour the square where they were bivouacked resembled a marketplace, replete with wines and liquors of all kinds, umpteen jars of conserved fruit, a "prodigious quantity of sugar loaves," and a few sacks of flour.

While various Grande Armée units were thus occupying the city, the disguised policemen and other Russian "patriots" who had agreed to stay behind were preparing to go into action. Rostopchin's remark to his son, "Salute Moscow for the last time, for within half an hour it will be in flames," was for once in his life only a slight exaggeration. Around midday a fire, reported to have been ignited by the bailiff of some unidentified "prince," broke out in the Chandlers Row of the Kitai-Gorod, consuming a few paint-and-wax shops and spreading an appalling stench throughout the area bordering the Kremlin.

Whether or not it was this initial blaze that later set fire to the labyrinthine shopping district of the Kitai-Gorod is not clear. But around five in the afternoon, Sergeant Bourgogne and his fellow grenadiers spotted columns of dense smoke swirling upward from the area of the bazaar, as they called it. They had already seen so many wooden towns and villages burst into flames during the long march to Moscow that they paid little heed, assuming that some Grande Armée marauders had accidentally started a fire while combing shops for foodstuffs. But at seven that evening, when another column of dark smoke was spotted behind the governor's palace, the colonel commanding Bourgogne's regiment ordered him to go out with a patrol of fifteen men and put out the blaze.

On the way they were fired upon by a number of drunken Russian soldiers and convicts, armed with pikes and muskets, who had set themselves up in an abandoned palace. The ensuing battle distracted the French grenadiers from their fire-fighting mission, as did the palace's magnificent furnishings, and in particular a collection of jewel-studded swords and pistols, which they promptly appropriated. A loud detonation, caused by an explosive device placed in the dining-room's porcelain stove, sent them running out to the street, in time to see clouds of black and reddish smoke pour from the upstairs windows and tongues of flame lick at the cornices. Fifteen minutes later the lacquered metal roofing caved in with a roar as the blazing walls collapsed.

Sometime between eleven and midnight a colossal explosion rocked the Yaouza River area, several miles east of the Kremlin. The detonation was so powerful, and the brief firework display so vivid, that it was heard and seen by Heinrich von Roos, whose Württemberg light-cavalry regiment was now bivouacked east of Moscow, by the road leading to Vladimir and Kazan. A munitions depot had just blown up. The shops of the Kitai-Gorod, filled with oils, fats, resins, silks and satins and other combustible materials, were now a mass of flames. Yet it still had not dawned on Bourgogne and his fellow grenadiers that they were confronted by a massive outbreak of arson. They saw several long-bearded men go by, their "sinister faces" illuminated by the torches they carried in their hands, and they made no attempt to stop them. But after meeting a couple of Imperial Guard chasseurs, who told them that the Russians were setting fire to their own city, Bourgogne and his grenadiers surprised three men trying to ignite a church. A little later, alerted by the desperate cries of two disheveled ladies—French actresses whose husbands had been forcibly deported from Moscow—they seized four Russian gendarmes who wanted to burn their house and all the stage costumes it contained.

Incidents like these became increasingly commonplace, as the prisoners whom Rostopchin had ordered released from jail now joined the rampage. Like Khomeini's fanatics in our time, they were persuaded that their "essential" work of destruction would win them remission of all past sins and a place of honor in the next world, if not in this one. Albert de Muralt, a Swiss officer serving with a Bavarian cavalry regiment, was walking up a street with two friends when they saw a French officer come racing toward them. "Run for it!" he cried to them. "There's a band of brigands behind me." Round the corner several hundred yards away a mob of fifty or sixty men suddenly appeared, carrying lit torches and uttering furious yells.

It was two in the morning (of Tuesday, September 15) when Bourgogne and his grenadiers finally made it back to the governor's palace with eight would-be arsonists caught more or less red-handed. Other soldiers of their Young Guard regiment had obviously not been idle. The square now teemed with a motley host of warriors sporting Kalmuk belts, Cossack boots, Tartar bonnets, Persian lambswool hats, Turkish scimitars and daggers, as well as a luxurious assortment of fur coats, gloves, and *shapkas*. Some had even got themselves up in French Court dress, with steel-handled rapiers gleaming at their sides. The stock of foodstuffs, too, had been considerably expanded, with generous additions of hams, fresh meat, and fish. The whole scene seemed utterly unreal, as unreal as the flames illuminating the night, which seemed to have been specially planned as part of the theatrical décor.

Inside the guardroom, near the foot of the staircase of the governor's mansion, the mood was less casual. The accumulating evidence—that many embittered Muscovites were now out to burn their city—was too glaring to be ignored. One of the first to warn about what was brewing was a French dressmaker named Madame Aubert-Chalmais, whose husband had been deported by Rostopchin and who had barely managed to escape the same fate by going into hiding. She called on General Durosnel at the governor's palace and implored him to stay in her house, which would thus be officially protected. For days, she said, the strangest rumors had been circulating about the Russians' intentions. There was talk of a gigantic balloon they had built, which was to explode over the heads of the invading French, destroying their entire army in an apocalyptic flash. No one knew just what it was, but Governor Rostopchin had been preparing some nefarious *grand coup*—he had had all the fire-fighting pumps removed from Moscow, the jails had been emptied and six hundred prisoners had been let loose upon the city.

Napoleon, to whom this information was quickly relayed, probably thought that it was the hysterical effusion of a frightened woman. Moscow's sheer immensity, the width of its larger avenues and squares, the number of its gardens, were bound to frustrate any systematic attempt at destruction. Barbaric though the Russians were, they could not be insane enough to want to disfigure their oldest, largest, most venerable city.

Anatole de Montesquiou—who was delighted to be able to spend the night between sheets, his first since Vilna—went to bed in the same tranquil disposition. But at two in the morning he was awakened by the French painter (an acquaintance of Madame Aubert's) with whom he had found lodgings.

"That's the beginning of the fire," said the painter, pointing at the luridly illuminated windowpanes. "Just what I feared. It's one of the dreadful plots they've mysteriously prepared."

Leaping out of bed, Montesquiou went to the window and saw flames rising some distance away, behind a building on the opposite side of the square. Beyond it, the painter explained, was the vast outer wall of the Kremlin, which is where the fire had started.

"It's a mishap common to warfare," suggested Montesquiou blithely. "Our soldiers are so careless."

"Don't you believe it," corrected the painter. "This terrible fire has broken out precisely where for almost three months the goods and provisions that could be most useful to the French army have been transported. Look, it's the stock market and the bazaar that are burning."

At six in the morning an exhausted General Durosnel, who had spent a sleepless night with Marshal Mortier trying to save the shops of the Kitai-Gorod from being totally consumed by flames, returned to the Dorogomilov suburb and asked Napoleon to name Mortier governor general of the city. It was decided that Marshal Lefebvre would garrison the Kremlin with his Old Guard veterans, while the maintenance of law and order in the rest of Moscow would be the task of Marshal Mortier's Young Guard soldiers. The normally jolly marshal may have felt flattered to be given this new responsibility, but it was soon to prove more than he could cope with. Not all of his three Young Guard divisions, now numbering fewer than 15,000 men, were stationed in Moscow—which made the policing of this vast city that much more difficult.

Napoleon's decision to have most of his Grande Armée stationed *around* the city's periphery—Prince Eugène's Fourth Corps to the north, Ney's Third Corps to the east, Davout's First Corps to the west, Murat's cavalrymen and Poniatowski's Poles to the south—merely exacerbated the universal thirst for loot, and far from saving the city from plunder and plunderers, it greatly facilitated the movements of Rostopchin's arsonists.

It was not until later, however, that this became apparent. By the early morning of this Tuesday, September 15, Mortier's Young Guardsmen, by emptying many Kitai-Gorod shops of their carpets, furs, clothes, meat, fish, and assorted liquors and piling them up along the arcades of Red Square, had halted the progression of the blaze. A few columns of dirty smoke continued to rise from the partly gutted area, but the conflagration seemed to have been extinguished. Napoleon, mounted on a white horse and preceded by the trumpeters and drummers of the Imperial Guard, was able to make a solemn, if not exactly triumphal, entry past the two eagle-topped obelisks of the Dorogomilov Gate into the abandoned city. He took up his residence in the main Kremlin palace, in the very apartments that Tsar Alexander had occupied seven weeks before, with windows facing southward over the Moskva River, and beyond it over "an immense horizon of houses, domes, and palaces" (in the words of his secretary, Baron Fain). Gérard's painting of his cradled son was hung up on the bedroom wall to make him feel less distant from the Tuileries Palace and Saint-Cloud. He had reached his destination, or at any rate one of them. But the satisfaction he might have derived from this pleasing thought was spoiled by the realization that the Turks were not lifting a finger to regain the Crimea, while Bernadotte, who should by all good logic have been laying siege to Petersburg, was quietly spending the autumn in Stockholm.

In the evening, Napoleon, who had got little sleep during his previous night's stay at the Dorogomilov inn, decided to retire early. At eight o'clock a new fire had been reported in an eastern suburb; once again it was attributed to the carelessness of Grande Armée soldiers. But then two bigger blazes sprang up to the west, along the Arbat and the long avenue leading to the Dorogomilov barrier, up which the imperial suite had ridden in the morning. Within an hour these fires, fanned by a strong northwest wind, had spawned a score of others. Flames shot up from the grain stores near the Moskva River, while flying sparks set fire to a military depot full of grenades, which for a fraction of a second illuminated the entire sky like a flash of lightning.

Awakened by eddies of light flowing back and forth across the ceiling, Napoleon's faithful Mameluke, Roustam, sprang out of bed and, going to the window, was confronted by an unbroken sea of flames. Caulaincourt, who was roused shortly afterward by his valet, had him go wake up Duroc. As the fires for the time being seemed some distance away and presented no immediate threat to the Kremlin, they decided not to disturb the emperor's sleep.

The first consequence of this renewed outbreak of fires, which soon seemed to be engulfing all of Moscow, was the legitimization of the plundering, which had begun almost from the moment the Grande Armée's far-flung units settled down in and around the city. Napoleon's decision to have most of his divisions *logées militairement*—consigned to bivouacs beyond the city walls—in the hope that this would save Moscow from being pitilessly ransacked, had almost the opposite effect. Had more units been billeted in the hundreds of more or less empty palaces and townhouses that were available, many more of these edifices could have been saved from the flames that eventually devoured them. (The French shops of the fashionable Kuznetsky Most were saved in this manner by the strenuous efforts of a company of French grenadiers, who laboriously carried pails of water up flights of stairs to douse threatened roofs.) But with nobody to guard them, all those palaces and townhouses were easy targets for Rostopchin's incendiaries; and once the fires had started, there was every incentive to empty them of everything that could be dragged out into the streets.

The methodical Heinrich von Brandt has left us a graphic account of this paradoxical phenomenon, which manifested itself just as the first fires were being lit. After spending their first night camped near a windmill just beyond the walls of the Semyonovsky Gate, on Moscow's southern periphery, he and other officers and soldiers of General Claparède's Young Guard division met some fellow Poles from an uhlan cavalry regiment who were returning from an officially ordered food-finding mission with plentiful supplies of wine, rum, tea, sugar, and preserved delicacies of every kind. They had been sent in to Moscow to find food for their hungry colleagues, only to discover that thousands of other Grande Armée soldiers were already busy looting every house they could break into. Soon the entire bivouac area, like a Tower of Babel, was abuzz with the polyglottic clamor of Portuguese, Spanish, German, Croatian, Italian, Polish, and French voices demanding the right to plunder, too. The movement was irresistible. "Everyone who was not under arms or standing duty," Heinrich von Brandt later recalled, "stole or slipped away under some pretext. Stewpots remained without cooks or fire. Anyone sent out for wood, straw, or water simply failed to return."

Soldiers who might have shown some respect and been prepared to defend houses in which they were billeted now went on a rampage. Churches as well as palaces were ruthlessly looted of everything that shone or glistened. Silver-framed ikons, china and cutlery, armchairs of every size and shape, necklaces and jewels in daintily embossed caskets or exquisitely lacquered boxes, precious furs, damask hangings, rugs, and curtains were trundled out in cartloads to the bivouac encampment beyond the walls, which was turned overnight into a fleamarket filled with amateur vendors peddling purloined goods. While truly valuable objects could often be obtained at bargain-basement prices, the meanest nag could fetch twice or three times its real price, and Russian stud horses changed hands for astronomical sums.

As though by magic, all shortages of food disappeared and there was a sudden glut of edibles. "Meat, raw and salted"—to quote again from Brandt —"smoked fish of every kind, salmon, sturgeon, hake, filled the caldrons. Wine, rum, vodka, schnapps could be found in plentiful supply in all the huts. There was a sizzling of meat and a brewing of soups over every campfire in the evening, and everywhere there was wild carousing. A cheer went up each time a new convoy of plunderers came into view—usually they were drunken Russians, forced to carry the stolen goods. Wounded civilians were also brought in as prisoners. Probably they were unfortunate individuals who had tried to defend their belongings, or perhaps also looters who had been involved in fights—they were treated as mutineers who had allegedly attacked our men with weapons and who had been disarmed and dispatched to the camp only after a fierce struggle."

One of the reasons why the fires spread with such rapidity, leaping from house to house and from street to street, was, as Boniface de Castellane noted in his diary, the presence of extensive stables, mews, and coachhouses next to each palace. Being made of wood, they acted as kindling for the flames, igniting the adjoining buildings. But what Castellane and probably the majority of Napoleon's staff officers did not suspect was that most of these splendid townhouses and palaces, with their brilliantly whitewashed pillars and sculpted architraves and pediments, were, like Mount Vernon and so many of the stately homes of Virginia, built of wood. The facades alone were plastered, overlaid with stucco, marble, or alabaster—providing shields too thin to protect the interior woodwork and wainscoting from the fiery heat of blazing forecourts and serf-servant outbuildings.

At four o'clock on the morning of the sixteenth the wind-fanned fire was so fierce and extensive—"it moaned, it boiled like the waves of the tempest," in Baron Fain's words—that Duroc and Caulaincourt decided to wake the sleeping emperor. By this time enough torch-bearing arsonists—women as well as men, many of them drunk—had been spotted, caught red-handed, and interrogated to make it clear that these raging flames had not started accidentally. Immediately Napoleon began issuing orders—patrols were to be sent out, more sentinels posted, greater vigilance exercised—as though his battle-scarred soldiers could somehow beat back the flames with their bayonets and musket butts. Faced with a situation beyond his control, he kept sitting down and getting up, stalked restlessly from window to window, as though to make sure he was not dreaming, and kept repeating, half in anger, half in admiration, "What a dreadful sight! So many palaces! What extraordinary resolution! What men!"

The wind, shifting from north to west, now began to blow with gale force, probably sucked in by the rising air and the ever-increasing heat. Waves of fire seemed to be advancing relentlessly on the Kremlin, as though determined to consume it, too. The windowpanes of the palace began to heat up ominously. Red-hot strips of wood and flaming pine twigs came sailing over the battlements and landed on the kitchen's roof, which would have caught fire had Old Guard soldiers not climbed up on ladders and swept them off with brooms and pails of water.

Using two partly damaged fire pumps that had been repaired during the night, Caulaincourt with his grooms and ostlers fought a grim battle to save the Kremlin stables, which now housed many of Napoleon's jittery horses as well as the equipages used for tsarist coronations. Similar efforts were made to save the nearby Golitsyn Palace, where Old Guard soldiers were actively assisted by the prince's servants, who had remained behind. For by a curious twist of fate it was now the French who had become Moscow's protectors and who were trying to save what could be saved from the ravenous holocaust. The scorching air was so full of smoke and flying cinders that men found it difficult to breathe, even down by the Moskva River, where other Old Guard soldiers and sappers beat out the fires that kept erupting along the planks of the wooden bridge. Many mustachioed grenadiers had their busbies singed.

At noon the clock face of the Troitsky Gate tower caught fire, while scraps of flaming wood rained down on the nearby Kremlin arsenal and ignited heaps of wadding used for the priming of Russian cannon. Four hundred French caissons had recently been brought in, along with 100,000 pounds of gunpowder. Climbing onto the arsenal's long roof, with brooms, French gunners swept furiously to keep the hot sheet-iron from igniting the wooden beams beneath, while other cannoneers struggled desperately to move the caissons to areas that seemed less exposed to bombardment from the flaming heavens. Informed of the danger, Napoleon insisted on coming over to watch and to stimulate their efforts—to the confused embarrassment of many gunners and to the horror of many of the officers of the imperial suite, who were afraid that the arsenal might blow up at any moment, taking not only the Kremlin but their emperor with it.

General Baston de La Riboisière, inspector general of the Grande Armée's artillery, pleaded with Napoleon to withdraw. Berthier, Bessières, and crusty old Marshal Lefebvre added their own earnest supplications. But Napoleon would not budge. The mere thought of having to abandon this mighty fortress he had conquered—the first foreigner to do so in two hundred years—was mortifying in the extreme. He was not going to beat a panicky retreat, and he was not going to move until he had seen for himself just how great the danger really was, by climbing the Kremlin's highest tower, that of Ivan Vyeliki.

Accompanied by Berthier, Caulaincourt, and others, the emperor climbed the hundreds of stone steps of the spiral staircase. Finally they reached the belfry, where they could feel the rush of hot wind and from which they could contemplate the semicircular ring of fire now hemming in the Kremlin.

"The barbarians, the savages, to burn their city like this!" exclaimed Napoleon. "What could their enemies do that was worse than this? They will earn the curses of posterity."

He was immediately parroted by Berthier, who, speaking in his usual nasal voice, admonished Anatole de Montesquiou, standing a step or two lower down on the circular stairwell, with a slit in the stone wall to peer through: "Monsieur, the Russians are barbarians, savages! This is no way to wage war. One doesn't burn cities, particularly one's own. . . . Monsieur, they will earn the maledictions of posterity!"

Caulaincourt, for his part, preferred to hold his peace.

They had hardly descended to ground level when there was a new alert. The Kremlin, someone said, had been mined! The fuse had been set and the explosion could be expected at any moment! Napoleon paid no heed to these reports, which turned out to be mere rumor. But reluctantly he now decided that he had better leave the Kremlin. Berthier had found the argument needed to overcome his stubborn reluctance. "Sire, if the enemy attacks the army corps which are outside of Moscow, Your Majesty has no way of communicating with them."

If the emperor left the Kremlin, where else could he reside? Someone suggested the Petrovsky Palace. Situated by the main road to Petersburg, a mile or two northwest of the Tver gate, it was sufficiently removed from Moscow to be in no danger of burning. Built by Mathias Kazakov for Catherine the Great, it had been used by Emperor Paul and by his son Alexander when they had journeyed to Moscow for their respective coronations. It was an imperial palace, and thus worthy of Napoleon.

More troubling was the question of how to get there. The direct route lay through the northern part of Moscow, which was now a sea of flames. It was therefore decided to proceed in a westerly direction, where the fire, having begun earlier, seemed to be burning itself out.

It was five-thirty when Napoleon finally emerged from the Kremlin via a small postern door opening onto the embankment of the Moskva River. He then walked as far as the stone bridge, where one of his white saddle horses was waiting for him. A battalion of Old Guard grenadiers was left to guard the Kremlin, but everyone else was evacuated.

For Napoleon and his imperial suite, the march westward from the Kremlin proved even more harrowing than the desperate battle against flying sparks and burning matter they had been carrying on inside its walls. For many, the passage ahead looked more "like an entrance into hellfire" than an issue from the inferno. To keep from getting lost in the blinding whirl of smoke and flame they had to enlist the cooperation of a Moscow policeman, whom they happened to encounter and who was asked to act as guide, with the promise that he would subsequently be given his freedom. On both sides of the street up which they hurried, the houses were ablaze with flames, which arched and swayed over their heads, slapped by howling guests of wind. "We were walking on an earth of fire, under a sky of fire, between two walls of fire" was the way Philippe de Ségur described it. "We were obliged to protect our cheeks, hands, and eyes with our handkerchiefs, hats, and the tailcoats of our uniforms," Anatole de Montesquiou later recalled. "The extreme heat stirred up the horses so much that we had trouble keeping them at a walking pace."

At one point Napoleon and his suite had to overtake a slow-moving column of Imperial Guard artillery, which was being hastily evacuated to the suburbs. All kept their fingers crossed, hoping that the powder-laden caissons would not explode just as the emperor passed. As the fire intensified, many of the following cavalrymen paused, then raced through at a gallop, while the less fortunate foot soldiers had to run as fast as their white-trousered legs could carry them. "Everywhere the air we were breathing seemed about to asphyxiate us by its heat," wrote Fantin des Odoards, noting that "many an old mustache" was singed during this infernal journey. Sergeant Bourgogne's Young Guard detachment, which was trying to follow, found the way blocked by houses that had collapsed into the street in a blazing heap. They had no choice but to grope their way back to Tversky Square, in front of the governor general's palace, using strips of corrugated roofing to shield their eyes from the hot, blinding cinders blown into their faces by the wind.

Finally, after many detours, the imperial column snaked its way out of the burning city. The sun had long since set when Napoleon and his marshals finally reached the Petrovsky Palace, on the northwest road to Tver. This extraordinary red-brick and stucco edifice, built in what the French immediately labeled a "Tartar style" to celebrate Catherine the Great's victories over the Turks, must have looked even more exotic as the dancing flames of burning Moscow garishly lit up its rococo-gothic windows, its Byzantine rotunda, and the bulbous, pawn-like pillars holding up the façade like bloated bowling pins. But the cool, Moorish interior, filled with arcades and pillars that seemed to have been copied from the Alhambra in Granada, and above all the large English-style garden—where staff officers could make themselves at home in artificial grottos, miniature Greek temples, Chinese pagodas, and Ottoman kiosks; where the soldiers could bivouac in leafy arbors; and where the horses were attached to the unscarred trunks of linden trees and acacias—seemed an oasis of tranquillity after the flame-defying siege they had experienced behind the massive ramparts of the Kremlin.

The palace, though sparsely furnished and abandoned by its servants, was not entirely empty, as was soon discovered. For when Anatole de Montesquiou, worn out by ceaseless vigils, decided to take a quick catnap in the window embrasure of a salon where Napoleon had been carrying on a monologue with his favorite audience, Berthier, he found a wounded Russian soldier cringing behind a curtain. A meticulous search flushed out a dozen more. The wretched, ill-clad fellows were not incendiaries, but simply fugitives who had sought shelter here from the cataclysm to the south.

That evening the wind momentarily abated, but the flames rose ever higher. Occasionally they would be obscured by a dense cloud of smoke rising like a column of volcanic ash. Sometimes the flames would part, almost like theater curtains, revealing the luridly lit pediment of one more forlorn palace, before it too was swallowed up forever. Like many other officers at Petrovsky, Fantin des Odoards spent several hours watching the awesome spectacle before turning in for the night. "The sound reached us like the distant howling of a hurricane. Every now and then a palace, in collapsing, shot sheaves of sparks up toward the heavens, while the metal mass which had formed its roofing fell with a roar, and then a salvo of cannon fire seemed to interrupt the lugubrious murmur of the infernal storm." The clouds, as though reflecting a gory sunset, seemed to magnify the effulgence of the blaze, radiating so much light that one could easily read a letter or a book five or six miles beyond the city's walls in all directions.

The next morning—Thursday, September 17—the wind rose again, blowing from yet another direction, as though determined to complete its fiery work of destruction. To Abbé Surugue, rector of the Church of Saint-Louis and the man who had converted Rostopchin's wife to Catholicism, it seemed that "the hand of divine vengeance" had come to the aid of the incendiaries, "so super-natural seemed the cause of this fire." This time the flames, engulfing the eastern part of Moscow, licked at the Kremlin's Red Gate, partly devoured the famous wood market, and finally drove the foreign merchants inhabiting the "German suburb" to seek refuge in church graveyards, where their forlorn figures, eerily illuminated in the night, looked like ghostly spirits risen from the tombstones.

Napoleon's restless brain, meanwhile, had not been idle. No one was more acutely aware of the formidable blow to his prestige and to the morale of his army that had been struck by this new and unexpected development. There was little glory to be derived from the occupation and administration of an abandoned city that was gradually being reduced to ashes. Inevitably French and allied soldiers would be accused of having set fire to Moscow through callous carelessness or satanic malevolence—further exacerbating the fanatical patriotism of the Russians. These were disturbing prospects. Something had to be done, and done fast, to refurbish his hideously smudged prestige.

Bent over his maps, he calculated that St. Petersburg was only fifteen march-days distant along the main highway through Tver. The only Russian soldiers on this road were a negligible force of several thousand men, com-manded by General Wintzingerode, who invariably retreated each time they encountered the soldiers of Prince Eugène's Fourth Corps. From Murat, whose cavalry forces were now bivouacked south of Moscow, Napoleon had been receiving encouraging reports saying that Kutuzov's army was disinte-grating, that Russian soldiers were deserting in droves, and that the Cossacks, with whom the king of Naples was on the best of terms, were as war-weary as the rest. Such being the case, a strong rearguard force should suffice to hold Moscow and the Kremlin, while the other corps of the Grande Armée began a curving march along several roads seemingly aimed at Petersburg. Veering westward before they reached Alexander's capital, they would strike at the rear of General Wittgenstein's forces, destroying them or sending them reeling back in panicky confusion. By joining up with Marshal Macdonald's Tenth Corps, still besieging Riga, with Oudinot's Second Corps, and Saint-Cyr's Sixth Corps, solidly entrenched around Polotsk, and with the 30,000 men of Marshal Victor's recently arrived Ninth Corps, the Grande Armée could hold a line stretching from Riga along part of the Dvina River all the way to Vitebsk and on to Smolensk. All this could be accomplished by October 15—enough to scare the wits out of the inhabitants of Petersburg and to bring a trembling Alexander to the negotiating table.

Of the marshals and generals with whom Napoleon discussed this plan, only Prince Eugène reacted at all favorably—perhaps because he sensed that his troops would be spearheading the attack. But no one else in the emperor's entourage felt the slightest enthusiasm for this bold northward plunge. It looked too much like a gamble. They were far enough north as it was, and if they ventured up the road to Petersburg at this season of the year, the army's artillery might get hopelessly bogged down in autumnal rains and swampy marshlands. Above all, men and horses needed several weeks of rest; although many of Moscow's finest palaces and houses were now reduced to cinders, there were still enough foodstuffs in the cellars to keep the army happily supplied for months.

Sensing that his marshals, like most of his soldiers, felt worn out by endless marches and skirmishes, Napoleon did not press the matter further. Now that the tsar's main army had been forced to yield Russia's ancient capital without a fight, Alexander, he was convinced, would have to sue for peace. But what better means could be found to force his stubborn hand than to threaten his nobility by suspending a revolutionary sword of Damocles over their frightened heads? Here, in the heart of Russia, Napoleon was no longer hampered, as he had been in Lithuania, by his need to pamper the land-owning aristocracy. From the very outset he had been persuaded—and no one, not even Caulaincourt, had been able to wean him from this idée fixe—that the mere threat of a French decree emancipating the country's serfs would suffice to spur Russia's aristocrats to put pressure on their tsar to sue for peace. Better a quick though inglorious conclusion to a war with a foreign power than the incalculable convulsions of a civil war at home!

When he heard that Marie-Rose Aubert-Chalmais, the fashionable dressmaker whose warnings about Rostopchin and his incendiary machinations had been so dramatically confirmed, had taken refuge with her children in Prince Eugène's nearby Fourth Corps camp, Napoleon had her summoned to Petrovsky. Marshal Mortier was waiting on the steps to greet this newly recognized "authority" as she stepped out of a shabby droshky with a fur-lined riding coat incongruously draped over her feminine dress. Ushered in to the imperial presence, she was accorded a private audience which lasted a full hour. Napoleon asked her how she thought the Russians would react to a decree emancipating the serfs. She replied "in all frankness" that one-third of the peasant serfs "would appreciate this good deed, but the other two-thirds would not know what was meant by it. . . . Here it is not the same as in the south of Europe. The Russian is moody, hard to stir up. The nobles would not fail to take advantage of their serfs' hesitation: these new ideas would be represented as antireligious and impious; stirring up the others would prove difficult, indeed impossible." The decree announcing the emancipation of Russia's serfs was accordingly shelved, exactly as had been the plans for a lightning advance on Petersburg.

At three o'clock the following morning (Friday, September 18), the first raindrops began to fall, and there was a downpour later in the day, which turned the ravaged gardens of the Petrovsky Palace into a sea of mud. Columns of dirty smoke rose from the charred skeletons and hissing stumps of burned-out houses, covering the city with an enormous pall, which—in the words of Armand Domergue, the manager of Moscow's French Theater—"seemed to envelop it like funereal crape. . . . In the midst of the ruins one saw emaciated horses, wandering aimlessly about, as well as packs of famished dogs, which emitted the most dreadful howls. Raising your eyes, you saw thousands of strung-up corpses, swaying to and fro above your head in the wind, while at your feet lay the shapeless and half-charred remains of muzhiks and animals of every kind . . . Unable to recognize the quarters they had once dwelt in, the former inhabitants haunted their residential districts like haggard ghosts. The air was foul, and one could hardly breathe in this atmosphere vitiated by putrefaction."

That there were "thousands" of strung-up corpses was an exaggeration, but that hundreds of Russian incendiaries were caught, summarily tried, and executed is certain. For days after the first rains began to fall the dedicated arsonists continued their infernal work, as undeterred by the weather as by the risks they ran if caught. Some went about their grim business with baskets filled with fuses of all kinds. Any house occupied by a French general or his staff was singled out for destruction. Marshal Davout, after moving into a suburb containing some thirty intact townhouses and palaces, had to change his place of residence three times, as each one mysteriously caught fire. The even more ill-starred Marshal Mortier was forced by fire to move five times in almost as many days. Some houses were found to have been cleverly booby-trapped with flint-primed mechanisms calculated to ignite a charge of powder or a bundle of dry straw the moment a door was opened. In Rostopchin's governor's mansion the chimneys leading up from the enormous porcelain stoves used to heat the rooms were found to be stuffed with nine-inch-long cylinders of hollowed-out pinewood filled with gunpowder, which surely would have exploded and brought the inner walls tumbling down had some of the count's serf-servants, who had developed a liking for General Durosnel, not extracted them for their new French masters before the stoves were lit. General Grouchy, commander of the Third Cavalry Corps, was almost roasted in his bed when an incendiary was caught by the general's son as he was about to put a torch to the curtains of his four-poster.

CHAPTER 20

A HANDFUL
OF ASHES

NAPOLEON'S RETURN to the Kremlin, which began at nine in the morning on September 18, offered him a sobering view of the dramatically altered aspect of his Grande Armée and of the charred city it had come so far to seize. On both sides of the Tver highroad leading into Moscow the troops of Prince Eugène's Fourth Corps were grouped around vast campfires fed by strips of window frames, gilt doors torn from their hinges, and pieces of mahogany furniture. "Around those fires," as Philippe de Ségur later described them, "on beddings of wet straw, badly sheltered by a few boards, soldiers and their officers could be seen, all splattered with mud and blackened by smoke, seated in armchairs or stretched out on silk divans. At their feet were spread out or heaped up cashmere shawls, the rarest furs from Siberia, gold-embroidered silks from Persia, and silver plates, on which all they had to eat was a black paste, cooked under the ashes, and chunks of horse flesh, half grilled and bloody: a singular assemblage of abundance and want, of wealth and filth, of luxury and poverty!"

Caulaincourt, who had been unable to crack a smile since his brother's death at Borodino, found the return journey to the Kremlin even grimmer than had been their forced departure. "I was crushed! Happy are those who did not see this hideous spectacle, this picture of destruction!" The city was now a wilderness of gutted ruins, in which men and women dressed in smoke-smudged and often half-burned clothes could be seen frantically digging the ground for potatoes, carrots, and other vegetables, or tearing at the remains of a dead horse with knives, watched from a distance by protesting crows. As they advanced, behind a fanfare of trumpets that now seemed grotesquely out of place, the chasseurs of the Imperial Guard had to clear the way through bands of Grande Armée soldiers, pulling carts full of booty, or forcing some downtrodden muzhiks to carry it for them. The pavement was everywhere littered with the debris of broken pieces of furniture, tossed from the windows of burning houses to save them from the flames. Each square they came to resembled a marketplace—to which flour was brought wrapped up in damask hangings, sugar loaves in ballroom dresses, vat-tapped liquors in ornate china basins and chamber pots. Fantin des Odoards had the impression of witnessing a burlesque masquerade as he watched drunken soldiers parading around in sacerdotal vestments and canteen girls strutting about in minks and sables and delicately spangled Indian saris.

Distasteful to Napoleon's tidy mind though such scenes were, he knew that there was little he could do about them. The only way to restrain the wholesale looting was to organize it—something that was started a few days later, when specific Grande Armée units were assigned different city quarters and ordered to amass in regular military depots everything of value that could be found in stores and cellars.

Back in the palace of the tsars—which, like the other buildings of the Kremlin, had survived the fire, thanks to the vigilant activity of the grenadier battalion left to guard them—Napoleon dashed off another letter to Marie-Louise. "I had no idea what this city was like. It had 500 palaces as beautiful as the Elysée . . . furnished à la française with incredible luxury, several imperial palaces, barracks, magnificent hospitals. Everything has disappeared, the fire for the last four days has been consuming everything. Since all the small houses of the bourgeois are of wood, they catch fire like matches."

Later Napoleon slightly revised his earlier reckoning, when he wrote again to Marie-Louise: "We have shot so many incendiaries that they have stopped. One-quarter of the city remains, 3/4 of it are burned." This estimate was probably not far from the somber truth. The Abbé Surugue later calculated that of the 9,300 private houses and 800 palaces and townhouses that Moscow had boasted before the outbreak of the fire, only 2,000 had survived.

One of the edifices that had survived was the huge Foundling Hospital, located on the northern bank of the Moskva River, east of the Kitai-Gorod shopping area and the Kremlin. The largest of its kind in Europe, this hospital for parentless waifs had been placed by Emperor Alexander under the patronage of his mother, Dowager Empress Maria Feodorovna. Impressed by its sheer size, Napoleon had dispatched a battalion of Young Guard soldiers to protect it. They were led by an enterprising colonel, who, refusing to be daunted by the ring of flame hemming them in from three sides, had had the adjacent wooden sheds and fences knocked down, thus helping to save some two hundred orphans who had remained behind with their septuagenarian director, Ivan Akinfievich Toutolmin.

When Napoleon heard that Toutolmin was a personal friend of Dowager Empress Maria Feodorovna, and that he had once been grand marshal of Alexander's (grand ducal) court, he had him summoned to the Kremlin. The old soldier was questioned about his hospital with Napoleonic thoroughness, then treated to a brief tirade directed against that "wretched man," that "stupid savage" Rostopchin, who, in launching a campaign of "pitiless destruction," had now superseded every other Russian as the French emperor's most despised bête noire.

There is little doubt that this outburst was carefully planned. Napoleon wanted the Russian emperor to know that the destruction of Moscow had never been his aim, that this was not the way he had wanted to wage war against his "dear brother." And so, when a little later Toutolmin asked if he could write a letter to the dowager empress in Petersburg to let her know that the Foundling Hospital was intact and the children well, Napoleon could not have been more obliging. Not only was Toutolmin free to write the letter, but there was a sentence or two Napoleon very much wanted him to add. Toutolmin did so in the letter that he brought back the next day: "Madame, the Emperor Napoleon shudders at seeing our capital almost entirely destroyed by means which are not, he says, those one employs in a proper war. He seems convinced that if no one interposed himself between him and our august Emperor Alexander, their former friendship would soon regain its rights, and all our misfortunes would be ended."

This, of course, was a plea for a return to the "spirit of Tilsit." It betrayed, with almost pathetic clarity, Napoleon's deep-seated conviction that Alexander was a man too much influenced by his entourage—in particular, "intriguing foreigners" and the notoriously pro-British elements of Petersburg's high society.

Napoleon probably harbored few illusions about the success of this indirect approach to Alexander. For the very next day he summoned another Moscow notable to the Kremlin to see if he could persuade him to carry a personal message to the tsar. This second notable was Ivan Alexeyevich Yakovlev, a well-to-do member of the Moscow nobility who, like so many others, had spent many years abroad. Some of them had been spent in Paris, where he had met Marshal Mortier—in a Masonic lodge. Yakovlev had been so slow and casual about packing up his belongings that before he and his family knew what was happening, French dragoons were trotting up the street on which they lived. Driven out of his home by fire and forced to take refuge in other houses, courtyards, and gardens, he had finally managed to get a message through to Mortier, who had immediately sent for him and then reported this "find" to Napoleon.

Without wasting a moment Napoleon summoned Yakovlev to the Kremlin. "A great stickler for convention and the rules of propriety"—as his illegitimate son, the future radical Alexander Herzen (then barely six months old), was later to write—Ivan Alexeyevich Yakovlev presented himself in the throne room of the Kremlin wearing an old brass-buttoned hunting jacket, a shirt with mud-splattered ruffles, boots that had not been cleaned in several days, and a two-day growth of beard.

Asked if, in exchange for a safe-conduct pass for himself and his family, Yakovlev would agree to carry a letter to Emperor Alexander in Petersburg, the Russian said he would do his best, but he could not guarantee the success of such a mission.

The next morning Yakovlev was summoned back to the Kremlin and handed a sealed envelope containing a personal letter which Napoleon had written during the night. It was addressed: "*A mon frère, l'Empereur Alexandre.*"

Armed with a safe-conduct pass signed by Marshal Mortier, Yakovlev left

Moscow on foot, walking alongside the open carriage in which his German paramour, Luisa Haag, his six-month-old son, a nurse, and a wounded brother-in-law were seated. They were escorted out of Moscow by a detachment of French cavalrymen, who saluted, wished them well, and then galloped back to Moscow when they came within sight of a Cossack patrol.

The Cossacks escorted Yakovlev and his family to the headquarters of their commander, General Wintzingerode. When this handsome, Viking-featured warrior heard that Yakovlev had been given a letter by Napoleon personally addressed to the tsar, he had him sent to Petersburg in a courier's cart escorted by two dragoons.

When the courier's cart reached Petersburg, Yakovlev was taken directly to the house of General Alexei Arakcheyev. Recently appointed head of the Imperial Chancellery, Arakcheyev was already carving out for himself a new and formidable base of power as the nation's supreme watchdog. The sweeping powers he had assumed included the right to see all incoming messages from the various war "fronts" before they were transmitted to the tsar. Instead of being escorted directly to the imperial dacha on Kamenny Island, where Alexander spent most of this September, Yakovlev was retained as a virtual captive in Arakcheyev's house for an entire month. He knew that the tsar had received Napoleon's letter, for Admiral Shishkov came to see him on the sovereign's behalf to hear Yakovlev's account of the Moscow fire, of how the entering French had behaved, and of his interview with the French emperor in the Kremlin. But for most of the time he was treated as a suspect for having agreed to carry a letter written by Bonaparte.

The suspect emissary was finally pardoned for having, under conditions of duress, agreed to act as a go-between for the French. But he was ordered to leave Petersburg immediately. The treatment accorded him showed how sensitive Alexander had become to all questions of "treasonous behavior." Having ordered Kutuzov not under any circumstances to enter into negotiations with Napoleon, he was not going to run the risk, as sovereign of all the Russias, of maintaining clandestine contacts of his own with the detested invader.

It was Rostopchin's hurried letter, written during the hectic evening of September 13, that had given Alexander the first inkling of the news that Moscow was being abandoned without a fight. Kutuzov, after dictating his first dispatch on the outcome of Borodino, had followed up with a self-congratulatory communiqué—on the lines of Napoleon's "Bulletins de la Grande Armée"—in which it was reported that the Cossack general Platov, "having been sent in pursuit of the enemy," had driven Napoleon's rear guard "eleven versts from the village of Borodino"—a superlative fib which Kutuzov's admirer Liubomir Beskrovny later explained away as "destined for foreign consumption." Two days later (September 10) the generalissimo had again written to Alexander to say that because so many of his "most needed generals" had been severely wounded at Borodino, he had been obliged to continue his retreat in the face of superior forces. Thereafter the sly fox had lapsed into silence.

Outraged by the casualness of his supreme commander, the normally placid

Alexander wrote him a tart note saying that it was thanks to a letter from Rostopchin that he had learned the sad news that Moscow was being abandoned; that Kutuzov's silence "aggravates my astonishment"; and that he was sending his aide-de-camp Prince Pyotr Volkonsky to ascertain at first hand the present situation of the generalissimo's army "and the reasons that impelled you to such an unfortunate resolution."

The day after this note was dispatched, Colonel Michaud reached Petersburg with an explanatory letter which Kutuzov had dictated on September 16. After being escorted out over the bridge of boats to the tsar's summer residence, Michaud was ushered into Alexander's study. The glum look on the colonel's face made it clear that he was not the bearer of glad tidings, but the news he brought—that Moscow had been occupied by Napoleon's Grande Armée and that it was now a mass of flames—surpassed Alexander's bleakest apprehensions. The tsar reassured Michaud that under no conditions would he make peace with Napoleon. He would, if necessary, use up the last resources of the empire to continue the struggle, and were Divine Providence to decree "that my dynasty should cease to reign on the throne of my ancestors, then, having exhausted all the means in my power, I will let my beard grow down to here"—he put his hand on his chest—"and I will eat potatoes with the lowliest of my peasants rather than sign the dishonor of my country and of the dear nation, whose sacrifices I know how to appreciate."

While a greatly relieved Michaud had himself driven back across the Neva, Alexander was left on his summer island to ponder the contents of Kutuzov's letter. In it the generalissimo explained that because of the "disarray" of his forces and in particular the serious weakening of his Second Army after "the so bloody but victorious battle" of Borodino, he had been forced to withdraw toward Moscow without receiving the reinforcements he needed or being able to find a suitable place for fighting a successful battle. With his two wings threatened by the enemy's enveloping movements, he could only have fought a battle which would have resulted not only in "the destruction of the remains of the army, but in the bloodiest destruction and reduction to ashes of Moscow itself." To extricate the army from this precarious pass he had decided—after consulting "our most prominent generals," some of whom had been "of a contrary opinion"—to allow the enemy to enter Moscow, from which, he hastened to add, "all the treasures, the arsenal, and practically all belongings, both state and private, had been removed, and in which not a single gentleman remained." .

Then, deftly moving from the negative to the positive, the generalissimo went on to point out that "the enemy's entry into Moscow is not yet the subjugation of Russia." His units, now being steadily reinforced by new arrivals and positioned athwart the roads to Tula and Kaluga, would soon be in a position to cut the enemy's main communication line along the Smolensk–Moscow highroad. He was now prepared to face Napoleon "on a firm footing" and with an army that was still intact. "However," he added, "Your Imperial and Most Gracious Majesty will allow that these consequences are indivisibly bound up with the loss of Smolensk and with that thoroughly disordered state of the armies in which I found them."

Alexander was sufficiently impressed by this cleverly couched dispatch as to have it later printed, with only minor changes, in the *Sanktpeterburgskiye Vyedomosti* (St. Petersburg News). He did not even take the trouble to eliminate the next-to-the-last sentence about the loss of Smolensk and the "disordered state" the armies were in when Kutuzov had assumed command—two nasty barbs aimed at Barclay de Tolly. Probably Kutuzov knew, from the conversation they had had in the tsar's office before he had left Petersburg, that Alexander had not forgiven Barclay for evacuating Smolensk, instead of digging in for an all-out battle—which he still assumed Barclay could have won.

Two days after the tsar's conversation with Michaud, the Council of Ministers met at Alexander's instigation and drafted a resolution which complained of the cursory nature of Kutuzov's reports from the field. The ministers wanted to know why a retreat had been ordered after the "victory" of Borodino, and why Moscow had been left unprotected. They insisted on seeing the minutes of the Fili meeting at which the decision to abandon Moscow had been taken, and they further demanded that Kutuzov be required in future to provide full and explicit accounts of his military movements and actions.

This bluntly worded resolution, signed by fourteen ministers, was the start of a ground swell of incredulity and revulsion, which now swept over the dazed capital in the wake of the dreadful news from Moscow. For Emperor Alexander this was a supremely trying moment. Taken in by Kutuzov's first dispatch from Borodino, he had hurriedly had it celebrated as a major victory —only to discover ten days later that his generalissimo had not told him the full truth. This time he would have to exercise greater caution—even if it meant leaving the Petersburgers in the dark as to the full extent of the Moscow fire disaster.

On September 24 and again on the twenty-fifth John Quincy Adams noted in his diary that the Russian government had still not issued any official declaration regarding the recent events in Moscow. "The English are all preparing to leave the country; . . . My landlord, Strogolshikoff, also came to me much alarmed, and mortified at the present condition of his country— hinting, but afraid expressly to say, that Moscow is in the hands of the French, and still reposing confidence in the cunning of General Koutouzof. Nothing official has yet been published by the Government concerning the occupation of Moscow, and the rumors are innumerable. Several persons, it is said, have been made to sweep the streets for having said that Moscow was taken; so the people are afraid of talking."

The "people," yes; but not the members of the Court and the nobility, who knew they ran no such risks so long as they exchanged the latest scraps of gossip among themselves, and preferably in French—a language unintelligible to most of their serf-servants. For we know from the reminiscences of Count Fyodor Tolstoy that the moment the news leaked out about Moscow's abandonment, there was a strong backlash in the salons of Petersburg. Many of those who only yesterday had hailed Kutuzov's elevation to the rank of supreme commander as a profoundly wise and God-inspired choice now denounced their former idol as a scoundrel and a renegade who had wretchedly betrayed their ardent expectations. The fainthearted, led once again by the unstable Grand Duke Constantine, found new arguments for their contention that Napoleon was invincible, and that, such being the case, they had better make the best of a bad situation and reach an accommodation with Bonaparte before he marched on Petersburg.

So fearful indeed was General Arakcheyev that he had all of his most precious possessions, including his finest china and silverware, shipped north by barge to Lake Ladoga and beyond—with the result that he was left (in the words of one contemporary) with "no more than three spoons" at home to dine with. The innumerable paintings in Catherine the Great's Hermitage palace, entire libraries and scientific collections, and voluminous state archives, all stuffed into enormous chests, followed over the same watery route. As frightened as Arakcheyev, Ossip Petrovich Kozadavlev, the minister of the interior, had his servants pack his prize belongings into eighteen huge trunks, which were transported for safekeeping to the Tikhvin monastery (near Tver)—to the great embarrassment of the archimandrite to whose custody they were entrusted, and to the even greater annoyance of the monks, who groaned and grunted as they pushed and shoved the trunks into the sacristy, the wooden floor of which sagged and then collapsed under the excessive weight of these unwanted treasures. At the new lycée which had recently been founded in the "imperial village" of Tsarskoye Syelo, south of Petersburg, the thirteen-year-old Alexander Pushkin and other privileged students of this select establishment received visits from the tsar's French tailors, who had orders to have them all fitted out with short, Chinese-style sheepskin coats lined with fur, in preparation for the journey eastward.

"Everyone lived, as the saying has it, on axle-grease," Vassily Marchenko, who was then working for Arakcheyev, was later to recall. "Whoever could do so kept at least two horses in reserve, while others had hidden boats ready to leave via the canals, which were especially diked up for their use." All Court banquets and official receptions were canceled.

One person who refused to be downcast by the news from Moscow was the petite, delicate, but admirably stouthearted Empress Elisabeth. Unwilling to yield to the panicky fretfulness that had overtaken her mother-in-law, Alexander's wife let it be known that she was not going to pack up any of her belongings. "Since," she proudly declared, "there is no possibility of saving the property of all the inhabitants of Petersburg down to the last and poorest, I must endure an identical lot with them."

Unlike his wife, who was reduced to living off deceptive rumors and reports, Alexander had access to two vital pieces of inside information. The first was the indirect peace overture Napoleon had sent him via Toutolmin's letter to the dowager empress; the second was the personal letter the French emperor had entrusted to Yakovlev. In this letter Napoleon explained in some detail how the burning of Moscow had been ordered by Rostopchin and how it had encouraged the looting of the city. As a result Moscow had suffered a fate that Berlin, Madrid, and Vienna had all been spared. Napoleon could not bring himself to believe that all these deliberate conflagrations—which since Smolensk had left 600,000 Russians homeless—had been ordered by Alexander;

which was why he was writing this letter, among other things to inform him that "at a time when one was removing the fire-pumps of Moscow, one hundred and fifty field cannon, 60,000 new muskets, 1,600,000 infantry cartridges, more than 400 thousands of powder, 300 thousands of saltpeter, as much sulphur, etc., were left behind. I made war against Your Majesty without animosity," he continued; "a letter before or after the latest battle would have halted my march, and I would have been able to sacrifice the advantage of entering Moscow."

The idea that the sovereign of all the Russias might appreciate being informed of what was happening in Moscow by the commander of a foreign army that had just occupied it was a tactless miscalculation. Alexander probably regarded Napoleon's letter as an admission of weakness rather than as a sign of strength.

This is not to say that Alexander was not profoundly shaken by the news from Moscow. It was some days, indeed probably weeks, before he realized the full scope of Rostopchin's program of destruction—which he never formally approved, nor for that matter condemned. During his long, solitary walks through the autumnal, leaf-littered alleys of his Kamenny Island park, he indulged in gloomy and morose ruminations. His grandmother Catherine the Great had refused to panic in 1788, when Gustav III's Swedes were advancing on her frightened capital; but she had not had to face an adversary like Napoleon, still less live down a disaster comparable to the fall and destruction of Moscow.

Determined though he was to avoid all official ceremonies during these tense days, there was one he could not avoid: the commemoration of his imperial coronation, celebrated each year on September 27. This time the usual manifestations were cut to an absolute minimum, and as John Quincy Adams noted in his diary, "there was one yacht upon the river dressed out with colors, and in the evening an illumination." The tsar, however, had no choice but to leave his island retreat for a few hours in order to attend the commemorative service at the Holy Mother of Kazan Cathedral. Normally careless to the point of recklessness about his personal security—there were footmen but no sentinels at his Kamenny Island palace—Alexander had to abandon all thought of riding in to Petersburg on horseback, as had been his habit in the past. Instead, yielding "for the first and last time . . . to the counsels of a timid prudence," he rode in the same coach with the two empresses. Roxandra Stourdza, who had recently been appointed lady-in-waiting to Empress Elisabeth, has left us a vivid account of the ensuing scene, as the imperial coach, followed by a number of other glassed-in carriages, made its way through "a huge crowd, whose gloomy silence and irritated faces contrasted with the festival that was being celebrated. Never in my life will I forget the instant when we walked up the steps of the cathedral, between two hedgerows of people who did not utter a sound of acclamation. One could have distinguished the sound of our footsteps, and I have never doubted that a spark at this moment could have set off a general conflagration. A glance at the Emperor told me what was going on in his soul, and I felt my own knees sagging beneath me."

The religious ceremony, however, passed off without an incident. Two days later the tsar felt confident enough to let his subjects know the bitter truth; he had Kutuzov's personal apologia published with only minor changes in the text, along with an official governmental proclamation in which the generalissimo's decision to abandon Moscow was defended on the grounds that it was designed to "convert the enemy's short-lived triumph into an inescapable disaster." The proclamation, drafted in Admiral Shishkov's exalted style, ended by invoking the aid of Almighty God on behalf of his Russian Church, and on behalf of the Russian people's righteous struggle against the enemy; for in triumphing over him "and in saving itself, it will save the freedom and independence of rulers and their realms."

This text was in effect Alexander's reply to Napoleon's overtures. It made clear that there would be no peace with the French emperor, and that the goal of Russian policy from now on was the liberation not only of its national territory, but also of that of all the oppressed peoples of the continent from the servitude of the Napoleonic yoke.

CHAPTER 21

A DECEPTIVE
INDIAN SUMMER

O N S E P T E M B E R 1 6, while a disgruntled Napoleon was pacing up and down the ill-furnished halls of the Petrovsky Palace, wondering what to do next, a number of Russian staff officers and generals had persuaded Kutuzov to alter the direction of their retreat. Instead of continuing down the road to Ryazan, they suggested, the Russian army should veer west toward Podolsk. This town, situated almost due south of Moscow, straddled the road leading to Tula—a vital center which had to be defended at all costs, since it was the home of Russia's largest arms factory.

Certain Russian historians have argued that this "brilliant maneuver" was part of a premeditated plan worked out in advance by Kutuzov's unaided genius. More likely it was the result of a rapidly formed consensus. The generalissimo's most trusted adviser, Colonel Toll, had from the start proposed that the Russian army place itself southwest rather than southeast of Moscow, across or near one of the two roads leading to Kaluga: a suggestion endorsed by Kutuzov's chief quartermaster officer, General Lanskoy, for the simple reason that Kaluga had become the main center for the storage of munitions and of food supplies brought up from the grain-rich provinces of the Ukraine. When the idea was revived after the nerve-racking march through Moscow, it met with the immediate approval of Barclay de Tolly, of Bennigsen (who would have liked to claim it as his own), and of the pipe-smoking Konovnitsyn, an increasingly influential general who was shortly to become Kutuzov's chief duty officer.

So close to the withdrawing Russians were the cavalrymen of Murat's vanguard that not until they had retreated another eleven miles down the Ryazan road could Kutuzov's men begin their sideward march. On reaching a point where the road crossed the winding Moskva, they made a momentary halt by the riverside to let the baggage trains and the seemingly endless stream of fleeing carriages and refugee pedestrians pass on ahead, while the engineers put together several pontoon bridges. Then, at four the next morning (September 17) and under cover of darkness, they crossed the river, marched up the inclined slope, and veered to the right beyond the crest of the hill, continuing their march in two columns along cross-country roads. These, under the pelting of the rain, were soon turned into long ribbons of mud.

This arduous side-march—much of it conducted at night and fitfully illuminated by the cloud-reflected glare of still-flaming Moscow—was not completed until September 18: the day on which Napoleon, completely misled, informed Maret that the Russians were withdrawing behind the Volga. The sudden change of direction was cleverly masked by several rearguard Cossack regiments, which continued to retreat down the Ryazan road far beyond the points where the rest of the army had veered off. For three full days they managed to sustain the illusion of an orderly retreat, until at last the French cavalrymen of Murat's vanguard realized that they were pursuing a phantom host.

On September 21, when he received news that the Russian army had suddenly disappeared, Napoleon ordered the Third Cavalry Corps and Poniatowski's Poles to move southward from Moscow down the Tula road. He showed Caulaincourt several dispatches he had received from Murat in which he quoted the Cossack officers he had talked to as expressing not only an extreme war-weariness but a readiness to desert their uninspiring Russian commanders and to serve under his far more flamboyant leadership. "Murat, king of the Cossacks! What folly!" the French emperor scoffed.

The Cossacks, by assiduously flattering Murat's ego, had clearly been pulling the wool over his eyes. Even more irksome for Napoleon was the realization that the tacit cease-fire agreed to one week earlier between the French vanguard and the Russian rear guard was of strictly limited scope. While several "friendly" Cossack regiments had been taking General Sébastiani and his horsemen for a long ride down the Ryazan road, others, in a surprise attack mounted against a munitions convoy that was only fifteen miles from Moscow on the Smolensk highroad, had destroyed fifteen French artillery caissons and made off with two hundred horses.

All this angered Napoleon so much that for the next twenty-four hours he seriously considered interrupting his army's looting binge in Moscow and launching it southward in a general offensive. Marshal Bessières was actually ordered to carry out the first phase of this operation with the help of two infantry divisions, added to Poniatowski's Poles and his own Imperial Guard cavalry.

Had the commander of the Russian army at this point been Bennigsen rather than Kutuzov, it is likely that a major battle would have resulted once Napoleon had ascertained exactly where his adversary was to be found. The result might have been another victory, which, if it had been followed by the French occupation of Tula and Kaluga, might have saved the Grande Armée from the grim fate that eventually overtook it.

Kutuzov, however, was a good deal smarter than the impulsive Hanoverian. Six thousand demoralized Russian soldiers had managed to break ranks and disappear during the grim march through Moscow, further weakening an army which had suffered an almost crippling loss of able front-line officers (needed to train and lead replacements) at Borodino. There was consequently no point in rashly provoking Bonaparte at a time when his Grande Armée was scattered all over the Moscow landscape. Time, as well as geography, was on Russia's side, and with new troop reinforcements pouring in or due to arrive soon, each day gained without a major battle was in reality a victory for his country and himself, no matter how inglorious or even cowardly further withdrawals might seem.

So cautious had Kutuzov by now become that Toll had trouble persuading him not to halt his sideward movement around Borovsk, but to move on eleven miles westward. The purpose of this movement was to place the Russian army closer to the Smolensk–Moscow highway. Kutuzov did, however, agree to Barclay's suggestion that General Dorokhov be dispatched northwestward with a roving force of Cossacks, backed up by horse-artillery and light-infantry Jaegers, to prey on French convoys and supply trains. The result was a second, even more devastating raid, carried out on the Smolensk–Moscow highroad on September 24, when a mixed force of Cossacks and hussars overwhelmed 150 French Imperial Guard dragoons—a feat that provoked more consternation among Napoleon's staff officers than "the loss of fifty generals" at Borodino, as Caulaincourt caustically noted.

Two days later, when Murat's, Bessières's, and Poniatowski's joint forces—close to 25,000 men in all—began a general advance southward, another council of war was held at Kutuzov's headquarters. There was a feeling, shared by a number of officers, that this was the start of a general French offensive. Bennigsen was all for mounting a counterattack by moving the bulk of the army back toward Podolsk for a decisive showdown. This proposal was finally rejected on the grounds that it might play into Napoleon's hands, offering him a chance to outmaneuver and destroy Russia's main army at one stroke and to open the road to Tula, Kaluga, and the rich provinces of the south. It seemed more prudent, therefore, to adopt Colonel Toll's new plan, which called for an orderly withdrawal to Tarutino, some fifty miles southwest of Moscow. This would further distend Napoleon's already dispersed divisions, give Kutuzov's army time to beef up its seriously depleted regiments, cover the vital armaments-manufacturing and supply centers of Tula, Kaluga, and Briansk, and maintain communications with Kiev and Admiral Chichagov's forces advancing northward from Moldavia.

This new withdrawal before the advancing French provoked a lot of grumbling among senior Russian officers, as well as among the uncomprehending rank and file. Also less than pleased was the British military observer, General Sir Robert Wilson, who, having been away in Petersburg while Borodino was being fought, had let himself be persuaded that its real hero was General Bennigsen—a man after his own heart, since he had wanted to fight rather than to abandon Moscow. Whereas Kutuzov, as he noted in his diary, "is very unequal to much exertion in society," Bennigsen maintained an excellent dinner table, where Wilson now enjoyed a "regular cover"—an honor which also prejudiced him in favor of the chief of staff.

Wilson was impressed by what the Cossacks and other Russian light-cavalry and infantry forces were already achieving. "Every day since we have been here," he noted on September 27, "prisoners in parties of fifty, and even of a hundred, have been brought in, chiefly wounded. Of course many more are killed; for such is the inveteracy of the peasants that they buy prisoners of the Cossacks for several roubles to *put them to death.* Two guns have been taken by the peasants; vast quantities of baggage, &c., going both to and from Moscow; much melted silver, which I myself have seen. . . . In brief, the Spanish guerrilla warfare never was more successful, and certainly was not so formidable to the enemy."

The difference between the Iberian precedent and what was now happening in Russia was that in the latter case there were several large indigenous armies to contend with, which had never been the case in Spain. It was precisely for this reason that the war in Spain had dragged on inconclusively for four years. Left to themselves, neither Russia's peasants, nor the Cossacks, nor the free-booting partisans who were beginning to prey on French supply trains and isolated outposts could have brought about the annihilation of Napoleon's Grande Armée. For a war of attrition to succeed, it was imperative that Russia's main army not be prematurely destroyed by being rashly rushed into battle with the French invaders.

Another person who was even more irritated by Kutuzov's decision to pull the bulk of his forces back to Tarutino was Count Fyodor Rostopchin, in whose magnificent country estate at Voronovo, located by the old Kaluga road, both General Bennigsen and Sir Robert Wilson were frequent guests. "What is maddening," Rostopchin wrote in a letter to his wife, "is that our troops have everywhere the upper hand, but the general [to lead them] is missing. . . . The morale of our army is so bad that I fear a revolt. Kutuzov never shows himself, he eats and sleeps alone, he drags around with him a young girl dressed as a Cossack, and he lets two scoundrels"—he probably meant Kaissarov and Kudashev—"carry out his functions for him. At times the soldiers call him a traitor, at other times the 'murky one' "—the opposite of *svetleishy* ("brightest" or "most illustrious"), the adjective associated with the generalissimo's princely title.

Ostracized by Kutuzov, who refused to receive him, shunned by most officers, who regarded him as an idiosyncratic maverick suddenly landed in their midst, an unemployed and unwanted Rostopchin was left to vent his atrabilious rage against the sleep-loving commander in chief, whom, in another letter to his wife, he described as being "like a dead man, whom one doesn't dare wake up." The final straw was added when a number of senior staff officers invaded Rostopchin's country house. Forcing him to move to quarters above the stables, they pushed out his horses to make room for their own.

On the last day of September, it became clear that Voronovo too would have to be abandoned to the advancing French in accordance with Kutuzov's withdrawal plan. That evening a number of Russian generals and senior officers were invited, along with Sir Robert Wilson, to join Rostopchin around a bivouac fire that had been built in front of the stables. Rostopchin treated the company to a bitter litany of complaints against Kutuzov, who had failed to give him the promised warning as to his intentions and who had thus deprived the authorities and inhabitants of Moscow of the opportunity of displaying a more than Roman, that is, a *Russian,* dignity in setting fire to their city *before* it was sullied by the boots of the invaders. For this he would never forgive Kutuzov. But since this time he had been forewarned of the planned withdrawal, he was going to put the torch to his property with his own hands.

The men seated around the campfire knew the military governor well enough to realize that this was no empty threat. And sure enough, at dawn Rostopchin asked his guests to join him on the porch, where flaming torches were distributed to all of them. The reluctant arsonists were then led upstairs by the master of the house, who invited them to follow his example in setting fire to curtains, draperies, and other combustible materials. A dumbfounded Sir Robert Wilson watched, torn between awe and admiration. "Each apartment was ignited as the party proceeded, and in a quarter of an hour the whole was one blazing mass. Rostopchin then proceeded to the stables, which were quickly in flames, and afterwards stood in front contemplating the progress of the fire and the falling fragments." The Saracen towers of the stables, designed on the same monumental scale as the rest of this palatial estate, were surmounted by copies of the famous Monte Cavallo equestrian group in Rome —grooms holding rampant horses—and the shuddering plunge of one of them into the spark-projecting blaze was not the least spectacular moment of this miniature holocaust.

Having made sure that all of the wine, beer, and vodka barrels in the spacious cellars had been staved in, the lord of Voronovo added a final, highly personal seal to this heroic act of self-deprivation. Over the door of the nearby church he placed a sign on which he defiantly proclaimed in French, so that the hated "brigands" could read it when they swarmed over the premises:

> For eight years I embellished this country estate, and I lived there happily in the bosom of my family. The inhabitants of this property, 1720 in number, are leaving at your approach, and I am setting fire to my own house, so that it should not be sullied by your presence. Frenchmen, I abandoned my two Moscow houses to you with furniture worth half a million rubles: here you will find nothing but ashes.

A day or two later a sullen Rostopchin wrote to Kutuzov to say that since the army was now evacuating the province of Moscow (of which he was still the military governor), he felt that his official duties were terminated: "Not wishing to be unemployed, nor to watch the ravaging of the province of Kaluga, nor to hear all day long that you have been engaged in sleep," he was leaving for Yaroslavl and Petersburg.

If Rostopchin's disappearance from the scene aroused few regrets, such was not the case with Barclay de Tolly's abrupt departure, which took place at roughly the same moment. No general in Kutuzov's army had done more to restore the sagging morale of its rank and file than Barclay, who had made a point of visiting as many units as possible to explain the tactical reasons for their westward march. But gratitude was the last quality Kutuzov was prepared to display toward a general who was now regarded by many as the man who had saved the army from total rout at Borodino.

Barclay for his part could not forgive Kutuzov for having abandoned the excellent defensive site of Tsarevo-Zaimishche. He was appalled by the casualness of Kutuzov's operating methods, which relied so much on oral rather than written and duly registered orders. With two different command centers—Kutuzov's and Bennigsen's—often operating at cross-purposes, there was endless confusion in troop movements and in the coordination of supply deliveries, with the result that the rank and file had actually gone for two days without food.

These accumulated grievances did nothing to improve Barclay's health, which had been intermittently feverish for the past couple of weeks. Accordingly, on September 30, he wrote a letter to Kutuzov requesting sick leave, adding as a kind of postscript a blunt itemization of the "bad things that have surreptitiously crept into the army either without your sanction or without your being able to notice them. The administration of the army, previously so well set up, no longer exists." A crazy, two-headed system of command—Kutuzov's and Bennigsen's—was engendering endless confusion. The corps of engineers responsible for road and bridge maintenance had been needlessly disorganized, and the quartermaster system was a shambles. Orders to attack were issued and then immediately retracted. As he bluntly concluded: "An army that does not find itself under the command of one person, but of many, cannot fail to head toward complete decomposition."

Even for the thick-skinned Kutuzov this was pretty strong medicine. He lost no time accepting Barclay's resignation of his command—to the chagrin of a number of senior officers, led by Konovnitsyn, who pleaded vainly with Barclay to stay on. No one was more assiduous in manifesting his regret than his chief of staff, Yermolov, who shed crocodile tears as he bent down to kiss Barclay on each shoulder, in the traditional Russian fashion.

After bidding farewell to his fellow officers at Tarutino on October 4, Barclay journeyed to Kaluga with a doctor and two aides-de-camp. There he completed a letter he had begun writing to the tsar, in which he painted a bleak picture of the disorder reigning at Kutuzov's headquarters. At a relay station in the province of Vladimir, now crowded with anguished as well as angry refugees from gutted Moscow, a mob of "patriots" appeared, yelling for the blood of the "traitor" who, they had learned, was inside the coach-inn. Fortunately the horses were already hitched up. Even so one of the aides-de-camp had to draw his sword and clear a path through the fist-waving throng so that Barclay could climb back into the carriage and be driven to safety.

Shortly afterward he learned that the *Sanktpeterburgskiye Vyedomosti* (St. Petersburg News) had published the text of Kutuzov's September 16 report to the tsar, in which Barclay was implicitly held responsible for the "disordered state" in which the generalissimo had found the army and for the loss of Smolensk, which had led inevitably to the later abandonment of Moscow. This was not the behavior that Barclay had expected from his former protector,

Alexander; and the realization that he had been sacrificed by the tsar came as such a shock that he came down with a new and even more serious bout of fever. Weeks were to pass before he could appear again in public without being hissed or booed, and not once during that depressing time did the tsar care or dare to calm the wave of mindless animosity he had, perhaps unwittingly, done so much to encourage.

At the palace of the tsars, inside the Kremlin, Napoleon was meanwhile trying to restore a semblance of law and order to the gutted city of Moscow. Partly to combat the belief that his troops had set fire to it, partly to impress everyone with his determination to stay put in Moscow until peace was signed, he tried to set up a municipal administration headed by Muscovites. But General Toutolmin explained that he had more than enough to keep him busy at the Foundling Hospital, while Count Nikolai Zagriasky, who had once served as court chamberlain under Emperor Paul I, bowed out on account of his excessive age (all of two-and-eighty years). So ruined by the great inferno were the few remaining noblemen that there was hardly one of them who still possessed a velvet coat and satin breeches in which to be fittingly presented to the French emperor.

The sole exception was a Prince Visapur, a small, swarthy man of Indian extraction who had married the daughter of a wealthy sugar merchant. An eccentric with a prodigious gift for improvising verses for every possible occasion, Visapur had first joined the panicky exodus, but then, unable to resist the temptation of beholding this extraordinary man who had turned the continent upside down, he had returned to Moscow. Napoleon, believing that here at last was a Muscovite boyar who was willing to collaborate, immediately granted him an audience. But his surprise turned to indignation on seeing the swarthy little man with the huge jewel-like eyes and the black shoulder-length locks raise his dark hands as he stopped on the threshold and proclaimed: "O great man! O truly great man! The humblest and most ardent of your admirers has at last the happiness of contemplating you!" Realizing that he was dealing with a gifted buffoon, Napoleon soon calmed down and agreed to have his eccentric admirer sent back to Paris as a kind of human trophy. (The carriage was intercepted on the way by Cossacks, and notwithstanding his poetic supplications poured out in classic Alexandrine verses, the diminutive dark-haired prince was shot as a traitor to his country.)

Napoleon finally appointed the former French consul in Petersburg, Jean-Baptiste de Lesseps, to head an interim administration. Police commissariats were set up in each of the city's twenty precincts to help round up roaming bands of homeless Muscovites, who were lodged in the Academy of Medicine and in Prince Adrianov's palace. Using his fluent knowledge of Russian, Lesseps was even able to enlist the active assistance of a number of local citizens, who agreed to help him in his humanitarian efforts.

From the fields and vegetable gardens surrounding Moscow thousands of potatoes and cabbages were brought in every day on carts to supply the Old Guard garrison in the Kremlin, Marshal Mortier's Young Guard units, the hospitalized sick and wounded, and the homeless. But the attempt to set up regular markets, on which Napoleon set such store, proved a dismal failure. The sight of the gutted city sufficed to fill most peasants with fear and trembling, while the rapacity of Napoleon's lawless soldiers, who heartlessly despoiled them at Grande Armée checkpoints, dissuaded them from making a second trip.

Incredible as it may sound, Napoleon seems for a while to have believed that he and his Grande Armée could, if necessary, spend the winter in Moscow, blithely disregarding the difference between the occupation of a friendly and of a massively hostile country. To maintain the morale of his soldiers he had his valet light two candles by his window every night, so that they should exclaim, "Look, he sleeps neither at night nor in daytime; the Emperor works continually!" All sorts of hopeful rumors were floated, which, as they spread from mouth to mouth, assumed the most extraordinary dimensions. It was reported that immense stocks of flour had been found in Moscow—enough to keep the army going for six months. Marshal Victor had just reached Smolensk with endless convoys of foodstuffs and supplies of winter clothing. Marshal Macdonald for his part had finally occupied Riga and was now closing in on Petersburg.

Two factors contributed greatly to sustaining these fanciful illusions. The first was a period of exceptionally clement weather—a kind of Russian Indian summer lasting well into October, which caused Napoleon to claim that the autumn was "warmer in Moscow than at Fontainebleau" and to scoff at "the terrible Russian winter with which Monsieur de Caulaincourt likes to frighten children." The other was the regularity in the arrival of couriers and mail from Paris—eighteen days was the norm—which for the first couple of weeks suffered no interruptions. The posting of garrisons at all the relay stations along the Smolensk–Moscow highroad seemed to have reduced the Cossack threat, encouraging Napoleon to believe that he could rule his empire from Moscow almost as easily as from Paris.

The members of his staff were accordingly encouraged to gather up any pieces of furniture they could salvage from gutted townhouses in order to fill out the more or less empty chambers in the Kremlin's Palace of the Tsars (where only the imperial apartments were adequately furnished). Others managed to find billets in merchants' houses that had happily survived. For officers who had spent so many weeks in the field it was a strange sensation to be suddenly seated next to elegantly dressed ladies and to have to indulge in genteel conversation.

For evening meals a few restaurants were set up, where the wine was plentiful but where, increasingly, the officers had to bring their own foodstuffs to be cooked by the chefs. The actors and actresses of the city's French theater, most of whom had remained in Moscow, were rounded up by Bausset, the prefect of the imperial palace, and persuaded to resume their playing. Moscow's main theater had been burned to the ground, but a new home was found for them in the relatively small but exquisitely decorated private theater of General Posniakov's townhouse.

Other officers preferred to spend their evenings gambling—on the same restaurant tables which had earlier provided a somewhat meager dinner— while the gallant Louis de Narbonne, notwithstanding his carefully powdered white hair and his seven-and-sixty years, was happy to celebrate his occupation of Prince Alexander Kurakin's portrait-filled palace by starting an affair with a flirtatious lady of Creole origin who was roughly half his age.

Napoleon himself had little time for such urbane distractions, although an Italian tenor named Tarquinio was twice invited to the Kremlin to sing a few of his favorite operatic airs. But these various amenities and the attempt to reestablish a semblance of "normal" social life seem to have acted as a kind of soporific, lulling the vigilance of those lucky enough to be stationed in some part of Moscow. Not only the rank and file, but even senior officers paid little or no heed to the morrow, as though this sun-blessed Indian summer could last forever. Soldiers who had callously torn the boots or shoes off burned-out Muscovites to replace their own worn-out footwear made no effort to fit themselves out with a second pair.

It was almost as though, from the moment it had entered Moscow, the Grande Armée had succumbed to a kind of spell. Murat's reports of cavalry losses, due to constant skirmishing and the daily collapse of hundreds of undernourished horses, were dismissed by Napoleon as Gascon exaggerations. When General Mouton presented him with the latest troop strengths of different corps and divisions, Napoleon contested the figures, claiming that the head-counts had not been properly effected. As early as July Foreign Minister Maret had suggested to Berthier in Vilna that the hides of sheep slaughtered to feed the Grande Armée be preserved and tanned, so that the soldiers could have warm sheepskin jackets readily available for the coming winter. Berthier had paid no heed to this proposal, simply because all of Napoleon's attention was then concentrated on the job of feeding his enormous forces. Not until the very eve of the French evacuation of Moscow did Berthier belatedly order a distribution of the stocks of shoe leather that had been carefully husbanded by the quartermaster service.

In every corps, officers and soldiers were left to pick up whatever furs or woolens they could find, buy, or barter for. Too many of them seemed to think that the pleasantest way to protect themselves against the coming frosts was to amass as much wine, brandy, and vodka as they could. Even the meticulous Davout seems to have lapsed into an extraordinary state of listlessness and to have done little to prepare his men for the ordeals they were soon to have to face. Caulaincourt alone decided to take no chances. As grand equerry and thus responsible for the imperial household's horse-and-carriage service, he had all of the officers and soldiers under his command paid their salaries and wages so that they could buy furs or have their hooded cloaks lined with fur. He ordered them to procure wool-lined gloves and fur bonnets, or to have them made by local tailors and seamstresses (most of them foreigners living in the "German" suburb). He had several blacksmith forges set up and he had every one of the 715 saddle and draft horses in his equestrian service roughshod with crampons to be able to plod, trot, or canter over frozen ground and icy slopes.

He even had sleighs fashioned in advance, so that his men could continue to operate in any kind of weather.

If Napoleon had displayed this kind of foresight, there is little doubt that it would have mitigated the extent of the catastrophe that was soon to swallow up the Grande Armée. But his will to take such elementary precautions—for the moment, the mere idea of a "retreat" was taboo—seems to have been paralyzed by the illusion he was bent on fostering: that peace with the Russians was just around the corner.

By early October, however, even Napoleon was beginning to have misgivings. Almost two weeks had elapsed without a word from Petersburg. With each passing day it was becoming more difficult for the wide-ranging foraging parties to find the fodder needed to keep their starving mounts alive. Barns and villages had been ruthlessly ransacked over an ever-widening area. Cavalry and artillery horses were dying by the scores, while the number of horseless horsemen—cavaliers démontés, they were called—was now up in the thousands. With swarms of pike-wielding Cossacks now coursing over the landscape, each convoy along the Smolensk highroad had to be protected by a contingent of 1,500 men, including some mounted units; and the farther afield they had to roam in search of fodder, the more their hungry horses needed to consume.

In an effort to think his way out of this dilemma Napoleon dictated a detailed memorandum examining the three courses of action open to him. To reach its winter quarters "in the middle of a friendly people"—by which was meant Lithuania—the Grande Armée could strike southward at Kaluga and then veer west toward Smolensk, or it could return to Smolensk along the same highroad it had used to reach Moscow. There was also a third and much bolder possibility: this would be to have Marshal Victor march with his four Ninth Corps divisions—close to 40,000 men—from the region of Smolensk, where they were now concentrated, to the key road junction of Vyeliki Luki, one hundred miles north of Vitebsk, while Napoleon, with the bulk of his Moscow army, headed for the same point.

Of the three routes examined in this fascinating memorandum, it was clearly the third that enjoyed Napoleon's favor. The trouble with the first—via Kaluga —was that it would mean advancing in the direction from which Kutuzov's forces were receiving their reinforcements (Russia's southern provinces and the Ukraine), with the result that they would be constantly adding to their strength as they pursued Napoleon's forces toward Smolensk, while the Grande Armée would be losing men in ceaseless rearguard actions.

The second possible solution—a withdrawal along the main Smolensk highroad—might present difficulties for finding fodder for the horses, though fifteen days' worth of flour rations and the supply depots established along the way should suffice to carry the soldiers as far as their winter quarters in Smolensk. The trouble with this course, however, was that the regions of Smolensk and Vitebsk, being relatively poor agricultural regions compared with the East Prussian lands surrounding Elbing and Koenigsberg, could not sustain a large army for a defensive war that would then drag on for months.

The third possible solution, aimed at strengthening Marshal Saint-Cyr's two corps at Polotsk and at concentrating Marshal Victor's Ninth Corps and the bulk of Napoleon's forces around the key road junction of Vyeliki Luki, was on the other hand an essentially offensive operation, which no one could mistake for a retreat. It would tax Kutuzov's forces to the limit, since they would be moving ever farther from their supply depots in the south and from Admiral Chichagov's army in Moldavia. Five days after effecting the planned junction with the Second, Sixth, and Ninth Corps, Napoleon could advance boldly on Novgorod and thus threaten Petersburg directly.

On October 3, after "a night of anxiety and anger" (Ségur's description) provoked by the continuing silence from Petersburg, Napoleon summoned his marshals to a meeting in the Kremlin, where he had Prince Eugène read out his new plan. The reception was glacial. Davout, who from the start had favored a bold southward thrust aimed at seizing Kaluga and destroying the arms factory at Tula, and then heading for the fertile regions of the Ukraine, where fodder and grain were available in abundance, argued forcefully against this "leap into the unknown." Even assuming that they found all the food and fodder they needed along an unfamiliar route, which would take them through woods and marshes, and even if they were able to join up with Marshal Victor's forces at Vyeliki Luki, they were likely to find themselves snowed in and surrounded when they got there.

Pierre Daru, with whom Napoleon had been spending more and more time because of his long experience of quartermaster problems, was equally dubious about this audacious attack plan, which might have had a chance of success six weeks earlier, but which it was now too late to try.

Irritated by this absence of enthusiasm for a project which struck him as grandiose ("What will the world say when it learns that in three months we have conquered the two great capitals of the North?"), Napoleon dismissed his chicken-hearted marshals and returned to his somber brooding. All this was Tsar Alexander's fault and the consequence of his obtuse obstinacy.

Later that same day Napoleon summoned Caulaincourt to his office. After explaining how anxious he was to bring this war to an end, he asked him if he would be willing to carry a letter to Emperor Alexander in Petersburg. Caulaincourt said that such an initiative would be pointless, that Alexander would refuse to receive him—particularly now that Napoleon was installed among the ruins of Moscow, which was humiliation enough, and at a moment when time and climatic conditions were clearly on his side. The emperor then asked him if he would at least consent to undertake a peace mission to Kutuzov's headquarters. Again Caulaincourt refused, pointing out that it would be wiser to avoid an overture which was certain to be interpreted as a sign of weakness.

Annoyed, Napoleon turned on his heel. "All right," he snapped, "I will send Lauriston. He will have the honor of making peace and of saving the crown of your friend, Alexander."

Lauriston, though a more pliable individual than the rock-ribbed Caulaincourt, seems to have been equally reluctant to undertake such a mission. He is even reported to have suggested that instead of vainly tendering an olive branch, Napoleon should set out immediately for Kaluga with his Grande Armée, smashing through Kutuzov's lines if he tried to stop him.

"I like simple plans, and roads without detours, main roads!" exclaimed Napoleon with some heat. "I intend to return by the one I came on, but I will not set out on it until I have peace." He then told Lauriston—this was not a request but a command—that he was to go to Kutuzov's headquarters and ask for a safe-conduct pass for St. Petersburg. "I want peace, I must have peace, I want it absolutely!" were the emperor's concluding words.

October 4—the day on which Lauriston left Moscow on this desperate mission—proved to be a singularly hot one for Murat. With the flamboyant insouciance his men so much admired but which many of his officers deplored —"He is a fabulous soldier, but he has ruined our cavalry, which will soon be dismounted!"—Murat trotted boldly down into a river valley near the newly occupied village of Vinkova and was suddenly ambushed by the Russians, who opened fire from a wood with forty cannon. Only by taking refuge inside an infantry square quickly formed by the seasoned Polish veterans of General Claparède's division was he able to escape capture.

Murat's new command post was now located some 45 miles from Moscow, near the river valley where he had narrowly escaped capture. The main Russian camp lay half a dozen miles beyond, established between the Nara River and a forest. So close was it to the front-line outposts of the French that Murat's soldiers could clearly hear the target-practice gunfire with which the veterans of Kutuzov's army were training raw recruits and militiamen. Nearby was the town of Tarutino, which the Russian forces—roughly 60,000 strong —were in the process of dismantling to feed their bivouac fires; so thoroughly indeed that Kutuzov himself was soon forced to move to a peasant hut in another village, as yet undestroyed.

It was already evening when Lauriston reached Murat's command post. Murat enthusiastically endorsed the idea of arranging a cease-fire with the Russians.

Early the next morning, Lauriston, accompanied by a number of senior French officers from Murat's staff, rode up to the Russian lines and handed over a letter addressed by Marshal Berthier to Field Marshal Prince Kutuzov. It was about ten in the morning when the generalissimo received it. He had been conferring with the tsar's close friend and aide-de-camp Prince Pyotr Volkonsky, who had been sent from Petersburg with a copy of the just published imperial proclamation, intended to dispel all lingering doubts about the Russian government's determination to pursue the war to the bitter end. Kutuzov was understandably intrigued to know why Napoleon was sending one of his own aides-de-camp to see him. He sent word back to Lauriston to say that he would meet him at midnight in the no-man's-land between the two armies. In this way, as Kutuzov explained to Volkonsky, they would gain a full day, Lauriston would see nothing of the Russian camp, and the meeting could take place with a maximum of discretion.

By this time, however, the "secret" of Lauriston's arrival had begun to spread far beyond the outposts, creating something of an uproar in the Russian camp. A dozen disgruntled officers, who felt that Kutuzov had been deliberately shirking battle, converged on General Bennigsen, who needed little prodding to be persuaded that Kutuzov was preparing to negotiate a cease-fire with the enemy, who would thus be able to withdraw gracefully from Russia. A messenger was immediately dispatched to Sir Robert Wilson, who, since he had recently seen the tsar, seemed well qualified to lodge a vigorous protest.

Flattered to be the instrument of destiny and in the proud belief that he was going to alter the course of human history by nipping an impending accommodation in the bud, Sir Robert hurried over to Kutuzov's log cabin to deliver himself of a forceful remonstrance. He reminded Kutuzov of the solemn pledge he had made to the emperor in Petersburg not to enter into any negotiations with Napoleon, adding that Alexander had personally charged him to intervene as soon as he saw "the pledge and the connecting interests endangered by anyone, of whatever rank he might be." He then launched into a little speech of explanation designed to open the generalissimo's eyes to the fact that Napoleon's forces, with a ruined cavalry and an inadequately horsed artillery, were on their last legs.

By the time this incredible harangue was over, Kutuzov must have been in a boiling rage. He had little sympathy for this brash British meddler, who was forever egging on his generals to attack and keep attacking. Volkonsky, who was brought into the discussion, seems to have been considerably embarrassed, doubtless because he knew better than anyone of the tsar's adamant opposition to any peace dealings with Napoleon. But he was intelligent enough to realize that there are times when one must be prepared to break the letter of the law while respecting its spirit.

Since Volkonsky had got to know Lauriston well during his year as French ambassador in Petersburg, he was chosen to drive up to the Russian outposts to meet him. Informed that Lauriston was the bearer of a letter addressed by Napoleon to Kutuzov, Volkonsky volunteered to carry it back to the commander in chief, but the French general said that he had been instructed to deliver it in person to the field marshal. Volkonsky then ordered one of his aides-de-camp to return to Kutuzov's headquarters. He added a few words in Russian, telling his aide-de-camp to gallop off for the first hundred yards or so, but to slow down to a walking pace once he was out of Lauriston's sight. The idea was to gain time and to make sure that the French general's meeting with Kutuzov took place after dark.

At that moment Murat trotted up, looking grander than ever in his brilliant red trousers, yellow boots, and emerald-green pelisse. On the Russian side Bennigsen appeared, accompanied by the commander of the Russian vanguard forces, General Miloradovich. Although he could not compare in stature with the towering king of Naples, the short, broad-shouldered, stockily built Miloradovich was almost a match for Murat in the elegant originality of his attire, for he obstinately sported a plumed tricorne, which was thirty years out of date, and a resplendent Turkish shawl which he wore crossed over his chest and sashed around his waist—two distinctive ornaments that enabled his men to distinguish him a hundred yards away. Like Murat, he was as inordinately vain as he was inordinately brave, his good humor seeming to increase, the hotter the fire to which he was exposed. A meeting between these two extraordinary individualists—the Gascon of the South (Murat), the Gascon of the North (Miloradovich), as Philippe de Ségur dubbed them—was almost invariably an occasion, marked by outlandish compliments and the ceremonious doffing of splendidly plumed hats. But this time their exchange seems to have been a bit cramped by the presence of so many curious eyes and ears.

"How much longer is this war going to last?" complained the Gascon of the South.

"It is not we who started it," retorted the Gascon of the North.

"This is no climate for a King of Naples," the southern Gascon again complained.

What the other Gascon replied to this, History has unfortunately not recorded, and it is just possible that Miloradovich kept his sharp tongue from adding that this was no place either for a King of Naples.

After this brief exchange of civilities, the French returned to their outposts, the Russians to theirs. It must have been a long wait for the impatient Lauriston. Not until dusk did Volkonsky's ambling aide-de-camp finally reappear, spurring his horse into a deceptive last-minute canter before delivering the news that the commander in chief, Field Marshal Prince Kutuzov, was pleased to receive General Lauriston at his headquarters.

The shrewd generalissimo had decided to make the most of this opportunity. He had issued orders to have as many campfires lit as possible, even in places where there were no troops. The soldiers were to fill their stewpots with succulent meat and *kasha* gruel, and they were to sing long and lustily to the accompaniment of their regimental bands, in order to impress the French emissary with their multitudinous strength and cheerful dispositions. The Russian commander in chief even donned a full-dress uniform, complete with feathered half-moon hat and a pair of epaulets, which he had to borrow from General Konovnitsyn, his own, unused pair being too tarnished for public display.

The meeting itself, which lasted little more than a quarter of an hour, took place tête-à-tête between the two men, after Sir Robert Wilson and the others had been ushered out of the simply furnished log cabin. Inside the candlelit room Lauriston began by declaring that the French had been dismayed by the burning of Moscow, for which they could not be held responsible, since it had been started by Russians who had remained in the city. The burning of captured cities was not a French habit, it was not in keeping with the French character, as they had shown in Berlin, Vienna, and other European cities. To this Kutuzov replied that he was well enough informed about what had been going on in Moscow to be sure that the Russians, who revered their ancient capital, had not set fire to it. The damage, however, had been done, and the Russian people were now persuaded that the burning of Moscow was the work of the French invaders.

Lauriston went on to complain of the "barbaric" turn the present war had taken, with Russian peasants displaying extreme cruelty toward any French soldiers who happened to fall into their hands, and apparently deriving a strange delight from burning their own houses and food supplies. These, he claimed, were "unheard-of" actions, and he wondered if something could not be done to temper their ferocity. Kutuzov, after duly noting that Lauriston was not directing his complaints at the behavior of his army or of regular Russian troops, pointed out that he had no control over the actions of simple peasants, who considered this war to be as devastating as another Tartar invasion.

This evoked a protest from Lauriston, who felt that comparing Napoleon and the Grande Armée to the hordes of Genghis Khan was a bit too much. "After all, there is a difference." Kutuzov conceded that there might indeed be a difference, but it was anything but evident to the Russian people, whom he could not hope to reeducate, even if he wanted to.

Lauriston proposed that, to mitigate the hardships of this cruel war, both sides should agree to an exchange of prisoners. The request was refused.

Napoleon's emissary then broached the central issue, the one that had motivated his visit. "Must this singular, this unheard-of war drag on interminably?" he asked. "The Emperor, my master, has a sincere desire to terminate this quarrel between two great and generous nations, and to terminate it forever." Kutuzov replied that he had no mandate to negotiate a peace. Whether the sentiments he had just heard expressed were the general's own or came from "higher up" (i.e., from Napoleon), he had no burning desire to transmit them to his sovereign. For, he added, "I would be cursed by posterity if I were regarded as the prime mover of any sort of accommodation, such being the present state of mind of my nation."

Lauriston, who by this time must have been grinding his teeth in frustration, now pulled out the letter that Napoleon had written to Kutuzov and asked if he could be granted a safe-conduct pass and allowed to proceed to St. Petersburg. Kutuzov replied that for this they would have to wait for an official authorization.

While waiting for the answer from St. Petersburg, would it not be possible to conclude an armistice? suggested Lauriston, only to be informed that this would not be possible.

"Well, then," cried Lauriston impatiently, "how long will we have to wait?"

Kutuzov, at his most evasive, simply shrugged his shoulders. "But I promise that I will make the desires of your emperor known to our sovereign as soon as possible," he added suavely.

After a few more exchanges of this kind, Kutuzov opened the door and asked Volkonsky to join them. He briefly recapitulated what had been discussed, pointedly stressing the fact that he was commander in chief of an army, not of a people, and that he had been forbidden by his sovereign to pronounce the words "peace" and "armistice."

When Lauriston heard that Volkonsky was about to return to Petersburg with his request for a safe-conduct pass, he suggested that he travel directly through Moscow, so as not to have to make a lengthy detour around the city. This suggestion met with a quiet refusal. So too did another Lauriston suggestion: that his request for a safe-conduct pass be carried to Petersburg by an express courier, thereby gaining precious time.

When Lauriston finally emerged from the generalissimo's peasant cottage, the expression on his face was glum. Or so at least it seemed to the Russian officers gathered outside. But even they could hardly have realized the extent of the victory Kutuzov had just won, without a shot being fired. For when Lauriston returned to Moscow on October 6, he told Napoleon that the tsar's own aide-de-camp was taking his request for a safe-conduct pass back to Petersburg with him. Had he returned to say that Kutuzov had simply refused to receive him—which is what the generalissimo should have done, in strict accordance with Tsar Alexander's instructions—Napoleon would have been stung to the quick, and he would have lost no time hastening his departure. Instead, the news that Lauriston's request was being transmitted to St. Petersburg revived all of Napoleon's flagging hopes—with fateful consequences for himself and his Grande Armée.

Kutuzov's behavior on this occasion fully substantiated his own modest self-appraisal, made at the time of his appointment to the post of commander in chief: "Bonaparte may well defeat me, but he will never fool me." His constant reminder that "Winter is our greatest ally" and that his steadily growing army had everything to gain by not awakening the giant from his pleasant Moscow siesta was finally taken to heart, and from October 5 on, a virtual cease-fire came into effect all along this front.

CHAPTER 22

BELATED EXODUS

IT IS NOT EASY to say when Napoleon finally decided that he could not prolong his stay in Moscow. His dictated orders attest his hesitations and divided state of mind right up to the last moment. As early as October 1 he gave orders to have thirty cannon installed in various Kremlin towers and at points along its walls, while defensive *tambours* (drum-shaped palisades) were built in front of four of the five gates: measures which could only mean that he was contemplating a partial evacuation.

On October 6, the day Lauriston returned from his mission to Kutuzov's headquarters, Napoleon ordered Junot, whose Eighth Corps was guarding the main road between Moscow and Mozhaisk, and General Baraguey-d'Hilliers, the military governor of Smolensk, to "ransack the countryside" for miles around in order to collect all available carts and wagons for the prompt evacuation of the wounded toward Smolensk. His staff officers were encouraged to contribute their private carriages, and three days later General Etienne Nansouty, commander of the First Cavalry Corps, who had been wounded at Borodino, was ordered to lead a first convoy of 1,500 wounded men out of Moscow.

On October 8 the French emperor instructed the various corps commanders to stock up six months' supplies of cabbages, three months' of potatoes, two months' of flour, and one month's of biscuits. The convent-fortresses (originally built to withstand Tartar sieges) on the roads to Kaluga, Tula, and Vladimir, like the convict prison used by Prince Eugène's Fourth Corps, were all to be strengthened and turned into fortified encampments.

At this point it looked as though Napoleon had agreed to the bold proposal put forward by Daru, who suggested that a massive roundup of livestock, horses, and fodder be undertaken on a wide-ranging scale by entire divisions, and that the Grande Armée then gradually withdraw back into Moscow and its outskirts, killing and salting all the undernourished horses so as to have enough food to carry it through the winter. Once the spring snows had melted, Victor, reinforced by Marshal Charles Augereau's Eleventh Corps (which was gradually being moved eastward from Pomerania) and local troops raised in Lithuania and Poland, would march to raise the siege of Moscow, destroying what remained of Kutuzov's army in the process.

Typically enough, it was not the news from either the southern or the northern "front" which finally dissuaded Napoleon from heeding this "lion-like" advice. He remained stubbornly convinced that Admiral Chichagov had not been able to withdraw more than 20,000 soldiers from the region of the lower Danube, always threatened by the unpredictable Turks, and that by having Marshal Victor concentrate most of his Ninth Corps around Orsha, rather than Smolensk, he could, as occasion demanded, march southwestward to aid Schwarzenberg, or northwestward to help Gouvion Saint-Cyr, who was now having trouble holding Polotsk against the assaults of General Wittgenstein's considerably expanded forces.

According to Caulaincourt, whose testimony can be trusted, what upset Napoleon more than anything else was the growing difficulty the daily *estafettes* were having outracing the pursuing Cossacks, as their valiant postilions whipped on their horses and tried to get their swift mail carriages to the next Grande Armée relay post before they were overtaken. The thought of being cut off for months without news from Paris was more than he could face, though he neatly reversed this bitter truth by objecting to Daru: "But what would Paris say? What would they do? Look what happens when they go three weeks without news of me! Who can foresee the effect of six months without communication? No, France would not get used to my absence, and Prussia and Austria would take advantage of it."

On the other hand, the fact that his reserve cavalry was quite simply wasting away seems to have left him remarkably unconcerned. Shortly after the French entry into Moscow, Murat's chief of staff, Belliard, had conducted an official tally, which indicated that there were now only 11,400 horsemen left in the four cavalry corps, which had numbered close to 30,000 at the time of the Niemen crossing. They had since been combined and sent south to confront Kutuzov's army—an ill-inspired move that had depleted them still further. By October 10 their number had declined well below the 9,000 level, and it was continuing to decrease. Yet Murat, who though fearless in battle seemed to cringe in the presence of his brother-in-law, could not bring himself to tell Napoleon bluntly just how desperate his cavalrymen's condition was.

By October 12, however, the situation had grown so critical that Murat sent one of his aides-de-camp to Moscow to explain to Napoleon that for lack of oats and proper fodder his cavalry's horses were dying like flies. "Bah!" replied Napoleon. "With light cavalry one can live anywhere; the entire countryside around him has not yet been devastated."

At ten o'clock that evening Napoleon startled the members of his staff by announcing that he would be leaving Moscow the next morning at nine and heading southward to join Murat. It was the first time since his return to the Kremlin on September 18 that he had shown any inclination to leave Moscow to visit his soldiers in the field. But perhaps because of the thick autumn fog which had suddenly descended on Moscow, he changed his mind during the night. Instead, he sent Murat a follow-up message the next morning, saying that he would be joining him in four to five days' time to launch a major attack on Kutuzov's forces. Until then Murat would simply have to sit tight, though he was authorized to pull back as far as Voronovo if he felt that there was any danger of a Russian attack in the interim.

It was now October 13, and the first snow began to fall. The Imperial Guard, the quartermaster service, and the three corps stationed in and around Moscow were placed on the alert. "Let us hurry, in twenty days we must be in winter quarters!" Napoleon declared to his secretary, Baron Fain, and others. But once again there was no follow-up.

The French emperor, it was clear, could not bring himself to issue the final order to abandon Moscow, knowing that this would shatter his lingering hopes of concluding a negotiated peace from a position of strength. Never before, save perhaps at Vitebsk, had he displayed such extraordinary irresolution. The members of his staff, used to seeing him bolt his meals in twenty minutes, were surprised to see him deliberately prolong them, just as they had been amazed to see him devote three full evenings to correcting the new statutes for the Comédie Française repertory company, which had been prepared for him by the members of his Conseil d'Etat in Paris. He seemed eager to clutch at anything—even the perusal of a novel—that offered him distraction from the pressing problems of the moment. As Philippe de Ségur was to write, with his customary elegance: "Having reached the peak of his glory, he doubtless foresaw that from this moment would date his decrease; and this is why he remained immobile, holding himself back and clinging for a few more instants to this summit!" Besides, to display excessive haste would have been an admission of weakness! He had had a study made of the weather in Russia over the past twenty years, and it had revealed that not until mid-November did the temperature in Moscow generally descend below zero and the Moskva freeze over. This left him another month in which to reach Smolensk, or for that matter Vitebsk.

That same evening Napoleon changed his mind yet again. Prince Eugène, Davout, and Ney were summoned to the Kremlin by Napoleon for another council of war with Berthier, Mortier, and Daru. All those present except Daru agreed that a withdrawal from Moscow was imperative, but the proposed attack on Kutuzov was suddenly shelved. Instead, Napoleon announced his intention of leaving Moscow by the northwestern route and heading for Vitebsk. The reasons for this sudden shift of plan were almost certainly of a psychological order. Although to the members of his entourage Napoleon scoffed at the state of Kutuzov's army, claiming that it was now reduced to 15,000 infantrymen, supported by newly arrived militiamen who would be a pushover in a battle, he shrank from a major new engagement, knowing that for an army that was no longer advancing but instead retreating, every wounded soldier would be irretrievably lost. By setting out along the northwestern route to Byeloye and Vitebsk he could avoid a costly battle, gain a head start of at least two and possibly three days on the bulk of Kutuzov's army, and appear to be *advancing* on Petersburg rather than *retreating* from Moscow.

Two more precious days were lost, as Napoleon continued to debate with himself which route to choose. Late in the afternoon of the fifteenth, he finally decided that the northern route was too fraught with perilous unknowns, and that he would have to try the southern route via Kaluga, trying to bypass Kutuzov if he could. One of Prince Eugène's divisions was ordered to start down the new Kaluga road toward Fominskoye; Junot was instructed to turn back all reinforcements moving up from Smolensk and to prepare the evacuation of Mozhaisk and the nearby Kolotsky monastery; and General Baraguey-d'Hilliers was told to march out from his headquarters and to establish a new garrison and supply base at Yelnya, fifty miles east of Smolensk on the road leading to Kaluga.

To find out if, by some miracle, word had been received from Petersburg, Lauriston was sent back to Kutuzov's headquarters, where he was politely told that no answer had been forthcoming. On October 16 Maret was informed, in a carefully ciphered letter, that Napoleon was going to leave Moscow on October 19 and head for Kaluga. If the Russians tried to stop him, he would defeat them, move on Tula or Briansk if the weather was fine, or head straight for Smolensk if it suddenly became "rigorous." It was the emperor's intention to have his army reach the area of its winter quarters—the region between Smolensk, Mogilev, and Minsk—by the first week of November, and once there and "supported by a friendly land which will cover all its needs," its commander would be able to prepare for the next phase: "the Petersburg campaign."

While his Imperial Guard sappers began dismantling the imperial eagles from the tops of the Kremlin turrets—to be transported westward as war trophies—the situation for Murat's cavalrymen was growing daily more grim. The giddy euphoria with which most of them had greeted the misleading news of a cease-fire had by now largely evaporated, even though the outposts of the two armies were not firing at each other. In most cavalry companies—drastically reduced in strength from an initial campaign strength of 130 to between 18 and 24 officers and men—the prime concern was how to keep body and soul together. For the Cossacks, who were not a party to any truce, continued to prey daily on forage parties and supply wagons bringing flour and other foodstuffs from Moscow. Kutuzov's sullen vow, made immediately after the Fili conference—"By God, I will make them eat horseflesh!"—was now being fulfilled. Even Murat and his staff officers were reduced to such a diet, and it was considered a great treat when they could obtain an ox or a sheep from the Prussian hussars or the 3rd Württemberg Light Cavalry Regiment, whose "meat on the hoof"—now no more than skin and bones—had finally caught up with them after a trek of five hundred miles from the Niemen.

Heinrich von Roos, the only surviving doctor among the seven originally assigned to General Sébastiani's light-cavalry division (3,500 strong when they had entered Vilna, but now little more than 800), later wrote that there was such a shortage of carriages and personnel to drive them that many of those who had been wounded by Cossack pikes preferred to remain with their detachments rather than risk disappearing forever during the trip back to Moscow. (The record-holder in this respect was a German cavalryman named

Haegele who had received twenty-four Cossack pike wounds without giving up the ghost.) Many of the horses were so weak that they could no longer be spurred into a gallop.

Although the days were pleasantly warm, the nights were already distinctly cold, and often, after burying themselves as deeply as they could under the straw, the men would wake to find themselves covered with a shining chrysalis of hoarfrost, which snapped like an eggshell when they got up. The horses that had lain down were frequently too weak to rise and were simply left to die, while those that had remained standing were often covered with thin crusts of frost, which only gradually dissolved under the warm rays of the sun.

The Russians would have had to be blind not to perceive that all was not well with Murat's advance-guard forces. But such was still the awe inspired by the mere mention of Napoleon's name that when Kutuzov's willful factotum, Colonel Toll, told a group of young staff officers that Bonaparte could not remain much longer in Moscow, they listened open-mouthed. And when he went on to outline what should be the Russians' strategy—to force the French to return via the ravaged Smolensk–Moscow highroad over which they had come, harried by a pursuing Russian vanguard while the main Russian army headed for Vyazma, in an effort to cut the Grande Armée's retreat—most of the young officers had the impression that the overconfident colonel was indulging in moonstruck fantasies!

In terms of numerical expansion the two weeks spent at Tarutino saw a dramatic improvement. In late September Kutuzov's army numbered little more than 60,000 all told—52,000 veterans (including more than 15,000 cavalrymen), plus 8,000 hastily trained recruits recently sent up from Ryazan and Kaluga. In addition, there were more than 15,000 militiamen, mostly armed with pikes, who formed the third rank of each battalion. By mid-October the number of militiamen had shrunk to 6,000—which meant that 9,000 had by then been properly armed with muskets and integrated into regular line regiments, along with newly arrived recruits. The number of available infantry thus leapt from around 35,000 in late September to over 60,000 two weeks later: four times the figure which Napoleon was so contemptuously bandying about, in his conversations, as in his letters. The 9,000 artillerymen could put 620 cannon in the field, only 20 fewer than at Borodino, while the Cossacks, a mere 6,000 during that bloody battle, now numbered 20,000—more than three times as many.

The Cossacks, not being subject to conscription (like the Russian peasant serfs), were all volunteers. Traditionally, in times of peace, it was the younger of these ardent horsemen who joined the army's elite Cossack units or the regiments that were used for frontier patrolling under the command of their *ataman* (headman), who in 1812 was General Matvei Platov. But once the tocsin of war began sounding through the villages of Russia, the old-timers were roused from their hunting, fishing, and flock-guarding retirement in the regions of the lower Don and the Kuban, and arming themselves with pikes, they again sallied forth on horseback to do battle with the enemy. Many of them had served under Suvorov and Prince Repnin in Italy or Poland, or in the wars against the Turks, and with their silver chains and decorations, their graying beards and whiskers, they looked even more impressive than their juniors. "The Don regiments are welcome guests *sous tous les rapports,*" commented Sir Robert Wilson in his diary. "They bring us the most agreeable wines, sturgeon, caviare, and large barrels of red and white grapes, of which Platov has given me a superabundant share."

It would be a mistake, however, to believe that it was patriotism alone which brought these bearded warriors to the Tarutino camp in such prancing swarms. They were drawn above all by a restless love of adventure and the lure of loot, which Napoleon's Grande Armée was certain to offer in vast abundance.

In a remarkable critique of the errors committed by both the French and the Russian supreme commanders during this stage of the campaign, Georges de Chambray (in 1812 a captain in the Imperial Guard artillery) argued that Kutuzov would have been better inspired if he had sent two large contingents —each composed of at least 5,000 infantrymen, as well as of cavalry and highly mobile horse-artillery detachments—to prey on the Smolensk–Moscow highroad, rather than leaving this task to small "partisan" forces which, notwithstanding the lavish praise later expended on their freebooting commanders by Russian historians, were unable to overpower a single one of the Grande Armée's relay-post garrisons along the 250-mile stretch of highroad prior to Napoleon's departure from Moscow. The point is well taken and confirmed by General Dorokhov's spectacular October 10 coup at Vereya, where, with the help of the local inhabitants, his five infantry battalions, four hussar squadrons, three Cossack regiments, and eight horse-artillery cannon—more than 5,000 men in all—captured an entire Westphalian battalion. But it is no less true that if Kutuzov had struck with real force at the Grande Armée's military lifeline, Napoleon would have stormed out of Moscow days, perhaps even a week, before he finally and so reluctantly moved, and Kutuzov's whole strategy was aimed at prolonging, rather than abbreviating, the French emperor's slumbers.

This Russian Fabius Cunctator now found himself, however, increasingly at odds with many of his senior staff officers, who cared little for the commander in chief's dilatory tactics. This time the "activists" were led not by that inveterate troublemaker General Bennigsen, but by Kutuzov's protégé, Colonel Toll, who had found time to indulge in a bit of front-line reconnaissance. Accompanied only by a lieutenant and a single Cossack, so as not to attract the enemy's attention, Toll spent several days carefully examining the positions of Murat's forces. It was soon evident to him that the swashbuckling king of Naples had placed his men in an exceedingly exposed position. His left wing rested on a wood that was not properly guarded or patrolled, and worse still, there was a kind of bottleneck, or *défilé,* about six miles behind the front-line outposts at Vinkova, where the old Kaluga road was hemmed in between two forests. Murat's vanguard forces were spread out like a broccoli head, the stem of which extended back past this narrow point. Within this forward area were concentrated 7,000 to 8,000 poorly fed horsemen—all that was left of Murat's once resplendent reserve cavalry—more than 10,000 infantry, and scores of artillery pieces.

This, argued Toll, was the chance of a lifetime. By sending a strong force behind the screening wood on the French left flank, it would be possible to sweep in and pinch off the escape route, cutting the only road over which Murat's forces could retreat. His men would be helplessly trapped, and even if a few riders and infantrymen managed to filter through the woods on each side of the main road, they would be an easy prey for the Cossacks as they straggled back toward Moscow.

Most of Kutuzov's generals were emphatically in favor of Toll's proposal —beginning with the chief duty officer (already a chief of staff in all but name), the pipe-smoking Konovnitsyn, and the jovial commander of the Second Corps, General Baggovut, whose impressive girth exceeded the generalissimo's generous rotundity. From the information now being brought in by Cossack scouts, who spoke of long French convoys proceeding west along the Smolensk highroad, it was clear that Napoleon was getting ready to leave Moscow in any case. It was therefore in the Russians' interest, argued Toll, to strike quickly and to annihilate or capture all or most of the enemy's reserve cavalry and what was left of four infantry divisions.

Faced with this clamor from his impatient generals, Kutuzov was forced to yield. Bennigsen was given command of the Russians' right-wing forces, consisting of three army corps and a dozen Cossack regiments, which were to execute the outflanking movement and to pounce on the key bottleneck village of Spas-Kuplya, while Kutuzov took personal charge of the center and the left.

To formulate a plan is one thing, to execute it quite another. For something now happened that would have been inconceivable under Barclay de Tolly's tidy leadership. (With General Barclay, as Loewenstern later wrote, "one roughed it like a pauper and risked one's life every day. With the prince [i.e., Kutuzov], on the other hand, one risked living eternally.") The attack, planned for the early hours of October 17, had to be preceded by a night march undertaken by the three right-wing corps. Some troops actually began moving out of their bivouac positions. But on the evening of the sixteenth General Yermolov was in such a hurry to be off to attend a dinner party given by one of his general friends in the pleasant décor of a nearby country house that he could not be bothered to wait for General Konovnitsyn's written instructions. "Have a courier bring them to me!" he shouted, as he climbed onto his horse and galloped away. Although the chroniclers are silent on this point, it seems probable that quite a few of Yermolov's officer friends were in their cups by the time the weary courier found them in the wee hours of the morning of October 17, when it was much too late to issue the necessary orders to various unit commanders.

Kutuzov, after a good night's sleep, rose long before the dawn and had himself driven in a light cabriolet from his peasant hut in the village of Letashovka to the main Tarutino camp. He found everyone fast asleep. No horses had been saddled, no guns were moving, and except for a few sentinels and officers on guard duty, there was no sign of activity. The Cossacks, who should by this time have been moving forward behind the cover of a forest to attack the French from behind, had spent an enjoyable evening entertaining Sir Robert Wilson "with all their luxuries, amusements, honours" and a rousing rendition of the Volga boat-song, which apparently was clearly heard, though not much appreciated, by the French outposts, situated only 600 yards from these boisterous festivities.

Kutuzov immediately blew up. "Who is the senior staff officer here?" he bellowed in a voice loud enough to rouse half the camp.

There was a momentary halt in the lava-flow of insults when a man oddly clad in a soldier's uniform and with a simple forage cap on his head rode up on a small, fat horse.

"Eto chto za kanalya?" (What kind of riffraff is that?) roared Kutuzov at the sight of this slovenly apparition, only to be informed by a sheepish voice: "Captain of the General Staff Brozin, chief of staff of the First Cavalry Corps."

The assault on Murat's forces had to be postponed until the following evening. Kutuzov, understandably, wanted to send Yermolov packing, but was finally talked out of it by Konovnitsyn, who argued that his performance at Borodino made him too valuable an officer to lose.

While an unsuspecting Murat sallied forth once again beyond the outposts, eager to strike up a conversation with any willing Russian general, Kutuzov's men girded themselves for the looming onslaught, now planned for the early hours of the eighteenth. This time the troops moved out on schedule, sometime after seven at night, while a few soldiers remained behind to sing songs and to keep the bivouac fires deceptively burning.

If a skilled battlefield tactician like Barclay de Tolly had been in charge of operations, there can be no doubt that the result would have been the destruction of Murat's cavalry, the annihilation of Poniatowski's Fifth Corps (now reduced to about 5,500), the overpowering of the 1,500 veterans of General Claparède's Polish division and of the 4,000 remaining foot-sloggers of Davout's 2nd Infantry Division, as well as the loss of 180 cannon (a far larger number than the ill-informed Russians thought were located in this broccoli-shaped "trap"). But the man directing the crucial right-wing enveloping movement was the sixty-seven-year-old Bennigsen, who spoiled Toll's carefully calculated attack plan by issuing a series of contradictory orders. These so delayed the night march of General Baggovut's Second Corps that it took them thirteen hours to cover a distance of eleven miles! Instead of jumping off at dawn in an attack aimed at storming a powerful French artillery battery anchoring Murat's left wing, Baggovut's men did not reach their attack positions until seven, by which time it was broad daylight. Just to complicate matters, Count Ostermann-Tolstoy's Fourth Corps, which was supposed to advance simultaneously with Baggovut's Second Corps in a coordinated assault, somehow lost its way—with the exception of one regiment belonging to Prince Eugen of Württemberg's division.

What should have been a massive assault, simultaneously launched from three angles, thus got off to a chaotic start. A strong Cossack detachment, led by Colonel Orlov-Denisov, swept in around the French left flank, as planned, taking General Sébastiani's careless cavalrymen completely by surprise; but then, instead of continuing their devastating behind-the-lines rampage, they began looting the hastily abandoned bivouac area, indiscriminately slaughtering French and Polish prisoners. The portly Baggovut—so fat that he had to be heaved into the saddle by his grooms—got into a violent shouting match with an irate Toll, saying that when the attack was over he would have the insolent colonel trussed up and tied to one of the enemy's gun barrels for daring to suggest that his friend Prince Eugen of Württemberg lacked guts; and to show his own fearless mettle he led his Second Corps men in a frontal assault on a now wide-awake French artillery battery and was struck down by a piece of grapeshot, which shattered one of his hips. The soldiers of his Second Corps, unnerved by the fall of their beloved commander, hesitated and broke ranks, giving Murat a chance to lead his carabineers in a spirited charge, which made mincemeat of a Russian light-infantry regiment. Bennigsen, rattled by what he thought was a major French counterattack (something that Murat's undernourished cavalrymen and foot-sloggers were utterly incapable of mounting), had the uncommitted troops of Baggovut's Second Corps halt their advance, while General Stroganov's Third Corps, which was supposed to swing in behind Orlov-Denisov's Cossacks to deliver the coup de grâce, was ordered to backtrack in a hurry to plug the gaping "hole" that had supposedly opened up in the center of the Russian line. Kutuzov, in the absence of Toll and Konovnitsyn—who were galloping all over the landscape trying to salvage something from the wreckage—stubbornly refused for hours to let Miloradovich lead his two corps in a strong left-wing assault, which would have sealed off Murat's escape route; and by the time a breathless Konovnitsyn rode up and persuaded the generalissimo to give the necessary order, it was too late.

Although Murat was slightly wounded in the ribs, and although Poniatowski lost his able chief of staff, General Fiszer, they were able to retreat through the hourglass défilé of Spas-Kuplya with the loss of only 3,000 men and 38 cannon—roughly one-fifth of what the Russians could have trapped had the surprise assault been properly carried out. The five Russian corps, who outnumbered their adversaries five to one, had to content themselves with occupying an area strewn with smoking embers and the remains of thousands of devoured horses—the sickening sight of which filled the hippophilic General Wilson with disgust and the less squeamish Russians with a mixture of contempt and admiration for the dire straits to which their hard-fighting adversaries had been reduced.

Neither Bennigsen nor Kutuzov had much to congratulate himself about when the day was over, but of the two, Bennigsen seems to have been the more aggrieved. The generalissimo was seated on a magnificent carpet, which Ataman Platov had spread out for him, when Bennigsen rode up on a horse, followed by a standard captured from a French cuirassier regiment and the first of the close to forty cannon that had been taken from General Sébastiani. Kutuzov heaved himself politely to his feet and advanced to congratulate his chief of staff on a "fine victory," though he probably did not mean a word of what he said. Bennigsen bowed coldly, acknowledging the compliment on behalf of his men. Then, complaining of a "contusion" caused by a passing cannonball, he asked to be allowed to retire and rode off without dismounting. If looks could kill, both of them would have died on the spot.

The next day the miracle-working ikon of the Madonna of Smolensk was once again paraded through kneeling ranks and then brought to the Imperial Guards' "campaign chapel," where a special thanksgiving service was attended by Kutuzov and all of his senior officers. Thousands of Russian soldiers flocked to gape at the 38 captured cannon, more than had ever been seized in a single engagement with the French. The peaked look of the hundreds of prisoners, like the woeful disorder of their positions, and the dung-filled litter in the nearby churches, where these sacrilegious invaders had stabled their emaciated horses, were enough to kill the myth of French invincibility and to persuade the credulous rank and file that God was on their side. Throughout the Tarutino camp there was a new feeling of elation, born of the realization that for the first time in this campaign the Russians had gone over to the offensive and forced Napoleon's soldiers to retreat. This, it was instinctively felt, was a decisive turning point, and from now on it would be they, not the enemy, who would be doing the pursuing.

If the "victory" of Vinkova marked a turning point in the war, it was so for another reason as well. This bold slap in the face administered to the naïve king of Naples by his "charming" Russian friends stung Napoleon into immediate, and as it turned out, disorderly action. On the morning of October 18 he was reviewing the three divisions of Ney's Third Corps, now reduced to about 9,600 infantrymen and about 900 cavalrymen, in the tree-lined parade ground of the Kremlin. They had been ordered into Moscow from their bivouac areas to the east, to be ready to take part in the southward advance planned to begin two days later. But while the French emperor was making the rounds, talking to officers and men, and distributing coveted decorations, the rumble of distant cannon fire could be heard coming from the south. Shortly after midday one of Murat's aides-de-camp came galloping in to the Kremlin to report that the king of Naples had suffered a surprise attack by the Russians and had been forced to retreat after losing a few cannon and several generals, and suffering a considerable number of other casualties. The tense, preoccupied look on the emperor's face and the haste with which he completed the review made it clear to all present that the tidings were disturbing.

Back in the Kremlin Palace of the Tsars, as Philippe de Ségur was to write, Napoleon seemed to have refound "the fire of his earliest years. A thousand general and detailed orders, all different, all concording, all necessary, gushed all of a sudden from his impetuous genius! Night had not yet fallen when already the entire army was in movement towards Voronovo."

Compared with Napoleon's recent lethargy, this sudden blaze of orders— to Davout, to Ney, to Prince Eugène, to the marshals commanding the Old Guard and Young Guard—was indeed like a firework display. But it is no less true that this accelerated departure compounded the accumulated ill effects of his cross-purposes. The quartermasters, who for weeks had been instructed to hoard as many provisions as they could in anticipation of a long, possibly all-winter, stay, were given no advance warning of a sudden change of plan —and this at a moment when their chief, General Mathieu Dumas, was incapacitated by pneumonia. A huge supply of oats—enough, according to General Gijsbert van Dedem, to feed 20,000 horses for a period of six months —was thus left behind. He also saw an immensely long magazine, filled to the vaulted ceiling with sacks of flour, being pillaged at the last moment by soldiers who had gone for days without bread. Colonel Raymond de Fezensac, who had been ordered to rendezvous with his regiment in front of the Semyonov monastery near the Kaluga city barrier early the next morning, spent a hectic night overseeing the last-minute preparations. But when, after a lugubrious march through dark streets and past the spectral walls of roofless buildings, they finally reached their Third Corps assembly area, they found the Semyonov monastery in flames. Some overhasty officer had given the order to burn the stocks of foodstuffs that could not be carried off, "and by an oversight worthy of those times, the colonels had not been forewarned. There was still room in several of our covered wagons, and we saw provisions burn before our eyes that might perhaps have saved some of our lives."

According to a roll-call tally undertaken shortly after Napoleon's return to the Kremlin, some 80,000 infantrymen and close to 16,000 cavalrymen either had entered Moscow or were encamped around it by September 20. During the next four weeks at least 15,000 Grande Armée officers and soldiers are estimated to have been lost in engagements and skirmishes with Russian troops, Cossack warriors, and (in a few isolated cases) armed Russian peasants. But thanks to the reinforcements sent up from Smolensk, the number of fighting men who left Moscow and its vicinity from October 18 on was about 104,000, while the number of cannon and howitzers—607 at the moment of Napoleon's entry into Moscow—was just short of 570 and thus not much smaller than the number that had been arrayed for the battle of Borodino. The number of noncombatant paymasters, ambulance men, gendarmes, sappers, engineers, bakers, blacksmiths, sutlers, and so on may have been as high as 12,000, while the carriages and wagons (including almost 2,000 artillery caissons) numbered anywhere from 5,000 to 15,000.

To disguise the fact that this was the start of a retreat, Napoleon instructed Mortier to remain behind in the Kremlin with one Young Guard division and 4,000 horseless cavalrymen (outraged to be treated as mere foot-sloggers); he was to issue a proclamation informing all remaining Muscovites that the Grande Armée was going to attack "Kaluga, Tula, and Briansk in order to seize these important points and the arms factories to be found there." To General Baston de La Riboisière, whose remaining artillery detachments were instructed not to blow up the Kremlin's sizable stock of gunpowder for the time being, Napoleon was even more specific in declaring, "I may possibly return to Moscow." It is just conceivable that he really meant it; for he had long cherished the idea of using Moscow as a base from which to launch attacks against the enemy, and he was clearly reluctant to abandon it. But because he was not sure of being able to return to Moscow, his troops were instructed to fill their knapsacks and to load their wagons with as many provisions as possible.

It was this inherent contradiction between his announced intention of waging a hard, fast campaign to knock out Kutuzov's army and to push on to Kaluga and Tula, and his secret desire to avoid another bloody battle by bypassing Kutuzov and reaching what he imagined to be the "safety" of Smolensk via Kaluga, Znamenskoye, Mossalsk, and Yelnya, which precipitated his undoing. To sustain the illusion that his army was marching on Kutuzov to avenge Murat's defeat, Napoleon sent the bulk of his divisions southward along the old Kaluga road, rather than the new road, which would have permitted a more rapid advance; and to prepare them for any eventuality, he allowed his troops to leave Moscow with an extravagant number of carriages and baggage wagons—what the Romans rightly called *impedimenta*—which fatally slowed the speed of their advance.

As the sun rose on October 19 in a clear, crisp, radiantly blue sky—prolonging the happy illusion that Napoleon "could command the seasons as he could command men"—it illuminated an extraordinary scene. While the marching infantry columns still bore some resemblance to an army of conquering warriors, the rest of the interminable procession of vehicles and pedestrians looked more like an extensive Oriental caravan, as exotic in its polymorphic variety as the onion-bulb domes of Moscow they were leaving behind. Philippe de Ségur likened it to "a Tartar horde after a felicitous invasion," Eugène Labaume was reminded of Agamemnon's Greeks after the sack of Troy, while the surgeon Dominique Larrey was convinced that the riches carried off outdid all that Darius and his Persians were able to remove from ransacked Babylon. Georges de Chambray (captain in the Imperial Guard artillery) was struck by the vast number of new, deluxe carriages. "Many generals who until then had contented themselves with only one, now left with several, while a large number of officers who had not had any on reaching Moscow had procured some for themselves." Anatole de Montesquiou later wrote that the "multitude of small vehicles which the army dragged behind it" beggared all possible description. "Charabancs, droshkies, wurts, calèches, kibitkas, contending with each other in elegance and speed, covered the road, overflowed everywhere and inundated the plain. The orders of the commanders had not put an end to these abuses, because these vehicles were supposed to be carrying foodstuffs."

Buried beneath the foodstuffs was every imaginable form of booty. The bon vivant Sergeant Bourgogne, whose grenadier regiment did not leave Moscow until the late afternoon of the nineteenth, had time to fill his detachment's canteen wagon with bottles of various liquors as well as a splendid silver vase that he and other Young Guard revelers and a couple of compliant Russian "washerwomen" had been using for the past several weeks to serve a hot rum punch, which had added greatly to the gaiety of their Moscow evenings. In addition to some basic rations of sugar, rice, and biscuits, he had managed to stuff into his bulging knapsack a Chinese woman's robe with gold and silver embroidery, a hooded riding cape with a green velvet lining (also tailored for a woman), two small silver-framed paintings, representing the Judgment of Paris and Neptune riding through the waves on a shell behind a team of seahorses, several medallions, and a diamond-studded decoration (belonging to a "boyar")—all of which he had picked up in various cellars and abandoned houses.

Bourgogne's haul was probably average, at any rate, for those who were fortunate enough to be posted near the center of Moscow, and his choice of loot was certainly more discriminating than that of the soldiers who stuffed their knapsacks with heavy ingots, believing them to be of solid silver when they were nothing more than a mixture of tin and zinc. The officers, having helped themselves to any carriages they could find in Moscow, had more space in which to stuff everything from cases of quinquina liqueurs to rolled-up canvases by the great masters and scores of exquisitely bound books. Louis-François Lejeune, recently promoted to the rank of general and now acting as Davout's chief of staff, had, by his own admission, five saddle horses, a calèche drawn by three horses for his furs and "personal belongings," a covered wagon (pulled by four horses) full of maps and cooking utensils for his staff, three small Russian troikas (three horses apiece) for the cook and more kitchen supplies, a horse for his secretary, as well as three spare horses he had obtained from a sister he had found in Moscow and whom he had wisely sent ahead to Smolensk—yet, even so, they were not enough to pull all of those carriages and wagons over the marshy and later icy roads that lay ahead of them. In addition to the numerous *cantinières* (sutlers), some of whom were accompanied by husbands and even children, the "camp followers" included a number of French civilians—like the actors and actresses of the Théâtre Français —who were now too compromised and frightened of being lynched by vengeful "patriots" to dare stay on in Moscow after the Grande Armée's departure. Quite a few soldiers who had been unable to lay hands on a cart or a carriage of their own had pressed bearded muzhiks into service, forcing them to carry their booty on their shoulders or to wheel it along in barrows!

Such was the motley host that streamed out of Moscow on October 19 with a maximum of loot and a minimum of discipline and order. Sergeant Bourgogne has left us a vivid description of this chaotic march, during which, above the sound of wailing babies, one heard "people shouting in French, swearing in German, invoking the Good Lord in Italian, and the Holy Virgin in Spanish and Portuguese." The dusty uproar and confusion might even have seemed comic had it not been the opening scene of a drama that was to end in stark tragedy. For even before this first day was up, many of the flimsy vehicles that had been rounded up for this long overland trek had been urged on so wildly by their inexperienced drivers that they collided, overturned, smashed their wheels or axles, and were finally "abandoned in the ditches and underbrush" (as Montesquiou noted) with the riches their avid owners had wanted to remove from Russia.

If Napoleon made so little effort to limit this chaotic profusion, it was perhaps most of all because he wanted to punish the city that had been willfully burned by its "barbaric" governor, and the country whose emperor had stubbornly declined to make peace. For the foremost of all the ravaged city's plunderers was Napoleon himself. To have melted down a large number of silver bowls, trays, and chalices—supposedly "saved" from gutted palaces or pillaged churches, including those of the Kremlin—in order to mint them into silver coins to replenish the coffers of the imperial *trésor* (which had accompanied the Grande Armée to Moscow) might perhaps be justified as an act of military expediency, though it was bound to exacerbate the anti-French feelings of Russia's God-fearing peasantry. But to have insisted on removing some of the regalia used in tsarist coronations, as well as all the Turkish standards captured during the past three centuries, to have ordered the taking down of the imperial eagles from the tops of the Kremlin turrets, and—supreme sacrilege—the dismantling of the thirty-foot-high cross surmounting the Ivan Vyeliki tower can only be regarded as acts of spite. The cross was so solidly imbedded in the top of the shining cupola that it had to be sawed away from its base; though held by gilded chains and even ropes, it tore itself loose, almost carrying the workers with it, and fell with a crash to the ground, where it splintered. A semblance of wanton destruction was thus added to the injury of desecration.

Shortly after General Roguet, commander of a Young Guard division, had pulled out of the Kremlin with the broken Ivan Vyeliki cross and other Russian treasures, Napoleon dispatched a colonel to Kutuzov's headquarters to find out if an answer had been received from St. Petersburg and if something could not still be done to give the war "a character more in keeping with the established rules." This request for a cessation of a scorched-earth policy which could only be "harmful to Russia" met with a polite but firm refusal from Kutuzov.

It has been argued that the main purpose of Colonel Berthemy's trip to Kutuzov's headquarters was to allay the generalissimo's suspicions and to make him believe that Napoleon was continuing his autumn holiday in the Kremlin. If this was the calculation, it failed of its purpose. Given the ubiquity of Ataman Platov's Cossacks, it was a foregone conclusion that no large-scale military movement could go unobserved for long. All that was accomplished by Napoleon's laborious feint—having most of his Moscow troops march down the old Kaluga road as though advancing to attack Kutuzov's army, then veer right after crossing the Pakhra River to reach the new Kaluga road —was to delay their progress. If they had moved straight down the new Kaluga road, the time thus gained would have greatly benefited the divisions of Davout's First Corps, and particularly of Ney's Third Corps, which were enormously delayed by the rain that began to fall on October 21 on the slippery clay road they had to follow, and by the dozens of narrow wooden bridges which kept collapsing and had to be repaired to get the cannon and caissons across small streams and gullies.

Georges de Chambray later claimed that if the rain had continued for another twenty-four hours, Ney would have been forced to abandon a good part of his artillery and baggage trains—"an event which would have been judged disastrous and yet which would have procured great advantages." For it was Chambray's considered judgment, based on his on-the-spot experience as an artillery officer, that one of Napoleon's gravest mistakes was not to have reduced the number of cannon to six per division—a measure which, if it had been accompanied by a drastic reduction in the number of carriages and wagons, would have given his forces a reasonable chance to outmarch Kutuzov's Russians. What is certain is that the unexpected rain, after such a sunlit start, further held up a leisurely advance—so slow and lacking in real impetus that it took the lead division of Prince Eugène's Fourth Corps a full day to cover the twenty miles from Fominskoye to Borovsk, and another day to reach Maloyaroslavets, only fifteen miles beyond.

Kutuzov's celebrated love of sleep may possibly have misled Napoleon into believing that he could steal past the Tarutino camp before his somnolent opponent woke up to what was happening, and that he could then outmarch him in a race to reach Kaluga. Given the far better condition of the well-fed Russian cavalry, this was at best a wild gamble. It could have succeeded only if Napoleon had ordered Prince Eugène to have his lead division cross the small Luzha River in force and occupy the key road junction of Maloyaroslavets. Instead, in accordance with his orders, which were not to take risks and to proceed with caution, General Delzons decided to halt his 13th Infantry Division just north of the Luzha River, which at this point describes an irregular loop. Since it was already late afternoon of the twenty-third and there was only a single bridge (which the retiring Cossacks had wrecked and which had to be repaired), he judged it wiser to send just two battalions over to invest the hillside town, while he bivouacked with the rest of his soldiers on an open stretch of ground along the river's northern bank. This proved a fatal error, which was soon to cost the general his life and to impose yet one more shift of plan on a strangely irresolute Napoleon.

For the Russians, though belatedly, had at last waked up to what was happening. Shortly after midnight on October 23 a breathless staff officer from General Dokhturov's Sixth Corps galloped into the village of Letashovka, where Kutuzov was lodged, with the news that a 500-man partisan detachment, commanded by Colonel Seslavin, had just captured several French officers, who had admitted, under interrogation, that their emperor had left Moscow three days earlier and was at present encamped with his Imperial Guard near the road junction of Fominskoye, which the Russians had been planning to attack. Konovnitsyn was immediately awakened and handed the report, after which Toll too was alerted. Together they proceeded to Kutuzov's peasant hut. Sitting up in his bed, the generalissimo, who had not bothered to get undressed, received the news with tears of joy. Turning toward the ikon in the corner of the room, he said: "O Lord, my Creator! At last you harkened to our prayer, and from this minute Russia is saved!"

The generalissimo had more than one reason for feeling satisfaction. His prediction that Napoleon would soon have to leave Moscow was now fully confirmed and justified; so too, he felt, his prudence in calling off the pursuit of Murat's forces after the battle of Vinkova. Any northern movement of his main army would have facilitated the execution of Napoleon's maneuver—if he was really trying to outflank him down the new Kaluga road.

Like an oyster stubbornly clinging to its protective shell, Kutuzov was, however, loath to abandon the security of the well-defended Tarutino camp. Dokhturov, who had prudently decided to postpone his projected attack on Fominskoye, was instructed to change the direction of his march and to head southwest toward Maloyaroslavets. Miloradovich was ordered to push northward to Voronovo, to see if Murat's forces were really moving west toward the new Kaluga road—a pointless maneuver that further distended the already dispersed Russian forces. The remaining Russian corps simply marked time in the Tarutino camp. The explanation later offered was that Kutuzov had to wait for the return of the many cavalry and artillery horses that had been sent to forage some miles away before he could put his army into motion. But this is clearly face-saving nonsense, since the generalissimo did not have to wait for his faster-moving cavalry and could have sent at least one infantry corps marching down the curving road to Maloyaroslavets, barely fifteen miles from Tarutino. Dokhturov's Sixth Corps and Dorokhov's flying contingent—some 20,000 men in all—were thus left to flounder across an almost roadless, waterlogged countryside with their more than 90 cannon and accompanying caissons, while the bulk of Kutuzov's army wasted most of this Friday, October 23, waiting for the foragers to return with the horses. In this clumsy fashion Napoleon's grievous error in overburdening his caravanlike host was matched by Kutuzov's extraordinary sluggishness.

Not until the early morning of October 24 did Dokhturov's men finally reach Maloyaroslavets, where they had little trouble dislodging the two French battalions that had been sent across the Luzha River to occupy the town. But instead of driving the French all the way back to the bridge, 500 yards beyond, they contented themselves with simply driving them back from the town's last houses. This gave General Delzons time to move other battalions across the bridge and to push the Russians back up the hill on which the town was built.

It seems well-nigh incredible that the Russians, who at the start of this bloody battle were vastly superior in numbers—12,000 infantrymen, compared with Delzons's 5,500—should not have made mincemeat of the French division and have established a firm grip on the town. For with more than 80 cannon finally ringing the town in a kind of irregular horseshoe arc across the plateau south of it, they enjoyed a great advantage of terrain, since the French had first to cross the Luzha River and the 500 intervening yards and then fight their way *up* through the town's inclined streets toward the crest of the hill. There was indeed a critical moment when General Delzons, who had been ordered by Prince Eugène to retake the town, galloped forward to rally his hard-pressed men, only to be hit in the forehead by a bullet fired by a Russian fusilier entrenched behind a cemetery wall. But Delzons was soon replaced by Prince Eugène's chief of staff General Guilleminot, an able tactical commander, who had a church and several adjacent houses near the upper edge of the town occupied by stalwart grenadiers, who were ordered to stay put and go down firing, no matter what happened. Guilleminot's men were several times forced to retreat, but each time the grenadiers' lethal fire, catching the incautious Russians from behind, threw them into confusion, allowing the French to mount successful counterattacks.

To assist the hard-pressed 13th Division, Prince Eugène, who was now personally directing the battle from a meadow north of the Luzha River, sent in the 14th Division, commanded by General Broussier; and when his soldiers too were thrown back in disorder, he committed some of the grenadiers of his Royal Guard to rally and lead them up through the town again. Each time the French foot-sloggers battled their way to the crest of the hill, they were forced to duck back under its brow to avoid the lethal fire of Russian artillery pieces guarding the Kaluga road, and each time the Russians tried to attack the bridge spanning the Luzha River in the valley below, they were driven back by the batteries that French Fourth Corps gunners had set up beyond the escarpment along the northern bank of the river. Since the ravines and gullies on both sides of the town were too steep and exposed to French cannon fire to be descended by the Russians, the fighting was limited to the town of Maloyaroslavets, which was soon a mass of blazing houses.

Wondering if he had done the right thing in thus engaging most of his corps in an increasingly bloody battle, Prince Eugène sent a Polish captain, Roman Soltyk (who had come forward to interrogate Russian prisoners), galloping back to the command post Napoleon had established some distance away on a kind of upland. Napoleon listened to Soltyk's report with a frown. Things were obviously not going as he had hoped. But his reply to Prince Eugène's request for reinforcements struck Soltyk as particularly harsh: "Return to the Viceroy and tell him that since he has begun to drink of the cup, he must swallow all of it."

The criticism—revealing how touchy Napoleon could sometimes be when his commanders acted on their own initiative—stung Prince Eugène to the quick. He now flung his last remaining division into the battle. This was the 15th, composed mostly of Italians, who felt frustrated because they had missed Borodino and had not yet taken part in any major action. Led by their intrepid commander, General Pino—who returned a little later, covered with blood and mourning a brother who had just been killed—the eager Italians poured across the bridge and charged up the hill. The town by this time was an inferno, so that they had to make their way through choking smoke and flames to battle the Russians hand to hand. A kind of suicidal fury possessed both sides, in the desperate realization that since the flames would probably consume them, they might as well die fighting. The air was filled with the hideous shrieks of wounded men, unable to move their crippled bodies clear of blazing logs and timbers. Soon what had once been streets were so covered with dead and still-writhing bodies that the advancing French gunners had to press their horses and gun carriages forward over cracking skulls and crushed rib cages.

In many French accounts of the 1812 campaign the battle of Maloyaroslavets is hailed as an extraordinary victory, won against overwhelming odds. But it could more accurately be described as a battle lost by the casual default of the Russian supreme commander. It was one more demonstration of Kutuzov's extreme reluctance to involve himself in another showdown with Napoleon. Instead of proceeding by forced marches to Dokhturov's rescue and throwing in all of his available forces, Kutuzov gave his infantrymen a rest after a march of just 12 miles, and only with reluctance could he be persuaded to send Rayevsky's Seventh Corps to the relief of Dokhturov's worn-out soldiers. Rayevsky's men joined the battle around three in the afternoon, by which time two of Davout's elite divisions—the 3rd, commanded by General Gérard, and the 5th, led by General Compans (who had recovered from his Borodino wound)—had been ordered to fight their way up through the blazing town and to anchor the left and right wings of a crescent-shaped front. This they succeeded in doing by ruthlessly dragging their horse-artillery pieces up over the bodies of the dead and dying, and by setting up batteries on the crest of the hill. That the Russians, with their superior artillery capacity, should have allowed this to happen is proof of how right Waldemar von Loewenstern was when he later described Kutuzov as a "detestable battlefield tactician."

Instead of vigorously taking the offensive, which is what the situation called for, Kutuzov drew up his forces on both sides of the Kaluga road about a mile and a half from Maloyaroslavets, well beyond the range of French artillery batteries. As dusk fell, Miloradovich arrived with the Second and Fourth infantry corps and the two cavalry corps that had been assigned to probe Murat's now abandoned lines at Voronovo. His men, marching at more than twice the speed of Kutuzov's slow-moving host, had covered 34 miles in one day—an achievement which earned him a warm commendation from the surprised generalissimo: "You walk more quickly than the angels fly." Kutuzov now had four corps to back up the three that had been committed piecemeal to the Maloyaroslavets battle. He had an impressive cavalry force, consisting of 10,000 cuirassiers, dragoons, and hussars, assisted by 20,000 Cossacks. Even more important for the outcome of a pitched battle, Kutuzov could count on the concerted fire of more than 600 cannon.

Over and against him were arrayed the battle-weary remnants of Prince Eugène's Fourth Corps, now reduced from 24,000 to about 19,000 men, and the two First Corps divisions that had been committed to the fray, which probably numbered about 11,000 (allowing for 1,000 battle casualties). Together the two corps had about 230 artillery pieces, most of them outranged by the Russians' 12-pounders. Many, particularly those assigned to Davout's three other divisions, were positioned in the loop north of the Luzha River, or even farther back, from where they could cover the town of Maloyaroslavets but not reach more than a quarter of a mile beyond it. The Russians' superiority in front-line artillery at this point was thus at least three to one.

Toll, who always believed in taking the offensive whenever it was feasible, now implored Kutuzov to launch a full-scale assault. But there was no budging the generalissimo from his defensive dispositions. "My dear Toll," he said, "don't be so stubborn—so for once and for my sake do what I desire." But the stubborn Toll, who knew he was right and that they were throwing away a golden opportunity for seriously mauling Napoleon's army, refused to write out any further orders.

At this moment the even more pig-headed Bennigsen appeared with a smug smile on his face. "Monsieur le Maréchal," he began, speaking as usual in French, "I congratulate you on the second round of the battle of Eylau, which Napoleon will furnish you tomorrow. The French intend to force matters and to hold on to the position of Maloyaroslavets at all costs, in order to do battle tomorrow."

This fatuous assessment, with its complacent invitation to Kutuzov to repeat Benningsen's own exploit of February 1807, was just what the generalissimo wanted to hear. He turned with a sardonic smile to Toll. "Well now, you heard him. Here is an experienced general who announces that the enemy will attack tomorrow. How do you expect me to show the recklessness of a hussar? You see well that I must prepare to receive him." With that he gave his protégé a friendly pat on the back. "So now go, go, and do as I told you."

And so the eighteen-hour battle, which should have lasted longer and ended in a Russian triumph, gradually petered out into random exchanges of musketry and cannon fire lasting late into the evening. Both sides had time to lick their wounds and to estimate their losses: about 6,000 for the French and Italians, 6,700 for the Russians. Only a handful of prisoners had been taken, so furious was the fighting.

CHAPTER 23

THE START OF
THE DEBACLE

WHILE TOLL ARGUED vainly with Kutuzov, Napoleon left his observation post and rode back along the main road as far as the village of Gorodnya, some six and a half miles from Maloyaroslavets, where quarters had been found for him in a ramshackle hut belonging to a weaver. He was baffled by the Russians' inability to hold an "inexpugnable" position, and by the astonishing inertia they had displayed in not pressing their attacks more vigorously. Militarily it made no sense, since the terrain greatly favored them. The French and Italians, holding the front-line crescent, had their backs to a ravine, with just two bridges (the old one, now repaired, and a new trestle-bridge some distance to the right) to use in case of a retreat. The new Kaluga road, on which they depended for supplies of munitions, was by now so rutted and full of potholes that the Fourth Corps' artillery officers had been able to get only part of their cannon across the river and into Maloyaroslavets. But it was too late to pull these forces back. Were he to do so, it would look like a second French defeat, similar to the one suffered at Vinkova, and this Napoleon's already shaken prestige could not afford.

Murat, whose four cavalry corps had caught up with the Imperial Guard, was now summoned to a council of war along with Berthier and Bessières. To the astonishment of all three, the emperor, after inviting them to sit down, spent the next hour with his elbows on the table, staring fixedly at the map spread out in front of him and not uttering a word. After which they were brusquely dismissed.

It is not difficult to guess what was going on in Napoleon's mind. His hope of being able to sneak past Kutuzov's Russians and of reaching Kaluga before them had been shattered. This left him with a choice between risking a pitched battle in order to push on down the road to Kaluga, or finding an alternative route to Smolensk. The first course, although it was what he had confidently told his generals he would, if necessary, do, was fraught with hazards. Whereas Kutuzov had been able to concentrate almost all of his troops south of Maloyaroslavets, Napoleon at this point could bring only about two-thirds of his scattered forces into action. The 5,500 Westphalians of Junot's Eighth Corps were dispersed over 100 miles of Smolensk highroad as far as Vyazma. Poniatowski's 5,000 Polish infantrymen, 850 cavalrymen, and 50 cannon had been sent to recapture the road junction of Vereya and to push on from there toward the town of Medyn, situated west of Maloyaroslavets on an important secondary road eventually leading on to Smolensk. Marshal Mortier was covering the withdrawal from Moscow with almost 10,000 Young Guard soldiers, horseless cavalrymen, cannoneers, and sappers. The 900 surviving Württembergers from Marshal Ney's Third Corps were needed to hold Fominskoye, while the 1,300 Poles of General Claparède's Young Guard division garrisoned Borovsk against surprise Cossack attacks. Assuming that Ney could bring his two main divisions up from Borovsk, Napoleon could count on a maximum of 72,000 men available for a major battle. This was more than 40,000 less than he had been able to muster for Borodino. With luck he could bring 400 cannon and howitzers into action—roughly two-thirds of the Borodino total. But this time he would have to use all of the available ammunition—enough for one major battle—and throw all five of the Old Guard grenadier regiments into action, something Napoleon had so far carefully refrained from doing.

Napoleon again summoned Murat, then Bessières, and finally General Mouton to solicit their opinions. The king of Naples and the more cautious commander of the Imperial Guard cavalry were both convinced that with his superior infantry forces Napoleon could defeat Kutuzov's "militiamen." But they also felt that given the woefully underfed condition of the Grande Armée's artillery and cavalry horses, they would have difficulty pursuing Kutuzov's routed forces and thus finishing off his army.

"And you, Mouton, what is your opinion?" asked Napoleon after he had heard what his brother-in-law and Marshal Bessières had to say. The general aide-de-camp responsible for recommending promotions and decorations and for keeping the emperor informed of the latest casualty figures did not mince his words. "Sire, my opinion is to retire toward the Niemen by the shortest and best-known route—via Mozhaisk, and as promptly as possible."

The news, brought by a messenger from Prince Eugène's headquarters, that Kutuzov's forces had begun to withdraw down the road to Kaluga, leaving a screen of Cossack horsemen to tend the bivouac fires near Maloyaroslavets, increased the emperor's impatience. Duroc and Bessières had trouble dissuading him from leaving immediately for a front-line inspection. But half an hour later, Napoleon, refusing to heed their sage advice to wait till daylight, climbed onto his horse and set off down the road toward Maloyaroslavets. He and his small escort had not proceeded very far when they heard shouting and the sounds of scuffling in the dark some distance in front of them.

Napoleon, thinking that a mere handful of Cossacks were involved, told General Rapp to take the advance "picket" of chasseurs (about a dozen cavalrymen) and to clear the road. Galloping forward with his customary fearlessness, Rapp suddenly went down with his horse, speared in the dark by an enemy lance. From the wild cries and the sound of blows being exchanged, it was clear that the Cossacks were pushing ever closer. Napoleon, Berthier, and Caulaincourt all drew their swords, expecting to be assaulted at any moment. Two squadrons of Imperial Guard cavalry galloped forward to join the confused mêlée, soon followed by Marshal Bessières at the head of two other squadrons.

The "Cossacks" were in fact a troop of Tartar hussars whom Kutuzov's son-in-law, Prince Kudashev, had led across the Luzha River during the night to prey on the enemy's communications. They had fallen on an artillery train that was moving up the road toward Maloyaroslavets. Had Napoleon not delayed his early-morning departure, he and his suite of eight generals would have been caught in the middle of the mêlée and might well have been killed or captured.

Once Bessières had made sure that the Kaluga road was secure, Napoleon set out again for Maloyaroslavets. He spent the rest of this Sunday, October 25, carefully inspecting the site of the previous day's battle and trying to fathom his opponent's incomprehensible intentions. The Russians had indeed retreated from their first position near Maloyaroslavets, but they had moved only a couple of miles farther down the road to Kaluga, halting to form new battle lines. Here they seemed to be waiting to see what the French were going to do.

During this fateful Sunday, which—though no one on either side could have guessed it—was to seal the fate of the Grande Armée, two things happened to spur Kutuzov's determination to withdraw even farther to the south. The first was the triumphal return of one of Ataman Platov's raiding parties. In a bold hit-and-run raid on a French convoy near Borovsk they had made off with several wagons containing a printing press and a quantity of maps and other documents. Among the papers seized was a Berthier memorandum instructing the head of the topographical service to provide him with detailed information about the roads leading westward from Maloyaroslavets and Kaluga. Next Kutuzov received word that General Ilovaisky, leading a large Cossack force, had ambushed the vanguard of Poniatowski's corps as it moved south toward Medyn, capturing five cannon and a general, and forcing the Poles to flee in confusion.

Instead of being encouraged to stand fast by these two promising actions, Kutuzov decided that there was now clear evidence that Napoleon was aiming to outflank him by mounting a strong thrust down the Vereya–Medyn road. That night (October 25–26), to the consternation of his staff, orders for a new withdrawal were issued. At the crack of dawn the next morning the Russian army was to resume its march down the Kaluga road and not to stop until it reached the hills of Goncharovo, a dozen miles away.

By a supreme irony Kutuzov, in ordering this additional retreat, thought that Napoleon was doing what Napoleon should have done. In ordering his first withdrawal he had committed the grave mistake of uncovering the transversal road from Maloyaroslavets to Medyn, from where there was a secondary road leading southwest to Yukhnov, and from there by a better road to Mossalsk, Yelnya, and Smolensk. But the Russian generalissimo having made this extraordinary gift to his adversary, Napoleon chose to turn his back on it, thereby sealing the doom of his Grande Armée.

We unfortunately know little of what was actually said by Napoleon, Prince Eugène, Berthier, Bessières, and Davout during their long afternoon postmortem inspection of the Maloyaroslavets battleground. Napoleon's secretary, Baron Fain, later claimed that the sight of so many French casualties (roughly 4,000 killed, 2,000 wounded) affected everyone, strengthening the hand of those, like Bessières, who felt that from now on the Grande Armée's main task should be to avoid all major engagements with the enemy. Murat, on the other hand, was above all impressed by the fact that more than half of the Russian corpses were wearing the gray blouses of the militia rather than the green uniforms of the regular army—a dramatic confirmation of his contention that Kutuzov's army had been destroyed at Borodino.

During the evening council of war, once again held in the tumbledown weaver's hut in the village of Gorodnya, Murat boldly declared that there are moments when temerity is the wisest course. Burning to avenge the surprise defeat he had suffered at Vinkova, he asked for permission to lead his four cavalry corps and the horsemen of the Imperial Guard in a massive attack on the Russians, who, he claimed, would be swept into oblivion by the sheer fury of this equine avalanche. Wearily raising his eyes from the contemplation of the map that was once again spread out before him, Napoleon told Murat that it was ridiculous to speak of "temerity" and "glory" at a time when they should be considering ways of saving the Grande Armée. Marshal Bessières, who had no intention of letting the fatuous king of Naples destroy his carefully husbanded Imperial Guard cavalry, chimed in to say that the one thing they now had to decide was not how to win new battles, but how best to effect the Grande Armée's *retreat*.

The marshals probably glanced at each other in surprise on hearing this hitherto taboo word uttered in the emperor's presence. But Napoleon, his head still buried in his hands, said nothing. Davout, taking this silence for assent, then declared that since it was now a question of retreating, they should choose the road leading from Medyn to Smolensk. To this proposed solution Murat took immediate exception, saying that if it was a question of retreating, the thing to do was to cut across by Borovsk and Vereya to the main Smolensk highroad, "where supplies have been assembled, everything is known to us, and no traitor will lead us astray." Davout, who had difficulty controlling his temper, retorted that he was proposing that they follow a route that would take the Grande Armée through a "fat, fertile, nourishing" countryside, whereas the other route was one of "sand and cinders," where their march would be slowed by long convoys of wounded, and they would be stalked by famine and demoralized by the sight of ruined villages.

Berthier and Bessières immediately intervened to keep the heated argument from assuming an even more bitter tone. But Napoleon, as though wearied to hear arguments expounded which he had been turning over and over in his mind, finally put an end to this vital altercation by declaring curtly, "That's enough, gentlemen. I will decide."

It is difficult to find a rational explanation for Napoleon's failure to support

Davout on this occasion. The emperor had recently sent a ciphered message to Marshal Victor, telling him to set out with one of his divisions for Yelnya, where he would be only five days' marching distance from Kaluga. General Teste, the former second-in-command of Davout's 5th Infantry Division, had previously been ordered to march from Vyazma with 4,000 men and to occupy the key road junction of Yukhnov, southwest of Medyn. A series of antennae or filaments had thus been thrown out, like buoys or lifelines, to help the Grande Armée across the intervening *mare incognitum.*

The road from Medyn to Yukhnov and Mossalsk was not as broad as the Smolensk–Moscow highway, where three columns could march abreast, with the slower-moving artillery and supply trains occupying the middle lane. The columns using the narrower road were bound to be more extended and consequently more vulnerable to attacks by the increasingly omnipresent and hardy Cossacks. On the other hand, there was yet another road, roughly intermediate between the main Smolensk–Moscow highway and the Medyn–Yelnya road, which could have been used by the remnants of Poniatowski's Polish corps and the 10,000 men under Marshal Mortier who were now on their way to Vereya. The retreat from Moscow could thus have been accomplished simultaneously along three different routes—which would greatly have reduced the human and equine pressure on the Smolensk–Moscow highroad, with its swathe of ravaged villages and ruined peasants, thousands of whom were now armed and thirsting for French blood.

In finally turning his back on his initial plan and opting for what Georges de Chambray later described as the worst of the three choices open to him, Napoleon revealed that he was still living in a dream world. The French emperor was still unwilling to admit that he might have to sacrifice part of his army to save the rest. Still believing in his lucky star, he assumed that the horses pulling his numerous artillery pieces would be capable of superequine efforts, comparable to the superhuman efforts the men he commanded were capable of making. He assumed, with equal rashness, that because he had given orders to have the Smolensk–Moscow highroad garrisoned, it would be safe from Cossack attacks, and that the supplies he had ordered stocked at several points along it would suffice to carry his Grande Armée all the way to Smolensk. He conveniently forgot that it had taken his troops the better part of a week to reach Maloyaroslavets, and that they had been obliged to consume almost half of their fifteen-days' rations. By the time they reached Mozhaisk, in three to four days' time, the most sparing and disciplined among them would have at most six days' worth of foodstuffs for a march likely to take a dozen days or more.

At three in the morning of Monday, October 26, Kutuzov's army began to leave its campsite near Maloyaroslavets and to trudge southward in the direction of Kaluga. By daybreak the news was known to the scouts of General Grouchy's Third Cavalry Corps, which had been sent across the Luzha River to assist the infantry divisions in Maloyaroslavets, now commanded by Davout. Napoleon received it shortly afterward, as he set out from Gorodnya. He experienced a feeling of relief not far from jubilation. This grievous error on

Kutuzov's part was like a gift from the gods. Since the Russians were in *full retreat* he could announce to the world in another of his bulletins that the minor setback of Vinkova had been fully avenged by the glorious victory of Maloyaroslavets. No less important, he could now steal several marches on the Russians, since it would take Kutuzov time to realize that he was headed in the wrong direction and to reverse the line of his army's march.

Stopping to warm himself by a roadside campfire, Napoleon sent his aides-de-camp galloping off in all directions with new orders for his corps commanders. Poniatowski was to halt his advance toward Medyn and to backtrack toward Vereya. Ney was to concentrate his Third Corps around Borovsk and be prepared to follow Prince Eugène's Fourth Corps and the Imperial Guard along the transversal road via Vereya to Mozhaisk. Davout, now in command of the rear guard, was to send some light-cavalry and infantry detachments a mile or two down the road to Kaluga in order to fool the Russians for as long as possible and to disguise the Grande Armée's retreat from Maloyaroslavets.

And so, for a psychological reason (on Napoleon's part) that Colonel Toll could not possibly have foreseen, Kutuzov's retreat, which Toll so rightly deplored as a tactical error, helped to achieve the end he was bent on pursuing: forcing the French to return to Smolensk by the ravaged road over which they had come.

Friedrich von Schubert, who as chief of staff of the Russian Second Cavalry Corps, witnessed but did not participate in the final stages of the hideous struggle for Maloyaroslavets, later wrote that it was the last real battle of the 1812 campaign. It was the last time that the forces pitted against each other were roughly equal in numbers. From then on, the engagements fought were more like holding actions, fought by various segments of a deeply wounded and desperate Grande Armée to facilitate the escape of the rest. "The magnificent French army," as Schubert noted, "which we hated but respected, became for us after a couple of weeks an object of pity, of repugnance, of disgust."

Virtually all of the eyewitness accounts later written by Frenchmen, Germans, or others serving with the Grande Armée agree that until they reached Mozhaisk things did not go too badly. But thereafter the army began to fall apart, fatally weakened and demoralized by ever-growing hunger.

After withdrawing from Maloyaroslavets up the new Kaluga road, Napoleon spent his first night at Borovsk, branching off from there in a northwesterly direction to Vereya. It was here, in the late afternoon of October 27, that Marshal Mortier reported to him on the accomplishment of his rearguard assignments. He had, or so at least he fancied, carried out Napoleon's orders —which were to have the Kremlin blown up with its large stock of gunpowder. The main detonation had been so violent that it had been heard scores of miles away by thousands of Grande Armée officers and soldiers. But what Mortier did not know was that much of the Kremlin had miraculously survived. The arsenal had been blown up and the Granovitaya Palata (Faceted Chamber) had been damaged by fire. Several turrets along the Moskva riverfront had subsided into heaps of masonry, leaving gaping breaches in the walls, but the

Ivan Vyeliki tower was still standing. Thanks to the providential rain which began to fall during that explosive night, some of the powder fuses lit by French sappers before their departure had been soaked and fizzled out, greatly reducing the number and power of the planned explosions.

Mortier brought with him a noteworthy captive: General Wintzingerode, commander of the light-infantry and cavalry contingent that had been assigned the task of guarding the highroad leading northwest from Moscow to Tver and Petersburg. Informed by his Cossack scouts that the French had abandoned Moscow, he had imprudently ridden into the ruined city, accompanied by a single aide-de-camp, Prince Lev Naryshkin. Near the Kremlin they had stumbled on a Young Guard outpost and had been taken into custody by a French lieutenant.

The unexpected sight of this bête noire threw the French emperor into a violent tantrum. He accused Wintzingerode of being one of the most ardent fomentors of the present war, although neither an Austrian nor a Russian subject. For as a Württemberger he owed loyalty to his king, now an ally of Napoleon, and consequently to his emperor. "You are my subject!" he cried. "You are not an ordinary enemy, you are a rebel, and I have the right to have you tried and shot as a traitor to your country!"

The handsome general tried to protest, pointing out that Württemberg had not been part of the French Empire or even allied to France when he had been born, and that he had long since left his native land to serve his benefactor, Emperor Alexander. This mention of Alexander's name made Napoleon even angrier. He accused Wintzingerode of being one of "fifty adventurers, bribed by England," which had flung them upon the continent to wreak havoc and destruction. "But the weight of this war will fall back on those who provoked it! In six months I shall be in Petersburg, and then we shall have done with all this posturing!"

Caulaincourt later wrote that he had never seen Napoleon so worked up. After the prisoner had been led out, Berthier sent one of his aides-de-camp to tell the gendarmes to treat Wintzingerode with the respect due to a general. But such was Napoleon's rage (and Murat's inability to calm it) that, pointing to a nearby country house, he ordered two squadrons of his Imperial Guard cavalry to go forage there and then to burn it.

"Since *messieurs les barbares* deem it proper to burn their cities, one must help them!" he declared.

This order was carried out with ruthless efficiency. Wintzingerode, on the other hand, was not tried for espionage or subversion, still less shot. Once his anger had died down, Napoleon even envisaged the possibility of releasing the aide-de-camp Naryshkin, in the hope that he would return to Petersburg to inform his sovereign of how generous and truly peace-desiring the French emperor really was. Most of the members of the imperial staff went out of their way to treat Wintzingerode well. (Later he and the young Naryshkin were entrusted to the care of an officer and a gendarme and sent on ahead to France. They were, however, freed near Borissov, on the Berezina River, by a party of Cossacks led by Colonel Alexander Chernyshov, who had been sent from

Admiral Chichagov's headquarters to establish contact with General Wittgenstein's army.)

Vereya, which had seemed to Boniface de Castellane "quite a pretty town" when he had entered it on the morning of October 26, had been reduced to ashes by that evening, if not through the negligence of Grande Armée soldiers, then by the clandestine action of Russian partisans. Borovsk apparently suffered the same fate.

To slow the progress of the pursuing Russians, who also needed food and fodder, both Ney and Davout had been instructed to burn all the villages through which their rearguard forces passed. "Never," wrote Raymond de Fezensac of the methodical Davout, "was an order executed with greater exactitude and even scruple. Detachments sent out to right and left of the road set fire to country houses and villages for as far as the pursuit of the enemy permitted." Thus to the summer devastations of a scorched-earth policy, haphazardly practiced by a retreating army to hamper the advance of the invaders, was added the autumnal ravages of the retreaters hoping to delay the progress of their pursuers.

Nothing more graphically illustrates the rapid disintegration of the loot-laden host that had left Moscow on October 19 than the litter it left in its receding wake. Within five days an extraordinary array of carpets, tapestries, silk and satin gowns was spread out along the roadside near Borovsk by Grande Armée "merchants" who were ready to sell their "treasures" at cut-rate prices in order to lighten their overladen carriages and carts. Forty-eight hours later the first wagons were burned by soldiers who were glad to find some ready firewood for the cooking of the evening meal. An ever-growing number of exhausted horses were similarly hacked to pieces, and then roasted on campfire spits or saber points to supplement the meager rations of flour and biscuits.

At Mozhaisk, past whose gutted ruins Napoleon rode on the twenty-eighth, some supplies of rice had been amassed by the men of Junot's Eighth Corps, but they barely sufficed to nourish Marshal Mortier's Young Guard and Marshal Lefebvre's Old Guard and the 5,000 horseless riders who were now marching with them. For lack of draft horses, eighty artillery caissons had to be burned and blown up—from now on an almost nightly spectacle. But when his senior artillery commander, General Baston de La Riboisière, suggested to Napoleon that a number of cannon be deliberately spiked and left behind, to allow larger teams of horses to haul the rest at a faster pace, Napoleon rejected the idea as *déshonorante* for a "victorious" army!

By this time General Grouchy's Third Cavalry Corps, assigned to guard the flanks of Davout's rear guard, had virtually ceased to exist. The Cossacks, who had not taken long to discover the new direction of the Grande Armée's withdrawal, swarmed in ever closer, picking up foragers and stragglers and forcing Davout's men to form squares and unlimber cannon. This slowed the rate of march of an army further encumbered by the need to heave 500 more French wounded (from the "hospitals" of Mozhaisk and the Kolotsky monastery) onto already overloaded carriages and wagons, so as not to leave them to the mercies of roaming Cossacks, or even worse, of infuriated Russian peasants, who were quite ready to burn them or bury them alive. This humanitarian concern for the wounded did little to alleviate the lot of these unfortunates, most of whom were too weak to endure the rigors of a journey spent on the swaying tops of stagecoaches, on outdoor seats, on trunk tops, in forage carts, or even on the canvas tops of covered wagons, from which, after a more than usually brutal jolt, they often fell, and were left lying in the roadway. Many drivers deliberately guided their horses over as many ruts and bumps as possible in order to shake off this human baggage, often pitilessly run over by the horses and the carriage following immediately behind.

Increasingly, in all units of the Grande Armée, it was *chacun pour soi,* as soldiers carefully hoarded their rations and sought shelter at night against the biting wind and the frost. Having no food to give them, a company of Portuguese soldiers charged with escorting Russian prisoners westward finished each one off with a musket shot when he could no longer walk. A contingent of German soldiers, to save precious powder and bullets, preferred to bash in the heads of their captives with their gun butts. The impossibility of freeing prisoners who had seen too much of the Grande Armée's famished and disordered state condemned them to be parked at night in guarded enclosures, where those who died were cut up and eaten by the ravenous survivors.

Those who were fortunate enough to pass through the ruined village of Borodino at night saw nothing more than the vague glint of hundreds of breastplates and helmets still littering the frost-covered battlefield. But those who passed it when the sun was high in the autumn sky were nauseated by the stench of thirty thousand partly buried, decomposing human bodies, as well as the countless carcasses of rotting horses, not all of which had been picked clean by vultures.

In the once charmingly canal-filled but now devastated town of Gzhatsk, which Napoleon reached on October 29, he and his imperial suite found the remains of a foodstuffs convoy that had come all the way from France. The Cossacks had made off with part of it, but there were enough wagons filled with vintage Clos Vougeot and Chambertin wines from Burgundy to put new spirit into the members of Napoleon's entourage. But there was no such cheer for the rest of the Grande Armée, increasingly chilled by freezing nights.

The steady drop in the nocturnal temperature could be measured by the increase in the number of Moscow "treasures"—paintings, candelabra, beautifully bound books—which had been discarded along the wayside by carriage owners anxious to lighten the load for their increasingly emaciated nags. Being improperly shod with ordinary horseshoes, they were often helplessly propelled down frozen slopes by the weight of their carriages or wagons. Many thus ended up in swampy gullies, from whose chill waters they vainly strove to drag their vehicles, gradually subsiding on the slippery uphill slope in a pathetic flurry of skidding hoofbeats.

Far from seeming to be calamities, such roadway accidents seemed providential dispensations to a steadily growing number of starving soldiers. "It was a stroke of luck to see a horse stumble and fall," Bernard Duverger, a horseless rider from General Nansouty's First Cavalry Corps, later recalled. "The poor animal was carved up and the pieces were fought over"—as often as not before the horse was completely dead.

Napoleon, now that he was leading the retreat—with Junot's Westphalians just behind his Imperial Guard, followed by Ney's, Prince Eugène's, Poniatowski's, and Davout's corps—seems to have been only vaguely aware of what was going on behind him. Most of his attention was concentrated on what was happening in front of him, and in particular in and around the region of Polotsk and the Dvina River. While passing by Mozhaisk, on the twenty-eighth, he had been jolted by the news that Marshal Gouvion Saint-Cyr—"my most capable lieutenant," as he remarked to Caulaincourt—had been wounded while overseeing the evacuation of Polotsk nine days before. But not until the late afternoon of October 31, when he reached Vyazma, dressed in a fur-lined bonnet, green pelisse, and fur-lined boots, and traveling for the first time in his closed berlin to shield himself from the biting wind and snow flurries, did he begin to realize how critical the situation along the Dvina really was.

In two reports, dated October 19 and 20, Gouvion Saint-Cyr explained why he had been forced to evacuate Polotsk. His Sixth Corps, composed mostly of Bavarians, who seemed unable to "endure the fatigues and privations of this war," had been reduced to 5,000 men. When added to the 18,000 infantrymen and 4,000 cavalrymen of Oudinot's Second Corps, they gave him a total of 27,000 soldiers over and against a vastly superior force commanded by General Wittgenstein. Massively reinforced by 10,000 soldiers from Finland and other contingents from Petersburg and Novgorod, the commander of Russia's First Corps (now in effect an army) had decided to launch a frontal assault on Polotsk. The battle had cost the Russians an estimated 12,000 casualties, compared with 6,000 killed and wounded for the French and the Bavarians, but the latter had been forced to retreat southward to keep from being encircled.

This jarring news was only partially counterbalanced by several other dispatches. The first was from Marshal Oudinot, whose plucky wife had hurried from Paris to take care of him at Vilna and who was now sufficiently recovered from his wound to be able to take the field again at the head of his Second Corps. The others were several reports from Victor, saying that he had left the Smolensk-Orsha region and was marching northeastward with two of his divisions to effect a junction with Saint-Cyr's retreating forces, now commanded by General Merle. To guard the region of Smolensk the commander of the Grande Armée's Ninth Corps had left behind 15,000 infantrymen and 12,000 cavalrymen commanded by General Baraguey-d'Hilliers. Victor, as Napoleon could see, had done the right thing. But his northward march had left the region west of Smolensk dangerously unguarded—save for Dombrowski's Polish division, stationed around Mogilev to watch the Russian forces at Bobruisk, and another Polish garrison (5,000 to 6,000 men) to guard the major supply base of Minsk. Baraguey-d'Hilliers, furthermore, had been ordered to proceed to Yelnya, fifty miles southeast of Smolensk—so there was an urgent need to have him recalled, with his soldiers and the supplies that had been

stocked there in anticipation of the Grande Armée's now abandoned withdrawal via Medyn, Yukhnov, and Mossalsk.

For Napoleon the one truly encouraging development was Kutuzov's failure
to reach Vyazma before him. The Russian generalissimo was now paying for
the error he had made in retreating southward from Maloyaroslavets, along
the road to Kaluga. He had thus lost several days—which should be enough
to enable the Grande Armée to reach Smolensk without being cut off at some
point by the Russians. But the progress of Davout's rear guard struck Napoleon as being excessively slow—so slow that he finally ordered Ney to replace
him as commander of the rear guard.

Davout's progress had been retarded not only by the need to fight repeated
rearguard actions, but by the steadily growing horde of dropouts from the
other corps that had preceded his still fairly well-disciplined divisions. Although hundreds of stragglers disappeared every day, captured by Cossacks
or burned to death or otherwise tortured by furious peasants as they roamed
the countryside in marauding bands in desperate search of food, their numbers
kept increasing, so that Davout had the impression of pushing along a snow-
ball, which kept growing ever bigger and more onerous. As many of them had
already thrown away their weapons, these undisciplined stragglers were a
deadweight, contributing nothing in the way of firepower to the Grande
Armée, while they helped to deplete the ravaged highroad's scarce resources.
The little fodder that was available for the first units marching toward Smolensk had long since been consumed by the time Davout's rearguard corpsmen
reached the scene. The fears and reservations he had expressed at Gorodnya
about the perils of this route were now confirmed with a vengeance.

There can be little doubt that, if he had wished to, Kutuzov, proceeding
westward from Medyn, could have outstripped Napoleon's slow-moving army
and have intercepted it near the Dnieper crossing-point of Dorogobuzh. But
instead of pressing the pursuit, Kutuzov had begun by retiring in a southwesterly direction to the cloth-manufacturing center of Polotnyaniye Zavody,
where he had found the comfort of the local textile magnate's residence such
an agreeable change from the cramped peasant huts he had been living in for
the past few weeks that he had given his forces a one-day rest after a march
of 14 miles! The exasperated Colonel Toll finally had to solicit Konovnitsyn's
assistance, saying, "Pyotr Petrovich, if together we can't put the marshal into
motion, we shall spend the winter here!"

To keep his forces properly fed, Kutuzov split them into three advancing
prongs. The northernmost was composed of twenty Cossack regiments, followed along the Moscow–Smolensk highroad by the infantrymen of General
Paskevich's 26th Division. General Miloradovich commanded the central
prong, advancing along a more or less parallel route with his Second and
Fourth infantry corps and two cavalry corps, while Kutuzov himself marched
with the main body of the Russian army some distance farther to the south.

On the evening of November 2, Miloradovich, riding forward with the
commanders of his two cavalry corps, reached a village that was only a few
miles east of Vyazma. A mile and a half to the north they could see the

Smolensk highroad, with Davout's men settling down for the night around the village of Fedorovskoye. Some distance to the west were the soldiers of Prince Eugène's Fourth Corps, and closer still to Vyazma were Prince Poniatowski's Poles. The three Russian commanders decided to strike early the next morning —by which time, they hoped, the infantry divisions of the Second and Fourth Russian corps would have arrived to finish off Davout's encircled rear guard.

It was this miscalculation which finally saved Davout, although for ten critical hours it was touch and go. Early the next morning (November 3) two Russian dragoon regiments came charging out of the mist, taking the baggage trains of Prince Eugène's Fourth Corps and the horde of accompanying stragglers completely by surprise. They were followed by the infantrymen of Prince Eugen of Württemberg's 4th Division, who brought up their horse-artillery batteries and placed themselves across the highroad. While a horde of wagoners and dropouts began a panicky stampede toward Vyazma, Davout and his five divisions found themselves cut off from the rest of the Grande Armée.

A confused artillery battle followed, as Davout's cannoneers set up their own pieces, while the infantrymen formed into squares to ward off attacks from all points of the compass. Firing steady volleys, the rearmost troops repulsed General Paskevich's 26th Division as it approached up the Moscow highroad with Platov's war-whooping Cossacks. Meanwhile, realizing that Davout's men were cut off, Prince Eugène de Beauharnais ordered his Fourth Corps men to do an about-face and to deploy for battle, followed by Poniatowski's Poles. Setting up artillery batteries of their own, they bore down on the Russian 4th infantry division, forcing Miloradovich to pull it back southward and reform parallel to the Smolensk–Moscow highroad.

Davout's trapped divisions were at last able to resume their march, having to run the gauntlet of the fire of two Russian infantry divisions (the 17th and the 4th). Two other Russian divisions, from Ostermann-Tolstoy's Fourth Corps, finally turned up, but too late to deliver a decisive blow. Ney, after posting one of his divisions on the heights around Vyazma to guard it from a Russian attack from the south, personally led his other division to the aid of the three embattled corps. A semicircular defense line was thus formed to keep Platov's Cossacks and Seslavin's partisans from penetrating Vyazma from the north, and Ouvarov's two cuirassier divisions from riding up the river valleys to the south. Behind this screen, Davout's corpsmen began an increasingly disorderly retreat, caused by the unmanageable torrent of panic-stricken dropouts and baggage-train wagoners trying to stampede their way across the single bridge over the Vyazma River. The retreat continued through the early hours of the evening and into the night, illuminated by the flames of burning houses, as French, Italian, and Polish infantrymen and cannoneers kept up a determined fire.

The tail end of the battle was witnessed by Sir Robert Wilson, who had been traveling with Kutuzov's headquarters staff some distance to the south. Hearing the sound of cannon fire, he came galloping northward with his British dragoon escort and three Cossacks, arriving in time to appreciate the wreckage left behind by the French. "The enemy, obliged to give way incessantly for twelve versts, blew up a number of powder-wagons, and abandoned carriages, cars and baggage of every description and all his wounded that could not walk. The route and the fields were covered with their ruins, and for many years the French have not seen such an unhappy day; they could not have lost less than six thousand men."

Most of this was probably true. But Davout, Prince Eugène, and Poniatowski, while deploring their losses, probably felt that they had snatched a hard-won victory from the yawning jaws of disaster. For this Miloradovich might be regarded as to blame, for not coordinating better the movements of his somewhat weaker infantry but far more formidable cavalry forces. But the real culprit was Kutuzov, as General Wilson had already noted: "Had we moved on Yukhnov after we quitted Maloyaroslavets, as we all besought the Marshal to do, we should now have been in an impregnable position facing Vyazma, and the golden, glorious opportunity lost at Maloyaroslavets might have been retrieved." To which he now added, "The misconduct of the Marshal quite makes me wild."

Napoleon meanwhile had moved on ahead to the village of Slavkovo, where he decided to spend the night in a kind of palisaded fort, built to guard the relay post from Cossack and partisan attacks. Informed by a messenger that the Russians had come close to cutting off Davout's First Corps, he decided to halt his own retreat, to concentrate his forces, and, using Ney's rearguard troops as a decoy, to lure Kutuzov into a battle on ground of his own choosing.

Ney now began bombarding Napoleon with alarming messages describing the truly desperate condition of his army. They confirmed what the emperor was soon able to see with his own eyes as units farther down the road began to catch up with his better-fed Imperial Guard. The First Cavalry Corps, like the Third, had ceased to exist; together they could muster barely 200 horses, although the Second Cavalry Corps still numbered 1,300. The mass of horseless riders had leapt from 4,000 to 8,000, and like Murat's chief of staff, General Belliard, who insisted on setting an example despite his wounded foot, they had to tramp along in high-heeled boots rather than in the more comfortable marching shoes used by the infantrymen. General Marchand's 25th Division now totaled 450 Württembergers, while Poniatowski's Polish corps, still 5,000 strong when it had marched through Moscow, was now down to 700. The valiant prince himself had been thrown from his horse while undertaking a battlefield reconnaissance near Vyazma, so severely wrenching one knee and ankle that he could no longer ride or walk; he had been forced to turn over his command to one of his division generals (Joseph Zayonczek), while he and a wounded aide-de-camp (Arthur Potocki) were driven along in a carriage at the head of his remaining troops. It had taken just ten days of skirmishing, marching, and frantic foraging to reduce most of Napoleon's forces to this skeletal condition, and as Ney put it in his typically blunt fashion, "Sire, you no longer have an army!"

Realizing the hazards of waiting any longer, Napoleon sent Junot's Eighth Corps down the road ahead of him, and early on November 5 he set out himself for Dorogobuzh. The weather, which for the past two days had been exceptionally mild, turned bitter, as a harsh wind began to blow, driving along low clouds and flakes of melting snow. Dorogobuzh—*la ville aux choux,* as it was known to many because of the vast quantities of cabbages that had been picked up here during the eastward march—now seemed less hospitable, and, as Sergeant Bourgogne noted, the soldiers of the Young Guard were so worn out on reaching it that "one didn't even have the strength to go steal a horse and eat it."

Napoleon by this time was three days behind his originally planned schedule and still fifty miles from Smolensk. To reduce the strain on the highroad's remaining resources he decided to send Prince Eugène's Fourth Corps along the northwestern road to Dukhovshchina, from where it could march on through an unravaged countryside to Vitebsk, and eventually join forces with Victor's Ninth Corps. He even considered sending Davout's First Corps on a southwestern route toward Yelnya, where supplies had been stocked up in anticipation of his own arrival, but he finally countermanded this order, realizing that this would leave Davout at the mercy of Kutuzov's still mostly invisible army, which was apparently dogging them some distance to the south.

By the afternoon of the sixth it was snowing in earnest, further aggravating the sufferings of a shivering as well as famished host. "The Moscow winter," as Philippe de Ségur was to write, using the historic present, now attacks in force. "It penetrates their light clothes and the torn shoes. Their wet clothes are frozen stiff; this envelope of ice grips their bodies and stiffens all their limbs; a bitter, violent wind cuts their breath; it seizes it as they exhale, forming icicles which hang from around their mouths and down their beards. The unhappy creatures drag themselves on, shivering until the stone-like lumps of snow sticking to the soles of their feet, or some piece of wreckage, a branch, or the body of one of their companions causes them to trip and fall. There they groan in vain; soon the snow covers them. . . . these are their sepulchres! The road is covered with these undulations, like a burial ground." But when, shuffling past these mounds, the hardier soldiers looked up toward the horizon, all that met their eyes was a great shroud of snow, and "somber pines, trees made for tombs, with their funereal evergreenness and the gigantic immobility of their black stems."

At Mikhailevska, fifteen miles farther on, one of Victor's aides-de-camp was waiting to inform Napoleon that the short, blond marshal—so radiantly golden-haired that his soldiers called him "Beau Soleil"—had met up with the Second and Sixth corps, withdrawing from Polotsk. But instead of immediately taking the offensive, Victor too had started to retreat before Wittgenstein's advancing Russians. The news threw the emperor into a rage. Hurriedly he dictated two more dispatches: one intended for Victor, telling him that victory over Wittgenstein's poor infantry troops was "indubitable" if only he went over to the attack; the other addressed to Oudinot, urging him to take immediate command of his "six divisions" (those of the Second and Sixth corps, which the wounded Gouvion Saint-Cyr had had to abandon), to push Wittgenstein back behind the Dvina, and to retake Polotsk!

No less upsetting for Napoleon was the news, brought to him by his efficient but increasingly intercepted relay-team courier service, that during the night of October 22–23 in Paris a disgruntled French general named Malet, previously arrested for plotting and finally consigned to a mental home, had spread the word that the emperor had died in Russia and thus persuaded two other equally obscure generals to join him in a revolt against the established authorities. They had surprised the minister of police (Savary, now officially known as the duc de Rovigo), and Baron Pasquier, the Paris prefect of police, and had had them locked up for a few hours in one of the capital's largest prisons. The farcical plot had come to nothing, thanks to the quick-wittedness of several loyal officers, who had had the conspirators arrested in their turn. Order had been restored barely twelve hours after it had been first disturbed. But the facts that his minister of police should have been taken so completely by surprise; that his minister of war (General Clarke) should not have bothered to rush to the barracks to have the Paris garrison swear immediate allegiance to Napoleon's designated heir, the eighteen-month-old king of Rome; and last but not least, that the gullible prefect of the Seine should so compliantly have placed the gilded chambers of the Hôtel de Ville at the disposal of the "new rulers" left the emperor in a state of outraged agitation.

"Well, and what if we had stayed in Moscow!" were his first words to Daru. To Caulaincourt, with whom he had already privately discussed the possibility of leaving the army in order to return to Paris, he was more explicit: "With the French, as with women, one must not make too long absences. In truth there is no telling what intriguers might not be able to convince people of, and what might not happen if they were left for a while without news of me!"

There could be no question, however, of his leaving the army at such a moment and before he had guided it to the presumed haven of Smolensk. Ney, barely one day's march behind, had wanted to hold the high ground overlooking Dorogobuzh and the Dnieper bridge below, but after five hours of battling (often in knee-deep snow), he had been forced to heed the insistence of his generals and other officers—now filled with a "frantic desire to reach Smolensk"—and had retreated to the other side of the river, relentlessly harried by the Cossacks on their small frisky horses.

"The soldiers, living off horse meat only, are attacked by a singular malady," noted Boniface de Castellane, sent back to find out how Ney and his rearguard men were faring. "They seem drunk, go through precipitated movements, and fall down saying, 'I have no strength left,' and die. . . . A horrible thing," he added, "is to be obliged to abandon the wounded who can no longer walk." It was indeed a horrible thing, but even grimmer than the visiting aide-de-camp imagined. His friend Raymond de Fezensac, who had had two Russian bullets whiz through his fur-lined pelisse while leading his 4th Infantry Regiment in a charge across the snow, later noted that his famished soldiers "forcibly grabbed all the foodstuffs from the isolated men they met, who were lucky not to have their clothes torn from them as well. After having ravaged the countryside, we were reduced to destroying one another. . . . It was essential to preserve the soldiers who had remained faithful to their flags and who, as the rear guard, had to bear the full brunt of the enemy's attack; the isolated soldiers, no longer belonging to any regiment and incapable of rendering further service, had no right to any pity whatsoever."

And so the desperate march continued, leaving behind it a pathetic wake of human wreckage and the remains of crudely carved-up horses. To save Ney's men from complete collapse Napoleon had a few wagons full of food-stuffs and brandy from Smolensk, and a few oxen from the Imperial Guard's dwindling reserve of livestock, sent back to the rear guard. But so widespread by now was the hunger and so rapid the rate of march that often Sergeant Bourgogne's Young Guard companions barely had time to empty a horse's blood into a caldron—for the cooking of the daily stew—before they were off again down the road; each soldier would have to hurry up and plunge his hand into the tepid stew as his companions marched along, smearing his bloodied face as he darted a piece or two of meat into his mouth. Many were the famished soldiers, even in the most disciplined units, who could not bear to abandon the horse they were cutting up and grilling on their saber tips, and who for that reason fell behind, never to be seen again by their companions. The sight of a dead horse was a treat, but only for a few hours. Once a horse was frozen solid, it was practically impossible to hack away the flesh.

On the seventh a trickle of supplies moving up from Smolensk put new cheer into the dispirited marchers, heartened to see the sun make its warming appearance. A number of stragglers even rejoined their units, in anticipation of a regular distribution of food (which failed to materialize). But on the eighth the cold returned more bitterly than ever, freezing the thawed snow and enormously delaying the progress of this tattered host. The improperly shod horses kept slipping and falling on the ice, from which many of them were too weak to rise again. The horsemen were all forced to dismount, and Napoleon himself climbed out of his carriage several times and walked along, supported by Berthier or Caulaincourt or one of his aides-de-camp, in order to quicken the circulation of his blood and to send a little heat pulsing through his half-frozen limbs.

That night (November 8–9), as though bent on destroying the remnants of the once proud Grande Armée before it could reach the haven of Smolensk, a fiendish northern wind came howling through the pine forests, over the rolling hills, and down across the highroad, freezing thousands of exposed soldiers, many of them as they groped, blinded by scudding snow, in vain search of shelter. To save their young commander, the twenty-year-old Prince Emil of Hessen-Kassel, a number of Hessian dragoons closed in around him like a rugby scrum to protect him with the warmth of their bodies from the piercing wind. By the next morning three-quarters of these white-cloaked warriors were frozen stiff.

Sergeant Bourgogne later claimed that 10,000 men and horses perished in the course of this dreadful night, and this may well have been the case. The survivors, plodding out of the woods or crawling out from under the pine-branch shelters where they had huddled, looked more like haggard cavemen, with their frosted beards and the animal skins in which they were enveloped. The roadway, not only on both sides but also in the middle, was so littered with the bodies of "wounded men dead of hunger, cold, and misery" that Caulaincourt was later moved to write: "Never did a battlefield present so much horror." They had used up every ounce of failing energy in the desperate hope of making it to Smolensk, only to collapse a few miles short of the goal. And even as they began to lean forward and to stumble prior to the final fall, the beady eyes and avid hands of others were waiting for the moment when they could rush forward and rip off shoes, stockings, trousers, scarves, jackets, furry bonnets, gloves—anything that could improve their own defective insulation against the wintry cold.

The next morning the air, clear of flying snow particles because the wind had suddenly abated, seemed almost blissfully soft, as the Imperial Guard lurched forward through the deep cut of the Valutina Gora hills. On the other side of the frozen Dnieper thousands of soldiers could be seen streaming across the snowy landscape toward the bastioned ramparts and gleaming domes of Smolensk. The march now degenerated into a disorderly rush as famished officers and soldiers pushed and elbowed their way across the bridge in their frantic determination to get inside the town before their weak legs buckled under them. General Charpentier, the military governor of Smolensk, had ordered the main gate closed in order to keep out the horde of gaunt, grimy-faced stragglers who had preceded the rest of the army; and it was not until Napoleon himself was sighted trying to move forward with his Old Guard chasseurs through the shouting and hammering throng that the guards finally consented to open the gate.

Inside the walls the main north-south street leading up over the hill on which Smolensk was built was like a river of ice, and many were the exhausted soldiers who had to be helped up the treacherous slope by their comrades, to keep from expiring on the spot. One of Napoleon's first actions after installing himself in one of the few remaining stone houses was to designate bivouac areas for the various army corps beyond the walls, the Old Guard alone being allowed to camp in the town itself. But there was no way of controlling the famished horde that clawed its way into Smolensk, taking the commissary stores by storm and hungrily devouring many of the draft horses that had been assembled in and around the town to help pull guns and wagons.

All day exhausted soldiers continued to stagger across the snow-powdered bridge, many of them expiring from the combined effect of cold and hunger before they could collapse into the arms of their regimental comrades. By evening the churches were crammed with the sick, the wounded, and the dying, and in the graveyard near one of them—where Sergeant Bourgogne spent a crazy night listening to tipsy Young Guard musicians singing and playing the organ—there were two hundred corpses. The terrible fire of the previous August had gutted most of the wooden houses, leaving heaps of charred logs, which, though useful for campfires, often concealed trapdoor holes, through which unwary soldiers would suddenly drop to their more or less rapid death in a dark, freezing cellar.

CHAPTER 24

THE DEBACLE

IT TOOK FIVE DAYS to concentrate what was left of Napoleon's Grande Armée in and around Smolensk. On November 13 the remnants of the Fourth Corps came staggering down the snowy hillside north of the town, having lost most of their artillery and virtually all of their baggage. On their way to Dukhovshchina Prince Eugène's men had been held up by the Vop— in August, when they had crossed it, an easily fordable river, but now a glacial torrent full of chunks of ice. Numbed by the foggy cold and chilling water, the sappers had been unable to complete their trestle-bridge in time to get the first carriages and carts across before a panicky stampede, caused by the approach of Platov's Cossacks, undid their fragile handiwork. For ten hours cannoneers and baggage-train drivers had struggled, with only limited success, to find fords and to urge their shivering horses to drag artillery pieces and wagons up slippery ramps; and in the evening, when it became clear that many wagons containing precious foodstuffs would have to be left behind, all discipline had broken down as soldiers and officers' servants indulged in an orgy of wild plundering. Relentlessly harried by the Cossacks, who were now using sleigh-borne cannon to fire at them across the snow, they had made it to Dukhovsh-china, where they had rested for a day, before veering south and marching night and day on empty stomachs to reach Smolensk. The corps, which still numbered 25,000 men when it had left Moscow, was now down to 6,000, and of its 92 artillery pieces exactly 12 remained.

The loss of more than half of his Moscow army, now reduced to 45,000 men and 220 artillery pieces, was only one of several mishaps confronting Napoleon. The afternoon of his arrival in Smolensk one of Marshal Victor's aides-de-camp rode in with the disturbing news that the Russians, taking advantage of their numerical superiority, had managed to seize Vitebsk with all the foodstuffs that had been stored there. This destroyed all hope of marching northwest to join Victor's Ninth Corps, since Napoleon's hungry army would now have nothing to sustain it at the end of a four- to six-day march. Nor was this all. Wittgenstein's forces, moving southward from Polotsk, had already reached the lake- and swamp-filled region of Lepel and Chasniki, from which they were within striking distance of the upper waters of the Berezina River. The route Napoleon had used in July to move from Vilna to Vitebsk (via Glubokoye) was now cut—unless Victor's Ninth Corps, acting in conjunction with the Second and Sixth corps, commanded by Oudinot, threw the Russians back. This he was ordered to do immediately in the firmest language.

That Victor, who had distinguished himself at Friedland, only to suffer a series of humiliating reverses in Spain, was not up to the task confronting him is certain. But it is only fair to add that he had been given the impossible assignment of defending a kite-shaped quadrilateral extending from Smolensk to Vitebsk to Minsk to Mogilev—each between 80 and 160 miles distant from the next—with exactly four divisions.

Even more important than Vitebsk from the point of view of supplies was Minsk, at the westernmost point of the kite-shaped lozenge. Its defense had been entrusted to a Polish commandant, General Bronikowski, most of whose 3,500 men were newly conscripted Lithuanian recruits. Bronikowski was himself subordinated to General Dombrowski, commander of the second Polish division in Poniatowski's Polish corps, who had been given the job of watching the Dnieper River, and in particular the fortress of Bobruisk, from which the Russians might emerge at any moment. Both Victor and Dombrowski seem to have been obsessed with the possibility of such a northward thrust—which, interestingly enough, was what Kutuzov had originally wanted Admiral Chichagov to undertake with his Army of the Danube by bypassing the Pripet Marshes to the east (via Kiev, Mozyr, and Bobruisk) rather than via Brest Litovsk, Kobryn, and Slonim to the west. Considering the defense of the Dnieper in the region of Mogilev to be more important than the defense of Minsk, Victor in late October authorized Dombrowski to have Minsk evacuated if it was threatened by Wittgenstein's forces advancing southward. Not realizing the famished state in which Napoleon's soldiers were going to reach Smolensk, Victor probably assumed at that moment that Vitebsk could be held, and that once Napoleon had joined his and Oudinot's forces, they could take care of Wittgenstein together.

As far as can be judged from Napoleon's written orders—of which a steadily increasing number were now intercepted by Cossacks or otherwise lost in transit—it was not until November 11, his third day in Smolensk, that the French emperor became aware of a new menace, posed by Admiral Chichagov's forces, moving northeastward from Slonim. (General Tormassov, on Tsar Alexander's specific instructions, had relinquished his command of the Third Army of the West and had gone to join the main body of Kutuzov's army. As a result the admiral now commanded two armies, totaling 58,000 men.) An order was immediately dispatched to Dombrowski, telling him to take over the defense of Minsk. It reached Dombrowski only on the fourteenth, and by that time it was too late. The vanguard of Chichagov's army, close to 30,000 strong, had crossed the upper Niemen, destroying two-thirds of Bronikowski's forces in the process, and the fate of Minsk was sealed.

Throughout his four-day stay in Smolensk Napoleon maintained an appearance of granitic calm, apparently afraid that any betrayal of his inner anxieties would further demoralize his now deeply discouraged generals. He blew up, however, on learning that one of Baraguey-d'Hilliers's brigade commanders had carelessly let himself be surrounded southeast of Smolensk by a mixed Russian infantry and cavalry force, and had surrendered to General Orlov-Denisov. Another 2,000 men were thus lost, along with precious stocks of food and fodder, and a large number of draft horses that had been sent out along the road to Yelnya in anticipation of the Grande Armée's arrival via the Yukhnov–Mossalsk route.

Two days after his arrival in Smolensk Poniatowski was ordered to march out with his 700 surviving Polish infantrymen in the direction of Mogilev, from where he was to proceed to Warsaw to round up new recruits and to fill the gaping holes in his terribly depleted corps. Napoleon by this time had decided to lead the rest of his army down the same Smolensk–Minsk highroad up which it had marched in August. But only with extreme reluctance would he let Caulaincourt burn carriages for which there were no longer draft horses in reasonably fit condition, and he flatly refused General Baston de La Riboisière's reiterated suggestion that a few artillery pieces be spiked and left behind to lighten the burden for the remaining horses. There could be no question either of abandoning the "trophies" that had been removed from the Kremlin.

When Napoleon left Smolensk at five in the morning on November 14, many of the Grande Armée's artillery horses were still not properly shod. Because of recent variations in the temperature—daytime thaws and nighttime frosts —the undulating road leading southwest to Krasnoye was covered with ice, and the upward slopes of the successive hills they had to cross were already littered with abandoned vehicles and dead or dying horses.

The marching order once again was much the same, with the 700 Westphalians of Junot's Eighth Corps in the van, followed by the Imperial Guard. Murat, no longer having a reserve cavalry to command, was allowed to take his place next to his brother-in-law in the imperial coach. Immediately behind came three sleighs—one occupied by Berthier, the second by Caulaincourt, the third by the aide-de-camp on duty.

One hour after reaching Korytnya, where Napoleon decided to spend the night, he learned that the Cossacks, only three miles farther back, had attacked a small artillery convoy and part of the baggage train belonging to the imperial headquarters staff. A number of panicky drivers had raced their wagons headlong down a hill and into ditches on both sides of the road, where they were quickly rifled. Berthier lost many of his maps, casually strewn over the snow —first by the war-whooping Cossacks and then by a horde of equally undisciplined Grande Armée stragglers. Two other wagons, laden with Kremlin trophies, were driven by their frightened coachmen out onto a frozen lake. The ice suddenly gave way, and horses, wagons, and trophies—including the broken Ivan Vyeliki cross—disappeared, more or less forever, for the treasures have remained there, buried somewhere in the murky ooze, to this day.

After sundown Caulaincourt was summoned to the peasant hut where the emperor was spending the night. Once again Napoleon spoke of the necessity of his returning soon to France. Although painfully aware of the weakness of his army, he looked forward to a dramatic change once he had effected a junction with the fresh troops of Victor's corps, and particularly with those of Schwarzenberg's Austrian contingent. New squadrons of "Polish Cossacks," he claimed, were now on their way from Vilna to provide them with a vitally needed cavalry screen, and beyond Orsha they would be able to replenish their strength with the plentiful foodstuffs stocked at Minsk. "I shall find reinforcements at every step, whereas Kutuzov will wear himself out like me by marches that will take him away from his reserves. He remains in a land we have exhausted. The magazines are there for us. The Russians will die of hunger."

At this very moment, though Napoleon did not realize it, Minsk was on the point of falling to Admiral Chichagov's Russians, while Kutuzov's not yet starving army, which had been advancing south of Smolensk by a converging road, was preparing to pounce on the Grande Armée at Krasnoye. No longer having a cavalry to provide it with advance reconnaissance scouts, what was left of Napoleon's army was now advancing blindly across a landscape of blindingly white snow.

If the Russians at this point had been commanded by a less lethargic generalissimo, Napoleon's fate would have been sealed. As General Wilson (once again traveling with Miloradovich's vanguard) noted in his diary, "Had the [Russian] army not halted yesterday [November 14], Poniatowski and his corps must have been taken; he passed last night ten versts from hence. Why he halted the Marshal only knows. . . ."

Perhaps because he wanted to give the late-arriving soldiers a badly needed rest, Napoleon in setting out had imprudently ordered Prince Eugène's Fourth Corps to leave Smolensk on November 15, and Davout's First Corps on the sixteenth; Ney's Third Corps, though supposed to retain contact with Davout's, was even authorized to delay its departure until the seventeenth. As a result, between the various corps there were enormous gaps, which, though filled by some thirty thousand stragglers, made, or at least should have made, the separately marching corps an easy prey for Kutuzov's Russians.

On November 15, when the first engagements of the "battle" of Krasnoye were fought, Napoleon had at most 20,000 men available, Prince Eugène's Fourth Corps (6,000 strong) being too far behind to help. Kutuzov, approaching up the converging road only a few miles to the south, had close to 80,000, with 600 cannon and an equally crushing superiority in cavalry.

Instead of boldly seizing and holding the key road junction of Krasnoye, which could easily have been done on November 15, Kutuzov had it occupied by a partly Cossack advance-guard force commanded by General Ozharovsky. This force was driven from the town by the Poles of General Claparède's Young Guard division. Shortly afterward a dozen Cossack regiments—so numerous that they seemed to form a dark, unbroken line extending from the hills to the left down across the highroad ahead—were dispersed with the firing of a few cannonballs. Napoleon's grenadiers then marched into Krasnoye, while two divisions of Ostermann-Tolstoy's Fourth Corps stood watching on the line of hills, as though petrified by the thought of having to challenge the veterans of the Imperial Guard.

That night Napoleon, in the mistaken belief that he had only the vanguard of Kutuzov's army to deal with, ordered General Roguet to lead his Young Guard division in a midnight assault on the closest Russian troops, whose bivouac fires to the south were clearly visible across the snow. A fierce struggle ensued, with a lot of hand-to-hand fighting over knee-deep snow in and around two burning villages. Losses on the French side were heavy, but their objective —to "teach the Russians a lesson"—was fully achieved. For the fear inspired among Ozharovsky's retreating soldiers by this unexpected attack seems to have convinced Miloradovich as well as Kutuzov that Napoleon's army was still formidably strong.

By the morning of the sixteenth Napoleon knew from interrogated Russian prisoners that he was now confronted by the bulk of Kutuzov's army. Couriers were immediately dispatched to the following corps commanders urging them to press their pace, while he halted the march of his own Imperial Guard to allow the 6,000 men of Prince Eugène's Fourth Corps to catch up. In an effort to facilitate the linkup 800 busbied veterans of the Old Guard were sent eastward to clear the way. They would have been doomed but for the ponderous immobility of the Russian infantry lined up south of the highroad, and though bombarded by cannon and engulfed by successive waves of enemy cavalry, they managed to make it back to Krasnoye.

Kutuzov's comportment on this occasion is not difficult to understand, given his extreme reluctance to be drawn into a major battle with Napoleon. Far more difficult to fathom is the extraordinary behavior of the once fearless Miloradovich, who at Borodino had ostentatiously courted danger by exposing himself to French cannon fire. Now that he had a golden chance to destroy an entire enemy corps, the vainglorious "Gascon of the South" deliberately scuttled the effort.

Once again the main initiative was taken by the enterprising Prince Eugen of Württemberg, who placed 700 infantrymen of his 4th Division across the highroad and began bombarding the vanguard of Prince Eugène's Fourth Corps with more than 40 cannon. The attack took the corps' headquarters staff (carelessly traveling up ahead) so completely by surprise that the prince had to gallop back to form the rest of his marching columns into fighting squares. But now, instead of releasing the rest of Prince Eugen's division (stationed in a nearby ravine) to help him finish the job he had so forcefully begun, Miloradovich ordered him to pull his men back off the highroad and refused to commit two other available divisions to the fray. The 4,000 survivors of Prince Eugène's Fourth Corps, after abandoning their 12 remaining guns and all their baggage wagons, were thus able to make it to Krasnoye after effecting a nighttime detour to the right across the snowy fields to circumvent Miloradovich's 20,000 Russians and their more than 150 cannon!

That night Toll and Konovnitsyn were fit to be tied. Their feelings of frustrated rage at such spineless ineptitude must have been shared by many others at Kutuzov's headquarters. Reluctantly, under their relentless prodding, the generalissimo agreed to let Toll prepare a plan for surrounding the town of Krasnoye, but only because he thought that Napoleon and his Imperial Guard had already marched out in the direction of Orsha. Had the plan been carried out as Toll intended, it would have resulted in the destruction not only of most of Davout's corps, but of the entire Imperial Guard, including Napoleon—who would have had to surrender or go down fighting.

In the early hours of November 17 a captured Bavarian officer was brought to Kutuzov, who, being fluent in German, decided to interrogate him personally. The worried generalissimo wanted to know who exactly was in command of the French forces in Krasnoye. Was he short and plump? Did he have dark brown hair? Oh no, said the Bavarian, the man in command was very tall. (Not having seen Napoleon, he was probably referring to Mortier, the towering commander of the Young Guard.) Kutuzov greeted the news with undisguised relief: *"Non, ce n'est pas lui!"* But shortly thereafter a local peasant was brought in who asserted that the town was still swarming with soldiers wearing bearskin hats. Bearskin busbies? That meant—the famous grenadiers of Napoleon's Imperial Guard. There could no longer be a doubt that the French emperor himself was still in Krasnoye, and that he had not yet left the town, as earlier reported. Toll's plan was promptly shelved.

Napoleon, with some 25,000 men, was by this time almost completely surrounded by Kutuzov's Russians. But without losing his sang froid he sent the survivors of Prince Eugène's Fourth Corps westward down the road to Liady and Orsha, behind Junot's Westphalians, while he himself faced about in the opposite direction. At dawn Mortier was ordered to head eastward to establish contact with Davout's corpsmen, marching as fast as they could from Smolensk. Climbing out of his coupé, the emperor, armed with a birch-branch walking stick, placed himself at the head of his busbied grenadiers as they marched back along the highroad toward Smolensk!

This sudden backward movement may not have taken Kutuzov by surprise, as so many rhapsodic French chroniclers have claimed. But it gave him the excuse he was looking for. Hastily he recalled the three infantry corps that had been sent westward to complete Napoleon's encirclement, on the grounds that the French were preparing to attack the "weak" center of the Russian line south of Krasnoye, and that it urgently needed to be reinforced. This move, reopening the escape route to the west, was quite unnecessary, given the Russians' crushing superiority in men and guns. As Philippe de Ségur later wrote: "The Russians had only to march forward, without maneuvers or even cannon fire; their mass sufficed; they would have crushed Napoleon and his feeble troop; but they did not dare assail him! The sight of the conqueror of Egypt and Europe cowed them!"

Although there was too much rhetoric here—as so often in Ségur's prose —it was basically a statement of the simple truth. Kutuzov's Russians, instead of closing in with their infantry, contented themselves with bombarding Mortier's Young Guard soldiers with repeated rounds of cannon fire and grapeshot, which took a heavy toll of life. The remnants of Davout's First Corps, hurriedly marching from Smolensk, were subjected to a similar treatment, when logically they should have been annihilated. Shortly after midday they appeared, surrounded by swarms of yelling Cossacks, and were able to join forces with Mortier's Young Guard troopers. Like Prince Eugène, Davout had lost most of his baggage, but what remained of his First Corps was saved—for the nonce, at any rate.

Once he was certain that Davout's corpsmen had linked up with Mortier's Young Guard, Napoleon turned and led his Old Guard veterans back through Krasnoye and out along the road leading westward toward Liady and Orsha. He did so reluctantly, knowing that he could no longer save Ney's Third Corps, now cut off from the rest of the retreating army. But it was a case of saving what could still be saved; for as it was, in holding Krasnoye until the last of Davout's men had passed, Mortier's Young Guard divisions (now little more than regiments) lost half their men.

The stage was thus set for the most spectacular feat of this entire campaign, pulled off by the indomitable Marshal Ney. His harassed soldiers had finally made it to Smolensk on the morning of November 14—the day Napoleon left it—only to find its streets full of animal carcasses, the windowless and doorless houses filled with dead and dying men, and most of the remaining supplies of food pillaged by a horde of dropouts and stragglers. On the seventeenth, reinforced by a French and a Croatian regiment, they left Smolensk in their turn, after firing the remaining caissons and blowing up several bastions, thus completing the once picturesque town's hideous disfigurement. Though harassed by Cossacks, they reached Korytnya without difficulty, and it was only the following day—the eighteenth—when they overtook and absorbed one of Davout's divisions, which had been unable to get through, that they realized that the highroad was solidly blocked by the Russians.

In the belief that he could ram his way through and join the tail end of Davout's corps, Ney disregarded a summons to surrender brought to him from General Miloradovich, who pointed out that the marshal was confronted by an army of 80,000 men. Instead, he had his cannoneers (handling 12 guns) fire a few rounds and then he sent two of his divisions down the highroad in a three-column attack on the Russians, who were drawn up on both sides of a broad ravine. The two divisions were cut to pieces by Russian cannonballs, grapeshot, musketry, and a cavalry charge which would have destroyed them entirely had the retreating survivors not used birch trunks to defend themselves against lances and swinging sabers.

Miloradovich sent another emissary to Ney, calling on him to lay down his arms. "A Marshal of France does not surrender" was the proud reply. Using his remaining division and his artillery pieces as a defensive screen, Ney began retreating toward Smolensk. One hour later, as dusk was falling, they reached a small, frozen stream, which, Ney realized, was flowing northward toward the Dnieper. The ginger-haired marshal decided to move across the snow-covered fields in that direction.

An extraordinary cross-country chase now began, as the Cossacks pursued Ney's tired infantrymen across the snow, firing carbine shots (which usually missed) and wheeling away on their swift horses each time the French formed a fighting square. After night had fallen, Ney had his men light bivouac fires around a deserted village, as though they were going to settle down. A little later, while the Cossacks slept, the marshal and his men were led onto the Dnieper by a peasant guide. Several points were found where the ice was strong enough to enable the infantry to cross, but the two remaining guns and the few baggage wagons had to be left on the bank. The Polish cavalrymen managed to find another place where they were able to cross on their small light horses. The ice, however, finally gave way in several places, plunging a few soldiers into the frigid water. One of them, General Freytag, would have perished, had Ney, seeing his distress, not swiftly hacked down a willow branch with his saber and used it to drag the dripping officer up the frozen bank.

Ney's men thus won a small head start on their pursuers. The next day the Cossacks reappeared in force, bombarding the foot-sloggers with their sleigh-borne cannon and forcing Ney and his men to duck around hills or to plunge boldly into pine and birch forests to keep from being peppered with grapeshot. Two days were thus spent in an astonishing forced march, which was finally ended when Ney's exhausted men were met some distance west of Orsha by one of Prince Eugène's divisions, sent out to meet them. Of the 6,000 men who had been stopped short of Krasnoye by the Russians not many more than 1,000 remained.

Napoleon meanwhile had continued toward the Lithuanian town of Liady, reached by a steep incline that was so slippery that the emperor, like his soldiers, had to let himself slide down the icy slope on his bottom. The next day it began to snow again, and a sudden rise in temperature, turning the ice into slush, made the journey to Dubrovna somewhat less arduous for the weary, mud-splattered horses. Here Napoleon was able to pass the night in Princess Lubomirska's splendid country mansion. But the pleasure this gave him was more than offset by the presumed loss of Ney's Third Corps.

Even more worrying was the devastating news, brought to him by a Polish officer, that Minsk had been captured by Admiral Chichagov's Russians just two days before. Forty-seven hundred French and Polish wounded had fallen into Russian hands, along with plentiful supplies of clothing, enough foodstuffs to feed an army of 100,000 for several months, and immense quantities of gunpowder, cannonballs, artillery pieces, and munitions. There was now noth-ing to stop Chichagov from advancing to Borissov—save for the remnants of General Bronikowski's forces and some 4,000 Poles from Dombrowski's 17th Infantry Division.

The grim news cost Napoleon a sleepless night. He paced up and down, wondering what on earth Prince Schwarzenberg, whom he had got to know so well in Paris, could have been doing to allow Chichagov to advance on Minsk without lifting a finger to stop him. Maret, from Vilna, had been bombarding Schwarzenberg with urgent dispatches, instructing him to head for Minsk, but they had apparently had not the slightest effect.

What neither Maret nor his imperial master realized was that Schwarzen-berg had grown increasingly fed up with the offhand manner with which

Napoleon had treated his repeated warnings about the combined strength of the Danubian army and the Third Russian Army of the West—in all close to 60,000 men. As he wrote in one of his letters to Vienna, quoting an old Austrian field marshal: "He who fears his foe is a dog; he who despises him is a fool." The fool in this case was Napoleon, who had so rashly marched on Moscow and who had only himself to blame for the mess he had got himself into. Schwarzenberg didn't see why he should sacrifice his entire Austrian corps—already reduced from 34,000 to 26,000 men—in a problematic attempt to save Napoleon's Grande Armée, particularly since his government in Vienna had made it clear that it was adamantly opposed to the dispatch of reinforcements. Having been given the job of defending the Grand Duchy of Warsaw, the prince, recently promoted to field marshal, decided to carry out this assignment to the letter by helping General Reynier and his 8,500 Saxons defeat a Russian corps commanded by General Sacken near Volkovysk. This surprise victory could not, however, compensate for the catastrophic loss of Minsk. Napoleon could no longer count on the Austrians to delay Chichagov's further advance toward the tricky marshlands of the Berezina. More than eighty miles still separated his Imperial Guard from the main crossing-point at Borissov—twice the distance Chichagov's forces would have to cover, moving northeast from Minsk.

At three in the morning of November 19 Napoleon dictated two important dispatches to his two northern-front commanders. The first, addressed to Oudinot, ordered him to march southward immediately with his Second Corps, a cuirassier division, and 100 cannon in order to secure the bridge over the Berezina at Borissov, and to march on from there to occupy Minsk! The second dispatch, sent to Marshal Victor, ordered him to mask the sudden departure of Oudinot's troops by maneuvering the various units of his own Ninth Corps into new positions, placing them closer to Vilna, Borissov, and Orsha than those of the enemy. Victor was also to do his best to persuade Wittgenstein that Napoleon and his Moscow army were going to march northwestward to meet him head-on, whereas in reality they were headed due west.

From Dubrovna, where the only sign of the enemy was an early morning appearance of a dozen Cossacks—enough to throw 6,000 stragglers into a crazy panic—the Imperial Guard and headquarters staff moved on to Orsha, where they crossed the Dnieper once again. Napoleon had decided to slow the pace of his retreat in the desperate hope that Ney might somehow catch up with them. A thaw had set in, turning the unpaved streets into seas of mud, but there were substantial supplies of food on hand—enough to persuade a few of the dropouts to rejoin fighting units to benefit from distributions of food rations by officials of the quartermaster corps. There were also welcome stocks of ammunition, 40 sorely needed artillery pieces, as well as 60 pontoon boats. Having only a limited number of draft horses left, Napoleon finally decided to use them to haul the cannon and to abandon the boats, which were burned the next morning, along with a number of carriages and excess baggage wagons. It was a decision he was soon to have cause to regret.

Still hoping against hope for news of Marshal Ney, Napoleon delayed his next day's departure until noon. Then he set out with his Imperial Guard chasseurs for Baranouy, less than ten miles farther on, where he stopped for the night in another country house. Here, while he was dining with Berthier and General Rapp, an aide-de-camp arrived with news that Ney and the survivors of his Third Corps had made it to Orsha. "Never did a battle won cause such a sensation," the normally sober Caulaincourt was later moved to write. "The joy was general; everyone was drunk with happiness. . . . It was a national event; one felt obliged to announce it even to one's ostlers."

It was almost with a feeling of elation that the headquarters staff and Imperial Guard set out the next morning on the next lap, which carried them seventeen miles farther on to the wood-surrounded town of Kokhanovo, where Napoleon again spent the night in a manor house. As punishment for having left Ney in the lurch, the unpopular Davout was reassigned the thankless task of commanding the rear guard, behind the skeletal remains of the Third and Fourth corps.

In Borissov, sixty miles to the west, all hell meanwhile had broken loose as General Bronikowski arrived with the 800 survivors of his small Minsk garrison. The town was suddenly inundated with hundreds of Polish "fugitive patriots" and camp-following opportunists, as Captain Heinrich von Brandt (who had been sent ahead with a convoy of wounded men) noted in dismay. "The household personnel of fleeing noblemen—scribes, bailiffs, cooks, lackeys, and gardeners—who had streamed down from Warsaw and its surroundings, their heads filled with nostalgic notions of the golden freedom of the former Polish aristocracy, had brought their unruliness with them and filled every nook and cranny of the town. The taverns and public houses in particular were all filled with these people, who spent their days and nights playing cards and drinking."

Late in the evening of November 20 the human crush was augmented by the belated arrival of General Dombrowski, who had led the 4,000 soldiers of his Polish division on a roundabout march in order to enable his wife to reach the relative safety of Mogilev. Having insufficient time to reconnoiter the western approaches to the bridge across the Berezina, he stationed his men in a bridgehead arc ("which did not cover the bridge," as Brandt noted), and left the direct defense of the bridge to Bronikowski and the survivors of the Minsk garrison. The relations between the two were strained, for Bronikowski regarded the prestigious commander of the Grande Armée's 17th Division as responsible for the fall of Minsk, in not coming to his rescue. Now, instead of coordinating their efforts, the two Polish generals acted independently, enabling the French émigré commander of Chichagov's leading division, Count Charles de Lambert, to seize the 600-yard trestle-bridge after an all-day battle on November 21.

Harried by the pursuing Russians, the retreating Poles did not have time to destroy the eastern end of the bridge. Although wounded in the shoulder, Lambert insisted on accompanying his soldiers into Borisov, where he installed himself in the elegant house that General Bronikowski had hurriedly vacated. Still smoldering in a fireplace were partly burned papers, including a letter that Marshal Victor had sent to Bronikowski, informing him that Napoleon would reach Borissov on November 23 and would be in Minsk by the twenty-fifth. This letter, which Lambert had a young aide-de-camp carry across the river to Chichagov, was the first inkling the admiral had that he might soon be meeting Napoleon and his Grande Armée.

Napoleon received news of this new hammer blow during the early morning of the twenty-second, shortly before reaching Toloczin. He was still fifty miles from Borissov, and his adversary this time was the same idiosyncratic and once rabidly pro-French sea captain whom he had so cordially welcomed at the Tuileries and at Empress Josephine's country house at Malmaison in 1807. "The navy," as the emperor remarked wistfully, thinking of Nelson's victories in the past, "always brings me bad luck."

A temporary halt was called, partly to enable Napoleon to study his serious situation, partly to allow the gendarmes and corps commanders to regroup as many soldiers as possible into units capable of fighting. In the middle of this stream of tattered soldiers, many of whom, though wounded, continued to plod forward, Marshal Lefebvre, the commander of the Old Guard, could be seen advancing along the road with a stick and shouting in his thick Germanic accent, "Come now, my friends, let us band together! It is better to have numerous battalions than brigands and cowards!"

The next day (November 23) Napoleon advanced to the town of Bobr, which first had to be cleared of the weirdly costumed rabble that had taken the town hall by storm and installed itself in the mayor's administrative offices. The chaos was compounded by the collision of two streams of more or less disorganized humanity: one composed of soldiers fleeing eastward from Borissov, the other of Grande Armée stragglers who were being pushed westward by units of the Imperial Guard. Here, in a modest one-story house graced by a small two-pillared porch, Napoleon received the first piece of really good news to have reached him in almost a month. Marshal Oudinot, who had proceeded southward by forced marches from the Lake Dolgoye region with 8,000 soldiers of his Second Corps, had surprised the advance guard of Chichagov's army. Disregarding the protests and warnings of his generals, the impatient admiral had ordered a new and unfamiliar commander, Count Pahlen, who had replaced the wounded Lambert, to lead the Russian vanguard eastward out of Borissov—the idea being (at least initially) that Chichagov was to follow with the main bulk of his army, thus crushing Napoleon's forces between his own and those of Kutuzov. Suddenly set upon by French cuirassiers, the startled and disoriented Russians had fled back in wild confusion through the town, shouting *"Frantsoozy! Frantsoozy!"* Lambert's wife had managed to persuade four hussars to carry her wounded husband across the "interminable" bridge, and Admiral Chichagov, who was about to sit down with his staff officers to a fine dinner served on silver plates, had also been forced to decamp in a hurry, fleeing on horseback and on foot to reach the safety of the farther bank. The Russians, in their panicky flight, had abandoned six cannon, hundreds of carriages and baggage wagons (many of them laden with clothes and precious foodstuffs), as well a thousand prisoners. But they had managed to keep Oudinot's saber-slashing cavalrymen from crossing the Berezina in their turn by cutting the 600-yard-long bridge in two places.

By the early morning of the twenty-second another way across the Berezina had been found, thanks to one of Oudinot's cavalry commanders, General Jean-Baptiste Corbineau, whose brigade had been stationed at Glubokoye. Ordered to establish contact with Napoleon's army, he had headed south for Zembin, where he learned that Chichagov's Russians had seized Borissov and its long bridge, twenty-five miles to the southeast. A Lithuanian peasant had then led him, under cover of a dimly moonlit night, to a ford across the Berezina between the villages of Vesselovo and Studyenka. The river, wider though shallower than the Dnieper, had not yet frozen over, and Corbineau's cavalrymen had managed to cross from the western to the eastern bank between ghostly slabs of ice.

Napoleon, however, was not apprised of Corbineau's exploit until the late afternoon of the twenty-third—by which time a precious twenty-four hours had been lost. He immediately summoned the cavalry general, and after hearing his description of the crossing-point, he ordered him to return and to do everything he could to help General Chasseloup, chief of the Grande Armée's engineers, and General Eblé, the chief of its *pontonniers,* gather materials for the construction of several bridges. (This meant tearing down all the nearby peasant houses for logs and planks.) Many regimental eagles were buried. Flags were removed from their staffs and wound around the standard-bearers' chests beneath their uniforms, so as to be invisible and thus not liable to capture by the enemy. The 1,800 *cavaliers démontés* of Marshal Bessières's once proud Imperial Guard cavalry were formed into two battalions armed with muskets, carbines, and sabers, while the officers among the few hundred horsemen under General Latour-Maubourg's command were formed into a "sacred squadron" to defend the emperor.

The next morning Napoleon and his Imperial Guard advanced another twenty miles through falling snowflakes as far as the forest-surrounded village of Losnitsa, where they could hear the distant growl of Marshal Victor's cannon, fighting one more rearguard action against Wittgenstein's inexorably advancing forces, barely twenty miles to the north. The French emperor was hoping to get his first fighting men across the Berezina by the twenty-fifth—his intention being to drive south along the right bank to deal with Chichagov's army, to free the bridge, and then to march on to Minsk. But the ominous thunder from the north must have made him realize that this would now be difficult to achieve.

It was once again Kutuzov who—this time inadvertently—came to the rescue of Napoleon's half-trapped forces. On November 16 he had written to Wittgenstein to say that Chichagov's projected capture of Minsk would probably force Napoleon to leave the Orsha–Borissov road and to head northward for Senno, from where he could be expected to move eastward toward Vilna. Afraid that he might miss Napoleon if such was the French emperor's intention, Wittgenstein halted his southward march and had his men mark time for three days (November 18–20). Not until the twenty-first did he venture to move his vanguard beyond Lake Dolgoye, and not until the twenty-fifth did the bulk of his forces reach Kolopenitchi, which was a mere twenty-five miles from the point finally chosen for the Grande Armée's crossing of the Berezina. But for those four or five wasted days—a real gift for the French—it is fair to say that Napoleon would never have made it across the Berezina with the tattered remnants of his army.

On November 22 Kutuzov made another gift to the French—again inadvertently. He sent Chichagov instructions to watch his southern flank. The admiral was urged to have his partisan scouts keep a sharp lookout for French movements toward the south along the eastern bank of the Berezina, aimed at crossing the river and bypassing Minsk.

The next day it was Wittgenstein's turn to sow confusion as to Napoleon's real intentions, in a dispatch to Chichagov in which he aired his own surmise: that Napoleon, though ostensibly headed for Borissov, was going to head southward in the direction of Bobruisk. The admiral was impressed by the concordance of these two opinions, emanating from generals (one of them now commander in chief) who were considerably better versed in ground operations than he was. Victor, in his letter to Bronikowski, had indicated that Napoleon intended to cross the Berezina and then to head for Minsk; and if such was his intention, as Chichagov assumed, he was far more likely to try to cross the river in the region of Berezino, seventeen miles south of Borissov, where there was a solid bridge and a good road, than to try to find a fordable passage to the north, where he and his men risked bogging down in the swamps along the river's western bank. He accordingly discounted the first reports he received of French activity north of Borissov, deciding that Napoleon was resorting to a clever feint to conceal his real intentions. Oudinot's exploit in routing a Russian advance-guard division meant that the Grande Armée was still a force to be reckoned with. There was only one way to keep it from crossing the Berezina—by concentrating virtually all of his Danubian army opposite the chosen point of passage. That point, Chichagov decided, was Berezino; and so, without hesitating any longer and again disregarding the protests of his dumbfounded generals, the impulsive admiral set out southward during the bitterly cold evening of the twenty-fourth with three of his divisions. Another French émigré general, Comte de Langeron—whom Chichagov could not abide (the feeling was fully reciprocated)—was left with his division to cover the riverside area immediately opposite Borissov, while a number of loosely linked detachments, scattered as far as Zembin under the command of General Chaplits, continued to observe French movements to the north.

Early on the morning of November 25 Oudinot rode out to the village of Losnitsa (ten miles from Borissov) to discuss the problems of the crossing with Napoleon. His cavalrymen had been ranging up and down the eastern bank of the Berezina looking for possible fords, and a strong force of cuirassiers, accompanied by a few hundred infantrymen and rounded-up stragglers, had been sent a mile or two south of Borissov to make a show of assembling bridge-building logs and planks in order to fool the Russians into believing that this was where a crossing was going to be attempted. (When their presence was reported to Chichagov, he assumed that these men were part of Napoleon's vanguard and that the rest of his army would soon follow.)

Borissov, which Napoleon reached around five in the afternoon—by which time it was almost dark—was crammed with thousands of stragglers and a huge cluster of carriages. Reaching the waterside, the emperor walked out onto the wooden bridge to see for himself how much of it had been destroyed and how strong the Russian forces seemed to be on the opposite bank, to judge by their bivouac fires. The river here, reflecting the last glimmers of sunset, looked like a half-frozen lake, and since it was three times wider than it was farther north, Napoleon decided that he had been well inspired to choose another, less well defended crossing-point.

After night had fallen he proceeded northward for a distance of five miles to the hamlet of Novy Borissov, where he installed himself in a large farm-house on a property belonging to Prince Radziwill. The chances of being able to get across the river—a good 150 yards at the selected point—seemed to have dimmed during the course of this day. Deprived of the boats that had been burned at Orsha, Eblé's *pontonniers* had been entrusted with the task of con-structing three makeshift bridges. Putting together solid trestles with the few tools and nails available proved an arduous job, even though the black-smiths had been working nonstop to hammer out more nails and clamps on their two portable forges. Finally, for lack of nails and time to assemble logs and planks, they had to limit themselves to the construction of just two bridges —one destined for infantry and pedestrians, the other for carriages, wagons, and artillery.

At five the next morning (November 26) Napoleon climbed onto a horse and rode five miles farther north to the chosen crossing-point, between the villages of Studyenka and Vesselovo. Covered by forty artillery pieces, which had been lined up along the crest of the embankment on the eastern side, Eblé's *ponton-niers,* many of them up to their shoulders in freezing water, were valiantly struggling to put together their two trestle-bridges. Though the river's turgid water was fortunately sluggish, the slimy bottom offered a precarious foothold to the shivering men, who had to hold on to one another and to keep warding off slabs of floating ice, which threatened to push them and their shaky handi-work downstream.

The ground on the farther bank was soggy marshland, which had partly frozen over during the preceding night. Some 500 yards beyond, there was a line of woods, from which a Russian artillery captain had brought out a battery of four guns, intending to bombard one of the bridges as soon as it was halfway across the river. But his gunners had hardly fired their first round when they were silenced by a formidable salvo from the forty French guns on the escarp-ment.

Napoleon, who had reckoned from the start that he would meet stiff opposi-tion from the other side, now ordered a squadron of Polish lancers from Corbineau's brigade to ford the river. Their bruised and occasionally bloodied horses had to weave their way past knife-edge slabs of ice and to swim across passages where the frigid water was more than five feet deep. They were followed by a squadron of French chasseurs, each horse carrying a musket-wielding tirailleur behind the rider, and by three rafts, which were used to paddle over infantrymen from Dombrowski's Polish division.

In trying to follow what was happening on the eastern bank, General Chaplits's Russians were handicapped by the fact that it was higher than their own, so that they could not see over the crest of the embankment, where Eblé's men had been assembling their bridge-building stocks of wood. Already on the twenty-fourth Chaplits's attention had been drawn to the unusual number of French officers who kept riding down to the river's edge, supposedly to water their horses. But the next day he was ordered by his immediate superior, Langeron, to move his men southward in order to take up the positions his division had been occupying opposite Borissov. When Chaplits protested this order and asked to be allowed to delay its execution, he was treated to a reprimand and ordered to carry out the movement without delay.

On the morning of the twenty-fifth Admiral Chichagov reached the town of Berezino—only to discover that there was no trace of Napoleon's army on the opposite bank! Already worn out by a thirty-mile trek over "execrable" roads, the dog-tired Russian regiments had to face about and start marching back, leaving behind a long trail of stragglers, many of whom were put to work pushing and pulling artillery pieces mired in bogs of snowy mud.

That evening, while Chichagov's frustrated infantrymen were backtracking toward Borissov, General Chaplits, some ten miles farther north, spotted numerous bivouac fires and a sizable concentration of enemy troops on the eastern bank. He ordered one of his colonels to lead 300 Cossacks across the Berezina and to bring back several French prisoners and the village bailiff at Vesselovo, which they did. He thus learned, at around one o'clock in the afternoon of the twenty-sixth, that the French had been preparing two bridges for a crossing that was to take place sometime during that day.

Had Chaplits been more courageous, he would have risked defying Langeron's two orders in order to deal with the threat that was building up before his eyes. Instead, he withdrew most of his troops precisely at the moment when Napoleon's men began to cross the river. When Rapp and Oudinot broke into the little hut where the emperor once again was pondering his maps, he scoffed at the idea that a long column of Russians was clearly visible in the distance, headed south. But after Ney and Murat had come in to confirm the news, he came out, lifted his spyglass, and sure enough, there were Chaplits's men moving off toward the left. Napoleon could hardly believe his good luck. "Gentlemen," he announced, "I have fooled the Admiral!"

Shortly after one in the afternoon the first bridge was finished. Shouting *"Vive l'empereur!"* Oudinot's cavalrymen rode across the uneven planks, followed by the French infantrymen of General Legrand's division, the Swiss and Croatians of General Merle's division, and two light-artillery pieces—all that could be transported across this uneven, rickety structure, primarily destined for pedestrians. Three hours later the second bridge was completed, and the four-horse teams began hauling the 40 cannon and the more than 100 artillery caissons of Oudinot's Second Corps to the other side. They were followed by some of the cannon of the Imperial Guard and the remaining guns of most of the other corps, lined up in the woods in a long column comprising close to 250 artillery pieces in all.

That evening the snow began to fall in thick flakes—another boon to the French, since it reduced visibility. Around eight the second bridge broke down under the lumbering of heavy cannon and artillery caissons. Once again Eblé's heroic *pontonniers* had to lower themselves into the frigid and now dark water, and struggle to wedge new trestles into position, covering them with logs and planks in the hope that they would withstand the more or less vertical weight of heavy wheels and the horizontal pressure of slabs of ice, continuing to float downstream. Twice more during this same night—at two and again at six (November 27)—several trestles collapsed with the planks attached to them, and the bridge-builders, who had been warming themselves and their dripping clothes by the campfires, had to wade out again into the freezing water to repair the damage so that the movement of the all-important artillery pieces and caissons could continue.

At dawn the remnants of Ney's Third Corps were ordered across to help Oudinot's soldiers. Heinrich von Brandt, who had rejoined his fellow Poles in General Claparède's division, marveled at the flaming redness of the beard which now covered the lower part of Marshal Ney's squarish, almost "impertinent" face. Equally spectacular was the "wonderfully old-fashioned hairdo" of Louis de Narbonne, who had lost none of his imperturbable urbanity in the midst of the recent disasters. Napoleon, near whom they were standing on the embankment overlooking the river, was dressed in a fur coat, which he had left deliberately unbuttoned so that his familiar black boots and white breeches were clearly visible to the soldiers advancing toward the bridges. Murat had stuck a heron plume into his fur-lined headgear, and as though to prove to everyone that he was not afraid of the cold, even though it had noticeably darkened the scar wound on his chin, he ostentatiously sported his short velvet pelisse, which, barely covering his waist, enabled him to display the splendidly curved saber hanging from his belt by a gold-threaded *cordon d'Egypte*. But the hero of the hour was the already gray-haired General Eblé, who courteously doffed his hat each time he came up to report to the emperor on how his courageous bridge-builders were faring.

Access to the two bridges was controlled by a semicircle of *gendarmes d'élite,* mounted on emaciated nags. Their still tidy uniforms contrasted sharply with those of the armed rabble that was waiting to cross the river, among which many curiously club-footed creatures could be seen who had wound woolen scarfs, strips of sheepskin, or animal furs around their threadbare shoes to keep the snow from penetrating through the holed leather. Discipline at first was strict, and the order having been given to let no unarmed person cross, Heinrich von Brandt had some difficulty obtaining permission to follow his regiment as one of its wounded officers. But later, after Junot's Westphalians, Poniatowski's Poles, the regiments of the Young Guard and the Old Guard, and Napoleon himself had crossed to the other side, the gendarmes and bridge-builders had to use force to hold back the surging multitude of gaunt, grisly, hollow-cheeked, dirty-bearded, and lice-ridden men who tried to push their way onto the bridges, only to be shoved back, trodden underfoot, or swept by the human pressure into the icy river water.

Paradoxical as it may sound, it was the cold—so numbing to Eblé's toiling bridge-builders (some of whom drowned, while others finally died of exposure) —that saved what remained of Napoleon's army during these two critical days of November 26–27. But for the frozen crust that had formed over the 500 yards of marshlands on the western side, not a single French artillery piece, caisson, or carriage could have been hauled to the safety of the nearest woodlands. As it was, fascines of faggots had continually to be laid down over the veinlike network of tracks, which gradually branched out in all directions as postilions and drivers broke new ground to avoid the quagmires into which a few unlucky caissons had finally bogged down for good.

Perhaps the most extraordinary feature of the crossing was the eerie calm that descended on the eastern bank during the evening and night of the twenty-seventh, even though hundreds of jumbled carts and carriages still remained to be trundled across the stouter left-hand bridge. The sound of approaching cannon fire seemed to have no effect on the thousands of soldiers and sutlers who were content to remain where they were, huddled in the woods around campfires that had been left behind by others. After the few thousand survivors of Prince Eugène's Fourth and Davout's First corps had crossed to the other side, the bridges remained virtually unused, so that anyone who wished to could get across. Their senses numbed by prolonged cold and hunger, the dropouts and camp followers had lost all sense of danger and no longer had the will to drag themselves from the life-giving warmth of their bivouac fires to the shelterless cold of the other bank.

While General Chaplits's remaining infantrymen, cavalrymen, and outnumbered cannoneers skirmished with Oudinot's troopers during the eight daylight hours of this crucial November 27, Admiral Chichagov was obliged to give his worn-out men a rest some distance to the south after the fruitless sixty-mile march they had made to Berezino and back. An attempt to ferry a few Russians across the river for a frontal assault on Borissov was beaten back by the infantrymen of one of Victor's divisions, commanded by General Parthouneaux, who had been ordered to hold the town for as long as possible— against Platov's Cossacks, who now began to appear (several days too late) on the main road from Orsha, and the advance guard of Wittgenstein's army.

On the early morning of the twenty-seventh Wittgenstein was belatedly informed of exactly where Napoleon's forces were crossing the Berezina. One of his divisions managed to advance through wooded paths north of Borissov until they were near the eastern bank of the Berezina. Finding himself surrounded, the commander of Victor's rearguard, General Parthouneaux, now found his progress impeded by a horde of Grande Armée stragglers, fleeing southward from the Russians. Soon realizing that he was surrounded, Parthouneaux ordered his battalion commanders to try to sneak past the Russian campfires and to reach Studyenka, but only one battalion, which had accidentally followed a different route through the woods closer to the river, finally rejoined the rest of Victor's corps, which now straddled the Berezina. The rest of Parthouneaux's division, now reduced to several thousand tracked and harassed soldiers, were finally forced to surrender during the morning of November 28.

In the hope of rescuing Parthouneaux's missing division, Napoleon, during another almost sleepless night (November 27–28) held up his advance and had one of Victor's divisions, which had moved over to the western bank, recross the river to join the rest of the marshal's forces around Studyenka.

Having occupied Borissov (during the evening of the twenty-seventh), Wittgenstein's soldiers were able to repair the long, broken bridge and to establish contact with Chichagov's army on the western bank of the Berezina. Kutuzov's forces, which had been slowly lumbering up from the southeast, could now cross the river and join Chichagov's divisions in harrying the retreating French.

At seven o'clock on the morning of the twenty-eighth the vanguard of Admiral Chichagov's 30,000 men began attacking the French, Poles, Swiss, and Croatians who, under Oudinot's command, were guarding the wooded hills and the escape route to Zembin. In the course of the cannonade Oudinot was wounded—for the second time in this year of 1812. Ney was immediately ordered to take command of the Second Corps in addition to his own. Simultaneously Wittgenstein's Russians began bombarding the bridgehead held by Victor's two remaining divisions between Studyenka and Vesselovo. Panic seized the thousands of stragglers who had so carelessly spent the night huddled around campfires on the eastern bank, and who now began to stampede across the two flimsy trestle-bridges, along with a number of carriages and wagons. There was wild shouting and scuffling, as the terrified rabble sought to cross, the weaker and less ruthless often being pushed into the freezing river. Callous drivers drove their carriages or carts over the bodies of the fallen, while those who had missed their footing and who struggled to clamber back onto the crowded planks were pushed into the water. At the height of the uproar the trestles gave way again and part of the vehicle bridge collapsed, plunging scores of horses and drivers into the glacial river. It was minutes before the lawless horde ceased its blind shoving. Then, flooding back to the eastern bank, it took the other bridge by assault, sweeping along the venerable, white-bearded Marshal Lefebvre, who had planted himself near the access and sought to control this impetuous human flood. "Around the bridges there rose hill-like mounds of men and horses trampled underfoot or killed by enemy fire," noted Faber du Faur, one of the 150 survivors of the 25th (Württemberg) Division. "To gain the bridges one had to pass over their bodies while fighting; the current and the ice-slabs propelled by the river carried them away from time to time, but it was only to make room for others."

To the west Ney's soldiers held off Chichagov's men for several hours, and a French cuirassier regiment even managed to decimate a Russian infantry column and take 1,500 prisoners. But two of the three division generals in the Polish corps—Dombrowski and Zayonczek—had to be carried wounded from the field, as were Oudinot and one of his own generals. On the eastern side

Wittgenstein's first assault was likewise repulsed by Marshal Victor's soldiers, even though the Russians had been reinforced by a few units from Kutuzov's army led by Yermolov, and though the French, Poles, and Germans composing the Ninth Corps were outnumbered five to one.

With the onset of night the cannonade and musket fire died down, and Victor's soldiers could at last resume their retreat over the body-strewn bridges. Wittgenstein's Russians made little effort to impede this nighttime movement, preferring to remain comfortably grouped around their warm campfires rather than to be exposed to the harsh, snow-driving wind. The next morning, after the last artillery pieces had lumbered their way over the heaps of corpses, there was a final crazy surge of terrified humanity across the bridges, again jam-packed, as General Eblé's *pontonniers* prepared to burn what they had so heroically put together. Some sought to cross the river on the passing ice slabs, others rushed desperately through the rising flames, hoping to make it to the other side by the sheer force of momentum, only to drop with a smoking splash into the chilling water. "Burned and frozen at the same time, they perished by two contrary torments," as Philippe de Ségur noted.

Ten thousand stragglers, sutlers, and assorted camp followers, some of them with little children and many of them too weak to move, were thus left behind amid the hideous wreckage of burned or shattered carts and wagons (many of them still loaded with Moscow plunder). Thirteen generals had been wounded during the desperate fighting of the previous day, an entire division had been lost, but 40,000 men and a handful of women had made it across the two flimsy bridges with more than 200 artillery pieces. Like a vessel that had lost two masts but was still afloat, the Grande Armée had narrowly escaped total shipwreck once again. But its tribulations were still very far from over.

CHAPTER 25

THE FLIGHT

IN PETERSBURG a dramatic change of mood had set in since the somber days of late September, when so many precious possessions had been packed up and transported out of the capital in expectation of a French assault, and when in all government offices, as the witty Joseph de Maistre put it, enough administrative paper had been burned "to roast all the livestock of the Ukraine." The welcome delivery in early October of 50,000 English muskets, followed by generous quantities of gold, had given the subjects of King George III a popularity they had not enjoyed in years. But it was not until the end of the month that the public began to realize that the tide had really turned in the fortunes of this war. On October 26—the dowager empress's birthday —a special Te Deum service was held in the chapel of the Winter Palace to celebrate General Wittgenstein's capture of the fortified city of Polotsk. The next day the cannon of the Peter and Paul Fortress boomed again—this time to announce the Russian "victory" at Vinkova and the recapture of Moscow. The city was festively illuminated and there was wild enthusiasm in the streets, as in the salons.

There was one person, however, who refused to be carried away on this surging tide of jubilation, even though he saw fit to award Bennigsen—hailed as the "victor" of the battle of Vinkova—the diamond-studded decoration of the Order of Saint Andrew and 100,000 paper rubles (twice what Barclay de Tolly had received for his performance at Borodino). Tsar Alexander was still not satisfied by Kutuzov's explanations as to why he had abandoned Moscow without a fight, and he was none too happy to be informed by his returning friend and aide-de-camp Pyotr Volkonsky that the generalissimo, disregarding his instructions, had consented to receive Napoleon's emissary, Lauriston.

On October 20 his aide-de-camp Major Ludwig von Wolzogen, who had left the Tarutino camp shortly after Barclay de Tolly, and returned to Petersburg, was at last able to give Alexander a detailed account of everything that had happened at army headquarters from the moment he himself had left it the previous July to go to Moscow. During Wolzogen's description of the battle of Borodino the tsar broke in angrily, exclaiming, "About all these details the *scoundrel* who at present leads my army has written nothing to me, but rather reports mere lies!" After Wolzogen had finished explaining the many services Barclay had rendered to the army and to the nation as a whole, the Russian sovereign made this comment: "You know that Barclay is somewhat ponderous and that sometimes he does not understand me properly; but I still share the conviction that he is an honorable and capable man, who devoted all of his energies to me and to the Nation, and that as a man he towers above the depraved Kutuzov." But having said this, Alexander went on to explain that he would have to leave Barclay for a little while longer in his present "exile . . . since even the most absolute monarch is obliged to subordinate his personal sentiments to imperative circumstances."

It is one of the many ironies of the 1812 campaign that the general who could most surely have brought about the annihilation of Napoleon's dwindling forces was allowed to languish in retirement, while others—Kutuzov by his slothful inertia, Chichagov by his excessive impulsiveness and lack of experience, Wittgenstein by his indolence and lack of imagination—bungled the job and let the French emperor slip through their fingers. Afraid to brave the virulent animosity with which Barclay was regarded by a militarily ignorant public, Alexander refrained from replying to the letter sent to him by his former minister of war, requesting that he be allowed to return to the capital to convalesce. Barclay had no choice but to spend these crucial weeks at his aide-de-camp Zakrevsky's country house in the province of Vladimir, where with his usual diligence and care he composed a masterly analysis of the campaign. This "tableau," as he called it, was dispatched on November 21 along with a personal letter to the tsar, who this time sent Barclay a short, affectionate note, while carefully refraining from specifically inviting him to come to Petersburg to see him.

Wolzogen's intercession on Barclay's behalf, though it failed to end the exile of the former minister of war, did at least have one salutary consequence. If there was one general in the Russian army whom the tsar disliked even more than Kutuzov, it was Bennigsen—the man who had strangled his father (Emperor Paul I) with a scarf during the palace revolution of March 1801. Now made considerably wiser by Wolzogen about Bennigsen's responsibility for the poor troop alignments and the consequent bloodbath at Borodino, Alexander wrote to Kutuzov on October 21 to say that he had heard that the generalissimo had grounds for being dissatisfied with the behavior of his chief of staff; if such was really the case, then he should dismiss him and have him sent to Vladimir (east of Moscow). Lethargic as ever, Kutuzov let almost a month go by before finally acting. But on discovering that Bennigsen had been criticizing him behind his back to Arakcheyev and wanted to have Colonel Toll dismissed from his staff job, he issued a blunt four-line order informing Bennigsen that because of his "attacks of illness" he was to leave his headquarters and proceed to Kaluga, there to await a new assignment from His Imperial Majesty. The outmaneuvered Hanoverian had no choice but to pack his bags and to bid good-bye to his friend Sir Robert Wilson, who was probably one of the very few officers at Kutuzov's headquarters who were genuinely sorry to see him leave.

Long before this the first snows had begun to fall in Petersburg, the fur-lined sleighs had reappeared, and the two pontoon bridges across the Neva had been dismantled as slabs of ice began to form. The bright, white-frosted capital was beginning to display some of its usual wintry jollity, but its better-informed sovereign was still anything but pleased by the way the war was going. To Kutuzov he dispatched another stiff reprimand on November 11, berating the generalissimo's "incomprehensible inactivity after the happily concluded battle near Tarutino," and his subsequent failure to trap Davout's, Ney's, and Prince Eugène's army corps at Vyazma. Alexander by this time had lost all faith in his dawdling commander in chief, but having personally appointed him to this supreme position and made him a prince and field marshal, he could not now get rid of him without unleashing another storm of bewildered discontent.

Two weeks later another thanksgiving service was held at the Holy Mother of Kazan Cathedral, again attended by the imperial family. Also present was the dashing, dark-eyed aide-de-camp Alexander Chernyshov, suddenly promoted from colonel to the rank of major general for having rescued Wintzingerode and his young aide-de-camp Lev Naryshkin as they were being escorted toward Vilna by two French gendarmes. A number of captured trophies—including Davout's marshal's baton—were on display, as tangible evidence of the French debacle at Krasnoye.

Before long the Russian commanders in the field again demonstrated their tactical incompetence. Once it was known that the French were crossing the Berezina north of Borissov, it should have been obvious that Napoleon intended to head for Vilna via Zembin rather than Minsk. Beyond Zembin the road leading northwest was carried by a series of wooden bridges, some of them half a mile long, over an extensive marshland area, which was not yet frozen solid. The planks were made of highly inflammable pinewood, and, as Caulaincourt noted, "six Cossacks with burning torches" would have sufficed to cut this escape route, had they been more intelligently led.

After passing this dangerously marshy *défilé* on November 29, Napoleon began to breathe more freely, confident that from now on he had little to fear from Chichagov's pursuing Russians. The next night—the first of the wintry month of December—was spent at Staiki, promptly renamed Miserovo by the French officers of the imperial staff, who had to pack themselves into stifling huts and hay-filled barns to protect themselves from the bitter cold. The problem for virtually everyone was how to keep moving on a more or less empty stomach. Unless one was near a roadside campfire, the slightest pause, particularly at night—and the nights now lasted fifteen hours—was lethal, engendering a soporific sense of relief. Numbed by the persistent cold, many soldiers were seized by a kind of dizziness, which made them lose all sense of direction as they swayed and staggered forward like drunkards. As the army's chief surgeon, Dominique Larrey, later wrote, "Death was preceded by a paleness of the face, by a kind of idiocy, by a difficulty of speaking, and a feebleness of eyesight." The cold, no respecter of persons, thus leveled all ranks to the same dazed, half-dozing, suffering condition.

To keep from being separated from the rest, as had happened during the march to Krasnoye, Ney and the survivors of the Third and Second corps, after igniting several of the marshland bridges they had crossed to delay the advance of the pursuing Russians, marched almost nonstop for two days and three nights, sustaining themselves on the foodstuffs they forcibly tore or stole from the stragglers they overtook. They finally caught up with the bearded veterans of the Old Guard, still recognizable by their busbies but otherwise looking as shaggy, unkempt, and disorderly as the rest.

At Molodechno, which he reached on the evening of December 3 after coming out onto the main Minsk–Vilna highroad, Napoleon was able to spend a relatively comfortable though largely sleepless night in the country house belonging to the pro-Russian Lithuanian nobleman Count Mihal Oginski. Here twenty carriages, filled with mail from Paris, were waiting to be emptied, having been stopped by the French relay-post authorities after they had received news that Minsk had fallen to the Russians. Napoleon had originally hoped to make this little town an outpost for the defense of Lithuania. But lack of food and the increasingly haggard aspect of his frozen-cheeked, frozen-fingered, frozen-footed soldiers made him realize that this was hopeless and that they would have to stumble on to Vilna, with its plentiful supplies of food and munitions.

More than three weeks had gone by without official word about his activities or whereabouts, and the Parisians, Napoleon realized, must by now be growing anxious. Sooner or later news of the Grande Armée's vicissitudes would begin to filter out. It would therefore be better if he himself broke the bitter truth —by issuing another Bulletin de l'Armée, describing his soldiers' tribulations, but also their triumphs in the field.

Little did Napoleon guess, as he was putting the final touches to this 29th Bulletin (destined to be so famous), just how precarious his position really was. That same night several thousand Cossacks, egged on by the reward which a mortified Admiral Chichagov was offering for the capture of "the author of Europe's ills"—"He is short and squat of build, has a pale complexion, a short, thick neck, a strong head and black hair," the description went—tried to cross a frozen river and a marshland pond less than a mile away. But their attempt to take Oginski's country house by storm was thwarted by the brittle thinness of the ice crust, and several hundred of them perished while trying to cross the insufficiently frozen pond. The next night it was frozen solid.

And so the desperate march continued—through blinding snow to the little town of Bienitsa, in whose well-furnished castle the fortunate members of the imperial headquarters staff were able to play billiards and to feast off beans, potatoes, porridge, and that unheard-of luxury, beef! There was a promise of more to come in Vilna, now only sixty miles away. But the next day (December 5) the temperature dropped to 20 degrees below zero, and in the evening, at another country house in the famous bear-taming town of Smorgonye, all but a handful of previously initiated souls were dumbfounded by the disheartening news that the emperor was leaving them.

The secret had been well kept by Napoleon's closest aides, and particularly by Caulaincourt, who had to make preparations in advance to make sure that the emperor's carriage would be properly protected by an escort and readily equipped with teams of fresh horses at the relay stations ahead. (So commonplace had thievery become in an army where there was now little trace of discipline that the grand equerry had been forced, since Smolensk, to keep a special sack of coal locked up in one of his wagons in order to be able to supply his blacksmiths, who often had to work far into the night and with gloves on their half-frozen hands, hammering out new cramponed horseshoes.) At seven-thirty in the evening, when his marshals were summoned to be told the news, not one of them had received any advance warning. Napoleon explained that it was imperative that he return as quickly as possible to Paris in order to recruit a new army of 300,000 men and to deal with any restive movements and intrigues that might be brewing against him in Berlin or Vienna. Count Louis de Narbonne, whose imperturbable good humor he had gone out of his way to extol in the 29th Bulletin, was being sent to Berlin to placate King Frederick William III and his Prussian ministers. He was sending General Lauriston to Warsaw to help the Poles organize the defense of their capital against a possible Russian assault, and he was sending Rapp back to Danzig to hold that vital Baltic supply base and bastion. His foreign minister, the duke of Bassano, was to remain in Vilna, which it was to be the marshals' task to defend with the help of the reinforcements that had just reached it. Marshal Macdonald's Tenth Corps would continue to hold the line of the lower Niemen, guarding the approaches to Koenigsberg, while Schwarzenberg, whose Austrian contingent was due to be reinforced, covered the Grand Duchy of Warsaw with General Reynier's Saxon corps. His hope was that the Russians, already suffering from the cold as much as his own soldiers, would not be able to cross the Vistula before he was back at the head of a new and formidable army in the spring.

No one present dared to contest the wisdom of his returning forthwith to Paris. But Davout, looking more than usually surly, was dismayed to learn that he would have to take orders from the king of Naples, who was to command the Grande Armée in the emperor's absence. Berthier was even more upset, but for an entirely different reason: he could not bear the idea of being separated from the man he had served in every campaign for the past dozen years. He even broke down and wept when everyone else had left, in a pathetic plea to be allowed to accompany Napoleon back to Paris. This spectacle sickened Napoleon, who had often had to upbraid his chief of staff for having so little taste for war and such an uncontrollable passion for his beautiful mistress, Giuseppina Visconti. Now he told him bluntly that if he was unwilling to remain at his post, he would have him exiled from Paris for the rest of his days.

At ten that night the emperor's *dormeuse*—the mattress-equipped "sleeper" in which he and Caulaincourt could stretch out as though on a large couch —left Smorgonye, pulled by six small Lithuanian horses and guided by the

Mameluke, Roustam. They were escorted by a strong cavalry detachment, several outriders, and Count Dunin Wonsowicz, a colonel in the honor guard who had been chosen because he spoke fluent German as well as French and Polish. Behind them in another carriage were Duroc and General Mouton, and in a third Napoleon's valet and several footmen were seated next to General Lefebvre-Desnouettes, commander of the Imperial Guard chasseurs responsible for the emperor's protection.

So intense was the cold (more than 25 degrees below zero) that when they reached Oszmiana after a two-hour drive they found that most of the soldiers in the town had abandoned their bivouac fires and taken refuge indoors. A force of Cossack partisans (probably commanded by Colonel Seslavin) had just raided the town, killing and abducting a few sentinels and setting fire to several foodstuff stores before being driven off by the musketry of soldiers firing from open windows. These soldiers, for the most part German and Italian, were part of a recently arrived division on which Napoleon was greatly counting for the defense of Vilna. Its commander, fearing a Cossack ambush, sought to dissuade the emperor from continuing, but Napoleon (quite rightly, as it turned out) decided that there would be less risk if they traveled by night rather than waited for the dawn, when the Cossacks could spot them more easily. He then handed his two pistols to General Lefebvre-Desnouettes, saying, "In the event of certain danger, kill us rather than let us be captured."

With that they set off at a trot along the Minsk–Vilna highroad, trusting to the night and Napoleon's legendary star. The sky fortunately was clouded, reducing visibility for the Cossacks, whose campfires could be seen in the distance. As Napoleon had reckoned, they were in no mood to leave the warmth of their campfires during such a freezing night. By the time the emperor's berlin and the accompanying carriages reached the first relay post, only thirty-six of the one hundred escorting Polish lancers were left. The rest had been felled by the cold. At the following relay post the Poles were replaced by the crimson-clad horsemen of the Royal Neapolitan Guard, whom Murat had had the fatuity of summoning from Naples. Less well prepared than the Poles for such frigid temperatures, they had trouble keeping their improperly shod horses from slipping and falling on the road's icy snow, and by the time they reached the next relay post there were only fifteen riders left.

In the little town of Miedniki, fifteen miles from Vilna, the party was met by Foreign Minister Maret, who had been confidentially informed of Napoleon's arrival and had driven out in his carriage to meet him. The Lithuanian capital had been abuzz with alarming rumors ever since the fall of Polotsk and the Russian capture of Minsk, which had brought many panic-spreading refugees to the city. In an effort to counter the shattering effect of these successive reverses on local morale, Maret and his local French deputy, Baron Louis Bignon, had decided to stage a ball, as though everything were normal and life proceeding as usual. Caulaincourt, who drove into Vilna in Maret's calèche, was struck by the weird contrast between persons dancing unconcernedly in elegant ballroom attire and the thousands of soldiers who, not far away, were freezing to death. Nothing had been prepared for Napoleon's

incognito arrival, and Caulaincourt had great difficulty collecting ten cavalrymen to escort the emperor's carriage on its next lap. He managed, however,
to buy a few pairs of badly needed fur-lined boots, without which the other
members of the imperial party would probably never have made it to Paris.

From Miedniki Napoleon had meanwhile moved on with Maret to a Vilna
suburb, where they lunched. His foreign minister was apprised of the gravity
of the situation and told to be ready to have all the representatives of the
diplomatic corps sent back to Warsaw. Then, after Caulaincourt had rejoined
the party, the emperor said good-bye to Maret and continued on his way.
Wonsowicz, to keep from falling behind like the other horsemen, now took his
place on the front seat next to the coachman. Never, Caulaincourt later wrote,
had he suffered so much from the frost as during the sixty-mile journey from
Vilna to Kovno, on the Niemen. It was so cold inside the normally snug
dormeuse that their breath froze on their lips, forming tiny icicles under nose,
eyebrows, and eyelashes, while the closed carriage's cloth-lined ceiling became
white and crisp from congealed vapor.

After crossing the Niemen bridge at Kovno, they had to get out and help
push the berlin up an icy hill, which was so steep that several times the carriage
seemed about to slip backward out of control over the clifflike ledge. At
Marianpole a helpful Polish relay-post manager told Caulaincourt that the
roads, though snow-covered, were open and that they could obtain teams of
horses all the way to Warsaw.

At the next relay post they came upon a small, ramshackle coupé, which
a local lord had mounted on runners, like a sleigh. Wonsowicz and Caulaincourt had some difficulty persuading the owner to part with it, but when he
learned that it was for Napoleon, he asked to be introduced to the French
emperor and offered it to him for nothing. This rickety conveyance—which
vaguely resembled a square cage, with four large windowpanes encased in
peeling frames—was far less comfortable than the well-cushioned and
-equipped *dormeuse,* the faded red-lacquer doors being so warped that cold air
mixed with snow kept blowing in through the fissures. But the emperor was
pleased because it was far more rapid in running over the snow. They now
advanced at a pace which left Duroc and Mouton, in their unsteady calèche,
far, far behind.

For the next two days, as they traveled southwest toward Warsaw, Napoleon talked incessantly: about his plans for holding Vilna (provided that Murat
did nothing foolish) and his intention of "electrifying the Poles"; about his
Continental System and the marvels it had achieved in stimulating European
industry; about the insuperable difficulties he had encountered in trying to find
a hereditary monarch for a Poland forever torn by the jealous intrigues of its
leading families, the Czartoryskis, the Potockis, the Poniatowskis; about Tsar
Alexander, basically more intelligent than his generals and particularly more
so than "that old dowager of a Kutuzov," whose campaign was dismissed as
a model of ineptitude. And finally, recurring like a leitmotif, the supreme
self-justification, which was to be echoed and re-echoed later by thousands of
fanatical Bonapartists, dazzled by the tinsel glitter of this myth: "We are the

victims of climate. The good weather fooled me. If I had left [Moscow] fifteen days earlier, my army would be at Vitebsk. . . . All our disasters hinged on fifteen days and the inexecution of my orders concerning the levying of Polish Cossacks."

As they approached Warsaw, Napoleon insisted on climbing out of their drafty glass "cage." Floundering about in knee-deep snow, he visited the fortifications of Sierock and of the Praga suburb, on the eastern bank of the Vistula. He dismounted again after they had crossed the bridge linking the suburb to the capital, and walked most of the way to the Hôtel de l'Angleterre, where rooms had been reserved for him under the names of the duc de Vicence and his personal secretary, Monsieur de Rayneval. Although many passers-by stared at his green velvet pelisse with the golden brandenburg flourishes, the sable bonnet the emperor wore to protect his ears—for it was almost 20 degrees below zero—was pushed down so far over his forehead and eyes that it made "Monsieur de Rayneval" unrecognizable.

Normally, Napoleon should have put up at the residence of the French ambassador extraordinary—the Brühl Palace, now occupied by the archbishop of Malines. But the emperor was so displeased by his envoy's dismal performance that he preferred to spend his few hours in Warsaw in a dingy ground-floor room looking out onto an inner court, inadequately warmed by a hissing and spitting fire of excessively green wood.

After lunch had been ordered, Caulaincourt was dispatched to the Brühl Palace to fetch the French ambassador extraordinary. Napoleon lost no time making his displeasure felt when His Grandiloquent Grace was ushered into his presence. An acrimonious argument followed, while the ordered lunch cooled in an adjoining room. The emperor heaped reproaches on his ambassador for his failure to galvanize the Poles and to levy more than 80,000 new conscripts, and for dishonoring the name of France by making a public spectacle of his niggardliness in his desire to save money from his generous allowance. Far from being crushed by this avalanche of criticism, the glib prelate undertook to defend his record, even venturing to contest Napoleon's claim that vast numbers of "Polish Cossacks" could be raised to protect the winter quarters in which the new Polish recruits were to be housed.

After angrily bolting down a stone-cold lunch Napoleon was ready to receive Count Stanislaw Potocki, the urbane chairman of the Grand Duchy's Council of Ministers, and two of his colleagues, Thaddeus Mostowski, the minister of the interior, and Thaddeus Matuszewicz, the forceful minister of finance. News of the French retreat from Moscow had already begun to upset the inhabitants of Warsaw, and the scarcity of information thereafter had further increased the malaise in families worried about the fate of fathers, brothers, husbands, cousins who had so ardently volunteered for service in the Grande Armée. Even now the best informed—like Potocki and his ministerial colleagues—were far from imagining the magnitude of the disaster. While candidly admitting that his armies had suffered heavy losses, Napoleon claimed that he still had 150,000 fighting men in the field, and that in three months' time that figure would be doubled thanks to the levies being undertaken in France, where the arsenals were full, and so forth. He made light of the perils he had run, saying that repose was fit only for "do-nothing kings" and that he himself throve on fatigue. He deprecated the present fighting quality of Russian officers and soldiers, vastly inferior to those who had fought at Eylau and Friedland, and he stressed the fact that his forces had defeated them in every single battle, including that of the Berezina crossing.

The Polish ministers painted a bleak picture of the impoverished duchy, groaning under the burden of having to maintain an army of more than 80,000. Grudgingly Napoleon agreed to release several million more francs from various sources to help replenish the country's empty exchequer. He made it sound as though his resources were unlimited—provided that the Poles fulfilled their half of the bargain. His determination to "electrify the Poles," even though limited to an audience of three, seems to have been no vain boast—to judge, at any rate, from Anna Potocka's account of how this inspired harangue affected the chairman of the Council of Ministers. "The fascination which this extraordinary man exercised on all who listened to him was so powerful that my father-in-law, who had left us so depressed, returned full of hope."

At seven in the evening of December 11, Napoleon said good-bye to the Polish ministers and the archbishop of Malines in Warsaw. He climbed back into the coupé-sleigh with Caulaincourt, while Wonsowicz sat on the driver's bench up front next to the Mameluke, Roustam. Their next destination was Poznan. On the way they passed through the town of Lowicz, near which was Maria Walewska's estate. Napoleon had a sudden urge to see the tender, blue-eyed mistress who had borne him a son two years before, and Caulaincourt needed all his powers of persuasion to keep him from making this amorous detour—which would have been an affront to Marie-Louise, as well as to all the suffering survivors of the Grande Armée, and would have proved ruinous to his prestige if the news ever leaked out.

From Poznan, which they reached shortly before dawn on December 12, they sped on toward the fortress town of Glogau along the same road over which the imperial cavalcade had so proudly trotted six months before. The sandy earth was now invisible, the eyeball-grating dust of the summer replaced by the blinding glare of a faintly undulating sea of snow, amid whose swells half-buried farmhouses and white-capped woods seemed to ride like distant ships.

At Glogau, on the Oder, still occupied by a French-Saxon garrison, Napoleon and his grand equerry climbed into a carriage lent to them by the local commandant. But the deep snowdrifts of mountainous Silesia soon forced them to return to their drafty coupé-sleigh. Unable to sleep in this cramped, chilly "cage," Napoleon amused himself and Caulaincourt by imagining all the things that might happen to them if they were stopped at gunpoint by a party of French-detesting Prussians.

They suffered another breakdown at Bunzlau, and not until the wee hours of the morning of December 14 did they finally reach Dresden. No one was on hand to greet the duc de Vicence and his traveling companion, Monsieur de Rayneval, though the local French minister, who had received advance warning of the grand equerry's arrival, had had several rooms prepared for them at his residence. The Saxon coachman, who had rashly assured his passengers that he knew where he lived, spent an hour wandering aimlessly through the lifeless streets, and was rudely rebuffed when he pounded on the door of a house that still showed a gleam of candlelight in an upper window. Finally, thanks to a cooperative pedestrian, they found the French minister's house. Here, to make up for lost time, Napoleon began dictating letters: to Murat and Berthier in Vilna; to Foreign Minister Maret in Warsaw; for his father-in-law, Emperor Francis, in Vienna, who was asked to raise the Grande Armée's Austrian contingent to 60,000 men; for King Frederick William III in Berlin.

While Caulaincourt was dutifully taking down the emperor's exhortations and expostulations, Colonel Wonsowicz was dispatched to the royal castle to inform the king of Napoleon's arrival. Such a middle-of-the-night intrusion into the sedate, meticulously regulated life of the Saxon Court struck the somnolent sentinels as an unheard-of breach of etiquette, and it took a good half hour of arguing with the commander of the Guard and the on-duty aide-de-camp before Wonsowicz could persuade them to lead him upstairs to the sleeping monarch's bedroom. Woken up with a start, the sexagenarian sovereign had some trouble understanding that his suzerain and protector, the emperor Napoleon, was once again in Dresden. The royal horses being habitually stabled in the suburbs, the deferent Frederick Augustus decided that it would take too long to have them hitched to one of his carriages, so four porters were summoned to carry him to the French minister's residence in a sedan chair. Napoleon was by now fast asleep, so that he too had to be awakened, to entertain the visiting monarch in bed!

While the French emperor and his obsequious friend and ally were conversing tête-à-tête, the royal household was thrown into an unprecedented uproar by the disturbing news that His Majesty had disappeared in the middle of the night, after being pulled from his bed by a bearded stranger dressed in a tattered and distinctly un-Saxon uniform. The queen suffered a nervous fit, as aides-de-camp, court chamberlains, and pages were summoned and dispatched to various churches to see if by any chance the devout king might have decided to celebrate matins somewhere other than in the royal chapel. Not until the sedan-chair porters came back was the intense commotion finally appeased.

To replace the defective coupé, which had twice broken down, King Frederick Augustus lent Napoleon one of his own berlins, also mounted on runners for travel on the snow. It was stocked with food and bottles of wine from the castle cellars and escorted by two noncommissioned officers from the Royal Saxon Guard, who rode behind in a horse-drawn sleigh. The party now made such rapid progress that they overtook the outriders who had been sent ahead to order fresh teams of horses at the next relay station, reaching Leipzig before them. Here, during a three-hour stopover at the Hôtel de Prusse, Napoleon bought some newspapers and several "books of frivolous literature" (Wonsowicz's term for novels). He also had a long talk with the French consul, who, having been tipped off about the imperial incognito, quick-wittedly addressed him as *"mon général"* when answering his questions.

Beyond the town of Lützen (where the French emperor was destined to fight a major battle less than five months later) there was so little snow that one of the runners broke, and "Monsieur de Reyneval" and Caulaincourt had to leave King Frederick Augustus's elegant berlin to the care of their Saxon escort and climb into a relay-post calèche. This took them as far as Erfurt, where the local French minister, Saint-Agnan (who also happened to be Caulaincourt's brother-in-law), provided them with a landau equipped with mattress-and-cushions, in which Napoleon could stretch out and sleep.

At the next relay post, near Eisenach, in the heart of Lutheran Thuringia, the kind of unpleasant incident Caulaincourt had long been fearing occurred when the post's innkeeper, who seemed reluctant to provide them with fresh horses, got involved in a noisy altercation with the Mameluke, Roustam. Suspecting that this was part of a plot designed to hold them up and to have them seized by local "patriots," the grand equerry drew his sword; but it was the appearance of the local French commandant with a detachment of gendarmes which finally dispersed the overly curious and anything but friendly crowd.

It was with a distinct feeling of relief that they finally reached the Rhine, near Mainz—or rather Mayence, as the city was known to the French. The bridge of boats, over which Napoleon, Marie-Louise, and members of the imperial suite had driven with such grandiose solemnity in May, had been dismantled, and they had to cross on a ferry. Once across the river, Napoleon sent Wonsowicz to the governor's palace to fetch Marshal Kellermann. The crusty old soldier was giving a ball and he did not take at all kindly to the intrusion of this self-styled colonel in a shabby foreign uniform, whom he took to be some troublemaking imposter, out to spread false rumors—like the crackpot General Malet, fomentor of the abortive coup d'état of the previous October. Kellermann even ordered two gendarmes to escort Wonsowicz down to the relay post, and he had him released only after his own eyes had assured him that this was indeed no hoax, but the emperor Napoleon in person.

Having admitted candidly that much of his Moscow army had been lost in the campaign, Napoleon reassured the septuagenarian commandant, saying that he would soon have "800,000 bayonets" under his orders and that many of them would soon be marching eastward through the streets of Mainz and across the reconstructed bridge of boats in the spring. Caulaincourt later wrote that never had he seen the emperor in such radiant high spirits as at the moment when they found themselves again on French soil.

From now on there was no need to preserve his incognito, and at each relay post the presence of the emperor aroused the feverish enthusiasm of grooms and ostlers, as they hurried to unhitch the old and to hitch up fresh horses. At Château-Thierry, where they paused to dine, Napoleon climbed out of his green *chasseur-à-cheval* uniform (his usual campaign dress) and donned the blue-and-white uniform of the Imperial Guard's *grenadiers à pied,* which he normally wore in Paris. But at Meaux, after moving so fast that they left one of their two outriders behind them in the flying mud, the landau they had borrowed at Erfurt broke down, and they had to transfer to a humble post chaise. It was lent to them on credit, since Caulaincourt, like Napoleon and Wonsowicz, had by this time completely emptied his purse.

The single remaining outrider managed to make it to Paris just ahead of them, which was just as well. For when they finally rattled over the cobbles of the Place du Carrousel, in time to hear the third-quarter chime strike just before midnight, the Old Guard grenadier on duty would not have opened the grilled gate to let the mud-splattered post chaise pass if he had not been forewarned. The carriage was driven at a gallop through the Carrousel's diminutive Arch of Triumph, to the dismay of several guards, who knew that this was a privilege exclusively reserved for the emperor but who arrived too late to stop the outrage. When they finally drew up in front of the Tuileries Palace's main entrance, the sentinels took them for the bearers of urgent dispatches and let them by.

Exactly how Napoleon looked at this moment, Caulaincourt in his 145-page account of this extraordinary thirteen-day trip unfortunately did not say when he later came to record it. But his own appearance was so repellent that when the doorman at the end of the pillared gallery on the garden side came out in his nightclothes with a lamp and peered suspiciously at the tall stranger with the thick growth of uncouth beard and the outlandish fur-lined boots, he had to summon his wife to make sure that this really was the grand equerry.

It was now some time after midnight, on December 19. Napoleon was led by the overjoyed servants to his own and Marie-Louise's apartments. Caulaincourt, who had hardly slept a wink for the past fortnight, had to make one more trip—this time to the townhouse, just across the Seine, of the archchancellor, Cambacérès. The grand equerry's hollow-eyed and bearded appearance again caused surprise and consternation, followed by immense relief. For the emperor of the French a new day was beginning—typically enough in the middle of the night—with the news that he would be holding a formal *lever* at eleven in the morning. It was almost as though nothing of importance had really happened, notwithstanding the recent publication—in the December 16 number of the official *Moniteur*—of the 29th Bulletin de l'Armée, in which his wondering subjects had been informed of the sufferings of the Grande Armée, only to be reassured at the end: "His Majesty's health has never been better!"

CHAPTER 26

THE HECATOMB
OF VILNA

SOME 900 MILES to the east, the tattered army Napoleon had left behind continued to disintegrate under the combined effects of exhaustion, cold, hunger, and rampant indiscipline. The news that the emperor had abandoned them was greeted by some with apathy, by others with dismay. Inevitably, it had a profoundly demoralizing influence on officers as well as soldiers. As Raymond de Fezensac noted, "The opinion one had of the Emperor's genius gave confidence; . . . After his departure each did as he pleased, and the orders issued by the King of Naples only served to compromise his authority."

Murat began by setting a deplorable example during the 22-mile march from Smorgonye to Oszmiana, when the daytime temperature stubbornly refused to rise above 20 degrees of frost. He installed himself next to Berthier in the commander in chief's carriage and rode along in comfort, as Napoleon had done, while in front and behind soldiers with frozen faces, which their frozen hands could not even bring back to life by rubbing them with snow, kept tottering and falling by the snowy wayside.

That evening (December 6), when the Imperial Guard and headquarters staff reached Oszmiana, the still-smart soldiers of General Loison's recently arrived division were ordered out of all the houses they were occupying and told to find lodgings in neighboring villages, which, having been burned and pillaged, had ceased to exist. Dispatching the 10,000 men of this fresh division from Vilna, as the Dutch governor, General van Hogendorp, had done on instructions from Napoleon, was almost certainly a mistake. But Murat compounded this error by ordering them to bivouac around the town to "protect the army," rather than having them march straight back to Vilna. Several nights of exposure to the cold were enough to finish off two-thirds of the 10,000. Barely 3,000 made it back to Vilna still in fighting condition.

During the next day's six-hour march to Miedniki, fifteen miles farther on, the temperature dropped to 27 degrees below zero—some accounts say 30 degrees—claiming many more victims. ("A little blood begins to appear around the mouth, then it is over; on seeing this sign of approaching death appear on their lips, often their comrades give them a shoulder shove, push them to the ground, and strip them before they are completely dead," as Boniface de Castellane noted in his diary.) Soldiers still carrying weapons could no longer load their muskets in the open, and many were so afraid of not being able to rebutton their suspenders with their half-frozen fingers when they let their trousers down that they split open the backside seams (during the nighttime rest periods when they were huddled in barns or around campfires) in order to be able to answer the call of nature with a minimum of risk. Everything seemed to have been congealed by the intense cold—the frozen trees, the frozen birds, frozen horseflesh, frozen cheeks, ears, and noses, frozen lips, frozen tears, frozen whiskers with icicles dangling from them, frozen vocal cords crippling the powers of speech. As Philippe de Ségur noted, "The dull, monotonous sound of our footsteps, the crunching of the snow and the faint groans of the dying were all that interrupted this vast and lugubrious taciturnity." Sergeant Bourgogne, who had tramped along for days in a feverish daze, later noted: "He who was obliged to stop had no trouble refinding the way, for the quantity of men who kept falling, never to rise again, could serve as a guide."

That evening Marshal Victor caught up with the Imperial Guard, accompanied by fifty soldiers—all that was left of his Ninth Corps, which had by now dissolved like the rest into a leaderless mass of shuffling survivors. Murat and Berthier took him sternly to task for abandoning the rear guard to its fate, but he flatly refused to go back. It was one more symptom of the army's relentless breakdown.

During the night a number of Old Guard veterans died of cold while seated around their bivouac fires, and the next morning a sentinel was found standing upright—frozen stiff. A brilliant sun now rose over the glittering landscape like a "glowing globe," but, as Heinrich von Brandt noted, it provided no warmth, while the thousands of diamondlike particles of ice in the lung-chilling air blinded the bleary-eyed marchers, as with bent heads, frosted eyebrows, and bearded faces begrimed with campfire smoke they leaned on their pine-branch sticks and plodded and hobbled and shuffled on toward Vilna, now only eight hours away. (One of the hobblers was Brandt, the wounded captain from General Claparède's division, who, because of his bullet-stricken left foot, had been swinging himself on crutches since the crossing of the Berezina!)

In anticipation of the army's arrival, the governor, General van Hogendorp, had persuaded the monks in a number of Vilna's ecclesiastical establishments to crowd into one convent, leaving the other, roomy monasteries free to accommodate soldiers. He had also had signs posted in various parts of the city indicating which corps had been assigned to which monasteries. These precautionary measures, however, proved almost useless. The first to reach Vilna on the morning of December 8 were, as usual, the vanguard dropouts, so adept at keeping a march ahead of everyone else. The sight of this grimy horde of vagabonds, stumbling forward under layers of turbanlike rags, horse blankets, sheepskin pelts, woolen shawls and scarves, and fur-lined women's coats with dangling sleeves was so disconcerting that the commander of the battalion charged with maintaining law and order in Vilna reacted as had the authorities in Smolensk: he ordered the city gate to be closed to all except armed soldiers marching in formation.

When the gate was finally opened, the horde following the armed soldiers poured in like a torrent through a sluice, paying no heed to shouted or written instructions. The houses—fortunately made of stone, for otherwise they would surely have been destroyed in the crazy stampede—were taken by storm by all who could force their way inside. Several foodstuff storehouses were assaulted in the same rough fashion when the quartermaster officials demanded regular requisition slips. But the looting was not as wild as it might have been, partly because the assembled stocks were sufficient to feed an army of 100,000 for a period of three months, partly because few still had sufficient strength to indulge in wholesale plundering.

Outside the gate thousands of desperate soldiers, some of them dragging horses behind them, sought to force their way through the tunnellike vault in the walls. Scenes reminiscent of Smolensk and the Berezina crossing were relived by men who found themselves helplessly wedged in and squeezed forward inch by inch, like sausage meat, over mounds of dead and dying. The crush, which grew steadily more deadly during the afternoon and evening of December 8, became even more lethal the next day. When General Lubin Griois, commander of the Third Cavalry Corps artillery (which, like the corps, had ceased to exist), reached the scene, it took him a full, painful hour to be pushed and shoved into the city. To avoid the mindless, half-crazed mob, Marshal Davout, along with several of his generals, used a couple of ladders to scale several garden walls.

Throughout December 9 the sound of cannon fire could be heard coming from beyond the ring of hills to the east, where General von Wrede's Bavarian cavalrymen and what remained of the Loison division vainly sought to hold up the advancing Russians. Ney, who once again assumed the thankless task of commanding the rear guard, tried to round up as many soldiers as he could and to have them form ranks in the main square, but even he soon realized that it was hopeless. A good week at least would have been needed to restore the strength and will to fight of these thousands of disbanded soldiers, who were too busy trying to nurse themselves back to life with bread and beef and biscuits, wine, brandy, and sleep to be concerned about much else. But a week of rest was far more than Chichagov's frustrated Russians were prepared to grant them.

Around four in the afternoon General von Wrede came galloping into Vilna from the east with several hundred of his remaining Bavarian cavalrymen, shouting, "All is lost! We must leave! The Russians are surrounding the city!" An exasperated Hogendorp tried to calm him, but the nearby sound of gunfire lent urgency to his alarm. Shortly afterward a general staff officer informed Murat and Berthier that many Cossacks had been sighted, approaching up different roads. Murat, as commander in chief, immediately ordered a general call to arms to be sounded by the drummers. Afraid that their escape route was going to be cut if they remained in Vilna any longer, the conspicuous king of Naples and the unimposing prince de Wagram et de Neuchâtel pushed through the milling throng of wondering officers and soldiers in front of the governor's residence and made for the western gate and the road leading to Kovno and the Niemen.

From his new headquarters in the western suburbs Berthier issued orders to the various corps commanders, telling them that Vilna could no longer be defended and would have to be evacuated during the night. The news provoked consternation, particularly among the late arrivals, who had barely had time to warm their frozen bodies and to extract their swollen feet from boots they had not taken off in weeks. Marshal Lefebvre and several generals hurried through the streets, shouting, "To arms!" A few hastily formed platoons were marched toward the Smolensk gate to rout the Cossacks, who were trying to infiltrate their way in amid a horde of stragglers. "But most of the soldiers," as Raymond de Fezensac noted, "lying in the streets and in the houses they had been allowed to enter, declared that they could no longer fight and that they were staying put. The inhabitants, fearing pillage, hastened to close their houses and to barricade the doors." Shops, inns, and taverns had already boarded themselves up for the same reasons, and it was in a singularly sullen décor of bolted doors and shuttered windows—so different from the joyous Vilna of late June—that the Old Guard formed ranks once again on the main square, with their muskets cleaned, their cartridges and powder pouches filled, and their knapsacks replenished with biscuits, flour, rice, and salt. The air was filled with smoke as the torch was put to a number of imperial carriages and wagons, containing Napoleon's field tent, table linen, camp beds, and other items, including, it seems, a fragment of the broken Ivan Vyeliki cross, which, having been placed in another vehicle, had escaped the Semlyevo Lake disaster.

There was little semblance of order in the mass exodus that followed. Seven hundred carriages and wagons had recently been assembled in and around Vilna to speed the evacuation of sick and wounded soldiers. They were now used to hasten the evacuation of members of the diplomatic corps, who were to follow Foreign Minister Maret to Warsaw, as well as of many officials charged with administrative, financial, recruiting, and supply duties. It was only thanks to the commotion and congestion thus caused that Marshal Mortier, commanding the remnants of the Young Guard, first realized that Vilna was being abandoned. Many sleighs and wagons had no sooner been loaded up with foodstuffs and valuables by officials of the quartermaster service than they disappeared—brazenly stolen by quick-witted stragglers who had formed themselves into robber bands and who, for weeks past, had always been a march or two ahead of the army and thus the first to plunder and the last to fight. The still amply provisioned stores were left open to all comers, no one having the time or the heart to burn them in the midst of so much suffering and hunger.

It was once again a piercingly cold night, with myriads of twinkling stars. The late-rising moon shone so brightly on the snow that it seemed almost like daylight as the chaotic stream of Grande Armée fugitives poured out of Vilna.

Three miles to the west the road to Kovno led up a steep hill known as Ponary
—the same down which Murat's light-cavalry hussars and Polish lancers had
so lightheartedly galloped on June 28 to enter the city. Now the rutted roadway
was coated with ice, up which dozens of straining horses struggled in vain to
pull the heavier vehicles, the caissons and cannon of the Imperial Guard's
artillery, and wagons of the imperial baggage train, including several carrying
the coin-filled sacks of the paymasters' *trésor.* Many sleigh drivers managed
to circumvent the hill by branching off across the snow to the left, or by
following the frozen Vilia to the right for a mile or two. The heavy artillery
pieces and caissons, however, could not leave the roadway, and like the covered wagons of the paymasters' *trésor,* they were stuck at the foot of the frozen
hill.

As the shouting and swearing mounted and more and more horses were
forcibly "borrowed" from the furious artillerymen and their officers to be
hitched to the covered wagons of the top-priority imperial exchequer, an
ever-growing crowd of stragglers gathered. Finally, employing a familiar ruse
which had often been used in the past to unleash a profitable panic, one of them
shouted, "The Cossacks! The Cossacks!" Immediately the paymasters, the
assistant paymasters, and all the treasury officials fled across the snow and up
the hill on foot. Like a pack of wolves, the stragglers leapt on the stranded
wagons, using bayonets, gun butts, and knives to force the locks and break
open the chests. Sacks full of five-franc coins were hauled out, followed by
others filled with gold napoleons, as well as jewels, snuffboxes, watches, and
richly embroidered clothes (the latter being part of the booty collected in
Moscow and elsewhere). Soldiers, servants, and even officers with drawn
swords were soon scuffling to lay hands on the loot. Some of the first comers
staggered away with sacks so weighed down with gold and silver coins that
they fell in the snow. Many were attacked and divested of their purloined gains
by other robbers. A wild free-for-all ensued. The snow was bloodied as men
fought like beasts to carry off their booty or to wrest what they could from
others. Millions of francs in gold and silver coins were thus stolen in frenzied
plundering, which raged on until the light began to dawn, when another shout
went up: "The Cossacks! The Cossacks!" This time no one paid any attention,
as real riders galloped up in their distinctive pointed bonnets; using their pikes,
they speared some of the robbers before joining in the gold-grabbing spree
themselves. The Cossacks were later driven off, but only momentarily, by 300
rearguard infantrymen led by Marshal Ney, who let his soldiers help themselves to what was left of the "treasury," since it was lost in any case.

This sordid episode marked the final phase in the dissolution of an army that
had been undermined as much by indiscipline and the lure of loot as by heat,
hunger, freezing weather, and enemy attacks. Few of these plunderers made
it home with their loot. Most of them were caught by the Cossacks before they
reached the Niemen. The rest were pursued by a kind of malediction, the gold
or silver coin they offered for food arousing the cupidity of peasants, who
decided to kill them in order to divest them of the other riches they might be
carrying.

Hunger and cold, even more than General Chaplits's Cossacks, detained by the substantial quantities of booty to be picked up in and around Vilna, claimed many more victims along the sixty miles of frozen roadway leading to the Niemen. At Kovno, where the stores were ransacked by a horde of starved and exhausted soldiers, hundreds more died after drinking too much vodka, while many others expired around campfires lit in the streets, the jam-packed houses being unable to offer them another square foot of space. Here, to save the remnants of the army as it crossed the frozen Niemen, Marshal Ney decided to fight a final rearguard action on December 14 with a handful of Bavarian, Württemberg, and French infantrymen, and two remaining horse-drawn guns. The first salvo from the Cossacks' sleigh-borne cannon knocked out one of the French artillery pieces, and the infantrymen behind the earthwork "drum" barring the entrance to the town would all have fled had Ney not appeared, grabbed a musket, and begun firing at the enemy.

This heroic action, however, almost led to the loss of what remained of the rear guard. For when General Marchand's Württembergers and General Ledru's Frenchmen finally crossed the corpse-strewn bridge that afternoon they found 400 to 500 Cossacks, who had crossed the frozen river a few hundred yards downstream, solidly implanted on the summit of the long hill up which Napoleon, Caulaincourt, Wonsowicz, and their escort had had so much trouble pushing the imperial carriage a few days before. At the foot of this same icy slope were several caissons and the last of the Imperial Guard's artillery pieces, which Murat had had to abandon the day before. Ney, like his generals and all the other officers, again seized a musket and began blazing away at the enemy, but the Cossacks, who could bombard them with cannon from the height, were out of effective bullet range. Several officers in despair returned to Kovno. Ney, however, decided to repeat the ruse he had already employed near Krasnoye. A few campfires were lit at the foot of the hill, to make it look as though they were bivouacking for the night, and at seven o'clock Ney and his men plunged down the snowy escarpment as far as the iced-over Niemen, whose western bank they followed for four or five miles before climbing up again and cutting back through the pine forests to rejoin the main road to Gumbinnen.

This detour turned out to be a blessing, for it took them through undestroyed peasant villages, where they found food and sleighs and horses to pull them. They advanced so rapidly that they reached Gumbinnen before Murat. The surprised king of Naples thus discovered that the remains of his army had been moving along without a rear guard to protect it from the pursuing Cossacks, who had not hesitated to cross the Niemen into Polish territory, but who hesitated to cross the borders of East Prussia.

Murat took advantage of this unexpected respite and called a halt of several days in the retreat, hoping to achieve here what he had wanted to do in Vilna: reform the thousands of stragglers and disbanded soldiers into regular companies, battalions, and regiments. But the stragglers had but one desire—to reach their homes as soon as possible. Unnerved by the total breakdown of discipline, Murat, at a meeting attended by his fellow marshals, suddenly broke down and declared that the source of all their woes was the emperor Napoleon, who had rejected the peace terms offered by the British shortly before embarking on this ill-fated expedition. Only with regret had he left Naples to take part in it, and had he not done so, he would now be reigning over his Neapolitan subjects as serenely as the emperor of Austria and the king of Prussia over their own.

This singularly ill-timed statement was too much for Davout. He interrupted Murat harshly, pointing out that whereas the king of Prussia and the emperor of Austria were "princes by the grace of God and the habit of their peoples, you are king only by the grace of Napoleon and French blood." That, so far as we know, ended Murat's speech. It also finished him off in the eyes of his fellow marshals, even though he was nominally still commander in chief.

On December 18—the day their fleeing emperor reached Paris—Murat, Berthier, and the remains of the Imperial Guard moved on Koenigsberg. The East Prussian capital was already jam-packed with officers and soldiers, glad to be able to exchange what remained of their Moscow loot for wine, liquors, coffee, whipped cream, cakes, desserts, and all the other delicacies they had been denied for months. The spectacle of this horde of ragamuffins invading inns and taverns, and in some cases literally drinking themselves to death, was more than a little repugnant to the sedate inhabitants of Immanuel Kant's home town. Although some remained outwardly polite, many others seethed with indignation and made no secret of their contempt. Young urchins, and university students whose patriotism had been fired by Fichte's "Discourses to the German Nation" and who had enthusiastically joined the so-called Tugendbund (League of Virtue) dedicated to the renascence of their prostrate country, marched through the streets insolently chanting the latest "hit song":

> *Trommler ohne Trommstock,*
> *Kuirassier in Weiberrock,*
> *Ritter ohne Schwert,*
> *Reiter ohne Pferd!*
> *Mit Mann und Ross und Wagen*
> *So hat sie Gott geschlagen!*

> (Drummers without drumsticks,
> Cuirassiers in female garb,
> Knights without a sword,
> Riders without a horse!
> Man, nag, and wagon
> Thus has God struck them down!)

Even more infernal was the atmosphere in Vilna, following the departure of Ney's rear guard during the morning of December 10. Here between fifteen thousand and twenty thousand French and allied soldiers were left to the mercies of the local inhabitants and of the Cossacks. Thousands were already dead, thousands of others were dying, having been laid out like cordwood over the freezing floors of convent "hospitals," where they were kept vaguely alive on a diet of biscuits. So short was the available space that the dead were unceremoniously pitched out of the windows to make room for the still-living. Most of those who had taken refuge in private homes in the poorer quarters met a similar fate: after being poisoned or otherwise killed by their reluctant "hosts," who stripped them of their uniforms and belongings, they were pushed out of doors or heaved from the windows into the street, so as not to constitute a compromising proof that food and shelter had been offered to the "enemy."

The cold, which claimed so many victims among the retreating French and their allies, was no kinder to the better-clothed and better-nourished Russian infantrymen, who, as Waldemar von Loewenstern observed, could no longer be persuaded to leave "once they had managed to find a well-heated shelter or a warm cottage. They crowded around the stoves at the risk of being grilled alive." As a result Kutuzov, when he made his triumphal entry into Vilna on December 12, his chest beneath the fur-lined greatcoat covered with diamond-studded decorations, commanded an army that had shrunk to almost one-third of its former size—35,000 men and 250 cannon.

Sir Robert Wilson, who had suffered a frozen nose and cheek during the sleigh ride north from Minsk, was appalled by the spectacle confronting him when he reached Vilna in his turn. The road leading into the city was "covered with human carcasses, frozen in the contortions of expiring agonies. The entrance to the town was literally choked with the dead bodies of men and horses, tumbrils, guns, carts, &c. and the streets were crowded with traineaus carrying off the dead that still crowded the way. . . . The dead, however, are to be envied. With frost to twenty-eight and thirty degrees, naked bodies and infirm health offer but subjects for terrible torments: imagination cannot conceive the reality. One incident I must, however, note. *Yesterday I saw four men grouped together, hands and legs frozen, minds yet vigorous, and two dogs tearing their feet.*"

It was not days but weeks before the streets could be cleared of all the scruffily uniformed and nude corpses that littered them. Hundreds of laborers and militiamen were put to work digging a vast ditch beyond the walls—which was anything but easy, given the hardness of the frozen ground, the quantity of snow above it, and the packs of ravenous wolves that now roamed the landscape. This thankless task was necessitated by the dreadful stench that filled the city each time the temperature rose and there was a thaw. Particularly pestilential was the air around the Monastery of Saint Basil, now converted into a makeshift hospital, where, as Sir Robert Wilson discovered to his horror, 7,500 bodies were piled up "like pigs of lead over one another in the corridors." To keep the freezing outdoor air from sweeping in through the broken windows, those of the wounded inmates who were still alive had used the frozen limbs of the dead—feet, legs, hands, even torsoes and heads—to clog the apertures. "The putrefaction of the thawing flesh, where the parts touched and the process of decomposition was in action, emitted the most cadaverous smell." But the attempt to combat these pestilential odors—by igniting bonfires of often dung-filled straw in many streets—did no more than fill the air with acrid smoke, giving the fuming city the sulphurous aspect of a "Tartar hell-fire," as the German patriot-poet Ernst Moritz Arndt put it.

Tsar Alexander himself reached Vilna on December 22, his partly frozen nose reddened by the speed with which his coachman, Ilya, had driven their sleigh all the way from Petersburg in just three days. He was more than ever fed up with Kutuzov for having let Napoleon escape, and more than ever unable to dismiss the man who was now generally regarded as the "savior of the fatherland." He celebrated his arrival with a speech thanking Kutuzov and his officers for their achievements, and reproving the university professors for having so enthusiastically embraced the cause of Napoleon and the French. The next day, his birthday, he felt obliged to decorate the generalissimo with the Order of Saint George, First Class; but, as he explained to Sir Robert Wilson in a private conversation shortly before the official ceremony: "I will not ask you to be present. I should feel too much humiliated if you were."

Kutuzov, with equal hypocrisy, returned the compliment by offering a state banquet to the tsar. When the emperor appeared, a number of captured French standards were flung down on the parquet floor for him to tread on—to Alexander's visible dismay. This uncouth exhibition of military bravado was followed by a distinctly constrained ball, where the tactless Grand Duke Constantine made himself more than usually obnoxious by badgering and forcing reluctant officers who were not in a festive mood to dance with the thirty Lithuanian ladies present. Many other ladies had previously retired to their estates in the country, fleeing the horrors of war and fearing rebukes and reprisals because their menfolk had joined Napoleon's forces.

In honor of the tsar's arrival a transparent streamer had been strung across the façade of the illuminated town hall. Here the two-crowned imperial eagle of Russia was shown biting and clawing the many tentacular heads of the Bonapartist hydra. This symbolic representation of the war of 1812 faithfully depicted Alexander's conception of his personal duel with Napoleon and his determination to be the "liberator" of the oppressed peoples of Europe. This was the role that the forceful Baron vom Stein had long been insisting should be his, but it was not a mission Kutuzov felt any urgent desire to promote. He felt he had done his patriotic duty in expelling the French from Russian territory, and he foresaw nothing but trouble and added tribulations from trying to extend the war beyond the Niemen, or at any rate beyond the Vistula. All told, Chichagov's depleted forces (now about 15,500 men, with 180 cannon), Wittgenstein's corps (34,500 men, and 177 cannon), added to his own sadly shrunk army and various other units, totaled slightly more than 100,000 men —far too few, in the cautious generalissimo's opinion, to engage in operations far from the Russian heartland.

Such, Kutuzov was pleased to discover, was also the view of the superpatriotic Admiral Shishkov, the speech-writing factotum who had accompanied the tsar to Vilna along with the "bulldog" Arakcheyev, who now directed Alexander's private chancellery. It would be better, Shishkov argued, to negotiate a peace with Bonaparte on favorable terms than have to bear the brunt and burden of a war for the liberation of other European countries, which might prove extremely costly. Kutuzov was in full agreement. But, as he explained to the admiral, "the sovereign reasons differently, and so we are going to continue to advance. When he cannot contest my arguments, he embraces and kisses me; then I weep and agree with him."

Although they were agreed on the need to end the war as quickly as possible, Shishkov was dismayed to hear Kutuzov at the dinner table express the hope that His Majesty would not get rid of the French theater in Petersburg (an object of Shishkovian loathing) and that he would not discard the French language, thereby plunging Russia back into "ignorance and clumsiness." Like Napoleon, at the time when he was First Consul, Kutuzov had felt that France and Russia, being placed at the opposite ends of the continent, were made to be friends rather than enemies in Europe. He had always secretly regretted Russia's involvement in the basically Austrian war that had led to Austerlitz, and in 1806 he and the then rabidly pro-Bonapartist Chichagov had been the only two important officials in Petersburg who had had the courage to support the peace treaty with France that the Russian chargé d'affaires in Paris (Pierre d'Oubril) had worked out with Talleyrand. The rejection of that treaty had led to the bloody battles of Eylau and Friedland, to the phony peace of Tilsit, and ultimately to the war of 1812, with all of its blood-letting and fiery disasters. Like Chancellor Rumiantsev (now more than ever in disgrace), Kutuzov felt that Russia's natural enemy was Turkey and that Russia's mission in Europe should be to liberate the oppressed Christian populations of the Balkans from Ottoman rule rather than to restore the Kingdom of Prussia to her former greatness.

It would of course be going too far to suppose that Kutuzov, in this month of December 1812, could have foreseen what was to happen one hundred and one years later—in August 1914—when another foreign army began invading Russia, composed this time of Germans, who had been united at last under a Prussian emperor. But so opposed to the continuation of the war was the generalissimo that when, four months later, Tsar Alexander came to see him on his deathbed, saying, "Forgive me, Mikhail Hilarionovich!"—for having forced him to continue the winter campaign as far as German Silesia—Kutuzov replied, "I forgive you, Sire, but Russia never will!"

CHAPTER 27

THE AFTERMATH

S O E N D E D the "severest campaign of six months in the annals of the world," as Sir Robert Wilson was to write. Less given to hyperbole, John Quincy Adams claimed that "there has been nothing like it in history since the days of Xerxes." The losses Napoleon's forces had suffered were simply staggering: 125,000 killed in various battles; 48 generals, more than 3,000 officers, and 190,000 soldiers captured; another 100,000 killed by hunger, cold, or sickness; 75 imperial eagles and 929 cannon taken by the Russians—"exclusive of those thrown into rivers or buried," as General Wilson added.

From this shattering debacle Napoleon was unable to recover—even though in Spain Wellington was stopped at Burgos and the French managed to reoccupy Madrid. Replacing the more than 200,000 French soldiers who had been lost in Russia with raw recruits and some troops withdrawn from Spain proved relatively simple, though the inexperienced newcomers were no match for the veterans who had perished or disappeared. New infantry units were fashioned from the more than one hundred National Guard *"cohortes"* that had been formed to guard France from a possible British invasion while the emperor was off campaigning in the east, and one more manpower levy brought another 180,000 Frenchmen flocking (not always willingly) to the eagle-headed colors. (We should not forget that the population of France at this time was not far from 30 million, compared with 24 million in the Austrian Empire, 15 million in Great Britain, and less than 5 million in Prussia (stripped of its Polish lands).

The 158 million francs of gold that Napoleon had carefully husbanded in the cellars of the Tuileries Palace were sufficient to finance the new military effort, so energetically pursued at all levels that, as Caulaincourt put it, France had become "one vast workshop." The empire's arsenals and foundries, though technically fifteen years behind the British in efficiency, were able to replace the hundreds of thousands of muskets, bayonets, and sabers, and even the one thousand artillery pieces that had been lost in Russia. More difficult proved the task of finding horses to pull the cannon and caissons, an undertaking complicated by the need to create a new cavalry, virtually from scratch. A massive roundup of horses was launched in Germany, Italy, the Low Countries, as well as in France, to replace the more than one hundred thousand horses that had perished beyond the Niemen; but it proved impossible, in the short time available, to train new cavalrymen, and this was to prove a decisive factor in the next campaign.

Philippe de Ségur has left us a vivid account of the insuperable problems posed by a superhuman effort that was doomed from the outset. Recently promoted to general and sent to the region of Tours, he was given exactly two officers and four noncoms to help him whip 2,700 horsemen into shape—part of a new Garde d'Honneur, 10,000 strong, which was intended to bolster Marshal Bessières's sadly depleted Imperial Guard cavalry. Many of Ségur's "honor guards" turned out to be royalists from western France who had been pressured by departmental prefects into "enlisting." Faithful to their monarchist sympathies, they refused to utter the ritual shout of *"Vive l'Empereur!"* preferring instead to demonstrate their personal attachment to their harassed commander by crying *"Vive le général!"*

Although the 29th Bulletin of the Grande Armée, which Napoleon had dictated in the Lithuanian town of Molodechno, had exposed part of the bitter truth, it was months before the French, in Paris as elsewhere, really began to grasp the magnitude of the catastrophe. So universal had been the faith in the invincibility of Napoleon—*le conquérant,* or *l'ambitieux,* as he was known to the gossiping "old countesses" (George Sand's term) of the ultraroyalist and reactionary Saint-Germain suburb—that even the emperor's bitterest foes only gradually shed their disbelief.

A few royalist, as well as revolutionary, critics began spreading hostile anecdotes and cruel puns. One of them even managed to scrawl four nasty verses on the side wall of the Tuileries Palace nearest to the Place Vendôme, which was then (as now) dominated by the French emperor, atop his proud victory column:

> Tyran, juché sur cette échasse
> Si le sang que tu fis verser
> Pouvait tenir dans cette place,
> Tu le boirais sans te baisser.

> (Tyrant, hoisted on your stilt,
> If the blood you caused to be spilled
> Could hold in this square,
> You would drink it without bending down.)

This particular quatrain, according to Junot's wife, Laure d'Abrantès, greatly pained Napoleon and prompted an irritated outburst. (He was hurt by the idea that he was "bloodthirsty" as well as a "tyrant.") But there is little doubt that it expressed a minority rather than a majority sentiment. The Malet uprising of the previous October, as Napoleon was not long in discovering, had been the work of a handful of harebrained malcontents, and so limited had been its impact on Parisians that he did not in the end have to dismiss his "insufficiently vigilant" minister of police, General René Savary.

Black, as the Duchesse d'Abrantès also noted, gradually became the national color, as family after family went into mourning for their lost ones, but during the late winter and early spring of 1813 there was little trace of the deep discouragement into which the country sank a few months later. As another, more eloquent and above all more truthful, feminine eyewitness was later to recall—Aurore Dupin, alias George Sand—"The sufferings and misfortunes of this retreat were not officially known until some time later. With the emperor back in Paris, people thought that all was saved, that all was repaired. The bulletins of the Grande Armée and the newspapers told only part of the truth. It was through private letters, and from the accounts of those who had escaped the disaster, that one was able to form an idea of what had happened."

The Napoleonic call to arms, made in the name of an "enlightened," not to say "progressive," country that was once again threatened by reactionary forces, was only slightly less popular now than it had been during the years of the first *levées en masse* of the 1790s. As George Sand, again quite rightly, noted: "The authority of Napoleon began once again, from the moment of our disasters in Russia, to represent the individuality, the independence, and the dignity of France. Those who judged differently during the struggle of our armies with the coalition fell into a fatal error." Her own childish infatuation —she was less than nine years old at the time—was unquestionably shared by millions of compatriots, for as she recalled: "At that time one was weaned on the pride of victory with one's mother's milk. The myth of the nobility had enlarged itself, had communicated itself to all classes. To be born French was an illustration, a title. The eagle was the coat of arms of the country as a whole."

For the Russians the recapture of Vilna and Kovno was a first, important step toward the "liberation" of Lithuania. In concentrating most of their forces —Chichagov's, Kutuzov's, Wittgenstein's—on this central objective, they had been obliged to neglect Schwarzenberg on their southern flank, although General Tormassov had been left behind with more than 10,000 men to guard Minsk. The Austrian commander took advantage of this situation to seize the towns of Slutsk and Pinsk, on the northern and western fringes of the Pripet Marshes, with considerable stocks of badly needed food. But these were no more than token thrusts, undertaken to sustain the military prestige of the Austrian expeditionary force in the face of French accusations of "do-nothingness," and to mitigate the humiliation of a retreat back to the borders of the Grand Duchy of Warsaw, which Schwarzenberg now knew to be inevitable.

In the north, where news of the Grande Armée's debacle was very slow to reach him, Marshal Macdonald had considerable trouble moving the units of his Tenth Corps back over small, icy roads from the region of Riga (which they had been besieging) to that of the lower Niemen. A small advance-guard force of 1,400 Russian and Cossack horsemen, led by Wittgenstein's assistant chief of staff, a young Prussian general named Diebitsch, was too weak to stop the march of Macdonald's single French division. But Diebitsch managed to intercept the two retreating Prussian divisions, and with the aid of Lieutenant Carl von Clausewitz and of Scharnhorst's son-in-law, Count Friedrich Dohna (both now serving with the Russians), he was able to persuade the crusty Junker commander General von Yorck to sign a cease-fire agreement in a windmill near Tilsit on the penultimate day of the year.

Macdonald, true to his tolerant and gentlemanly form, took the news of this defection in his stride, even allowing a Prussian liaison officer on his staff to return to Yorck with thirty horses. At the same time he accelerated the pace of his retreat with his remaining 9,000 men along the road to Koenigsberg, so as not to be cut off (as he should have been) by Wittgenstein's slowly advancing Russians. His Tenth Corps, now reduced to one-third of its original strength, could no longer hope to hold Koenigsberg, in the midst of an East Prussian populace seething with anti-French feeling, whose once cringing subservience had changed almost overnight into insolent contempt.

On January 4 of the new year (1813) Murat, Berthier, and Macdonald had no choice but to evacuate Koenigsberg. The scattered remnants of the Grande Armée were pulled back to the line of the Vistula, in the hope that it could be held. When this hope began to fade, Murat turned over his command to Prince Eugène (on the grounds that his wife, Caroline, was up to more mischief) and hied himself in a hurry to the bright blue skies and lemon-scented air of Naples.

In mid-January Prince Poniatowski, still unable to walk on his painfully wrenched ankle, made a pathetic reappearance in Warsaw, one of the last to return of a decimated corps, which, because its small, sturdy horses had been properly crampon-shod, managed to bring back two-thirds of the sixty cannon with which it had started the campaign. By the end of the month it was clear that Schwarzenberg and his Austrian expeditionary force, who were supposed to defend Warsaw against the advancing Russians, had received secret instructions from the government in Vienna to abandon the city to its fate. To the consternation of the Poles and the fury of Poniatowski—who had a heated argument with his old friend Schwarzenberg (whose life he had once saved during a battle with the Turks)—the Austrian expeditionary force was drawn back west of the Vistula, leaving the capital defenseless. On February 4, Count Edouard Bignon, who had replaced the fatuous archbishop of Malines as French ambassador, was obliged to leave an anguished Warsaw, which was occupied four days later by Miloradovich's Russians.

The fall of Warsaw ended all hope of holding the line of the Vistula, even though the fortress of Thorn continued to resist, along with the Baltic bastion of Danzig, where the dauntless Jean Rapp was determined to hold out (and did—for ten months!).

On March 4 Wittgenstein, continuing his virtually unopposed advance, entered Berlin, to the delirious delight of its deeply humiliated inhabitants. Its sovereign, however, could not partake in the festivities. Still awed by Napoleon's military prestige and not realizing the scope of the disaster in Russia,

King Frederick William III had ordered General von Yorck to be dismissed from his command (for having signed a cease-fire with the Russians) and had then fled from Berlin to Breslau, the capital of Prussian Silesia.

After leaving Petersburg in late December, the former Prussian premier, Baron vom Stein, had journeyed in his turn to Vilna, proceeding from there to a recently liberated Koenigsberg. Several weeks later, at Kutuzov's headquarters at Kalisz (south of Warsaw), the forceful Prussian Freiherr had teamed up with Scharnhorst to obtain a preliminary agreement of military and diplomatic cooperation between Prussia and Russia. In late February he reached Breslau, where he spent several feverish weeks battling a typhus germ he had picked up in a Polish inn, while the frustrated French ambassador (who had followed King Frederick William to Silesia) tried to spy on him to see who were the patriotic Prussian "plotters" who came to visit him. The latter were now joined by August von Gneisenau, just returned from London, where he had persuaded an initially reluctant Conservative government, headed by Lord Liverpool, to finance the formation of a Swedish expeditionary force, to be landed under Bernadotte's command on the coast of Mecklenburg.

On March 15 it was the turn of Tsar Alexander to reach the Silesian capital. The Russian sovereign, already yielding to mystical "illuminations" in which he saw himself as the chosen instrument of Divine Providence, was greeted as a "savior" by the joyous populace, and with carefully concealed misgivings by Frederick William III, who was as suspicious as Metternich of Russia's designs and who was desperately anxious to regain all of previously Prussian Poland (which had included Warsaw). Two days later, completing what the now forgiven General Yorck had begun, the refugee Prussian monarch put his signature to a ringing declaration calling on all Germans to rise up against the French. The texts promulgated on this memorable March 17 covered the organization of a Prussian *Landwehr* militia, which was to buttress the rapid expansion of the army.

The next day—as though in answer to the king's appeal, a German-Russian force staged a raid on French-held Hamburg, and the two young dukes of Mecklenburg withdrew from the Confederation of the Rhine. The question now was not if the Oder could be held—it had long since been crossed—but if the French could keep their enemies east of the Elbe.

In January Napoleon had seriously aggravated his situation by responding coolly to Metternich's proposal that he mediate a settlement between France and Russia. Louis de Narbonne, who had returned to Paris after a brief stopover in Berlin, had astutely proposed that Napoleon offer Prussian Silesia to Austria as a bait to keep Emperor Francis's empire firmly attached to the French alliance. But Napoleon at that point was interested only in obtaining more Austrian cannon fodder—to the tune of 100,000 men! Neither Francis I nor Metternich was prepared to forgive this slight, though they were none too happy to see Russia occupy the Polish heartland.

In April Louis de Narbonne, who had been hurriedly dispatched to Vienna in a last-minute effort to patch things up, was at last authorized to offer Silesia to Austria. But by now it was too late. Metternich and his sovereign had lost all faith in promises the French emperor made only grudgingly and which he was in no hurry to honor—such as his pledge to return the Illyrian provinces, which was still unfulfilled. The time had come to punish the incorrigible upstart who had dared to destroy the Holy Roman Empire and to rob the Habsburgs of all their Italian possessions—by leaving him to his fate, prior to joining his enemies. As Prince Schwarzenberg, who had resumed his ambassadorial post in Paris, bluntly explained to Foreign Minister Maret, the future tranquillity of the world demanded many sacrifices, "and if it is necessary to undo a marriage to give peace to Europe, Austria would not hesitate to undo it, if forced to."

On April 11 Barclay de Tolly, who had finally been appointed to replace the militarily inexperienced Admiral Chichagov as commander of the Third Russian Army of the West, saw the white flag run up over the Vistula fortress of Thorn after a brief five-day bombardment with siege guns. Fifty-seven more French cannon were thus claimed by the Russians. Less than three weeks later Kutuzov died (at Bunzlau, in Silesia), and Wittgenstein was named nominal commander of an army which the mystically inclined tsar was more than ever anxious to command in person as the chosen "instrument of Destiny."

Meanwhile Napoleon, whose return to Paris had had an electrifying effect on ministers and subordinates—"the plodding march of affairs gave way to the élan of zeal," as his devoted secretary, Baron Fain, later put it—had managed by working twenty hours a day to forge a new army. But it was a truly pitiful host, compared with the resplendent Grande Armée that had set out for the east one year before.

Leaving Paris on April 15—almost four months to the day after his clandestine return to the Tuileries—Napoleon reached Mainz during the early hours of the seventeenth, only to find that he had outstripped most of his cavalry units and that the horsemen of the Imperial Guard were alone ready to accompany him eastward. Some infantry units had been formed from National Guard "cohortes," which had had from six months to one year of training, but many others were composed of raw recruits. The best trained of them, as Caulaincourt noted, had handled firearms for barely one month. Many others had received their flintlocks a week before crossing the Rhine, and some had to wait till they reached Erfurt, in Thuringia, before being properly armed.

That Napoleon was able to lead this ill-trained host into battle and even win several victories seems well-nigh incredible. It is unquestionably a tribute to the magnetism of his personality, as well as a commentary on the blundering incompetence of his adversaries.

On May 2, a combined Russian-Prussian force under Wittgenstein met Napoleon's multinational host of French, Dutch, Saxon, Westphalian, Bavarian, and Italian soldiery at Lützen, near Leipzig. The battle lasted all day, but the ill-coordinated Russians and Prussians were finally forced to retreat.

Greatly heartened by this success, which made them feel like veterans, Napoleon's ill-trained soldiers tramped through Leipzig and on to the Saxon capital of Dresden, whose war-weary inhabitants were forced to put up with one more foreign occupation. (In half a dozen years they had been successively occupied by the Prussians, the French, the Austrians, and the Russians.) The next encounter took place at Bautzen, some thirty-three miles to the northeast. Once again it resulted in a Napoleonic victory. But in the absence of Murat's roving cavalrymen—who had ranged over the landscape so brilliantly after Auerstädt and Jena in 1806—the French emperor was unable to exploit his advantage. His old adversary Barclay, who had not taken part in the earlier battle at Lützen, was this time present and thus able once again to live up to his reputation as the (unjustly) scorned *"général de la retraite"* by covering the Russian-Prussian withdrawal—for a greatly upset Alexander, a more than usually despondent Frederick William, and their querulous staffs.

Wittgenstein at this point decided that he had had enough of imperial interference, and asked to be subordinated to his former commander, Barclay de Tolly, who thus became, more or less by default and for a brief space only, supreme commander of the Russian and Prussian armies. He found himself having to resume the job of destroying Napoleon, which could so easily have been accomplished in Russia in 1812—if only he had been in charge! As Kutuzov had foreseen, it was to cost a great deal of effort and several hundred thousand Russian lives.

On June 15 Great Britain formally joined the anti-Napoleonic coalition, shortly followed by Austria, and three months later by King Maximilian's Bavaria. Napoleon now found himself confronted by a military alliance that included Russia, Prussia, Austria, Bavaria, Great Britain, and Sweden. No French ruler in history had ever had to face such a mobilization of European countries against him. Even for Napoleon this was too much. The result was a new campaign, culminating in the "Battle of the Nations" at Leipzig (mid-October 1813), which cost him another 200,000 men in killed, wounded, prisoners, and desertions.

The defection of several thousand unhappy Saxons, who joined the allies as they fought their way into the old university city, was the signal for a general scramble to leave the sinking Bonapartist ship on the part of German rulers who had once been members of the Confederation of the Rhine—Württemberg, Hessen-Darmstadt, Baden. The luxury-loving Jerome Bonaparte was forced to flee his capital at Kassel, as the "kingdom" of Westphalia collapsed like a house of cards.

In November it was the turn of the disgruntled Dutch to rise up in revolt. The Napoleonic Empire was now no more than a memory, and with more and more German soldiers joining the Russian-Prussian-Austrian host, it was simply a question of time before this new anti-Bonapartist "Grande Armée" rolled over the hopelessly outnumbered French. On the last day of March 1814, the poorly coordinated juggernaut finally marched into Paris—eleven days before Napoleon's abdication, which it was left to Armand de Caulaincourt (who had so vainly advised against the fateful invasion of 1812) to negotiate with his "dear friend," Emperor Alexander of Russia.

NOTES

The following abbreviations have been used:

ADB	*Allgemeine Deutsche Biographie*
AKV	*Arkhiv Knyazya Vorontsova* (40 vols., edited by P. B. Bartenev)
AMREP	Archives du Ministère des Relations Extérieures, Paris
ANP	Archives nationales, Paris
CEAS	*Correspondance de l'Empereur Alexandre avec sa soeur* (compiled and edited by Grand Duke Nicolas Mikhailovich)
Corr.	*Correspondance,* particularly of Napoleon (Nap.)
KSD	*Kutuzov: Sbornik Dokumentov* (references are to volume 4, part 1, unless part 2 is specified)
LIML	*Lettres inédites à Marie-Louise* (sent by Napoleon)
Loewenstern	References are to his *Mémoires* unless otherwise specified
MP Eugène	*Mémoires du Prince Eugène* (compiled and edited by A. Du Casse)
MR Jérôme	*Mémoires du Roi Jérôme* (compiled and edited by A. Du Casse)
NMR	(Grand Duke) Nicolas Mikhailovich of Russia
RA	*Russky Arkhiv* (periodical series edited by P. B. Bartenev)
RBS	*Russky Biographichesky Slovar* (edited by A. A. Polovtsov)
RDRF	*Relations diplomatiques de la Russie et de la France* (compiled and edited by Grand Duke Nicolas Mikhailovich)
REH	*Revue d'Etudes historiques*
RHA	*Revue historique de l'Armée*
RHD	*Revue d'histoire diplomatique*
RS	*Russkaya Starina* (periodical series dealing with Russian past)
Ségur	References are to Paul-Philippe de Ségur's *Histoire et Mémoires* unless otherwise specified
SIRIO	*Sbornik Imperatorskago Russkago Istoricheskago Obshchestva* (collection of periodicals published by the Imperial Russian Historical Society)

PAGE   LINES   1 **On the Eve: March 1812**

3   The laggard advent of spring in 1812 is noted by John Quincy Adams in April 9 diary entry (*Memoirs* 2, p. 356). Frame-supported ice hills are described in diary entries for 9 Jan. 1810, 7 Feb. 1811 (ibid., pp. 94, 228). For Lenten ban on marriages and theater performances, see NMR, *L'Impératrice Elisabeth* 1, pp. 146, 389. On the breakup of the ice, Adams 2, pp. 123–24; Adam Czartoryski, *Mémoires* 1, p. 94; L. E. Vigée-Lebrun, *Souvenirs* 1, pp. 350–52, and p. 318, on the "Venetian" animation of Petersburg's waterways during the late spring and summer months.

4   9–10   On "construction fever" in Paris, Pasquier, *Mémoires* 1, pp. 428–29.

PAGE   LINES

4   15–21   Adams, 5 Nov. 1809 entry (*Memoirs* 2, pp. 50–55).

4   22 ff.   Sir Robert Ker Porter, *Travelling Sketches* 1, pp. 19–20.

4   42 ff.   On the Admiralty, Winter Palace, and Kazanskoy Bozhey Materi Cathedral, see Carl Baedeker, *La Russie* (Leipzig, 1893), pp. 21–31, 64–65; Porter 1, pp. 6–9; Louis Réau, *L'Art russe de Pierre le Grand à nos jours*, pp. 90–96; Adams, 15 Oct. 1811 entry (*Memoirs* 2, pp. 317–18).

5   17–21   On the two comets, Adams 2, p. 329.

5   21–32   Countess Edling, in her *Mémoires*, p. 62, speaks of the *fêtes brillantes* that preceded the 1812 invasion, but Varvara Bakunin, in her reminiscences (*RS* 47, pp. 391–92), speaks of a glum atmosphere, officers being arrested for sloppy maneuvering, etc.

5   33 ff.   Chernyshov's dispatches to Tsar Alexander and Chancellor Rumiantsev can be found in *SIRIO* 21, pp. 1–110. Adams 2, pp. 352–53.

7   10–19   On the Luddite uprisings, see Elie Halévy, *England in 1815*, pp. 331–37.

7   42 ff.   On growth of Napoleonic empire, Jean Tulard, *Le Grand Empire*.

8   5–10   F. Masson, *Napoléon et sa famille* 1, pp. 319–21; Duchesse d'Abrantès, *Mémoires* 9, pp. 95–106, 321–23, 361; Madame de Rémusat, *Mémoires* 3, pp. 48, 120–21, 304–9.

8   10–12   Pasquier 1, pp. 472–88.

8–9   45   Tatichtchev, *Alexandre Ier et Napoléon*, pp. 265–6.

9   13 ff.   On hardships endured by famished provincial and suburban dwellers, Pasquier 1, pp. 497–509, 516; on insouciance of young French officers, Baron Fain, *Manuscrit de 1812* 1, pp. 45–46, and George Sand in part 3, ch. 14, of *Histoire de ma vie* (pp. 730–31 of the 1970 Pléiade ed.).

9   28–34   Albert Vandal, *Napoléon et Alexandre Ier* 3, p. 404; Senfft von Pilsach, *Mémoires*, pp. 163–64.

9   38–44   J. Tulard, "*Le 'Dépôt de Guerre' et la préparation de la campagne de Russie*," in *RHA* 1969, no. 3.

9–10   On warnings against the campaign, see Thiers, *Histoire du Consulat et de l'Empire* 13, pp. 458–59; Fouché, *Mémoires*, pp. 296–98; Caulaincourt, *Mémoires* 1, pp. 310–22; Jean Rapp, *Mémoires*, pp. 135, 160–61; Beugnot, *Mémoires* 1, pp. 496–97; *MR Jérôme* 5, pp. 127–28.

10   22 ff.   Paul-Philippe de Ségur, *Histoire et Mémoires* 4, pp. 66–74.

11   23 ff.   A. F. Villemain, *Souvenirs contemporains* 1, pp. 161–80.

PAGE	LINES	
II	36ff.	On Napoleon's attitude toward the Spaniards (contrasted with the Germans), see his 2 Dec. 1811 letter to Davout (*Corr.* 23, pp. 51–53, no. 18300).
12	3ff.	The word *braves* appears significantly in the 87th Bulletin de la Grande Armée, issued at Tilsit on 26 June 1807 (Nap., Corr. 15, p. 466, no. 12827). See also Las Cases, *Mémorial de Sainte-Hélène* 3, p. 123, and Marbot, *Mémoires* 3, p. 38, quoting General Bertrand.
12	16ff.	Nap., *Corr.* 23, and Vandal 3, pp. 322–32.
12	21ff.	Heinrich von Brandt, *Aus dem Leben,* pp. 273–75, 301–5.

2 Petersburg and the Polish Powder Keg

14	10ff.	Charles de Larivière, *Catherine II et la Révolution française,* pp. 34–36, 74–79, 204–14; A. Boethlingk, *Frédéric-César Laharpe,* pp. 57–69.
14	25–28	A. Palmer, *Alexander I,* pp. 6–21, and NMR, *L'Impératrice Elisabeth* 1.
14	14–15	On Emperor Paul's eccentricities, F. Golovkin, *La Cour et le règne de Paul Ier;* N. K. Schilder, *Imperator Pavel I;* E. D. Clarke, *Travels* 1, pp. 16–17; J. Niemcewicz, *Notes on My Captivity,* pp. 46–47; Vigée-Lebrun, *Souvenirs* 2, pp. 21–28.
15	13ff.	Palmer, *Alexander I,* pp. 42–46; Schilder, *Pavel I,* pp. 482–94.
15	29ff.	Vigée-Lebrun 2, pp. 73–80; Varvara Golovine, *Souvenirs,* pp. 265–66.
16	11ff.	Tatichtchev, pp. 42–43.
16	33ff.	On Russia's social and economic situation at this time, see R. Pipes, *Russia Under the Old Regime,* and W. Blackwell's *The Beginnings of Russian Industrialization.*
17	14ff.	On the abduction and execution of the Duc d'Enghien, see A. Rambaud, *Les Français sur le Rhin,* pp. 362–65; Caulaincourt's *Mémoires* 1, pp. 64–73, 252–56.
17	33ff.	Czartoryski, *Mémoires* 1, ch. 12; Golovine, pp. 190–91; Dirk van Hogendorp, *Mémoires,* pp. 153–54; Henri Troyat, *Alexandre Ier,* pp. 112–13.
18	36ff.	Tatichtchev, pp. 70–93; A. Potocka, *Mémoires,* pp. 90–93.
19	31–42	Tatichtchev, pp. 96–98.
20	9–15	Geoffrey Bruun, *Europe and the French Imperium,* p. 121.
20	16ff.	William Pierson, *Preussische Geschichte* 1, pp. 498–512; Hermann von Boyen, *Erinnerungen* 2, pp. 13–20.

PAGE	LINES	
20	39ff.	Pierson 1, pp. 513–15; Hardenberg, *Denkwürdigkeiten* 4, pp. 3–15.
21	3ff.	Princess Antoni Radziwill, *Quarante-cinq années de ma vie*, pp. 229–33; Pierson 1, pp. 515–21; Oskar von Lettow-Vorbeck, *Der Krieg von 1806 und 1807.*
21	8–10	M. Handelsman, *Napoléon et la Pologne*, pp. 34–44.
21	12ff.	Crane Brinton, *A Decade of Revolution*, pp. 90–91; Kukiel, *Czartoryski and European Unity*, pp. 3–6; M. Oginski, *Mémoires*, vols. 1 and 2; Szymon Askenazy, *Dantzig et la Pologne*; B. Engelmann, *Preussen*, pp. 144–46.
21	34ff.	Kukiel, pp. 4–14, 84–86; Potocka, pp. 96–108; Askenazy, *Poniatowski*, pp. 114–30, 297–303; Oginski 2, pp. 336–39; Handelsman, pp. 45–90.
22	8–25	Schilder, *Imperator Aleksandr I* 2, pp. 160–69; Radziwill, pp. 250–53; Rambaud, *L'Allemagne sous Napoléon*, pp. 177–79; Askenazy, *Dantzig*, pp. 90–98.
22	26ff.	Denis Davydov, *Voyenniye Zapiski*, pp. 115–21; Troyat, *Alexandre Ier*, pp. 140–42; Radziwill, pp. 260–64; Tatichtchev, pp. 116–23.
22	36ff.	Schilder, *Aleksandr I* 2, pp. 354–61; Palmer, *Alexander I*, ch. 8.
23	6–9	For Napoleon's piercing gaze, see Comtesse de Choiseul-Gouffier, *Réminiscences*, p. 144.
23	9–12	Tatichtchev, p. 153; Nap., *Corr.* 15, p. 464, no. 12825.
23	13–20	Tatichtchev, pp. 131ff.; Schilder, *Aleksandr I* 2, pp. 169–202, 291–97.
23	21–27	Hardenberg 4, pp. 93–97; Radziwill, pp. 256–57; Gräfin von Voss, *Neunundsechsig Jahre am Preussischen Hofe*, pp. 303–6; Nap., *Corr.* 15, pp. 490, 495, nos. 12869, 12875.
23	28ff.	Tatichtchev, pp. 140–44, 231; NMR, *RDRF* 4, pp. 270–72.
23	44–46	NMR, *CEAS*, pp. 17–18.
24	1ff.	Davydov, pp. 128–31; K. Waliszewski, *Le Règne d'Alexandre* 1, p. 242; Radziwill, pp. 256, 273.
24	8–14	P. A. Vyazemsky, *Polnoye Sobranye Sochinenii* 8, p. 255.
24	15ff.	NMR, *CEAS*, pp. 18–19; Tatichtchev, pp. 175–80; Clercq, *Recueil des Traités de la France* 2, pp. 207, 224; Bignon, *Histoire de France* 6, p. 335; Garden, *Histoire des traités* 10, p. 234; Thiers 7, p. 666.
25	1ff.	Tatichtchev, pp. 190–4; NMR, *L'Impératrice Elisabeth* 2, pp. 251–53; NMR, *RDRF* 4, p. 267.
25	9ff.	On Caulaincourt, see Jean Hanoteau's long introduction to *Mémoires* 1.

PAGE	LINES	
25	28–43	Tatichtchev, pp. 258–59; Caulaincourt, *Mémoires* 1, pp. 98–99; Oginski 3, pp. 45–46.
25	44 ff.	Tatichtchev, pp. 277–309.
26	5–11	Askenazy, *Poniatowski,* pp. 140–56.
26	18 ff.	On Rumiantsev, see P. Grimsted, *The Foreign Ministers of Alexander I,* pp. 167–87; J. Q. Adams, 30 Nov. 1810 diary entry (*Memoirs* 2, p. 191); Tatichtchev, pp. 324–28, 358–59, 364–67.
26	43 ff.	Caulaincourt 1, pp. 274–75; Talleyrand, *Mémoires* 1, pp. 447–51; J. Orieux, *Talleyrand,* pp. 484–88.
27	4 ff.	NMR, *CEAS,* pp. xxvi, 4, 6, 9–12, 14, 16–17, 21, 22; Edling, pp. 70–71.
27	23–29	NMR, *RDRF* 6, 47, 51.
27	32–35	NMR, *L'Impératrice Elisabeth* 2, pp. 253–54. It was probably Bagration's ugliness which had caused his beautiful wife, born Catherine Skavronska, to flee from his embraces to Vienna. (See NMR, *Portraits russes* 1, p. 49.)
27	35–41	NMR, *RDRF* 6, pp. 55–56.
28	2 ff.	NMR, *RDRF* 4, pp. 18–24; Askenazy, *Poniatowski* (German ed.), pp. 181–82.
28	17–27	Askenazy, *Poniatowski,* pp. 172–97, 321–23.
28	28 ff.	NMR, *RDRF* 4, pp. 50, 56–58.
28	41–45	Bruun, p. 170.
28–29		Tatichtchev, pp. 498–514; NMR, *RDRF* 4, pp. 52, 68–80, 111–12, 122–25, 129–30, 136–37, 144–46, 154–58.
29	8–12	Tatichtchev, pp. 513–14.
29	12–17	Czartoryski, *Mémoires* 2, p. 217.
29	18 ff.	NMR, *RDRF* 4, pp. 192–248, 297, 320; Tatichtchev, pp. 518–24.
29	37 ff.	NMR, *CEAS,* pp. 251–61.
30	15–19	NMR, *RDRF* 4, p. 234.
30	20–34	Tatichtchev, p. 519; NMR, *RDRF* pp. 249–80.
30	35 ff.	F. Masson, *Napoléon et sa famille* 5, pp. 5–12; L. Madelin, *La Contre-révolution,* pp. 288–91; Vandal 2, pp. 253–68; Thiers 2, pp. 322–80.
31	1 ff.	NMR, *RDRF* 4, pp. 298–319; Tatichtchev, pp. 524–28.
31	15 ff.	Adams 2, pp. 342–45.
31	33 ff.	On Napoleon's feeling that his marriage to one of Alexander's sisters

PAGE	LINES	

could have averted a rupture with Russia, see his 23 October 1810 conversation with Chernyshov (*SIRIO* 21, pp. 17–18).

3 The Looming Storm

32   **4–6**   On Alexander's casual treatment of his wife, see NMR, *L'Impératrice Elisabeth,* particularly vol. 1, and pp. 194–96, 436–38 of vol. 2. Their second daughter died in May 1808 (vol. 2, pp. 280–84).

32   **6–8**   On Maria Antonovna Naryshkin, see Golovine, pp. 246–47; Edling, 60–61; Count de Bray, *Aus dem Leben eines Diplomaten,* pp. 178–84, 192–93; NMR, *Portraits russes* 1, p. 105. Maria Antonovna Naryshkin had also given birth to a son who, according to Sophie von Tisenhaus (Choiseul-Gouffier, *Réminiscences,* pp. 200–7), was neither Emperor Alexander's nor her husband's.

33   **12ff.**   On the Continental System and its far-reaching consequences, see Vandal 2, pp. 441–45; Tulard, *Le Grand Empire,* pp. 141–53; Dunan, *Napoléon et l'Allemagne,* pp. 23–29; Madame de Rémusat, *Mémoires* 3, pp. 260–66.

33   **27ff.**   On the pope, see Tulard, *Napoléon,* p. 357, and on Adriatic "smuggling," Dunan, pp. 314–16.

34   **7–22**   Servières, *L'Allemagne française,* pp. 82–90, 110–28, 195–96; Dunan, pp. 285, 303–4, 695.

34   **24–31**   Vandal 2, pp. 443–44; Tulard, *Grand Empire,* pp. 179–81.

35   **10ff.**   Vandal 2, pp. 489–512; Servières, *L'Allemagne française,* p. 286; Nap., *Corr.* 21, pp. 268–69 (17062), p. 275 (17071).

35   **34ff.**   Tatichtchev, pp. 542–44; Nap. *Corr* 21, pp. 296–97 (17099), 349–50 (17179), 430 (17291).

35–36   Rambaud, *L'Allemagne sous Napoléon,* p. 96. According to the 1805 edition of the *Almanac de Gotha* (p. 46), Maria Feodorovna's sister died in Nov. 1775.

36   **6–17**   Vandal 2, pp. 521–31.

36   **35–38**   Caulaincourt 1, p. 282; J. de Maistre, *Corr. diplomatique* 1, p. 13.

36   **41–46**   Schilder, *Aleksandr I* 3, pp. 22–23.

37   **5ff.**   M. Josselson, *The Commander,* pp. 74–77; *La Guerre nationale* 1, part 2, pp. 15–21.

37   **22–27**   Toll, *Denkwürdigkeiten* 1, pp. 280–81.

37   **28ff.**   See pp. 10, 19, and chs. 6 and 7 of Josselson's *Commander,* a meticulously researched biography of Barclay de Tolly.

37   **38–42**   Ibid., pp. 76–77; Boutourlin, *Histoire militaire* 1, pp. 56–57; Mansuy, pp. 70–71.

PAGE	LINES	
37	43 ff.	Czartoryski, *Mémoires* 2, pp. 250–53, 271–70; Kukiel, pp. 85–96.
38	21 ff.	On Pulawy and its treasures, see Potocka, pp. 58–64; V. de Broglie, *Souvenirs* 1, pp. 189–91. On Alexander's 1805 visit, see M. Lempitski, "Aleksandr v Pulavakh," *RS* 55 (1887), pp. 165–73, and Caulaincourt's 15 Sept. 1809 dispatch to Foreign Minister Champagny (NMR, *RDRF* 4, p. 84).
38	43 ff.	Kukiel, pp. 81–84; NMR, *Le Comte Paul Stroganov* 1, pp. 256, 264–65.
39	11 ff.	Bignon, *Souvenirs d'un diplomate,* pp. 356–57; Potocka, pp. 10–13. On the Praga massacre, A. Potocka, pp. 11–13; Oginski 1, pp. 343–412.
39	23–30	In a March 1810 conversation recorded by Czartoryski (*Mémoires* 2, pp. 226–30), Alexander admitted that he had missed a "golden opportunity" in not having himself proclaimed king of Poland in the autumn of 1805.
39	31 ff.	Ibid., pp. 256–70.
40	10–16	Askenazy (*Poniatowski,* pp. 222–24, 337–38) takes Mazade to task for the grave omissions in his edition of Czartoryski's *Mémoires.* See also Kukiel, 92–95.
40	21–29	Nap., *Corr.* 21, p. 354 (17187); and nos. 17259, 17286, 17526.
40	35 ff.	Ibid., pp. 419–21, 427–28, 447–62, 468–69, 479–80, 483–85.
41	10–15	Ibid., pp. 570–73, 590–93.
41	16–19	Ibid., 17371, 17391, 17344.
41	20 ff.	Ibid., pp. 508–9, 544–45. 573–74; 18 March 1811 letters to Jerome of Westphalia and King Frederick of Württemberg (pp. 576–77); 583–85, 587, 591–92, 604–6, 623–24.
41	35–44	Ibid., 17372, 17454.
41–42		Ibid., pp. 593–88 (17515, 17516).
42	18–24	Ibid., 17 Feb. 1811 draft letter to Champagny (17316), pp. 477–78; letter to Tsar Alexander (17395), p. 497.
42	29 ff.	25 March 1811 letter from Alexander to Nap., Tatichtchev, pp. 547–52.
42	37 ff.	J. de Maistre, *Corr. diplomatique* 1, pp. 8–9; Adams 2, pp. 266–67.
43	17 ff.	L. Dupech and P. d'Espezel, *Histoire de Paris* 2 (Paris, 1931), pp. 76–80.
43	36–38	Potocka, pp. 200–1.
44	4 ff.	On change of atmosphere in Paris, see Abrantès 9, pp. 95, 102–6; Potocka, pp. 201–14; Tulard, *Napoléon,* pp. 325–34.

PAGE	LINES	
44	21–26	Rémusat 3, p. 282.
44	34–37	Abrantès 10, p. 76.
44	38ff.	Beugnot 2, pp. 400–2.
45	7ff.	Rémusat 3, pp. 234–38, 274–77; Castellane, *Journal* 1, p. 82; Abrantès 9, pp. 23–24; L. Madelin, *La Contre-révolution sous la révolution,* pp. 226–49; Tulard, *Napoléon et la noblesse d'Empire,* pp. 55–105.
45	18ff.	Georges Blond's *La Grande Armée* contains brief portraits of Berthier (pp. 98–100), Lefebvre (pp. 147–55), Ney (pp. 57–58), Davout (pp. 108–9).
45	25–32	Caulaincourt 1, pp. 281–82; Vandal 3, pp. 174–75.
46	21–34	This description of Napoleon is based on Fain, *Mémoires,* pp. 286–87, and Meneval, *Souvenirs historiques,* pp. 1–5.
46	35ff.	Caulaincourt 1, pp. 281–98.
50	30–32	Chernyshov, in a 17 June 1811 dispatch to Rumiantsev, claimed that Napoleon's conversation with Caulaincourt had begun at 1:00 P.M. and finished at 9:00 in the evening! *SIRIO* 21, p. 176.
50	32ff.	Caulaincourt 1, pp. 298–302; Madame de Rémusat (*Mémoires* 3, p. 53) also quotes Napoleon as often complaining to Talleyrand of the *"caractère passionné mais léger des Polonais."*
50–51		See Napoleon's remarks to Tsar Alexander's emissary General Shuvalov in May 1811 on the need to keep Poland weak, for a reconstituted "Poland might slip away from me, like other countries." *SIRIO* 21, pp. 411–20. On Napoleon and the Poles, see also Askenazy, *Napoléon et la Pologne* 1, pp. 175–90; Villemain, *Souvenirs contemporains* 1, pp. 161–80; Askenazy, *Ponitowski,* pp. 136–38, 217–30, 308, 341; Ernouf, *Maret,* p. 296; Bignon, *Souvenirs,* pp. 68–81, 112–5; Mansuy, pp. 247–78, 284–92.

4 The Final Squeeze

52	1–6	Caulaincourt 1, pp. 244–45, 254; Vandal 2, p. 207; *SIRIO* 21, pp. 280–82, 413–14, 419.
52	7ff.	Vandal 2, p. 295; *SIRIO* 21, p. 17; Waliszewski 1, pp. 269–70.
52	18–21	On Kurakin's vanity, see Caulaincourt's 5 February 1810 dispatch to Champagny (NMR, *RDRF* 4, p. 273).
52	21–24	Tatichtchev, pp. 137–38.
52	25–30	On Razumovsky in Vienna, see Prince A. Vassilchikov, *Semyeistvo Razumovskikh* 3 (in French edition, *Les Razoumovski* 2, parts 2 and 3); Waliszewski p. 259; A. Potocka, pp. 182–4.

PAGE	LINES	
53	1ff.	NMR, *Portraits russes* 1, p. 48; Vigée-Lebrun 2, pp. 64–65.
53	34–40	Schilder, *Aleksandr I,* 3, pp. 19–20; Bausset, *Mémoires anecdotiques* 2, pp. 49–55; Stanislas de Girardin, *Mémoires et Souvenirs* 2, pp. 397–401.
53	41–43	Nesselrode, K. R. V., *Lettres et Papiers* 2, pp. 72–73.
53–54		*SIRIO* 21, pp. 83–84.
54	5ff.	Vandal 3, pp. 209–17; Max Duncker, *Aus der Zeit,* pp. 374–75; Tatichtchev, pp. 572–73; AMREP, *Corr. politique—Russie,* vol. 153, pp. 139–44.
55	45ff.	Ernouf, *Maret,* pp. 301–5, and for a negative judgment on Maret, Pasquier 1, p. 470
56	27ff.	Vandal 3, pp. 217–26; Bignon, *Histoire de France* 10, p. 89; Ernouf, *Maret,* pp. 301–5; AMREP, *Corr. diplomatique—Russie,* vol. 153, pp. 145–56.
57	10ff.	Tulard, "Le 'Dépôt de la Guerre' et la préparation de la campagne de Russie," in *RHA* 1939, no. 3, pp. 104–9.
57	43ff.	B. Engelmann, *Preussen,* pp. 156–57.
58	9ff.	Voss, pp. 371–80; Beugnot 2, pp. 392–94; Servières, *L'Allemagne française,* p. 170.
58	27ff.	Max Lehmann, *Scharnhorst* 2, p. 424, fn.; F. de Martens, *Recueil des Traités* 7, pp. 16–19.
58	40ff.	Lehmann, *Scharnhorst* 2, pp. 155–65; Clercq, *Recueil des Traités* 2, pp. 270–72.
59	7ff.	Hardenberg, *Denkwürdigkeiten* 4, pp. 167–69.
59	18ff.	Lehmann, *Scharnhorst* 2, p. 400ff.; H. von Boyen, *Erinnerungen aus dem Leben des Feldmarshalls* 2, pp. 140–41.
60	13–21	Martens 7, pp. 23–37.
60	22ff.	Lehmann, *Scharnhorst* 2, pp. 418–20; Hardenberg 4, p. 276; and on the "war scare" atmosphere, Bignon, *Souvenirs,* pp. 99–101, 125–26.
60	33–38	F. von Ompteda, *Zur deutschen Geschichte* 3, p. 131.
60	39ff.	Hardenberg 4, p. 283; Lehmann, *Scharnhorst* 2, p. 426.
61	3–11	Ompteda 3, p. 135; Lehmann, *Scharnhorst* 2, 429–30.
61	17ff.	See Metternich's long 28 November 1811 (misdated December) memorandum to Emperor Francis in his *Mémoires* 2, pp. 422–35; also Emperor Francis's reaction (p. 435), and Schwarzenberg's subsequent (17 December) meeting with Napoleon (pp. 436–42).
61	26–27	Ompteda 3, pp. 124–25; Hardenberg 4, p. 298.

PAGE	LINES	
62	5 ff.	Lehmann, *Scharnhorst* 2, pp. 431–34; Ompteda 3, pp. 176–79.
62	25 ff.	Lehmann, *Scharnhorst* 2, pp. 436–37; Ompteda 3, pp. 221–22; Radziwill, pp. 316–18.
63	1 ff.	Clercq 2, pp. 354–59.
63	8–13	Lehmann, *Scharnhorst* 2, pp. 437–38.
63	14 ff.	Hardenberg 4, pp. 275–76.
63	23 ff.	Vandal 3, pp. 339–40; Radziwill, pp. 318–21.
63	32 ff.	Metternich 2, p. 439; C. A. Macartney, *The Habsburg Empire,* pp. 189–90.
63	40 ff.	Clercq 2, pp. 369–72.
64	12–18	Pasquier 1, pp. 497–509; Thiers 13, pp. 447–54; Tulard, *Napoléon,* pp. 378–81, and *Grand Empire,* pp. 246–52.
64	18–30	Pasquier 1, pp. 516–18; Abrantès 14, pp. 208–10.
64	31 ff.	On Chernyshov, *RBS,* pp. 293–305; NMR, *Portraits russes* 2, p. 56; Adams 2, p. 93. On his talent for waltzing, NMR, *L'Impératrice Elisabeth* 1, pp. 71–72, and Choiseul-Gouffier, *Réminiscences,* p. 11.
65	14–22	Abrantès 14, pp. 162–69.
65	23–26	Fouché, *Mémoires* 2, pp. 125–27; Savary, *Mémoires* 5, pp. 206–10.
65	27 ff.	*SIRIO* 21, pp. 110–24, and the many references to military matters in his dispatches to Rumiantsev, ibid., pp. 145–304. For his espionage activities, Josselson, p. 75, and *La Guerre nationale* 1, part 1, pp. 147–49, 154–55. Original source material concerning Chernyshov and his French contacts can be found at ANP, Ministère de la Justice file, carton BB 3-145; Police générale, carton F 7-6575. The "Acte d'accusation contre Michel Michel, etc." can also be found at AMREP, *Corr. politique—Russie,* vol. 154, item no. 131, pp. 287–94.
66	10–11	Schilder, *Aleksandr I,* 3, pp. 25, 365.
66	11 ff.	Metternich on Nesselrode, quoted by P. Grimsted, p. 198; and Nesselrode, *Lettres et Papiers* 2, pp. 69–75; also vol. 3 (containing his secret correspondence with Speransky), pp. 225–387.
66	21–26	Pasquier 1, pp. 518–19; Savary 5, p. 207.
66	42 ff.	Vandal 3, pp. 306–12; *SIRIO* 21, pp. 125–44.
67	12 ff.	Vandal 3, pp. 312–21; Savary 5, pp. 208 ff.; Pasquier 1, pp. 518–19.
67	33 ff.	Vandal 3, pp. 376–88; *SIRIO* 21, pp. 362–410.
68	10–18	Thiers 13, pp. 446–47; Vandal 3, p. 311.

PAGE	LINES	

5 Dresden

PAGE	LINES	
69	1–12	Caulaincourt 1, p. 330; Bausset 2, pp. 80–83; Denniée, *Itinéraire de l'Empereur Napoléon,* pp. 15–16; Fain, *Manuscrit de 1812* 1, pp. 61–62.
69	13ff.	Colonel Ponthon is mentioned by General Marbot, *Mémoires* 3, p. 6.
69	26–29	Pasquier 1, p. 525.
70	13–18	Nap., *Corr.* 22, pp. 494–97; pp. 529–30 (18089); pp. 539, 555–59; pp. 577–78 (18152); pp. 620–4 (18204).
70	23–26	On Germaine de Staël's flight from Paris, see Christopher Herold's scintillating biography *Mistress to an Age.*
71	10–16	Karl von Suckow, *Aus meinem Soldatenleben,* pp. 134–38.
71	17ff.	François Bourgogne, *Mémoires,* p. 29.
71	22–26	A. G. Macdonell, *Napoleon and His Marshals,* pp. 48–49.
71	34–41	Caulaincourt 1, pp. 330.
71	41ff.	On Mainz and the French invasion of the Rhineland, see A. Rambaud, *Les Français sur le Rhin,* pp. 162–279.
72	18ff.	Bausset 2, p. 86. On Dahlberg, see Rambaud, *Les Français,* pp. 207–8, 350, and his *L'Allemagne sous Napoleon,* pp. 138–42; Dunan, pp. 23–24; and biographical essay in ADB 6. On the treatment previously accorded to the ghetto Jews of Frankfurt, see Georg Brandes (quoting Ludwig Borne), *Main Currents in Nineteenth-Century Literature* 6 *(Young Germany),* pp. 40–43, 54–58.
72	36ff.	On unpaved state of German roads, Brandt, p. 318; on French roads, Tulard, *La Vie quotidienne sous Napoléon,* pp. 161–65; and on Archduke Ferdinand's cordial relations with the former commander of l'Armée d'Italie, Miot de Melito, *Mémoires* 1, ch. 4.
72	46ff.	Rambaud, *L'Allemagne,* pp. 41–45; C. T. Perthes, *Politische Zustände* 1, pp. 435–60; Rapp, *Mémoires,* pp. 148–49.
73	10ff.	Denniée, pp. 183–85; Caulaincourt 1, p. 331; Castellane, *Journal* 1, p. 92.
73	26–32	On the composition of Prince Eugène's Fourth and Sixth corps, see Denniée, pp. 183–84; J. C. Sauzey, *Les Allemands sous les aigles françaises* 5, subtitled *Nos Alliés bavarois,* and *De Munich à Vilna: Papiers du général d'Albignac.*
73	33ff.	Senfft von Pilsach, *Mémoires,* p. 166.
73–74		Napoleon's entry into Dresden, as described in M. Lindau's *Geschichte der Königlichen Haupt- und Residenzstadt Dresden,* p. 744.

PAGE	LINES	
74	10–17	Castellane 1, pp. 92–93. Royal Schloss is described in G. Servières's *Dresde, Freiberg et Meissen.*
74	29 ff.	André Bonnefons, *Un Allie de Napoléon: Frédéric Auguste, premier roi de Saxe,* pp. 15–28; Bignon, *Souvenirs,* pp. 7–8.
74	39–45	Senfft von Pilsach, p. 167.
74–75		Lindau, p. 744; Castellane 1, p. 92; Senfft von Pilsach, p. 168; Fain 1, pp. 65–66.
75	25 ff.	Senfft von Pilsach, pp. 168–69; Fain 1, p. 62; Lindau, pp. 744–45.
76	14 ff.	Fain 1, p. 65; Abbé de Pradt, *Histoire de l'ambassade dans le Grand-Duché de Varsovie,* pp. 52–53; Vandal 3, p. 413; Castellane 1, p. 93.
76	30 ff.	Pradt, pp. 66–67; Senfft von Pilsach, p. 171; Castellane 1, p. 94.
77	18 ff.	On vague promises made to the Austrians for the return of the "Illyrian provinces," see *MR Jérôme* 5, pp. 19, 63, 139, 161, 165, 167, 173; Abel Mansuy, *Jérôme Napoléon et la Pologne,* pp. 78, 85, 139; Metternich, *Mémoires* 1, pp. 120–23.
78	6 ff.	Senfft von Pilsach, pp. 172–3; Castellane 1, p. 95.
78	13 ff.	Thiers 13, pp. 513–14, 529–30; Nap., *Corr.* 23, pp. 525–26 (18739); Fain 1, p. 63; Gourgaud, *Napoléon et la Grande Armée* 1, pp. 84–85; Senfft von Pilsach, p. 171.
78	27–34	Fain 1, pp. 76–78; Caulaincourt 1, pp. 333–6.
78	35 ff.	This portrayal of Louis de Narbonne is based on Eile Dard's *Un confident de l'empereur, le comte de Narbonne,* and on frequent references in Jean Orieux's biography of Talleyrand, and Herold's *Mistress to an Age.*
79	3–10	Las Cases, *Mémorial de Sainte-Hélène,* pp. 121–22.
79	16–27	Vandal 3, pp. 384–87; Napoleon to Alexander, from St.-Cloud, 25 April 1812, in *Corr.* 23, p. 454 (18669).
79	28 ff.	On Narbonne in Vilna, see Schilder 3, pp. 79; V. Kharkevich, *Voina 1812 goda* 2, pp. 54–56; Dard, pp. 218–21; Choiseul-Gouffier, *Mémoires,* pp. 79–81; AMREP, *Corr. politique—Russie,* vol. 154, p. 393.
80	27–39	Senfft von Pilsach, pp. 174–75; Bausset 2, pp. 59–69.
80	40 ff.	On Frederick Augustus's somnolence, General Lubin Griois, *Mémoires* 2, p. 4; and on this forced nocturnal vigil, Senfft von Pilsach, pp. 173–74.
80–81		Castellane 1, pp. 96–97.

PAGE	LINES	

6 Onward to Danzig

82   1–12   Castellane 1, p. 97. On Napoleon's campaign carriages, Fain, *Mémoires,* pp. 223–25.

82   21–29   Fantin des Odoards, *Journal,* pp. 169–73; Griois 2, p. 5; Victor Dupuy, *Souvenirs militaires,* p. 158; Mansuy, pp. 165–66.

82–83   Nap., *LIML* (no. 24), 30 May 1812, pp. 28–29.

83   12ff.   Fain, p. 80; Castellane 1, p. 97; Caulaincurt 1, p. 337.

83   24ff.   Brandt, pp. 311–28.

84   34ff   Fain 1, p. 81.

84   42ff.   Brandt, pp. 326–28.

85   16–19   Fezensac, *Journal,* pp. 6–7.

85   34–38   Rambuteau, *Mémoires,* pp. 85–86; Caulaincourt 1, pp. 322–25.

85   41ff.   Bignon, *Souvenirs,* pp. 218–20; Askenazy, *Poniatowski,* p. 331.

86   21–31   Nap., *Corr.,* 23, pp. 516–23 (18734).

86   32ff.   Rémusat, *Mémoires* 3, pp. 373–4; Vandal 3, pp. 430–9.

86   41ff.   Beugnot 1, pp. 491–92; Bignon, *Souvenirs,* pp. 219–20; Thiers 13, pp. 525–26.

87   4ff.   Fain 1, pp. 82–83; Castellane 1, p. 98; Brandt, pp. 329–30.

87   20ff.   Fain 1, pp. 82–83; Karl von Suckow, pp. 138–46.

87   38ff.   On Ney during the winter campaign of 1806–1807, see Fantin des Odoards, pp. 112–45.

88   1ff.   Karl von Suckow, pp.139–40; Luwig von Wolzogen, *Memoiren,* pp. 23–24, 35.

88   17ff.   Suckow, pp. 133–36.

88   26ff.   Dunan, p. 431; A. G. Mcdonell, p.129.

89   8ff.   Metternich 1, pp. 122–23. The idea of using Jerome to "bait" the Russians is argued, I think convincingly, by Mansuy, pp. 335–36, 347–48, 557–59.

89   30ff.   Mansuy, pp. 298–99, 17–23.

89   35ff.   Masson, *Napoléon et sa famile* 4, pp.167–94, 288–305, 310–12; 7, pp. 295–97; Rambuteau, pp. 56–57; Kleinschmidt, *Geschichte des Königreichs Westfalen,* pp. 58–83; Rambaud, *L'Allemagne,* pp. 103–5; Bignon, *Histoire de France* 8, p. 229; *MR Jérôme* 5, p. 319; Mansuy, pp. 43–44, 399–400; and on Jerome's popularity with his army officers, F. Giesse, *Kassel–Moskau–Küstrin,* p. x of preface.

PAGE	LINES	

90   7ff.   *MR Jérôme* 5, pp. 49, 62, 127–28, 247–48; Mansuy, pp. 57, 67–68, 80–86; Du Casse, *Napoléon. Supplément à la Correspondance,* pp. 165–66.

90   16ff.   Mansuy, pp. 90–91, 98, 107–8.

90   24ff.   Ibid., pp. 135–55; *MR Jérôme* 5, pp. 291–92.

90   36ff.   Mansuy, pp. 159–68, 172–75.

91   7ff.   Ibid., 62–68, 379–89, 418–21, 437–60, 474–75, 645–46; A. Potocka, p. 320.

91   22ff.   Mansuy, pp. 332, 530; Niemcewicz, *Pamietniki* 1, p. 326.

91   37ff.   Brandt, p. 390; and on the composition and uniforms of the Imperial Guard, G. Blond, *Grande Armée,* pp. 52–53; Liane Funcken and Fred Funcken, *L'Uniforme et les armes des soldats du Premier Empire* 2, p. 34; F. Masson, *Cavaliers de Napoléon,* pp. 219–43.

92   12–22   Fantin des Odoards, pp. 296–97.

92   23ff.   Brandt, p. 330.

92   36ff.   Nap., *LIML,* pp. 33–34; Castellane 1, p. 99; Caulaincourt 1, pp. 337–38.

92   42ff.   Ségur 4, pp. 31, 115–6; Mathieu Dumas, *Souvenirs* 3, pp. 418–19; V. B. Derrécagaix, *Le maréchal Berthier* 2, pp. 229–330; H. Vigier, *Davout* 2, pp. 73–75.

93   10   Nap., *Corr.* 23 (18740, 28 May from Dresden), 18771, 18772, dated 5 June, p. 503; Fain 1, p. 90; Thiers 13, pp. 512–13; Dums 3, p. 419.

93   22ff.   Fain 1, pp. 85–87; Rapp, *Mémoires,* p. 163–64.

94   18ff.   On Murat as king of Naples, see Jean Lucas-Dubreton, *Murat,* pp. 170–81.

94–95   Caulaincourt 1, pp. 338–42; Fain 1, pp. 87–88.

95   4ff.   On Berthier, see A. F. de Marmont, *Mémoires* 1, pp. 150–51; C. F. de Meneval, *Mémoires* 3, pp. 47–49; Miot de Milito 1, p. 91; on Grosbois, Stanislas de Girardin, *Mémoires et Souvenirs,* 2, pp. 422–23; Castellane 1, p. 88; Rémusat 3, pp. 345–46.

95   24–36   Rapp, p. 166.

7   Plotters, Dreamers, and Intriguers

96   1ff.   NMR, *CEAS,* pp. 57–62.

96   20ff.   Ibid., pp. 45–46, 57, 59, 60; Gen. L. V. Rochechouart, *Souvenirs sur la Révolution,* pp. 144–45; Edling, pp. 60–63.

97   10–20   NMR, *CEAS,* p. 63; Palmer, *Alexander I,* p. 210; Raeff, *Speransky,* p. 187; Adams 2, pp. 348–51, 370.

PAGE	LINES	
97	21–26	V. Bakunina, *RS* 47 (1885), pp. 392–93; A. Potocka, p. 92.
97	27 ff.	Czartoryski, *Mémoires* 2, p. 282.
97	33–39	On Speransky's attempted reforms and what happened when they were shelved, see Bernard Pares, *A History of Russia,* pp. 293–96, 304–5; and for a more skeptical opinion, Edward Crankshaw, *The Shadow of the Winter Palace,* pp. 24–25. This is also the general tenor of Richard Pipes's *Russia Under the Old Regime.*
97	40 ff.	Raeff, pp. 10 ff.
98	21 ff.	Ibid., pp. 119–59.
98	36–40	Boguslavsky, "Zapiski," in *RS* 26 (1879), p. 109.
98	44 ff.	See, for example, Napoleon's remarks on his Senate and Conseil d'Etat during the Dresden congress, Metternich, *Mémoires* 1, pp. 120–21.
99	4 ff.	Raeff, pp. 170–76.
99	21 ff.	Narichkine, *Le comte Rostopchine et son temps,* pp. 76–79.
99	30–40	A French translation of this pamphlet, in Rostopchine's *Oeuvres inédites,* pp. 39–54.
99	41 ff.	Raeff, pp. 174–77.
100	14 ff.	NMR, *CEAS* 25, pp. 63–65; Raeff, p. 181–82; Armand d'Allonville, *Mémoires* 11, pp. 367–68; E. M. Arndt, *Meine Wanderungen,* pp. 48–51; Schilder, *Aleksandr I* 3, p. 23; Abrantès 17, pp. 190–203.
100	32–40	Oginski 3, pp. 84–85, 118, 153, 157–60.
100	41 ff.	Raeff, p. 181; Adams 2, p. 327.
101	3 ff.	Raeff, pp. 181 ff. On Balashov, NMR, *Portraits russes* 2, p. 175; Waliszewski 1, p. 383; NMR, *RDRF* 5, pp. 349–50.
101	18 ff.	Raeff, pp. 193–94.
101	27–39	Schilder 3, pp. 25, 64, 365, 367 (fn. 63), 494; Nesselrode 2, pp. 66–71, and in 3, pp. 225–387, his letters to Speransky from Paris.
101	39 ff.	Schilder 3, pp. 54–55; Raeff, pp. 183–84.
101–2		Schilder 3, pp. 46 ff.; Raeff, pp. 190–91.
102	11–15	Schilder 3, pp. 368–69 (fns. 75, 79); Raeff, p. 191; J. de Maistre, *Corr. diplomatique* 1, pp. 68–72.
102	16–22	NMR, *RDRF* 6, p. 254; Raeff, pp. 193–94; P. P. Viegel, *Zapiski* 2, p. 10; Schilder 3, p. 32; AMREP, *Corr. politique—Russie,* vol. 154 (letter 127), p. 279.
102	23 ff.	V. Bakunina, "Dvenadtsaty god," pp. 393–94.
102	32–39	Schilder 3, pp. 48–50, 369 (fn. 79), 50–52; Raeff, p. 193; Nesselrode,

PAGE	LINES	
		Lettres et Papiers 2, pp. 75–76; NMR, *L'Empereur Alexandre Ier,* pp. 90–91.
103	3–9	*SIRIO* 21, pp. 422–45.
103	10 ff.	Ibid., pp. 107–8, 269–70, 334–35, 437–39; Nesselrode 3, pp. 383–84.
103	33–37	P. Coquerelle, article on Sébastiani in *RHD* 18 (1904), pp. 575–93.
103	39–41	J. W. Zinkeisen, *Geschichte des Osmanischen Reiches* 7, pp. 455–56.
103	42 ff.	Coquerelle, *RHD* 18 (1904), pp. 598–607.
104	8–18	Juchereau de Saint-Denys, *Histoire de l'empire ottoman* 2, pp. 173–202. The news of Sultan Selim's overthrow reached Napoleon while he was negotiating at Tilsit. It upset him considerably. *Corr.* 21, pp. 505–6 (12886, dated 9 July 1807). The eventual result was Napoleon's renewed offer to Alexander (first made at Tilsit) to carve up the Ottoman Empire between them. See Tatichtchev, pp. 309–15.
104	19 ff.	Juchereau de Saint-Denys 2, pp. 207–72; and for text of Anglo-Ottoman Treaty of 5 January 1809, J. C. Hurewitz, *Diplomacy in the Near and Middle East* 1, pp. 81–84.
104	27 ff.	Juchereau de Saint-Denys 2, pp. 274–304; F. von Schubert, *Unter dem Doppeladler,* pp. 192–98.
104–5		Tchitchagov, *Mémoires inédits,* pp. 5–15, and in the Lahovary (1909) ed. of his *Mémoires,* pp. 370–73, 380–82; Juchereau de Saint-Denys 2, pp. 315–7; Zinkeisen 7, pp. 716–8.
105	10 ff.	Schubert, p. 197; Albert de Ligne, *Mémoires* 1, pp. 127–28, 188–91; Léonce Pingaud, *Les Français en Russie,* pp. 131, 139.
105	18–20	On the imperial silver favored by Kutuzov, see W. von Loewenstern's "Zapiski" in *RS* 105 (January-March 1901), p. 124; and on the Vallachian damsel, J. de Maistre, *Corr. diplomatique* 1, p. 100.
105	25–30	V. Bakunina, p. 394; Lebzeltern, *Mémoires,* pp. 216–17.
105	31 ff.	On Chichagov, article in *RBS* and the undated edition of his *Mémoires,* vol. 1.
105–6		On Chichagov's admiration for Napoleon, Edling, pp. 22–23, and Tatichtchev, pp. 321–22, 331–32.
106	3 ff.	NMR, *RDRF* 4, pp. 51, 194, 242, 269, 273.
106	10–14	Tchitchagov, undated *Mémoires,* pp. 281–82.
106	15 ff.	J. de Maistre, *Corr. diplomatique* 1, pp. 20–23.
106	28 ff.	Tchitchagov (*Mémoires inédits,* pp. 6–11) quotes at length from Tsar Alexander's written instructions of 19 April 1812. The idea of exploiting Slavic national sentiment against the Turks had long been an idée fixe with Chancellor Rumiantsev, but the spectacular

PAGE	LINES	
		new twist given to this idea—of using it simultaneously against the Turks and the French—was almost certainly Chichagov's rather than the tsar's.
107	1ff.	On idea of using Slavic uprising threat to put pressure on Austrian government in Vienna, see Alexander's 21 April 1812 letter to Bernadotte (Schilder 3, fn. 50, on pp. 365–66); Bogdanovich, *Istoria otechestvennoy voiny 1812 goda* 3, p. 411. Also Lebzeltern, *Mémoires,* pp. 222–29; and Lauriston's analysis in AMREP, *Corr. politique—Russie,* vol. 154, p. 407.
107	7ff.	AMREP, *Corr. politique—Russie,* vol. 154, p. 432; J. de Maistre, *Corr. diplomatique* I, pp. 99–100; V. Bakunina, p. 396.
107	17–26	Tchitchagov, *Mémoires inédits,* pp. 16–21.
107	27ff.	J. de Maistre, *Corr. diplomatique* I, pp. 99–100; Allonville II, pp. 365–67; Adams 2, pp. 364–65.

8 The Hornets' Nest of Vilna

PAGE	LINES	
109	1–11	Schilder, *Aleksandr I* 3, pp. 75–76; Bakunina, p. 395; NMR, *L'Impératrice Elisabeth* 2, p. 525.
109	43ff.	*SIRIO* 21, pp. 422–50.
110	9–14	NMR, *CEAS,* p. 69; Schilder 3, p. 76.
110	15ff.	This description of Vilna is based on article in Brockhaus & Ephron's *Entsiklopedichesky Slovar* 6, pp. 381–85; Baedeker, *West- und Mittel-Russland* (Leipzig, 1883), pp. 46–47; Hogendorp, *Mémoires,* pp. 310–11.
110	33–38	Choiseul-Gouffier, *Réminiscences,* p. 134.
110	38–44	Schilder 3, pp. 76, 399.
110	45ff.	Choiseul-Gouffier, *Mémoires historiques,* pp. 75–77.
111	20–24	NMR, *CEAS,* pp. 70, 73.
111	24–32	Nesselrode 2, p. 75; Schilder 3, pp. 63, 371 (fn. 102).
111	42–46	NMR, *Le comte Paul Stroganov* I, pp. 257–58; Radziwill, pp. 247–48.
112	4–16	NMR, *Stroganov* I, p. 258; Adams 2, p. 72.
112	18–19	On Ostermann-Tolstoy's superpatriotism, Josselson, pp. 99–100.
112	30ff.	Ibid., pp. 86–87; Wolzogen, *Memoiren,* pp. 63–77.
113	19ff.	Josselson, pp. 93–94, 31ff.
114	43–46	On Alexander's straw-stuffed mattress, see Choiseul-Gouffier, *Mémoires,* p. 63, and *Réminiscences,* p. 24.
114–15		J. de Maistre, *Corr. diplomatique* I, pp. 9–10.

PAGE	LINES	
115	5ff.	Josselson, pp. 60–61.
115	17–23	On Arakcheyev, see Michael Jenkins's biography.
115	27ff.	Josselson, pp. 81–84; Wolzogen, pp. 41, 18–19; on half-shaving of soldiers' heads, Niemcewicz, *Notes on My Captivity in Russia,* pp. 84–85.
116	2–10	J. de Maistre, *Corr. diplomatique* 1, pp. 9–10.
116	11–14	Wolzogen, pp. 78, 29; Sir Robert Wilson, *Brief Remarks,* p. 51; Schubert, p. 90; Tatichtchev, p. 491; NMR, *RDRF* 4, p. 84.
116	14ff.	NMR, *RDRF* 4, pp. 82–83; C. F. Toll, *Denkwürdigkeiten* 1, pp. 2–3, 124, 130–31; Czartoryski, *Mémoires* 1, pp. 78, 80.
116	23–27	Josselson, p. 78; NMR, *RDRF* 4, p. 209; Y. Tarlé, *Campagne de Russie,* pp. 66–67; P. A. Zhilin, *Ghibel Napoleonskoy Armii,* p. 79.
116	32ff.	Josselson, pp. 89–90; Mathieu Dumas, *Souvenirs* 3, pp. 416–17.
117	25ff.	Josselson, pp. 91, 96; D. P. Boutourlin, *Histoire militaire* 1, pp. 55ff.
117	37–45	Josselson, pp. 73–90.
117–18		Schilder 3, pp. 75–76.
118	5ff.	References to Paulucci can be found in J. de Maistre's *Corr. diplomatique* 1, pp. 129–32, and more acidly in Chichagov's undated *Mémoires* 1, pp. 321–23.
118	19ff.	Josselson, pp. 98–99; Nesselrode 2, pp. 79–80.
118	25–32	On Yermolov, see NMR, *Portraits russes* 3, no. 170; Loewenstern, *Mémoires* 1, pp. 203–4; Toll 1, pp. 347–48; Josselson, p. 100.
118	39–43	On Bennigsen, Wolzogen, pp. 40–41; Josselson, pp. 30–38, 100. Tarlé, in *Napoleon's Invasion of Russia,* p. 229 (p. 216 in Russian ed.), claims that Bennigsen was an unscrupulous taker of bribes from contractors and commissary officials in the quartermaster services.
119	1ff.	This description of Shishkov is based on article in *RBS,* pp. 316–20, and Arndt, *Erinnerungen,* pp. 145–46.
119	33–38	Schubert, p. 216.

9 Forward to the Niemen!

120	1ff.	V. Bakunina, pp. 396–98.
121	5ff.	Schubert, pp. 208–10; and p. 179 of Loewenstern's *Mémoires* 1, which contains many allusions to his own philandering in Petersburg.
121	20–26	Caulaincourt 1, pp. 388–89; Fain 1, pp. 90–92.
121	40ff.	Nap., *Corr.* 23, p. 583 (18800).

PAGE	LINES	
121	44ff.	Caulaincourt 1, pp. 342–43; A. Dedem de Gelder, *Mémoires*, pp. 211, 226–27.
124	5ff.	Eduard Rüppell, *Kriegsgefangene im Herzen Russlands*, pp. 13–26; H. von Roos, *Mit Napoleon in Russland*, pp. 14–17.
124	18–21	Ségur 4, pp. 111–12.
124	23–31	On the previous year's drought, see Roos, p. 1; Askenazy, *Poniatowski*, p. 339. On the lateness of the spring, Mansuy, p. 317 (fn. 71); *MP Eugène* 7, pp. 322, 345–46, 350, 364. On shortages of fodder, Castellane 1, p. 101; Roos, pp. 15–16; A. de Saint-Chamans, *Mémoires*, pp. 210–13.
124	33–39	Castellane 1, pp. 102–3; Caulaincourt 1, p. 339; Grenadier François Pils, *Journal de Marche*, p. 103.
124	40ff.	Fantin des Odoards, pp. 148, 302; Fain 1, pp. 92–93; AMREP, *Corr. politique—Russie*, vol. 154, pp. 402–5, 411–44.
125	3–12	Jomini, *Précis . . . des campagnes de 1812 à 1814* 1, pp. 53–54.
125	12ff.	Nap., *Corr.* 23, p. 581 (18799, dated 15 June, to Prince Eugène).
125	21–29	Nap., *Corr. inédite* 5, p. 439 (3rd Bulletin de la Grande Armée).
125	30ff.	Nap., *Corr.* 23, pp. 607–8 (18839, 20 June letter to Davout from Gumbinnen).
125	38ff.	Caulaincourt 1, pp. 339–42; Jomini, pp. 54–55; Dedem, pp. 210–12, 226–27.
126	17–29	Nap., *Corr. inédite* 5, pp. 435–36; and (less accurately) Ségur 4, pp. 131–32.
126	30ff.	Oginski 3, pp. 160–61; Choiseul-Gouffier, *Mémoires*, p. 97; A. Potocka, pp. 302–3; Dedem, p. 214.
126	40ff.	Askenazy, *Poniatowski*, pp. 229–31, 235; Brandt, pp. 312–13; Dumas 3, p. 414; Derrécagaix, V. B., *Les Etats-Majors de Napoléon: le Lieutenant-Général Comte Belliard*, pp. 485–86.
127	8ff.	Schubert, p. 212.
127	15–19	The figure of 14 million is given in Oginski 3, p. 63. The total population of Lithuania, Volhynia, and Podolia was around 8 million.
127	29ff.	Nap., *LIML* (no. 41), p. 43.
127	36ff.	Caulaincourt 1, p. 339–45; Castellane 1, pp. 103–5.
128	9–14	Caulaincourt 1, pp. 342–45, and the more detailed and probably more accurate description in Roman Soltyk, *Napoléon en 1812*, pp. 10–11.
128	27–31	Fain 1, p. 166.

PAGE	LINES	
128	32ff.	Saint-Chamans, pp. 213–14; Denniée, pp. 14–15; Nap., *Corr.* 23, pp. 622–26 (18857); Derrécagaix, *Belliard*, p. 487; Caulaincourt I, pp. 343–45.
129	19ff.	NMR, *Stroganov* 2, p. 258.
129	26ff.	Oginski 3, pp. 40–43; Choiseul-Gouffier, *Mémoires*, pp. 82–83.
129	34ff.	V. Bakunina, p. 391.
129	40ff.	Schubert, p. 209; Allonville II, pp. 376–77; Choiseul-Gouffier, *Mémoires*, pp. 84–86, and *Réminiscences*, pp. 20–21.
130	7ff.	Schilder 3, pp. 82–83; Choiseul-Gouffier, *Mémoires*, pp. 86–91.
130	14–23	Choiseul-Gouffier, *Réminiscences*, pp. 49–52; Schubert, pp. 216–17.
130	24ff.	Choiseul-Gouffier, *Réminiscences*, pp. 52–60; *Mémoires*, pp. 87–90. Schilder 3, p. 84; E. A. Komarovsky, "Zapiski," in *RA* 1867, pp. 766–67.
131	17ff.	Zhilin, *Ghibel*, p. 85.

10 An Ominous Beginning

PAGE	LINES	
132	1–5	Pils, p. 104; Faber du Faur, *Napoleons Feldzug in Russland*, pp. 33–35; Griois, *Mémoires* 2, p. 13.
132	6–9	Fain I, pp. 167–68.
132	9ff.	Ségur 4, pp. 138–39; and for a slightly different version of the Niemen crossing, Soltyk, pp. 20–21.
132	14ff.	Denniée, pp. 14–15; Caulaincourt I, p. 345; Nap., *Corr.* 23, p. 622 (18857).
132	19ff.	Fain I, pp. 168–70; Dedem, pp. 210–11; Castellane I, pp. 105–6; V. Dupuy, *Souvenirs militaires*, p. 166.
133	4–9	As described in the 3rd Bulletin (*Corr. inédite* 5, pp. 438–39).
133	10ff.	Denniée, pp. 15–16.
133	16–17	On the heat, see Castellane I, p. 107; Pils, p. 104.
133	17ff.	Dedem, p. 213–14; Ségur 4, p. 140.
133	32ff.	Jomini, pp. 56–57; Brandt, pp. 337–38.
133	40ff.	Pils, pp. 104–5; Roos, p. 18; Jomini, p. 57; Griois 2, p. 13; Castellane I, p. 107.
134	5–8	Ségur 4, pp. 141–43.
134	9–17	Jomini, pp. 55–56.
134	18ff.	*MR Jérôme* 4, p. 347.

PAGE	LINES					
134	24 ff.	The Grande Armée's official strength, as of June 1, 1812, was as follows:				

Davout's First Corps	66,719	men	9,641	horses
Oudinot's Second Corps	44,661	men	7,574	horses
Ney's Third Corps	42,908	men	8,089	horses
Prince Eugene's Fourth & Sixth Corps	77,033	men	15,107	horses
Jerome of Westphalia's Fifth, Seventh, Eighth Corps	78,687	men	18,626	horses
Macdonald's Tenth Corps	51,507	men	6,386	horses
Murat's reserve cavalry	44,451	men	45,829	horses
Imperial Guard	50,716	men	16,695	horses
Reserve artillery, sappers, engineers, etc.	20,248	men	11,005	horses
Total	476,930	men	138,952	horses

Figures given in Baron Danniée's *Itinéraire de 1812,* pp. 183–85. I have not included the official figures for Victor's Ninth Corps and Augereau's Eleventh Corps, which at this time were still far from the Niemen. The official figures were almost certainly inflated. Belliard, for example, claimed that Murat's reserve cavalry did not number more than 32,000 horses at the time of the Niemen crossing. (Derrécagaix, *Belliard,* pp. 483–85).

134	30 ff.	Nap., *Corr.* 23, p. 620 (18856), p. 625 (18857), pp. 635–36 (18871).
134	40 ff.	Dedem, p. 215; Brandt, p. 339; Saint-Chamans, p. 214.
134	43 ff.	Nap., *Corr.* 23, pp. 626–29 (18858, 18860), 633–34 (18869).
135	9–14	Derrécagaix, *Belliard,* p. 488; Soltyk, pp. 23–24; Nap., *Corr.* 23, p. 631 (18867).
135	16 ff.	Faber du Faur, pp. 44–45; Suckow, pp. 150–52.
135	22–25	Nap., *Corr.* 23, pp. 629–37 (18861, 18862, 18872).
135	26 ff.	Suckow, pp. 152–3.
135	43 ff.	Schilder 3, p. 83; Oginski 3, pp. 152–4.
136	8 ff.	Josselson, p. 93; L. G. Beskrovny, *Otechestvennaya voina,* p. 177.
136	25 ff.	Loewenstern 1, p. 187; Josselson, p. 96; Boutourlin 1, pp. 150–55.
137	1–6	M. Bogdanovich, *Istoria otechestvennoy voiny* 3, p. 108; Loewenstern 1, pp. 189–90.
137	7 ff.	Choiseul-Gouffier, *Mémoires,* pp. 92–95, and *Réminiscences,* p. 61; Oginski 3, p. 155.

PAGE   LINES

137   18ff.   F. W. von Weymarn, "Barclay de Tolly" in *RS* 151 (Sept. 1912), pp. 314÷15; Loewenstern 1, pp. 189–94.

137   26–28   Choiseul-Gouffier, *Mémoires,* p. 92.

137   30ff.   Caulaincourt 1, pp. 348–49; Castellane 1, pp. 108–9; Derrécagaix, *Belliard,* p. 488; Ségur 4, p. 145.

137   44ff.   Choiseul-Gouffier, *Réminiscences,* pp. 62–63; Askenazy, *Pohiatowski,* p. 234; Bignon, *Souvenirs,* pp. 120–22, 182, 213–14.

138   6–7   On excellence of Polish cavalrymen, see E. Rüppell's laudatory remarks in *Kriegsgefangene,* p. 23.

138   8ff.   Soltyk, pp. 35–37; Jomini, p. 59; Dedem, pp. 217–18; Choiseul-Gouffier, *Mémoires,* pp. 94–95, and *Réminiscences,* p. 62–63; Dupuy, pp. 166–67.

138   31ff.   Caulaincourt 1, p. 349; Choiseul-Gouffier, *Mémoires,* p. 95.

138   39ff.   Fantin des Odoards, p. 306; J. F. Boulart, *Mémoires militaires,* pp. 243–44; Chevalier, p. 181.

139   4ff.   J. R. Coignet, *Cahiers,* pp. 295–96.

139   18ff.   Brandt, p. 339; Derrécagaix, *Belliard,* p. 488; Caulaincourt 1, pp. 349–50; Griois 2, p. 14; Rapp, p. 175.

139   28ff.   Jomini, p. 62; Soltyk, pp. 59–60; Faber du Faur, pp. 50–52; Castellane 1, p. 111; Coignet, p. 296; E. Labaume, *Relation circonstanciée de la campagne de Russie en 1812,* pp. 32–34.

139   40ff.   Brandt, pp. 339–40; Choiseul-Gouffier, *Réminiscences,* p. 105, and *Mémoires,* pp. 113–14.

140   4ff.   Choiseul-Gouffier, *Mémoires,* pp. 97–98; Caulaincourt 1, pp. 349–50; Coignet, pp. 296–97; Choiseul-Gouffier, *Réminiscences,* pp. 64–65; Nap., *Corr.* 24, p. 55 (18942), p. 64 (18951).

140   12ff.   Soltyk, pp. 59–60; Choiseul-Gouffier, *Réminiscences,* pp. 64–65; Derrécagaix, *Belliard,* pp. 488–89; Jomini, pp. 61–62; Caulaincourt 1, pp. 353–55.

140   28ff.   Derrécagaix, *Belliard,* p. 488; Komarovsky, "Zapiski," *RA* 1867, pp. 769–70. Balashov's report for the tsar can be found in Tarlé's *Campagne de Russie,* pp. 54–59.

141   21ff.   Schilder 3, p. 373 (fn. 131).

141   31ff.   Caulaincourt 1, pp. 354–59.

142   35–38   Ségur 4, pp. 168–71. For Napoleon's written reply to Alexander, see *Corr.* 24, pp. 1–5 (18878).

142   40ff.   Caulaincourt 1, pp. 360–61; Nap., *Corr.* 23, pp. 637–38 (18874), 24, pp. 63 (18949), 65 (18951).

PAGE	LINES	
143	1ff.	Nap., *Corr.* 24, p. 25 (18907); Boutourlin 1, p. 329; Clausewitz (Eng. ed.), pp. 110–11; Schubert, pp. 219–20; Loewenstern 1, pp. 196–99; Suckow, p. 153.
143	27ff.	*MP Eugène* 7, p. 381 (Berthier to Prince Eugène, 1 July from Vilna), Nap., *Corr.* 24, p. 643 (18878).
143	36ff.	Tarlé, *Campagne,* pp. 76–77.
143–44		Boutourlin 1, pp. 170–75; Fain 1, pp. 186–87.
144	12ff.	Nap., *Corr.* 24, pp. 5–6 (18879, 18880); Brandt, pp. 341–42.
144	37ff.	Faber du Faur, pp. 53–54.
145	1–3	Nap., *Corr.* 24, pp. 18–19 (18899, 4 July order to Berthier for Ney).
145	3ff.	Suckow, pp. 153–55; Faber du Faur, pp. 68–69.
145	16ff.	Nap., Corr. 24, pp. 26–27 (18910), 9 (18886); *MP Eugène,* pp. 381–83; Labaume, pp. 32–33; Pini, *In Russia nel 1812,* p. 17.
145	26ff.	Labaume, pp. 34–36; Castellane 1, pp. 111–12.
146	1ff.	Jomini, p. 70. Nap., *Corr.* 23, p. 634 (18870), p. 638 (18876), and 24, pp. 10–11 (18887, 18888), pp. 33–34 (18918, 18919), p. 62 (18949), p. 64 (18950), p. 68 (18957), pp. 103–4 (18995); Hogendorp, *Mémoires,* pp. 307–8.
146	8–12	Soltyk, pp. 52–53; Oginski 3, pp. 205–15; Nap., *Corr.* 24, pp. 51–53 (18939); Mansuy, pp. 654–55; Hogendorp, pp. 314–16.
146	12ff.	Choiseul-Gouffier, *Mémoires,* pp. 106–10; *Réminiscences,* pp. 81–82, 87–93; Castellane 1, p. 112.
147	4ff.	Choiseul-Gouffier, *Mémoires,* pp. 78–79.
147	12ff.	V. de Broglie 1, p. 181; Potocka, pp. 302–3; Bignon, *Souvenirs,* pp. 224ff.; Mansuy, pp. 612ff.
148	6–15	Niemcewicz, *Pamietniki* 1, pp. 332–33; Mansuy, p. 626.
148	16ff.	Mansuy, p. 631; Bignon, *Souvenirs,* pp. 230–34.
148	23ff.	Niemczewicz, *Panietniki* 1, pp. 332–33; Mansuy. p. 631, and on Matuszewicz, pp. 221–27.
148	38ff.	V. de Broglie 1, pp. 191–92; Mansuy, pp. 281–82, 484–88, 564–68, 652; Soltyk, p. 51.
149	1ff.	Mansuy, pp. 642–48.
149	7ff.	Bignon, *Souvenirs,* pp. 232–39; A. Potocka, pp. 312–17.
150	15ff.	Soltyk, pp. 56–63; Oginski 3, pp. 199–200.
150	20ff.	On Wybicki, see Askenazy, *Poniatowski,* pp. 65–66, 126–27, and first volume of his *Napoléon et la Pologne,* pp. 98–108; Man-

11   The Elusive Foe

PAGE	LINES	
158	6 ff.	Clausewitz (Eng. ed.), pp. 18–25; Boutourlin 1, pp. 192–96.
158–59		A. de Montesquiou, *Souvenirs,* pp. 212–13.
159	4–11	Schubert, p. 219; E. A. Komarovsky, "Zapiski," *RA* 1867, pp. 772–73.
159	19 ff.	Toll 1, pp. 344, 350–52.
159	38 ff.	Toll 1, pp. 344–48, Tchitchagov, *Mémoires* (1909 ed.), p. 404; Bogdanovich 2, pp. 524–34.
160	3–9	Komarovsky, *RA* 1867, pp. 773–4; NMR, *CEAS,* pp. 76–77.
160	10 ff.	Josselson, pp. 104–5; Loewenstern 1, pp. 207–8.
160	24 ff.	Tarlé, *Campagne,* p. 71; Toll 1, p. 353.
160	38–46	Josselson, p. 104.
161	1–5	Castellane 1, p. 112.
161	11 ff.	Dumas 3, p. 415; Nap., *Corr.* 24, p. 44 (18935, 9 July, to Berthier), p. 50 (18938, 9 July, to Davout).
161	18–26	Pils, p. 105.
161	27 ff.	Nap., *Corr.* 24, pp. 48–49 (18937, to Prince Eugène), p. 50 (18938, to Davout), pp. 71–72 (18963, 18964, to Oudinot, both dated July 15), pp. 75–76 (18965, to Macdonald, July 16).
161	41 ff.	Boutourlin 1, pp. 191–92; Fain 1, p. 263; Nap., *Corr.* 24, pp. 77–78 (18967, 18969).
162	2–7	Nap., *Corr.* 24, pp. 82–84 (18972, 18973).
162	9 ff.	Caulaincourt 1, p. 362.
162	18–26	Castellane 1, p. 117; Nap., *Corr.* 24, p. 31 (18915, to Berthier).
162	33 ff.	Oginski 3, p. 165; H.-F. Biot, *Souvenirs,* pp. 11–12; Nap., *Corr.* 24, nos. 18961, 18963 (announcing captured arms and supplies).
162	42 ff.	Castellane 1, p. 120 (25 July entry); Suckow, pp. 153–55.
163	13 ff.	*MR Jérôme* 5, pp. 412–15; Nap., *Corr.* 24, p. 28 (18911, to Davout).
163	36–45	Nap., *Corr.* 24, pp. 92–93 (18984, to Davout, 20 July); Fain 1, p. 264.
164	1 ff.	Clausewitz (Eng. ed.), pp. 102–3.
164	23 ff.	Loewenstern 1, p. 209; Toll 1, pp. 354–60; Wolzogen, pp. 109–10.
164	40 ff.	Oginski 3, pp. 175–77; Josselson, pp. 108–9; Loewenstern 1, pp. 209–12; Boutourlin 1, pp. 214–8; Labaume, pp. 65–73.
165	26 ff.	Ségur 4, pp. 188–89.

PAGE	LINES	
165	35 ff.	Josselson, pp. 109–10.
166	3 ff.	Toll 1, pp. 361–64.
166	16 ff.	Labaume, pp. 72–73; Ségur 4, pp. 198–200; Caulaincourt 1, pp. 367–69; Castellane 1, pp. 122–23.
166	32 ff.	Roos, *Avec Napoléon*, pp. 45–46.

12 Let Us Plant Our Eagles Here!

168	7 ff.	Ségur 4, p. 201–3; Castellane 1, p. 123; Caulaincourt 1, p. 371; Boutourlin 1, pp. 224–25.
168	25 ff.	Castellane 1, pp. 123–24.
169	4–19	Montesquiou, pp. 213–14, Nap., *LIML*, pp. 54–55; Ségur 4, p. 183.
169	21–28	Nap., *LIML*, pp. 54–57; Ségur 4, pp. 217–18; Fain 1, pp. 303–7; Caulaincourt 1, pp. 375–78; Castellane 1, pp. 123–24.
169	45 ff.	Dumas 3, pp. 427–29; Fain 1, p. 305.
170	23 ff.	P. Bourgoing, *Souvenirs*, pp. 99–100; Blond, *Grande Armée*, pp. 90–94; Giesse, p. 42; André Soubiran, *Le baron Larrey*, p. 273.
171	7 ff.	D. Larrey, *Mémoires de chirurgie militaire* 4, pp. 24–26; Caulaincourt 1, p. 375; Ségur 4, pp. 214–15.
171	20 ff.	Caulaincourt (1, p. 380) notes a shortage of nails, and Ségur (4, p. 229) mentions a mash made of rye, which suggests that the French bakers lacked ovens for making rye bread.
171	25 ff.	Roos, *Avec Napoléon*, pp. 49, 51–53; also Rüppell, p. 46.
171	38 ff.	Derrécagaix, *Belliard*, p. 493; Faber du Faur, p. 102; Dedem, pp. 225–27.
172	2 ff.	Caulaincourt 1, p. 377. Aide-de-camp, chosen for cavalry, was General Antoine Durosnel.
172	22–27	Rüppell, p. 40; Schubert, pp. 214–15. Also Hogendorp, pp. 314–16.
172	31 ff.	Dedem, pp. 230–31; Villemain 1, ch. 14.
173	6–24	Caulaincourt 1, pp. 383–85; Villemain 1, pp. 167–75.
173	25 ff.	Dumas 3, pp. 427–29; Ségur 4, p. 212.
174	6 ff.	Fain 1, pp. 306, 319–25; Ségur 4, pp. 217–19.

13 The Battle for Smolensk

176	7–11	The point is well made by Josselson, pp. 112, 241 (fn. 77), quoting from Friedrich von Smitt's *Zur näheren Aufklärung*, pp. 65–66.
176	16–24	Wilson, *Private Diary*, pp. 146–47; also Wolzogen, pp. 110–3.
176	27 ff.	Loewenstern 1, p. 218; Wolzogen, pp. 114–15; Josselson, pp. 113–14.

PAGE	LINES	
177	7ff.	Arndt, *Erinnerungen,* pp. 136–38.
177	24ff.	Toll (I, pp. 386–91) gives August 6, Wolzogen (pp. 115–19) August 5, as date of this conference.
178	28–32	Roos, *Avec Napoléon,* pp. 55–59.
178	33–39	Clausewitz (Eng. ed.), pp. 111–121, 129–30.
179	4ff.	Wolzogen, pp. 119–20; Toll I, pp. 392–94.
179	20–27	Caulaincourt I, p. 388.
179	28ff.	Nap., *Corr.* 24, pp. 148–49 (19051, to Davout, 6 August).
179–80		Nap., *LIML,* pp. 59–61; Castellane I, p. 131; Fain I, pp. 353–54; Labaume, pp. 92–93; Faber du Faur, pp. 115–22; Brandt, pp. 367–69.
180	9ff.	Toll I, pp. 404–5; Boutourlin I, pp. 253–55; Brandt, pp. 355; 370–71; Castellane I, p. 132 (14 August entry), and on Murat as a cavalry leader, p. 121; Fain I, pp. 358–59; Faber du Faur, pp. 120–22; Soltyk, pp. 122–26.
181	11ff.	Toll I, pp. 406–7.
181	25–34	Brandt, p. 369; Chevalier, p. 186; Fain I, pp. 360–61.
181	35ff.	Castellane I, p. 133–34; Wolzogen, pp. 122–23; Fain I, p. 362; Brandt, pp. 370–71; Rüppell, pp. 75–78.
182	5ff.	Toll I, pp. 408–9; Soltyk, pp. 127–29; Faber du Faur, pp. 124–26; Baedeker, *La Russie* (Leipzig, 1893), pp. 239–40; Wolzogen, p. 125.
182	33ff.	Wolzogen, p. 123; Toll I, p. 414; Griois 2, pp. 19–20; Fain I, pp. 362–64; Castellane I, p. 135.
183	7–16	Faber du Faur, p. 126; Toll I, p. 409.
183	17ff.	Castellane (I, p. 133) gives time of Napoleon's arrival as 1:00 P.M. See also Montesquiou, pp. 214–15.
183	22–34	Toll I, p. 409; Wolzogen, pp. 123–25.
183	39–40	Toll I, p. 418. Barclay de Tolly, in his subsequent explanation to the tsar, claimed that his forces numbered 75,000, compared with Napoleon's 150,000.
183	41ff.	Fain I, p. 369.
184	8ff.	Wolzogen, pp. 124–25; Rüppell, pp. 77–79; Bourgoing, pp. 102–3; Soltyk, p. 135.
184	16ff.	Clausewitz (Eng. ed.), p. 130; Fain I, pp. 368–69; Brandt, pp. 373–74.
184	40ff.	Fantin des Odoards, pp. 318–20; Soltyk, p. 143; Gourgaud, p. 155.
185	11ff.	Fain I, pp. 368–72; Brandt, p. 374; Wolzogen, pp. 125–26; Loewenstern I, pp. 220–21; Fain I, pp. 370–2; Boutourlin I, p. 364.

PAGE	LINES	
185	26 ff.	Toll 1, pp. 417–18; Wilson, *Private Diary*, pp. 148–49; Weymarn, *RS*, Oct. 1912, p. 129; Josselson, p. 123.
185	41–45	Boutourlin 1, p. 267; Soltyk, p. 128.
186	5–9	Wilson, *Narrative of Events*, pp. 114–15.
186	10 ff.	Ivan S. Timiryazov, *RA* 1884, vol. 1, p. 166; Boulart, p. 248; F. W. von Lossberg, *Briefe*, p. 13; Griois 2, p. 22.
186	19–32	Brandt, p. 376; Coignet, pp. 314–15; Rüppell, p. 79; Faber du Faur, pp. 128–30.
186	32 ff.	Caulaincourt 1, pp. 393–95.
187	8 ff.	Lossberg, pp. 13–14; Soltyk, pp. 148–49; Rüppell, pp. 77, 80; Baedeker, *La Russie*, p. 240; Toll 1, pp. 420–422.

14 Blood and Dust

188	1–10	Fain 1, pp. 375–76; Larrey 4, p. 30; Suckow, p. 162; Chevalier, pp. 188–89; Labaume, pp. 99–100.
188	11 ff.	Laugier de Bellecour, as quoted by C. G. Pini, *In Russia nel 1812*, p. 47.
188	21 ff.	Caulaincourt 1, p. 295; Boulart, p. 249.
189	7 ff.	Suckow, pp. 162–65; Faber du Faur, pp. 132–34, 146–48.
189	34–40	Stendhal, *Corr.* 4 (1934 ed.), pp. 60–62.
189	41–46	Fain 1, pp. 376–77; Caulaincourt 1, p. 296.
190	1–14	Clausewitz (Eng. ed.), p. 128; Wilson, *Narrative*, pp. 106–7; Ségur 4, pp. 284–85; Toll 1, pp. 425–27.
190	15 ff.	Boutourlin 1, pp. 270–71.
190	27 ff.	Toll 1, pp. 429–31; Loewenstern 1, p. 227; Wilson, *Narrative*, pp. 114–15.
191	24 ff.	Loewenstern 1, p. 222–31; Toll 1, pp. 433–35.
192	8–23	Schubert, pp. 96–97; Wilson, *Narrative*, pp. 108–9.
192	24 ff.	Toll 1, pp. 435–39; Brandt, p. 380; Soltyk, pp. 162–63.
193	1–7	Brandt, pp. 385–86, in particular Lt. Col. Regulski's comment that already during siege of Zaragoza Junot had shown signs of madness.
193	8–16	Carl von Martens, *Denkwürdigkeiten*, pp. 151–52.
193	17 ff.	Caulaincourt 1, p. 398; Rüppell, pp. 80–92; and for two slightly different accounts, Lossberg, pp. 16–17, and Giesse, pp. 106–9.
193	34–41	Loewenstern 1, p. 229; Fain 1, p. 385; Larrey 4, p. 36; Castellane 1, p. 137; Gourgaud, pp. 171–73; Suckow, pp. 172–73.

PAGE	LINES	
194	11ff.	Ségur 4, p. 293; Brandt, pp. 383, 394; Dedem, p. 247; Gourgaud, pp. 175–76.
194	28–34	Labaume, p. 106; Larrey 4, p. 30.
194	35ff.	Wolzogen, pp. 125, 130; Clausewitz, *Feldzug*, pp. 121–25.
195	14ff.	Castellane 1, p. 139; Soltyk, p. 140; Brandt, p. 386.
195	32–42	Askenazy, *Poniatowski*, pp. 232, 236–37, 344.
195	43ff.	Ibid., pp. 14, 81, 100, 42–49, 280–284, 109–110.
196	20ff.	Ibid., pp. 240, 172–181, 321–23, 229–30; Brandt, pp. 386–88.
197	23ff.	Soltyk, pp. 177–79; G. de Chambray, *Histoire de l'Expédition de Russie* 2, p. 236; Nap., *Corr.* 24, pp. 58–59 (18946), pp. 135–37 (19035, 19036, 19038); P. Berthezène, *Souvenirs militaires* 2, pp. 4–8.
197	39ff.	Berthezène 2, pp. 1–3.
198	7ff.	Denniée, pp. 57–58; Dumas 3, pp. 432–33; Nap., *Corr.* 24, pp. 187–88 (19106, to Berthier about hospitals); Larrey 4, pp. 30–33; Castellane 1, p. 139; Fantin des Odoards, p. 321.
198	25–32	Boulart, p. 250; Montesquiou, p. 216.
198	40–46	Fain 1, pp. 397–402; Pils, pp. 122–26; Castellane 1, p. 141.
199	1ff.	Caulaincourt 1, p. 401; Denniée, p. 59; Nap., *Corr.* 24, no. 19124.
199	7ff.	Carl von Martens, p. 156; Ségur 4, p. 322; Fezensac, p. 36; Caulaincourt 1, p. 412.
199	27ff.	Denniée, pp. 59–60; Brandt, pp. 395–97. See also Suckow, p. 177.
200	3ff.	Fain 1, pp. 406–408.

15 The Two Capitals

201	1–6	A. D. Bestuzhev-Riumin, "Zapiski," *RA* 1896, vol. 5, p. 341.
201	7–14	A. F. de Beauchamp, quoted by Grunwald, *Campagne*, p. 183.
201	19–22	Daria Olivier, *L'Incendie de Moscou*, p. 29.
201–2		F. Rostopchin, "Zapiski," *RS* 64 (Oct.–Dec. 1889), pp. 655–66.
202	11ff.	Bestuzhev-Riumin, pp. 342–45; Daria Olivier, pp. 30–31.
202	26–29	Viegel, as quoted by A.N. Popov, "Moskva v. 1812 g.," *RA* 1875, vol. 2, pp. 274–75.
202	36ff.	Réau, *L'Art russe*, pp. 296–318; Grunwald, *Histoire de Moscou et des Moscovites;* Madame de Staël, *Dix Années d'exil*, pp. 278–285; Arndt, *Erinnerungen*, p. 140; Lyall, *Russians*, pp. 244ff.
203	29ff.	Réau, pp. 297–98, 314, 318; Grunwald, *Moscou*, pp. 123–33.

PAGE	LINES	
203	43–44	Grunwald, *Stein,* pp. 195–96.
204	1ff.	"Moskva v. 1812 godu," *RS* 151 (June-Sept. 1912), pp. 72ff.; and on the Sloboda Palace, M. I. Pyliayev, *Staraya Moskva,* pp. 482–84.
204	6ff.	E. A. Komarovsky, "Zapiski," in *RA* 1867, p. 775; "Moskva v. 1812 g.," *RS* 151, pp. 73ff.; Narichkine, *Rostopchine,* pp. 132–33; Rostopchin, "Zapiski," *RS* 64 (Oct.-Dec. 1889), pp. 670ff.
204	18ff.	Waliszewski 1, p.
204	30ff.	"Moskva v. 1812 g.," *RS* 151 (1912), pp. 74–75.
205	4ff.	Ibid, pp. 75–76; Komarovsky, *RA* 1867, pp. 776–77.
205	15ff.	"Moskva v. 1812 g.," pp. 77–79.
205	26–34	Ibid., pp. 82–84; Rostopchin, *RS* 64 (1889), pp. 674–76.
206	3ff.	J. de Maistre, *Corr. diplomatique* 1, p. 132; Komarovsky, *RA* 1867, pp. 778–79; de Staël, p. 279.
206	11–16	Bestuzhev-Riumin, *RA* 1896, p. 349.
206	17–24	"Moskva v. 1812 g.," *RS* 151 (1912), pp. 85–87.
206	26ff.	G. I. Villanov, *RS* 151 (1912), p. 92; Adams 2, pp. 394–95; Bakunina, p. 401.
206	32ff.	Tarlé, *Campagne,* pp. 133–34; Bakunina, pp. 401–2; Oginski 3, pp. 178–80.
206–7		NMR, *CEAS,* pp. 66–68.
207	7ff.	Bakunina, p. 403; Bogdanovich 2, pp. 53–54; Toll 1, pp. 4–5; Oginski 3, pp. 185–86; Wilson, *Narrative,* pp. 130–31.
207	30ff.	Schilder 3, p. 95; Toll 1, pp. 451–53; Edling, p. 76.
207	38–46	Adams 2, pp. 395–96; Clausewitz (Eng. ed.), p. 113; Tarlé, *Campagne,* pp. 133–34.
207–8		Tarlé, *Campagne,* pp. 135–36; N. Dubrovin, *Otechestvennaya Voina* (letter no. 65); Josselson, pp. 61, 129–30.
208	16ff.	Schilder 3, pp. 96–97; Toll 1, pp. 452–53; Wolzogen, p. 132; V. R. Marchenko, "Vospominaniya," *RS* 85 (1896), p. 492.
208	26–34	Tarlé, *Campagne,* pp. 136–37; NMR, *CEAS,* pp. 80–81, 87.
208	41ff.	Edling, p. 74; Komarovsky, *RA* 1867, pp. 779–80; Bagration's letter to Rostopchin, in "Zapiski," *RS* 64 (1889), p. 693; Schilder 3, p. 98.
209	7–19	Oginski 3, pp. 186–87; Toll 2, p. 4; I. P. Odenthal, writing to A. Y. Bulgakov, in *RS* 151 (1912), p. 170; Schilder 3, p. 99.
209	26ff.	Josselson, pp. 130–31; Ségur 4, pp. 344–45; Toll 1, pp. 463–64.

PAGE	LINES	
		16 Divisions and Dissensions
211	1ff.	Toll 1, p. 444, 450–51; Grunwald, *Campagne,* pp. 105–6; Dubrovin, pp. 95–96.
211	23ff.	Toll 1, pp. 448–49.
212	13–21	Ibid., pp. 454–55; Timiryazov, *RA* 1884, vol. 1, p. 166; Loewenstern 1, pp. 230–31.
212	22ff.	Toll 1, pp. 460–61; Tarlé, *Campagne,* pp. 134–35.
212	35–46	Fain 1, pp. 421–29; Castellane 1, p. 141.
213	1–5	Nap., *Corr.* 24, p. 213 (19149).
213	6–10	Fain 1, p. 421; Caulaincourt 1, p. 405; Castellane 1, p. 141.
213	22ff.	On the row between Davout and Murat, see Ségur 4, pp. 327–30; Derrécagaix, *Belliard,* p. 499; F. Dumonceau, *Mémoires* 2, p. 122; Vigier, *Davout* 2, pp. 90–91; N. Ternaux-Compans, *Le général Compans,* p. 170; Castellane 1, p. 143.
214	12ff.	Denniée, pp. 60–61; Fantin des Odoards, p. 323; Faber du Faur, pp. 175–77; Fain 1, pp. 437–38.
214	26–29	Brandt, p. 398; Castellane 1, p. 143; Bourgogne, p. 36.
214	30–33	Girod de l'Ain, *Dix ans de souvenirs militaires,* pp. 252–53.
214	35ff.	Toll 1, pp. 462–64; 2, pp. 11–12.
215	12ff.	Toll 2, pp. 8–9; Glinka's reminiscences, quoted by Grunwald, *Campagne,* p. 113.
215	31ff.	Schilder 3, p. 99; Toll 2, pp. 8–10.
216	4ff.	A. N. Muravyov, in *KSD,* p. 374 (no. 191); French version in Grunwald, *Campagne,* p. 114.
216	18–30	For differing versions of this "eagle" incident, see Toll 2, pp. 9–10; Timiryazov, *RA* 1884, vol. 1, p. 167; A. B. Golitsyn (*KSD,* p. 343), who claimed that the eagle followed Kutuzov around during his first troop review at Borodino; Rodozhitsky (*KSD,* p. 391), who also placed it at Borodino; and for the sensation that this auspicious omen created in Moscow, A. Popov, *RA* 1875, vol. 3, p. 17, and Narichkine, p. 150; and for its impact in Petersburg, J. de Maistre, 14 Sept. letter in *Oeuvres complètes* 12, pp. 217–19.
216	31ff.	Shcherbinin's reminiscences in *KSD,* p. 398 (no. 196); Toll 2, pp. 13–16; and on Kutuzov's dislike of written orders, S. Mayevsky in *RS* 8 (1873), pp. 153–54.
216	38ff.	Toll 2, pp. 10–17.
218	19ff.	Dubrovin, pp. 106–7 (letter no. 98).
218	30ff.	Ibid, p. 108 (letter no. 100).

PAGE	LINES	
218	40 ff.	Caulaincourt 1, pp. 415–18; Soltyk, pp. 196–97.

219 19 ff. Brandt, pp. 398–401; Larrey 4, p. 39; Castellane 1, pp. 143–44; Faber du Faur, pp. 179–82; Fain 1, pp. 444–46; Caulaincourt 1, pp. 418–19.

219 32 ff. Brandt, pp. 400–1; Nap., *Corr.* 24, pp. 225 (19164), 231–33 (19174), 235 (19176).

219 41 ff. Castellane 1, p. 146; also Chambray 1, p. 300.

220 16 ff. Roth von Schreckenstein, *Die Kavallerie*, p. 15; Brandt, pp. 400–1.

220 21 ff. Larrey 4, pp. 40–41; Nap., *Corr.* 24, pp. 237–38 (19178).

220 33 ff. Nap., *Corr.* 24, pp. 231 (19173), 235 (19176); Ségur 4, p. 324; Girod de l'Ain, p. 236.

220 38 ff. Nap., *Corr.* 24, p. 228 (19168); Caulaincourt 1, pp. 419–20; Castellane 1, pp. 218–20; Girod de l'Ain, p. 254.

221 22 ff. Denniée, pp. 61–63; Dumonceau 2, pp. 128–129.

17 Borodino

223 1 ff. Toll 2, pp. 19–23; Wolzogen, p. 134; Rodozhitsky, *KSD*, p. 383; P. Holzhausen, *Die Deutschen in Russland*, pp. 82–83; C. Duffy, *Borodino*, pp. 75–76.

224 1 ff. Toll 2, pp. 23–28; Wolzogen, pp. 137–38.

224 42 ff. Toll 2, pp. 29–30; Rodozhitsky, *KSD*, p. 384.

226 5–18 Mayevsky, *RS* 8 (August 1873), p. 137.

226 19 ff. Schubert, p. 232; Brandt, p. 402; Labaume, p. 128.

226 24 ff. Griois 2, pp. 27–28; Castellane 1, p. 147 (5 Sept. entry); Dumonceau 2, p. 130; Popov, *RA* 1875, vol. 3, pp. 156–58.

226 33 ff. Brandt, p. 402; Coignet, p. 317; Dumonceau 2, p. 131; Labaume, p. 129.

227 8 ff. Dumonceau 2, pp. 131–32; Soltyk, p. 204; Ternaux-Compans, pp. 175–76; Fain 2, pp. 1–2.

227 20 ff. Griois 2, p. 29; Ternaux-Compans, pp. 176–79; Brandt, pp. 405–6; Toll 2, pp. 34–36; Denniée, pp. 65–66; Soltyk, pp. 203–7; Fain 2, p. 3.

228 6 ff. Toll 2, pp. 37–38; Gorchakov, *KSD*, p. 345; A. Thirion, *Souvenirs militaires*, pp. 176–78.

228 23 ff. Barclay de Tolly, "Izobrazheniye . . . ," *KSD*, p. 331 (no. 179); Yermolov, *KSD*, pp. 350–51.

228 29 ff. Toll 2, pp. 41–42; Shcherbinin, *KSD*, pp. 395–96; Prince Eugen von Württemberg, *Erinnerungen*, p. 69.

PAGE	LINES	
228–29		Castellane 1, p. 146; Fain 2, pp. 5–6; Dumonceau 2, p. 133.
229	15ff.	Griois 2, p. 30; Caulaincourt 1, pp. 422–24; Castellane 1, p. 147 (statement that Napoleon rose at 1:00 A.M.); Fain 2, p. 7; Ségur 4, p. 355.
229	21ff.	Fain 2, pp. 6–8; Caulaincourt 1, p. 423; Griois 2, p. 31; Rodozhitsky, *KSD*, p. 385; Fezensac, p. 43.
229–30		Ségur 4, pp. 359–66; Caulaincourt 1, pp. 423–24; Fain 2, p. 11. Fezensac, p. 42. Daru apparently supported Davout, explaining to Napoleon that Davout, given his shortsightedness, must have undertaken a closer reconnaissance of the enemy's lines than the others. As told to Pasquier (*Mémoires* 2, p. 8).
230	31ff.	Bausset 2, pp. 76–77; Fezensac, p. 43; Denniée, pp. 67–70; Fain 2, pp. 8–10.
231	9ff.	Muravyov, *KSD*, p. 375; Rodozhitsky, *KSD*, p. 385; Eugen von Württemberg, p. 73.
231	17ff.	D. Bogdanov, *KSD*, p. 336; Muravyov, *KSD*, p. 375; Rodozhitsky, *KSD*, p. 384.
231	26ff.	Barclay de Tolly, *KSD*, p. 332; Shcherbinin, *KSD*, pp. 395–96.
231	40ff.	Kutuzov's final instructions, in *KSD*, p. 88 (no. 77); Barclay's, *KSD*, pp. 89–90 (no. 78); Bagration's, pp. 91–92 (no. 80); Kutaissov's, p. 139.
232	16ff.	Rodozhitsky, *KSD*, p. 386; D. Bogdanov, *KSD*, pp. 338–39.
232	28ff.	J.-M. Chevalier, *Souvenirs*, p. 195; Holzhausen, p. 82; Brandt, pp. 408–9; Roos, pp. 77–78; Castellane 1, p. 148.
232	37ff.	Griois 2, p. 32; Fain 1, pp. 17–18; Labaume, p. 138; Girod de l'Ain, p. 256.
233	13–24	Castellane 1, pp. 148–49; Caulaincourt 1, p. 424; Denniée, p. 74; Fain 2, pp. 22–23; Griois 2, p. 33.
233	25ff.	Labaume, p. 135; Nap., *Corr.* 24, p. 240 (19182); and Fain (2, p. 20), who sought to limit the Napoleonic hocus-pocus by altering the end of the text to read "at the great battle on the *plains* of Moscow." (Italics mine.)
233–34		Berthezène 2, p. 48; Labaume, p. 138; Captain François, quoted by G. Bertin, *Campagne de 1812*, pp. 90–91 (but with a "*six heures du soir*" misprint); Brandt, p. 409; Clausewitz, *Feldzug*, p. 145; L.-F. Lejeune (*Mémoires* 2, p. 209) and Denniée (p. 74) say that the cannonade began at 7:00 A.M. On the morning mist, see Loewenstern 1, pp. 253–54; Griois 2, p. 34; Fain 2, p. 19; and on Sorbier, Toll 2, pp. 67–68; Chambray 1, p. 312.
234	6ff.	Labaume, pp. 139–40; Lejeune 2, pp. 210–11; Toll 2, pp. 67–68.

PAGE	LINES	
234	17ff.	"*Bumaghi Zakrevskago*" in *SIRIO* 73 (1890), vi; Timiryazov, *RA* 1884, vol. 1, p. 167; Loewenstern 1, pp. 254–56.
234	35ff.	Toll 2, p. 68; Wolzogen, pp. 140–41; Barclay de Tolly, in *KSD*, p. 332; Ségur 4, pp. 374–75; Labaume, pp. 140–41; Thirion, pp. 182–83.
235	13–23	Toll 2, p. 55; Duffy, pp. 42–47; Golitsyn, *KSD*, p. 343 (no. 183).
235	24ff.	Schubert, pp. 233–34; Soltyk, p. 218; Mayevsky, *RS* 8 (August 1873), p. 138.
235	36ff.	For La Riboisiére's estimate, see Denniée, p. 81. Gourgaud (pp. 240–42) claims that French cannoneers fired off 91,000 rounds, but had enough left over for two more battles.
235	43ff.	Chevalier, p. 195; Boulart, p. 254; Brandt, p. 409.
236	12ff.	Ternaux-Compans, pp. 184–91; Toll 2, p. 67; Soltyk, pp. 217–22; Berthezène 2, pp. 48–49; Fain 1, pp. 24–26. Girod de l'Ain, p. 257.
237	4ff.	Fain 2, pp. 24–25; Rapp, p. 206; Girod de l'Ain, p. 258.
237	26ff.	Toll 2, pp. 69–73; Soltyk, p. 223; Vorontsov, *KSD*, p. 342 (no. 182); Girod de l'Ain, pp. 259–60; Konovnitsyn, *KSD*, p. 358 (no. 187); Barclay, *KSD*, p. 333; Mayevsky, *KSD*, p. 380.
238	12–22	Toll 2, pp. 76–77; Clausewitz, *Feldzug*, pp. 151–52.
238	23ff.	Suckow, pp. 189–91; Dumonceau 2, p. 123; Faber du Faur, pp. 193–94; Holzhausen, pp. 90–91.
238–39		Montesquiou, pp. 221–22; Dedem, pp. 238–40; Suckow, pp. 184–85.
239	10–21	Shcherbinin, *KSD*, p. 398; Toll 2, pp. 81–83.
239	22ff.	Yermolov, *KSD*, p. 352; and Konovnitsyn, *KSD*, p. 358; von Württemberg, pp. 76–78.
239	36ff.	Labaume, p. 140; Captain François, in G. Bertin's *Campagne*, pp. 91–92.
240	5ff.	Mayevsky, *KSD*, pp. 380–2; Loewenstern 1, pp. 257–58.
240	21–33	Yermolov, *KSD*, pp. 355, 359; Wolzogen, pp. 140–41; von Württemberg, pp. 80–81.
240	36ff.	Duffy, p. 109 (quoting Glinka, "Ocherki Borodinskogo Srazheniya," p. 69).
241	7–15	Loewenstern 1, p. 260.
241	16ff.	Clausewitz, *Feldzug*, pp. 151–59; Duffy, pp. 119–21; Labaume, pp. 147–48; Brandt, p. 410; Soltyk, p. 236.
241	30ff.	Toll 2, pp. 102–5; Schreckenstein, pp. 24–27; Yermolov, *KSD*, p. 356.
241–42		Mayevsky, *RS* 8 (August 1873), p. 137; Bogdanov, *KSD*, p. 336; Soltyk, pp. 230–32; Schreckenstein, p. 52; Lejeune 2, p. 211.

PAGE	LINES	
242	20 ff.	Holzhausen, pp. 92–96; Schreckenstein, pp. 51–66; Konovnitsyn, *KSD*, p. 358; Duffy, p. 114; Ségur 4, pp. 379–80.
242–43		Dedem, pp. 238–39; von Württemberg, pp. 81–83.
243	19 ff.	Toll 2, pp. 98–99; Brandt, pp. 410–12.
243	32–38	Soltyk, pp. 234–35; Dedem, p. 288.
243	39–43	Ségur 4, pp. 385–87; contradicted by Gourgaud (pp. 236–37), who says that Ney could not have uttered such words.
243–44		Various terms are used to describe the spot from which Napoleon directed most of the battle. Bausset (2, pp. 78–80) speaks of a "little space, where he came and went." Fantin des Odoards (p. 327) describes him as sometimes standing, sometimes "lying on the ground of a ditch of the conquered redoubt." Denniée (p. 75) calls it a "kind of ditch," which Dedem (pp. 236–37) places some 300 yards in front of the redoubt. Chambray (1, pp. 304–5) also speaks of the edge of a gully (*ravin*, in French) near Shevardino, while Lejeune (2, p. 218) describes him as "below his [Imperial] Guard, on an inclined slope, from where he could see everything." Coignet (p. 320) heard Napoleon ask for his bearskin, and adds: "as he found himself on the slope of a gully, he was lying and almost upright"—which may well be the most accurate description of them all. On Napoleon taking throat lozenges, see Soltyk, p. 218, and on his drinking a glass of Chambertin, Bausset 2, p. 81.
244	12 ff.	Lejeune 2, pp. 213–4 (in Bertin, p. 74).
244	23 ff.	Von Württemberg, pp. 81–84; Barclay, *KSD*, p. 334; Freiherr von Helldorff, *Aus dem Leben* 1, pp. 167–68.
244	43 ff.	Schubert, pp. 235–36; confirmed by Loewenstern 1, p. 265.
245	7 ff.	Yermolov, *KSD*, p. 355; Wolzogen, pp. 142–43; Loewenstern 1, p. 273.
245	25–33	Barclay, *KSD*, p. 334; von Württemberg, p. 84.
243	34 ff.	Schreckenstein, pp. 82–87; Chambray 1, p. 317; Lejeune 2, p. 207; Thirion, pp. 181–82; Griois 2, p. 36.
246	12 ff.	Schreckenstein, pp. 46–47, 70.
246	19–23	Roos, pp. 82–83; Larrey 4, pp. 47–48; Brandt, p. 410.
246	24 ff.	Caulaincourt 1, pp. 425–26; Derrécagaix, *Belliard*, p. 503.
247	1 ff.	Griois 2, pp. 37–38; Schreckenstein, pp. 37, 90–94, 109; Holzhausen, p. 98.
247	13–24	Griois 2, pp. 37–38; Holzhausen (quoting Leissnig), p. 98; Lejeune 2, pp. 212–13 (in Bertin, p. 73). Also Labaume, p. 144.

PAGE	LINES	
247	25–31	Schreckenstein, pp. 95–97, 119–23; Chambray I, pp. 311–12.

247   32 ff.   Toll 2, pp. 90, 98–99 106–8; Barclay, *KSD*, p. 334; Holzhausen (quoting Meerheim), pp. 100–1.

247–48   Dumonceau 2, p. 147; Toll 2, pp. 107–8; Berthezène 2, p. 53; Labaume, pp. 144–45; Loewenstern I, p. 268.

248   18 ff.   Barclay de Tolly, report on the battle sent to Kutuzov from Kaluga, *KSD*, pp. 175–76 (no. 151); Loewenstern I, pp. 261–62, 265.

248   32 ff.   Barclay de Tolly, "Izobrazheniye" (later sent to the tsar), *KSD*, pp. 334–35; Schreckenstein, p. 110; and in a special tribute to these elite Russian horsemen, Labaume, p. 145. Also Loewenstern I, pp. 262–65; Wolzogen, p. 144.

248   42 ff.   Toll 2, p. 109; Barclay to Kutuzov, *KSD*, p. 176.

249   5 ff.   Brandt, pp. 412–14; Griois 2, p. 39; Labaume, pp. 149–52; Toll 2, p. 105.

249   37–43   Fain 2 (p. 37), Berthezène 2 (pp. 55–57), Boulart (p. 255), and Denniée (p. 78) describe the initial advance of Bessières' Imperial Guard cavalry, suddenly halted by a counterorder from Napoleon. Denniée, without naming him, says that one of Napoleon's marshals reminded him: "Sire, Your Majesty is eight hundred leagues from his capital." Gourgaud (p. 243) undertook to ridicule Ségur's claim that Daru had sought to persuade Napoleon to "*donner la garde*," but Denniée was told that same evening by Daru that he regretted the "council of prudence" that had been given to the French emperor—almost certainly by Berthier, and probably by Bessières as well.

249   43 ff.   The point is well made by Chambray (I, pp. 316–17). Soltyk (pp. 234–36) rightly believed that the chance for a decisive breakthrough in the center was spoiled by the diversion of two Young Guard divisions toward Prince Eugène's supposedly threatened left flank. See also Loewenstern (I, p. 270) on Barclay de Tolly's intended knock-out below.

250   17 ff.   Bausset 2, p. 84; Roos, p. 84; Chambray I, p. 314; Brandt, p. 414.

250   31 ff.   Muravyov, *KSD*, p. 377; Loewenstern I, p. 269; Wolzogen, pp. 145–46; Shcherbinin, *KSD*, pp. 396–98.

251   13 ff.   Kutuzov's angry reaction was ably translated by M. Josselson, in *Commander*, p. 144.

251   31–38   Toll's penciled order, signed by Kutuzov, is no. 85, *KSD*, p. 95.

251   39 ff.   Wolzogen, pp. 146–47; Barclay de Tolly, *KSD*, pp. 335–36; Muravyov, *KSD*, p. 378; Loewenstern I, p. 275.

252   8–21   Timiryazov, *RA* 1884, vol. I, p. 167; Muravyov, *KSD*, p. 378.

252   22–26   Schreckenstein, p. 116.

PAGE   LINES

18 The Torrent and the Sponge

253   1–21   Brandt, p. 415. See also Dumonceau 2, pp. 142–43.

253–54   A. B. Golitsyn, *KSD*, pp. 343–44; Toll 2, pp. 113–14.

254   8 ff.   *KSD*, pp. 114–15 (no. 189), pp. 156–57; Wolzogen, pp. 147–48; Loewenstern 1, pp. 276–77; Barclay de Tolly, "Izobrazheniye", in *RA* 1893, vol. 2, p. 489; Josselson, p. 146.

254   14 ff.   Brandt, p. 418; Toll 2, pp. 122–23; Shcherbinin, *KSD*, p. 399.

254   16–22   Kutuzov to Alexander, *KSD*, pp. 101–2 (no. 89), and to Rostopchin, *KSD*, pp. 151, 155–56 (nos. 185, 188). Also Wolzogen, p. 150.

254   30 ff.   Labaume, p. 153; Castellane 1, pp. 151–52; Brandt, p. 417; Bausset 2, pp. 86–87; Denniée, p. 81.

255   7–17   Captain François, in Bertin, pp. 94–96; Brandt, pp. 420–21; Suckow, p. 192.

255   18 ff.   Schreckenstein, pp. 128–29. In a letter sent to S. R. Vorontsov in London, and dated 28 April 1813 (OS), Rostopchin wrote that he had had 58,630 human corpses and the cadavers of 32,765 horses burned "on the fields of Borodino." In a later letter, in which he spoke of bodies being buried as well as burned, he increased the figures to 67,000 men and the cadavers of 37,000 horses (*AKV* 8, p. 314).

255   26 ff.   Castellane 1, p. 152; Brandt, pp. 417–18; Soltyk, pp. 249–50; Yermolov, *KSD*, p. 357; Dedem, pp. 82–83; Schreckenstein, p. 4; Fantin des Odoards, pp. 318–19; Denniée, pp. 82–83.

255   41 ff.   Rostopchin to Balashov, no. 102, in Dubrovin, p. 110.

256   5 ff.   Dedem, pp. 241–42; Brandt, pp. 417–18; Larrey 4, pp. 59–61.

256   12 ff.   Fain 2, pp. 45–46; Caulaincourt 1, p. 437; Dedem, pp. 242–45; Brandt, pp. 419–21.

256   26 ff.   NMR, *CEAS*, pp. 83, 88; Narichkine, p. 149.

256   33 ff.   Bogdanovich 2, pp. 26–30; Schilder 3, pp. 105–6; Alexander's rescript to Kutuzov (concerning Gen. Steinheil), in *KSD*, p. 194.

257   14 ff.   J. Q. Adams (2, p. 399) noted that Alexander returned to Petersburg "quite charmed" with Bernadotte.

257   17 ff.   J. de Maistre, *Oeuvres* 12, p. 204; Edling, pp. 66–69; V. Bakunina, pp. 409–10.

257   24 ff.   Wilson, *Private Diary* (30 August entry), p. 155; Adams 2, pp. 399–401; Arndt, *Erinnerungen*, pp. 162–63. But according to *Meine Wanderungen* (pp. 57–60), Germaine de Staël herself went to the theater.

258   7 ff.   Wilson, *Narative*, pp. 116–19.

PAGE	LINES	
258	22 ff.	Bogdanovich 2, pp. 229–31. No mention of Kutuzov's "necessary" withdrawal from the battlefield of Borodino was made in the carefully censored text published in the *Severnaya Pochta*. See also Toll 2, p. 128, about the fake Napoleonic *Ordre du Jour* that was circulated in the salons of Petersburg, and also reported (in a slightly different version) by J. de Maistre, *Oeuvres* 12, p. 224.
258	29 ff.	Wilson, *Private Diary*, p. 162; Arndt, *Meine Wanderungen*, p. 85; NMR, *L'Impératrice Elisabeth* 2, pp. 535–36.
258–59		Kutuzov's letter to his wife, no. 220 in *KSD*, p. 181; and for its impact on Petersburg's *haute société*, J. de Maistre 12, pp. 222–25.
259	12 ff.	Bestuzhev-Riumin, *RA* 1896, pp. 351–52; Narichkine, pp. 138–40.
259	36 ff.	Popov, *RA* 1875, vol. 2, pp. 270–71; F. Rostopchin, "Zapiski," pp. 667–68; Narichkine, p. 148.
260	20–30	Bestuzhev-Riumin, pp. 351–54.
260	31 ff.	A. de Ségur, *Vie du Comte Rostopchine*, pp. 195–96.
260	43 ff.	Tarlé, *Campagne*, p. 151.
261	5 ff.	Bestuzhev-Riumin, p. 354; Narichkine, pp. 141–42.
261	21 ff.	*AKV* 8, p. 315; Bestuzhev-Riumin, p. 355; Narichkine, p. 151.
261	29 ff.	Popov, *RA* 1875, vol. 3, pp. 18–19.
261	35 ff.	Bestuzhev-Riumin, p. 355; *KSD*, pp. 150, 151 (nos. 183, 185).
261	42 ff.	A. de Ségur, *Rostopchine*, p. 198; *KSD* pp. 155–56, 158–59 (nos. 188, 191, 192).
262	14 ff.	Popov, *RA* 1875, vol. 3, p. 191. Text of this Rostopchin exhortation is given in Bestuzhev-Riumin, pp. 356–57; in French translation by D. Olivier, p. 41; and in a garbled version by Baron Fain (2, p. 79).
262	26 ff.	Bestuzhev-Riumin, pp. 357–58; A. de Ségur, *Rostopchine*, pp. 196–97.
262	32 ff.	*KSD*, p. 181 (no. 200). On the Moscow militia, see Popov, *RA* 1875, vol. 3, pp. 189–91, and for the spectacular results obtained in Petersburg, Bogdanovich 2, pp. 53–57. Other Kutuzov messages to Rostopchin in *KSD*, pp. 184–85 (nos. 223, 224, 225, 227) and Barclay's, p. 187 (no. 230).
263–64		Popov, *RA* 1875, vol. 3, pp. 192–95.
264	3 ff.	Bestuzhev-Riumin, p. 358.
264	29 ff.	Dubrovin, p. 114; Narichkine, pp. 158–61.
265	5–12	Popov, *RA* 1875, vol. 3, p. 195.
265	14–17	Beskrovny, *Otechestvennaya voina*, pp. 73–74; Tarlé, *Campagne*, p. 143.

PAGE	LINES	
265	23–30	Yermolov, "Zapiski," *RS* 151 (1912), p. 75; Carl von Martens, p. 161; Barclay de Tolly, "Izobrazheniye," in *RA* 1893, vol. 2, pp. 489–90.
265	31ff.	*RA* 1893, vol. 2, pp. 490–91; Wolzogen, p. 153. Even Wilson, normally an admirer of Bennigsen, had to admit that the "position could not have been worse" (*Narrative*, p. 160).
265	37ff.	Yermolov, *RS* 151 (1912), p. 78; Josselson, p. 148.
266	11ff.	J.-B. de Crossard, *Mémoires militaires et historiques* 4, pp. 360–65.
266	26ff.	Popov, *RA* 1875, vol. 3, pp. 257ff.
266–67		Rostopchin, *Oeuvres inédites*, pp. 214–15. See also Narichkine, pp. 161–62; Yermolov, *RS* 151 (1912), p. 80; Dubrovin, letter no. 80, p. 110.
267	4ff.	Rostopchin, *Oeuvres inédites*, p. 217; Yermolov, *RS* 151 (1912), p. 79; Popov, *RA* 1875, vol. 3, pp. 262–63; Helldorff 2, pp. 58–59.
267	38ff.	The four primary sources of information about the Fili conference are Barclay de Tolly's later report (to Emperor Alexander) in his "Izobrazheniye" (*RA* 1893, vol. 2, pp. 191–92); Kutuzov's succinct report to Tsar (*KSD*, pp. 220–21, no. 250); Toll's notes, later written up and commented upon by General Theodor von Bernhardi (Toll 2, pp. 143–48); and Yermolov's own, not very reliable, reminiscences, written much later ("Zapiski," as published in *RS* 151 [1912], pp. 80–82). Like Michael Josselson (*Commander*, pp. 149–51), I have drawn what seems most truthful from all four.
268	1–2	Tarlé, without citing his source, claims that Platov and General Lanskoy, responsible for supplies, were also present (*Nashestviye*, p. 143).
269	1–9	According to Yermolov, both Dokhturov and Ouvarov supported the retreat, while according to Wolzogen (p. 153), who was not present, Konovnitsyn and Ostermann-Tolstoy, like Yermolov, wanted to attack.
269	20–29	On consternation felt by most Russian officers, see Mayevsky's reminiscences, *RS* 8 (1873), p. 143; Tarlé, *Nashestviye*, p. 144–45.
269	30ff.	Popov, *RA* 1875, vol. 3, p. 272; Toll 2, p. 148; Kutuzov to Rostopchin, *KSD*, pp. 221–22.
269	35ff.	Yermolov, *RS* 151 (1912), pp. 82–83; Popov, *RA* 1875, vol. 3, p. 272. Bernhardi (Toll 2, p. 148) claims that Kutuzov was prevented from heading for Nizhny Novgorod by Colonel Michaud's warning that they could then be cut off from the vital supply depots in the south by the autumn flooding of the Moskva and Oka rivers.
270	6–10	Tarlé, *Napoleon's Invasion*, p. 152. As source references for torrent-and-sponge simile, Tarlé (*Nashestviye*, p. 144) cites Prince A. B.

Golitsyn's *Zapiski* (autobiographical notes), as collected by the military historian Mikhailovsky-Danilevsky.

19   The Holocaust

271   1 ff.   Popov, *RA* 1875, vol. 3, pp. 263, 274–76.

271   16–22   Narichkine, pp. 162–68.

272   25 ff.   Popov, *RA* 1875, vol. 3, pp. 275–76.

272   32 ff.   Rostopchin, *Oeuvres inédites,* pp. 194–96; Narichkine, p. 165; D. Olivier, p. 236.

272–73   Popov, *RA* 1875, vol. 3, pp. 278–82; Narichkine, pp. 168–69.

273   31–33   Kutuzov order in *KSD,* pp. 224–25 (no. 258), and contrast with its actual execution, no. 259 (report dated 2 Sept., OS), describing march through Moscow, pp. 225–26. Also Wolzogen, pp. 154–55; Popov, RA 1875, vol. 3, p. 280.

273   33 ff.   Wolzogen, p. 155; Crossard 4, pp. 368–69; Chicherin, quoted by Grunwald, *Campagne,* pp. 185–86; Mayevsky, *RS* 8 (1873), p. 143; Popov, *RA* 1875, vol. 3, p. 281.

274   10 ff.   Barclay de Tolly, *RA* 1893, vol. 2, p. 192; Loewenstern 1, pp. 282–83; Mayevsky, *RS* 8 (1873), p. 143; Wolzogen, p. 155.

274   17–26   Popov, *RA* 1875, vol. 3, p. 280; Grunwald, quoting A. Golitsyn, in *Campagne,* p. 186.

274   39 ff.   On the Vereshchaghin episode, see Narichkine, pp. 171–74; A. de Ségur, *Rostopchine,* pp. 211–12; Popov, *RA* 1875, vol. 3, pp. 285–86; Bestuzhev-Riumin, pp. 160–61; Tarlé, *Nashestviye,* pp. 150–54 (Eng. ed., pp. 158–63); Abbé Surugue, *Lettres sur l'incendie de Moscou,* pp. 12–14. That the Moscow populace were by no means hostile to Rostopchin is stressed by Prince Vyazemsky in his interesting comments on Tolstoy's *War and Peace* (*RA* 1869, vol. 1, pp. 011–016).

276   28 ff.   Narichkine, p. 174; Rostopchine, *Oeuvres inédites,* p. 200. For different version of Yaouza bridge encounter, see A. B. Golitsyn's reminiscences, quoted by Popov, *RA* 1875, vol. 3, pp. 287–88, and by Grunwald in his *Campagne,* p. 186.

277   1–4   Jean de Bonnefou, in preface to Rostopchin's *Oeuvres inédites* (p. xvii), quotes this remark, not included in Rostopchin's own (largely bogus) disclaimer of having organized the Moscow holocaust (p. 221).

277   5 ff.   Wolzogen, p. 156; Popov, *RA* 1875, vol. 3, p. 286.

277   21 ff.   Montesquiou, pp. 222–24; Castellane 1, p. 142; Toll 2, pp. 153–54; Wolzogen, p. 156; Grunwald, *Campagne,* pp. 191–92.

278   10–17   Caulaincourt 1, pp. 440–41.

PAGE	LINES	
278	18ff.	See, for example, Brandt's description of Moscow, p. 424.
278	31ff.	Montesquiou, pp. 225–26; Chevalier, pp. 204–5. Other descriptions are offered by Denniée, pp. 86–87; Caulaincourt 2, pp. 3–4; Ségur 5, p. 33.
278–79		Fantin des Odoards, p. 331; Ségur 5, pp. 29–32; Fantin des Odoards, p. 332; Montesquiou, pp. 226–27; Fain 2, p. 53.
280	13ff.	Castellane 1, p. 143; Caulaincourt 2, pp. 4–6. General Durosnel had succeeded Auguste de Caulaincourt, killed at Borodino, as imperial headquarters commandant.
280	20ff.	Montesquiou, p. 228; Brandt, p. 425.
280	29ff.	Bestuzhev-Riumin, RA 1896, pp. 363–64; Montesquiou, p. 229–30; Ségur 5, pp. 34–38; Dumas 3, pp. 444–45.
281	23–30	Caulaincourt 2, pp. 5–6; Bausset 2, pp. 88–89.
281	31ff.	Bourgogne, pp. 45–54.
282	21–28	Bestuzhev-Riumin, p. 362.
283	4ff.	Surugue, p. 17; Roos, Avec Napoléon, pp. 105–7.
283	26ff.	A. de Muralt, in Grunwald, Campagne, p. 199; Bourgogne, pp. 53–54.
284	1ff.	Montesquiou, pp. 230–33.
285	1ff.	Brandt, pp. 431–32.
285	11ff.	Fain 2, pp. 55–56, 84–85.
285	27–36	Caulaincourt 2, p. 11; Roustam, in Grunwald, Campagne, p. 205.
285–86		Brandt, pp. 427–32; Surugue, pp. 24–25.
287	8ff.	Castellane 1, p. 156 (18 Sept. entry); Brandt, pp. 434–35.
287	20ff.	Fain 2, p. 88; Ségur 5, p. 47; Caulaincourt 2, pp. 12–13.
288	8ff.	Bestuzhev-Riumin, p. 372; Bourgogne, p. 58.
288	21ff.	Gourgaud, pp. 283–84; Montesquiou, pp. 234–35.
289	5ff.	On Petrovsky Palace, see Grunwald, Histoire de Moscou, p. 192; Golovine, p. 160.
289	16ff.	Caulaincourt 2, pp. 15–16; Bestuzhev-Riumin, p. 372.
289	30ff.	Segur 5, pp. 50–51; Montesquiou, p. 235; Boulart, p. 261; Fantin des Odoards, p. 334; Bourgogne, pp. 59–62.
290	5–29	Grunwald, Moscow; Fantin des Odoards, p. 335; Fezensac, p. 244; Labaume, p. 227; Castellane 1, p. 155; Bausset 2, pp. 97–98; Montesquiou, pp. 236–37.
290	30ff.	Brandt, p. 433; Fantin des Odoards, p. 335; Surugue, pp. 22–23.

PAGE	LINES	
291	8 ff.	Fain 2, pp. 93–95.
292	17 ff.	A. Domergue, *La Russie pendant les guerres de l'Empire* 2, pp. 73–75.
292	36 ff.	Ibid., p. 88.
293	5 ff.	Nap., *LIML,* p. 82 (no. 98); Lejeune 2, pp. 222–26; Bausset 2, pp. 90–91; Bourgoing, pp. 116–17.

20 A Handful of Ashes

294	1 ff.	Caulaincourt 2, pp. 19–21; Ségur 5, pp. 56–68; Fantin des Odoards, p. 337.
295	12 ff.	Nap., *LIML,* pp. 78–82 (nos. 94, 95, 98); Surugue, pp. 39–40.
295	26 ff.	Larrey 4, p. 70; Dumas 3, pp. 449–50; Fain 2, pp. 99–103.
296	24 ff.	On Yakovlev, see his son's memoirs: Alexander Herzen, *Childhood, Youth, and Exile,* pp. 3–9.
297	11 ff.	One of the victims of Arakcheyev's letter-opening snoopiness was Kutuzov's wife. See V. R. Marchenko, "Vospominaniya," in *RS* 85 (1896), p. 500.
297	33 ff.	Bogdanovich 2, pp. 287–88; *KSD,* pp. 151–53 (no. 186), and pp. 175–76 (no. 240); *CEAS,* p. 84.
298	3 ff.	*KSD,* pp. 233–34; Bogdanovich 2, pp. 288, 597–99.
298	22 ff.	*KSD,* pp. 233–34 (no. 270); Bogdanovich 2, pp. 290–91.
299	10–17	Bogdanovich 2, pp. 300–1
299	18 ff.	J. de Maistre, *Oeuvres* 12, pp. 231–33; Adams 2, pp. 404–5.
299	38 ff.	"Zapiski Grafa F.P. Tolstogo," *RS* 1873, p. 138; Schilder 3, p. 112.
300	5 ff.	V. Bakunina, p. 407; F. P. Tolstoy, *RS* 1873, pp. 124–37.
300	19 ff.	Henri Troyat, *Pouchkine* 1, p. 106; Marchenko, *RS* 85 (1896), pp. 500–1; V. Bakunina, pp. 409–10.
300	30–36	F. P. Tolstoy, *RS* 1873, p. 137.
300	41 ff.	Nap., *Corr.* 24 (19123) pp. 256–57.
301	9 ff.	Schilder 3, p. 112; Edling, pp. 76–77.
301	27 ff.	Adams 2, p. 405; Edling, pp. 79–80.
302	1 ff.	Adams 2, p. 408 (29 Sept. entry); Bogdanovich 2, pp. 294–96.

21 A Deceptive Indian Summer

303	1–8	Toll 2, pp. 172–75, 182–83; Wolzogen, pp. 158–59. Crossard (4, pp. 371 ff.) even claimed that the westward march toward Borovsk was his idea.

PAGE	LINES	
303	9–11	Mikhailovsky-Danilevsky 3, pp. 1–2.
303	18–22	*KSD*, p. 248 (no. 291).
303	23 ff.	Toll 2, p. 182; Crossard 4, p. 374; *KSD*, pp. 236–40, nos. 273, 275, 276 (journal of military operations); Popov, *"Dvizheniye russkikh voisk to Moskvy do Krasnoy Pakhry,"* in *RS*, July 1897, pp. 516–17; Loewenstern 1, pp. 286–87.
304	4 ff.	On this phantom pursuit, see Brandt, pp. 436–37.
304	14 ff.	Nap., *Corr.* 24, p. 259 (19216); Caulaincourt 2, p. 31–34; Denniée, pp. 99–100; Ségur 5, pp. 79–80; Castellane 1, pp. 158–59; Fain 2, pp. 177–79.
305	11 ff.	Toll 2, pp. 185–91; Josselson, pp. 154–55; Fain 2, p. 112; Ségur 5, pp. 79–80; Castellane 1, p. 161; Bourgogne, p. 83; Caulaincourt 2, pp. 56–57.
305	20 ff.	Toll 2, pp. 196–99; Josselson, pp. 152–54.
305	36 ff.	Soltyk, pp. 322–24; Brandt, p. 445; Toll 2, pp. 205–6; Tarlé, *Nashestviye,* p. 204 (Eng. ed. pp. 215–6).
305	38 ff.	Wilson, *Private Diary,* pp. 173–75.
306	14–19	Loewenstern 1, p. 288.
306	24 ff.	Narichkine, pp. 186–90.
306	43 ff.	Wilson, *Narrative,* pp. 178–80, and *Private Diary,* pp. 167, 177–78.
307	23 ff.	Michel Combe, *Mémoires,* p. 115.
307	29–34	Narichkine, p. 191. Brandt (pp. 447–48) also saw the sign, as well as one of the Saracen towers.
307	36–41	Tarlé, *Nashestviye,* p. 205 (Eng. ed. pp. 216–17).
307	42 ff.	Popov, *RS,* July 1897, p. 119.
308	4 ff.	Ibid., p. 115; *KSD*, pp. 241–42 (no. 280); Josselson, p. 156, and fn. p. 256; Toll 2, p. 209; Wolzogen, p. 160.
308	12 ff.	Popov, *RS,* July 1897, pp. 115–16; Josselson, pp. 156–57.
308	25 ff.	Wolzogen, pp. 160–61; Loewenstern 1, pp. 289–90.
308	31 ff.	*SIRIO*, no. 73 (1890), *"Bumaghi Grafa Zakrevskogo,"* p. vi; Josselson, pp. 158–61.
309	8 ff.	Caulaincourt 2, pp. 39–40; Domergue 2, pp. 102–9.
309	37–43	Berthezène 2, p. 83; Domergue 2, pp. 90–92.
309–10		Caulaincourt 2, p. 27; Nap., *Corr.* 24, pp. 289–90 (19253); Fezensac, pp. 248–49; Soltyk, pp. 300–3; Mikhailovsky-Danilevsky 3, pp. 157–58. Both Lesseps and Caulaincourt opposed the circulation of a Napoleonic proclamation emancipating Russia's serfs, the

printed text of which had already been prepared (Caulaincourt 2, pp. 80–82; Chambray 2, pp. 160–1). Berthezène 2, p. 83; Denniée, p. 97; Larrey 4, p. 77. Dumas (3, pp. 446–47, 454) speaks of 6,000 Grande Armée wounded arriving from Mozhaisk.

310   7 ff.   Fezensac, p. 249; Caulaincourt 2, pp. 23–25; Castellane 1, pp. 161–63 (entries of 27, 29 September); Domergue 2, pp. 92–93.

310   20 ff.   Caulaincourt 2, pp. 42–43; Soltyk, p. 318.

310   39 ff.   Bausset 2, pp. 100–2; Bourgoing, pp. 119–20, 137–38; Combe, pp. 125–27.

311   1–6   Domergue 2, p. 101; Castellane 1, pp. 166–67.

311   7 ff.   Bausset 2, pp. 102–3; Domergue 2, pp. 77–79; Fezensac, pp. 247–49; Holzhausen, p. 123.

311   17 ff.   Denniée, p. 101; Soltyk, p. 189; Ségur 5, pp. 88, 95–96.

311   33 ff.   Bourgoing, pp. 126–29; Larrey 4, pp. 76–77; Berthezène 2, pp. 79–80; Soltyk, p. 376; Joseph Grabowski, *Mémoires militaires*, pp. 8–9; Caulaincourt 2, pp. 26–28.

312   9 ff.   Bausset 2, p. 99; Nap., *Corr.* 24, pp. 270–72 (19234), p. 263 (19220).

312   20 ff.   Nap., *Corr.* 24, pp. 273–76 (19237).

313   9 ff.   Ségur 5, pp. 72–73; Dedem, pp. 258–59.

313   30 ff.   Caulaincourt 2, pp. 40–41, 46–47.

313–14   Ségur 5, p. 75. Ségur's claim that Napoleon gave Lauriston a letter for Alexander has never been substantiated. Caulaincourt also thought that he had been given such a letter, but it has never been found (*Mémoires* 2, p. 48, and J. Hanoteau's fn. 1).

314   9 ff.   Brandt, pp. 450–53, also describing how he was wounded in the leg; Griois 2, pp. 63–67; Combe, pp. 16–17.

314   31 ff.   Loewenstern 1, pp. 297–98; Mikhailovsky-Danilevsky 3, pp. 80–82; Wilson's *Private Diary*, pp. 183–86, and the less disjointed account offered in his *Narrative of Events*, pp. 182–91.

315   28 ff.   Mikhailovsky-Danilevsky 3, pp. 82–86; Helldorff 2, pp. 87–88; Loewenstern 2, pp. 299–300.

316   17–31   Mikhailovsky-Danilevsky 3, p. 85; Toll 2, p. 212.

316   32 ff.   Sources used for a description of this conversation *à deux* are: Kutuzov's report to the tsar (*KSD*, pp. 367–68) and also the highly fanciful account later published for propaganda purposes in a Nov. 1812 issue of *Russky Vestnik*, Appendix 2, pp. 472–73; Wilson, *Private Diary*, and his letters to Lord Cathcart, published

in a Russian translation by Dubrovin (nos. 146, 147, 148, 150—pp. 176–85); Mikhailovsky-Danilevsky 3, pp. 86–90.

318 · 13ff. · Kutuzov to Nadezhda Nikitichna, quoted by Count Fyodor Tolstoy in his "Zapiski," *RS* 1873, p. 137.

22 Belated Exodus

319 · 1–7 · Nap., *Corr.* 24, p. 277 (19328); Bourgogne, pp. 86–87; Castellane 1, pp. 164–65.

319 · 8ff. · Nap., *Corr.* 24, p. 288 (19251). Denniée (pp. 103–4) claims that a serious concern for his army's wounded—15,000, according to Chambray (2, p. 231)—had been a major factor in deterring Napoleon from marching on Petersburg. See also Caulaincourt 2, p. 54; Castellane 1, p. 166 (9 Oct. entry); Brandt, p. 457.

319 · 18ff. · Nap., *Corr.* 24, p. 301 (19264); Chambray 2, pp. 154–55; Berthezène 2, p. 86; Fantin des Odoards, p. 340; Ségur 5, pp. 91–92.

320 · 14–24 · Caulaincourt 2, p. 52; Ségur 5, p. 92.

320 · 25ff. · Derrécagaix, *Belliard,* pp. 505–10.

320 · 36ff. · Chambray 2, pp. 205–10; Castellane 1, p. 168; Fain 2, pp. 205–6.

321 · 5–7 · Castellane 1, pp 168–69; Fezensac, pp. 249–50.

321 · 8ff. · Fain 2, pp. 151–53; Ségur 5, p. 93; Soltyk, p. 331.

321 · 30ff. · Derrécagaix, *Belliard,* p. 510; Chambray 2, p. 208; Tarlé, *Nashestviye,* p. 213 (Eng. ed., pp. 225–26).

321 · 42–46 · For an intelligent discussion of the northern route plan, see Bernhardi (Toll 2, p. 227); also Denniée, pp. 103–4; Loewenstern 1, p. 315.

321–22 · Chambray 2, p. 211.

322 · 11–13 · Castellane 1, p. 170; Nap., *Corr.* 24, p. 310 (19277, addressed to Kutuzov).

322 · 14ff. · Napoleon to Maret, *Corr.* 24, p. 308 (19275, dated 16 Oct.).

322 · 22–24 · Castellane 1, p. 170 (16 Oct. entry).

322 · 25ff. · Combe, pp. 118–31; Griois 2, pp. 64–75; Thirion, pp. 214–19; Roos, *Avec Napoléon,* pp. 115–35; Dupuy, pp. 185–86.

323 · 12–22 · Wilson, *Private Diary,* pp. 187–90; Toll 2, pp. 221–23, 184, 211.

323 · 23ff. · Toll 2, pp. 206–8, 218–20; Loewenstern 1, p. 302.

323 · 38ff. · Wilson, *Private Diary,* pp. 193–96; Wolzogen, p. 159.

324 · 13ff. · Chambray 2, pp. 195–203.

PAGE	LINES	
324	23–27	On Dorokhov's Vereya coup, Toll 2, p. 218; Chambray 2, p. 204.

324   33ff.   Toll 2, pp. 228–30.

324–25   The figure of 8,000 Grande Armée cavalrymen was Bennigsen's, but it was probably 1,000 too many (Loewenstern 1, p. 300). See also Chambray 2, p. 230.

325   21ff.   Toll 2, p. 230ff.; Loewenstern 1, p. 292.

326   1ff.   Wilson, *Private Diary,* pp. 196–97; Toll 2, pp. 231–34.

326   26ff.   Von Württemberg, *Erinnerungen* 1, pp. 110–16; Toll 2, pp. 235–41; Helldorff 2, pp. 72–79. Chambray (2, pp. 216–19) estimated the number of cannon available to Murat at 187.

327   22–27   Griois (*Mémoires* 2, p. 80) claimed that the Russians could have outflanked the French right wing even more easily than the left. See also Loewenstern 1, p. 304.

327   28ff.   On Murat's wound, Thirion, p. 218, and on the death of his chief of staff (General Déry), Combe, p. 137. In a fn. to p. 305 of Loewenstern's *Mémoires* 1, the editor, M. H. Weil, lists the total of allied losses (as reckoned by Berthier) at 790 killed, 854 wounded, 310 "missing."

327   34–38   Wilson's *Private Diary,* p. 198; Schubert, p. 266; Loewenstern 1, p. 301; Mikhailovsky-Danilevsky 3, pp. 255–61.

328   21ff.   Fezensac, p. 251; Ségur 5, p. 97; Montesquiou, pp. 242–43; Fain 2, pp. 158–59; Lejeune 2, p. 231; Castellane 1, p. 191.

328   38–42   Ségur 5, p. 98.

328   43ff.   Dumas 3, pp. 457–58; Dedem, p. 253 (confirmation by Berthezène 2, p. 80); Fezensac, pp. 254–55.

329   20ff.   Chambray 2, pp. 230–31. His figures do not include the Westphalians of Junot's Eighth Corps, assigned to guard the Smolensk –Moscow highroad. Caulaincourt's figures for the numbers setting out from Moscow concord more or less with Chambray's: 87,500 infantry (including 4,000 horseless cavalrymen), 14,700 cavalry, and 533 cannon—a figure that probably takes into account the 38 lost by Sébastiani at Vinkova (Caulaincourt 2, p. 83). Berthezène, on the other hand (2, pp. 84–85), felt that the official figures had been greatly inflated and that the total fighting force reaching Moscow did not exceed 71,000.

329   30–34   Chambray put the number of carriages and wagons at 5,000; Soltyk (p. 332) at 10,000; Castellane (1, p. 173, Oct. 19 entry) at 15,000; and Ségur (5, p. 100), in a wild flight of fancy, at 40,000.

329   35ff.   Nap., *Corr.* 24, pp. 316–18 (19285), p. 319 (19287).

PAGE	LINES	
329	44 ff.	Derrécagaix, *Belliard,* pp. 506–7.
330	44 ff.	See Bernhardi's pertinent critique of these confused tactics (Toll 2, pp. 251–54).
330	16 ff.	Ségur 5, p. 102; Labaume, p. 247; Larrey 4, p. 80; Chambray 2, p. 316; Montesquiou, pp. 243–44.
330	38 ff.	Bourgogne, pp. 77, 88–91.
331	7 ff.	Griois 2, pp. 57–58; B. T. Duverger, *Mes aventures,* p. 12; Lejeune 2, pp. 234–35; Bourgogne, p. 89; Ségur 5, p. 103; Montesquiou, p. 224.
331–32		Napoleon's last written order to Berthier from Moscow (*Corr.* 24, pp. 321–22, no. 19290) called for a count of all vehicles to be undertaken by each corps commander, so that one or two wounded soldiers could be placed in each. All unnumbered vehicles were to be confiscated, and those traveling without any wounded were to be burned. But as Castellane noted in his journal on Oct. 19 (1, p. 173), it was already too late to implement this well-meant directive.
332	2 ff.	On Napoleon the looter, see Castellane 1, pp. 170–71 (diary entries of 14 and 16 Oct.); Wilson, *Private Diary,* pp. 194–95; and C. M. Roguet, *Mémoires militaires* 4, pp. 497–98.
332	9 ff.	Berthier was appalled by the dismantling of the Ivan Vyeliki cross. See Dumas 3, pp. 455–56; Bourgogne, p. 80.
332	20–27	Fain 2, pp. 221–23; Chambray 2, pp. 319–20; Wilson, *Private Diary,* p. 201.
332	28 ff.	Bernhardi (Toll 2, pp. 254–55) demolishes Gourgaud's not very intelligent claim that Napoleon's indirect line of march was a *"manoeuvre habile."* See also Soltyk, p. 343; Chambray 2, pp. 321–23.
333	19 ff.	Labaume, pp. 254–55.
333	29 ff.	Toll 2, pp. 255–58; Wilson, *Private Diary,* p. 201; Loewenstern 1, p. 307; Mikhailovsky-Danilevsky 3, pp. 299–304; Soltyk (pp. 350–51) confirms that one of the French captives was an Imperial Guard officer.
333	43 ff.	Helldorf (2, pp. 80–81) defends Kutuzov's caution.
334	3 ff.	Toll 2, p. 259; Wilson, *Private Diary,* pp. 201–2; Mikhailovsky-Danilevsky 3, 325–27.
334	24 ff.	Toll 2, p. 262.
334	31 ff.	Labaume, pp. 255–58; Chambray 2, pp. 330–33; Caulaincourt 2, pp. 90–91; Bogdanovich 3, pp. 32–38; Soltyk, pp. 356–57; Ségur 5, pp. 121–22; Griois 2, p. 89.

PAGE	LINES	
336	2 ff.	Mikhailovsky-Danilevsky 3, pp. 318–9.
336	13–15	Loewenstern 1, pp. 300–1; a judgment which concorded with that of Wilson, *Private Diary,* pp. 203–4.
336	16–29	Crossard 5, pp. 51–52; Helldorff 2, pp. 81–82; Bogdanovich 3, p. 38; Mikhailovsky-Danilevsky 3, pp. 321–23.
336	30 ff.	According to Chambray (2, p. 314), Davout's First Corps had 144, and Prince Eugène's Fourth Corps had 92 artillery pieces—a total of 236—when they left Moscow. Caulaincourt's figures (2, p. 83) are slightly lower: for the First, 130, for the Fourth Corps, 80 cannon—a total of 218.
336	40 ff.	Loewenstern 1, pp. 309–11.
337	14 ff.	On Russian losses, Loewenstern 1, pp. 307–8; Bogdanovich 3, p. 38; Mikhailovsky-Danilevsky 3, pp. 323–24. On French losses, Chambrey 2, pp. 333–34; Ségur 5, pp. 115–16; Larrey 4, p. 81.

23 The Start of the Debacle

338	1–4	Caulaincourt 2, pp. 91–93; Ségur 5, p. 116.
338	17 ff.	Chambray 2, pp. 334–5; Ségur 5, 116–17.
339	1 ff.	Toll 2, p. 266; Suckow, p. 216; Fezensac, p. 256.
339	19 ff.	Ségur 5, pp. 117–19; Caulaincourt 2, pp. 93–96.
339	33 ff.	Gourgaud, pp. 328–30; Caulaincourt 2, pp. 96–98.
339	38 ff.	Rapp, pp. 225–28; Segur 5, pp. 119–21.
340	5–11	Grunwald, *Campagne,* pp. 269–70; Loewenstern 1, pp. 312–13.
340	15–18	Crossard 5, pp. 51–54; Wilson, *Private Diary,* p. 204.
340	20 ff.	Toll 2, p. 270; Grunwald, *Campagne,* pp. 261–62; Wilson, *Private Diary,* p. 205; Mikhailovsky-Danilevsky 3, pp. 333–35.
340	33 ff.	Toll 2, pp. 271 ff.; Loewenstern 1, p. 313; Crossard 5, pp. 54–72.
341	2 ff.	Fain 2, pp. 252–53. Ségur's account (5, pp. 124–27) is the only fairly detailed description we have of this crucial conference.
341–42		Nap., *Corr.* 24, pp. 337–38 (19305); Soltyk, p. 366.
342	23 ff.	Chambray 2, pp. 341–47; Ségur 5, p. 146.
342	40 ff.	Griois 2, pp. 89–90; Fain 2, p. 255.
343	16–20	The point is well made by Bernhardi (Toll 2, p. 276).
343	22–30	Schubert, p. 270.
343	35–39	Caulaincourt 2, pp. 100–4; Fain 2, p. 257; Nap., *Corr.* 24 (to Mortier via Berthier), pp. 323–24.

PAGE	LINES	
343	39 ff.	Tarlé, *Nashestviye,* pp. 218–9 (Eng. ed. pp. 231–32); Olivier, pp. 214–15; and Labaume, pp. 251–52, severely criticizing Napoleon's attempt to retard Russian civilization by one hundred years.
344	5 ff.	On Wintzingerode's capture, see Kharkevich 2, pp. 117–20; Ségur 5, pp. 143–45; Caulaincourt 2, pp. 103–8.
345	3 ff.	Castellane 1, p. 177 (26 Oct. entry); Ségur 5, p. 142.
345	8 ff.	Fezensac, pp. 256, 258–59; Lejeune 2, pp. 232–33.
345	18–24	Roos, *Avec Napoléon,* pp. 142–44.
345	25 ff.	Caulaincourt 2, p. 108; Denniée, p. 121; Chambray 2, p. 367.
345	39–43	Derrécagaix, *Belliard,* p. 513; Griois 2, pp. 93–94.
345	43 ff.	Nap., *Corr.* 24, p. 340 (19308), Chambray 2, pp. 355–56; Bourgogne, p. 95; Ségur 5, pp. 153–54. Caulaincourt (2, pp. 109–12) claims that not more than a score of the wounded transported in carriages or on the wagons of the better-fed Imperial Guard finally made it to Vilna.
346	11 ff.	Bourgogne, pp. 95–97; Griois 2, pp. 97–98; Castellane 1, pp. 176–77; Fezensac, p. 259; Ségur 5, pp. 154–55; Toll 2, pp. 283–86. Wilson (*Private Diary,* p. 207) claimed that the returning Russians massacred some 4,000 French wounded left behind in Moscow, adding: "The French also have habitually shot all the Russian soldiers who from wounds etc. could not keep up with the line of march."
346	21–27	Ségur 5, p. 48; Griois 2, p. 96; Roos, *Avec Napoléon,* p. 129.
346	35–43	Bourgogne, pp. 95–96; Ségur 5, p. 160; Caulaincourt 2, p. 113; Duverger, p. 13.
347	4–16	Fain 2, p. 259; Caulaincourt 2, p. 113; Castellane 1, p. 179 (31 Oct. entry); Denniée, pp. 121–22; Chambray 2, pp. 178–82, 257.
347	17 ff.	Fain 2, pp. 261–68; Chambray 2, pp. 164–82.
347	30 ff.	Fain 2, pp. 267–68; Oudinot, *Souvenirs inédits,* pp. 168–203; Nap., *Corr.* 24, pp. 342–43 (19312, to Berthier for Oudinot, from Vyazma, 2 Nov.).
348	8–10	Fain 2, p. 269; Ségur 5, p. 161.
348	11 ff.	Wilson, *Private Diary,* p. 209 (18 Nov. entry).
348	22–25	Castellane 1, pp. 180–81 (entries of Nov. 2, 4).
348	26 ff.	Toll 2, pp. 288–91; Wilson, *Private Diary,* pp. 206–7.
348–49		Mikhailovsky-Danilevsky 3, pp. 369–71; Toll 2, pp. 290–91.
349	7 ff.	Griois 2, p. 101; Ségur 5, pp. 163–65; Fain 2, pp. 278–80; Labaume, pp. 283–90; Mikhailovsky-Danilevsky 3, pp. 372–79; Frezensac, pp. 259–61; Toll 2, pp. 294 ff.; von Württemberg 1, pp. 131–46.

PAGE	LINES	
349–50		Wilson, *Private Diary* (5 Nov. entry), pp. 210–11.

350 | 10–16 | Wilson, *Private Diary,* pp. 205, 208–9. See also Bernhardi's critique (Toll 2, pp. 299–300) of Mikhailovsky-Danilevsky's attempt to justify Kutuzov's sloth (3, pp. 380–82).

350 | 17ff. | Fain 2, p. 280; Nap., *Corr.* 24, pp. 346–47 (19320).

350 | 23ff. | Fezensac, pp. 263–64; Caulaincourt 2, p. 121; Fain 2, pp. 280–81; Derrécagaix, *Belliard,* p. 523; Castellane 1, p. 181; Askenazy, *Poniatowski,* p. 243; Denniée, p. 124.

350–51 | | Griois 2, pp. 104–5; Bourgogne, pp. 99–100; Ségur 5, p. 175; Lejeune 2, pp. 250–51.

351 | 8ff. | Nap., *Corr.* 24, pp. 348–50 (19322, 19324).

351 | 18–33 | Ségur 5, pp. 170–71.

351 | 34ff. | Fain 2, pp. 283–84; Caulaincourt 2, p. 122; Marbot 3, p. 177; Nap., *Corr.* 24, nos. 19325, 19326; Fain 2, p. 340.

351–52 | | Caulaincourt 2, pp. 125–26; Ségur 5, pp. 175–76; Pasquier 2, pp. 12–41; Savary, *Mémoires* 6 pp. 1–45.

352 | 33ff. | Fain 2, pp. 286–87; Fezensac, pp. 266–68; Ségur 5, p. 181; Castellane 1, pp. 182–83.

353 | 3ff. | Castellane 1, p. 183; Ségur 5, p. 180; Caulaincourt 2, pp. 130–31; Bourgogne, pp. 102–13; Chambray 2, p. 144; Fain 2, p. 287.

353 | 31ff. | Bourgogne, pp. 117–20; Fain 2, pp. 287–88; Caulaincourt 2, pp. 131–32; Duverger, p. 15.

354 | 10ff. | Ségur 5, pp. 193–94; Chambray 2, pp. 148–49. Junot's Westphalians had reached Smolensk one day before Napoleon and his Imperial Guard.

354 | 24–33 | Bourgogne, pp. 122ff.; Caulaincourt 2, pp. 132–33; Fain 2, pp. 289–90; Roguet 4, pp. 508–9; Ségur 5, pp. 205–15; Chambray 2, p. 241. According to Chambray (2, p. 189), the temperature on Nov. 9 was minus 12 degrees and on Nov. 12–13 it was 17 degrees below zero.

354 | 34ff. | Bourgogne, pp. 135–40.

24 The Debacle

355 | 1ff. | Griois 2, pp. 113–25; Labaume, pp. 302–30; Chambray 2, pp. 153–54.

355 | 22–24 | Chambray (2, p. 195) gives a figure of 37,000 infantry and 5,000 cavalry, but he does not include artillerymen, engineers, and others.

355 | 24ff. | On the Russian capture of Vitebsk, ibid., pp. 175–84; Fain 2, p. 290; Castellane 1, p. 184 (9 Nov. entry).

PAGE	LINES	
356	7ff.	For a detailed analysis of Victor's formidable problems, see L.G. Fabry's preface to Langeron's *Mémoires,* pp. xxi–xxiii.
356	13ff.	Chambray 2, pp. 160–62; Fabry, preface to Langeron, pp. xxiii–xxxii.
356	21–25	*KSD,* pp. 265–66.
356	25–32	Chambray (2, pp. 184–86) quotes Berthier's dispatch to Victor of Nov. 11, in which Napoleon spoke of establishing winter quarters in the region of Vitebsk, Orsha, and Mogilev.
356	33–37	Nap., *Corr.* 24, pp. 356–57 (19322, to Dombrowski, via Berthier). On Napoleon's stubborn conviction that Tormassov's (and later Chicagov's) Third Army was a negligible force posing no serious threat to his southern flank, see Chambray 2, pp. 190–96, and Caulaincourt 2, p. 51, in which Schwarzenberg's misgivings were dismissed as *"niaiserie sentimentale."*
356	37–40	*KSD,* p. 224 (257); *KSD,* part 2, pp. 179–80 (170); Chichagov, *Mémoires inédits,* p. 44
356	40–45	Fabry, preface to Langeron, pp. xxx–xxxi; Chambray 2, pp. 160–61.
356–57		Fain 2, pp. 290–96; Caulaincourt 2, pp. 133–39; Chambray 2, p. 154. On Berthier's responsibility in sending the withdrawal order to Victor rather than directly to Baraguey d'Hilliers, see Toll 2, pp. 274, 306. See also Wilson's revealing entry in *Private Diary,* p. 222: "Bonaparte did not let his people in the neighbourhood know of his retreat from Moscow. The prisoners taken, including General Augereau's party, were reposing in perfect security." There is no trace in Napoleon's published correspondence of a letter addressed either to Victor or to General Charpentier, the governor of Smolensk, to let them know that the original southern march route via Yukhnov and Mossalsk was being abandoned. Not until Nov. 1, five days after he had radically altered his army's line of march, did he bother to inform General Charpentier that Junot's Eighth Corps would be reaching Dorogobuzh the next day (*Corr.* 24, pp. 341–42, no. 19310, sent from Viazma).
357	10ff.	Nap., *Corr.* 24, pp. 357–58 (19334); Caulaincourt 2, pp. 136–39.
357	23–26	Castellane 1, p. 186 (14 Nov. entry); Ségur 5, pp. 223–28; Bourgogne, p. 144.
357	33ff.	Caulaincourt 2, p. 140; Castellane 1, p. 187 (15 Nov. entry); Roguet 4, pp. 506–7. The lake was apparently called Semlyovskoye Ozero, misleading Ségur (5, p. 174) into believing that the Kremlin trophies had been jettisoned in a lake near Semlevo, between Vyazma and Dorogobuzh.
357–58		Caulaincourt 2, p. 141.
358	19–24	Wilson, *Private Diary,* p. 222.

PAGE	LINES	
358	25 ff.	Chambray 2, pp. 190–94; Lejeune 2, p. 257.
358	38 ff.	Toll 2, pp. 312–18; Chambray 2, pp. 197–98; Ségur 5, pp. 225–26; Bourgogne, pp. 145–46.
359	3 ff.	Roguet 4, pp. 508 ff.; Bourgogne, pp. 148–53; Ségur 5, pp. 239–40; Chambray 2, pp. 198–99.
359	13 ff.	Caulaincourt 2, pp. 148–49; Fain 2, pp. 304–5; Castellane 1, p. 187; Ségur 5, pp. 229–37.
359	23 ff.	On Miloradovich's usual fearlessness, see Wilson, *Narrative,* p. 129; NMR, *Portraits russes* 1, p. 183. Also Madame de Staël's interesting impressions of his energetic and forthright personality in *Dix Années d'exil,* pp. 259–60.
359	30 ff.	Toll 2, pp. 319–28; von Württemberg 1, pp. 162–67; Chambray 2, pp. 202–4; Labaume, pp. 337–45.
360	20 ff.	Caulaincourt 2, pp. 151–52; Fain 2, pp. 306–8; Castellane 1, p. 188; Bourgogne, pp. 154–59; Ségur 5, pp. 244–49.
360	41 ff.	Lejeune 2, pp. 259–61; Loewenstern 1, p. 344; Wilson, *Private Diary,* pp. 225–27.
361	6 ff.	Fain 2, pp. 308–9; Ségur 5, pp. 249–50; Bourgogne, pp. 159–60.
361	14–26	Fezensac, pp. 267–75. On the night of Ney's arrival in Smolensk the thermometer registered 25 degrees of frost.
361	27 ff.	Ibid., pp. 276–83; P. Pelleport, *Souvenirs militaires* 2, pp. 46–52. Loewenstern 1, pp. 345–7.
362	4–11	J.-D. Freytag, *Mémoires* 2, pp. 171–72.
362	22–24	Caulaincourt 2, p. 154; Labaume, p. 363.
362	24–29	Fain 2, pp. 315–16; Castellane 1, pp. 189–90 (18. Nov. entry); Brandt, p. 465; Caulaincourt 2, pp. 155–60.
362	30 ff.	Fain 2, pp. 319–20; Ségur 5, p. 252; Chambray 2, pp. 166–67.
362–63		K. Schwarzenberg, pp. 168–75.
363	21–31	Fain 2, pp. 320–21; Nap., *Corr.* 24, pp. 361–62 (19342).
363	32 ff.	Fain 2, pp. 322–23; Castellane 1, p. 190; Bourgogne, p. 167; Ségur 5, pp. 253–54, 301.
363–64		Fain 2, pp. 323–24; Bourgoing, pp. 152–54; Caulaincourt 2, pp. 162–64; Castellane 1, p. 191 (20 Nov. entry).
364	9–15	Fain 2, pp. 325–26; Castellane 1, p. 191; Caulaincourt 2, p. 164.
364	16 ff.	Brandt, p. 463.
364	35–37	Brandt (p. 463) claimed that Bronikowski owed his appointment to the (unjustified) recommendation of Marshal Suchet in Spain.

PAGE LINES

Ségur (5, p. 299) blamed Maret for not having ordered the Du-
rutte and Loison divisions, from Augereau's Eleventh (reserve)
Corps to head for Minsk.

364 42 ff. Langeron (*Mémoires,* pp. 47–48) praises the vain courage of Dombrowski's Polish soldiers. The young aide-de-camp was Victor de
Rochechouart (*Souvenirs,* pp. 185–87).

365 6 ff. Castellane (1, p. 192) indicates that the news reached Napoleon
during the night of Nov. 21–22, while Fain (2, p. 327) claims that
he received it after he had left Tolochin. Caulaincourt's assertion
(2, pp. 168–69) that Napoleon received the news on Nov. 24 is
almost certainly a mistake.

365 13–20 Caulaincourt 2, pp. 169–72; Fain 2, pp. 355–60; Bourgogne, p. 172.

365 21 ff. Brandt, p. 465; Chambray 2, pp. 178–79; Langeron, pp. 31–33; Rochechouart, pp. 188–89; Ségur 5, p. 302; Marbot 3, pp. 184–88.

366 3–14 Caulaincourt 2, pp. 177–78; Ségur 5, p. 313; Fain 2, pp. 361–63.

366 15 ff. Fain 2, pp. 363–64; Ségur 5, pp. 306–7.

366 29 ff. Castellane 1, p. 193; Fain 2, p. 363; Caulaincourt 2, p. 179.

366 39 ff. *KSD,* part 2, p. 230 (293); Fabry, preface to Langeron, p. xliii.

367 7 ff. *KSD,* part 2, pp. 344–45 (363); Fabry, note in Langeron, p. 133, for
the French text of Kutuzov's dispatch to Wittgenstein. A German
translation in Toll 2, p. 503. See also Wilson, *Private Diary,* p. 235
(1 Dec. entry); Chichagov, *Mémoires inédits,* pp. 61–63; Rochechouart's justification of Chichagov's southward movement
(*Souvenirs,* pp. 192–93); and Langeron's critique (pp. 54–55).

367 39 ff. Castellane 1, p. 193; Fain 2, pp. 364–65; Ségur 5, pp. 312–14.

368 3 ff. Fain 2, pp. 372–74; Caulaincourt 2, pp. 178–80; Castellane 1, p. 194;
Ségur 5, pp. 317–19.

368 35–41 See Captain Ivan Arnoldi's account in Grunwald, *Campagne,* pp.
337–38.

368 42 ff. Ségur 5, pp. 320–21; Castellane 1, p. 194; Fain 2, pp. 375–76; Brandt,
p. 476; Oudinot's reports to Berthier, in Grunwald, *Campagne,*
pp. 330–31.

369 4–14 Fabry, preface to Langeron, pp. xlv–xlviii; Rochechouart, pp. 194–
95.

369 21–28 Fabry, preface to Langeron, pp. xlviiiff.; Chichagov, *Mémoires,* p.
66; Ségur 5, pp. 319–21.

369 39 ff. Bourgogne, p. 251; Caulaincourt 2, p. 180; Castellane 1, pp. 194–95;
Brandt, p. 477; Fain 2, pp. 376–77.

370 4 ff. Brandt, p. 473; Ségur 5, pp. 321–25; Bourgogne, pp. 252–54.

PAGE	LINES	
370	17 ff.	Brandt, pp. 474–75. On Narbonne's hairdo, Ségur 5, pp. 348–49.
370	35 ff.	Brandt, pp. 474–75; Ségur 5, pp. 332–34; Faber du Faur, *Journal,* pp. 269–75; *Napoleon's Feldzug,* pp. 293–98; Dumonceau 2, pp. 221–22.
371	4 ff.	Caulaincourt 2, pp. 181–82.
371	27 ff.	Rochechouart, pp. 193–94; Fabry, preface to Langeron, pp. xlvi–xlix; Fain 2, p. 389, 405–7; Ségur 5, pp. 336–38; Caulaincourt 2, p. 183.
372	9–14	Langeron, pp. 666–68; Rochchouart, pp. 193–94; Chichagov, *Mémoires inédits,* pp. 70–77; Brandt, p. 478; Fain 2, pp. 339–40; Bourgogne, pp. 255–60; Ségur 5, pp. 339–40; Faber du Faur, *Journal,* p. 282, and *Napoleons Feldzug,* p. 304.
372	42 ff.	Fain 2, pp. 400–3; Brandt, p. 478; Pelleport 2, pp. 53–56; Ségur 5, pp. 344–47.
373	5 ff.	Bourgogne, pp. 260–62; Fain 2, pp. 408–9; Ségur 5, pp. 344–47.
373	19 ff.	Wilson, *Private Diary,* pp. 236–37; Loewenstern 1, pp. 354–55.

25 The Flight

374	1 ff.	Tarlé, *Nashestviye,* p. 207 (Eng. ed., p. 218); J. de Maistre 12, pp. 194, 241; Adams 2, pp. 416–19.
374	17–25	Toll 2, p. 245; *KSD,* pp. 320–21 (413) and pp. 431–32 (531); *KSD,* part 2, p. 68 (54); Tarlé, *Nashestviye,* p. 222 (Eng. ed., p. 235); Oginski 3, p. 219.
374	26 ff.	Wolzogen, pp. 162–63.
375	15–17	On Napoleon's poor opinion of Wittgenstein, whom he had previously respected, see Caulaincourt 2, p. 188.
375	22–28	On the composition of this "Izobrazheniye," see Josselson, p. 247, fn. 77, and for Alexander's answering letter, Toll 2, pp. 505–7.
375	29 ff.	Bogdanovich 3, pp. 285–87, 482 (fn. 51); *KSD,* part 2, pp. 237–38 (238), pp. 390–91 (405 and 406); Wilson, *Private Diary,* p. 232.
376	3 ff.	Adams 2, pp. 419–20; Tarlé, *Nashestviye,* p. 222 (Eng. ed., p. 235).
376	17 ff.	Adams 2, pp. 422–23.
376	26 ff.	Brandt, p. 479; Fezensac, p. 312; Castellane 1, p. 197; Caulaincourt 2, p. 188; Segur 5, pp. 346–47.
376	35 ff.	Castellane 1, pp. 197–98; Caulaincourt 2, pp. 193–94; Fain 2, p. 412; Larrey 4, pp. 106–7, 127.
377	4–11	Ségur 5, pp. 356–57; Fezensac, pp. 314–15; Pelleport 2, p. 56.
377	13 ff.	Oginski 3, p. 163; Castellane 1, p. 200; Fain 2, pp. 413–17.

PAGE	LINES	
377	24–29	Caulaincourt 2, p. 193. The text of the 29th Bulletin can be found in Nap., *Recueil de Pièces authentiques* 9, pp. 124–28.
377	30 ff.	The text promising a reward for Napoleon's capture was apparently issued by Chichagov as an order to Langeron. It can be found in the preface to NMR's *Stroganov* (Fr. ed., pp. xlvi–xlvii); and Langeron, p. 134 (n. 19).
377	40 ff.	Castellane 1, pp. 200–2; Ségur 5, p. 356; Lejeune 2, pp. 288–89; Brandt, p. 487.
378	3 ff.	Caulaincourt 2, pp. 198–203; Fain 2, pp. 421–23; Castellane 1, p. 201.
378	28–31	Ségur (5, pp. 364–65), almost certainly exaggerating, claimed that Napoleon spoke of commanding an army of 1,200,000 men!
378	32–43	Ibid., pp. 354–55; Castellane 1, p. 202; Roustam, *Souvenirs,* pp. 242–43.
378–79		Caulaincourt 2, pp. 205–6; Bourgoing, pp. 172–77.
379	8 ff.	Caulaincourt 2, pp. 206–7; Ségur 5, pp. 370–71; Hogendorp, p. 334; Grunwald, *Campagne,* p. 360.
379	22–34	Bourgoing, pp. 179–83.
379	35 ff.	Bignon, *Souvenirs,* pp. 246–47; Caulaincourt 2, pp. 208–9; Hogendorp, pp. 330–31.
380	5–8	Ségur 5, p. 370; Choiseul-Gouffier, *Réminiscences,* pp. 128–29; Bourgoing, p. 183.
380	8 ff.	Caulaincourt 2, pp. 209 ff. From here on I have followed Caulaincourt's lengthy account of his extraordinary journey with Napoleon, adding a few details from Baron Paul Bourgoing's *Souvenirs* (pp. 183 ff.). His version was based on a French text prepared by Count Dunin Wonsowicz, who later married Countess Anna Potocka. See also Roustam, pp. 216–26.
381	5–15	Caulaincourt 2, pp. 261 ff.; A. Potocka, pp. 331, 334.
381	16 ff.	Caulaincourt 2, pp. 273 ff.; Bignon, *Souvenirs,* pp. 236–37.
381	34 ff.	Anna Potocka pp. 331–32; Caulaincourt 2, 271–72; Nap., *Recueil de pièces* 9, p. 129.
382	12–17	Potocka, pp. 332–33.
382	23–29	Potocka, pp. 335–36; Caulaincourt 2, pp. 275–76.
382–83		Caulaincourt 2, pp. 323 ff.
383	8–12	Letter to Emperor Francis of Austria can be found in Nap., *Corr.* 24, no. 19385, dated December 14.
383	13 ff.	Bourgoing (Wonsowicz's account), pp. 197 ff.
385	17 ff.	Caulaincourt 2, pp. 349–351.

PAGE	LINES	
		26 The Hecatomb of Vilna

PAGE	LINES	
386	1–9	Brandt, p. 491; Lejeune 2, p. 289; Fezensac, p. 317.
386	10 ff.	Ségur 5, pp. 375–76; Bourgogne, pp. 273–75.
386	17–27	Hogendorp, p. 336; Pelleport 2, p. 59; Lemoine-Montigny, *Souvenirs anecdotiques,* pp. 225–26; Fezensac, p. 317; Bourgogne, p. 275.
386–87		Castellane 1, p. 203; Grois 2, p. 179; Bourgogne, p. 302.
387	10 ff.	Bourgogne, pp. 266–71; Ségur 5, p. 377; Brandt, p. 490.
387	10 ff.	Castellane 1, pp. 205–6; Ségur 5, p. 373.
387	26 ff.	Brandt, pp. 491–92; Ségur 5, pp. 378–79; Griois 2, pp. 177–78; Bourgogne, p. 271.
387	37 ff.	Hogendorp, p. 335; Gervais, *A la conquête de l'Europe,* pp. 264–65; Brandt, p. 492.
388	5 ff.	Hogendorp, p. 337; Fezensac, p. 331; Gervais, p. 265; Brandt, pp. 493–94.
388	15–26	Ségur 5, pp. 385–86; Brandt, pp. 492–93; Griois 2, pp. 182–83; Lejeune 2, pp. 292–94; Bourgoing, p. 222.
388	27 ff.	Hogendorp, p. 338; Bourgogne, p. 276; Fezensac, pp. 324–25; Brandt, p. 493.
388	39 ff.	Hogendorp, p. 340; Ségur 5, p. 389; Bourgogne, p. 278; Labaume, pp. 404–5; Castellane 1, p. 208; Brandt, p. 494.
389	5 ff.	Griois 2, pp. 185–86; Brandt, p. 495; Gervais, p. 265; Bourgogne, pp. 285, 303; Choiseul-Gouffier, *Réminiscences,* pp. 136–37; Wilson, *Private Diary,* p. 258.
389	28 ff.	Bignon, *Souvenirs,* p. 251; Fezensac, pp. 325–26; Bourgogne, pp. 279–80.
389–90		Brandt, p. 495; Captain Lyautey (quoted by Grunwald, *Campagne,* pp. 365–66); Fezensac, pp. 327–28; Bignon, *Souvenirs,* p. 252; Bourgogne, p. 296.
390	13 ff.	Brandt, p. 496; and on *"pillage du trésor,"* Lemoine-Montigny, pp. 229–38; J. Grabowski, pp. 8–12; Fezensac, p. 328. Bourgogne (pp. 296–99) valued the stolen goods at 7 million francs; Ségur (5, pp. 394–95) put them at 10 million. Other estimates range all the way from 12 million to 20 million francs.
390	39 ff.	Brandt, pp. 496–97; Grabowski, pp. 9–10; Gervais, p. 267.
390	1–14	Ségur 5, p. 396–404; Castellane 1, pp. 210–13; Bourgogne, pp. 301–26; Brandt, p. 499.
391	15 ff.	Pelleport 2, pp. 61 ff.; Bourgogne, p. 327; Castellane 1, p. 213 (13 Dec. entry); Fezensac, p. 332 ff.

PAGE	LINES	
391	34 ff.	Ségur 5, pp. 405 ff.
392	27 ff.	Verses quoted by Harold Nicolson, *The Congress of Vienna*, pp. 23, 282.
392	40 ff.	Fezensac, p. 327; Ségur 5, pp. 390–1; Bourgogne, pp. 286, 303–4; Choiseul-Gouffier, *Mémoires*, pp. 131–32.
393	8–16	Loewenstern 1, p. 356. Choiseul-Gouffier, *Mémoires*, pp. 128–29. Tarlé (*Napoleon's Invasion*, p. 269) estimated the strength of Kutuzov's army at 27,000, with 200 cannon. Clausewitz (*Feldzug*, pp. 175–76) put it at 40,000; and Bernhardi (Toll 2, pp. 367–69) at 40,290, with 274 cannon.
393	17 ff.	Wilson, *Private Diary*, pp. 251–52; Shishkov, *Kratkiya Zapiski*, pp. 63–65.
393	29 ff.	Choiseul-Gouffier, *Mémoires*, pp. 129–31; Wilson, *Private Diary*, pp. 256–57, and *Narrative*, pp. 353–55; Arndt, *Erinnerungen*, pp. 172–74.
394	1 ff.	Choiseul-Gouffier, *Mémoires*, pp. 142–43, and *Reminiscences*, pp. 152–57; Wilson, *Private Diary*, pp. 254–55, and *Narrative*, pp. 356–57 (also quoted by Tarlé, *Napoleon's Invasion*, p. 284); Shishkov, *Kratkiya Zapiski*, p. 74.
394	33–39	Wilson, *Private Diary*, p. 242; Toll 2, pp. 369–72.
394	40 ff.	Shishkov, *Zapiski, Mneniya i Perepiska*, pp. 167–68; D. N. Sverbeyev, *RA* 1871, pp. 166–74; Tarlé, *Campagne*, pp. 321–22.
395	5–8	On Kutuzov's Francophilia, see Wilson, *Narrative*, p. 131; *Private Diary*, pp. 221–22.
395	8 ff.	See Bernhardi (Toll 2, p. 5) for his criticism of Toll's and Mikhailovsky-Danilevsky's excessive admiration of Kutuzov as a military leader, and the contrast he draws with the opinion of Eugen of Württemberg, who felt that Kutuzov was really more a statesman than a general.
394	24 ff.	Tarlé, *Nashestviye*, p. 272 (*Napoleon's Invasion*, p. 285); *Campagne de Russie*, pp. 323–24. Alexander's unusual statement and Kutuzov's frank reply were apparently overheard by one of Kutuzov's secretaries. The exchange, passed from mouth to mouth, finally reached the ears of Count Nikolai Tolstoy, grand marshal of the Russian imperial Court, and was later recorded in the archives of the historian H. K. Schilder, who did not dare use it in any of his published works for fear of the tsarist censorship.

27 The Aftermath

396	1 ff.	Wilson. *Narrative*, p. 368; Adams 2, p. 424.
396	14 ff.	Caulaincourt 2, p. 396; C. Ballot, *L'Introduction du machinisme en France*, pp. 8–14.

PAGE	LINES	
396	29ff.	Ségur 6, pp. 33–47.
398	30–41	Schwarzenberg, pp. 176–77; Toll 2, p. 366.
398	42ff.	Clausewitz, *Feldzug*, pp. 165–204; Ségur 5, pp. 412–19.
399	17–23	Ségur 5, pp. 431–37.
399	24ff.	Potocka, pp. 338–44; Bignon, *Souvenirs*, pp. 255–82; and on Poniatowski and Schwarzenberg, Askenazy, *Poniatowski*, pp. 17, 247–51.
399	43ff.	Pertz, G. H., *Das Leben des Ministers Freiherr vom Stein* 1, pp. 627–33.
400	18ff.	Schilder 3, p. 142; Shishkov, *Kratkiya Zapiski*, pp. 83–94; NMR, *L'Empereur Alexandre Ier*, pp. 141–43.
400	35ff.	Bignon, *Souvenirs*, pp. 402–18; and *Histoire de France* 12, Ch. 6; de Broglie 1, pp. 213–18.
400–1		Caulaincourt 2, p. 403.
401	11–18	Josselson, pp. 168–73.
401	19ff.	Fain, *Manuscrit de Mil Huit Cent Treize*, p. 8.
401	25ff.	Caulaincourt 2, pp. 404–5.

BIBLIOGRAPHY

Abrantès, Laure Junt, Duchesse d'. *Mémoires, ou souvenirs historiques sur Napoléon, la Révolution, le Directoire, le Consulat, l'Empire et la Restauration.* 18 vols. Paris: Ladvocat, 1831–1835.

Adams, John Quincy. *Memoirs.* 12 vols. J. B. Lippincott 1874–1877 ed. Reprint. New York: Aims Press, 1970.

Allonville, Comte Armand d'. *Mémoires tirés des papiers d'un homme d'Etat . . . de 1792 jusqu'en 1815.* 13 vols. Paris, 1828–1838.

Arndt, Ernst Moritz. *Erinnerungen aus dem äusseren Leben.* Leipzig, 1840.

———. *Meine Wanderungen und Wandelungen.* Berlin, 1858.

Askenazy, Szimon. *Dantzig et la Pologne.* Paris: Alcan, n.d.

———. *Napoléon et la Pologne.* French translation of the first volume of his three-volume *Napoleon a Polska,* Warsaw, 1918. Brussels: Flambeau, 1925.

———. *Fürst Joseph Poniatowski, 1763–1813.* Authorized German translation of the original Polish edition, Warsaw, 1906. Gotha, 1912.

Bakunina, Varvara Ivanovna. "Dvenadtsaty god." (Reminiscences of 1812.) *Russkaya Starina* 47 (1885), pp. 391–410.

Bartenev, Pyotr B., ed. *Arkhiv Knyazya Vorontsova.* 40 vols. Moscow, 1870–1895.

———, ed. *Russky Arkhiv.* 75 vols. 1869–1899.

Bausset, Louis François Joseph, Baron de. *Mémoires anecdotiques sur l'intérieur du palais. . . .* 2 vols. Paris: Baudoin, 1827–1829.

Beauharnais, Prince Eugène de. *Mémoires et correspondance militaire et politique.* Edited by A. Du Casse. 10 vols. Paris, 1858–1860.

Bennigsen, General Levin August Gottlieb, Count. *Mémoires.* Introduction and notes by Captain E. Cazalas. Paris: Lavauzelle, 1907–1908.

Bernhardi, General Theodor von. *See* Toll.

Berthezène, General Baron Pierre. *Souvenirs militaires de la République et de l'Empire.* 2 vols. Paris: Dumaine, 1855.

Bertin, Georges. *La campagne de 1812 d'après des temoins oculaires.* Paris, n.d.

Beskrovny, Liubomir Grigorievich. *Borodinskoye Srazheniye.* Moscow, 1971.

———. *Otechestvennaya voina 1812 goda, i kontranastupleniye Kutuzova.* Moscow, 1951.

———. *Kutuzov, Sbornik Dokumentov.* 4 vols. Moscow, 1951–1960.

Bestuzhev-Riumin, Alexei Dimitrievich. "Zapiski." *Russky Arkhiv* 1896.

Beugnot, Jacques-Claude, Comte. *Mémoires du comte Beugnot, ancien ministre 1783–1815.* 2 vols. Paris: Dentu, 1866.

Bignon, Baron Louis Pierre Edouard. *Souvenirs d'un diplomate. La Pologne (1811–1813).* Paris: Dentu, 1864.

————. *Histoire de France, depuis le 18 brumaire (Novembre 1799) jusqu'à la paix de Tilsitt (Juillet 1807).* Vols. 1–6. Paris: Bechet, Didot, 1829–1830.

————. *Histoire de France sous Napoléon. Deuxième époque, depuis la paix de Tilsitt en 1807 jusqu'en 1812.* Vols. 7–10. Paris: Firmin Didot, 1838.

————. *Histoire de France sous Napoléon. Dernière époque, depuis le commencement de la guerre de Russie jusqu'à la deuxième Restauration.* Vols. 11–14. Paris: Didot, 1845–1850.

Biot, Colonel Hubert-François. *Campagnes et garnisons. Souvenirs anecdotiques et militaires.* Introduction and notes by Comte Fleury. Paris: Vivien, 1901.

Blackwell, William L. *The Beginnings of Russian Industrialization, 1800–1860.* Princeton, N.J.: Princeton University Press, 1968.

Blocqueville, Adélaide-Louise d'Eckmühl, marquise de. *Le Maréchal Davout, prince d'Eckmühl.* 4 vols. Paris: Didier, 1879–1880.

Blond, Georges. *La Grande Armée.* Paris: Laffont, 1979.

Boehtlingk, Arthur. *Frédéric-César Laharpe, 1754–1838.* Neuchâtel: La Baconnière, 1969.

Bogdanovich, Major General Modest Ivanovich. *Istoria otechestvennoy voiny 1812 goda.* 3 vols. St. Petersburg, 1859–1860.

Bonaparte, Jérôme. *Mémoires et correspondance politique du roi Jérôme et de la reine Catherine.* Edited by A. Du Casse. 7 vols. Paris: Dentu, 1861–1868.

Bonnefons, André. *Un Allié de Napoléon: Frédéric-Auguste, premier roi de Saxe et grand-duc de Varsovie, 1763–1827.* Paris: Perrin, 1902.

Boulart, General Jean-François. *Mémoires militaires.* Paris, 1892.

Bourgogne, François. *Mémoires du sergent Bourgogne.* Paris: Hachette, 1978.

Bourgoing, Paul. *Souvenirs militaires, 1791–1815.* Paris, 1897.

Boutourlin, Dmitri Petrovitch. *Histoire militaire de la campagne de Russie.* 2 vols. Paris, 1824.

Boyen, Hermann von. *Erinnerungen aus dem Leben des Feldmarschals. Aus seinem Nachlass.* 2 vols. Leipzig: Hirzel, 1889.

Brandes, Georg. *Main Currents in Nineteenth-Century Literature.* 7 vols. London, 1924.

Brandt, General Heinrich von. *Aus dem Leben des Generals H. v. B.* Berlin, 1869.

Bray, Count François Gabriel de. *Aus dem Leben eines Diplomaten alter Schule (1765–1832).* Leipzig: Hirzel, 1901.

Brett-James, Anthony. *Eyewitness Accounts of Napoleon's Defeat in Russia.* London: Macmillan, 1966.

Brinton, Crane. *A Decade of Revolution: 1789–1799.* New York: Harper, 1934.

Broglie, Achille Charles Léonce Victor, duc de. *Souvenirs.* 4 vols. Paris: C. Lévy, 1886.

Bruun, Geoffrey. *Europe and the French Imperium.* New York: Harper, 1938.

Castellane, E. V. E. Boniface, maréchal comte de. *Journal du maréchal de Castellane (1804–1862).* 2 vols. Paris: Plon-Nourrit, 1895–1897.

Caulaincourt, Armand de. *Mémoires du général de Caulaincourt, Duc de Vicence, Grand Ecuyer de l'Empereur.* Introduction and notes by Jean Hanoteau. 3 vols. Paris: Plon, 1933.

Chambray, General Georges, marquis de. *Histoire de l'expédition de Russie.* 3 vols. Paris: Pellet, 1823.

Chardigny, Louis. *Les maréchaux de Napoléon.* Paris: Tallandier, 1977.

Chevalier, Jean-Michel. *Souvenirs des guerres napoléoniennes.* Paris: Hachette, 1970.

Chichagov. *See* Tchitchagov.

Chlapowski, General Baron Adam Désiré. *Mémoires sur les guerres de Napoléon 1806–1813.* Paris: Plon-Nourrit, 1908.

Choiseul-Gouffier, Comtesse de [born Sophie von Tisenhaus]. *Mémoires historiques sur l'empereur Alexandre et la cour de Russie.* Paris: Leroux, 1829.

———. *Réminiscences sur l'empereur Alexandre et sur l'empereur Napoléon Ier.* Besançon: Bonvalot, 1862.

Christian, R. F. *Tolstoy's "War and Peace."* Oxford, 1962.

Chuquet, Arthur. *La Campagne de 1812: Mémoires du Margrave de Bade.* Paris: Fontemoing, 1912.

———. *La Guerre en Russie.* Paris, 1912.

Clarke, Edward Daniel. *Travels in Various Countries of Europe, Asia and Africa.* Vol. I, *Russia, Tartary and Turkey.* London: Cadell & Davies, 1813.

Clausewitz, General Carl von. *Hinterlassene Werke:* Vol. 7, *Der Feldzug von 1812 in Russland.* 2d ed. Berlin, 1862. In English (but shortened), *The Campaign of 1812 in Russia.* London: Murray, 1843.

Clercq, Alexandre J. H. de. *Recueil des Traités de la France.* 21 vols. Paris, 1864–1900.

Cogordan, Georges. *La Vie de Joseph de Maistre.* Paris: Hachette, 1894.

Coignet, Capitaine Jean-Roche. *Cahiers.* Paris: Hachette, 1883.

Combe, Colonel Michel. *Mémoires sur les campagnes de Russie (1812), de Saxe (1813), de France (1814 et 1815).* Paris: Blot, 1853.

Crankshaw, Edward. *The Shadow of the Winter Palace.* London: Macmillan, 1976.

Crossard, Jean-Baptiste Louis, Baron de. *Mémoires militaires et historiques.* 6 vols. Paris, 1829.

Czartoryski, Prince Adam. *Mémoires.* Edited by Charles de Mazade. 2 vols. Paris, 1887.

———. *Memoirs.* Edited by Adam Gielgud. 2 vols. London: Remington, 1888.

Dard, Emile. *Un confident de l'empereur, le comte de Narbonne (1755–1813).* Paris: Plon, 1943.

Davydov, Denis Vassilievich. *Voyenniye Zapiski.* Moscow, 1940.

Dedem de Gelder, Anton Boudevijn Gijsbert, Baron van. *Mémoires. Un général hollandais sous le Premier Empire.* Paris: Plon-Nourrit, 1900.

Denniée, Baron Pierre-Paul. *Itinéraire de l'Empereur Napoléon.* Paris, 1842.

Derrécagaix, General Victor Bernard. *Les Etats-Majors de Napoléon: le Lieutenant-Général Comte Belliard, Chef d'Etat-Major de Murat.* Paris, 1908.

———. *Le maréchal Berthier.* 2 vols. Paris, 1904–1905.

Domergue, Armand. *La Russie pendant les guerres de l'Empire, 1805–1815.* 2 vols. Paris, 1935.

Dubrovin, Nikolai F. *Otechestvennaya voina v. pismakh sovremennikov (1812–1815).* Vol. 43 of *Zapiski* (Notes) of the Imperial Academy of Sciences. St. Petersburg, 1882.

Du Casse, Albert, Baron. *Le général Vandamme et sa correspondance.* 2 vols. Paris: Didier, 1870.

———. *Mémoires pour servir à l'histoire de la campagne de 1812 en Russie.* Paris, 1852.

———. *Napoléon: Supplément à la correspondance.* Paris, 1887.

———. *Catherine de Wurtemberg, princesse Jérôme. Correspondance inédite.* Paris, 1893.

See also his editions of the memoirs of Eugène de Beauharnais and of Jérôme Bonaparte.

Duffy, Christopher. *Borodino and the War of 1812.* London, 1972.

Dumas, General Mathieu, Comte, *Souvenirs* (1770–1836). 3 vols. Paris, 1839.

Dumonceau, François. *Mémoires.* 2 vols. Brussels, 1958, 1960.

Dunan, Marcel. *Napoléon et l'Allemagne: le système continental et le début de royaume de Bavière, 1806–1810.* Paris: Plon, 1942.

Duncker, Max. *Aus der Zeit Friedrichs des Grossen und Friedrich Wilhelms III.* 3 vols. Leipzig: Duncker & Humblot, 1876.

Dupont, Marcel. *Murat, cavalier.* Paris, 1934.

Dupuy, Victor. *Souvenirs militaires, 1794–1816.* Paris: C. Lévy, 1892.

Duverger, B. T. *Mes aventures pendant la campagne de Russie.* N.p., n.d.

Edling, Comtesse [born Roxandra Stourdza]. *Mémoires.* Moscow, 1888.

Engelmann, Berndt. *Preussen: Land der unbegrenzten Möglichkeiten.* Munich, 1979.

Ernouf, Baron Alfred Auguste. *Maret, Duc de Bassano.* Paris: Perrin, 1884.

Espitalier, Albert. *Napoléon et le roi Murat (1808–1815).* Paris, 1910.

Faber du Faur, G. G. de. *Napoleons Feldzug in Russland in 1812.* Engravings, with text by Major F. von Kaussler and introduction by Armand Dayot. Leipzig, 1897.

———. *Campagne de Russie, 1812.* Engravings, with text by F. von Kaussler. Paris: Flammarion, 1895.

———. *Blätter aus meinem Portefeuille, im Laufe des Feldzuges 1812 in Russland.* (Portfolio of engravings of the 1812 campaign.) Stuttgart, n.d.

Fain, Baron Agathon Jean-François. *Manuscrit de Mil Huit Cent Douze.* 2 vols. Paris: Delaunay, 1827.

———. *Manuscrit de Mil Huit Cent Treize.* 2 vols. Paris: Delaunay, 1824.

———. *Mémoires.* Introduction and notes by P. Fain. Paris: Plon, 1908.

Fantin des Odoards, General Louis Florimond. *Journal.* Paris, 1895.

Fezensac, Raymond Aimery Philippe Joseph de Montesquiou, Duc de. *Journal de la campagne de Russie.* Tours: Mame, 1849.

Fouché, Joseph, Duc d'Otrante. *Mémoires du Duc d'Otrante, Ministre de la Police général.* Edited by Alphonse de Beauchamp. 2 vols. Paris: Le Rouge, 1824.

François, Capitaine. *Journal.* Paris, 1903.

Freytag, General Jean-David. *Mémoires.* 2 vols. Paris: Nepveu, 1824.

Funcken, Liane, and Fred Funcken. *L'Uniforme et les armes des soldats du Premier Empire.* 2 vols. Paris: Casterman, 1968.

Garden, Comte Guillaume de. *Histoire des traités de paix . . .* 15 vols. Paris: Amyot, 1848–1887.

Garros, Louis. *Ney, le brave des braves.* Paris: Amiot-Dumont, 1955.

Gay de Vernon, Jean-Louis Camille, Baron. *Vie du maréchal Gouvion de Saint-Cyr.* Paris, 1856.

Gentz, Friedrich von. *Osterreichs Theilnahme an den Befreiungskriegen.* (Includes Schwarzenberg's correspondence with Metternich.) Vienna: Gerold, 1887.

Georgel, Abbé. *Voyage à Saint Petersbourg en 1799 et 1800.* Paris, 1818.

Gervais, Capitaine. *A la conquête de l'Europe.* Paris: Calmann-Levy, 1939.

Giesse, Friedrich. *Kassel–Moskau–Küstrin. Tagebuch während des russischen Feldzuges.* Leipzig, 1912.

Girardin, Stanislas de. *Mémoires, journal, et souvenirs.* 2 vols. Paris: Moutardier, 1829.

Girod de l'Ain, General Félix Jean-Marie. *Dix ans de souvenirs militaires.* Paris: Dumaine, 1873.

Glover, Michael. *A Very Slippery Fellow: A Life of Sir Robert Wilson.* Oxford, 1977.

Golovine, Countess Varvara Nikolayevna. *Souvenirs de la comtesse Golovine, née Princesse Galitzine, 1766–1821.* Introduction and notes by K. K. Waliszewski. Paris: Plon, 1910.

Golovkin, Comte Fédor. *La Cour et le règne de Paul Ier—Portraits, souvenirs et anecdotes.* Paris: Plon-Nourrit, 1905.

Gourgaud, General Baron Gaspard. *Napoléon et la Grande Armée en Russie.* Paris, 1825.

Gouvion Saint-Cyr, Marshal Laurent de. *Mémoires pour servir à l'histoire.* 4 vols. Paris: Anselin, 1831.

Grabowski, Jozef. *Mémoires militaires.* Paris, 1907.

Gretch, Nikolai Ivanovich. *Zapiski o moyei zhizni—Sochineniya.* 5 vols. St. Petersburg: Suvorin, 1880.

Grimsted, Patricia K. *The Foreign Ministers of Alexander I.* Berkeley, 1969.

Griois, General Lubin. *Mémoires.* 2 vols. Paris, 1909.

Grunwald, Constantin de. *Freiherr vom Stein: l'ennemi de Napoléon.* Paris, 1936.

———. *Alexandre Ier, le tsar mystique.* Paris: Amiot-Dumont, 1955.

———. *La Campagne de Russie.* Paris: Julliard, 1964.

———. *Moscou: Histoire de Moscou et des Moscovites.* Paris: Pont-Royal, 1963.

———. *La Guerre nationale en 1812.* Publication du comité scientifique du grand état-major russe. Translated from Russian by Captain E. Cazalas. 7 vols. Paris: Lavauzelle, 1903–1911.

Halévy, Elie. *England in 1815.* Translated by E. I. Watkin and D. A. Barker. London: Benn, 1949.

Handelsman, Marceli. *Napoléon et la Pologne, 1806–1807.* Paris: Alcan, 1909.

Hardenberg, Prince Carl August von. *Denkwürdigkeiten.* Edited and published by Leopold von Ranke. 5 vols. Leipzig: Duncker & Humblot, 1877.

Hastier, Louis. *Vielles histoires: étranges énigmes.* Vol. 5. "Napoléon faussaire." (On Napoleon's counterfeiting of English and Russian money.) Paris: Fayard, 1961.

Helldorff, Freiherr von. *Aus dem Leben des Kaiserlichen Russischen Generals der Infanterie Prinzen Eugen von Württemberg.* 4 vols. Berlin, 1861–1862.

Herold, Christopher. *Mistress to an Age: A Life of Madame de Staël.* New York, 1958.

Herzen, Alexander. *Childhood, Youth, and Exile.* London: Penguin, 1979.

Hogendorp, General Dirk van. *Mémoires.* The Hague: Martinis Nijhoff, 1887.

Holzhausen, Paul. *Die Deutschen in Russland.* Berlin, 1912.

Hourtoulle, François Guy. *Davout le terrible.* Paris, 1975.

Hurewitz, J. C. *Diplomacy in the Near and Middle East.* Vol. I. New York: Van Nostrand, 1956.

Jenkins, Michael. *Arakcheev: Grand-Vizir of the Russian Empire.* London, 1969.

Jomini, General A. H., Baron de. *Précis politique et militaire des campagnes de 1812 à 1814.* 2 vols. Lausanne, 1886.

Josselson, Michael, and Diana Josselson. *The Commander: A Life of Barclay de Tolly.* Oxford, 1980.

Juchereau de Saint-Denys, Baron Antoine. *Histoire de l'empire ottoman depuis 1792 jusqu'en 1844.* 4 vols. Paris, 1844.

Karnovich, Yevgheny Petrovich. *Tsesarevich Konstantin Pavlovich.* St. Petersburg, 1899.

Kharkevich, V. *Voina 1812 goda ot Nemana do Smolenska.* 2 vols. Vilna, 1901.

———. *1812 god v. dnevnikakh, zapiskakh i vospominaniakh sovremennikov.* Vilna, 1904.

Kleinschmidt, Arthur. *Geschichte des Königreichs Westfalen.* Gotha: Perthes, 1893.

Klippel, Georg Heinrich. *Das Leben des Generals von Scharnhorst.* Vol. 3. Leipzig, 1869.

Kügelen, Wilhelm von. *Erinnerungen eines alten Mannes.* Berlin, 1883.

Kukiel, Marion. *Czartoryski and European Unity*. Princeton, N.J.: Princeton University Press, 1955.

Labaume, Eugène. *Relation circonstanciée de la campagne de Russie en 1812*. Paris: Panckouke, 1814.

Langeron, Louis Alexandre Andrault, Comte de. *Mémoires*. Edited by L.-G. Fabry. Paris: Picard, 1902.

Larivière, Charles de. *Catherine II et la Révolution française*. Paris, 1895.

Larrey, Baron Dominique. *Mémoires de chirurgie militaire*. 4 vols. Paris, 1817.

Las Cases, Emmanuel Auguste Dieudonné, Comte de. *Mémorial de Sainte-Hélène*. 8 vols. Paris, 1823.

Laugier de Bellecour. See Pini.

Lebzeltern, Chevalier Ludwig von. *Lebzeltern: un collaborateur de Metternich. Mémoires et Papiers*. Publiés par Emmanuel de Levis-Mirepois, Prince de Robech. Paris: Plon, 1949.

Lehmann, Max. *Freiherr vom Stein*. Vol. 3. *Nach der Reform (1808–1831)*. Leipzig, 1905.

———. *Scharnhorst*. Vol. 2. *Seit dem Tilsiter Frieden*. Leipzig, 1887.

Lejeune, Louis François. *Mémoires*. Vol. 2. *En Prison et en Guerre*. Paris: Firmin-Didot, 1896.

Lemoine-Montigny, Adolphe. *Souvenirs anecdotiques d'un officier de la Grande Armée*. Paris: Gosselin, 1833.

Lettow-Vorbeck, Oskar von. *Der Krieg von 1806 und 1807*. Berlin, 1893.

Ligne, Albert de, Prince de Barbançon et d'Aremberg. *Mémoires et mélanges historiques et littéraires*. 3 vols. Paris: Dupont, 1827–1829.

Lindau, M. B. *Geschichte der Königlichen Haupt- und Residenzstadt Dresden*. Dresden: Grumbkow, 1885.

Loewenstern, General Waldemar Freiherr von. *Denkwürdigkeiten eines Livländers aus den Jahren 1790–1815*. Edited by Friedrich von Schmitt. 2 vols. Leipzig-Heidelberg, 1858.

———. *Mémoires (1776–1858)*. With notes by H. Weil. 2 vols. Paris, 1903.

Lossberg, Friedrich Wilhelm von. *Briefe des Westphälischen Stabsoffiziers F. W. von L., vom russischen Feldzug des Jahres 1812*. Berlin, 1910.

———. *Briefe in die Heimat geschrieben während des Feldzuges 1812*. Leipzig, 1911.

Lucas-Dubreton, Jean. *Murat*. Paris: Fayard, 1944.

———. *Ney*. Paris: Fayard, 1941.

Lyall, Robert. *The Character of the Russians and a Detailed History of Moscow*. London: Cadell, 1823.

Macartney, C. A. *The Hapsburg Empire, 1790–1918*. New York: Macmillan, 1969.

Macdonell, Archibald Gordon. *Napoleon and His Marshals*. London: Macmillan, 1934.

Madelin, Louis. *Histoire du Consulat et de l'Empire*. 15 vols. Vol. 12. *La Catastrophe de Russie*. Paris: Hachette, 1949.

———. *La contre-révolution sous la révolution, 1779–1815*. Paris, 1935.

Maistre, Comte Joseph de. *Correspondance diplomatique, 1811–1817*. Edited by A. Blanc. 2 vols. Paris: Lévy, 1860.

———. *Lettres et Opuscules inédits*. Edited by his son, Rodolphe de Maistre. 2 vols. Paris, 1851.

———. *Oeuvres complètes*. 14 vols. Paris, 1889–1893.

Mansuy, Abel. *Jérôme Napoléon et la Pologne en 1812*. Paris, 1931.

Marbot, General Jean-Baptiste Marcellin, Baron de. *Mémoires*. 3 vols. Paris, 1891.

Marchenko, Vassili Romanovich. "Autobiographicheskiye Vospominaniya." *Russkaya Starina* 85 (1896).

Marmont, Auguste Frédéric Louis Wiesse de. *Mémoires du maréchal Marmont.* 9 vols. Paris, 1857.

Martens, Carl von. *Denkwürdigkeiten aus dem kriegerischen und politischen Leben eines alten Offiziers.* Dresden: Arnoldi, 1848.

Martens, Fedor Fedorovitch. *Recueil de traités et conventions conclus par la Russie avec les puissance étrangères.* St. Petersburg: A. Böhmke 1892–1909. (Vols. 9–12 cover treaties with England from 1710 to 1895; vols. 13–15, treaties with France from 1717 to 1906.)

Masson, Frédéric. *Napoléon et sa famille.* 13 vols. Paris, 1897–1919.

———. *Cavaliers de Napoléon.* Paris, 1896.

———. *Marie Walewska.* (In series *Les Maîtresses de Napoléon.*) Paris: Borel, 1897.

Mayevsky, General. "Istoria General Mayevskago." *Russkaya Starina* 8 (August 1873).

Meneval, Baron Claude François de. *Mémoires de Napoléon Ier.* 3 vols. Paris, 1893–1894.

———. *Napoléon et Marie-Louise.* 3 vols. Vol. 3. *Souvenirs historiques.* Paris, 1935.

Metternich, Clemens Lothar Wenzel, Fürst von. *Mémoires, documents et écrits divers.* Collected and edited by Alphons von Klinkowstroem. Paris, 1880.

Mikhailovsky-Danilevsky, Lieutenant General Alexander. *Opisaniye otechestvennoy voiny v. 1812 godu.* 4 vols. St. Petersburg, 1839. A German translation by Carl Goldhammer was published in Riga and Leipzig under the title *Geschichte des vaterländischen Krieges im Jahre 1812.*

Miot de Melito, André François. *Mémoires.* 3 vols. Paris: Lévy, 1858.

Montesquiou, Ambroise Anatole Augustin, Comte de. *Souvenirs sur la Révolution, l'Empire, la Restauration, et le règne de Louis-Philippe.* Edited by Robert Barnaud. Paris, 1961.

Napoléon. Recueil de *Pièces authentiques sur le captif de Sainte-Hélène.* Vol. 9. (Bulletins de la Grande Armée for 1812.) Paris: Correard, 1822.

———. *Correspondance.* Compiled under the orders of his nephew Louis-Napoléon—Emperor Napoléon III. 32 vols. Paris: 1858–1869.

———. *Correspondance inédite.* Edited by Lieutenant Colonel E. Picard and L. Tuetey. 5 vols. Paris, 1912–1925.

———. *Lettres inédites de Napoléon Ier à Marie-Louise, écrites de 1810 à 1814.* Edited with introduction by Louis Madelin. Paris, 1935.

———. *Supplement à la correspondance de Napoléon Ier: L'Empereur et la Pologne.* Compiled by Adam Skalkowski. Paris, 1908.

Narichkine [Naryshkin], Nathalie. *Le comte Rostopchine et son temps.* St. Petersburg: Golicke & Willborg, 1912.

Nesselrode, Karl Robert Vassilievitch, Comte de. *Lettres et Papiers du Chancelier, Comte de Nesselrode, 1760–1856.* 11 vols. Paris: Lahure, 1905–1912.

Nicolas Mikhailovich Romanov, Grand Duke of Russia (NMR). *L'Empereur Alexandre Ier.* French translation by Baroness Wrangel of the original Russian text. Paris: Payot, 1931.

———. *L'Impératrice Elisabeth.* 3 vols. St. Petersburg, 1905–1908.

———. *Correspondance de l'Empereur Alexandre avec sa soeur, la Grande-Duchesse Catherine.* (Letters written in French.) St. Petersburg, 1910.

———. *Knyazya Dolgorukiye.* St. Petersburg, 1901. German translation, *Die Fürsten Dolgoroukij,* was published in Leipzig in 1902.

———. *Relations diplomatiques de la Russie et de la France.* (Reports from French ambassadors in St. Petersburg to Napoleon and his foreign ministers.) 6 vols. St. Petersburg, 1905–1908.

———. *Le Comte Paul Stroganov.* French translation by F. Billecocq of the Russian text, *Graf Pavel Alexandrovich Stroganov.* 3 vols. St. Petersburg, 1903. 3 vols. Paris: Imprimerie nationale, 1905.

———. *Portraits russes.* (Also entitled *Russkiye Portrety.* A collection of portraits of prominent Russian men and women of the 18th and 19th centuries, published in a fat-tomed 5-volume edition, with texts in French and Russian; and a 10-volume edition, with texts published separately from the plates.) St. Petersburg, 1905–1909.

———. *Voyennaya Gallereya 1812 goda.* (Contains some 330 portraits of Russian officers who took part in the war of 1812, most painted by George Dawe, with preface and biographical notes by NMR.) St. Petersburg, 1912.

Nicolson, Harold. *The Congress of Vienna.* London: Readers Union Constable, 1948.

Niemcewicz, Julian Ursyn. *Notes sur ma captivité à Saint-Petersbourg en 1794, 1795, et 1796.* Paris: Bibliothèque polonaise, 1843. Also available in English: *Notes on My Captivity in Russia.* Translated by Alexander Laski. Edinburgh: Tait, 1844.

———. *Pamietniki* [Diaries], *1809–1820.* 2 vols. Poznan: Zupanski, 1871.

Noël, Jean Nicolas Auguste. *Souvenirs d'un officier du Premier Empire.* Paris, 1895.

Nowakowski, Tadeusz. *Die Radziwills. Die Geschichte einer grossen europäischen Familie.* Munich: Piper, 1966.

Oginski, Count Mihal Kleofas. *Mémoires sur la Pologne et les Polonais, de 1788 à 1815.* 4 vols. Paris, 1826.

Olivier, Daria. *L'Incendie de Moscou.* Paris, 1962.

Ompteda, Freiherr Friedrich von. *Zur Deutschen Geschichte in dem Jahrzehnt von der Befreiungskriege.* 4 vols. Hanover and Jena, 1866–1869.

Orieux, Jean. *Talleyrand: Le sphinx incompris.* Paris: Flammarion, 1970.

Oudinot, Eugénie de Coucy, Maréchale. *Le Maréchal Oudinot, Duc de Reggio, d'après les souvenirs inédits de la maréchale.* Compiled by Gaston Stiegler. Paris: Plon, 1894.

Paixhans, General Henri-Joseph. *La Retraite de Moscou.* Metz, 1868.

Pajol, General Charles Pierre Victor. *Pajol, Général en Chef.* 3 vols. Paris: Firmin Didot, 1874.

Paléologue, Georges Maurice. *Alexandre Ier, un tsar enigmatique.* Paris, 1937.

Palmer, Alan. *Napoleon in Russia.* London: André Deutsch, 1967.

———. *Metternich.* London: Weidenfeld & Nicolson, 1972.

———. *Alexander I—The Tsar of War and Peace.* London: Weidenfeld & Nicolson, 1974.

Pares, Bernard. *A History of Russia.* New York: Knopf, 1946.

Pasquier, Etienne-Denis, Baron [later Duke]. *Histoire de mon temps. Mémoires.* 6 vols. Paris: Plon, 1893–1895.

Pelleport, General Vicomte Pierre de. *Souvenirs militaires.* 3 vols. Paris: Firmin-Didot, 1874.

Perthes, Clemens Theodor. *Politische Zustände und Personen in Deutschland zur Zeit der französischen Herrschaft.* 2 vols. Gotha, 1862, 1869.

Pertz, Georg Heinrich. *Das Leben des Feldmarschalls Grafen Neithardt von Gneisenau.* 3 vols. Berlin: Reimer, 1864–1869.

———. *Das Leben des Ministers Freiherr vom Stein.* 6 vols. Berlin: Reimer, 1849–1855.

Peyrusse, Baron Guillaume. *Lettres inédites écrites à son frère André, de 1809–1814.* Paris: Perrin, 1894.

Pierson, William. *Preussische Geschichte.* 2 vols. 7th ed. Berlin, 1898.

Pils, Grenadier François. *Journal de Marche.* Paris: Ollendorff, 1895.

Pingaud, Léonce. *Les Français en Russie, et les Russes en France. L'ancien régime, l'émigration, les invasions.* Paris: Perrin, 1886.

Pini, Cesare Guglielmo. *In Russia nel 1812. Memorie d'un officiale italiano, Conte Cesare de Laugier de Bellecour.* Livorno, 1913.

Pion des Loches, Colonel Antoine Augustin Flavien. *Mes Campagnes (1792–1815).* Paris: Firmin-Didot, 1889.

Pipes, Richard. *Russia Under the Old Regime.* London: Penguin, 1977.

Polovtsov, A. A. *Russky Biographichesky Slovar.* St. Petersburg, 1905.

Popov, A. N. "Moskva v. 1812 g." *Russky Arkhiv* 1875, nos. 7–11.

———. "Frantsuzy v. Moskve v. 1812 g." *Russky Arkhiv* 1876, nos. 1–8.

———. "Dvizheniye Russkikh voisk ot Moskvy do Krasnoy Pakhry." *Russkaya Starina,* July 1897.

Porter, Sir Robert Ker. *Travelling Sketches in Russia and Sweden.* 2 vols. London: John Stockdale, 1809–1813.

Potocka, Countess Anna. *Mémoires de la comtesse Potocka (1794–1820).* Paris, 1897.

Pradt, Dominique Georges Frédéric de Riom de Priolhiac de Forut, de, Archêvèque de Malines. *Histoire de l'ambassade dans le Grand Duché de Varsovie en 1812.* Paris: Pillet, 1815.

Pyliaev, Mikhail Ivanovich. *Staraya Moskva.* St. Petersburg: Suvorin, 1891.

Radziwill, Princess Antoni [born Frederike Luise Dorothea of Prussia]. *Quarante-cinq années de ma vie (1770–1815).* Paris: Plon, 1911.

Raeff, Marc. *Michael Speransky: Statesman of Imperial Russia, 1772–1839.* The Hague, 1969.

Rambaud, Alfred. *La Domination française en Allemagne.* Part I: *Les Français sur le Rhin.* Paris, 1873. Part II: *L'Allemagne sous Napoléon I.* Paris, 1874.

Rambuteau, Philibert M. E. S. Lombard de Buffières, Comte de. *Mémoires.* Paris, 1905.

Rapp, General Jean. *Mémoires.* Paris: Bossange, 1823.

Réau, Louis. *L'Art russe de Pierre le Grand à nos jours.* Paris: Laurens, 1922.

Rémusat, Claire Elisabeth Jeanne Gravier de Vergennes, Comtesse de. *Mémoires de Madame de Rémusat, 1802–1808.* Paris: Calmann-Levy, 1880.

Rochechouart, General Louis Victor Léon, Comte de. *Souvenirs sur la Révolution, l'Empire, et la Restauration.* Paris: Plon, 1889.

Roguet, General Comte Christophe Michel. *Mémoires militaires.* 4 vols. Paris, 1862–1865.

Roos, Heinrich von. *Mit Napoleon in Russland—Erinnerungen.* Introduction by Paul Holzhausen. Stuttgart, 1910. Also available in French: *Avec Napoléon en Russie—souvenirs d'un médecin de la Grande Armée* (Paris, 1913) and in a translation by Lieutenant Colonel Buat (Paris, 1913).

Rose, J. Holland. *Dispatches, Select Documents from the British Foreign Office Archives, Relating to the Formation of the Third Coalition.* London, 1904.

Rostopchin, Count Fyodor. "Zapiski." *Russkaya Starina* 64 (1889), pp. 643–725.

———. *Oeuvres inédites.* Published by Countess Lydie Rostopchine. Paris: Dentu, 1894.

———. Letters (in French) to Count S. R. Vorontsov. *Arkhiv Knyazya Vorontsova* 8 (1876).

Roustam [Raza]. *Souvenirs de Roustam, Mamelouck de Napoléon.* Paris: Ollendorff, 1911.

Rulhière, Claude Carloman de. *Histoire de l'anarchie en Pologne et du démembrement de cette république.* 4 vols. Paris: Desenne, 1807.

Rüppell, Eduard. *Kriegsgefangene im Herzen Russlands, 1812–1814.* Berlin: Poetel, 1912.

Saint-Chamans, Alfred de. *Mémoires, 1802–1832*. Paris: Plon-Nourrit, 1896.

Sand, George. *Histoire de ma vie*. (In *Oeuvres autobiographiques*.) Paris: Pléiade, 1970.

Sauzey, Lieutenant Colonel Jean Camille A. F. *Les Allemands sous les aigles françaises*. 6 vols. Paris, 1902–1912.

———. *De Munich à Vilna: Papiers du général d'Albignac*. Paris, 1911.

Savary, General A. J. M. René. *Mémoires du duc de Rovigo*. 8 vols. Paris: Bossange, 1828.

Schilder, Nikolai Karlovich. *Imperator Aleksandr I*. 4 vols. St. Petersburg, 1897–98.

———. *Imperator Pavel I*. St. Petersburg, 1901.

Schlossberger, August von. *Politische und militärische Correspondenz Koenigs Friedrich von Württemberg mit Kaiser Napoleon*. Stuttgart, 1889.

Schreckenstein, Roth von. *Die Kavallerie in der Schlacht an der Moskowa*. Münster, 1858.

Schubert, Friedrich von. *Unter dem Doppeladler: Erinnerungen eines Deutschen im russischen Offizierdienst (1789–1814)*. Stuttgart, 1962.

Schwarzenberg, Prince Karl. *Feldmarschall Fürst Schwarzenberg: der Sieger von Leipzig*. Vienna, 1964.

Ségur, Anatole de. *Vie du Comte Rostopchine, Gouverneur de Moscou en 1812*. Paris, 1871.

Ségur, Louis-Philippe, Comte de. *Mémoires, ou Souvenirs et anecdotes*. (First three volumes of his *Oeuvres complètes*.) Paris, 1824–1826.

Ségur, General Paul-Philippe, Comte de. *Histoire et Mémoires*. 7 vols. (Vols. 4 and 5 are entitled *Histoire de Napoléon et de la Grande Armée pendant l'année 1812*.) Paris: Firmin Didot, 1873.

Senfft von Pilsach. *Mémoires du comte de Senfft, ancien ministre de Saxe, 1806–1813*. Leipzig: Veit, 1863.

Servières, Georges. *L'Allemagne française sous Napoléon Ier*. Paris: Perrin, 1904.

———. *Dresde, Freiberg et Meissen*. Paris: Laurend, 1911.

Shishkov, Admiral Alexander Semyonovich. *Kratkiya Zapiski*. St. Petersburg, 1832.

———. *Zapiski, Mneniya i Perepiska*. 2 vols. Berlin: Beln & Bock, 1870.

SIRIO—contraction for *Sbornik Imperatorskago Russkago Istoricheskago Obshchestva*. (Collection of periodicals published by the Imperial Russian Historical Society.)

Six, Georges. *Dictionnaire biographique des généraux et amiraux français de la révolution et de l'Empire (1792–1814)*. 2 vols. Paris, 1934.

Smitt, Friedrich von. *Zur näheren Aufklärung über den Krieg von 1812, nach archivalischen Quellen*. Leipzig and Heidelberg, 1861.

Soltyk, General Roman. *Napoléon en 1812, mémoires historiques et militaires sur la campagne de Russie*. Paris: Bertrand, 1836.

Soubiran, Dr. André. *Le baron Larrey, chirurgien de Napoléon*. Paris, 1904.

Staël, Germaine de. *Dix Années d'exil*. Paris: Treuttel & Würtz, 1821.

Stendhal [Henri Beyle]. *Correspondance*. 10 vols. Edited by H. Martineau. Paris, 1933–1934.

Suckow, Colonel Karl Friedrich von. *Aus meinem Soldatenleben*. Leipzig, 1910.

Surugue, Abbé Adrien. *Lettres sur l'incendie de Moscou*. Paris: Plancher, 1823.

Sverbeyev, Dmitri Nikolayevich. *Zapiski*. 2 vols. Moscow, 1899.

Sybel, Heinrich Karl Ludolf von. *Geschichte der Revolutionszeit*. 7 vols. Stuttgart, 1897.

Talleyrand-Périgord, Charles Maurice, Duc de. *Mémoires*. 5 vols. Paris, 1891–1892.

Tarlé, Yevgheny. *Nashestviye Napoleona na Rossiyu—1812 god*. Moscow, 1938. *Napoleon's Invasion of Russia*. Translated by N. Guterman and R. Manheim. London:

Allen & Unwin, 1942. *Campagne de Russie.* Translated by Marc Slonim. Paris: Gallimard, 1950.

Tatichtchev, Serghei Spiridonovich. *Alexandre Ier et Napoléon, d'après leur correspondance inédite, 1801–1812.* Paris: Perrin, 1891.

Tchitchagov, Admiral Pavel Vassilievich. *Mémoires de l'amiral Paul Tchitchagof.* 2 vols. n.d.

———. *Mémoires inédits de l'amiral Tchitchagoff. Campagnes de Russie en 1812 contre le Turquie, l'Autriche et la France.* Berlin: F. Schneider, 1855.

———. *Mémoires de l'amiral Paul Tchitchagof, commandant en chef de l'armée du Danube.* Introduction by Charles Lahovary. Paris: Plon-Nourrit, 1909.

Tegner, Elof. *Gustaf Mauritz Armfelt.* 3 vols. Stockholm, 1883–1887.

Ternaux-Compans, Nicholas Dominique Maurice. *Le général Compans (1769–1845).* Paris: Plon, 1912.

Thiers, Adolphe. *Histoire du Consulat et de l'Empire.* Vols. 13 and 14. Paris, 1856.

Thirion, Auguste. *Souvenirs militaires.* Paris: Berger-Levrault, 1892.

Tisenhaus, Sophie von. *See* Choiseul-Gouffier.

Toll, Carl Friedrich, Graf von. *Denkwürdigkeiten aus dem Leben des Kaiserlichen Russischen Generals von der Infanterie, Carl Friedrich Grafen von Toll.* With introduction and notes by General Theodor von Bernhardi (the real author, who, in addition to drawing upon Toll's posthumous papers, talked to a number of Russian participants in the war of 1812). 5 vols. Leipzig, 1865.

Troyat, Henri. *Pouchkine.* 2 vols. Paris: Albin Michel, 1946.

———. *Alexandre Ier—Le sphinx du Nord.* Paris: Flammarion, 1980.

Tulard, Jean. *Napoléon, ou le mythe du Sauveur.* Paris: Fayard, 1977.

———. *Le Grand Empire, 1804–1815.* Paris: Albin Michel, 1982.

———. *La vie quotidienne des Français sous Napoléon.* Paris: Hachette, 1978.

———. *Napoléon et la noblesse d'Empire.* Paris: Tallandier, 1979.

———. *Murat, ou l'éveil des nations.* Paris: Hachette, 1983.

Vandal, Albert. *Napoléon et Alexandre Ier.* 3 vols. Paris, 1891–1896.

Vassilchikov, Prince Alexander Alexeyevich. *Semyeistvo Razumovskikh.* 5 vols. St. Petersburg: Stasiulevich, 1880–1894.

———. *Les Razoumovski.* Edited by Alexander Brückner. 3 vols. Halle, 1893–1894.

Viegel, Philip Philipovich. *Zapiski.* 2 vols. Moscow, 1891.

Vigée-Lebrun, Louise Elisabeth. *Souvenirs.* 3 vols. Paris: Fournier, 1835–1837.

Vigier, Henri. *Davout, maréchal d'Empire, duc d'Auerstädt, prince d'Eckmühl (1770–1823).* 2 vols. Paris: Ollendorff, 1898.

Villemain, Abel François. *Souvenirs contemporains d'histoire et de littérature.* 2 vols. Paris, 1854.

Voss, Sophie Wilhelmine Charlotte von Pannwitz, Gräfin von. *Neunundsechsig Jahre am preussischen Hofe.* Leipzig, 1876.

Vyazemsky, Prince Pyotr Andreyevich. *Polnoye Sobraniye Sochinenii.* 8 vols. St. Petersburg, 1878–1886.

Waliszewski, Kazimierz K. *La Russie il y a cent ans. Le Règne de'Alexandre I.* 3 vols. Paris, 1923–1925.

Weymarn, F. W. von. "Barclay de Tolly i otechestvennaya voina 1812 goda," *Russkaya Starina* 151 (1912).

Wilson, General Sir Robert. *Brief Remarks on the Character and Composition of the Russian Army.* London, 1810.

———. *Narrative of Events During the Invasion of Russia by Napoleon Bonaparte.* London: Murray, 1860.

————. *Private Diary of Travels, Personal Services and Public Events.* Vol. 1. London, 1861.

Wolzogen, Ludwig Freiherr von. *Memoiren der Königlichen preussischen Generals der Infanterie Ludwig Freiherr von Wolzogen.* Leipzig, 1951.

Württemberg, Eugen Prinz von. *Erinnerungen aus dem Feldzuge des Jahres 1812 in Russland.* 3 vols. Breslau, 1846. *See also* Helldorff, Freiherr von.

Yermolov, General Alexei Petrovich. *Materialy dlya istorii voiny 1812 g. Zapiski.* Moscow, 1863. (Parts concerning war of 1812 were reprinted in several commemorative issues of *Russkaya Starina* in 1912.)

Zhilin, P. A. *Ghibel Napoleonskoy Armii.* Moscow, 1974.

Zinkeisen, Johann Wilhelm. *Geschichte des Osmanischen Reiches.* 7 vols. Gotha, 1852–1863.

ACKNOWLEDGMENTS

THIS BOOK was begun at a time when my life was darkened by a kind of mini-Berezina. For his thoughtful encouragement at a moment when my morale had hit rock bottom I am much beholden to my editor, Robert Cowley, and even more to my devoted stepson, Michael Aminoff, and his wife, Jan, without whose extraordinary bounty and solicitude I could never have completed the work begun.

I also owe a deep debt of gratitude to Diana Hodgson and to Francis and Mona Fisher, who were more than loyal friends in an hour of need, as I do to others—like Margot Winnick, Françoise Mahieu, Marina Vlady, Hélène Vallier, Margaret Gallois-Montbrun, Michelle Lapautre, and Françoise Adelstain—who did so much in their various ways to offer me solace and support.

For their valuable advice on fine points of Russian history and geography I am indebted to Princess Zinaida Shakhovskoy, Prince Alexei Shcherbatov, and Professor Nikolai Riasanovsky, of the University of California at Berkeley; as I am also to the late Michael Josselson, who in his fine biography of Barclay de Tolly proved himself to be as remarkable a scholar as he had been an administrator, when helping to direct the Congress for Cultural Freedom.

Jerzy Peterkiewicz was particularly enlightening in his explanations of certain aspects of Polish history. Most helpful too were Georges Mond and his colleagues, Eduard Borowski and Dr. Xavier Deryng, of the Bibliothèque Polonaise in Paris, who provided me with a lithograph illustration of their illustrious compatriot Prince Joseph Poniatowski.

I would also like to thank Guy de Commines and Georges Dethan for kindly allowing me to consult certain French Foreign Ministry archives; Madame Laure Beaumont, of the Bibliothèque Nationale, for permission to reproduce a number of portraits preserved in the Département des Estampes' extensive print and rare-books collection; and Madame Paulette Strub for being so imperturbably good-humored in helping me to obtain the volumes I needed in the frequently overcrowded Salle des Imprimés.

To the Librairie Plon I am indebted for permission to quote from the first volume of Armand de Caulaincourt's fascinating memoirs; to Madame Gaubert, of the Bulloz photographic archives, for her exemplary efficiency and dispatch; and to Charles Otto Zieseniss for some useful pointers about the Paris of Napoleon.

It would be ungrateful of me not to add a word of personal appreciation for the courtesy displayed by the staff members of that invaluable institution the London Library, on St. James's Square, the likes of which, alas, I have never encountered in any other city.

Particularly helpful during the final stages of this book was Robert Cowley's assistant, Ruth Singleton.

Finally, no words could possibly convey what I owe to my loving and long-suffering wife, Elena, whose patience was often sorely tried but whose loyalty never wavered for an instant during those long, nerve-racking months of gestation.

C. C.

INDEX

Born in France of American parents, CURTIS CATE served for some years as European editor of the *Atlantic Monthly*, with headquarters in Paris. His first book, a biography of the French aviator-writer Antoine de Saint-Exupéry, which appeared in 1970, was later translated into French and awarded the Grand Prix Littéraire de l'Aéro-Club de France. His second biography, *George Sand*, was a Book-of-the-Month Club alternate selection in 1975. He has also written a dramatic account of the Berlin Wall crisis of 1961 and coauthored a book of reminiscences with the noted American opera director Boris Goldovsky. This is his fifth book.